The Southern Key

The Southern Key

Class, Race, and Radicalism in the 1930s and 1940s

MICHAEL GOLDFIELD

OXFORD
UNIVERSITY PRESS

Oxford University Press is a department of the University of Oxford. It furthers
the University's objective of excellence in research, scholarship, and education
by publishing worldwide. Oxford is a registered trade mark of Oxford University
Press in the UK and certain other countries.

Published in the United States of America by Oxford University Press
198 Madison Avenue, New York, NY 10016, United States of America.

First issued as an Oxford University Press paperback 2022

Library of Congress Cataloging-in-Publication Data
Names: Goldfield, Michael, author.
Title: The southern key : class, race, and radicalism in
the 1930s and 1940s / Michael Goldfield.
Description: New York, NY : Oxford University Press, [2020] |
Includes bibliographical references and index.
Identifiers: LCCN 2019044783 (print) | LCCN 2019044784 (ebook) |
ISBN 9780190079321 (hardback) | ISBN 9780190079345 (epub) |
ISBN 9780190079352 (online) | ISBN 9780197629987 (paperback)
Subjects: LCSH: Southern States—Social conditions—20th century. |
Southern States—Civilization—20th century. |
Southern States—Social life and customs—20th century. |
Equality—United States. | United States—Race relations.
Classification: LCC HN79.A13 G65 2020 (print) |
LCC HN79.A13 (ebook) | DDC 306.0975—dc23
LC record available at https://lccn.loc.gov/2019044783
LC ebook record available at https://lccn.loc.gov/2019044784

1 3 5 7 9 8 6 4 2

Paperback printed by Marquis, Canada

CONTENTS

PREFACE

This book represents a project I have been working on, off and on, for several decades. It is part of my attempt to understand the peculiarities of American politics and society, including why it is what it is today. My cut differs greatly from that of most analysts of American society and politics. As a political scientist (among my several hats), I certainly study elections and the actions of officials, elected or not, but it is my considered opinion that they are rarely the moving forces, especially in times of dramatic change, and are at best facilitators. The underlying factors, often ignored or minimized, are rooted in the economy and, in times of societal upheaval, as in the 1930s and 1940s, in the actions of social movements, particularly labor. It is my hypothesis that much of what is important in American politics today was largely shaped by the successes and failures of the labor movements of the 1930s and 1940s, and most notably the failures of southern labor organizing during this period. I give something of a synopsis in previous works (see, e.g., Goldfield 1997:chs. 6 and 8, 1998, 2001, 2008), and hope to expand it in this volume.[1] Here, I give a brief overview of the organization of the book and interwoven themes.

First, I wish to tell an important story of what I see as central events of the 1930s and 1940s, which, despite the enormous amount of important and useful scholarship, seems to me largely misinterpreted. Yet I discuss only a small piece of my research, focusing on just four industries: coal mining, steel, textiles, and wood. I have extensive archival material on virtually every industry in the South, and most other parts of the country, as well as a wide variety of other material that occasionally makes it into my accounts. Although I mention some of these other areas in passing, dealing extensively with them would have led to four thousand or more pages of text with many hundreds of pages of footnotes and references; the result would have been a work which interests me and perhaps one or two others, but certainly no

[1] For a careful analysis of the elite history of this period, especially that of the Roosevelt administration, see, e.g., Katznelson (2013).

publisher. So I have been highly selective and have attempted to tell an engaging story. If I have been at all successful, is, of course, for the reader to decide.

Second, I believe that the failure of southern organizing during this period, with its central themes of race, class, and radicalism, is the key to understanding America today. A good bit of what is significant about American politics, the political conservatism of certain segments of the U.S. working class, especially among whites, and the racial intransigence of the white South, as well much of the rest of the country, has its roots in this era. Although I have argued this point in other venues, I have changed my opinion about many facets of this thesis on the basis of deeper research and continued reflection.

Third, it will soon be obvious that this is a highly opinionated work, and its theoretical orientation goes against the grain of much of contemporary labor history and political analysis. While I had originally hoped to integrate these theoretical points into the ongoing narrative, my closest friends and colleagues have convinced me to elaborate my theoretical considerations in the first full chapter of the book.

Fourth, this work presents my view of how best to do careful social science. It is my opinion that research, no matter how illuminating and important, that focuses on single industries, towns, or even a single country is not easily subject to compelling generalizations or conclusions. The only valid type of deep analysis must be comparative and global, even if that is not the main spotlight of the work, or as Immanuel Wallerstein once said, the smallest viable unit of analysis is the world over the course of many centuries (1985:2, 2002:366, 2007:16, 19). In this sense, this work, although its focus is the United States of America, is allied with the contemporary focus on global labor history, as expressed, for example, in Marcel van der Linden's *Workers of the World* (2008). This explains, at least to some extent, what seem to be lengthy digressions from a focus on the South to national events and movements, and even international comparisons.

Fifth, although cultural factors can at times be important, I find a primary focus on these factors almost always misleading. Without a clear focus on the underlying structure of economic development, and in particular the economics of an industry, researchers are often led down the yellow brick road of fantasy. This will become clear in my analysis of struggles in the U.S. textile industry (Chapter 6), where I find the conclusions of much of the extant literature provincially presumptuous and mostly off-base. None of this is to belie the importance at times of issues of race, gender, and ethnicity (which I consider central to the U.S. experience), but to look at these factors as merely cultural artifacts seems to me mistaken.

Sixth, the analysis of social movements, and the models for how they grow, I also find generally wanting. Thus, I try to argue carefully against the preoccupation with laws, legal frameworks, and the agency of the state, at least with regard to their causal role in the growth of social movements, a position I have previously adopted in discussions of both the public sector and the 1935 National Labor Relations (Wagner) Act (Goldfield 1989a, b, 1990a, b; Goldfield and Bromsen

2013; Goldfield and Melcher 2019). In particular, in Chapter 2, I try to show how virtually all other researchers have been wrong on the causal importance of Section 7(a) of the National Industrial Recovery Act of 1933, and how liberal (and sometimes conservative) ideological biases have led researchers astray. And, to be fair, this uncomfortable conclusion cuts across ideological lines, from the far left to the far right, and is an erroneous assumption to which I also, at one point, succumbed.

Seventh, the use of data is key to understanding social phenomena, but I find much of its use analytically careless. For example, researchers at times cite strike statistics across industries with very few qualifications. I argue that these statistics must be interpreted in the context of the structure of an industry and the type of leverage workers might have. This latter theory is laid out initially in my theoretical chapter and addressed more specifically first in the discussion of coal miners. In addition, in my analysis of the development of unionism in steel, for example, I try to show why it makes no sense to compare strike statistics in steel with those in coal, at least not without a great deal of circumspection.

There is, of course, much more. Although I have published a number of articles and encyclopedia pieces on the U.S. Communist Party, I have revised my view of the Party and other radical groups, with respect both to their contributions and to their problems. I reject the general tendency in much contemporary work to lump all these groups together and to talk about "the left," a tendency that not only fails to highlight the differences concerning important issues, and the consequences for the successes and failures of various movements, but completely obfuscates the relative weight of each of these groups.

Finally, although I have argued in the past for the importance of Operation Dixie, the post–World War II failed effort by the Congress of Industrial Organizations (CIO) to unionize southern industries— I now view it as secondary, and merely a coda to the far more significant events that took place earlier, a theme on which I elaborate in Chapter 7.

The Southern Key

Introduction

America as the South and Alabama Exceptionalism

The South is today, as it always has been, the key to understanding American society, its politics, its constitutional anomalies and government structure, its culture, its social relations, its music and literature, its media focus and blind spots, and virtually everything else. The South is a distinctive, atypical part of the United States; it is also, however, America writ large, a contradiction I hope to illuminate further. The bedrock of this understanding begins not with the culture or social history of the South, but with its economy and the racial/social relations that have sustained it. W.E.B. Du Bois, perhaps the most penetrating—and, in my opinion, greatest—American social scientist of the twentieth century, understood this well. Du Bois argues implicitly that the answer to the old question, originally posed by Werner Sombart, "Why no socialism in the United States?" (by which he meant "Why was the United States unique among industrial countries in not having an electorally significant working class–supported labor, socialist, social democratic, or communist party?"), really reduces to "Why no liberalism in the South?" The South, according to Du Bois, was inherently reactionary, so there could be "no successful third party movement" in the country as a whole (by which he meant one with a left-wing labor focus) until the South changed dramatically ([1935] 1998:703–707).

In a parallel argument—with little acknowledgment of Du Bois's pathbreaking work—V. O. Key argues that control of the South and southern politics "revolves around the position of the Negro" (1984:5). Historically, it was not primarily culture or lower-class "racism" that maintained the system of white supremacy in the South (and by extension in the country as a whole) and led southern political representatives to play a highly unified and generally conservative role in national politics, but the material stake of cotton plantation owners in maintaining cheap African-American labor, first in the form of slaves, and later, sharecroppers. The plantation owners were allied with those who gained from having a ready pool of below-market-priced laborers (white, as well as Black, forced to compete in a labor market whose bottom was defined by the income of semi-chattel plantation

The Southern Key. Michael Goldfield, Oxford University Press (2020). © Michael Goldfield
DOI: 10.1093/oso/9780190079321.001.0001

labor) as extractive workers in coal, metal mining, lumber, and other industries, among which were the textile, tobacco, longshore, and steel industries. Finally, both were supported by a wellspring of financial and commercial interests (many in the North) that benefited derivatively from these arrangements, including Wall Street financiers, holders of mortgage and loan guarantees for cotton planters, and country stores. Thus, the South historically, and still today, has always billed itself as a cheap-labor, "business friendly, union free" place, currently the location of many foreign, non-union transplants (Bromsen 2019).

This story, of course, begins in colonial times, first with the development of to-bacco and sugar crops, later cotton, all produced largely with slave labor.[1] In this volume, I wish to probe the somewhat more recent history of the South, especially the failure during the 1930s, 1940s, and 1950s of organized labor to fully unionize the main southern industries (whose success, I will argue, would have had the po-tential to radically transform the South and, thus, the nation as a whole), a cen-tral factor in our understanding of America today. I argue further that the failure of unions to organize the South during this period was not at all predetermined.

What Is the South?

What exactly constitutes the South is a surprisingly contentious question. One of the more comprehensive attempts to address this question is that of Odum (1936). He criticizes the U.S. Census Bureau definition, which was based on climate and geography, leading the bureau to include, among other states, Maryland, Delaware, and the District of Columbia, clearly not part of the South even during the 1930s (1936:5). Odum presents literally hundreds of indicators in search of a definition (1936:4–9). Many others, including Kirby (1983), have attempted to tackle this question. I present my rough cut here. First, there is the generally agreed-upon Deep South, those states with the largest African-American populations and his-torically the most dependent on cotton agriculture: Mississippi, Alabama, South Carolina, Louisiana, and Georgia. Then, with a few qualifications, one would want to add the other six states of the former Confederacy—North Carolina, Florida, Texas, Arkansas, Tennessee, and Virginia—with the recognition that even during the 1930s, parts of Texas, Florida, and the District of Columbia suburbs in Virginia were often urban and did not share many commonalities with the rest of the South. Finally, for many purposes, I would add parts of Kentucky, Oklahoma, West Virginia, and Missouri because of their similarities of income, dependence on ex-tractive industries, and other factors, all the while indicating that no exact science for selection exists here.

---

[1] I give a broad overview of this tale in my *The Color of Politics* (1997); see especially chapters 1–4.

The South as Distinctive and Atypical

The distinctive nature of the South, of course, begins with the early dependence of its economy on enslaved African labor. Although slavery existed to varying degrees in the North throughout the colonial era, it was in the South that slave labor was the bedrock of the economy.[2] At the U.S. Constitutional Convention, South Carolina delegate Rawlin Lowdes argued, "Without slaves this state would degenerate into one of the most contemptible in the union . . . Negroes are our only wealth, our only natural resource" (Robinson 1979:141). Between 1815 and 1860, cotton formed a majority of the value of all domestic exports. By 1860, the twelve wealthiest counties in the country were all in the cotton South. Then as today, economic power equaled political power. A majority of the early presidents (for fifty of the first sixty-four years) were slave owners, as were Speakers of the House, Supreme Court justices, and president pro tems of the Senate (Goldfield 1997:113–20).

Southern elites controlled national politics up until the Civil War. This had great ramifications for the North. Slave owners hired vigilantes in the 1850s who engaged in the murder of white settlers in Kansas, the latter of whom wanted the territory to become a non-slave, homesteading, "free" state. Some argue that the Civil War really began not with the shots fired at Fort Sumter on April 12, 1861, but in 1854 in "Bloody Kansas." Slave owners sanctioned the beating, mutilation, lynching, and murder of those who challenged slavery, especially northern abolitionists. Southern national political representatives censored, muzzled, and punished even northern congressional representatives who attempted to present abolitionist petitions. On the Senate floor in 1856, southern elites cheered when South Carolina Congressman Preston Brookes beat the elderly Massachusetts Senator Charles Sumner into unconsciousness with a cane (crippling him for life) because of an abolitionist speech he had given, much to the disgust of many northerners. Although a federal crime, slave-owner-controlled state governments censored mail from the North, destroying not only abolitionist publications but northern newspapers they deemed not sufficiently pro-slavery. This censorship was still going strong in the 1960s as Mississippi television refused to show interviews with James Baldwin and Thurgood Marshall, or Nina Simone singing "Mississippi Goddam." They even attempted to censor the television series *Bewitched*, as romantic relationships between witches and ordinary humans seemed to their enchanted minds coded propaganda for interracial sex (Watson 2010:51).

[2] At the time of the American Revolution (or at least the first census in 1790), of the three million inhabitants of the United States, 600,000 were of African heritage. New York and New Jersey, home to more than three-quarters of northern slaves (20,000 and 10,000 respectively), were the only northern states with significant numbers. And these paled beside the figures for Virginia, Maryland, South Carolina, and Georgia, where well over 90% of African-Americans lived and worked.

The legacy of slavery and white supremacy have left a callous disregard for human dignity and the sanctity of human life (despite the strength of allegedly pious anti-abortion activists) in the South today. It is reflected among other places in the distribution of death penalty executions. More than 80% of the 1,460 executions since the death penalty was reinstated in 1976 have been in the South, with over half in three states alone: Texas, Oklahoma, and Virginia (DPIC 2017). This lack of respect for human life is itself the heritage of African slavery and the plantation system. The low levels of social support for those in need (be in the form of children's health care, unemployment insurance, workmen's compensation, or disability benefits) also perhaps reflects these attitudes.

The South continues to this day in general to have the lowest levels of unionization, the most anti-union laws (the overwhelming majority of anti-labor so-called "right to work" laws), and the most egregious violations of worker safety (Devinatz 2015). It is not surprising that it is the part of the country with the lowest level of, and lowest support for, public education and health care. And it is probably far from a coincidence that Texas today (which is relatively affluent) is the state with the largest percentage of people without health insurance. In the three-year period from 2010 to 2012, almost one-quarter of Texans had no health insurance coverage, over 55% more than the national average of 15.8%. In 2015, 17.1% of Texans had no health insurance, nearly double the national average of 9.4%. Of the twenty-two states with a higher proportion of uninsured than the national average, eleven were in the South (Barnett and Vornovitsky 2016).

The low levels of unionization, I would argue, are in good part the reason for so much ignorance and superstition. Lack of working-class organization leads to atomization, individualism, and an increased receptivity to manipulation by dominant economic interests. As a result, the South is the region where the largest percentage of people are birthers, reject evolution, and deny the existence of global warming, evidence to the contrary on these issues notwithstanding (National Center for Science Education 2013a, b; Porter 2013; Gallup 2012; Pew 2011; Ramsey 2013). It is in the South that there exists increased legislative pressure for teaching creationism in public schools—for instance, the Texas bill (HB 1485) that would effectively enable teachers to teach both creationism and climate change denial.

Still many people in this region continue to glorify the Confederate flag and the "Lost Cause," whose destruction was one of the great triumphs of human dignity in world history. It was not until 2013 that the state legislature in Mississippi finally ratified the Thirteenth Amendment to the U.S. Constitution, outlawing slavery (Chumley 2013). As recently as 2011, a Pew poll found that 52% of southern whites considered it appropriate for today's political leaders to praise the leaders of the Confederacy, and 22% had a positive reaction to the Confederate flag (Pew 2011). In 1972, the state of Mississippi amended its code to celebrate Martin Luther King's and Robert E. Lee's birthdays on the same day; to celebrate Jefferson Davis's birthday and the national Memorial Day on the same day; and a Confederate Memorial Day.

Until 2013, Mississippi even refused to honor July 4 as a holiday, since that was the day the Union army defeated the Confederates at Vicksburg, in 1863.

None of this is to argue that the South is all bad. The South has played a significant, enriching role in American culture, with its cuisine, its home as the birthplace of blues and jazz, and much more. American literature would not be as rich without our southern writers (some of them émigrés from their oppressive birthplaces).[3] It is more recently the site of many great universities and research centers, some of which produce far more African-American PhDs than institutions in the allegedly more liberal and racially tolerant North. Thirteen of the top twenty doctorate-granting institutions for Black PhDs are in the South (NSF 2017).

It also has been the area where some of the country's most valiant popular struggles have taken place. Whites and Blacks in many places fought slave owner–led secession before the Civil War, even engaging in guerrilla war against the Confederacy in Jones County, Mississippi.[4] Successful interracial labor organizing took place throughout the South in the late nineteenth and early twentieth centuries under the banner of first the Knights of Labor and later the Industrial Workers of the World. The interracial labor battles of the 1930s and 1940s, and the civil rights struggles of the 1950s to 1970s, in the South served as inspirational beacons in the twentieth century.

Nevertheless, the South remains, as Du Bois so poignantly argued, a distinct reactionary region of the country, and this has been the case since the colonial era.

The South as a Reactionary Drag on National Politics

The sticking point in the formation of the Union at the 1787 Constitutional Convention was, of course, slavery. Much attention has rightly been paid to the compromise that granted southern states the right both to pay taxes on only three-fifths the value of their slaves and to gain political representation, including on three-fifths of the number of their electorally disenfranchised chattel. But at least as important was a constitution that forbade the federal government from interfering with the use of slave labor— the buying and selling of slaves, the recapturing of runaway slaves by vigilante head hunters, and anything else that limited the "free" exercise of the southern elite's right to debase dark-skinned human beings. The issue of whether southern states had a right to reject, declaring null and void, federal policies

---

[3] The list of southern writers is itself overwhelming and includes Eudora Welty, Mark Twain, Alice Walker, William Faulkner, Maya Angelou, Tennessee Williams, Langston Hughes, Erskine Caldwell, Frederick Douglas, Thomas Wolfe, Flannery O'Connor, Zora Neale Hurston, and numerous others.

[4] Interestingly, this once obscure rebellion against the Confederacy in Mississippi has been the subject of a 2015 blockbuster movie, *The Free State of Jones*, starring Matthew McConaughey. See also Bynum 2016.

they did not like, or even to secede as independent political entities, was presumably decided by the Civil War, although secessionists in Alaska and Texas today still seem to be accorded a respectable hearing by the national media. The acceptance of the principle of "states' rights" as somehow sacrosanct (rather than as a ruse for the continued exploitation and oppression of African-Americans and other minorities, including immigrants today) has been an anchor in national politics. The history of states' rights is as good a case as any for rejecting the "strict constructionist" interpretations of American law.

The constraints that the South has placed on national politics have operated in a threefold way. First, national social policies that developed much earlier in most other industrialized capitalist countries were largely illegitimate in the United States. They had first to jump the hurdle that the laws were needed to promote interstate commerce, allegedly the only legitimate national constitutional concern of the federal government. Thus, national health care, social welfare, pensions, unemployment compensation, and other programs considered in most developed countries to be part of a humane national policy have been highly restricted in the United States. Second, the states' rights doctrine cast doubt on whether national programs should be put forth at all. Finally, the concept of universalism (which would have meant the equal treatment of African-Americans) was opposed absolutely. This meant that even when such programs were instituted during the 1930s, 1940s, 1950s, and 1960s (whether aid to farmers, social security, or Veterans Housing Administration and Federal Housing Administration federally supported mortgages), they were administered at the state and local levels by those committed to disadvantaging African-Americans (Katznelson 2005; Rothstein 2017).

Thus, the southern states were in general so anti-labor (especially toward African-American workers) and so inhospitable to universal programs that they made broad, national policies all but politically untenable. Attempts to form national labor-supported third parties, seemingly so initially successful during the 1930s—especially in the Midwest and West—foundered on their inability to gain any traction in the South. The low level of labor organization in the South also meant that unions in the North often had limited leverage when companies threatened to, and often did, move their facilities to lower-wage, non-union areas of the South (as Boeing, Ikea, and many others have recently done; Bromsen 2019). What was acceptable and possible for labor, and for national politics in general, was sharply circumscribed by the white supremacist South.

The South as America Writ Large

The continued oppression of African-Americans in the United States is not merely a legacy of slavery or something that existed only in the pre–civil rights era. The so-called plight of the inner cities, including poor and segregated housing, poor education, lack of job opportunities for less-educated African-American youth, the ghettos themselves, police brutality, and a racially biased criminal justice system, show few signs of changing in the immediate future. The racially based prison system in this country (with incarceration rates higher than in any other country in the world) is so extreme that it has been dubbed the "New Jim Crow" (Alexander 2010). As Malcolm X starkly put it, in the United States there is only Up South and Down South.

Rather than being merely a legacy or after effect of African-American slavery (now long gone), much of the present situation is a result of social policies pushed by southern elites and accepted either passively or enthusiastically by northern elites. Following Harry Haywood, one might call this "the shadow of the plantation" (1948:66). Historically, in order to justify the continued undemocratic suppression of African-American cotton agricultural labor in the South and the system of white supremacy that sustained it, as many of the discriminatory policies as possible needed to be nationalized. Segregation of government employment and the armed forces, universities, racial limitations on federal benefits, segregation in restaurants, resorts, motels, and hotels all needed to be as widespread as possible in the North. In this, southern elites were largely successful. During the New Deal period, federal programs in the South, run by southern political appointees, showed great disparities between the benefits given to Blacks and whites.

Even after World War II, as the armed forces were integrated, huge federal programs, including the GI Bill (Servicemen's Readjustment Act of 1944) and federal housing loan programs, left such large disparities between Blacks and whites that the educational and wealth differences between whites and African-Americans were not only accentuated but shaped racial opportunities for decades (Oliver and Shapiro 2006; Katznelson 2005; Rothstein 2017). Thus, white supremacy in the South, the main bulwark of the southern labor system, was extended to the North, with draconian racial results, whose effects are still with us today.

The Contradictions in the Upper South

All this having been said, in the end the North (which includes the West and Midwest) was and still is somewhat different than the South. First, African-Americans in the North, unlike those in the South, did have the franchise, even early in the twentieth century. Thus, as their numbers increased, their electoral and general political influence grew, even to the point of electing political representatives from the majority-Black areas of the nation's largest cities. Second, their entrance into certain segregated industrial and occupational channels meant that they had a strong influence in some labor venues, from the post office to steel mill coke plants, the killing floors of slaughterhouses, and eventually automobile assembly lines in Detroit. LeRoi Jones (né Amira Baraka) captures this duality well in *Blues*

People (1963), where he describes how the greater freedom (albeit in a segregated arena) of Chicago allowed the blues to develop in the 1920s and 1930s in a way it never could in Mississippi.

The Bottom Line

The importance of the South for America means that its political transformation holds the central lever for transforming the United States as a whole. The key, I argue, to transforming the South today as in the past lies in the ability of its workers to organize themselves collectively, especially across racial, ethnic, and gender lines. The last great chance to do this occurred during the 1930s, 1940s, and 1950s. It is this period that I propose we examine (at least in broad outline).

Could the South Have Been Organized During the 1930s, 1940s, and 1950s?

What difference would it have made? Well, the question, of course, gnaws at us. Perhaps I am engaged in a fool's errand and the South could not have been organized at all. Even if it had been organized, it might have had a character that was far from transformatory. These are, of course, possibilities to explore. I wish to begin by presenting some brief "stylized facts" that are at least suggestive of the possibilities. Some of these "facts" will be explored in greater detail later.

Alabama Exceptionalism

Alabama, along with Mississippi, South Carolina, Louisiana, and Georgia, was the heart of the Deep South. Controlled by Black Belt plantation owners and their industrial allies in Birmingham, voting for the white supremacist (read "racist") States' Rights "Dixiecrat" presidential candidate Strom Thurmond of South Carolina in 1948, and fervent supporter of its overtly racist governor George Wallace in 1964 and 1968, Alabama seems an unlikely place for interracial liberalism and radicalism to take root. The state was as gerrymandered or "gerry-rigged" in favor of rich white cotton owners—enshrined in the 1901 Alabama state constitution—as any state in the South, and hence the United States. Even in the 1960s, the sixteen hundred whites in Lowndes County (the twenty-three thousand Blacks there, as in much of Alabama, were completely disenfranchised), for example, had equal representation at the state level to the half-million citizens living in Jefferson County, which included Birmingham. Lynchings, chain gangs, and rigid segregation were part of the scene.

Yet in 1946, when the left populist James ("Big Jim") Folsom, endorsed by the Congress of Industrial Organizations (CIO), was elected governor, the ever-optimistic *Nation* declared Alabama "the most liberal state in the South" (Mezerik 1947). While Folsom was a bit unique, even in Alabama, he was not alone. Alabama had a history of electing relatively pro-labor, non-segregationist state-wide candidates, including Senators Hugo Black, Lester Hill, and John Sparkman. Folsom, even in this context, however, stood out. Calling himself the "little man's big friend" (he was six feet, eight inches tall and well over 270 pounds), he was rooted squarely in the tradition of Alabama's hill country radical populist tradition.

Folsom, in contrast to most other southern governors, not only argued for more opportunities for Blacks, but explicitly stated that "race was a phony issue, a ploy used by the rich and powerful to divide poor people and blind them to their common interests" (Carter 1995:75). He opposed the poll tax and argued that all African-Americans in Alabama should have the right to vote. He made a point of welcoming African-Americans to his campaign rallies, shaking hands with them the same as everyone else. And even as the storm of white backlash was enveloping Alabama, along with the rest of the South, in November 1955 Folsom (who had been elected for a second term as governor in 1954) not only invited flamboyant African-American Harlem Congressman Adam Clayton Powell to the statehouse, but had a limousine pick him up at the airport and was photographed in the governor's mansion drinking scotch with him. He called the nearly unanimous resolution of the Alabama legislature—declaring the 1954 *Brown vs. Board of Education Supreme Court* decision (which unanimously ruled that school segregation was unconstitutional) null and void in Alabama—to be "a bunch of hogwash" (Strong 1972:449–50). I am not, of course, suggesting that Folsom was a militant civil rights activist or consistent integrationist, but merely that he was well outside the Dixiecrat consensus that ruled much of southern politics at the time.

So why did Alabama—a hardcore, Deep South, Dixiecrat state—appear for a time to be so different from other southern states? It, of course, had its share of up-country whites, who chafed at the rule of their state by the Dixiecrats and their allies and who had no particular use for white supremacy. Many of these up-country areas had historically opposed the Black Belt plantation owners. They had opposed secession and often fought for the Union during the Civil War, supported the Populists in the 1890s, and even voted for the Socialist candidate Eugene Debs for president in 1912 and 1920. Yet this hardly made them unique in the South, nor were their numbers particularly high compared with those in other states. Let me suggest that what made Alabama exceptional was that in the 1940s it was the most unionized state in the South. Union membership had increased from approximately seventy-thousand in 1933 to over two hundred thousand in 1945, more than 25% of the labor force in that year. To put this in perspective, the percentage of workers unionized in Alabama in 1945 was higher than the percentage of union workers in any state in the United States today. The labor movement in Alabama was centered in the Birmingham area, the stronghold of the United Mine Workers of America (UMWA), who had already shown their strength in 1928 by leading a coalition that successfully abolished convict labor in the state. The roughly twenty-three thousand unionized coal miners in Alabama were clearly the vanguard of the labor movement, aiding the organization of all other workers across the state in the 1930s, including steelworkers, woodworkers, textile workers, schoolteachers, and even principals in one county. They were joined by others in the Birmingham area, including steelworkers and metal mine workers, tens of thousands strong. There were also industrial enclaves across the state where textile and other factory workers were organized, including Gadsden and Huntsville. Workers in shipbuilding and those who worked for the federally run Tennessee Valley Authority centered in Muscle Shoals, Alabama, were fully organized. Finally, longshoremen in Alabama—95% of whom were Black—were organized, including those in Mobile, Alabama's largest port. Unionized areas during the 1930s and 1940s consistently supported more liberal, pro-labor, non-segregationist candidates and voiced opposition to poll taxes. Thus, the high level of union membership in Alabama is suggestive of the degree to which further unionization of Alabama and the South as a whole might have politically transformed the region.

A similar story could be told of Louisiana, where the left populist-oriented Long regime rejected strong segregationist stances. Earl Long, who was reelected governor in 1950, opposed the White Citizen's Councils, had a position similar to Folsom's on racial issues, supported Black enfranchisement, and allowed Louisiana State University's New Orleans branch, opened in 1958, to enroll one thousand whites and two hundred Blacks, making it "the only educational institution in the South to be integrated" at the time (Bartley 1995:207–208). In 1956, the Long supporters successfully led the repeal of Louisiana's right-to-work law, making it the only former Confederate state without such legislation. Among the strongest supporters of the Long faction were workers in the highly unionized cities of New Orleans, Baton Rouge, and Bogalusa.

There are, of course, numerous other, perhaps lesser examples of similar activity. The point of these stories is twofold. First, they indicate that militant, often interracial unionism was possible during our period, even in the states of the Deep South. Second, they suggest that large-scale unionization often made an important political difference.

The real question is, then, why was the rest of the South not like Alabama? If it had been, what difference would that have made? My overriding thesis is that American politics today is understandable only in the context of—or to put it more strongly, is largely derivative from the failures of interracial labor organizing in the South as a whole during the 1930s to 1950s. The legacy of these failures is what makes the South distinctive today. It is the place where large numbers of whites, including many workers, are disproportionately racist; where large percentages of whites are birthers, believe President Barack Obama was a Muslim, and are anti-immigrant; where racial appeals have been most effective; and where people were

more likely than other Americans to have voted for Donald Trump. It is the transformation of the South that is the key, if you will, to transforming the United States
of America.

I wish to begin by giving a road map of the chapters that follow and my rationale
for the order in which they proceed. Chapter 1 is largely theoretical, exploring some
of the recurring themes in our story. It presents my view of how best to do careful social science in a rigorous manner, how to examine large-scale theories, why the unit
of analysis must be quite broad, as well as what role counterfactual analysis plays. It
also highlights and explains some of the key themes of the book. These include the
centrality of the economy, the importance of leadership for social movements, how
such movements tend to grow, and most centrally the ways that groups of workers
can potentially exert power in society.

Chapter 2, on the coal miners, places their struggles and attempts to form a stable
union in an international context. Coal miners everywhere were militant, prone to
strike, and open to radical political views, and they had broad class perspectives
about their role in supporting and developing the overall workers' movement. They
also had enormous structural power, which they used when they finally became
organized. Even so, the intense repression by employers and the state, especially
in West Virginia, undermined their organizations until the 1930s upsurge. When
coal miners finally did organize, they did not do so, contrary to the views of virtually all other analysts, because of the passage of laws (especially Section 7(a) of
the National Industrial Recovery Act) that allegedly facilitated their efforts, but
as a result of a nationwide explosion of mineworkers' organizing, based on their
experiences in the 1920s and their escalating strikes in the 1929–33 period, before
the New Deal. Coal miners, then, provided the stimulus and support to aid virtually every other group of workers. I analyze the seemingly enigmatic John L. Lewis,
president of the United Mine Workers of America (UMWA) and the CIO, in terms
of the economics of the coal industry, placing him in the context of other UMWA
presidents, finally showing how the degeneration of the UMWA into a thuggish
company union must be understood in terms of the changing economics of the industry and the leadership choices of a conservative Lewis.

Chapter 3 looks at the various social movements that gave added strength to
union organizing campaigns.

Chapter 4, on the woodworkers, examines how one of the largest industries
in the United States, whose workers had important structural power, was not organized in the South, due largely to the incompetence and backwardness of one of
the most provincial leadership groups of the 1930s. These leaders were installed
by the CIO national office, replacing a popular, democratically elected, left-wing
leadership group. This chapter also makes clear that attacks on the left, especially
on Communists, did not begin during the post–World War II period, as many
have claimed, but rather in the late 1930s. The possibilities for organizing southern
woodworkers, at least half of whom were African-American, were evident at the

time even to many more conservative activists. If organization had taken place, it might have dramatically strengthened and changed the orientation of the later southern civil rights movement.

Chapter 5, on the steelworkers, highlights several important points. Among these are the difficulties of takeoff in steel (compared with virtually all other industries), due mainly to the size of individual enterprises and the enormous power and resources that steel companies were willing to use to prevent unionism. Yet when breakthroughs did take place, steelworkers, contrary to the claims of many analysts, were among the most militant of union-minded workers. Complementing their structural power was the use of various allies to aid the initial organizing, the use of support from nearby, already organized coal miners, support and aid from organizations of African-Americans and ethnic and immigrant groups, and the formation of important strategic alliances with the Communist Party and its numerous working-class activists. The enigma that the chapter addresses is how a seemingly broad class view of organizing in the early period of the union was transformed into an authoritarian, repressive, racially backward organization under its president, Philip Murray, mirroring the subsequent fate of the labor movement as a whole.

Chapter 6 focuses on the textile industry, where workers usually had little structural power. Textile workers' struggles and attempts to form organizations are briefly examined internationally. It is found that textile workers were rarely successful except in those instances where they had broad associative power. Leadership groups historically failed to comprehend this situation, from the old American Federation of Labor, the Hillman leadership group of the 1930s, and later. These leaders drastically misread the situation. Their failures and strategies can fruitfully be compared with those in steel, which this chapter attempts to do.

Chapter 7 in part extends the analysis of the textile industry to the post–World War II attempt by the CIO to organize the South, Operation Dixie. In contrast to most other scholarship (including previous work of my own), the chapter makes a number of comparisons to fully understand the campaign and to flesh out its main characteristics. It argues that, contrary to previous claims, the resources committed to Operation Dixie were merely a fraction of those committed to the 1936–37 campaign to organize the steel industry and the campaign of the Textile Workers Organizing Committee (TWOC) in 1937–38. Thus, Operation Dixie is no longer considered an important turning point (as I suggest in my earlier work), but merely a coda indicating the failures and declining fortunes of the labor movement, already apparent in 1946 and 1947. The state of the labor movement is also reflected in that Operation Dixie presents itself as a manual on how *not* to organize workers successfully, a manual that most of today's unions have largely followed.

Chapter 8 looks at the Communist Party, its strengths and weaknesses, its major role in stimulating and leading many of the most important social movements and labor struggles, as well as its role in advancing the struggle against racial oppression. It also tries to understand how some of the Party's changing perspectives helped undermine and even at times destroy much of the work it had played such an important role in developing.

The concluding chapter looks at how the failures (and smaller successes) of southern labor organizing have helped shape the terrain in the present or, as the title of this book suggests, have provided a key to an in-depth understanding of the politics and much else that is important in the United States today. First and foremost was the shaping of the civil rights movement of the 1950s, 1960s, and 1970s in the South. Second was the special contour of post–World War II southern politics. The chapter tries to explain the major role these events and failures played in keeping the country mired in the politics and values of a racially backward South, and to speculate about how things might have been different. The chapter also offers some suggestions for the future.

1

Rigor in Historical Analysis

Who built the seven gates of Thebes?
The books are filled with names of kings.
Was it the kings who hauled the craggy blocks of stone?
Berthold Brecht, *A Worker Reads History*, 1935

Much of my previous research has been an attempt to understand the peculiarities of U.S. politics (e.g., Goldfield 1987, 1989, 1997). I have argued in the past that American politics and society in general were often shaped by critical turning points in American history. These critical turning points include (1) the colonial period, when African slavery became the dominant form of agricultural labor in the South; (2) the American Revolution/founding decades; (3) the Civil War and Reconstruction; (4) the defeat of the Populists in the 1890s; (5) the Depression/New Deal era; (6) and the 1950s to 1970s civil rights movement. Specifically, I have argued that questions of race and the successes and failures of labor movements were critical to each of the turning points (Goldfield 1997). It is my contention that much of what is important in American politics and society today, including many of the successes and failures of the civil rights movement, was shaped by events that took place during the 1930s and 1940s. It is the failure of interracial labor organizing to extend itself more fully in the U.S. South during this period that provides the framework for understanding the United States today.

I argue that the successes and failures, strengths and weaknesses of labor and social movements, as well as various leadership groupings, especially those on the left, are critical to understanding the sweep of history. This is not, however, a call for a mere "bottom-up" reading of history. In his *18th Brumaire of Louis Bonaparte*, an analysis of the French counterrevolution of 1848, Karl Marx asserts that "men make their own history, but they do not make it just as they please; they do not make it under circumstances chosen by themselves" (Marx [1852] 1963:103). What, then, are these circumstances that constrain and structure human action?

The Southern Key. Michael Goldfield, Oxford University Press (2020) © Michael Goldfield
DOI: 10.1093/oso/9780190079321.001.0001

The Centrality of the Economy

It is my hypothesis that one must first start with the economy—not merely the structure of capitalism itself, but both general and specific features. Some cases will illustrate the point. First, the ups and downs of the economy provide a framework in which mass movements grow and decline. To take one example, discussed in my chapter on social movements: Despite the hardships that unemployment imposed on many workers during the 1920s, Communist efforts to organize the unemployed met with meager results. After the collapse of the stock market in 1929, however, and with it the tremendous loss of jobs and wages, the struggles of unemployed workers and of other social movements grew rapidly and achieved mass proportions nationally. It was a confirmation of what Billie Holiday once said: "People do not know when they have had enough until they have had more than enough" (Holiday with Duffy 1956:155). Conversely, even in those industries that were difficult or virtually impossible to organize during normal times (e.g., the textile industry), full employment and labor shortages, as during World War I, provided the context of successful organizing of the textile industry, including throughout the South. Alternatively, the Roosevelt recession beginning in late 1937 sapped organizing in every industry, until the wartime recovery began in late 1939. Thus, the general state of the economy and labor markets is an important framework to be examined if one wants to fully understand the trajectory of mass movements.

Second, each of my industry chapters begins with a lengthy analysis of the structure of the industry, including a wide range of factors, among which are capital requirements, technology, skill levels, and mobility. Some may find such an emphasis diversionary. Yet in order to understand the possibilities for organizing, it is not culture, paternalism, religion, or individual attitudes that one must address first, however important they might or might not turn out to be. For instance, I have done a lengthy examination of the economics and structure of the textile industry over the course of several centuries in eight major countries (a brief summary of which appears in the chapter on the textile industry). I find that the nature of labor struggles in these countries follows similar patterns with a few noticeable exceptions. Southern U.S. textile labor struggles turn out to be typical of textile labor struggles worldwide, despite many enormous cultural differences between countries. Thus, those many hundreds of analysts who examine southern culture as a key determinant of the unionization (or not) of southern textile workers most likely have it backward. Similarly, U.S. coal miners, despite their existence in cultures that were often similar to those of textile workers, and who experienced repression at least as extreme, both in the South and nationally, were able to organize successfully, like their compatriots in numerous other countries. Looking at the economics and structure of an industry is the place to start. Not doing this leaves analysts trying to see the landscape through a permanent heavy fog. There are indeed peculiarities of southern culture, as my introduction has noted, but this is never the place to start. A materialist, structural analysis must take precedence.

Third, and most important, money interests dominate politics in all capitalist societies. As many have noted, they have disproportionate influence and ultimate control. Yet this is not a reform issue that can be solved by controlling campaign finance and lobbying or overturning Citizens United, as many liberals claim. This control is at the very center of capitalist societies; in Marx's prosaic words, the state functions as the "committee for managing the common affairs of the whole bourgeoisie" (Marx and Engels 1948:11). This also extends to the so-called free press or, as in a quote attributed to A. J. Liebling (1960) but cribbed from Socialist Party leader Eugene Debs, "Freedom of the press is guaranteed only to those who own one." Thus, in all capitalist societies, the terrain is shaped, except in very exceptional moments, by the dominance of capitalist interests.[1] The debates about whether this control is direct (i.e., instrumental), indirect, or peripheral I find distracting. It is exercised in various ways, sometimes easily, sometimes with great difficulty. In certain venues, as I show with the steel and wood industries, some of the influence is very direct. But even when it is not, there is often, as even Robert Dahl argued in his later work, a veto power of capital (Manley 1983:370, 380).

The role of the state is many-sided, involving not merely making society safe and hospitable for capital. Both liberals and conservatives tend to underplay its role in repressing democratic movements, especially with respect to labor. Many tend to see such events as the 1919 Palmer raids, the McCarthy period, and the targeting of radical and Black groups in the 1960s and 1970s as anomalies, exceptions, rather than systematic, regular occurrences (Goldstein 1978). Liberals and conservatives also tend to exaggerate the degree to which the state facilitates the flowering of mass movements, underplaying the ability of workers and others to organize without legal encouragement. My coal chapter illustrates both these points graphically, especially the growth of coal miner unionism, allegedly facilitated by New Deal legislation.

Methodology, Historical Analysis, and Philosophy of Social Science

With these preliminary remarks, I now want to address some methodological questions. Can there be rigor in examining broad social science questions, especially those that are historical? I would like to suggest that there can be. For our set of questions, there are two components.

---

[1] I find the targeting of the top 1% a populist distraction, for the overwhelming majority of those in this stratum, despite their affluence, have very little control over the economy or politics. Those with the real power—the capitalist class—are a tiny fraction of this category, and it is their role that must be understood (Manning 2017).

For the first, I draw on philosopher of science Imre Lakatos's notion of competing research programs. For the second, I look at counterfactual analysis, especially for the question of whether the South could have been organized. I also use this analysis to look at the counterfactual, if the South had been organized, what difference might that have made? And, finally, given that it was not, what conclusions can we draw?

Lakatos argues that paradigmatic theories in the physical sciences are essentially research programs, with a core and a series of interlocking supporting hypotheses. Theories or research programs are not proved or disproved by Popperian principles of falsification (Popper 2002). Rather, research programs are considered largely correct in their competition with other research programs, each of which thrives or eventually gets discarded due to its greater or lesser ability to account for accepted facts.

Thus, in the competition between the Ptolemaic (earth-centered) model of the universe and the Copernican model of the solar system (where the planets revolve around the sun), it became increasingly difficult for the former model to account for the new empirical observations of sixteenth-century astronomers. The Ptolemaic model became less and less useful as a heuristic for understanding and predicting, while the Copernican model became more and more efficient at explaining and predicting the findings of astronomers. Subhypotheses of the Ptolemaic system had to be continually rejected and replaced, while the Copernican model was sharpened and made more efficient (Lakatos 1970:132–38, 154–77 for his full argument). The research program that I offer is laid out in a series of interrelated hypotheses, which are tested to greater or lesser degrees in each chapter. Accordingly, the research program presented here is to be judged on whether it better fits and explains the facts than other approaches do.[2] My hypotheses are as follows.

First is the centrality of the economy for an analysis of the labor movement and society in general, as already discussed. An important caveat to be stressed, as Engels notes, is that just because the economy is primary does not mean that certain cultural factors do not at times take on a life of their own and even cause changes in the economy (this point is particularly salient when one is dealing with questions of race; Engels [1893] 1988). But, in general, I argue against the currently popular culturalism as a primary mode of analysis.

---

[2] There is, of course, a broad recent philosophy of social science literature from which I have gained important insights, many of whose issues I do not directly address here. Among this literature is the work of Kincaid (1996, 2012), who argues that social science research is based on principles similar to those in the natural sciences, and hence is open to rigorous causal analysis, and Little (2016), who argues that it is different, not subject to the same type of apodictic conclusions. Also useful is Groff (2008), especially her introduction, and Engelskirchen (2011). Much contemporary debate hinges on the existence of natural kinds (law-abiding entities with similar causal structures) and whether there are similar social kinds. The most penetrating writing in this genre is that of Richard Boyd (2010).

Second is the complex role of laws and the state under capitalism, whose influence on mass movements tends to be overemphasized, especially when accorded primary causality in the development and spread of mass labor and social movements.
In much of my previous work, I have suggested that those who give primacy to the
laws with respect to the importance of the 1935 National Labor Relations (Wagner)
Act for the growth of industrial unionism have it wrong (Goldfield 1989b, 1990a).
I have made an even stronger argument with respect to the growth of public sector
unions in the United States during the 1960s and 1970s (Goldfield 1989a, 1990b).
In my discussion of coal miners, I also argue, on the basis of archival evidence, that
those who give primacy to the importance of Section 7(a) of the National Industrial
Recovery Act have distorted history.

Third is my hypothesis about how movements grow, often requiring background
conditions and stimulating causes, but thereafter needing no further causal agents,
certainly not on a macro level, an approach I first attempted to lay out in detail in the
late 1980s (see, e.g., Goldfield 1989a, b).

Fourth is the role of leadership in determining the character of these movements,
how successful they are, and ultimately whether they continue to grow and become more radical, or whether they lapse into harmless or relatively mainstream
enterprises. As a subset of this analysis, I try to clarify, and extend earlier analysis in
previous writings, about the nature of trade unionism and the various competing
leadership camps within the labor movement, from narrow American Federation
of Labor (AFL) craft unions to the competition within the Congress of Industrial
Organizations (CIO) between liberal (self-proclaimed right-wing) leadership
groups and those farther left, especially the Communists.

Fifth is the question of causal analysis, related to the preceding hypothesis.

Sixth is the suggestion that broad analysis must have a large unit of analysis, often
the whole world over a long period of time, and that it must be comparative to be
compelling.

Seventh is the central role of the South, discussed earlier.

None of these hypotheses should be taken as systematic imperatives alone, nor
do they obviate the need for hard research and intellectual work. Science itself, according to Ernest Mandel in the introduction to his magisterial *Marxist Economic
Theory*, quoting a Dr. Bronowski, chair of the British Association, says, "Science is
not a set of facts but a way of giving order, and giving unity and intelligibility to the
facts of nature" (Mandel 1968:19), which is the goal here.

Counterfactuals

I have drawn selectively on the philosophical and social science literature on counterfactual analysis to provide a framework for examining the role played by southern

labor organizing in the shaping of U.S. politics and society. Some of this is suggested in the introduction, in my analysis of the state of Alabama.[3]

Hawthorne in particular argues compellingly that all historical explanations in the human sciences involve discussions of alternative "possibilities" (1991:xi). He examines a large variety of "What if?" scenarios, from what if the Moors had won in Spain in the fifteenth century?, to what if workers had won the 1926 general strike in the United Kingdom, to what if Trotsky had not fallen ill during his early struggles with Stalin, Kamenev, Zinoviev, and Bukharin in the Soviet Union? (1991:2–8). He also examines Fogel's arguments on the U.S. Civil War, including what if the North had allowed the South to secede?, or what if Lee had won at Gettysburg? This may be sufficient for a start, but it fails to deal with a differentiation of different types of causes. Certain causes are indeed serendipitous, like Trotsky's illness or the heavy storm that contributed to the defeat of the Spanish Armada in 1588. Other causes, however, go deeper. Max Weber in his *Methodology of the Social Sciences* (1949), for example, also argues for counterfactual analysis "if history is to be raised above the level of a mere chronicle of notable events and personalities" (1949:164). Yet Weber also makes the important distinction between proximal causes and deeper causes. He discusses the Berlin uprising that led to the 1848 revolution in Prussia. The spark or proximal cause was a rumor that a group of soldiers had fired into a peacefully protesting crowd, perhaps killing civilians. But this cause must be downgraded, according to Weber, since the situation was such that almost "any accident" would have caused the conflict to break out. A similar argument might be made about the 1967 Detroit rebellion/riot. The proximal cause of raiding a blind pig after hours was the spark, but the rebellion had deeper causes. I would also suggest that with respect to deeper causes, some possibilities are more plausible than others. Marx, for example, argues that the victory of the North in the Civil War was largely inevitable, despite the early ineptitude of its military leaders and the strategic skill of the Confederate generals. The overwhelming advantages of population and economic might of the North were sure to dominate in the end. And once the Emancipation Proclamation was issued by President Lincoln on January 1, 1863, the inevitable became even more so (Marx and Engels 1969).

In examining the possible "What ifs?" of southern labor organizing, I wish to separate out those factors that appear to be mere contingencies, those that are proximal causes, those that seem inevitable and unlikely to be reversed, and those that rely on decisions and approaches, especially of leaders, that could in principle have been different.

---

[3] In this respect, I have found especially useful philosophical discussions in Putnam (1978), Lewis (1973, 1986, esp. 1–80), and Hawthorne (1991). In addition, I have benefited greatly from Miller (1987, esp. 60–105). See also Morgan and Winship (2015).

Units of Analysis

An issue that arises concerns the proper unit of analysis for examining these questions. For many contemporary social sciences (among others, economics, political science, and behavioral psychology) the basic unit is often an idealized, rational-choice, decision-making individual. It is the accumulation of individual choices that determines larger aspects, including the development of labor and other social movements, as well as the broader movement of the economy. I have criticized this view in other places and do not plan to revisit it here (Goldfield and Gilbert 1995). To understand the particular fate of southern labor in the 1930s and 1940s, one must cast a broader net (Little 2016).

By necessity, we must stray a good bit from directly examining the immediate topic at hand. Labor movements cannot be examined effectively in one locale or area (as much of the labor history and sociology literature does, with certain notable exceptions). Southern labor struggles and unions must be analyzed within the context of the national movement as a whole, even, often the whole North American labor movement, and the broad organizing strategies of unions. Even Canada at times looms large, which is especially true for woodworkers. To truly comprehend labor organizing in the South, one must often put the situation in an international context, comparing industries across many countries, as well, of course, as studying the specificity of each situation. A tall order, to be sure. Thus, with respect to coal, I look at the worldwide struggles of coal miners. For textiles, I look at struggles in other countries, arguing that the structure of the industry places universal constraints on textile workers that shape outcomes, having little to do with culture, religion, southern paternalism, or the specific nature of southern repression. This approach, which, I suggest, is far more illuminating, implicitly targets what I consider the poverty of the highly popular cultural turn in historical analysis.

What Explains the Variance in Social Movements?

I wish to first examine the large degree of variance in social movements, especially labor movements, in different times and places. Deciding what is possible during periods of militant labor upsurge and extensive trade union growth requires a brief discussion of the nature of trade unions in capitalist societies.[4]

Contrary to the views of many neoclassical economists, individual workers, except under atypical circumstances, have little leverage with their employers. Conflicts of interests between workers and their employers are inherent and take place on numerous levels. Most fundamentally, employers, whatever their

---

[4] For my more extended analysis and further references, see Goldfield (1987:56–75).

intentions, however magnanimous their feelings toward their employees, are in intense competition with other employers. Employers each wish to expand their market share and increase their profits by offering comparable or superior products or services at competitive prices. To do this, they generally want more productivity and more work from their workers at less pay. This pressure from the market affects most industries and their workers directly but is especially pressing in more labor-intensive ones. Individual workers are usually at the mercy of their employers and quite often resort to forming unions to gain some degree of leverage.[5]

The early stages of capitalism have universally been characterized by what I have called "trade union illegality." Trade union illegality is a de facto state based on the unwillingness of companies and the government to fully accept the rights of workers to be represented collectively by an organization of their own, whatever the extent of de jure trade union rights. Under conditions of trade union illegality, not only do the laws often make it difficult for unions to function, but even companies' illegal actions against them are often overlooked by the government. These illegal actions by capitalists are accepted because unions are de facto illegal. Periods of trade union illegality have existed in the early phases of capitalist development in all major capitalist countries and continue to exist today in many places. In some countries, at certain times, the trade union rights demanded by workers (the right to organize, to bargain collectively, to be dealt with in a legal, non-arbitrary manner by the employer, the right to strike) have been insurrectionary.

Under conditions of trade union illegality, struggles are often quite intense. Organizational survival, the livelihoods of many leaders and activists, and some-times even their lives are at stake. The possibilities for class collaboration and trade union narrowness (i.e., narrow interest group activity) are more limited. Workers and their unions are often more willing to ally themselves with and take support from radical groups. One key dimension of the 1930s and 1940s in the United States was the struggle for trade union legality, what Antonio Gramsci calls the "industrial legal order."[6]

The acceptance of trade union legality marks a major change in the day-to-day relations between workers and capitalists. The establishment of the National Labor Relations Board (NLRB) in 1935 and its upholding in 1937 by the U.S. Supreme Court marked a legal turning point in the history of U.S. labor–capital relations. It reflected the emerging recognition by the government and major capitalists in the United States that trade unions were legitimate institutions. The establishment of the NLRB was the product of large-scale social unrest in general and of intense struggles by workers (Goldfield 1989b, 1990a). This de jure recognition of trade

[5] Much of what follows here, with some minor changes and enhancements, is cribbed from Goldfield (1987).

[6] See Gramsci's incisive discussion in L'Ordine Nuovo, June 5, 1920, reprinted in his *Political Writings* (1910–20); see also Lawrence and Wishart (1977:265–68).

union rights was not yet—but only the beginning of—de facto recognition of trade union legality in major industrial areas of the United States.

I use the term "trade union legality" to describe the general acceptance by both employers and employees (through their unions) of a certain degree of orderliness in their relations, involving both rights and obligations. The capitalist recognizes the union, bargains with it, and accepts grievance claims. The union guarantees that its members respect their contractual obligations, including the forgoing of the right to strike over every grievance.

It should be emphasized that trade union legality is related to, although not at all coincident with, the labor laws that govern labor–capital relations. This distinction is important. Coal miners, I argue in the next chapter, fully organized and largely gained acceptance of their unions in 1933, not merely before the 1935 National Labor Relations Act (NLRA), but even before the passage of the 1933 National Industrial Recovery Act, which included the largely symbolic section 7(a), asserting the right to form unions. On the other hand, southern textile owners (among others) refused to accept trade union legality, even during World War II, when the government unsuccessfully tried to demand it of them. That being said, it was the CIO upsurge from 1937 to 1941, the period of organizing of basic industry, that marked the general acceptance of trade union legality by U.S. capitalists.

In order for capitalists to accept trade union legality, unions must be organized on a national scale with demonstrated power to disrupt major sectors of the economy. This acceptance, however, is a compromise between workers (and their unions) and capitalists. The capitalists provide organizational stability for the union and, thus, some consistency in wages and benefits (the price of labor power) and working conditions. The unions in return restrain the disruptive tendencies of the organized workforce and help the capitalists discipline the workers in various ways. The contradictory nature of trade unions under capitalism arises from their dual role as joint upholders of the class compromise of trade union legality and as representatives of the trade union (and occasionally more radical) demands of their members.

This structure of ambivalence pervades the union hierarchy from top to bottom, albeit in different ways. Even without no-strike clauses and involvement in punitive discipline of workers (which weights the compromise even more heavily on the side of the capitalists), the union must attend to the "interests" of the company. The national leadership must know the "reservation price" of the company, both for normal bargaining situations and for strike confrontations (e.g., at contract times), being sure not to raise the stakes so high as to precipitate a fight to the death.

Accommodating leaderships aim much lower, often not to offend at all. Industrial legality requires the maintenance of the "goodwill" of the employer and the state.

At the local level, even the most militant shop steward is affected by this compromise. Aggressive stewards with organized constituents can often gain more for their members than passive representatives can. Yet even the militant steward knows or comes to know that there is a line somewhere, no matter how vague its exact location, beyond which the company will give in on nothing and will quickly respond with repression (often in alliance with local and even national union officials). This line, of course, may drastically change its location depending on the militancy of the national union, the degree of broader support, and the general level of working-class turbulence—but it is always there.

The winning of trade union legality is a highly positive, yet contradictory victory for workers. They undoubtedly gain more strength in the labor market, where their greater numbers allow them to obtain better terms in the sale of their labor power. Unionized workers in the United States, all other things being equal, have higher wages and benefits, as well as safer work environments (see Goldfield and Bromsen 2013; see also additional summaries of literature in Ahlquist 2017).

In general, unionized workers have more democratic rights, and consequently more dignity. The seniority that is written into virtually all union contracts regarding job promotions, job rights, layoffs, and vacations, despite its several flaws, gives unionized workers certain protections from arbitrary actions of management. One only has to read the stories of workers before industrial unions existed—about the type of favoritism given to obtain and keep better (easier, cleaner, higher-paying) jobs, to get toilet breaks, to keep one's job, to avoid being laid off—to understand the importance of seniority. In many workplaces, bringing the foreman a bottle of liquor, mowing his lawn, or washing his car on a weekend, and, for women, being subjected to sexual violation, were often regular occurrences. Seniority diminishes such indignities (among numerous sources, Stepan-Norris and Zeitlin 1996:54, 58; Bromsen 2011; Meyerowitz 1985: 240–41; Gabin 1990:12–13, 28; Korstad 2003:294–95).

The idea put forward by many free-market theorists (including "right-to-work" advocates), that individual workers have more freedom than unionized workers to deal with and negotiate with their employers, is unconvincing. Unionized workers not only have more bargaining power but are able to be more assertive. In many non-union workplaces, workers are often illegally discharged for filing complaints to government agencies (e.g., Occupational Safety and Health Administration, OSHA; or the Equal Employment Opportunity Commission, EEOC), filing for legally guaranteed workman's compensation when they are injured, or even just complaining, much less actually talking in favor of a union to their co-workers.[7] The greater voice unionized workers have in the workplace is undoubtedly reflected in

---

[7] The number of workers reinstated for being illegally discharged during an organizing campaign is a very substantial fraction of those voting for a union. In 2007, for example, a worker who just voted for a union had a one in seven chance of being discharged (assuming that those who voted against the union would not be illegally discharged). Thus, workers who spoke for the union publicly or who actively organized for a pro-union vote have a good chance of being illegally discharged in an organizing campaign (Goldfield and Bromsen 2013).

their turnover rates, which are lower than those of non-union workers (Freeman and Medoff 1984:103–107; Hirschman 1970).

Unions' inherently contradictory tendencies, however, depend on an aroused and vigilant membership to keep the organization and its leaders from continually narrowing their focus and from accommodating employers to a greater and greater extent. When southern textile workers, for example, voiced their main demand as opposition to the "stretchout" (i.e., huge increases in workloads) in the events leading up to the 1934 general textile strike, national union officials and their liberal allies continued to insist that the main issue was really wages and that "stretchout" was a myth (Irons 2000:106–107, passim).

On the other hand, unions are the most powerful force in counterbalancing the unrestrained rule of capital in all aspects of modern society. It is only labor upheavals that have brought us the eight-hour day, the NLRA, and other benefits to workers. And it was the strength and militancy of unionized West Virginia coal miners in 1970 that forced the expansion of coal mine safety, first on the state government and eventually on Congress and the Nixon White House (Fry 2010:7, 177, 248, 275).

More broadly, it is no accident that in those countries where labor unions and labor parties are stronger, social welfare benefits, including pensions, universal health care, fuller unemployment insurance, etc., exist. As unions weaken, OSHA and workers' safety are weakened, regulations on banks and financial institutions become lax, and taxes become more skewed toward the rich (Goldfield 1987:27–32; Wilensky 2002), phenomena that are the staple of current political life.

Dahl and Lindblom ([1953] 2017) suggest that unions play a democratic role in capitalist societies, that without a large organized working class, there is no challenge to the unrestrained control of business over all aspects of society, including the political arena. Paradoxically, it is only in the context of extensive union organization that broad forms of solidarity and class struggle can emerge. Unions give workers more self-assurance in speaking out, defying authority, and engaging in collective actions, even when their leaders are hesitant. This capability is especially apparent in times of crisis.

Workers' Power and Leverage: What Explains the Variance in Power and Leverage That Different Groups of Workers Have?

Workers' Power

Two central questions arise: what allows workers to have power in a capitalist society, and why do some groups of workers seem to have more leverage than others? By "power," I mean here the ability of individuals, groups of workers, or a whole class to realize their interests, either narrowly (e.g., a small wage increase or improved working conditions), broadly, or completely. As a starting point, I have drawn on the seminal works of Erik Olin Wright (2000) and Beverly Silver (2003).

Silver, following Wright, distinguishes between structural power and associational power (Silver 2003:13; Wright 2000:962). Structural power is that power that workers have solely on the basis of their relation to the economic system. Structural power consists of two main types. First is that power which results strictly from the labor market. How easily can workers be replaced? Certain highly skilled workers are difficult to replace, at any time. This would be true of skilled electricians and plumbers on construction projects, but also all-star home-run hitters and pro-bowl quarterbacks. The services of these workers become even more precious when there is competition for their labor. Competing sports leagues, for example, at times have created a premium for the most skilled athletes, often dramatically raising their salaries. As the sports labor market becomes international, this competition increases, as one can see today in sports like soccer and to a lesser extent in hockey, basketball, and baseball. Even workers with lower-level skills, however, may be difficult to replace when they stick together in full solidarity. Thus, when then-President Richard Nixon attempted to replace striking New York City postal workers in 1970 with National Guard troops, the ineffectiveness of the latter in handling the mail forced the president to capitulate. The skills of coal miners are difficult to replace, except by other miners. Thus, when large numbers strike and experienced miners cannot be found as replacements, strikers have a great deal of leverage. When coal miners struck during World War II, they declared correctly that one could not mine coal with bayonets. Less skilled workers can at times be easily replaced. Yet when the labor market is tight—that is, when there are few available workers due to very low unemployment (as was the case in many industries during World Wars I and II)—even these workers become difficult to replace, and the leverage of all organized workers increases.

While not absolutely distinct from labor market leverage, the type of leverage that workers have because of their location in the economic system, namely their workplace bargaining power, is worth identifying. This has several dimensions. Certain groups of workers have the ability, when they stop work, to cause their employers or even the whole society a great deal of grief. Manufacturing workers—for example, those making certain products, or even those in key departments—have the ability at times to shut down a whole employer, or even a whole manufacturing industry. Workers at Boeing in Seattle have had the ability to postpone the delivery of the latest aircraft, a reason the company has developed a backup non-union facility in South Carolina. This has also historically been true of automobile workers making certain components that are manufactured at only one location (sometimes brakes or engines). Then there are workers whose broad strikes would threaten to bring the whole economy to a standstill. In the nineteenth century, railroad workers occasionally exercised this power. Truck drivers and airline employees have this potential power but have never used it. Coal miners during the 1930s and 1940s had this power (which they no longer have today) and at times used it. At the other end of the spectrum, university professors—though they may have highly specialized, irreplaceable skills—have very little workplace leverage. When they go on strike, they may shut down a university (on the off-chance they all stick together), but the people they mainly inconvenience, at least in the short term, are their students, themselves not powerful economic actors. I use the concept of associational power in a slightly different way than Silver and Wright. Associational power comes from the support of various allies in one's struggles. These allies can be other workers and unions, outside groups, whether racial, ethnic, or immigrant organizations, students, community activists, political organizations, or a myriad of other forces. All workers gain additional power from having broader support. Some groups, however, need this outside support much more than others. For those workers without a large amount of structural leverage (be they easily replaced textile workers or others), associational power is essential.

In various chapters, I attempt to show how the support of other groups— whether other unions or various outside groups—was often critical to successful organizing. The support of unemployed groups in numerous workers' struggles was ubiquitous; it was of central importance, for example, in the 1934 strikes in Toledo, Ohio, Minneapolis, and San Francisco, as well as in the organizing of workers in the steel and wood industries. The support of organized coal miners—the vanguard of the 1930s movements—was important throughout the country, including the South, especially for workers' struggles in numerous industries in Alabama. And the unwillingness of more conservative union leaders to take advantage of potential allies was often a reason for the failures of the campaigns that they led. This unwillingness was decisive in the failure of the CIO's post–World War II Operation Dixie. These themes will be explored more fully with respect to specific industries in the chapter on social movements and throughout the book.

An Alternative Model of Union Growth

Large-scale union growth in the United States and in many other places usually takes place in waves, at times involving many workers across many industries, and led in most cases by those workers who have the most structural power. Such periods of large-scale growth are not well studied.

The methodological individualism assumptions of most social scientists who examine labor union growth tend to lead them astray, into a narrow, empirically dubious view of union growth. Most especially those who use linear regression models to study union growth tend to seek temporal correlates in an attempt to locate causes. Unionization is generally viewed as an unnatural process; one must explain why workers join them initially and why, once the organizations have become viable, workers continue to join and remain in them. Thus, the key task is to find the central explanatory covariates (usually economic) that correlate with periods of growth and decline. Behind this approach is a nagging question: Why do workers break with their normal patterns of life and "preference maximization"? Why do they take the risks that involve potentially high costs to join a union, become active, and go on strike, perhaps risking their jobs and livelihoods? These questions, seemingly plausible to ask, put an overwhelming emphasis on the calculation of costs and benefits by individual workers: though this paradigm is not without its grain of truth, the search for continuously active causal covariates, which are supposedly necessary to sustain the process of union growth, is, I argue, ultimately misplaced.

An alternative paradigm posits labor–management relations as inherently conflictual. It argues that workers generally want more wages and benefits and better working conditions. These natural desires are in opposition to what employers generally want, which is more work, more control, and inferior working conditions (at least when improvements cost money, as they often do) for less money. This calculus, mediated by intervening circumstances for public sector labor–management relations, ultimately applies to both. Thus, workers usually want and almost always need organization, except in the most unique situations of labor market shortage, the possession of rare sets of skills, etc. The question to ask with respect to this alternative paradigm is, hence, not why workers organize, but what holds them back when they do not. And when periodic bursts of organization do take place, the most important question is not necessarily what sustains the process, but rather what allowed it to take off.

What Holds Union Growth Back?

Two interrelated factors hold back the growth of unions. First, the initial development of unions is often thwarted by strong resistance from employers and the government. Unions historically have rarely been accepted initially, even under general conditions of trade union legality. Second, the effectiveness of opposition to unions is enhanced by the structural characteristics of union organizations. As some analysts have noted, unions are different from most other voluntary organizations (Wilson 1973:117). Unions, by their nature, claim either explicitly or implicitly to represent a majority of the workers in a particular unit, be it a skilled division, factory, university, enterprise, company, or industry. Whatever the sentiments of their potential constituency, organizers of new unions generally have problems breaking through the threshold barriers. Once these barriers have been broken, that is, when takeoff has taken place, growth often occurs more or less automatically. Steelworkers, in particular, faced especially high barriers to takeoff, due in good part to the power of the small number of employers in the industry, the large size of the individual workplaces, and the immense amount of resources and lawlessness employers were willing to expend to keep their workforces non-union. In contrast, coal miners faced much lower barriers, engaging in strikes and walkouts far more frequently. And it is for this reason primarily that comparisons of strike rates of miners with those of steelworkers must be done with a great deal of circumspection.

Other organizations (e.g., political parties, business organizations, and neighborhood groups) may have threshold problems too, especially in their attempt to attain initial legitimacy, but they do not have the demands for overwhelmingly majoritarian status built into the life and death of their organizations.

The organizational characteristics are what account for the often-explosive nature of union growth. As a small number of commentators have suggested, labor movements often grow and spread through a series of tremendous leaps, whose particular contours are only indirectly related to short-term economic and other background conditions. John Dunlop, for example, argues:

> Henri Sée, the French historian, used to emphasize that a social movement operates like the wave of the sea eating away at the base of a cliff. For years nothing seems to happen. Then, one day, the side of the cliff falls in. That's the way our labor movement has grown. I remember the day people said you couldn't organize government workers. Then, bingo, in the Sixties and early Seventies the unions got half the state and local employees and two-thirds of the federal employees. Just like that! The labor movement has always grown in surges. (Goldfield 1987:4)[8]

E. J. Hobsbawm comes to similar conclusions in comparing changes in the levels of trade union membership in the United States and Western Europe during the nineteenth and twentieth centuries. He argues that the "periodic and sudden expansions in the size, strength and activity of social movements" are almost always "'jumpy'" and "discontinuous" (1964:150). Often the combustible material and the stock of grievances accumulate over a long period of time; that is, the underlying causes must be separated from the proximal causes. Attempts to apply a cost/benefit analysis to the involvement of workers in these upsurges usually fail. Equally important, as Hobsbawm stresses, is the lack of any useful indices for important factors that affect working-class behavior, such as the intensity and discomfort of work, and the disrespect and arbitrariness of management. In addition, it is not always clear to what degree the accumulated grievances have to affect the whole potentially mobilized constituency. It is not necessary for all to be near the point of spontaneous ignition. Successful actions often stimulate and are imitated by constituencies whose stock of grievances is not nearly so strong. It is never obvious what determines whether a whole sector is ready to ignite (as with the whole public sector in the

---

[8] Thus, Dunlop is one of the few mainstream labor economists who seems to understand the nonlinear process of union growth.

1960s) or whether the upsurge will be limited to one local constituency, as with the highly militant 1946 Buffalo teachers' strike (Goldfield 1989a, 1990b).

The import of seeing the development of unions as a natural process with severe threshold problems is to change the emphasis of what aspect of union growth is considered most important. If unions are unnatural, then the whole process of development and growth is equally important. Yet if union growth is a natural process, held back by structural and oppositional constraints, then the process of takeoff is the most important aspect to examine.

The post-takeoff growth of unions can best be understood as a time-dependent process. Before takeoff actually begins, there is a store of accumulated grievances, desires, and pressures. The upsurge of unionization eventually "takes off," uncapping a large amount of pent-up social energy. A series of initial shocks—successful strikes, victories—starts the process forward, leading to imitation in other geographic areas and in other sectors. The post-takeoff process can be modeled as one of binary diffusion (similar in some respects to the spread of contagious diseases, an essentially exponential, time-dependent process, largely undetermined by other covariates), which is inadequately captured by linear models; union growth during the 1930s (as well as public sector union growth in the 1960s and 1970s) was continually propelled and occasionally set back by new shocks.

Despite their often seemingly rapid spread in times of mass upsurge, unions can take many forms. As suggested earlier, the pressures to accommodate employers are continuous and immense. Unions in all countries where trade union legality exists feel these pressures. But in the United States (where union leaders universally accept the alleged glories of capitalism), business unionism has reached a degree that is rare in other economically developed capitalist countries.

The term "business unionism" most assuredly originated in the United States, the land where the term finds its most ready application. Whether Hyman (1973) is right in attributing it to Hoxie is uncertain, for it was in common use before Hoxie's book on U.S. trade unions was published in 1915 (reprinted in 1966). The usage of this term, however, has varied.

Hoxie uses the term to refer to what many call pure and simple trade unionism, as opposed to either class or revolutionary unionism:

> Business unionism . . . is essentially trade-consciousness, rather than class-consciousness. That is to say, it expresses the viewpoint and interests of workers in a craft or industry rather than those of the working class as a whole. It aims chiefly at more, here and now, for the organized workers of a craft or industry, in terms mainly of higher wages, shorter hours, and better working conditions, regardless for the most part of the welfare of the workers outside the particular organic group, and regardless in general of political and social considerations, except in so far as these bear directly upon its own economic ends. It is conservative in the sense that

it professes belief in natural rights and accepts as inevitable, if not as just, the existing capitalistic organization, the wage system, as well as existing property rights and the binding force of contract. It regards unionism mainly as a bargaining institution. (1966:45)

This view is shared by Eugene Debs (1921), who calls it the "old unionism," contrasting it with the revolutionary industrial unionism of the Industrial Workers of the World (IWW). Daniel De Leon (1921) put forward a similar view in 1919.

With the establishment of widespread industrial unionism in the 1930s and 1940s, a derivative usage developed, which distinguished business unionism from pure and simple unionism. This usage refers to the literal running of a union as a business. Lens (1949, 1959) adopts this usage. There are several ways of running a union as a business. One is based on the view of union leaders that a union must be primarily a solvent financial organization; they see it as a dues collection entity whose major function is to preserve its income, and they discourage the unnecessary depletion of its resources. Such a stance may mean the avoidance of strikes, careful investment of funds, and even alliances with employers to preserve the union's solvency. If the preservation of the business union requires the bureaucratic domination of the membership, the submergence of the rights of the rank and file, whose desires might present organizational risks, then so be it. This view of the union is argued for explicitly in steelworker leaders Clint Golden and Harold Ruttenberg's *Dynamics of Industrial Democracy* (1942).

A second view of business unionism involves not merely the treatment of the union as a business by its leaders, but its operation as a business for the personal enrichment of the leaders, involving high salaries, expense accounts, and occasional swindles with money on the side. Here one sees the willingness of the leaders to sacrifice the business interests of the union for their personal aggrandizement. Gangster-dominated unions are, of course, a subset of this latter type of business unionism. Fitch (2006) argues at great length that gangster unionism is far more common in the United States than most critics acknowledge. None of these forms are pure. Even a gangster-dominated union must occasionally defend the interests of its members. When I refer to business unionism here, I use the term as Lens does, in the sense of running the union as a business. Most unions in the United States fall into this category.

Occasionally, unions see their identity and missions tied to fighting on classwide issues, even during quiescent times. Mosimann and Pontusson (2017) argue, in one of the few systemic studies on the topic, that unions engender solidaristic attitudes that lead members to support broad, pro–working class policies that need not necessarily serve their immediate self-interest. This is especially true in more democratic unions, like the United Electrical Workers (UE) and the International Longshoremen's and Warehouse Union (ILWU), where political debate and participation in the class struggle are actively encouraged (see Stepan-Norris and Zeitlin

2002, esp. 159–88; Ahlquist and Levi 2013). Relatively contemporary examples include the ILWU's opposition to the Vietnam War, its refusal to unload South African ships in protest of apartheid, and, most important, its emphatic support and promotion of interracial equality (Cole and Limb 2017; Cole 2018; ILWU 2014). In times of upheaval, especially when conditions of trade union illegality exist, many unions become quite radical in their pursuit of classwide issues. Examples abound but include the South African Congress of Trade Unions campaign against apartheid, the role of unions in instigating the ouster of Hosni Mubarak in Egypt (contrary to the liberal "internet revolution" narrative), and the recent support of Spanish unions for the Catalonian independence movement, including the Assembly of Stevedores' refusal to allow shiploads of Spanish soldiers and police to dock at the port of Barcelona and the subsequent general strike on October 7, 2017 (Kaboub 2013; Aouragh and Alexander 2011; Strange 2017).

Leadership

While circumstances from structural power to large-scale labor upsurges play a key role, the role of leadership is also important. During the 1930s and 1940s, various leadership groups vied for power and influence in trade unions, in the South and elsewhere. It is my contention that these different leadership groups were often the key to whether organizing was successful or not. These groups included the long-standing, narrow, often racially exclusionary craft unions that fought for control of their occupations, concentrated in the AFL. The latter, of course, occasionally contained more radical groupings, including segments of the teamsters, under the influence of the revolutionary Trotskyists centered in Minneapolis. On certain issues, one might add the majority–African-American longshoremen of the International Longshoremen's Association (ILA) in the Southeast, in Gulf of Mexico ports, and in towns along the Mississippi River.

Within the industrial union movement, there were leadership groups from the very beginning. These groups were not pure, although I reject as inaccurate the view that more conservative groups emerged and gained strength only during the late 1940s. There were, from the start, those centered around Sydney Hillman, leader of the Amalgamated Clothing Workers of America (ACWA), who preached cooperation with capitalists, no matter how unlikely this was in particular industries. In addition, he advocated reliance on the government, downgrading, even suppressing, mass struggles by workers. Hillman himself was something of a curious mixture, enslaved by his relationship with President Franklin D. Roosevelt and his close relation with non-labor figures. Yet he was also an early supporter of the Soviet Union and not viscerally anti-communist (like many of his allies in the CIO), at times openly allying with the Communist Party.

There were others who shared Hillman's general views but were more virulently anti-communist. These leaders often had the narrowest of business union visions. Although they came to dominate the CIO after World War II, they were central players well before the war. Walter Reuther, Philip Murray, and the steelworkers, despite occasional class rhetoric, clearly fit into this camp. And in certain periods, the Communists, especially at the national level, supported and were part of this grouping.

There were also some leaders, not always radicals, who recognized the need for mass struggle, not just in establishing their presence, but also in increasing the bargaining leverage of their unions. This group included John L. Lewis at times, although Lewis was a highly contradictory figure whose actions I attempt to explain in the chapter on coal miners. The early Reuther, at least before 1939 or 1940, undoubtedly fits here as well.

Then there were the Communists, central figures in the CIO and other mass movements, to whom I devote a whole chapter. At times, the Communists were the staunchest fighters for the rights of African-Americans, and often the most militant and impressive of trade union organizers. At other times, they subordinated themselves to the more reactionary and racially backward leadership groups in the labor movement, helping to strengthen and eventually pave the way for their gaining complete control of the CIO. I attempt to explain their alleged inconsistencies and their eventual destruction of the radical wing of the workers' movement, which they had played such an important role in helping develop.

Finally, there were a number of smaller left groups that at times played important roles at the local level; the most significant of these was the Socialist Workers Party with its stronghold in the Minneapolis Teamsters. There were the followers of A. J. Muste, who were for a short period influential in the left and within several mass movements. There were also some small groupings of the left wing of the Socialist Party, occasionally influential in auto and elsewhere, including in the South.

The pluses and minuses of all these groups will be examined in subsequent chapters, since they give further insights into what might have been possible and what was not. In looking at working-class leadership, there are several dimensions to be examined, not always distinct.

First, there exists the issue of successfully organizing unions. One is struck at times by the sheer incompetence and stupidity of many of the conservative leaders of the CIO. I will argue that this was largely ideological. Their reliance on the beneficence of the government and the potential for cooperation with employers, even when the likelihood of such cooperation was basically nonexistent, often made them incapable of preparing workers for struggle and strike actions when necessary. While examples are manifold, my chapters on textile organizing, Operation Dixie, and woodworker organizing explore these questions. In general, the more radical groupings were far better at these tasks.

Second, there is the necessity at times of building wide support for unionization campaigns, what I call "associative power." While the left was in general better than other groupings, I also note the degree to which the steelworkers' unionization, relying on Communist activists and leaders, mobilized support among ethnic organizations, civil rights groups, and others. These broad coalitions of support, associative power, were a feature of some of the most powerful efforts. I argue that the mineworkers in Alabama used these coalitions to organize large numbers of workers without leverage. The extraordinary work of the Communist-led United Electrical Workers, based in St. Louis, as described and highlighted in fine detail by Rosemary Feuer (1996, 2006), fits in this category. The campaign of the Trotskyist-led Minneapolis Teamsters, especially during their 1934 strike, was striking. They had the strong support of farmers' organizations (which donated food and supplied manpower), organizations of unemployed workers, women who were mobilized in their own groups, other local unions, and many others. They put out a daily newspaper during the strike that highlighted and linked the issues of diverse groups.

Third, in addition to associative power was the ability and willingness of labor leaders to emphasize broad solidarity, especially around issues affecting the more oppressed members of the working class, including African-Americans, women, immigrants, and ethnic minorities.

Fourth, there was the question of radical/revolutionary leadership, of which broad solidarity was a piece. Lenin and Trotsky both argued that the infusion of broad class issues, many not pertaining directly to the workplace, was a key to educating workers on the overall nature of the oppressiveness of capitalism and the need for socialism. Also important was not fostering illusions in capitalist politicians and more conservative trade union leaders, with whom radicals were often allied. The Communists at times failed abysmally on this. Even the Trotskyists, however, were criticized by Trotsky for being too uncritical of the contradictions in the Minnesota Farmer-Labor Party in which they were involved and for being too subordinate to Teamsters officials, with whom they were allied at times. The Trotskyist newspaper, The *Militant*, under the editorship of Art Preis, was extremely laudatory and uncritical of John L. Lewis, exemplified also in Preis's book on the history of the CIO (1964:40–43).[9]

It is important to stress here, as subsequent chapters document in detail, that radical groups, with, of course, some exceptions, and contrary to the claims of both the established trade union leaders and the dishonest and now-discredited Cold War scholarship that dominated through the 1960s, were far better as trade unionists than their more conservative (read: liberal) rivals. Those organizations that were most successful in struggles did two things in general. First, they foresaw

---

[9] These issues, worthy of in-depth discussion, are addressed at length in Lenin (1961), Palmer (2013:235–37), Trotsky (1946, 1969, 1975), and Cannon (1973a, b).

the intensity of major struggles and prepared their ranks with often meticulous organization and broad support. Second, in many cases, they mobilized important
allies to support their struggles, as did the Communist leaders of the ILWU in
California, the United Electrical Workers in St. Louis, and the Trotskyist organizers
in Minneapolis. Radical groups were, in general, most aware of the need for such
broad support.

   These discussions are intended to provide a framework for the more empirical
chapters that follow. Some of the issues will be amplified as the story is told. In
addition, several issues are best discussed toward the end. These include the historiography of Communism and anti-communism, an analysis of the Communist
Party, the nature of liberal anti-communism, and what I consider to be the poverty
of U.S. liberalism in the post–World War II period. But let us proceed now to the
story itself.

The Vanguard

Coal Miners and Structural Power

Introduction

Coal was a central industry both for the U.S. economy and for the growth of industrial unionism during the 1930s and 1940s, especially in the South. Coal miners were the leaders—the vanguard if you will—in the growth of industrial unions in the South and nationally. Further, they were one of the few groups in the old American Federation of Labor (AFL) that had a public commitment to racial equality and a record on that score with many pluses. Coal miners had the potential to spur even greater organization of workers in the South, but for various reasons this potential was only partially fulfilled.

The Growth of the Coal Industry and Its Importance

To understand coal mining in the South, one must begin with the national industry. Coal production in the United States, already a growing industry in the early nineteenth century, took off after the Civil War, spurred by the rapid growth of railroads, for which it supplied the main fuel, and expanded exponentially until the turn of the century. Railroads, aided by huge public subsidies and investments, were the largest, most highly capitalized, and most national of industries during the late nineteenth century. One indication of their phenomenal growth was the increase in miles of track from 35,000 in 1865 to over 200,000 in 1900 (Hughes 1990:268). Coal followed suit, increasing from less than 16 million tons produced in 1859 to more than 250 million tons in 1899.[1] From 1899 to 1918, growth in coal production

---

[1] As David Brody argues, "Among the forces driving America's remarkable industrial growth of the late nineteenth century, none was more powerful than the surging production of coal. By 1910 the 501 million short tons mined represented nearly 40 percent of the world's production and far exceeded the output of America's nearest European competitors. The coal industry provided 90 percent of

The Southern Key. Michael Goldfield, Oxford University Press (2020) © Michael Goldfield
DOI: 10.1093/oso/9780190079321.001.0001

was relatively constant. After this time, until the early 1970s, coal production fluctuated greatly, no longer increasing significantly over time. Spurred by World War I, it reached 678 million tons in 1918, but fell back to 500 million tons by 1921. Propelled by the next world war, it reached 656 million tons by 1948, but fell again by 1949 to 480 million tons (Table 2.1).[2]

The leveling off and later decline of coal usage and production after World War I was due to two factors. First, ships were already at this time beginning to abandon coal for oil, although the switch to oil and natural gas for home heating, and to diesel fuel for locomotives, was still on the horizon. Second, although coal remained the main fuel used by public utilities for electrical power and by households for heating, and coke—a coal byproduct—was a major ingredient of steel during the 1930s, there had been huge gains in the efficient use of coal, particularly in the production of energy and steel.

Despite these emerging trends, coal was still the essential fuel for the U.S. economy during the 1930s and 1940s, as railroads, home heating, electricity, and industrial power (including the all-important automobile and steel industries) were fueled by coal.

The South (broadly defined) was an important location for coal mining. While Pennsylvania had historically been the largest coalfield (in both tons mined and number of workers)—still 35–40% during the 1930s—parts of the South were also important producers, especially West Virginia, Alabama, Tennessee, Kentucky, and Virginia, together almost equaling the output and employment in Pennsylvania.[3] By 1933, West Virginia had surpassed Pennsylvania in bituminous (soft) coal production. Alabama and West Virginia also had large percentages of African-American miners, while the other southern states had lower percentages, although still substantial numbers.

West Virginia was central to the economics of coal and the competition among coal companies. It was also central to the fortunes of the miners' union, so it is appropriate that we start there.

West Virginia Coal Miners

West Virginia miners, for various reasons, were slower to unionize than their counterparts in other states. This was true not only in comparison with northern

the nation's energy, operated at a per-worker productivity rate three times that of either Germany's or Britain's, and by every measure—cheapness, quality, availability—amply met the needs of the burgeoning economy" (1993a:131). See Fogel and Engerman (1974) for a counterargument.

[2] I have relied heavily on Risser (1958) for information on the economics of the coal industry. Other data and information from other sources are documented in the footnotes and tables.

[3] It could also be argued that the Appalachian parts of several northern states, including southern Ohio, Illinois, Indiana, and Pennsylvania, were in a sense southern.

Table 2.1 **Coal Production, 1859–2017, Selected Years**

YEAR	COAL PRODUCED *(thousands of short tons)*		
	Total	*Anthracite*	*Bituminous and Lignite*
1859	15,633	9,619	6,013
1869	32,904	17,083	15,821
1879	68,105	30,207	37,898
1889	141,229	45,546	95,682
1899	253,741	60,418	193,323
1903	357,356	74,607	282,749
1910	501,596	84,485	417,111
1915	531,619	88,995	442,624
1918	678,211	98,826	579,385
1919	553,952	88,092	465,860
1920	658,264	89,598	568,666
1921	506,395	90,473	415,921
1923	657,903	93,339	564,564
1929	608,816	73,828	534,988
1930	536,911	69,385	467,526
1931	441,735	59,646	382,089
1932	359,565	49,855	309,710
1935	424,532	52,159	372,373
1936	493,668	54,580	439,088
1938	394,644	46,099	348,545
1941	570,517	56,368	514,149
1944	683,277	63,701	619,576
1945	632,551	54,934	577,617
1949	480,570	42,702	437,868
1955	490,838	26,205	464,633
1960	458,214	42,702	415,512
1970	612,661	9,729	602,932
1985	883,638	4,703	878,930
2000	1,073,610	4,572	1,069,038
2017	774,609	1,912	772,697

Source: "Mines and Quarries," Fifteenth Census of the U.S., 1929, 257, table 7, U.S. Department of Commerce, Bureau of the Census (Washington, DC: Government Printing Office, 1933).

Historical Statistics of the United States: Colonial Times to 1970, part 1, pp. 589–90, 592–93, U.S. Department of Commerce, Bureau of the Census.

1989–2017: U.S. Energy Information Administration, *Coal Industry Annual*, annual reports.

Appalachian miners in the states of Pennsylvania, Illinois, Ohio, and Indiana (labeled the Central Competitive Field), but also in comparison with those in Alabama and other parts of southern Appalachia. They gave only partial support at best to national strikes in 1894, 1897, and 1902–1903 (Corbin 1981, Uchimura 2007, Singer 1982).[4] However, as many analysts have noted, they were eventually to become the most fervent of union supporters.[5] There were several interrelated reasons for these two characteristics. First, a larger percentage of West Virginia miners in the early 1930s lived in small, isolated towns (93% in towns with fewer than twenty-five hundred residents) and in company housing (75%) than in other coal mining states (Rochester 1931:83). Second, fear of the union led coal miner associations to hire hundreds of Baldwin-Felts guards and "detectives," so that by 1910, there was not a coal town in West Virginia in which they were not stationed (Corbin 1981:50). Whereas in earlier periods, union organizers moved around relatively freely in West Virginia, by this time not only union organizers but sympathetic miners were commonly harassed, brutalized, and murdered.

The growing militancy and solidarity of West Virginia miners was on full display when, in April 1912, Paint Creek and Cabin Creek miners struck. It was objective conditions (unsafe work, cheating on pay, company control, and sheer brutality), not southern or mountaineer culture, that led them to become a model of solidarity (a class solidarity so paradigmatic that it stimulated IWW (Industrial Workers of the World or Wobblies) songwriter Ralph Chapin to write the union anthem "Solidarity Forever" (Corbin 1981:92). The mine owners were determined to crush the 1912 strike with force. Baldwin-Felts guards "built iron and concrete forts that they equipped with machine guns throughout the strike districts," evicting miners from company housing and destroying their furniture. They then began to murder striking miners singly and in groups. In the most celebrated instance, they drove an armored train, dubbed the "Bull Moose Special," through the mining districts, machine-gunning strikers and their families in tent colonies near the tracks (Corbin 1981:88). The miners, to be sure, fought back in kind, shooting mine guards and detectives with six machine guns and one thousand high-powered rifles supplied by the national union. Women in the company towns were equally combative, engaging in gun battles alongside the men. It was women who prevented the "Bull Moose Special" from returning by tearing up the railroad tracks and who often attacked

[4] There are numerous detailed accounts of the struggles of West Virginia miners during these early periods. Except where otherwise noted, I rely most heavily on the careful accounts of Corbin (1981, 2011) and Shogan (2004).

[5] As Corbin notes, "The spiritual significance and moral fervor that the southern West Virginia coal miners came to attach to the UMWA was formed over a long period of time" (1981:146).

strikebreakers, driving them away (Corbin 1981:92). According to Wobbly Ralph Chapin, this was the appeal of famed United Mine Workers of America (UMWA) organizer Mother Jones, "who might have been any coal miner's wife ablaze with righteous fury" (Corbin 1981:93). Mineworker families not only fought, but in the tent colonies sang and danced, creating a new union solidarity culture, making the union "an intense, emotional unity" (1981:93).

The Paint Creek/Cabin Creek strike lasted a year and was never broken, despite the declaration of martial law and the arrest and jailing, without trial, of hundreds of miners, while the mine operator and gunmen who drove the "Bull Moose Special" were never even questioned, much less indicted (Corbin 1981:95). Rank-and-file coal miners and their local leaders rejected a settlement brokered by district officials, UMWA national president John White, and Governor Henry Hatfield, continuing to strike until all their demands were met. They then demanded the replacement of all their district leaders, finally forcing the national union to call elections. In 1916, they elected their strike leaders: outspoken socialist Frank Keeney as president of District 17, William Mooney as secretary-treasurer, and Bill Blizzard as a subdistrict leader.

During World War I, West Virginia miners, like workers around the country, including other coal miners in the South, joined the union en masse. By 1919, they had substantially organized Mingo County, which, along with Logan, was the most brutally repressive area in the state; in many unionized towns, they then elected sympathetic officials. On May 19, 1920, Baldwin-Felts gunman arrived in Matewan in Mingo County to evict striking miners from the company houses of the Red Jacket Coal Company. The gunmen were met by the pro-union Matewan mayor, Cabel Testerman, his sheriff, Sid Hatfield (himself a former miner and UMWA member), and a group of deputies. The mayor informed them that the evictions were illegal and would not be allowed. A gunfight broke out and ten people were killed, including the mayor and two other townspeople, as well as seven Baldwin-Felts gunmen, including Albert and Lee Felts, brothers of the agency head, Thomas Felts (Corbin 1981:201). The Felts brothers were allegedly shot by Sid Hatfield. The Matewan Massacre became a cause célèbre among miners throughout the state, who flocked into the union, and Hatfield, not surprisingly, became a hero for the miners. Hatfield was tried and acquitted by a Mingo County jury, which accepted his claim of self-defense.[6]

---

[6] There are numerous books on Matewan and Blair Mountain, in addition to a movie (Sayles 1987) and a fascinating historical novel by Giardina (1987). Aside from Corbin (1981, 2011), one might usefully consult Shogan (2004), Bailey (2008), Blizzard (2004), Harris (2012), Swain (2009), Green (2015), and Barkey (2012). Even so, there is much that is still not fully documented.

Blair Mountain, West Virginia (1921)

Hatfield himself and a companion (unarmed and in the company of their wives) were gunned down and murdered by Baldwin-Felts gunmen on August 1, 1921, on the steps of the McDowell County, West Virginia, courthouse, where they had arrived to answer a trumped-up indictment. The gunmen were acquitted, claiming self-defense, although this claim seemed preposterous. The murder of Hatfield, already a hero to the miners, enraged mining communities throughout the state.

Armed miners began to pour out of the mountains to end the police state that kept them from organizing in the two counties. By August 24, 1921,more than ten thousand armed miners in Charleston, the state capital, were preparing to march. Labor marches throughout Appalachia had a long history, much like earlier revival meetings. Workers and their families would often rally, listen to speeches, and march for days, agitating in large areas on behalf of unions. As mine owner violence worsened, the marches became armed. Corbin claims that a conservative estimate of the number of armed coal miners who took part in the eventual march was between fifteen and twenty thousand (1981:219). The miners were well organized, led by hundreds of miners who were World War I veterans. They had commissary, food support, and hundreds of medical personnel to take care of the wounded, and above all they had weapons, including numerous large machine guns seized from coal mine supplies. Corresponding to their proportions among miners in the state, roughly 25% of the marchers were African-American.

The main battle took place on Blair Mountain, where armed miners did battle with a private army led by Sheriff Don Chafin, the coal-company-financed dictator of Logan County. As the miners fought their way to Logan County, President Calvin Coolidge sent federal troops into West Virginia, allowing coal companies and their minions to destroy the union. Then–UMWA vice president, Philip Murray, claimed that if the army had not intervened, the state would have been rid of the mine gunmen. This is by no means certain, as Shogan argues (2004:211). What is certain, however, is that the arrival of federal troops ensured that the miners and their union would suffer a monumental defeat. By the end of the decade, union membership in the state, which had been many tens of thousands, had dwindled to the hundreds. The spirit and remembrance of Blair Mountain, however, was a factor in making West Virginia coal miners among the first workers to mobilize and organize in the early 1930s. So let us get beyond the romanticism of this heroic struggle and defeat, and try to understand why the struggle in West Virginia was so intense.

As Risser (1958) notes, the location of coal mining is a result of the interplay of several factors, including the richness of the coal deposits, the proximity to markets, the state of mining technology, and the development of transportation.

The early development of the Illinois coalfields, for example, was based not merely on the abundance of coal there, but on the nearness of the mines to the Chicago markets, the city being both the hub of the nation's railroad system and a focal point for the inexpensive Great Lakes shipping of iron ore to the Chicago/Indiana and Pittsburgh steel mills. The importance of this market led to the early rapid growth of the Illinois coal industry and the early subsequent organization of Illinois coal miners, who still remained the majority of unionized coal miners in the early 1930s. Alabama coal also served a local and regional market, with both coal and iron ore plentiful in the Birmingham region, thus making the area an important secondary producer of steel. Neither Alabama coal nor iron ore, however, was of sufficiently high quality to make it a principal national production center. Alabama operators tried to make up for these deficiencies by using the white supremacist labor market to pay miners, both Black and white, substantially lower wages than anywhere else in the country.

West Virginia coal seams, on the other hand, were richer (i.e., thicker) than those in Illinois and other states of the Central Competitive Field. However, it was only when the railroads extended their tracks throughout West Virginia and technological advances allowed for the efficient mining of the state's richer deposits that the state could become competitive.[7] Even so, the longer distances made shipping coal to the Midwest markets more expensive, despite the best efforts of the Interstate Commerce Commission (ICC) to diminish the differences in rates.[8] West Virginia coal companies tried to make large-scale inroads into the markets of more northern producers (who were nearer to primary markets) by paying substantially lower wages and by brutally keeping out the union. As a result, West Virginia was by far the fastest-growing coal producer in the early twentieth century, starting as a small producer in 1903, slightly surpassing Illinois in 1913, tripling its production, and ultimately surpassing Pennsylvania in the mining of bituminous coal in 1933 (Risser 1958:133) (Table 2.2).

West Virginia's huge increase in market share in the first part of the twentieth century relied on lower non-union wages, which made it possible to offer cheaper prices that more than offset the slightly higher transportation costs. Northern union operators (appreciating the ability of the UMWA to stabilize wages and limit spontaneous stoppages of work) continually complained to the union about the latter's inability or unwillingness to organize the non-union fields, especially those in West Virginia

---

[7] For a detailed discussion of the extension of railroads from West Virginia coal mines to Midwestern markets, see Lambie (1954), esp. 289–94.

[8] The ICC had a policy of encouraging competition from the non-union southern fields, in effect making those mines closest to the markets subsidize the more distant ones. Kanawha, West Virginia, coal companies (348 miles from Chicago), for example, paid 0.0056 cents/mile per ton, while Pittsburgh operators (166 miles away) paid 0.01 per ton (Singer 1982:43).

Table 2.2 **Coal Production by State, Selected Years**

State	1903	1913	1923	1933	1943	1953
Alabama	11.39	18.1	20.91	8.58	18.08	12.5
Colorado	7.42	9.08	10.31	5.07	8.46	3.58
Illinois	34.81	61.73	63.2	38.19	72.9	47.81
Indiana	9.61	17.13	27.54	11.48	22.79	15.39
Iowa	6.42	7.53	5.71	3.2	2.69	1.89
Kansas	5.55	7.04	4.37	2.1	3.38	1.72
Kentucky	7.21	19.2	41.12	36.19	64.25	63.39
Maryland	5.52	4.78	2.29	1.52	1.91	0.51
Missouri	4.24	4.32	3.4	3.43	4.56	2.96
Ohio	24.84	36.2	40.55	19.59	33.94	37.76
Oklahoma	3.52	4.17	2.89	1.24	4.71	17.67
Pennsylvania	102.45	173.49	166.89	78.37	133.79	87.61
Tennessee	4.8	6.9	6.04	3.78	7.4	5.07
Utah	1.68	3.25	4.72	2.68	7.12	6.67
Virginia	3.45	8.83	11.76	8.18	19.9	0.83
West Virginia	24.53	67.68	92.49	93.81	159.16	122.9
Wyoming	4.64	7.39	7.58	4.01	9.67	6.35

Source: Hubert E. Risser, *The Economics of the Coal Industry* (Lawrence: University of Kansas Press, 1958), 133, table 53.

(Gowaskie 1976:686–87).[9] Not only did the West Virginia operators resist with unusual violence, but they often regarded the union itself as a tool of northern operators.

To understand why these operators were so brutally anti-union and why miners in West Virginia were so militant and solidaristic, one needs to look more closely at the overall economics of the coal industry.

The Economics of Coal Production in the United States

Types of Coal Mined Historically in the United States

While there are numerous types of coal in the United States, and subdivisions among them, only two are important for our purposes here. The first is anthracite

[9] Certain of this angst must be taken with a grain of salt, since a number of large northern mine owners also owned mines in non-union areas of West Virginia (Singer 1982:102).

(or hard coal), originally the main fuel for home heating. Found almost exclusively in the Appalachian region of Pennsylvania, it constituted during the 1930s a significant percentage of U.S. mined coal. The second is bituminous (or soft coal), the most plentiful form of coal in the United States. It was used during the 1930s to power railroads, electricity, industry, and some ships. Related to anthracite is smokeless (i.e., cleaner-burning) bituminous coal (Howard 2001, Uchimura 2007), and was the preferred fuel for navy ships at the time and some electrical power plants.[10]

Crisis and Chronic Overproduction in the Coal Industry

As Anna Rochester noted in 1931, "In spite of the differences peculiar to each country and each industry, the underlying process of capitalist development is everywhere the same: chaotic over-expansion of markets; price-cutting; reduction of labor costs; technical improvements displacing workers . . . aggressive attack on workers' organization to prevent resistance as unemployment increases" (31). These trends were often more extreme in industries that were not dominated by a small number of large producers. The coal industry, in addition, had distinctive characteristics. While coal had a greater concentration of ownership than the wood industry, it still had thousands of small companies, which produced the majority of U.S. coal.[11] The labor-intensive nature of the industry also meant that there was an ease of entry, especially during boom periods. Further, small companies often had certain advantages in local, isolated, or seasonal markets.[12] During boom times, when prices per ton of coal often rose significantly, there was an expansion both in the number of producers and in coal production capacity, sometimes bearing little relation, even to the expanded market. When the market contracted, as it inevitably did, prices at times dropped substantially, leading to huge financial losses. After World War I, for example, as demand dropped, prices for bituminous coal declined, from 3.75 dollars per ton in 1920 to 2.68 in 1923 and 1.34 in 1933. During World War I, hundreds of companies made huge profits. Even during the worst of times, there were always those making profits in coal. These included not only some coal companies, but those who leased the land, those who received royalties for

[10] For more information on the types of coal, including their wide range and current locations, see the U.S. Mining Associations' "Facts about Coal" (1996–97:11) and the American Coal Foundation's "Types of Coal" (2014).

[11] As Gowaskie notes, there were also many smaller, sometimes family-worked mines, which were too small or remote to be captured in census figures (estimated to be almost ten thousand in the 1902 census), which often provided competition for the larger mines (1976:670).

[12] The U.S. Bureau of Mines reported that after the 1919 coal strike, as many as twelve thousand new mines opened to meet consumer demand (Singer 1982:94).

coal mined, and those who took depreciation and depletion allowances; there were also the lenders who earned interest for money advanced to the coal companies (Rochester 1931:34–41).

Finally, the coal mining industry had the peculiar trait that a significant percentage of the mines were not owned by independent companies but were rather the "captive" mines for companies that consumed coal as an important input for their final product. U.S. Steel, for example, owned important facilities in West Virginia, even naming one coal town they built "Gary," as they did for their modern steel production center in Gary, Indiana (see Uchimura 2007).[13] Ford Motor Company also owned its own mines, as did much of the steel industry. According to Rochester, steel plants, railroads, public utilities, and coke producers in 1930 used nearly 60% of the yearly output of bituminous coal in the United States and mined 20% of the total output of U.S. coal themselves (1931:67). Coal miners in captive mines thus faced conglomerates with considerably more leverage than those companies that primarily produced and sold coal on the open market. Certain whole coal mining districts were dominated by these captive mines, including the Birmingham and Pittsburgh areas and most of the state of Utah.[14]

Labor Cost and Productivity

As in the production of wood and certain other raw materials (but in sharp contrast to the technologically advanced and highly capital-intensive oil industry, for example), labor was a large component of the cost of coal production, averaging as much as 60% of costs during the 1930s.[15] In contrast to that in wood, however, productivity increased over time, particularly in bituminous coal (Table 2.3).

Among the many factors that led to increases in productivity were the following: mechanical loading, mechanical cutters, and the growth in strip mining. These factors especially affected bituminous coal mining. Other factors led to decreases as well as increases in inefficiency; among these were the depth and width of the coal seams and the sparseness of coal, which held back productivity gains in the Pennsylvania anthracite coalfields, whose richest fields were rapidly depleted, while no important new ones were discovered.

---

[13] Both towns were named after Judge Elbert Henry Gary, a founder of U.S. Steel, along with J. P. Morgan, and its first president and CEO, beginning in 1901.

[14] Note the role of the railroads, which controlled, by both direct and complex means, a significant percentage of coal operations (Singer 1982:91–92).

[15] For an earlier study, see Lubin (1924).

Table 2.3 **Total Value of Coal Produced and Percent Value Paid in Wages**

Year	Wages (millions of dollars)	Value of net shipments and receipts (millions of dollars)	% Wages
1889	103	160	64.38
1902	220	367	59.95
1909	363	551	65.88
1919	894	1,510	59.21
1929	805	1,352	59.54
1935	523	869	60.18
1939	540	933	57.88
1954	881	2,104	41.87
1958	842	2,333	36.09
1963	701	2,273	30.84
1967	812	2,740	29.64

Source: *Historical Statistics of the United States: Colonial Times to 1970*, Bicentennial Edition, part 1, series M 1-12, U.S. Department of Census, Bureau of the Census.

*Mineral Industries,*1963, vol. 1; Summary and Industry Statistics, table 1, U.S. Department of Commerce.

Demand for Coal and Its Variations

In general, the demand for and consumption of coal—which created the major (although not the sole) impetus for the production and supply of coal—was determined by three factors: (1) the general state of the economy, (2) increased uses for coal, and (3) the replacement of coal by other fuels. These factors governed its annual fluctuations, as well as its general trajectory of growth. Formally, we might view the relationship as follows:

Demand for coal $= f$ (state of the economy, increased uses, replacement) $+ U$

where U represents false expectations of various competitors for potential sales and market opportunities, often an enormous factor in the large-scale overproduction of coal.

Employment Numbers

In 1930, coal employed more workers than any other industry besides transportation or agriculture. Yet aggregate employment figures only begin to tell the story.

Declines in demand led coal companies not only to reduce the number of workers they employed, but to sharply cut down on the number of days per year those employed worked. The fluctuations in the number of workers was not merely related to the changes in the amount of coal consumed. Rather, boom periods led the many producers to overproduce, opening numerous new mines, then having to drastically reduce the number of days that miners worked as demand slackened. Note in Table 2.4, for example, the increase in the number of mines during and immediately after World War I and the sharp drop in 1921 in the average number of days worked, a low figure being maintained until 1941.[16]

The volatility of the market, both demand and prices for coal, the intense nature of competition, and the high percentage of costs that went to labor led to the brutal repression of coal miners and their unions, especially in those fields where quality or transportation issues reigned but existing at times in all fields. In addition, the conditions of work and life, and the type of leverage coal miners were able to exert, led to the intensity of their struggles.

Coal Miners' Culture

Coal miners have been immortalized in numerous films, including *Matewan* (about the 1920–21 strikes) (Sayles, 1987), *Coal Miner's Daughter*, with Loretta Lynn and Levon Helm (as her father) (Apted 1980), among others. There is also a gripping novel by Denise Giardina about Blair Mountain, *Storming Heaven* (1987). However, perhaps the most bizarre story of a tribute to coal miners centers on the songs written by country guitar legend Merle Travis.

In August 1946, Cliffie Stone, an assistant producer for Capital Records, asked Travis to write some new folk songs for a recording session the next day. That night Travis, from a family of coal miners in Muhlenberg County, Kentucky (also the hometown of the Everly brothers, Don and Phil, who Travis helped mentor), wrote three songs. Two of these, "Sixteen Tons" and "Dark as a Dungeon," are still commonly known. The chorus of "Sixteen Tons" came from a line in a letter from Merle's brother John Travis: "You load sixteen tons and what do you get, another day older and deeper in debt." Another line came from his father's frequent lament, "St. Peter, don't you call me, cause I can't go, I owe my soul to the company sto." These songs were later released in 1947 by Capital, on an album titled *Folk Songs from the Hills*. Travis himself, a somewhat apolitical patriot, was immediately branded as a Communist. Some in the government saw any sympathy for workers' oppression as "communistic." Capital producer Ken Nelson, who was a radio announcer

---

[16] A. J. Muste estimated that by 1930, capacity for coal production was already more than three hundred million tons per year higher than could be consumed (roughly 60% above demand) (1930:4).

Table 2.4 **Employment in the Bituminous and Lignite and Pennsylvania Anthracite Coal Mining Industry, 1890–2017**

Year	Bituminous and Lignite, Avg. men employed	Anthracite, Avg. men employed	Total	Year	Bituminous and Lignite Avg. men employed	Anthracite Avg. men employed	Total
1890	192,204	126,000	318,204	1932	406,380	121,243	527,623
1894	244,603	131,603	376,206	1933	418,703	104,633	523,336
1899	271,027	139,608	410,635	1934	458,011	109,050	567,061
1900	304,375	144,206	448,581	1935	462,403	103,269	565,672
1901	340,235	145,309	485,544	1937	491,864	99,085	590,949
1902	370,056	148,141	518,197	1938	441,333	96,417	537,750
1903	415,777	150,483	566,260	1939	421,788	93,138	514,926
1905	460,629	165,406	626,035	1941	456,981	88,054	545,035
1907	513,258	167,234	680,492	1943	416,007	79,153	495,160
1908	516,264	174,174	690,438	1944	393,347	77,591	470,938
1909	543,152	171,195	714,347	1945	383,100	72,842	455,942
1910	555,533	169,497	725,030	1947	419,182	78,600	497,782
1914	583,506	179,679	763,185	1948	441,631	76,215	517,846
1915	557,456	176,552	734,008	1950	415,582	72,624	488,206
1917	603,143	154,174	757,317	1951	372,897	68,995	441,892
1928	522,150	160,681	682,831	1952	335,217	65,923	401,140
1929	502,993	151,501	654,494	1953	293,106	57,862	350,968
1930	493,202	150,804	644,006	1954	227,397	43,996	271,393
1931	450,213	139,431	589,644	1955	225,093	33,523	258,616
				2017	52,137	914	53,051

Sources: *Minerals Yearbook,* 1960, vol. 2: *Fuels,* 154, 155, table 3; *Minerals Yearbook,* 1966, *Fuels,* 620, table 2; 705, table 1; *Minerals Yearbook,* 1950, 280, table 12.

"EIA Employment by State, Region and Method of Mining," 2017.

in Chicago in the late 1940s, recalls FBI agents coming around the station, advising it not to play the song of a Communist sympathizer. "Sixteen Tons" quickly, quietly disappeared.

In 1955, Tennessee Ernie Ford, who had worked with Travis, sang the song on his NBC radio show, then again in front of thirty thousand people at the Indiana State Fair. The response was overwhelming, with large numbers of people demanding to hear the song. Capital then released it as the B side of a Ford single. DJs around the country began flipping the record, which quickly sold more than two million copies, making it the greatest-selling single ever. Later, when Travis sang the song himself, he would change the last line during performances to "I owe my soul to Tennessee Ernie Ford."[17] In a further ironic twist, this song, such a biting critique of coal owners' brutality and ruthlessness, plays in the background of a recent twenty-first-century General Electric ad about clean coal.

Dark as a Dungeon: Conditions of the Work and Life of Coal Miners

Fourty [sic] years I worked with pick & drill
Down in the mines against my will
The Coal Kings slave, but now it's passed
Thanks be to God I am free at last.[18]

Work conditions for coal miners varied greatly by mine, region, and type of work. One thing, however, was certain during the 1930s: the work was harsh. In only a slight exaggeration, Lewis Mumford says, "No one entered the mine in civilized states until relatively modern times except as a prisoner of war, a criminal, or a slave . . . It was a form of punishment: it combined the terrors of the dungeon with the physical exacerbation of the galley" (1934:67).[19] In keeping with Mumford's remarks, much of southern coal was originally mined by African-American slaves. This legacy continued after Emancipation, as most southern states initially used overwhelmingly African-American convict labor in many of their mines. Even in West Virginia (which had seceded from Virginia during the Civil War and fought for the Union), until late in the nineteenth century, the majority of coal miners were African-American. It should be stressed, however, that onerous conditions were not incompatible with pride in work. Both Friedrich Engels ([1845] 2009:230) and E. P. Thompson (1966:328) make this point with respect to English knife and fork grinders, who often died in their mid-thirties from inhaling metal dust in their work. More recently, sports writer Dave Zirin (2018) makes this point about professional football players, whose injury rate is nearly 100%; though they take great pride in their craft, none (at least not among those Zirin interviewed) want their children to follow in their footsteps.

By the late nineteenth century, mining throughout the United States had become highly skilled work, and it was virtually all underground. In the 1930s,

---

[17] This account is based on notes from Rick Kienzle (2012), on ernieford.com.

[18] From the tombstone of Condy Brislin, Hazelton, Pennsylvania, who died of black lung disease (Derickson 1988:33).

[19] I was led to this quote by Miller and Sharpless (1985:xix).

mechanization was beginning to take place in some of the larger mines. Without mechanization, small groups of miners, often in twos, threes, or occasionally fours, would pick and drill coal to form a room, usually using explosives to loosen the coal. At the same time, they would brace the ceilings to make sure there was not a collapse. The coal, once it had been loosened by pick and explosives, would be broken into pieces of manageable size and loaded onto coal cars for transport. The miners might also lay track for the cars that would carry the coal to the mine face at the surface. All this required a great deal of skill and strength, including properly setting the explosives, building the support structures, and loading coal when there was often little clearance between the top of the car and the roof.

Minework was divided between those underground miners who dug the coal and those who worked primarily above ground. Underground miners generally got paid by the ton. Disputes often arose over pay for dead time (i.e., when extra time was needed to build support structures, or when the quality of the coal was not such as to yield much output, or when the miner had to wait a long time for another car or for the delivery of additional timber) or over the degree of debris in the coal. Often miners were defrauded by short-weighing of their coal, leading to a consistent union demand for a union check-weight man at the mine face. In addition to the tonnage miners, the company employed a large number of miners who were paid by the hour: those who moved the coal cars, brought the timber, pumped water, installed ventilation, and performed a variety of other tasks. The above-ground workers often included young children who cleaned slate and other debris from the coal (Derickson 1998:26–28).

Initial mechanization involved power winches to pull out the loaded cars, power drills, and electric or pneumatic cutting machines, eventually power loaders, and finally "the continuous miner." Whether there was mechanization or not, workers labored in semi-dark conditions, away from the sunlight, usually breathing varying degrees of dust from the mined coal or broken rocks, often in crouched positions for many hours with low overhangs, sometimes knee deep in water from underground streams, always with the fear that a gas leak or an explosion from gas or coal dust might prematurely snuff out their lives. Workers depended on the skill and safety consciousness of their fellow workers, and also on management, the latter for overall planning of the mine's development and safety provisions, but also for safety equipment and escape routes should a disaster occur. Such disasters were an ever-present possibility both for the workers in the mines and for their families, friends, and neighbors above ground, who never knew when those below might be buried alive, never to return.

In addition, there were diseases that usually afflicted any miner who spent decades in the mines breathing coal dust. Coal workers' pneumoconiosis (CWP), colloquially referred to as black lung disease, is caused by long exposure to coal dust. It is a common affliction of coal miners, similar both to silicosis from inhaling silica dust and to the long-term effects of tobacco smoking.

Inhaled coal dust progressively builds up in the lungs and cannot be removed by the body, leading to inflammation, fibrosis, and, in the worst case, necrosis. Estimates of the prevalence of severe cases of black lung disease among long-term miners vary greatly, ranging from 25% to more than two-thirds. It is a common affliction among veteran coal miners. In Alabama, especially among coal miners in the Birmingham area, dust-related diseases were quite common. As a sign of the strength of the labor movement, the UMWA Alabama's District 20 sponsored a number of successful suits against coal companies on behalf of victims, eventually (with the support of the rest of the labor movement and labor-friendly Governor Jim Folsom) amending the state's worker compensation law in June 1951 to include CWP (Dérickson 1996:235–36). None of the other UMWA districts or the national leadership took advantage of this breakthrough in Alabama to promote the identification, prevention, and compensation of respiratory diseases at this time. In response, Alabama operators began to lower the concentration of dust particles in their mines. Thus, Alabama was among the most progressive states in the country at this time in terms of worker safety, one of the facets of "Alabama exceptionalism."

Despite later reforms, coal mining has always had, and continues to have, among the highest death tolls and injury rates of any U.S. industry. Nevertheless, despite the dangers inherent in coal mining (highlighted by the continuing dramatic mine disasters in this country and elsewhere), coal mining in the United States has always had far more injuries and deaths per ton of coal mined than that in the United Kingdom or European countries (Brody 1993a:137). Fatality rates were 4 per 1,000 in the United States, 3 in Germany, 1.5 in Belgium, and 1 in Britain and France (Table 2.5).[20]

Living Conditions, Company Towns

> At least if there is a war they won't bomb us. The planes will look down
> and think we've already been bombed.
>
> Darryl Ponicsan, Androshen, Pennsylvania
> (Miller and Sharpless 1985:xix)

In the many thousands of mining communities that existed during the 1930s and 1940s, living conditions varied widely, not only by region but also often between communities that were in close proximity. As well as noting the variations, one can also highlight certain similarities. As much as possible, I begin with certain objective, describable conditions, then note the ones that most

---

[20] A disputed literature suggests that fatality rates are far lower in union than non-union mines. See, e.g., Uchimora (2007:106); Fishback (1996:205). Morantz (2013) perhaps gives the definitive assessment.

Table 2.5 **Fatalities, Coal Mining Industry, 1906–55**

	Underground Total	*Surface Total*	*Grand Total*
1906	1,960	178	2,138
1907	3,024	218	3,242
1908	2,286	159	2,445
1910	2,637	184	2,821
1912	2,220	199	2,419
1913	2,624	161	2,785
1915	2,109	160	2,269
1917	2,435	261	2,696
1918	2,333	247	2,580
1920	2,077	195	2,272
1921	1,875	120	1,995
1923	2,304	158	2,462
1925	2,107	127	2,234
1926	2,400	118	2,518
1928	2,092	84	2,176
1930	1,950	113	2,063
1931	1,378	85	1,463
1932	1,130	77	1,207
1933	976	88	1,064
1935	1,144	98	1,242
1936	1,256	86	1,342
1937	1,318	95	1,413
1939	1,014	64	1,078
1940	1,308	80	1,388
1941	1,166	100	1,266
1942	1,353	118	1,471
1943	1,327	124	1,451
1944	1,166	132	1,298
1945	960	108	1,068
1946	863	105	968
1947	1,047	111	1,158

(*continued*)

Table 2.5 **Continued**

	Underground Total	Surface Total	Grand Total
1948	880	119	999
1950	547	96	643
1951	707	78	785
1952	474	74	548
1954	342	54	396
1955	352	68	420

Source: *Injury Experience in Coal Mining*, 1977, U.S. Department of Labor, Mine Safety and Health Administration, Informational Report,138, 139, table 55.

bothered miners and their families, which they also hoped to change during their struggles.[21]

Environmental degradation and unhealthy conditions created by coal mining existed from the very beginning, even before surface mining and mountaintop removal began. Miller and Sharpless describe early coal mining in northern Pennsylvania:

> On the eve of the Civil War, only thirty years after the opening of the coal fields, the region's forests had been stripped completely of their timber stands. Streams and rivers had been dangerously contaminated by raw sewage from coal settlements and by acid seepage from the mines . . . busier towns [were] . . . blanketed by far-reaching clouds of coal dust and grit. After the war, the growth and devastation really began. (1985:xx–xxi)

Conditions were especially bad in company-owned towns, where a majority of the country's miners lived during the 1920s and 1930s, and remained that way to a large degree into the 1940s. Brian Kelly notes that in Alabama, epidemics caused by unsanitary conditions and unsafe drinking water ended up affecting productivity

---

[21] Having read thousands of oral history interviews, I would not disagree that one can occasionally find useful nuggets or things to explore in them. Nevertheless, as a basis for establishing facts or getting an overall picture, even of people's attitudes and values, oral history must be considered unreliable, and this is especially true when people are talking about things that happened decades before. The reason for this is that memory is selective and fallible. Even those with the purest motives and best of intentions (and this does not apply to many of those interviewed) get things wrong and construct narratives that have little basis in reality. Thus, the researcher who relies to any great extent on oral history (no matter how skillfully gathered) is more than likely to be substantially misled. (For suggestions about why this may be so, see Lippman 1922; Kahneman 2011). I have tried to cite oral history interviews only to add to established facts.

(1999:40). Hevener describes conditions in Harlan County, Kentucky, an important coal mining area. While housing varied considerably from camp to camp, "the county's provisions for sanitation, disease prevention, and health care were generally poor" (1978:19). Few of the outdoor privies were sanitary. Since these towns were controlled by coal companies, the responsibility and decisions were theirs. Hevener notes that it was only during World War II, when one-third of Harlan County's military draftees were rejected because of venereal disease, that the county became the last in Kentucky to form a health department (1978:19).[22]

However, the biggest grievances of miners and their families were over company control of all facets of non-working life. Company stores and payment in scrip rather than cash were major issues, especially in West Virginia and Alabama mining towns. Boyd notes that they played only a small role in Ohio and Illinois, places where mining camps tended to be closer to established towns (1993:28–31). Although company stores were illegal in Pennsylvania, Rochester claims that many companies there got around the law by setting up subsidiaries. As John Brophy relates in his description of his upbringing in Pennsylvania coal country, prices were considerably higher at the company stores, "and if a miner got caught bringing in things he had bought out of town, he might get fired" (1964:35).

Company housing was also a central issue, even in those rare instances when its quality was good. Shifflett (1991), whose work leans heavily on company-sponsored oral history (see Uchimura 2007:9–10), misses the point when he describes the physical conditions as often superior to those that rural families had experienced before they came to the mines. Yes, and slaves before the Civil War often ate better than northern urban workers—a "fact" that apologists for slavery often asserted in defense of the institution—though this did little to diminish slaves' desire for freedom (Fogel and Engerman 1974; Calhoun 1837). Company leases were draconian, although judges always ruled that they had been signed freely. If a worker went on strike, had visitors (especially unionists), died, went looking for another job, or did not buy enough at a company store, he was liable to eviction (Rochester 1931:97–102, passim). The company always knew where you were. Occasionally, company agents and thugs pulled sick miners out of bed and sent them to work. In Alabama mining towns, they were called "Shack Rousters" (Kelly 1999:54).

In virtually all mining towns, the control by the companies was absolute. The political offices of the towns, including that of the police chief, were almost always controlled by the mine owners. Policemen themselves were often subsidized by the mining companies. Police and company guards would force any stranger who could not explain his or her business sufficiently to leave town. In Verna, Harlan County, Kentucky, for example, the sheriff pistol-whipped a job applicant because

---

[22] Fishback sees conditions in company towns and independent towns with respect to sanitation as similar (1996:210).

he came from an adjacent union community. Companies also often controlled the post office. During a 1931–32 Harlan County coal miners' strike, owners cut off the delivery of "the miners' favorite newspaper, the *Knoxville News-Sentinel*, because it was critical of local operators" (Hevener 1978:20). Companies also often selected the teachers, social workers, and ministers. Many company towns were surrounded by barbed wire with a single gate manned by guards. Union organizers when discovered were occasionally murdered. Needless to say, prominent among the stated demands of many mining strikes were the abolition of this pervasive control and the mine-guard system.[23]

Propensity of Coal Miners to Organize: Coal Miners' Power

Just as economic cycles have their leading and trailing indicators, cycles of trade union growth, militancy, and political radicalism have had their vanguard groups of workers. During the nineteenth and early twentieth centuries, in virtually every geographic location, in every part of the world, in almost any time period, coal miners (where they existed in significant numbers) were in the lead when it came to labor struggles. Coal miners played this role so often, so many different times, in so many different types of societies that statements about their vanguard status are relatively uncontroversial.[24] However, why and even how they played such a role is hardly ever examined systematically.

One of the early studies—considered by many *the* seminal study—by Kerr and Siegel examines a large amount of data from thirteen developed countries.

---

[23] Note, for example, Corbin's discussion of the demands of the 1912–13 Cabin Creek, West Virginia, strike, in which many of these issues were more prominent than those concerning wages (1981:33). Thus, one must be highly suspicious of Shifflett's remarks drawn from interviews with retired miners and their families: "Most surprising about former miners and their families are their positive recollections of life and work in a company town" (1991:150). Shifflett further remarks, echoing the views of coal company elected judges, that "unless they were convicts, most miners were not forced to reside in company towns against their will. In other words, miners were not 'wage slaves'" (1991:19). Such a remark not only displays a complete lack of understanding of the traditional socialist argument of what it means to be a "wage slave," but perhaps even defies comment. Pope, in his incisive description of a 1922 strike by thirty thousand western Pennsylvania coke miners, says that the strikers "subordinated wage demands and other economic issues to the pursuit of basic rights of free speech, assembly, and association. The official strike call proclaimed, 'This is a Strike to End Fear'" (2003:35).

[24] Typical comments include the following: "In almost every country where coal is mined, labor protest among the workers in this industry has been frequent and intense in comparison with industrial workers generally" (Rimlinger 1959:389). And with respect to miners generally, they are "the most active revolutionary force in Chilean society. Their political radicalism is in line with the radicalism of miners all over the world" (Petras and Zeitlin 1967:580).

Kerr and Siegel argue that miners, along with longshoremen, sailors, and loggers (and "to a much lesser extent" textile workers), formed "isolated masses," a "race apart," living in isolated communities, with common grievances and values (1954:191). Their supposedly one-dimensional communities allegedly created sharp class polarizations, without the other occupational and class groupings that might mitigate class antagonisms. Further, the employees all do the same type of work and have the same work experiences, thus forming "a largely homogeneous, undifferentiated mass" (1954:192). While correctly identifying the high strike rates of miners, their explanation is far from compelling. As a general thesis, Shorter and Tilly (1974) find their argument lacking, noting that in France, at least, it is the multi-industry cosmopolitan cities, not the smaller, single-industry ones, that have the highest strike rates. Gary Marks (1989) extends the critique by arguing that Kerr and Siegel's description of the coal industry and coal mining communities is inaccurate. He notes that industrial growth (in England, Germany, and the United States—the three largest nineteenth- and early-twentieth-century coal producers) led to a rapid expansion of coal mining. Rather than leading to stable, isolated mining communities, the demand for labor led to a rapid influx of newcomers and a high level of transience of experienced miners (Marks 1989:158). In those few isolated areas, miners were, if anything, more provincial than in the more open locales (Marks 1989:157).

However, several studies have also shown that the strike militancy of miners varies considerably by country and even by mining districts within the same country. Numerous investigators have shown that coal miners in the United States and Great Britain, for example, have had significantly higher strike rates than miners in Western Europe, especially France and Germany, the largest Continental coal-producing countries (Rimlinger 1959:389; Marks 1989:154–94, passim; Church and Outram 1998:241–44).

Lipset, in a nuanced study of political proclivities of groups of workers, finds miners among those most predisposed to left-wing political support and activity, although, like Shorter and Tilly, he also lists larger cities, larger plants, and more "economically advanced regions" as similarly inclined (1981:242–46). In contrast to the variations in strike militancy, investigators have found coal miners consistently more likely to be left-wing in virtually all countries.

Investigators mention a number of hypotheses that might have led to increased militancy and radicalism on the part of miners. First, the sheer size of the coal industry and the large number of miners may have been a factor (see, e.g., Marks 1989:192). Second, the centrality of coal to the national economy gave coal miners decisive economic leverage in major battles. Third, miners' solidarity and sense of common grievances did not develop from the isolated community or lack of occupational hierarchy. Rather, it was due to the unique working conditions underground, "dark as a dungeon," the miners often on their hands and knees, deep in the bowels of the earth. Coal had seeped into the pores of all who came up at the end of a shift, whatever their occupation, age, or color. Fourth, coal mining had high accident and death rates, with the threat of being buried alive always present. When cave-ins and explosions did occur, it was not isolation that created broad solidarity, but the community-wide mobilizations and vigils that still accompany rescue efforts. Fifth, given the high percentage of the cost of coal that went to labor and the intense competition between the many producers, opposition to workers organizing for more pay and for better working conditions was inevitably intense.

These factors, of course, provide useful starting points. But to look at the conditions that create vanguard sectors of the working class, one must take a broader view. To get some initial suggestions, we need to look at a wide range of leading sectors. We also need to expand our indicators. Strike militancy—although important—is only one criterion. We ought also to include whether a group of workers was among the first to strike, as well as to organize, and whether they stimulated others to come out and organize (whether they participated during the early part of a wave or cycle). Willingness to support others in their own industries, in related industries, in nearby locales, as well as locales and industries far away is an additional criterion. Finally, we need to look at the readiness of workers to engage in classwide political activity, especially of the more radical variety. This is my initial cut on these questions.

Early Organizing of U.S. Coal Miners

They say in Harlan County, there are no neutrals there.[25]

With the dawn of the coal industry in this country, coal miners began to organize. Local unions came and vanished. One of the first was the Pennsylvania Bates local in anthracite (hard coal) in 1849. The first national union originated in 1861 from the Belleville, Illinois, mining area. In that same year the American Miners' Association held its first meeting in St. Louis. By 1868, the association was gone (Rochester 1931:163). Anthracite miners continued to organize in Pennsylvania. In the post–Civil War period, there were numerous armed skirmishes between mine gunmen and miners. In 1868, twenty thousand Pennsylvania anthracite miners struck and were defeated.[26]

---

[25] "Which Side Are You On?," written by Florence Reece in 1931, during a UMWA organizing drive.
[26] There is no comprehensive history of coal miner unionism, although there now exist numerous local histories and many detailed studies. Among those useful for the earlier period are Andrew Roy (1907), Trauger (2002), Suffern (1926), and Aurand (1971). On the Knights of Labor in the South, McLaurin (1971) and Fink (1985) are particularly useful.

Repression was initially so severe in Pennsylvania that miners were forced to organize in secret. Mine owners and the government invented an alleged underground organization called the Molly Maguires, to which they attributed murder and sabotage. Despite the flagrant fabrication of evidence based on the testimony of dubious undercover agents, mineworker organizers were framed and convicted, with many of the leaders hanged in 1877 and 1878. The myth of the Molly Maguires is perpetrated by John Commons et al. (1918:181–85) and seconded by the more left-wing labor historian Bimba (1932:155). The myth is debunked and ably explained by Foner (1947:460–63).

Local struggles continued to break out in coalfields all over the country, including among southern coal miners in the 1870s and 1880s. Virtually all of these struggles met with defeat, often by state militias. By 1878, Knights of Labor assemblies of miners had been set up in Pittsburgh, Maryland, West Virginia, Ohio, Indiana, and Illinois. Within a few years miners in Colorado, New Mexico, Alabama, Tennessee, Kansas, and Kentucky, among other places, had joined their ranks. In 1885, two national coal organizations formed, including Knights of Labor National Trades Assembly 135 and the National Federation of Miners and Mine Laborers (NFMML), both of whose avowed goals were to develop peaceful relations with the coal operators. In 1886, the NFMML helped to organize the AFL, and in 1888 it changed its name to the Miners' Progressive Union. In 1890, the two coal miner organizations merged to form the United Mine Workers of America (UMWA), which was affiliated with the AFL and, until 1894, also with the Knights of Labor.

Nationally, coal miners continually played a vanguard role. In 1897, although perhaps as few as four thousand miners belonged to the national union (Gowaskie 1976:676), two hundred thousand miners answered the UMWA call and struck, stopping 70% of national soft coal production, resulting in a national agreement with a 33% wage increase and an eight-hour day. This victory, by many accounts, spurred other workers in the United States and Canada to organize (Foner 1955:345). The leadership of the union, conservative in temperament, with an extremely militant constituency generally sympathetic to radicalism, was often of two minds. This is revealed, among other ways, by how it went about mobilizing support for the 1897 strike. Foner emphasizes that President M. D. Ratchford requested aid from Socialist Party (SP) leader Eugene V. Debs, especially in Pennsylvania, where SP organizers played an important role in aiding the strike (1955:345). Taft chooses to highlight the degree to which Gompers and the AFL contributed money and organizers, playing a particularly active role in the formerly non-union fields in West Virginia (Taft 1957:140), continuing to aid the union financially, even after the strike. Both emphases, of course, are one-sided, although each is factually accurate as far as it goes. Miners continually chafed at the conservative, class-collaborationist orientation of the national leadership, never, however, succeeding in overthrowing it. At the 1910 UMWA convention, for example, they opposed the alliance of the AFL and former president John Mitchell with the business-dominated National Civic Federation (NCF), forcing Mitchell to resign from the NCF or lose his union membership (Taft 1957: 228). Although an exception had been made regarding the industrial jurisdiction of the UMWA in the 1901 Scranton Declaration by the AFL, the miners' organization as a whole continually agitated against the craft orientation of the parent organization, sponsoring resolutions, at AFL conventions, sheltering the radical Western Federation of Miners from craft union assaults, and even running John L. Lewis for AFL president against Gompers in 1921 (Taft 1957:194–200, 367). Hatred for Lewis, however, was so intense among many radicals that some even supported Gompers against Lewis for president. The schizophrenic nature of the UMWA, exceptional militancy of miners, classwide feelings of solidarity, and sympathy for radical ideology, combined with a conservative class-collaborationist leadership who sometimes expressed the more radical strains of the mineworkers, form a continual thread in the history of the union, playing an especially important role in the labor upsurge of the 1930s and 1940s, a legacy in which John L. Lewis fits comfortably—which many mistakenly attribute to his idiosyncratic personality.

Miners were among the first southern industrial workers to organize. The Knights of Labor was active in coal in Texas, Alabama, Tennessee, Kentucky, and West Virginia (Marshall 1967:71). Their struggles were as militant and dramatic as those we have come to expect of miners everywhere. The 1891 Coal Creek Rebellion in Tennessee epitomizes this. When the Knights of Labor contract expired at the Briceville mine near the town of Coal Creek, the company attempted to break the union, locking out the miners, evicting them from company housing, and bringing in convicts to work the mines. Merchants and property owners who depended on miners for their livelihood, along with miners, armed themselves. When the government called out the state militia, armed miners and other workers from around the state converged on Coal Creek, disarmed the militia, freed the convicts, and burned the stockade to the ground. Armed confrontations continued to occur, including one at Oliver Springs in 1892, where train crews refused to move troop trains to the mine areas. When Jake Witsen, a Black mine leader was killed, thousands of white miners and neighbors attended his funeral. Although these struggles were eventually defeated by the mobilization of the U.S. Army and the deputizing of large numbers of vigilantes, public opinion was so aroused against the use of convict labor that the legislature—which had initially supported convict labor by a large majority—was forced to abolish it (see Foner 220–29 for a detailed account). The specter of armed miners converging from around the state, supported by farmers and townspeople, and the overwhelming majority of public opinion in the state constituted one of those rare situations in which the need for social stability trumped the extra profits to be gained from the use of prison labor in the mines. Both structural and associative power reinforced each other to gain this victory.

Several newer studies (along with several seminal older works) have added greatly to our knowledge of the organization of coal miners in Alabama. From the late 1870s through the statewide strike in 1920, Alabama coal miners continually organized and struck locally, at the state level, and in conjunction with national initiatives. Statewide strikes took place in 1894, 1908, and 1919. What many of the studies find especially interesting is the degree to which Black and white miners, even during the heyday of white supremacy in the Deep South, found the means to sustain an unyielding interracial solidarity and a certain degree of racial egalitarianism.

By the early 1920s, coal unionism in the South, including organization in Alabama, Tennessee, and West Virginia, had largely been destroyed, with membership previously in the tens of thousands being reduced to irrelevancy in each state. The union remained largely dormant in the South until the onset of the Great Depression in late 1929.

How the Miners Actually Organized: The Myth of Section 7(a)

In a matter of months, or perhaps weeks, in 1933, the United Mine Workers of America went from an organization that seemed on the verge of disintegration, with coal miners largely un-unionized in most major coalfields, to an organization that had enrolled almost all its potential constituency across the country. Walter Galenson describes it as "one of the most rapid and successful organizing campaigns in American labor history" (1960:194). How did this dramatic result come about? The standard story, echoed in literally thousands of pieces of secondary material, is the following. John L. Lewis, along with other AFL leaders, forced Congress to include Section 7(a) in the National Industrial Recovery Act, signed into law on June 16, 1933. Section 7(a), with no intended enforcement powers, asserted: "Employees shall have the right to organize and bargain collectively through representatives of their own choosing." This symbolic statement was used, particularly by the mineworkers and the clothing workers, to encourage, nay empower, reticent workers to join unions en masse. John L. Lewis allegedly staked the remaining resources of his union on the campaign. Lewis put out posters throughout the coalfields, opportunistically claiming, "The President wants you to join. Your government says, 'Join the United Mine Workers.'" There was an "instantaneous mass response" (Galenson 1960:194). Thus, 7(a) and its clever use by Lewis were the key to the great organizing campaign of the mineworkers. Or as Irving Bernstein states: "The passage of Section 7(a) of the National Industrial Recovery Act was the spark that rekindled the spirit of unionism within American labor" (1969:37). Taft gives a similar account (1959:45–46). Even Robert Zieger, in less stark terms, concurs (1995:17;

Zieger, Minchin, and Gall 2014: 29).[27] From such authority, citing some of the most esteemed historians of the period, thousands of others have fallen in line.

While the story is not a total fabrication, it is overall false, a myth that does not fit well with the archival record of what happened. The myth can also be debunked by examining the facts presented and the interpretation of several of the more careful researchers studying the miners' union, although none of them makes a big deal of this point. In attempting to understand what really happened, I will focus on certain material from the archival record, then supplement it with the material of other researchers.

I begin by briefly reviewing what 7(a) was and why it passed. In the early days of the Roosevelt administration, the Black-Connery Bill (named after its sponsors, Senator Hugo L. Black and Congressman William Connery), or just the Black Bill, was moving through the Senate. The bill, mandating a five-day, thirty-hour workweek designed to spread work and reduce unemployment, passed the Senate on April 6, 1933, in a 53 to 30 vote. Subsequently, President Roosevelt, clearly chagrined by the radical nature of the bill, introduced a substitute while the Black-Connery Bill was still pending in the House. FDR's withdrawal of support led to the Black Bill being buried in the House Rules Committee. The new bill was the National Industrial Recovery Act (NIRA). In exchange for support of the NIRA, organized labor demanded a provision guaranteeing the rights of workers to organize, Section 7(a). Taft sees the hand of AFL President William Green and the AFL Executive Board both in the writing and in forcing the acceptance of 7(a). Taft argues that Lewis did not play the major role (1957:42).

However, Taft seems clearly to have let his sympathies for the AFL and antipathy for Lewis and the CIO get in the way of his judgment. A fuller, more convincing account is given by Irving Bernstein (1950). He traces the long history of the attempts to keep employers from interfering with the rights of employees to organize. Mineworkers had pushed for the Watson-Rathbone Bill in 1928, which sought to stabilize the coal industry and guarantee labor rights at a time when the AFL in general was not pursuing legislative remedies (Bernstein 1950:23). The UMWA continued heavy lobbying in 1932 for the Davis-Kelly coal stabilization bill. In the January 1933 hearings in the Senate on the Black Bill, the UMWA successfully demanded labor provisions similar to those in previous bills (Bernstein 1950:29).

[27] Such views range across the political spectrum and academic landscape: Taft and Fink (1981:83), Northrup (1944:165, 294, 378–79), Millis (1942), and Rowan (1982:14). Nyden presents the same timeline (1974:44). According to Northrup, "The organizing opportunity afforded by the NRA was taken advantage of by the UMW as by no other union" (1944:165). Even Philip Foner, who certainly should have known better, asserts—with no documentation: "In 1933, armed with the National [Industrial] Recovery Act's Section 7(a), the United Mine Workers surged into the coal fields to organize the miners of West Virginia" (1991:228). See also Lens (1949:272).

Lewis testified that collective bargaining was necessary to fight Communism, which he saw as potentially making huge gains in the labor movement (Bernstein 1950:24). The AFL was hardly on the radar and "did not discard voluntarism in overt policy until the spring of 1933" (1950:25). Though the mineworkers had taken the lead, other unions backed the labor provisions of the Black Bill. Thus, labor had proven its political influence in gaining passage of the bill. The Chamber of Commerce and the AFL had privately agreed to accept each other's provisions in the NIRA, although the National Association of Manufacturers refused to go along with 7(a) and denounced it (Bernstein 1950:34, 35). Bernstein concludes, "The impetus for including it in the Act came from the union movement, spearheaded by the Mine Workers. The principles of 7(a), in fact, closely resembled those in the Watson-Rathbone and Davis-Kelly coal bills" (1950:37). Despite the contention over its inclusion, 7(a) was largely viewed as a purely symbolic statement, with no enforcement powers.[28]

My account will now shift venues to review what the coal miners were doing prior to the passage of the NIRA. As was to be expected, the massive layoffs and record unemployment levels after the onset of the Depression dampened most worker militancy and union organizing efforts. Such was not the case, however, in the coal industry. As Dubofsky and Van Tine note, coal miners did not accept "their misery in silence or apathy . . . The years 1930, 1931, and especially 1932 saw mass violent strikes scar the coalfields" (1977:170). These strikes were for the most part led by Communists and independent radicals.

Theodore Draper describes the Communist Party (CP) activity in detail. Its organizational base was the National Miners' Union (NMU), whose September 9–10, 1928, founding convention was attended by 675 delegates. John Watt of Illinois was elected president; William Boyce, a Black miner, was elected vice president; while CP coal miners' leader, Pat Toohey, was named secretary-treasurer (Draper 1972:375). In 1929 and 1930, there were numerous spontaneous strikes, in which participants sometimes called in the NMU after they were out (1972:376). In 1931, there were four large strikes in different coal regions. In March, twenty thousand Pennsylvania anthracite miners struck under the leadership of non-Communist oppositionists. In July, twenty thousand West Virginia miners in the Kanawha Valley, led by Frank Keeney, a Lewis opponent supported by the left-wing

---

[28] "In fact, neither the drafters of the NIRA nor President Roosevelt regarded its labor provisions as more than a restatement of progressive homilies" (Zieger 1995:17). Alan Dawley describes Section 7(a) as a "political bone" thrown to labor and concludes that "[i]t may have been all a misunderstanding, but by seeming to remove government objections to labor unions, section 7(a) contributed to the most significant mobilization of wage earners since the war" (1991:372). In contrast, James Pope argues that the bill as written had exceedingly strong enforcement powers, enough to mandate a "death sentence" to corporations that did not comply. Of course, it was a sentence unlikely ever to be executed given the political parameters.

Musteites, went out on a prolonged strike.[29] From May to June, four thousand miners in western Pennsylvania, eastern Ohio, and northern West Virginia struck under NMU leadership. These strikes spread quickly because the miners were in "such an explosive mood." According to Draper, thousands joined the NMU, many of whom also joined the Communist Party. In the Pittsburgh area, the Pittsburgh Terminal Coal Company signed contracts with the UMWA to avoid the CP (Draper 1972:377–79).

The most dramatic 1931 strike took place in Harlan County, Kentucky, where thousands of miners worked in a state of peonage and company-sponsored terror. When ten thousand Kentucky coal miners struck, the UMWA sent in Philip Murray to organize. The violence became so great that the union abandoned the area. In one gun battle at Ewarts, three deputies and a miner were killed, and thirty-four miners were indicted for murder. In July, the NMU finally moved in, while the CP's International Labor Defense (ILD) took up the defense of the indicted miners. Draper, hardly sympathetic to the Communists, claims that "the circumstances in Harlan were so adverse that whatever the Communists did there seems somewhat incredible" (1972:385).

Draper also notes the extraordinary commitment of the CP to racial egalitarianism. He describes the white Harlan miners as fundamentalists, highly individualist, and racist. With less than 14% of Kentucky miners being Black (Draper claims only a few percent in Harlan County were African-American), racial solidarity was hardly the strategic issue that it was in Alabama or West Virginia. Thus, when the issue arose about whether Black miners should eat at the same soup kitchens and tables as white miners, there was quite a bit of resistance from white strikers. "On this point, however, the Communists were adamant. After six or seven hours of discussion, they succeeded in convincing the miners that all of them, irrespective of color, should eat in the same kitchen" (Draper 1972:386). "It is fair to say that only the Communists in that period, in the heat of battle, would have taken such a firm stand on this issue" (1972:387). Although the strikers were badly defeated, the Communists did manage to gain worldwide publicity for the Harlan miners' plight, mobilizing leading intellectuals, including Theodore Dreiser and John Dos Passos, to go to Kentucky to conduct hearings (*Harlan Miners Speak*, 1932).This case helped focus attention on the plight and repression faced by southern workers, especially in the coal mines.

By 1932, there was a new wave of strikes, this time led by the UMWA, involving as many as a hundred thousand miners by the summer, some fifty thousand in Illinois. So while it may have been true that the onset of the Depression temporarily dampened workplace militancy in many industries, with much of the national discontent being

---

[29] The Musteites were followers and members of A. J. Muste's American Workers Party, an independent radical, socialist organization. For a fuller discussion, see Chapter 3.

channeled into social movements, especially the nationwide unemployed and farmers' movements, such was not the case among coal miners.

With this background of militancy and activity, it was perhaps not necessary to suggest that Section 7(a) of the NIRA is what empowered workers to organize. Yet even John Brophy, a former CIO leader and earlier opponent of Lewis—having been expelled by Lewis from the UMWA in 1928—writes in his 1964 autobiography that the NIRA "transformed everything for the miners and their union. The miners, relying on the government's promise to protect the right to organize, flooded into the union. Within ninety days, the industry was organized. There was no need to campaign; an organizer only had to see that he had a good supply of application blanks and a place to file them, and the rank and file did the rest" (1964:236). However, as always, the best information, particularly on dating and exact timing, is to be found in the archival records.

How the Miners Actually Organized in 1933

Union activities and correspondence from 1930 until 1933 clearly suggest that union leaders did not want to commit themselves to new organizing, especially in the South. They felt that anti-union repression was so strong and labor market conditions so deplorable that it would be a waste of the dwindling resources of the union to make such an attempt. In 1930, as southern miners, particularly in Alabama, began to hold meetings and organize, District 20 (Alabama) director George Hargrove and President Lewis agreed that there would be no "bread wagon" (i.e., financial support) from the UMWA and no help for those discharged in such campaigns.[30] They also agreed that organizing would have no positive effect at this time and would only result in discharges. As Lewis wrote to John Lillich of Carbon Hill, Alabama, "Under present circumstances the International Union is disinclined to spend any money in Alabama."[31] Instead, union leaders' strategy in the early 1930s was to put their efforts into lobbying for support of the Davis-Kelly coal bill, which they believed might make organizing coal miners easier. In attempting to mobilize such support, they also made appeals, and exposed the highly repressive conditions, to other AFL unions, which generally supported, at least on paper, the UMWA's legislative efforts.[32] Lewis's lobbying emphasis switched, first in late 1932, to strengthening the labor provisions of the Black Bill, then to including 7(a) in the NIRA.

---

[30] Hargrove to Lewis, February 3, 1930, Lewis to Hargrove, February 6, 1930, Hargrove to Lewis, April 27, 1930, District 20 files, Correspondence, 1929–30, Penn State University (PSU).

[31] Lewis to Lillich, November 14, 1930, District 20 files, Correspondence, 1929–30, PSU.

[32] See, e.g., the circular letter "To All Affiliated Local Unions and Central Bodies" of the Alabama Federation of Labor, February 14, 1933, from Robert Moore, President, UMWA, District 20, in Dalrymple Correspondence folder.

But a strange thing happened while the UMWA leaders were lobbying for their provisions. Miners throughout the country began to organize and form vibrant locals on their own. On May 27, 1933, Lewis appointed his loyal follower Van Bittner as the new president of District 17 (West Virginia), as well as other new districts in West Virginia, Virginia, and Maryland. Lewis regularly informed Bittner of the progress of the NIRA and occasionally asked, almost incidentally, how things were going. At one point, Bittner replies that the miners have been organizing on their own, and there are no organizers to help and service them. Lewis telegrams back to say that he is reassigning organizers and that money is on the way. Van Bittner replies that miners have already organized a local in Ethel, the "heart of Logan County" (the most notoriously repressive of West Virginia counties).[33]

While Lewis was telling his officials that they would be in good stead to organize once the NIRA and 7(a) passed, the miners had already organized. Bittner describes this process in a report to Lewis on June 17. By June 22, 1933, Bittner writes to Lewis: "As I have reported to you heretofore, the work of organizing the miners in West Virginia is progressing more rapidly than I had ever dreamed of. The entire Northern field, as well as the New River, Winding Gulf, Kanawha field, Mingo and Logan are all completely organized. We will finish up in McDowell, Mercer and Wyoming counties this week." The same was true for Maryland and Virginia. "I feel that by the end of the week we can report a complete organization of these fields."[34]

A similar process and timeline can be seen in Alabama. Van Bittner writes to his fellow district director William Mitch in response to Mitch's report that they have organized Alabama: "Am surely pleased to learn of the wonderful progress you are making in Alabama," especially with the DeBardeleben Coal Company, "probably the worst company we had to deal with in the last big strike in Alabama." Their ancestors "came to this country as officers of the Hessian army in the pay of King George Third" during the American Revolution. "So far as our work in West Virginia is concerned . . . it is like a dream and seems too good to be true."[35]

Thus, much of the organizing had already taken place before the NIRA even passed. Mitch, for example, writes to Lewis as such on June 10. Two days later he sends an ecstatic telegram: "We held a large mass meeting at Sumiton Alabama today and organized two local unions[;] over 300 men signed up . . . progressing good in other areas."[36]

[33] Telegram of June 10, 1933; telegram of June 14, 1933.

[34] District 17 files, Correspondence, June 1933.

[35] Bittner to Mitch, June 23, 1933, Mitch papers, box 1, file 11, PSU.

[36] Letter, Mitch to Lewis, June 10, 1933; telegram, Mitch to Lewis, June 12, 1933, PSU, UMWA, District 20 files, Correspondence, June–August 1933.

But there seems to be a disjunction between the reports to Lewis and the information he is actually receiving. It is almost as if Lewis is not hearing that the workers have organized. At the same time that Lewis is reporting on the progress of the NIRA through Congress, he states, "This creates wonderful opportunity for workers in industry to organize. Can you report progress in Alabama?"

But it is not just Lewis who is out of touch. On June 5, 1933, the *Birmingham Age Herald* reports that Mitch is the newly appointed District 20 director (having come from Indiana) and plans to reorganize the UMWA in Alabama. And he has just set up an office. On June 8, Mitch sends Lewis a copy of letter to miners that he has just drawn up.[37] The leaflet is a preliminary one asking for names and information, completely out of touch with the degree of organizing that has already taken place. We have a continuing comedy of inappropriateness. The Birmingham district UMWA office prepares a flyer for a meeting on June 21 to discuss company unions and the meaning of the NIRA (when the battle is virtually over). Yet it is not just the district officials and organizers who are reporting that the workers have organized themselves. The *Birmingham News* of June 16–23, for example, reports a large upsurge and organization of new locals. The activity is so great that operators, even in the depth of the Depression, are proposing increased wages and shorter hours, among other things.

The ironies never cease. At the time that Mitch, following Lewis's advice, is preparing for a meeting with coal miners the next week to explain the benefits of the NIRA, he sends a telegram to Lewis. "We are having fine success. Over three thousand signed up . . . six new locals organized today. We are proceeding fast."[38]

Such events, including the mismatch between the legislative lobbying by the union leaders, the belated sending of money and organizers to already mobilized miners, and the seeing and not seeing by district officials of the massive upsurge taking place before their eyes, take place in virtually every coal mining district in the country. Dubofsky and Van Tine conclude that Lewis's role and that of the NIRA were "tangential in the sense that the coal miners seemed to organize themselves in June and July 1933, even in the absence of UMW funds and organizers" (1977:185). Alan Singer suggests that Lewis and the UMWA leadership "did not grasp the possibilities, involved in the rank-and-file upsurge" while it was going on, even as Philip Murray was attending one of the rank-and-file rallies in Pennsylvania at the time. As Singer notes, on June 17, 1933, a day after the NIRA had passed, UMWA leader John Cinque reported that 80% of Ohio miners had already signed up as members (1982:118). On June 23, 1933, Sam Caddy wrote that all of the main mines in Kentucky were organized. By the end of June,

[37] Letter, Mitch to Lewis, June 10, 1933; telegram, Mitch to Lewis, June 12, 1933, PSU, UMWA, District 20 files, Correspondence June 8, 1933.

[38] Telegram, Mitch to Lewis, June 16, 1933.

128,000 new members had been enrolled from the Pennsylvania bituminous coal mines (Singer 1982:119).[39]

The situation in the largest coalfields in the country, in western Pennsylvania, was if anything more dramatic. The struggle of miners to organize there is carefully documented and incisively analyzed by James Pope, in work that convincingly goes against the grain of virtually all the established scholarship.[40] Some of the earlier strikes in Pennsylvania led by Communists and other oppositionists have already been discussed. On March 5, 1933, long before there was even a draft of the NIRA, a group of between eighteen hundred and three thousand soft coal miners in Portage, Pennsylvania, held an organizing rally at a local theater. Delegations arrived from as far as fifty miles away. At this meeting, they decided to organize the district. In mid-April, fifty miles to the southwest, the NMU led a strike at the Republic Mine of the Republic Iron and Steel Corporation. Management sat down with the union and settled the strike. Several weeks later, miners at the R. B. Hays Company struck for union recognition. The regional UMWA organizer, William Feeney, claimed he was not authorized to help. Nevertheless, the strikers won recognition (Pope 2003a:18–19). Pope argues that by mid-April, miners were "flocking to mass meetings" and forming unions all over Pennsylvania. The upsurge was so immense that local and regional union leaders began to claim credit (Pope 2003b:261).

It should also be noted that in the two other industries, whose organization, many scholars argue, relied heavily on Section 7(a), similar activities took place. Pope claims that "the miners were not alone in their pre-NIRA organizing success." Philadelphia dressmakers, whose union had been reduced to "a mere skeleton," won a three-day strike, including recognition of the International Ladies' Garment Workers' Union (ILGWU), which "electrified the whole International." Shirtmakers outside New York, historically non-union, signed up "en masse," struck, and won union recognition in the main shirtmaking centers of Connecticut and Pennsylvania. As Pope shows, before FDR signed the NIRA on June 16, 1933, organization was virtually complete in many areas in both the garment and coal industries (2003a:20). Pope further concludes that the biggest impact of Section 7(a) was to spur companies all across the country to set up company-controlled unions. Thus, 7(a) may have been, rather than a stimulus, a roadblock to union organization, a point also argued by Preis (1964).

One can, of course, fruitlessly debate which factors were most important in stimulating the miners to act when they did: their general historical tendency toward militancy; the desperation that they, along with the general population, felt; or the growing solidarity of broad social movements around the country,

---

[39] It is important to note that "signing up" (especially by overwhelming majorities) is generally a process that takes place well after locals are already organized. Paid membership dues almost always lag behind actual organizing (Goldfield 1990b).

[40] In discussions of western Pennsylvania, I rely heavily on Pope's research and analysis.

including, among others, those of unemployed workers, farmers, students, African-Americans, and retirees. Singer claims the most important factor was the election and inauguration of FDR. However, he gives no evidence to back up this assertion.[41] He also fails to explain why the coal miners, and few others, were so stimulated (for the full argument see Singer 1996:117–19).To attribute all or most of the impetus for miner organizing to Section 7(a), which was not passed and signed into law until the organizing was just about over, even if the mine union leaders themselves tended to do so, is to substitute myths for facts and to falsify history.

The Vanguard Role of U.S. Coal Miners

When miners finally organized, gaining substantially higher wages, much in the way of democratic rights vis-à-vis their employers, and some slight respite from their onerous working conditions, their solidarity and willingness to defy authorities, whether county sheriffs, state militias, or even the federal government, were breath-taking. By their example and active aid to others, mineworkers set the table for the rest of the labor movement. Some selected examples will paint the picture.

"Wall to Wall" in Alabama

Coal miners not only struggled for themselves, but took a broad view of their role and responsibilities within the labor movement as a whole. This was certainly evident in the coal mining counties of northern Alabama. In Walker Country, just northwest of Jefferson County (the latter containing Birmingham), coal miners like their compatriots elsewhere became fully organized in 1933. They then proceeded to organize workers in virtually every other industry and occupation, "wall to wall." Not only coal miners but the many woodworkers, hod carriers, washerwomen, preachers, and schoolteachers all became organized. According to the *Union News*, the Walker County CIO newspaper, the county was the most highly unionized in the country, with, at least according to one report, even school principals unionized (U.S. Department of Labor 1945:291). What was the case in Walker Country was also so in many other counties in northern Alabama where coal miners were organized. Coal miners were also the strongest supporters of the Farmers' Union, which

---

[41] Singer also argues that Lewis and other mine union leaders did not grasp at first the strength of the early 1933 massive organizing. Only on June 15 did the *United Mine Workers Journal* (*UMWJ*) recognize the upsurge, claiming it was being led by Lewis. Belatedly Lewis gave his version of the role of 7(a) in the *UMWJ* (Singer 1996:117; *UMWJ*, October 15, 1933; see also Bernstein 1969:41–43). Singer argues, "Neither John L. Lewis nor the NIRA created this surge" (1996:118).

was successful in northern Alabama in organizing Black and white sharecroppers and renters, not merely in Walker County, but in Bibb, Tuscaloosa, Marion, and Shelby Counties.[42]

The coal miners in Alabama provided leadership and support for all other workers in their struggles. Textile workers in Alabama were among the earliest to organize in the South. Among southern textile workers they were the vanguard, if you will, of the events leading up to the 1934 textile general strike and by far the strongest contingent in the South. They were strengthened by their ability to count on the ready support of the more than twenty-three thousand organized coal miners in the state, as well as a state government more reluctant than many others, especially in the South, to mobilize its repressive powers in support of textile company owners, whose political strength they had to weigh against that of the highly unionized workforce.[43] I would call this the "Folsom effect," described in the introduction, or "Alabama exceptionalism."

Organizing U.S. Steelworkers

Miners were also critical in many places to the organizing of the nation's steelworkers. This was clearly the case in the steel center of Birmingham, Alabama, with its approximately twenty thousand steelworkers. First, it should be noted that the mineworkers' union contributed millions of dollars and scores of organizers to the overall national campaign in steel. While miners protested many things about the union, including its lack of democracy under the dictatorial Lewis regime, and successfully fought against the leadership in 1936 for a convention resolution in support of a labor party, I have found no record of any complaints in any archive or newspaper about the use of their dues money or paid officials being given to help aid the organization of steel. Mineworkers themselves were far from passive supporters. In Pennsylvania steel towns, especially in the Pittsburgh area, police-state conditions prevailed before 1936. Public speech and the calling of rallies in support of the Steel Workers Organizing Committee minimally meant loss of jobs, arrest, and occasionally death. At times, armed contingents of coal miners, sometimes numbering in the many thousands, marched into steel towns to ensure that allegedly constitutionally guaranteed rights of free speech and assembly would be peacefully respected. To an important, although somewhat lesser degree, the UMWA also lent money and staff to the early organizing efforts in the automobile industry.

---

[42] *The Union News*, May 6, 1937, which made this claim, reported fifteen thousand unionized workers and thirty-eight hundred members of the Farmers Union in Walker County alone (cited in U.S. Department of Labor 1945:291).

[43] The 1934 textile strike and the role of the Alabama contingent will be discussed more fully in Chapter 6.

Mineworkers, for various reasons, have always had a broad view of their struggles. The UMWA began the CIO era by bankrolling the new industrial organization and lending its own staff and leaders to assist with efforts both to staff the new organization and to organize in other industries.

Philip Murray and other assistants were in charge of the steel organizing; Van Bittner took control of the meatpacking drive, among other assignments. Mineworkers themselves helped organize and aid the struggles of other workers in their locales, including those in the wood and textile industries.

The leadership role of coal miners and their power to attract workers in other industries were a constant worry of mainstream CIO leaders after Lewis and the UMWA distanced themselves from the CIO. The untapped potential and fear that Lewis and the mineworkers would take the rest of the labor movement with them, away from the established leaders of the CIO, resurfaced numerous times during the 1940s and 1950s. The possibilities for taking the labor movement in a more militant, solidaristic direction, and undermining the class-collaborationist CIO leaders, struck fear into their hearts. This potential was never a real strategy for Lewis, but something with which he occasionally verbally toyed.

One potential vehicle for raiding CIO members after Lewis and the mineworkers left the organization in 1941 was UMWA District 50. In August 1936, District 50 had its first convention in Boston, to draw in utility workers originally affiliated with the AFL (Galenson 1960:200). Its initial claimed jurisdiction was in industries that used coal-derived chemicals, but this was to soon change (Zieger 1995:78). In August 1941, Lewis reorganized District 50, appointed his daughter Kathryn Lewis as secretary-treasurer, and began to give it large amounts of money from the UMWA treasury. He also pulled all the UMWA organizers off of CIO work and reassigned them to District 50. As Zieger notes, "It began to appear that Lewis was creating a sort of second CIO that was beginning to challenge the official CIO for the allegiance of workers in chemicals, paper, utilities and other areas" (1995:137).[44] Although District 50 was to reach well over two hundred thousand members by 1972, the year it officially merged with the United Steelworkers of America (USWA)—a number that then exceeded that of its original parent—it never quite fulfilled the hopes of Lewis or the fears of its enemies. However, the concerns of top CIO leaders after the break with Lewis were apparent in many situations.

The activities around the factional fights in the Packinghouse Workers Organizing Committee (PWOC) in 1940 suggest the depth of these fears on the part of national CIO leaders. In 1939, the national leadership of the PWOC, led by the highly bureaucratic, conservative former mineworkers' official Van Bittner,

---

[44] The most complete account of District 50 is the short encyclopedia entry by Donald Sofchalk (1977:76–79), while small tidbits can be gleaned from Zieger (1995) and Galenson (1960). There is also an in-house history by James Nelson (1955), its first president.

purged Communist activists—many of whom had played a major role in organizing the union, especially in the industry's Chicago center—from their positions within the organization. As Roger Horowitz describes, those eliminated included PWOC national director Don Harris, Chicago director Herb March (the center of the industry was located in Chicago), and a number of other regional organizers and staffers (1997:127). In 1940, however, when John L. Lewis effectively split himself off from the rest of the top CIO leadership by announcing his support for Republican presidential candidate Wendell Willkie in the upcoming election, a number of top PWOC leaders decided to throw in their lot with Lewis. These included some of the most prominent African-American leaders, led by assistant national director Hank Johnson and organizers Arthell Shelton and Frank Alsup. Although they enjoyed enormous prestige and support, especially among Black workers, those in the Johnson group were dismissed from their positions. They subsequently were hired by Lewis's UMWA District 50 and began encouraging the packinghouse workers to affiliate with it. Because of the fear that packinghouse workers, particularly African-Americans, who rightly suspected that the firing of the Johnson group signified a weakened commitment to fighting racial discrimination, might abandon them and follow Lewis, CIO leaders were forced to bring the Communists back into responsible positions, particularly in the key and high-percentage-Black district of Chicago, and eventually even to abandon the highly unpopular Bittner (Horowitz 1997:130–35). Such was the fear that Lewis and the UMWA inspired.

Rouge Event

It was not just politically and socially marginalized workers who looked to the miners for leadership and inspiration. In 1941, militant Ford workers, "often led by Communists and their allies," had been firmly supported by Lewis in their successful struggle to organize the strongly anti-union Ford Motor Company (Zieger 1990:49). At the heart of the Ford industrial empire was the River Rouge complex, whose United Auto Workers (UAW)Local 600 in 1951 still had more than sixty-two thousand members. Local 600 was a center for shop floor militancy, civil rights mobilizations, left-wing activity, and opposition to the bureaucratic Reuther machine, detested not only by union activists but by Lewis as well, who subjected Reuther to "widely publicized . . . scathing attacks" and viewed him as "the personification of what had gone wrong with the American labor movement since the Second World War" (Zieger 1990:49, 53). It seemed a marriage of convenience, if not a master stroke, when Local 600 invited Lewis to be the keynote speaker at its tenth anniversary celebration. National UAW leaders were up in arms, seeing the invitation to Lewis as just a bit short of treason, forbidding staffers to attend, and urging national and state political leaders to boycott the event. The appearance of Lewis, however, in the UAW heartland was too much for the media and politicians, no less workers, to resist. Tens of thousands of autoworkers and others left work and came to Cadillac Square and Grand Circus Park, the legendary site of mass working-class demonstrations in Detroit, often involving hundreds of thousands of workers. Though large numbers of workers and activists hoped the Lewis visit would help rekindle the spirit of the 1930s, it was not to be. In the UAW, the Reuther machine continued to tighten its authoritarian hold, making elections and control even more farcical and less competitive than Soviet-style elections during the same time period. As the bituminous coal industry continued to decline, Lewis—rather than being a beacon of class struggle and mass action—engaged in more and more collaborative arrangements with coal operators, including the virtual elimination of Black workers from the industry. Nonetheless, in good part because of their own lack of rapport with rank-and-file workers, UAW and CIO leaders for several years after the Rouge rally "kept a wary eye on Lewis" (Zieger 1990:55).

How the Miners Were Able to Play the Vanguard Role

Of special importance was the mineworkers' ability to mobilize their own constituency for broad-based, solidaristic, militant actions. During normal times, when there was not broad mobilization of all miners, this was not simple. The miners themselves were not uniform in their structural power; they had leading sectors within the industry that pulled along the rest. It was only during full mobilizations and national strikes that they were able to do this. Western Pennsylvania, Illinois, and Alabama miners often led the way. In general, it was miners in the larger mines who took the decisive initiatives. During normal times, miners in small installations, mostly "truck" miners, did not automatically join the union or strike. These non-union miners were the weak link in the industry. Their leverage in fragile, low-tech, relatively peripheral operations was relatively minimal. However, their grievances over wages, and especially safety, were similar to those of the rest of the country's coal miners. During the mass strike waves, they tended to get swept up in the mass movement, occasionally coerced by flying squadrons from the larger mines, but most often voluntarily joining the movement (on the importance of large workplaces, see Goldfield 1987:149–52).

In 1897, with a union membership of less than ten thousand, more than two hundred thousand coal miners answered the union call and struck. In 1933, before the passage of the NIRA, virtually all the nation's coal miners were swept up into the union. The 1943 and 1950 strikes, when the union was still at the height of its powers, exhibited these features also. After the bombing of Pearl Harbor, on December 7, 1941, FDR called together U.S. labor leaders and received a no-strike pledge in return for what would be called the National War Labor Board, which would have the power to adjudicate and enforce contracts, as well as ensure that workers in unionized facilities would "maintain" their membership. In July 1942, steelworkers received a 15% wage increase from the War Labor Board (WLB). The administration then made this the maximum raise, referred to as the "Little Steel Formula," for all industrial workers. However, as businesses received cost-plus contracts and continual permission to raise prices, the real wages of workers declined significantly, with cost of living rising, by some calculations, by as much as 30%. Unions complained bitterly, but to no avail (Reed 1982:90).

On January 2, 1943, twenty thousand anthracite miners went on strike, initially against a dues increase.[45] The strike, however, quickly morphed into one whose demand was a wage increase of two dollars a day, against the Little Steel Formula, as other miners began to join. On January 15, 1943, the WLB ordered the miners to return to work, and the strike then spread to virtually all of the country's over half million miners. On January 22, the miners finally went back to work at the urging of their leaders. Then, on January 30, the government's Office of Price Administration (OPA) approved a price increase for coal sales. On April 8, FDR ordered a general wage freeze (Reed 1982:91). When, on April 24, the WLB ordered a freeze on mineworkers' wages, coal miners in western Pennsylvania and Alabama stopped work. On May 1, President Roosevelt delivered an ultimatum to these miners, and every soft coal miner in the country left the pits, whereupon the government seized control of the mines. While virtually all non-coal union leaders opposed the strike, that was not the case among rank-and-file workers. Miners refused to go back to work, until they finally returned on June 3, only to strike again en masse on June 20. With a new contract deadline approaching on November 1, President Roosevelt threatened on October 13 to draft any coal miner who left work; thereafter, all twenty-three thousand Alabama miners stopped work. By November 1, every coal miner in the country was on strike. At this point, the government gave in; Secretary of the Interior Harold Ickes (with Roosevelt's concurrence) conceded to the mineworkers' main demands. The strikes of the mineworkers and their successful struggle emboldened workers in virtually all other industries.[46]

Despite the almost universal chorus of opposition from outside the union, Lewis and the mineworkers not only had 100% support within their own ranks but seemed to have the sympathy of large numbers of other U.S. workers, whose grievances they tended to reflect. When the miners struck on May 1, 1943, they were denounced

---

[45] There is some debate about the initial cause of the dispute (Dubofsky and Van Tine 1977). Singer argues that it was a 50% dues increase and was organized by Lewis oppositionists (1996:141). Preis (1964) argues that this was not the case.

[46] There are numerous detailed accounts of the 1943 coal strike (see, e.g., Preis 1964:174–97; Lichtenstein 1982; Dubofsky and Van Tine 1977; Singer 1996). It may also be the case that while many workers across the country were enthused by the strike, it also contributed to the backlash against labor that ultimately led to Taft-Hartley.

by AFL and CIO officials, including UAW president R. J. Thomas. Nevertheless, on May 2, in Detroit, one thousand UAW delegates representing 350,000 autoworkers in Michigan overwhelmingly voted to support the strike. Despite the appeals of Thomas and Walter Reuther at the convention, only a half dozen voted against the coal strike (Glaberman 1980:95). Thus, according to Martin Glaberman, "The ability and willingness of the miners to take on the government in a series of battles and emerging with a significant victory was evident to everyone in the country, not least of all the autoworkers ... it lent legitimacy and strength to those who opposed the no-strike pledge" (1980:97; for a different analysis, see Laslett 1996:140–45).

The same phenomenon was in evidence during the 1950 coal strikes.[47] After World War II, coal miners and the union became more and more focused on health and safety, with the union negotiating employer contributions to a union-administered health program, complete with union-run health centers and hospitals and union-paid physicians. However, mine disasters continued to occur. One of the biggest took place on March 25, 1947, when a mine explosion in Centralia, Illinois, killed 111. Investigators determined that the cause was a failure by the company to take certain safety measures (Phillips 2002:9).

Concerns over safety were not confined to mineworkers. On May 6, 1949, sixty-two thousand Ford Rouge workers, for example, wildcatted over speedup and safety issues (Phillips 2002:12). On the same date, the continuous miner was introduced at Bethlehem Steel's Carolina-Idamay captive mine in Marion County, West Virginia. The amount of dust and heat generated by this new machinery was so extreme that it could no longer be controlled by the existing sprinkler systems, and miners saw their health and safety conditions deteriorating. Meanwhile, a number of National Labor Relations Board (NLRB) decisions challenged the union. The Taft-Hartley Act of 1947 mandated that union shops could be achieved only by a workplace vote run by the NLRB. Since the coal miners had refused, however, to sign the anti-communist pledges of Taft-Hartley, they were not eligible for NLRB elections. The union shop provisions of their contracts were ruled illegal. Then questions were raised about whether the health and welfare royalty payments to the union were legal contractual issues. Companies began to refrain from making their contractual contributions, and the union health care system approached insolvency (Philips 2002:15).

On September 19, 1950, the largest captive mine in West Virginia, Barrackbille, and largest commercial mine, Grant Town, voted to strike until companies paid into the health and welfare fund. The rest of West Virginia and southwestern Pennsylvania miners immediately followed; roving pickets covered the whole region, including many "small unorganized mines." Most scab operators immediately closed their mines when they saw union pickets (Philips 2002:16–17).

---

[47] There is a paucity of material on the 1950 strike. The best account is Phillips (2002).

On October 1, 1950, steelworkers also went out on strike, followed shortly by workers at Ford, Chrysler, and General Motors. These strikes together almost certainly stalled efforts to repeal the Taft-Hartley Act, creating an anti-union public opinion backlash (Phillips 2002:19). John L. Lewis then ordered the West Virginia miners back to work, but they refused to comply. Finally, district officials called a meeting on January 19, 1950 to try to get the miners back. Two thousand showed up and chased the international reps from the stage; Lewis's name was booed from the floor (Philips 2002:20–21). The coal miners again had support from the rest of the labor movement. Autoworkers in Detroit donated money and food. Tommy Thompson, president of UAW Local 600, came to Pursglove, West Virginia, with a food caravan and relief money, pledging the support of the sixty thousand auto workers at his Ford local (Philips 2002:30). The 1950 strike, however, was the last one that Lewis was to lead.

Lessons Drawn from the National Coal Strikes

Both strikes mobilized and had the support of virtually every coal miner in the country, from those in the larger, more militant mines and the vanguard regions of the country, especially Alabama, almost always an area that led the way in struggle (of great relevance to our thesis on the South), to those in the smaller, more difficult to organize areas. However, without mass mobilizations and mass strikes, miners in the small mines could not be mobilized and brought into the union. This was to become a long-term problem for the United Mine Workers. During the 1950s, Lewis and the union turned to a very narrow, collaborationist, bureaucratic style of business unionism. The union declined dramatically as membership went from more than 500,000 in 1950 to 175,000 in 1960. Lewis became a "labor statesman" who was largely adverse to conflict, aiding mine owners in providing stability to the industry (Dubofsky and Van Tine 1977:502).

Mechanization was in good part responsible for the decline in miner employment numbers. Coal usage had been declining since the end of World War II. In 1940, it constituted 30.3% of the nation's fuel. By 1964, it was only 23.1%. Coal production, 688 million tons in 1947, was only 516 million tons in 1950, and down to 392 in 1954 (Dubofsky and Van Tine 1977:494).

Combined with mechanization was the increased proliferation of small non-union "truck" mines. By 1953, up to 20% of working miners were not UMWA members, many working for small non-union mines in hundreds of "truck" mines, encouraged in their growth by the government-run Tennessee Valley Authority (TVA), which rapidly became the largest user of coal. Unlike the traditional government policies established during the 1930s and applied most consistently in the construction industry, TVA did not favor unionized suppliers that paid the "prevailing wages" and benefits. Rather, they favored the lowest bidders, those employing miners in the most oppressive, least remunerative conditions. Dubofsky and Van Tine suggest that liberals and radicals favored these "price-cutting, non-union operators" because they were merely "little guys trying to make good" (1977:504). The largest number of these mines were concentrated in still violently anti-union counties in Kentucky and Tennessee. The existence of such a large number of non-union mines began to jeopardize the UMWA's national agreements with the large mining companies, and Lewis was told as much by the operators (Dubofsky and Van Tine 1977:503). Small non-union mines could compete with large mechanized mines not merely by paying much lower wages, but by avoiding royalty payments to the health and retirement funds, and not having to enforce union and government safety practices, the latter of which were not applicable to companies with fewer than sixteen employees (Dubofsky and Van Tine 1977:495). Given the repressive conditions, small mines could not be organized without being tied to a militant insurgent union movement. By the early 1960s, it was estimated that the non-union mines accounted for as much as 25% of all coal production (Dubofsky and Van Tine 1977:495).

Unable or unwilling to organize these mines by traditional bureaucratic means, Lewis turned the "problem" over to his assistant, William Anthony ("Tony") Boyle, who set up guerrilla armies and covert activities to deal with the situation. The Boyle operation often roamed the mining districts with armed groups, coercing miners to join and dynamiting the equipment of recalcitrant owners. This process helped transform the union from a militant, solidaristic—albeit highly authoritarian—organization into a violent, gangster-style organization. It was three of Boyle's lieutenants who would be convicted in the 1970s of the murder of Boyle's challenger for union president, "Jock" Yablonski (Dubofsky and Van Tine 1977:503–504).

What are we to make of this degeneration of the UMWA from its leading role in the upsurge in the 1930s and 1940s to its sinking into a largely criminal organization that abandoned its constituency even on the crucial issues of mine safety and black lung disease? How much of the trajectory of the union was due to John L. Lewis's unique personality (a claim made in much of the literature on the subject), and how much was due to the structural imperatives of the industry and union? And could things have been largely different? I will offer some preliminary assessments here. I begin by looking at Lewis and how he compared with previous leaders of the mineworkers, since much discussion of the CIO and the UMWA focuses on Lewis's personality.

John L. Lewis, the Miners' Union, and the CIO

No twentieth century American labor leader preached class struggle more loudly than John L. Lewis—nor practiced class collaboration more cunningly.

Dubofsky and Van Tine (1977:xiv–xv)

In assessing how the mineworkers led the formation of the CIO and how they set a standard for organization, worker militancy, and broad solidarity, one must inevitably evaluate the role of John L. Lewis. To say the least, Lewis was a contradictory figure, for some an anomaly, a baffling contradiction, whose actions can be explained by his idiosyncratic personality. On the one hand, Lewis seemed to be the unflinching head of the miners and the CIO, winning pathbreaking deals for the miners, including higher wages, benefits, and health care. On the other hand, he was personally corrupt: he was friends with bankers and mine operators, at times selling out miners, even receiving payoffs to restrict organizing. He brutally repressed his union opponents, was at times aggressively anti-communist, and periodically supported conservative Republicans. At other times, he collaborated with Communists wholeheartedly, claimed to be a radical leftist, and preached class struggle. Sometimes he exhibited these characteristics in different situations; sometimes he did so simultaneously.

Differing assessments of Lewis do not necessarily depend on where the writer stands on the political spectrum. He had his defenders and detractors, both among conservatives and coal operators and among those on the left.

In 1964, Art Preis, former editor of the Trotskyist Socialist Workers' Party newspaper, the *Militant*, wrote:

> It is doubtful if the CIO would have been formed, or if the industrial union movement would have arrived as quickly as it did, if not for the exceptional qualities of Lewis. There has been a vile campaign to denigrate and discredit Lewis, to low-rate his real role. Lewis has many weaknesses—political conservatism, blind belief in capitalism, contempt for union democracy—which he shares with virtually all other top union officials. But it was Lewis, with his boldness, his self-reliance, his aggressiveness and courage, stamping him as a man of superior character and moral fibre, who pushed through the CIO's formation. When his detractors are long dead and forgotten, the American working class will remember and honor Lewis as the founder of the CIO. (1964:43)

Before the formation of the CIO in 1935, most radicals had a far more negative view of Lewis. Anna Rochester, for example, in describing Lewis's tenure from his ascendancy to the UMWA presidency in 1919 until 1931, said that he followed the business union tradition (as opposed to a "militant union policy") "that kept the favor of the operators by playing into their hands."

> He and his lieutenants have accomplished more bald betrayals of the miners to the operators and more autocratic suppressing of a militant rank and file than are revealed in the annals of any earlier regime. (1931:199)

Rochester then went on to compellingly document the long list of sellouts by Lewis throughout the 1920s.

Because Lewis was so central to the mineworkers and the formation of the CIO, it is worth examining his activities in detail, trying to separate his personal characteristics from the structural imperatives of his union, distinguishing necessity from alternative possibilities.

One question for us, of course, is whether Lewis changed during the 1930s and perhaps the 1940s. Another question is whether—regardless of any change he may or may not have undergone—was he a boon to the formation of industrial unions during the 1930s, someone who helped empower the labor movement, or was merely an opportunistic con man, along for the ride, who kept the labor movement from realizing a fuller potential. Or, as others have argued, was he a bit of both, contradictory to the end?

This question has a particular importance for us about what was possible during the 1930s, whether Lewis helped the labor movement realize its full potential, especially in the South. A deeper understanding of Lewis will also allow us to more fully evaluate the other key players in the labor movement, in particular in the attempt to organize the South (many of whom were originally protégés of Lewis). I begin with something of a balance sheet of pros and cons; on the basis of this material, I will then strive for a more nuanced assessment.[48]

Skills and Dedication

Orator

Lewis was clearly one of the compelling orators of his time; he had a deep baritone voice and was an amateur thespian in his younger days before he became fully immersed in union activities. He was able to use biblical, Shakespearean, and other classic material to great advantage and borrowed freely from Bartlett's quotations. As a speaker, he was by all accounts charismatic.

Tireless Worker

Lewis subordinated virtually everything else in his life, personal and otherwise, to his labor activities. He had a distaste for alcohol, did not hang out in barrooms or at parties, led a prudish sexual life, and seemed to have no interest or preferences with

---

[48] While I have looked at numerous sources for material on Lewis, including much of the hagiography as well as extensive archival material, I rely heavily on the biography of Lewis by Dubofsky and Van Tine (1977), unquestionably the most in-depth, careful account. I supplement their account with other material at critical junctures.

respect to religion. In order to carry out his union responsibilities, he was often away from his family for long periods of time (Dubofsky and Van Tine 1977:7, passim).

Skilled Negotiator

He was a skilled negotiator, often winning important benefits for his members, maintaining wage rates, equalizing northern and southern wage scales, winning portal- to-portal pay during World War II, and gaining employer-funded, union-run health facilities (Dubofsky and Van Tine 1977:38). Even when the 1919 strike was broken by the government, Lewis won substantial concessions from mine operators (1977:48). Lewis also often understood, as many other moderate and business union leaders did not, that it was the militancy of the miners that allowed him to take strong negotiating positions (1977:192). He frequently used leading academic experts, especially his chief economic adviser, economist W. Jett Lauck. Lewis always displayed detailed knowledge of the industry and the working conditions of miners, especially when testifying at congressional hearings, but also during contract negotiations, at union conventions, and in talking to the media.

Skilled Administrator

Lewis was, by all accounts, a skilled administrator of the union, building alliances with key leaders in all districts, running an adequate newspaper, carefully controlling and accounting for the union's finances, and keeping in touch regularly with his subordinates in every district. He held to certain principles, which he pushed aggressively throughout his career. He believed in high wages for his constituents: he held that the nature of their work, and the dangers and diseases to which they were subjected, entitled them to good pay. He did not believe that government had a right to interfere within unions. For this reason, he adamantly opposed Taft-Hartley, and continued to oppose it long after other union leaders (some with more undeserved radical reputations) had accepted it or, like the UAW's Walter Reuther, had used it opportunistically from the beginning to attack their leftist rivals. Under Lewis, the UMWA worked tirelessly to defeat those congressmen and senators who had supported Taft-Hartley. As a result of the union's 1948 campaign, forty-one congressmen and six senators who had supported the bill, and who resided in coal mining areas, were not reelected. When Robert Taft successfully ran for reelection in 1950, two of the four Ohio counties he lost had large numbers of unionized miners (Dubofsky and Van Tine 1977:475). As late as 1953, Lewis and the mineworkers' union still had not signed the government affidavits stating that they were not Communists (Dubofsky and Van Tine 1977:503).

On the Other Side of the Ledger

Corruption

As Dubofsky and Van Tine document extensively, a history of corruption and self-aggrandizement, either through deals based on his union positions or actual enrichment from union funds, were signature traits of John L. Lewis, long before he emerged as a figure in national mine union politics. Much of this initial corruption involved his five brothers, who were also involved, beginning in 1910, in union politics in Panama, Illinois. When Lewis resigned as president of the Panama UMWA local, his brother Thomas took over, having no problem being both president of the local and manager of the mine where his constituents worked. Thomas, another brother Denny, and their father were later cited by auditors appointed by the union district for embezzlement in "one of the widest conspiracy cases in the United Mine Workers on record" (Dubofsky and Van Tine 1977:23). Although Lewis was not directly implicated, he continued to appoint his brothers and other family members to important positions within the union. By 1917, Lewis was a union lobbyist in Washington, DC, then business manager of the *UMW Journal*.

Lewis became close friends with and gambled with key coal operators at this time, accepting payments on the side during negotiations. As Dubofsky and Van Tine conclude, rather mildly, "By 1917, then, Lewis was deeply involved with the shady entrepreneurial characters and the peculiar style of bargaining that would shadow his entire trade union career" (1977:36). Or more succinctly, he engaged in graft and business dealings with operators for his personal benefit, while allegedly representing the interests of coal miners, all of whom would most likely have considered such activities treason (Finley 1972). During the 1920s, Lewis worked with financier and publisher Al Hamilton to negotiate sweetheart deals with mine owners and got personal kickbacks (Singer 1996:106).

Like a number of his immediate predecessors, Lewis enjoyed a rich lifestyle and amassed a considerable amount of wealth during his presidency. John Mitchell (1898–1907), Tom Lewis (1907–10), John P. White (1911–17), and Frank Hayes (1917–19) were all well paid, traveled first class, and imitated the lifestyle of the corporate elite (Dubofsky and Van Tine 1977:95–96). Lewis (1919–60), when he traveled, stayed at the finest hotels, including the Waldorf-Astoria in New York City and the Willard in Washington, DC. Not only his wife, Myrta, but other members of the family often accompanied him at union expense. Most members of his and his wife's families earned their livings either directly or indirectly from the UMWA. Lewis sported the most expensive, finely tailored business suits, often with a gold chain and silk ties. Myrta wore an extravagant, high-priced mink coat. For his personal use, he drove costly Cadillac roadsters. He purchased gravestones for his daughter Mary Margaret and his father at a cost of $1,000, a third of his annual salary.

Myrta Lewis's lifelong passion was collecting fine, delicate, and expensive antiques, and she spent thousands of dollars on her obsession during the 1920s and 1930s (Dubofsky and Van Tine 1977:97). The Lewises had numerous prestigious country club memberships and a vacation home on an island off the Florida Gulf Coast. He was also a regular visitor to a Jackson Hole resort, a favorite of wealthy business executives (1977:97). All these possessions and activities were well outside the means of even a well-paid union president. His social friends (including the Harrimans and Cyrus Eaton) were all members of the wealthy business ruling class. Not one of his union associates, including his most faithful servant for decades, Philip Murray, ever met the Lewises socially.

Anti-Democracy

Although it was true that other industrial unions were authoritarian like the miners' union under Lewis, few approached Lewis's level of repression and brutality. Here, Preis's apology is clearly disconnected from the facts.[49] As Singer notes, Lewis ruled the union "with an iron hand," despite Lewis's claim that "we have more democracy in the United Mine Workers of America than any other labor organization that I know." Singer adds, "Lewis's conception of democracy permitted him, as president of the union, to deny autonomy to UMWA districts, to use International Union organizers to impose central decisions on the union's membership, to rig election results, and to suppress dissidents by branding them as Communists and barring them from the UMWA as dual unionists" (1996:146–47).

The degree of violence used by Lewis against his opponents within the union was unprecedented among the mineworkers, and perhaps far exceeded that of any other major union leadership against its factional opponents. At the 1923 convention, Lewis, previously portraying himself as a radical allied with Communism, became a leading force in the fight against radicalism. He demanded that William

---

[49] Contrary to Preis's blithe and caustic assessment, and his unqualified, virulent anti-communism, many unions, especially left-led ones, were more democratic, as Stepan-Norris and Zeitlin (1996) make clear. Zieger, no friend of the Communist Party, cites the large presence and influence of a "large and well-led Communist contingent" and "vigorous internal democracy" in UAW Local 600 in opposition to the authoritarian Reuther regime (1996:157). The same was also true of the woodworkers' union when they were led by Communists, whose leadership changed control at the national level from Communist to non-Communist and whose districts were relatively independent. While the UAW (under Walter Reuther) and the steelworkers were as undemocratic as the UMWA, and their districts and regions were as tightly controlled, neither used excessive violence and repression, or extended it to the local level, the way the UMWA did under Lewis. Paradoxically, contrary to assertions, both by Preis and much Cold War scholarship, authoritarian control of unions and repression were more characteristic of liberal- and conservative-led unions than left-wing ones.

Z. Foster's son-in-law, Joseph Manley (Foster being one of the country's leading Communists), who had been invited to the convention as an observer, immediately leave and return to his "beloved Russia." Once outside the convention hall, Manley and an associate were severely beaten (Dubofsky and Van Tine 1977:99). When non-Communist radical and Lewis oppositionist John Brophy, former president of Pennsylvania District 12, ran for union president against Lewis in 1926, it is almost certain that Lewis lost the election. Brophy's supporters arrived at the 1927 convention with dozens of documented examples of voter fraud. Led by Powers Hapsgood, they went among the delegates, spreading the information. A group of Lewis thugs cornered Hapsgood in a hallway and beat him into unconsciousness, necessitating a trip to the hospital, and the effort collapsed (Finley 1972: 64–5; Dubofsky and Van Tine 1977:129–30). Lewis thugs also murdered four NMU activists leading up to the 1928 founding NMU convention. In 1930, when then–Lewis opponent Adolph Germer went to address a local of oppositionists in Illinois, Lewis sent three hundred armed supporters to ensure that the meeting never took place (Dubofsky and Van Tine 1977:69). These thugs were led by Bill Blizzard, former leader and hero of the battle of Blair Mountain, now turned Lewis hatchet man and gangster (1977:69).

Lewis and Radicalism

Beginning in 1933, however, as the upsurge of workers was taking place, his own union now fully organized, Lewis seemed to go through a transformation, seemingly more open to radicalism and broad class struggle, as was noted even in the changing assessments of his most trenchant detractors. In a letter to Oscar Ameringer dated October 25, 1929, John Brophy wrote about Lewis that "his presence in the Union is an insult to every honest man."[50] However, in 1935, Brophy, Powers Hapsgood, a Brophy disciple, and other radicals decided to work with Lewis, and agreed to rejoin the union and support him. They did not believe he had changed, but, Hapsgood argued, he saw Lewis at the 1935 AFL convention, "fighting for the things that we in the opposition had long been contending for. What is more, I saw him fighting with an effectiveness that none of us could muster" (Singer 1996:123). Brophy agreed (1964:124).

However, this seeming schizophrenia, this oscillation between extreme class collaboration and personal corruption, and willingness to embrace radicalism and help mobilize broad class struggles, was a feature of the union from the beginning, not just an idiosyncrasy of Lewis. One can also see these characteristics in John Mitchell (president, 1898–1908), perhaps the most important UMWA president

---

[50] Brophy Papers, correspondence folder; see also Singer (1996:115).

before Lewis and a man who in certain ways was even more conservative than Lewis in temperament and politics.

The push for centralization and the elimination of rank-and-file influence and control were, in good part, a result of the economic imperatives of national collective bargaining. Lewis, in this respect, was merely following in the footsteps of his predecessors. Phelan notes that the success of a national trade agreement depended on a tightly controlled national union (1996;73). In order for this to happen, Mitchell was "quite ruthless in asserting his authority and subduing his rivals, and he laid the foundations of a union in which rank-and-file sentiment would exercise limited influence" (1996:73). It also meant that he spent large amounts of time "with large-scale operators who purchased . . . labor . . . and national political figures" (1996:73). "By the time he stepped down as UMWA president, his speech, his clothing, his associations . . . his outlook more closely resembled those of the employers than the rank-and-file" (1996:73–74). Phelan asserts, "There is no evidence that Mitchell, like his successor Tom L. Lewis, pursued centralization merely to enhance personal power. For Mitchell, centralization was a prerequisite to the proper functioning of the interstate agreement" (1996:79). In order to ensure stable collective bargaining benefits and guarantee stability to the operators, he virtually eliminated local and district autonomy, an autonomy that often allowed locals and districts to call strikes against the wishes of the national leadership (1996:80). "Only strikes approved by the president and the national board received strike funds" (1996:80). Like Lewis in later years, Mitchell had great skill as a negotiator and marshaled an "impressive arsenal of facts" (1996:80). At the 1901 AFL Scranton convention, Mitchell successfully fought to gain an industrial charter for the UMWA, yet (unlike what Lewis was to do later) he stood with Gompers against resolutions advocating industrial unionism (1996:86). Cutting his spurs as an organizer during the 1897 national coal strike, he competently led the 1902 anthracite strike to an impressive victory. However, he saw publicity, arguments based on carefully researched facts and figures, and his political alliances and public opinion as more important than rank-and-file militancy (1996:90).

Union Strategy and the Structure of the Industry

Coal miners had enormous structural power, since the coal mine workforce consisted of workers whose skills could not be easily replaced, except by other miners. Their conditions of work and life and the structural power they enjoyed (because of both their centrality to the economy and the difficulty of replacing them) led to high levels of militancy. As Gowaskie suggests, "Mine owners persistently complained about their miners leaving the pits over the slightest provocation and smallest grievances. They also angrily maintained that miners refused to work while various disputes were being settled and that they frequently took off paydays and unofficial holidays" (1976:673). Operators thus depended on the union, once it was organized, to control most of this volatility. John Mitchell promised to do just that. While there was still intense opposition to the union in many arenas, including Colorado, Kentucky, West Virginia, and Alabama, many operators depended on the Mitchell-led UMWA to maintain "organization restraint" in return for acceptance of the UMWA and its union pay scale (Gowaskie 1976:680).

This agreement is part of the nature of trade unions under capitalism, what I have called the trade union legality (Chapter 1). This compromise was most effective when a militant workforce was fully organized in an industry, and wages and other conditions were taken out of competition. This situation, however, existed for only a brief period, from 1933 to 1950, when the miners were fully mobilized.

As Gowaskie argues, there were an enormous number of small operators, though this was understated in the census. "Many smaller operators were able to undersell larger competitors with higher fixed costs and operating expenses by paying low wages to their miners" (1976:686). The full unionization of the coalfields would eliminate this problem. From the beginning, large operators complained pub-licly that the UMWA was remiss in organizing non-union miners rapidly enough (1976:687).

We can conclude, then, that Lewis fits squarely within the tradition of leader-ship in the union, that he was not an iconoclastic outlier. John L. Lewis led the union during certain periods of mobilization, the full organization of the industry in 1933–38, and the 1943 and 1950 strikes. His personal corruption and author-itarian grip on the union, which largely stifled rank-and-file democracy and mili-tancy, eventually undermined the union.[51]

Tentative Assessments

Let me end this chapter with an assessment of Lewis and the coal miners' union and give some tentative conclusions about the possibilities grasped and missed during the 1930s, 1940s, and beyond. First, to a large extent Lewis must be understood in the context of the structure of the coal industry and the history of his predecessors. Although the coal miners were highly militant, solidaristic, and prone to radicalism, it is a mistake to view them as a uniform group. Companies and mines varied con-siderably. Some were clustered together in militant, solidaristic fields; others were small, isolated, or greatly constrained by powerful companies. In an overwhelming upsurge, many of the latter were swept along and received a great deal of help from more militant miners. In normal times, they were weak, with little leverage, and depended on the largesse of the national organization.

---

[51] "[T]oo often, Lewis's primary loyalty, his broader purpose, appears to have been self-advancement, personal aggrandizement, and power" (Singer 1996:146).

Thus, the strength of the union as a whole was in good part dependent on the ability of the more militant, structurally powerful groups of miners to offer associational power and support to those who were weaker; the latter were in turn necessary to ensure complete control of the industry and maximize their trade union leverage.

John Mitchell illuminates the parameters union leaders faced and the types of choices to be made. Mine operators were willing to make concessions to a union whose members had proved themselves willing and able to disrupt production on a large scale. They were willing to recognize the union and give benefits in return for a commitment to harmony and class collaboration (including a union that looked out for the interests of the operators in certain respects, for example by offering an assurance of the quality and timeliness of production). Continued collaboration with operators, however, also depended on the organizing of unorganized areas, even in times of low levels of class struggle. This was the dilemma for the union: either militant class struggle or extension of its network of class collaboration. It was an especially difficult dilemma for the miners' union.

Mitchell exemplifies a choice union leaders face again and again. Do they rely on the mobilization of the rank and file to engage in the broadest possible struggle with employers, gaining allies from other segments of the working class or the more downtrodden segments of the population (and in the process risking or even undermining the class compromise), or do they rely on their relations with capitalists and important politicians, using the facts about their industry and the conditions of their constituency, as well as their own reasonableness to compromise, as the basis for winning improvements for their followers?

Even within the context of mass mobilization and trade union compromise, leaders like Mitchell, no less Lewis, had choices to make. They could have aligned themselves with the more militant, radical segments of the labor force, even during the bleakest times. Rather than relying on government assistance and the largesse of operators, which often disappeared once the economic leverage of the union disintegrated, the mineworkers' union could have joined with others in the 1920s who were pushing more strongly for industrial unionism and a labor party, demands that many miners already fully embraced.

When the Depression began, the national union should have embraced the struggles of the miners that broke out across the coalfields and given strong support to the social movements that were sweeping the country, including the unemployed workers and farmers movements, as well as the struggle for African-American equality. In many places, including the South, miners were often inclined to do this. In turn, these movements in certain cases could have provided broader associational power to the miners, strengthening their struggles, as they did in auto plants in Toledo, Ohio, and in other auto plants, among Minneapolis teamsters, and during the San Francisco general strike. The strong unemployed, civil rights, and Black and ethnic movements, as well as the Communist Party, which existed in Pittsburgh, Chicago, and Birmingham (all of which were utilized surreptitiously later in the 1930s in steel and other industries), could have been exploited to greatly strengthen coalworkers' leverage, something that partially happened in Alabama. The push for a labor party, supported broadly in the labor movement, even among many members of more conservative unions, would have received a tremendous boost from stronger support by the mineworkers.

When the CIO was formed, Lewis and the mineworkers gave mixed support to more radical segments of the labor movement, but in the end often undermined them. Lewis was, of course, less narrow-minded at times than his more ideologically conservative colleagues, and gave early support to the CP-led United Cannery, Agricultural, Packing and Allied Workers of America (UCAPAWA) and the United Electrical Workers (UE). At other times, however, he helped destroy more radical forces. The woodworkers, under their early left-wing leadership, wanted to organize Black and white southern woodworkers, which would have given a tremendous boost to labor/civil rights activism in the South. As we shall see, this was eminently possible. Lewis, however, presided over the first anti-communist purge in 1938–39, sending in his operatives to support a right wing, which not only did not want to organize the South, but which even liberal/right CIO leaders came to view as totally provincial and incompetent. The same scenario almost played out in meat slaughtering and packing. In steel, Lewis and Murray used the Communists, especially their Black organizers, to organize the industry, then eliminated all democracy, leaving the union under the firm control of the anti-democratic, unimaginative, racially oppressive Philip Murray. There were other possibilities that a more radical mineworkers' union might have pursued. It could have sought broader alliances with the Trotskyist-led insurgency in the teamsters and strengthened rather than tried to eclipse the power of the West Coast longshoremen. Had they had been willing to force a direct confrontation within the CIO, they could have pushed for a militant campaign among southern textile workers in 1937, when the possibilities for organizing the industry looked real, rather than letting the Hillman-led Textile Workers Organizing Committee pursue its self-defeating Gompers-esque approach.

As the structural power of the union declined, especially in the 1950s, miners might have allied more closely with the radical wing of the labor movement. Interestingly, at times Lewis was not averse to this, as his support of UAW Local 600 suggests, as did his overtures to the United Electrical Workers (UE) and the Food, Tobacco, Agricultural, and Allied Workers (FTA) in 1947 to call a joint general strike against Taft-Hartley. The UMWA's refusal to sign the Taft-Hartley anti-communist affidavits did in the beginning lead Lewis to explore alliances with the CP-led UE and FTA. Lewis and the union might have taken a more aggressive stance on saving the jobs of Black miners, especially in West Virginia, as mechanization all but eliminated them from the industry. Although the ILWA on the West Coast largely capitulated to employers on the issue of jobs as the companies switched to containerization, the ILWA did not do so at the expense of Black and Latino workers. The example of the United Packinghouse Workers Union, which transformed itself both internally and externally into a militant civil rights organization, could have been followed. Lewis, a vocal advocate of civil rights, leading the union to be active in the CP-influenced National Negro Congress during the late 1930s and early 1940s, might have joined with or even transformed the National Negro Labor Alliance of the 1950s in pursuing such aims. Broader associational power during the 1950s might well have aided the mineworkers in their own struggles.

These, of course, are mere conjectures, but they are choices that Lewis did not make. His lifestyle, corruption, personal aggrandizement, and close relations with major bankers and industrialists, as well as his brutal authoritarian rule (which went hand in hand with these latter attributes), foreclosed these possibilities. Lewis, of course, was not the only obstacle to the development of much a broader, class-struggle labor movement, but he was an important one.

3

Social Movement Upsurge

Associative Power

Introduction

I have argued that workplace struggles and unionization are central to the politics
of modern capitalist societies. And this was especially true of the 1930s and 1940s
in the United States. More days were lost during both the 1918–21 and 1946 strike
waves than were lost in the 1930s and 1940s (as Melvyn Dubofsky 1979:12 likes to
point out). Yet the strike waves of the 1930s and 1940s were far more powerful and
consequential. One reason for this was the rise of massive social movements, which
were more extensive than those in the other two periods.

As various industry-specific chapters indicate, these social movements often
gave important associative power to labor struggles, as well as being important
movements in their own right. I do not wish to fully revisit these movements (many
of which are the subject of important and extensive scholarship and a few of which
are discussed in some detail in later chapters). I wish here merely to sketch some
of the general contours and suggest some of the influence they may have had. For
analytic purposes, I wish to distinguish these movements (although in certain cases
they were closely intertwined) according to the type of influence they had and support they gave to various labor struggles.

First, I wish to underscore those movements that were often closely allied with
and gave strong support to various labor struggles. Of first rank were the struggles
of the unemployed, invariably (or at least overwhelmingly) led by radicals, most
often, at least initially (1929–33), Communists. Organizations and struggles of
unemployed workers existed in virtually every large city and in literally thousands
of industrial areas, often giving important support to labor struggles, as evidenced
in Detroit, Chicago, New York, and Pittsburgh, and adding associative power to
the semi-insurrectionary union struggles of 1934 in Minneapolis, Toledo, Ohio,
and San Francisco. They played critical supportive roles in certain industries (as
documented in subsequent chapters on steel and wood especially). In addition,

The Southern Key. Michael Goldfield, Oxford University Press (2020) © Michael Goldfield
DOI: 10.1093/oso/9780190079321.001.0001

they often served as training arenas for many future labor leaders. Though they were important and extensive in many areas of the South, they are overlooked in much of the literature, which focuses largely on the North. These sometimes massive struggles also forced governments at the local, state, and federal levels to address the problems of the unemployed.

Second, three other types of organizations, often if not always led by radicals, gave important support and impetus to workers' struggles. These included civil rights organizations of various sorts, farmers' organizations, and ethnic and immigrant organizations.

Third, these and many other organizations also played a major role in providing an insurgent, often radical context during the 1930s. They included organizations of seniors demanding guaranteed pensions, students, and some that are hard to characterize, including Louisiana Senator Huey Long's Share the Wealth movement (sometimes improperly characterized as right-wing and accused of bearing some resemblance to that of Nazi sympathizer and anti-Semite Father Coughlin). Finally, the 1930s saw a proliferation of state and local third parties, including some that elected U.S. senators and members of Congress, and even governors. There were also an array of other groups, including artists, intellectuals, veterans, and jazz musicians, adding to the ferment and occasionally playing a supportive role.

The Unemployed

While the 1920s had seen robust economic growth, it had not been kind to the majority of workers. Although industrial production grew dramatically, especially between 1926 and 1929 (auto production increasing from 4.3 to 5.36 million vehicles per year during this period; Galbraith 1988:2), millions of farmers were in crisis, income inequality increased, wages declined, and unemployment often reached double digits (Bernstein 1960:47, 59). Communists during this period, although highlighting these issues, had been largely unsuccessful at mobilizing the unemployed, suggesting that while determined, competent leadership may be, as I argue, the crucial variable at times, the right context is certainly a prerequisite. From October 21, 1929, to Black Thursday, October 29, 1929, the stock market suffered a series of major crashes that signaled the collapse of the U.S. economy; investment stopped, and unemployment steadily rose to as high as 25% by early 1933 (perhaps as high as 37% of the non-agricultural labor force).[1] The economic conditions of the employed were also dismal, with hours shortened and wages cut, initially as much as 10–20% (Commons and Associates 1935:88–92).

---

[1] Government unemployment figures were not reliably kept during this period. For discussion of various estimates and some conservative assessments, see Darby (1976); Smiley (1983).

With the collapse of both the rural and urban economies, millions, including many children, took to riding the rails. In 1932, Southern Pacific, just one of many railroads, threw almost seven hundred thousand people off its trains (Folsom 1991:239). Shantytowns, aptly dubbed "Hoovervilles," emerged in major cities around the country, especially in those like Chicago that were transportation centers (Bernstein 1960:254, 155, 197). Spontaneous struggles, including group raids on food stores, emerged. And into this environment stepped the Unemployed Councils (UC), led by the Communist Party (CP). In a matter of months, hundreds of militant mass organizations had been organized around the country. On March 6, 1930, Communists worldwide took part in unemployment demonstrations. In the United States, where more than a million demonstrated, it is estimated that fifty thousand protestors turned out in Boston, thirty thousand in Philadelphia, twenty-five thousand in Cleveland, twenty thousand in Pittsburgh and Youngstown, and one hundred thousand each in New York City and Detroit (Folsom 1991:255). Active UCs existed around the country, including the South; Atlanta, Birmingham, Richmond, and Chattanooga were early centers. Yet isolated areas were not immune. Especially militant and well organized were groups in Michigan's Upper Peninsula. In the iron mining town of Crosby, Minnesota, the Communist leader of the UC won election as mayor, began hiring unemployed miners, and led a hunger march on the state capital (Folsom 1991:272). Yet as Lorence (1966) notes, although Michigan was among the most active places, with large, influential unemployed movements not only in Detroit and the Upper Peninsula, but in Flint, Saginaw and Bay City, and Pontiac, the more conservative western part of the state was less militant and confrontational.

Piven and Cloward call it the "largest movement of the unemployed the country has known" (1977:41). As a contemporary social scientist, Helen Seymour, argues, "Every large city, most small cities and towns, practically all states ... witnessed the growth, with tremendous variation as to type, duration, method of accomplishment, of relief pressure groups" (1940:1). The Musteite Unemployed Leagues claimed a hundred thousand members in 187 branches in Ohio alone, and another forty to fifty thousand members in Pennsylvania in 1933, and they were dwarfed by the much larger Communist-led Unemployed Councils in members and branches (Rosenzweig 1975:60). Of course, some areas were passed over, and even when they did emerge, they did not approach high levels of militancy. Nevertheless, what is most striking is the ubiquity and range of unemployed struggles and active groups.[2]

---

[2] Virtually the only writer who attempts to minimize the extent of the struggles and organizations of the unemployed is Theda Skocpol, in a piece co-written with Kenneth Feingold (1990), where they assert inaccurately that these movements were important only in Detroit, Chicago, and New York, a statement that defies all available scholarship. For my critique of this view, see Goldfield (1989).

One of the richest accounts of early unemployed activity is given by Nathaniel Weyl (1932:117–20). The UCs were organized by blocks and in tenements, and also in breadlines, flophouses, and relief centers, all with their particular demands and forms of action. One of the major activities of the neighborhood committees was to fight evictions: they amassed crowds, fought evictors, including police, moved furniture back when it had been removed, and re-hooked up utilities. By 1932, in some cities evictions had all but ended. All over the country, unemployed groups organized marches on relief stations, city halls, and even state capitals, demanding greater relief. In Chicago, where the Socialist Party (SP) was especially strong, the UC initiated a joint demonstration of tens of thousands of unemployed, demanding no cut in relief and an end to evictions. Chicago and Illinois officials rushed to Washington, DC, to borrow 6.3 million dollars from the Reconstruction Finance Corporation in order to meet the demands. Mayor Anton Cermak responded to critics by highlighting the seriousness of the growing radicalization of the masses: "I say to the men who object to this public relief because it will add to the tax burden on their property, they should be glad to pay for it, for it is the best way of ensuring that they keep their property" (Weyl 1932:118). The central national demand of the UCs was unemployment insurance at the expense of employers and the state, embodied in the Frazier-Lundeen Bill and eventually supported by unions as well as all unemployed groups.

In addition, many of the unemployed groups were industrially oriented. United Mine Workers of America (UMWA) locals in West Virginia, Ohio, and Pennsylvania established active unemployed organizations of their laid-off members (Feeley 1983:38, 101; Seymour 1940:20; Rosenzweig 1975:56). Communists organized unemployed stockyard workers for hunger marches (Rosenzweig 1976:51). The CP-led Auto Workers Union (AWU) led marches and picket lines at auto plants protesting layoffs, the most famous of which was the March 7, 1932, Ford Hunger March in Detroit and Dearborn, Michigan (Sugar 1980; Baskin 2001; on the AWU, Lorence 1996:21–23). As the subsequent chapters demonstrate, active, mass-supported groups of unemployed in steel towns and wood centers were widespread and played important roles in union organizing.

Unemployed worker organizing was also extensive throughout the South, especially in many of its industrial centers. There were active unemployed groups in cities in the border states, including Richmond, Virginia (Folsom 1991:263), Chattanooga, Tennessee (Rosenzweig 1976:41), St. Louis, Missouri (see the careful work of Feurer 2006:31–34, 39), Charleston, South Carolina (Feeley 1983:38), and Baltimore, Maryland (Feeley 1983:27; Skotnes 1991; 2013). Communists organized sustained interracial unemployed struggles in medium-sized Georgia cities, including Columbus, Macon, Augusta, and Savannah. In Atlanta, the organizing of the unemployed culminated in 1932 in a "mass demonstration led by the charismatic Angelo Herndon" (for quote, Lorence 2009:5, 9; see also Herndon 1969:188–92). The biggest, most continuously operating center of unemployed organizing in the South was Birmingham, Alabama. In May 1930, seven hundred Blacks and one hundred whites gathered to demand relief. Later the CP-led Metal Workers Industrial Union had a meeting of twenty-five hundred unemployed steelworkers, demanding relief, an end to evictions, and support for the CP-sponsored social insurance bill. On December 16, 1930, five thousand workers led by Joe Burton, an eighteen-year-old Young Communist League (YCL) activist, stormed the lobby of Birmingham's Hotel Morris, demanding jobs or relief and an end to evictions. Demonstrations continued throughout 1931 (Kelley 1990:15–20; Hudson 1972:54–58). On November 7, 1931, an interracial crowd estimated to be seven thousand strong, demonstrated at the Jefferson County courthouse, demanding relief (Kelley 1990:30). Kelley argues that "the unemployed campaign was the key to the Party's growth and consolidation in Birmingham; by the end of 1933, the Party's dues-paying membership in Birmingham rose to nearly five hundred, and its mass organizations encompassed twice that number" (1990:32).

Trajectory of Organizing During the 1930s

The organizing and struggles of the unemployed are inherently volatile and unstable. The situation of the jobless is far from secure, and their location is often less permanent than that of the employed. Thus, I find various critiques of the instability of their organizations, or the later deradicalization of their movement, that place the blame for these conditions exclusively on the radical organizations (note here Piven and Cloward 1977 and Vallocci 1990, both of whom have otherwise useful information and analysis) or lack of radicalization of participants (Dubofsky 1979:13) largely unconvincing. This being said, a rough periodization of the trajectory of unemployed struggles is useful.

First, the 1929–33 period was clearly the more radical and militant. The groups and struggles during this period were overwhelming led by Communists, whose early Unemployed Councils often remained the only viable groups in many locations throughout the 1930s. Although there were numerous self-help organizations, most notably in Seattle (for information on self-help groups, including Seattle's Unemployed Citizens' League, see Feeley 1983:14–16), the tone of this early period was set by the CP-led UCs, their mass demonstrations often leading to confrontations with the police and eviction battles, which were strident and often successful. This was also the period in which local, state, and federal authorities were most resistant (Weyl 1932; Leab 1967; Piven and Cloward 1977:68–69; Rosenzweig 1976; Folsom 1991:241–76).

Second, the 1933–36 period, while certainly not without its large-scale confrontations, eviction battles, and labor support, was more nuanced. With the election of FDR and New Deal Democrats in Congress, more aid and employment on government projects began to flow. Other left-led organizations also emerged into prominence, including the SP-led diverse collection of unemployed groups and the Musteite Unemployed Leagues, sometimes in direct competition with the UCs, other times in completely different locations, as with the Musteites who established organizations in the coalfields and small industrial towns in Ohio, Pennsylvania, and West Virginia (Seymour 1940:17–20). By March 1933, nine states had placed moratoriums on evictions or mortgage repossessions (Feeley 1983:75). Many public relief officials recognized and worked with the unemployed groups, at times allying to gain more relief funds. New Deal liberal Democrat Frank Murphy, first as Detroit mayor, then as Michigan governor, for example, publicly supported many of the groups' demands. As a consequence, differing degrees of deradicalization took place as many groups became absorbed into the New Deal framework.[3]

Finally, the 1936–39 period began with the Spring 1936 fusion of the main un-employed groups into the Workers Alliance (WA), with David Lesser of the Socialist Party as president and Herbert Benjamin of the Communist Party as organization secretary. The WA shifted much of its attention to the union organizing of the several million Works Project Administration (WPA) federal employees. And in many areas, industrial unions took over the organizing of their own unemployed workers, leaving less space for the WA, especially in industrial strongholds like southeastern Michigan. In addition, as industrial unions grew, left groups shifted their priorities, even moving many of their most capable organizers from work for the unemployed into the labor movement. The main left groups, the CP, the SP, the Musteites, and the smaller grouping of Trotskyists, all evolved in their work, something I will not dwell on at length here.[4] The work of the CP, so important for understanding the 1930s, I focus on in a separate chapter.

The Socialist Party had been relatively moribund during the 1920s. It was dominated by a racially backward, virulently anti-communist, rather detached old guard, who tended to support the most narrow-minded leaders in the AFL. As traditional right-wing social democrats, their ideological belief was that socialism would appear eventually as an evolutionary development under capitalism, its arrival required educational work but not mass struggle. They believed that un-employment (and racial inequities) could be resolved only after socialism was es-tablished. Thus, not surprisingly, they were alarmed and repelled by the emerging mass insurgencies of the early Depression (Rosenzweig 1979, passim, esp. 488–89 for an incisive summary).

---

[3] Rosenzweig asserts that this process affected all left-wing groups (1976:47). This is in contrast to the situation in Canada, where opposition by public officials and repression continued throughout the 1930s, partially accounting for the continued militancy of unemployed movements there in the latter part of the decade (Palmer and Heroux 2016).

[4] Lengthy discussions of the differences and similarities of the work of all groups can be found in Feeley (1983) and various articles by Rosenzweig (1975, 1976, 1979).

Yet, like many cautious political organizations (which included the National Association for the Advancement of Colored People, NAACP; and the National Urban League, NUL), the SP developed a militant, activist youth wing, beginning perhaps with the campaign for president of SP candidate Norman Thomas in 1928.[5] Around Norman Thomas an amorphous activist, left-leaning majority coalition emerged that included young people, many associated with the Student League for Industrial Democracy (SLID) and the Young People's Socialist League (YPSL), further energized by the 1932 Thomas presidential campaign. Many of these young activists threw themselves into organizing the unemployed, the highpoint of their work being in Chicago (Weyl 1932; Rosenzweig 1979). By June 1934, the old guard had been ousted from the leadership and had left the Party, at which point SP unemployed organizing became a dominant thrust around the country.

Finally, there was a small, much more radical grouping in the Socialist Party, the Revolutionary Policy Committee (RPC), which was not particularly influential nationally but of special importance to us, because a number of its members were to play significant roles in the movement in the South. Many of these southern radicals were involved with the Highlander Folk School in Monteagle, Tennessee. The group included James Dombrowski, Zilla Hawes, and Howard Kester, the latter three signers of the 1934 RPC manifesto, as well as Miles Horton and others, some of whom would eventually join the Communist Party, including Don West, his sister Belle West, and Claude and Joyce Williams. Many of them started as Christian radicals. All believed that the fight against white supremacy in the South (from lynching to disenfranchisement to employment discrimination), along with labor rights, was central to the fight for justice. They opposed most New Deal programs, sympathized with the Soviet Union, believed in the necessity of an anti-capitalist revolution and in working with Communists, certainly anathema to most Socialists at the time, especially in the South. Horton believed that "the best radical work in the South was the exceptional work being done by the CP in the Birmingham area" (for the quote Kelley 1990:120; see also Dunbar 1981:60–63).

As the CP's unemployed organizing tended to be scaled back after 1933, the Socialists came to dominate much of the organizing nationally, setting up the Workers Alliance in 1935, eventually drawing in other groups in 1936. While Rosenzweig (1979) has a valid point that much of the traditional scholarship on the SP tends to ignore the party's unemployed work, see the well-researched, highly informative work by Lorence (1996), which carefully documents the SP resurgence both in Michigan and nationally.[6]

---

[5] For an excellent account of this phenomenon, see Bates (1997).

[6] On the other hand, Prago (1976) devotes over one hundred pages to the CP unemployed work, but barely a few pages to that of the SP.

The Musteites

The Musteites, so named because of their leader, A. J. Muste, had a lengthy evolutionary history. Muste started out as a Dutch Reform minister, but by 1919 had become a labor organizer, leading the 1919 Lawrence, Massachusetts, textile strike. For the next two years he was the head of the Amalgamated Textile Union, when in 1921, he accepted the deanship of the newly formed Brookwood Labor College in Katonah, New York. The school graduated hundreds of labor organizers and educators during the 1920s, all loyal to Muste, many ready to organize and hoping to change the labor movement.[7]

In May 1929, Muste and his followers, along with various Socialists, labor organizers, and educators, met to form the Conference for Progressive Labor Action (CPLA), which was highly critical of the American Federation of Labor (AFL) leadership. They sent organizers to labor hot spots, including the 1929–31 textile battles in the southern Piedmont. By 1931, they had adopted a much more activist program, to the left of the SP. Although some of their members had been involved in unemployed organizing previously, by 1932 the CPLA as a whole began to aggressively organize unemployed workers, with a majority of their efforts centered in small industrial towns and rural areas in Ohio. Like the CP, they engaged in eviction fights, and in August 1933, they led a march of seven thousand on the state capital in Columbus.

Their biggest and most successful action, however, took place in Toledo, Ohio, in April 1934 when the CPLA-led Lucas County Unemployed League mobilized tens of thousands to support the Toledo Autolite workers' strike, helping rout the national guard and gain victory (among numerous accounts see Preis 1964:19–24 and Bernstein 1960:218–29).

Their radicalization proceeded, and in December,1934, CPLA merged with the Trotskyist Communist League of America to form the American Workers Party (AWP), the U.S. branch of international Trotskyism.[8] By 1936, the Unemployed Leagues of the AWP, like all other independent unemployed organizations, merged into the Socialist-led Workers Alliance.

Features of the Unemployed Movement

As I have suggested, the unemployed movement of the early and middle 1930s was massive and ubiquitous. Yet it is important to attempt to evaluate how important

[7] Much of my account here follows that of Rosenzwieg (1975).

[8] Accounts of their activities among the unemployed can be found in Prago (1976:189– 206); Feeley (1983); Weyl (1932:119); Seymour (1940), as well as Rosenzweig (1976).

it was to the general upsurge, especially for the growth and strength of the labor movement.

Compared with the labor unions, which were generally stable, unemployed movements historically have often been mercurial and ephemeral. James Cannon captures some of these features in stark terms:

> Unemployed organizations can be built and expanded rapidly in times of economic crisis and it is quite possible for one to get illusory ideas about their stability and revolutionary potentialities. At the very best they are loose and easily scattered formations . . . The minute the average unemployed worker gets a job he wants to forget about the unemployed organization. He doesn't want to be reminded of the misery of the former time . . . chronically unemployed workers very often give way to demoralization and despair. (1972:206)

This is one of the reasons I disagree with those critics who think that the growing bureaucratization, deradicalization, and diminution of militant unemployed struggles in the latter part of the 1930s can be blamed largely on the left groups that led the unemployed movement (e.g., Piven and Cloward 1977; Valloci 1990; Rosenzweig 1975, 1976).

Despite these inherent problems of unemployed movements, I will argue that they were the most important of the 1930s social movements. They gave immense power and stimulation to the upsurge in general and were a contributor to the strength of the labor upsurge. So let us begin our examination of these movements.

Social movements usually grow by leaps and often through contagion and "demonstration effects."[9] In certain important respects, they played a role similar to that of the portside mobilizations ("riots") that preceded the American Revolution.[10] These earlier mobilizations were largely directed against British navy press gangs. Impressment was the method that the British Royal Navy used to solve its manpower shortage. It was a form of brutal kidnaping whereby navy press gangs came to a port (in North America, this meant Boston, New York, Philadelphia, and Charleston) and seized able-bodied males, some even preadolescent, to work on their ships. Impressment affected all classes in colonial society, since the press gangs were indiscriminate, seizing slaves and legislators, sailors, fishermen, and servants. They were perversely egalitarian, never discriminating by race, class, nationality,

---

[9] See the argument in Dunlop (1982), discussed more fully in Goldfield (1987:4, 1990a, 1990b:ch. 1); Goldfield and Bromsen (2013).

[10] The *New York Times*, historically and consistently conservative (as it is today, with its putatively liberal veneer), insisted on calling the mostly peaceful unemployed protests "riots," especially when the protesters were attacked by the police (*New York Times*, October 17, 1930; also cited in Piven and Cloward 1977:52).

or even age, forging a common solidarity among potential victims. The protests too were universal, involving the poorest members of society, women, free Blacks, slaves, and bond servants, as well as artisans and professionals. These colonial mobs thus had a universal character, implicitly giving meaning to a new definition of "all men" being equal, as opposed merely to the rights of male Englishmen (Goldfield 1987:52–56, passim).

Similarly, the unemployed struggles exemplified a broader sense of class solidarity. While there were certainly enclaves, which were predominantly one or another ethnic or religious group, many struggles, especially those in urban areas, solidified a broad sense of class. As Feeley notes, "Both in the north and in the south the first time Black and white workers participated in joint campaigns to fight for their common needs often occurred in these unemployed organizations" (1983:58). In the South, in Atlanta, Savannah, and Columbia, Georgia, Birmingham, Alabama, Richmond, Virginia, Chattanooga, Tennessee, and Oxford, Mississippi, Communists organized large interracial Unemployed Councils (Lorence 2009:4–6; Folsom 1991:263; Kelley 1990:4–6).

One must be clear that leadership played an important role. The CP was unwavering in its support for racial equality in the unemployed movement. As is indicated in other chapters, it often went to extraordinary lengths. The UCs also made equal relief for Blacks central to their demands, certainly rattling the white supremacist ruling class in the South.[11] While a radical wing of the SP, including the previously mentioned grouping affiliated with Highlander, was equally committed, its members were a tiny minority among Socialists. Yet the Musteites, with their abiding belief in local autonomy and rank-and-file control, harbored racists in certain areas. At the national convention of the Musteite Unemployed Leagues on July 3, 1933, in Columbus, Ohio, for example, nativists, racists, and patriotic flag wavers seized control. Although the Musteites eventually regained dominant leadership and asserted their own political perspective, the fact that they had harbored such a large number of these Trump-like forces is not without significance. Thus, while the unemployed movement had a strong tendency toward interracialism, it did not necessarily happen automatically (Rosenzweig 1975:61).

While the Communists and to a lesser extent other leftists were formally committed to equality for women, they approached the issue with much less fervor than their stance on racial equality, with some notable exceptions.[12] Yet in place after

---

[11] Katznelson et al. (1993) argue that while southern Dixiecrats in Congress early in the New Deal supported social welfare policies, they were particularly chagrined when they were applied to southern African-Americans (see also Farhang and Katznelson 2005; Katznelson 2013).

[12] The United Electrical Workers (UE), with its large female base, was perhaps an outlier (see Schatz 1983; Filippelli and McColloch 1995; Feurer 2006). Even in the left-wing United Packinghouse Workers of America (UPWA), women often felt like second-class citizens (see scattered interviews with Black female packinghouse workers in Honey's *Black Workers Remember*, 2001). And iron ore miners in the Mesabi range in Minnesota, originally organized by the CP-led Mine Mill, were not sufficiently

place, women were in many cases the driving forces, the shock troops for the most militant activities of the unemployed organizing. This was true not only in large cities like Chicago, New York, Detroit, and Boston. It was also true among over-whelmingly white women in Lackawanna County and Scranton, Pennsylvania. As CP leader Steve Nelson reported, women there had "shown a remarkable interest" and were "the driving forces" (1934:9). This was true also in southern cities, in-cluding Chattanooga, Tennessee. In Birmingham, neighborhood relief committees attracted large numbers of Black women to the CP, as well as the UCs. Kelley reports that women were key, but often invisible, virtually never appointed to lead-ership positions. Even white women in Birmingham entered the CP through work with the unemployed (1990:21, 22, 32, 45–46). The same was true in St. Louis and Minneapolis (Feurer 1996; Faue 1991:65, 115–16, 132–34).

As in the portside riots of the pre-revolutionary period in the North American colonies, the broadest notions of "all men" and of class solidarity were not to sur-vive. In the aftermath of the Revolution and written into the U.S. Constitution, it was white supremacy that trumped the broadest definitions of humanity. And in the labor movement, the unions, the incorporation of labor and unemployed organiza-tions into the New Deal, reverted by the late 1930s to the standard definitions of male bread winners and female supporters.

Impact on the Labor Movement of Unemployed Struggles

All that being said, the unemployed movement had a number of important influences on and support for labor struggles. First, it was among the earliest expressions of discontent by working-class people, and thus had an important dem-onstration effect. Its actions were widespread across the country, involved large numbers of participants, and were aggressive, providing important examples and inspiration. The movement also at times shook the foundations of authority to the core. Elsewhere, I have argued that social movements and labor organization usually

conscious of women's issues to protect the small number of female miners from vicious harassment, as described by Clara Bingham and Laura Leedy Gansler (2002) in *Class Action* and portrayed in the film *North Country* (Caro 2005). In Michigan in 1941, although 70% of those on the Wayne County WPA assignment list were women, only 36% of project workers were women. Union unemployed organizer Alex McKay argued that women were not getting a fair opportunity. When the UAW's all-male leaders were challenged, the UAW showed little concern, with left-wing ally and union leader George Addes telling female unionists "not to make an issue . . . of women's rights" (Lorence 1996:283–84). The CP work was to change substantially after World War II, as noted in Chapter 8, with the strong emphasis on Black women in the work of the National Negro Labor Alliance, work that compares favorably with other radical organizations during the 1950s and 1960s (note the especially penetrating analysis in Lang 2009b).

proceed in waves, as if by contagion (Goldfield 1987; Goldfield and Bromsen 2013). As the earliest expression of radical, militant demands and actions, the unemployed struggles served as one of the initial stimuli.

Second, the unemployed movement planted the seeds and experience of solidarity.

Third, in numerous instances, the mobility of the unemployed made them readily available as picketers and gave associative power to the later struggles of employed workers. The highpoint was undoubtedly the 1934 Autolite strike, where tens of thousands of unemployed workers, led by the CPLA-organized Lucas County Unemployed Leagues, recued a failed strike and led the strikers to victory. The unemployed organizations, however, played critical roles, in hundreds of other strikes.

Fourth, the unemployed organizations were a major source of recruitment for radical organizations, especially the Communists. Kelley describes this process in Birmingham (1990:32). Other area-specific studies confirm these accounts. For what it is worth, I was told in the 1970s by former and then-current members of the Communist Party in Chicago that virtually all their in-plant cadre from the 1930s had been recruited through the unemployed movement.

Fifth, when work relief was established and expanded under the New Deal's Works Progress Administration (WPA), it was the activists in the unemployed movement who led the unionization of WPA workers.

Finally, as the economy began to pick up, unionized activists in the WPA projects played critical roles in organizing hitherto repressed and hesitant workers. This was perhaps no more dramatic than in Michigan, when laid-off Ford workers organized WPA unions involving hundreds if not thousands of former Ford workers. When they were eventually called back to work, these Ford workers often played a leading role in unionizing Ford (Lorence 1996:265). Thus, unemployed workers and their organizations, mercurial, ephemeral, and militant, were to play a central role in the 1930s upsurge and the formation of stable unions.

The Farm Revolt

In 1930, of a total U.S. population of 123 million, 30.5 million were farmers, who made up 21% of the labor force (Spielmaker 2014). By that time, the farm economy had completely collapsed. In 1925, corn sold for $1.07 per bushel; by 1932, it sold for 13 cents, well below the cost of production. One farmer shipped hogs to Omaha by truck. By the time the auction house deducted the cost of shipping and its fees, $1 was left for 1,300 pounds of hogs (Ganzel 2003). And banks were attempting to foreclose on hundreds of thousands of small farms, since farmers without income could not afford to make their mortgage payments.

The agricultural sector had been depressed since at least the mid-1920s. Thus, farmers' protests emerged rapidly early in the Depression. They were often entwined with the unemployed movement, occasionally involved with and supporting labor struggles. Farm struggles were at times massive, often dramatic. The two main issues were the collapse of prices and the stopping of foreclosures.

The farm protest movement had multiple dimensions. The largest traditional farm organization, the National Farmers Union (NFU), was dominated by wealthy farmers and had substantial business interests, and it opposed protests (Shover 1965:34). The most widely known protest group was the Farmers' Holiday Association (FHA), led by Milo Reno, who had been head of the Iowa Farmers Union. In May 1932, the FHA was launched in Iowa and rapidly established branches in Minnesota, Missouri, Illinois, Montana, Wisconsin, Nebraska, and North and South Dakota. In an effort to raise prices, hundreds, sometimes thousands of farmers blocked highways around major distribution centers, including initially Sioux City, Iowa, to stop deliveries of their products. The farmers had weapons, including farm tools, threshing machine belts, and chains. They were often supported by the AFL and the railroad brotherhoods. Few trucks crossed their lines (Shover 1965:46). Although these protests did not immediately affect farm produce prices, their dramatic, lawless activities got national publicity.

Mortgage protests also emerged early in the Depression (Pratt 1989:63, 1988:131–32). By 1930, the CP-led United Farmers Leagues were leading protests against foreclosures, initiating the tactic of "Penny" or "Sears Roebuck" sales (Shover 1965:79). Hundreds of farmers, often armed with guns, would show up at the bank auctions of foreclosed properties, tractors, farm equipment, or whole farms. Someone from the group would bid a penny or a nickel. It would be made clear that other bids were discouraged, sometimes by threats of death. Often a noose hung from a tree. When the sales were moved to banks or courthouses, farmers moved to these venues. The Senate testimony of John Simpson, president of the NFU, is suggestive: "They have taken courts by the arm and led them into a room where there is no telephone. . . . They have thrown ropes around the necks of the attorneys that brought the foreclosure proceedings until they begged for mercy" (Shover 1965:97). By 1933, nine states had passed into law moratoriums on farm foreclosures (Feeley 1983:75; Goldstein 1978:207). In Nebraska, a moratorium law was passed immediately after three thousand farmers marched inside the state capital building (Goldstein 1978:207). The Communists sometimes competed and sometimes worked with other farm organizations, including the FHA. During the Popular Front period, they dissolved their own organizations, merging into first the FHA, then eventually into the NFU. Yet they continued to maintain strongholds for long periods of time. Sheridan County, Minnesota, for example, was a red stronghold where every "pool hall and barbershop" carried the *Daily Worker*, and the sheriff "peddled" it "throughout the countryside" (Dyson 1982:31–33).

In more than a few labor struggles, farm organizations donated and shipped food to union strike kitchens. One of the more famous such venues was the 1934 Minneapolis teamsters strike (Palmer (2014); Dobbs (2004); Bernstein

1969:239–52). In sum, farm protests were an important dimension of the 1930s upsurge, giving additional breadth to the movement, with occasional significant support for protracted labor organizing struggles. The large, often law-defying, uncompromising protests added to the insurrectionary character of the era.

Sharecroppers and Tenants

The organization of sharecroppers was largely a southern phenomenon, involving two separate organizations. First was the CP-led, overwhelmingly African-American Sharecroppers Union (SU), originating and most firmly rooted in Alabama. Second was the interracial Southern Tenants Farmers' Union (STFU), whose early strength was in Arkansas. It was started by the SP, but also included Communists and radical preachers in the leadership; the three groups were intertwined, often consisting of the same people. The STFU, in particular, has had numerous researchers and chroniclers, with enormous disputes between them. I do not discuss these disputes here, but merely want to highlight the role of these movements in the general 1930s upsurge.[13] To begin with, one must note that organizing sharecroppers in the 1930s, especially African-Americans, in the South, particularly in the Black Belt counties, was a project with few avenues for success. Perhaps the most incisive analysis can be found in one of the earlier works, a student thesis by Dale Rosen (1969). As Rosen notes, by 1930, sharecroppers were a "declining class." By the mid-1930s, three-quarters of U.S. cotton was already being grown west of the Mississippi River, with half in Texas and Oklahoma alone (1969:22). Foreign markets for U.S.-grown cotton (markets that the United States had earlier dominated; Beckert 2015) were receding rapidly, while the price of cotton on the world market had dropped from seventeen cents per pound in 1929 to five or six cents per pound in 1932, a good deal below the U.S. cost of production. In certain areas, mechanization was well under way. And under the New Deal, beginning with the passage of the Agricultural Adjustment Act (AAA, signed into law May 12, 1933), in order to lower the amount of crops produced, thereby raising market prices, landowners (but rarely tenants) were being paid to withdraw their lands from cultivation, causing the eviction of tens of thousands more sharecroppers and tenants. These factors gave southern sharecroppers little leverage or structural power.[14]

---

[13] One of these disputes, about whether the STFU was a radical, interracial organization with a socialist perspective for restructuring modern society, or merely a conservative response to progressive agricultural programs of the New Deal, is well summarized in Ross (2004:3–5). There are also intense disputes about the ideological conflicts in the union, especially involving H. L. Mitchell, the CP, and the CIO. And there is even one writer who takes opposite positions in different articles, without ever explaining his changing assessment (see Naison 1968, 1996 and a quite different view in Naison 1973).

[14] In a carefully researched, data-rich book, *Sharecroppers All*, Arthur Raper and Ira De A. Reid (1941) describe the situation of sharecroppers as affecting all elements of the southern working

On the other hand, the horrors of white supremacy were at their worst in the Black Belt cotton areas; among these were disenfranchisement, lynching, chain gangs, the unpunished rape and murder of Blacks, absolute segregation, and brutal forced labor. Yet the Communists, because of their belief in a potentially revolutionary "Negro Nation" in the South, thought that the African-American peasantry in the South could be a revolutionary force. Thus, the CP, beginning in 1930, gave priority to organizing these sharecroppers, even though the combination of little leverage and horrific repression gave the Party's efforts minimal chances of success. As Rosen suggests, "The odds against organizing rural Blacks" seemed insurmountable, especially in conjunction with the problems of organizing isolated rural communities (1969:25).[15]

The SU was able to focus both on basic issues of sharecroppers, including higher wages, larger pay per weight of cotton, payment in cash, and the ability to grow and sell one's own crops, and on schools and school transportation for their children, many of whom were forced to work as young as seven years old. The SU did at times achieve some limited victories, including in some places an increase in wages and the right to sell their own cotton (Rosen 1969:40, 63; Johnson 2011). The SU, in contrast to the STFU, was militant and confrontational. Yet repression was severe, and numerous members and organizers were killed. At Reeltown and Camp Hill, both in Alabama, sharecroppers engaged in shootouts with local law enforcement officials. Members showed intense loyalty to the union, sending large delegations to national meetings, including a relief conference in the District of Columbia in 1932 and a large anti-war meeting in 1934 (Rosen 1969:40). At the beginning of the Popular Front period, the SU was disbanded and its members and locals joined the NFU, supposedly so they could participate in a broader movement.

The union and its activities, including the defense of its members, were highly publicized in the union's own publications and often received favorable publicity in the most important African-American newspapers. So one side effect was that Reeltown and Camp Hill helped convince African-Americans in urban areas that the CP was absolutely sincere in its willingness to do battle with white supremacy. Along with unemployed organizing and the CP-led Scottsboro defense, the CP-led sharecropper gun battles bolstered the CP's reputation in Black communities. Nowhere was this truer than in Birmingham (Kelley 1990:23). After Reeltown, three thousand people marched in the funeral procession there (Rosen 1969:55).

population, which they characterize as feudal. Ross gives detailed background on both cotton production and sharecropping into the 1930s, with focused statistics (2004:ch. 1).

[15] For a limited, relatively unsuccessful attempt to highlight this relationship (although it is not without certain useful pieces of information), see Johnson (2011). On the centrality of rape to the struggle of Black women, see McGuire (2010). For the fullest, most careful argument for the Black Belt nation thesis, see Haywood (1948).

Liberal whites organized in Montgomery, Alabama, to support the sharecroppers, with Mary Speed and her daughter Jane both joining the CP, the former eventually becoming the editor of the women's page of the CP's *Southern Worker* (Rosen 1969:54).

The STFU was organized in 1934 (1933 according to Ross 2004) by SP activists in the Mississippi Delta. They were supported and advised by Norman Thomas, who was looking for more organizational support to attack the New Deal. Unlike the CP-led SU, the SP and the STFU focused on legal and educational work, opposing mass actions. The SP and the leaders of the union spent time on national campaigns to expose the horrors of plantation life and the defects of New Deal programs (Naison 1996:103–104). The union grew quickly, having ten thousand members by the beginning of 1935 and perhaps twenty-five thousand by the end of that year. Despite the reticence of the SP leadership, croppers (like others devastated by the Depression) demanded seizure of the plantations and expropriation of the landowners. Mass activities, including a Delta-wide strike, gained higher pay for tens of thousands and helped spread the union to Oklahoma, Missouri, Tennessee, and Mississippi. Northern reporters publicized the violence directed against the union, helping bring the "plight of the sharecroppers" to national attention. So far, this account is generally shared by researchers and commentators, although Ross (2004) argues that the interracialism was not nearly so deep among whites as its enthusiastic proponents claimed.

Particularly after 1937, the accounts are highly disputed. Ideological conflict wracked the union. Its decision to join the CIO in 1937, first as a branch of the CP-led United Cannery, Agricultural, Packing, and Allied Workers of America (UCAPAWA), then to leave the CIO in 1939, and its eventual disintegration during the next year or so is the subject of myriad interpretations.

Nevertheless, the struggles of sharecroppers, carried out through both the SU and the STFU, added to the general social upsurge and focused additional attention on the oppression faced by rural workers in the South. Some have argued that these two sharecropper unions laid the basis for the emerging civil rights struggles on the 1940s, 1950s, and 1960s, but this is perhaps another story.[16]

Civil Rights Struggles: North and South

Of special importance for the emergence of a militant civil rights struggle, as well as the recruitment of thousands of African-Americans to the Communist Party, was the mass mobilization around the defense of the Scottsboro boys, led by the CP and

---

[16] For an in-depth look at the interracial African-American song tradition of the STFU and its continuity with the civil rights movement, see Honey (2013).

its defense organization, the International Labor Defense (ILD).[17] On March 25, 1931, nine Black youths were pulled off a freight train near Scottsboro, Alabama, and accused of raping two young white women who were traveling with them. In a hastily organized trial, with a large lynch mob outside the courtroom, they were quickly convicted and sentenced to death. While the NAACP hesitated to get involved, in part because of the explosive nature of the case and their desire to maintain relations with white southern moderates and northern philanthropists, the CP's ILD moved in, gained the support of the mothers and their sons, and quickly took charge of the defense. The ILD not only brought in its own high-level lawyers, but enlisted competent, respectable southern white lawyers as well. The CP argued that the case could not be won in the courtroom alone, but that millions had to be mobilized outside the courtroom. In northern ghettoes, it organized large-scale support. As Carter notes, "Unquestionably, the ILD captured the imagination of the nation's Negroes as Communist orators spoke in churches, conventions, union halls, and on street corners." Baltimore's Reverend Ashbury Smith, an executive board member of the National Urban League, said that it was almost entirely the CP's Scottsboro campaign that moved African-Americans from traditionally conservative positions (Carter 1969:147). By 1932, the ILD had appointed William Patterson, an African-American attorney from Harlem, as the national secretary and had chosen Harlem CP leader James Ford as the vice presidential candidate running with William Z. Foster as the 1932 presidential candidate on the CP ticket. In Harlem and across the North, thousands marched with the CP and ILD. Such notoriety also helped the CP in the South. As Kelley notes, the Scottsboro case "boosted Party popularity in Birmingham's black communities almost overnight" (1990:23). And what was true in Birmingham was true in numerous other places.

The case garnered worldwide attention as CPs in other countries linked their own protests to freedom for the Scottsboro boys (Carter 1969:142–43). The CP also gained public support for the Scottsboro case from a wide array of intellectuals and public figures, including Theodore Dreiser, Lincoln Steffens, Upton Sinclair, John Dos Passos, Albert Einstein, Thomas Mann, H. G. Wells and thirty-three members of the British Parliament (Carter 1969:146).While Scottsboro was by far the most important case, hundreds of other civil rights struggles took place, most led by the CP, which both mobilized Black communities and their white supporters and brought the issue of equality for African-Americans to the fore.

I do not wish to imply that the CP was the only show in town. The Brotherhood of Sleeping Car Porters led by A. Philip Randolph certainly played an important role (Harris 1977; Bates 2001; in St. Louis, Lang 2009b). White Socialists around

---

[17] For further information and references on the origins of the ILD, see Chapter 8 on the Communist Party. Of the numerous accounts of the Scottsboro case, one of the most thorough is that of Dan Carter (1969), whose information I largely draw on here; see Howard (2007) for additional material.

Highlander were aggressive about civil rights issues, as were numerous Harlem activists, including Frank R. Crosswaith and his various labor committees, such as the Harlem Labor Committee, founded in 1934, and remnants of Marcus Garvey's Universal Negro Improvement Association. As Beth Bates (1997) documents persuasively, even the NAACP and the NUL were not immune to the radicalism of the 1930s. Nevertheless, it was the CP and its various mass organizations whose activities were the most widespread. The National Negro Congress (NNC) was formed in February 1935 as an umbrella organization committed to a broad struggle for civil rights and the unionization of all workers, specifically Blacks. The precursors of the NNC were the Negro Industrial League (1932–33) and the Joint Committee on National Recovery, both led by John P. Davis, who was to be the national executive secretary and effective leader of the NNC (Randolph being the first chair but largely serving a titular role) from 1935 to1943.[18] The initial organization of the NNC included a broad range of Black leaders, ranging from liberals like Lester Granger of the Urban League, A. Philip Randolph, John P. Davis, and Ralph Bunche, and many Communists and Socialists. The NNC coordinated local struggles, including battles to open up jobs for Black workers. It also played a major role in assisting and supplying organizers, especially African-Americans, to various CIO organizing campaigns. As the chapter on steel indicates, it played a major role there. And contrary to the interpretation of Meier and Rudwick, whose Cold War anti-communist perspective gives undue credit to the NAACP in the organization of Ford in 1940 and 1941, it was the NNC and the CP, with their extensive contacts with Black workers, through Scottsboro, their activities in support of the unemployed, and their involvement in the organization of laid-off Ford workers in the WPA, that were key, especially in winning Black workers to the drive (Bates 2012:238; Meier and Rudwick 1979).

Ethnic and Religious Organizations

Though of more limited importance in the South, where Catholics and Eastern European immigrants were less numerous than in the industrial areas of the North and Midwest, organized religious and ethnic working-class organizations played a major role in the 1930s upsurge. I have discussed some of these issues in more detail in the chapter on steel. As many analysts have noted, the emergence of second-generation ethnic voters was an important part of the 1930s realignment, giving

[18] The two most comprehensive early works on the NNC are Hughes (1982) and Streater (1981), the latter giving by far the best account of the internal conflicts in the organization as well as the disputed scholarship. Gellman (2012) adds valuable new information on the activities of some of the most important local chapters. I also rely on the papers of the NNC in the New York City Public Library's Schomburg Center for Research in Black Culture.

majority status to the Roosevelt coalition (Anderson 1979; Sundquist 1983). There were millions of members of the large array of religious and ethnic organizations, and the Communists played a major role in this milieu. The foundation of their influence was the International Workers Order (IWO), led by CP central committee member Bronislav Konstantine ("Bill") Gebert, the central figure of the Polonia Society. The IWO had halls and activities throughout the industrial Midwest and Northeast. Gebert, as well as being a key staff figure for the Steel Workers Organizing Committee, was responsible for pulling together a large consortium of ethnic and foreign-born organizations into the Fraternal Orders Committee, of which he became the head. These organizations helped mobilize their constituents to support the CIO, playing an important constitutive and supportive role in the development of industrial unionism (Lizabeth Cohen 1990).

The Student Movement

The student movement of the 1930s was also a vital component of the 1930s social movement venue, giving both additional breadth to the general movement and at times important associative power to both the civil rights and industrial union movement.[19] During the 1920s, college students overwhelmingly voted Republican, and left activities were minuscule or nonexistent among students. This all changed in 1931 with the formation of the CP-led National Student League. The group was to share the stage in the first half of the decade with the Left-moving SP youth groups, YPSL and SLID. The NSL set the tone, prodding campus activists, including the SPers, to become more militant, pro-labor, and pro–civil rights. In March 1932, the NSL led a large student delegation to Harlan County, Kentucky, in support of a miners' strike, attempting unsuccessfully to bring food and clothing to miners' families. The attack by police and vigilantes on the peaceful group received national publicity, stimulating campus protests in support and even eventually leading to a Senate investigation of the conditions of coal miners. Later at Columbia University, they launched protests and a strike over the expulsion of Reed Harris, the activist editor of the *Spectator*, the campus newspaper. When Columbia was forced to reinstate him, the NSL gained much support. Among students, CPers and SPers worked together throughout the 1930s, even during the sectarian Third Period.

A southern activist youth organization, the Southern Negro Youth Congress (SNYC), was formed in 1937 as a spinoff of the NNC. It initially had the support of Mary McCleod Bethune, Charlotte Hawkins Brown, Franklin D. Roosevelt, Paul Robeson, A. Philip Randolph, and W.E.B. Du Bois. SNYC agitated against lynching,

---

[19] There is only a small amount of focused literature on the 1930s student movement. Aside from other works and certain archival material, a useful summary can be found in Robert Cohen (1992); R. Cohen (1987), Rawick (1957); H. Draper (1967); Pierce (2013).

attempted to get Blacks registered to vote, and fought to open more jobs to African-Americans. Soon after the group's official founding in 1937, SNYC activists were to play an important role in the organization of tobacco workers, an industry largely centered in the South. And as noted in the chapter on the Communist Party, large numbers of the nation's most prominent intellectuals, writers, artists, and others added their voices and support to the 1930s labor and social movements.

Third Party Organizations and Movements

Many agrarian, labor, and farmer-labor parties emerged during the 1930s. Most eventually disintegrated or became integrated into the New Deal coalition. Yet, especially in the early 1930s, they added to the ferment and upheaval to the left of the Democratic Party. Many had roots in protests before the 1930s. State-level movements existed in numerous places. The most important were the Minnesota Farmer-Labor Party (which for a while claimed to be anti-capitalist) and the Wisconsin Progressive Party, both of which elected senators, congress members, and governors. Others included South Dakota's Non-Partisan League, led by former Socialists, who for a while seized control of the South Dakota Republican Party; New York's American Labor Party; and Upton Sinclair's short-lived EPIC (End Poverty in California) party, which attempted to elect him governor. At the local level, there were hundreds, if not thousands, of local labor parties, which suggested the possibility of organizing a mass labor party in the United States (Davin and Lynd 1979–80).

More Ambiguous Social Movements

Finally, there were three mass movements, each led by a charismatic figure, whose character has been a matter of public dispute. These movements were based on the mass followings of Dr. Francis Townsend's plan for old age insurance, Father Charles Coughlin's evolving populism, and Huey Long's "Share the Wealth" movement. Some have labeled all three movements "proto-fascist," and others have seen them as left progressive movements (at least until Coughlin turned his sympathies toward anti-Semitism and fascism).[20]

The Townsend Movement

The Townsend movement was the least radical of these three, but there is much disputed territory.[21] The Townsend plan was quite simple. It called for $200 a month

---

[20] The conflicting scholarship is critically discussed in McElvaine (1974:217–18).
[21] The most comprehensive study is that of Amenta (2006), who argues strongly for its efficacy.

for all those over sixty who would stop working and promise to spend their money within thirty days. It was not opposed to capitalism or capitalists, nor did it propose to disproportionately tax the rich. It was to be financed by a 2% sales or "transaction" tax. It was deemed impractical or regressive by almost every other group. In 1935, while a retired couple would get $4,800 a year, 87% of families had incomes below $2,500. Although 89% of the population favored some form of old age insurance, "the Townsend Plan had the distinction of being opposed by the Liberty League, the Socialist Party, the Communist Party, the National Association of Manufacturers, and the American Federation of Labor" (for quote and useful summaries, see McElvaine 1984:241–43, 1974:231–37).

In 1936, the Townsend Clubs claimed over three million members, and said it had between twenty and thirty million signatures of those supporting its plan, which it was ready to deliver to Congress.

Although some clubs proposed marches, the organization as a whole opposed any form of action aside from letter writing and petition signing. Its constituency was not especially lower-class, but instead middle-class, white, and over sixty. Amenta tends to see the number of members and signatures as the basis for its important influence, also citing its popularity in public opinion polls over the more radical Lundeen Bill supported by the CP, SP, many unions, and others on the left (2006:97, 115). The Lundeen Bill included taxes on corporations and the rich to finance the bill.

Nevertheless, the demands for old age insurance from both the Townsend Clubs and the supporters of the more radical Lundeen Bill added to the ferment of the 1930s and to the pressure for a broader safety net and comprehensive retirement benefits.

The "Radio Priest"

Perhaps the most controversial of the odd figures to emerge during the Depression with a mass following was Father Charles Coughlin. His politics ran the gamut seemingly from liberal Catholicism to anti-capitalist criticism and eventually to pro-Nazi, anti-Semitic fascism by the late 1930s. Some saw him as an incipient fascist from the beginning, espousing populist rhetoric, while others saw him initially as part of the left, until he turned.[22]

Coughlin in the late 1920s was a priest at a small parish in Royal Oak, Michigan, a near suburb of Detroit, and was relatively unknown outside the area. He had a local radio program, but gradually expanded his broadcasts to include Chicago and

---

[22] The most sympathetic account of the early Coughlin and his followers is that of McElvaine, who traces the arguments of his accusers (1974:219). The most careful treatment is Brinkley's (1982:82–142).

Cincinnati. In 1930, he started focusing on the conditions of the Depression, the Detroit area being among the hardest hit in the country. He began first by attacking Communists, then switched to President Hoover and bankers. He developed his own national network of radio stations, having the largest radio audience in the country and perhaps the world, estimated at one point to be as many as forty million listeners. He had more than one hundred clerks and four secretaries to answer his roughly eighty thousand letters a week. By late 1930, he was denouncing "predatory capitalism" and espousing a "vague radicalism" (Brinkley 1982:96, 97; McElvaine 1984:238). He encouraged the political career of pro-union left-liberal Democrat Frank Murphy, who was elected mayor of Detroit in 1930 and later governor of Michigan. In 1931 and 1932, he was allied and worked with noted "progressives" in Congress, including George Norris of Nebraska (an author of the 1930 pro-labor anti-injunction Norris-La Guardia Act) and Senator Burton Wheeler, prairie radical from Montana. Yet he also had acquaintances with men like the rabid anti-communist Hamilton Fish and some noted anti-Semites at the time. In 1935, he was giving vigorous support to the Automotive Industrial Workers Association, based largely at Chrysler, headed by future UAW leader Richard Frankensteen. He was also opposed to the two major parties, as he became more and more critical of the New Deal, arguing that capitalism needed to be eliminated. Yet by 1938, he had become a supporter of Mussolini's corporate state and a rabid anti-Semite, and by 1940, he was praising Hitler.

While he may indeed have added to and ridden the crest of radical ferment, he at best represented the double-edged sword of radical populism. My own opinion is that McElvaine (1974:225, 1984:237–40) is wrong in his assessment of Coughlin's career in the first half of the 1930s. His focus on bankers (especially Jewish bankers), but more particularly his consistent anti-communism, marked him from the beginning as an anti-democratic proto-fascist. And here I concur with Nick Fischer's conclusion that in the end, there was no substantive, functional difference between anti-communism of the liberal or religious variety in the United States and that of the most xenophobic, anti-labor, racist, pro-Nazi variety (2016:xviii, 273–79). Yet it is also telling that as his right-wing views became more explicit, the overwhelming majority of his followers deserted him.

"The Kingfish," Huey Long

Huey Long was also a controversial figure, both when he was alive and in the historiography that emerged after his death.[23] Brinkley describes Long as a dictator with

---

[23] Unlike Townsend and Coughlin, Huey Long is the subject of many dozens of books and hundreds of articles. Most regard him as a typical anti-democratic southern populist demagogue. The most comprehensive book, and one of the more sympathetic, is T. Harry Williams's biography (1969). Useful summaries can be found in McElvaine (1974, 1984) and Brinkley (1982).

a "vision of ruthless, brutal power . . . reckless ambition" (1982:x). He argues that neither he nor Coughlin was among "the vanguards of a great, progressive social transformation" (1982:xi). A liberal contemporary saw Long as more contradic-tory: authoritarian at home but helping the lower class there, to the left nation-ally, criticizing FDR, while advocating taxing the rich to "Share the Wealth" (Allen 1939:187–92). McElvaine, in contrast, claims, "Huey Long's Share Our Wealth Society was perhaps the most striking expression of left-wing discontent in America of the 1930s" (1974:237).

Huey P. Long was from Winn County, Louisiana, a northern hill country area with a long history of radicalism, like the area from which Alabama's Jim Folsom emerged. It had refused to support secession or the Confederacy, was a stronghold of populism in the 1890s, and in 1912 Winn County had voted 35% for SP leader Eugene Debs for president while electing a number of SP local officials. Long ran from the beginning as an advocate for poor farmers and workers. When elected governor in 1928, he invested in infrastructure, dispro-portionately helping the poor, paving hundreds of miles of highways, building schools, bridges, and hospitals, supporting a major university, expanding care for the mentally ill, and providing free textbooks. He revised the tax codes so that Standard Oil and other large employers would pay more. He forced the building of a pipeline to supply cheap natural gas to New Orleans, against the wishes of the state's energy companies and their supporters. In these and many other ways, he was quite distinct from the usual southern demagogues. While not espe-cially a civil rights advocate, there was little racist cant in his campaigns, and he often claimed that his policies were for the benefit of all in his state. He ensured that at least some jobs in the new state hospitals and on road projects went to African-Americans. When Hiram Evans, Ku Klux Klan imperial wizard, threat-ened to campaign there against Long, he was told that if he did, he would leave with "his toes turned up" (Brinkley 1982:32). It is often claimed in criticism of Long that he did little substantively to help Blacks in his state and that he never fought against disenfranchisement. These things are true, but he was certainly in a somewhat different world than the Bilbos and Rankens of Mississippi. He also increased workmen's compensation and opposed "yellow dog" contracts, earning him some degree of labor support.

While still controlling Louisiana politics, his election to the Senate in 1932 gave him a national platform. He blocked with and was friends with a number of congressional liberal/leftists, including Burton Wheeler, George Norris, and Robert La Follette, Jr. He had a contentious relationship with FDR, supporting the Tennessee Valley Authority (TVA) and the Civilian Conservation Corps (CCC), and successfully fighting for the Federal Deposit Insurance Corporation (FDIC). He found Carter-Glass insufficient and thought FDR should have just nationalized the banks (Brinkley 1982:59, 61). In early 1934, he established his "Share the Wealth" clubs. By 1935, he claimed twenty-seven clubs with four million members. He was especially strong in the Deep South, with the most clubs in Louisiana, followed by Mississippi and Arkansas. Yet he also had many clubs in California, New York, and Minnesota. He was supported by numerous unions, including the left-leaning Chicago Federation of Labor. Secret polling by the Democratic National Committee suggested that he would gain many millions of votes (virtually all taken from FDR) if he ran as an independent. He described himself as a "leftist," and despite his flamboyant dress, his colorful demeanor and talk, he appealed to the radical, anti-capitalist sentiment of the lower classes, which existed in abundance during the 1930s.

Certainly, Long had tendencies toward megalomania, self-aggrandizement, and dictatorial control. Yet his attempts to raise public revenue from the oil companies led to legislative defeats and a massive counteroffensive against him. With the Standard Oil Company and its allies leading the charge, he was nearly impeached in 1929. Barely avoiding being driven from office, he tightened the screws, taking complete control of the patronage system and ruthlessly eliminating his enemies. In order to destroy Long's base, FDR refused to allow him senatorial courtesy, instead appointing his enemies to federal positions in Louisiana. With such enemies, it is hard to say what would have happened if Long had not achieved absolute control in his home state. My own sense is that there is a rather large dose of hypocrisy among his liberal critics, who gave free passes to racially discriminatory, thuggish authoritarians because of their loyalty and anti-communism while going so hard on Long. This was certainly the case with John L. Lewis, but even more so, as the chapter on steel will show, with Philip Murray, whose anti-democratic, thuggish rule and racist behavior were completely whitewashed by his liberal champions. Huey Long was assassinated on September 10, 1935, so what his ultimate influence on national politics would have been is difficult to evaluate. Nevertheless, without sharing the extravagant enthusiasm of McElvaine mentioned above, one can definitely say that he was representative of the social movement ferment, and may even have been a major contributor, especially in the South.

Conclusion

Let me try to summarize and pull together some of these disparate activities and topics, giving an initial argument for why I consider the wide array of social movements during the 1930s so important, both in general and especially for the trajectory of the labor movement. First, the sheer breath and diversity of these movements is unique in U.S. history. Their direct interaction and indirect synergy provide important contextual, contagion, demonstration, and multiplier effects. The unemployed, farmers and sharecroppers, ethnic and racial minorities, civil rights organizations, students, and middle-class retirees, among many others, all played their part.

Second, given the audacity, militancy, and aggressive nature of many of these movements, they fed on one another, escalating the "moments of madness" during the 1930s when almost anything seemed possible and contributing to feelings among many that a revolutionary or pre-revolutionary situation was in the air (Bernstein 1969).

Third, the mobilization most pointedly of farmers and the unemployed, especially at the onset of the Depression, created a demonstration and contagion effect for the later development of the labor movement. Such activities in the South were both catalytic and supportive of future labor organization. They were also to provide training grounds for militant labor-organizing cadres.

Fourth, and perhaps most important, the unemployed, farmers, ethnic and racial organizations, civil rights groups, students, and intellectuals provided key and often necessary associative power to the developing labor movement. The failure at times to take advantage of this support (as I attempt to show with Operation Dixie) weakened and occasionally doomed labor organizing, undermining greater possibilities for labor in the South.

Social upheavals develop in fits and starts, and often with huge breakthroughs in formerly quiescent arenas. And the percentages of those directly involved is often not indicative of the broad impact that these struggles might have. These factors have led certain analysts to argue that the 1930s were not so turbulent, a conclusion I regard as erroneous.

4

Class Struggle in Steel

The steel industry might not seem, at first glance, as important to the southern economy as textiles, woodworking, longshore, or even coal, although it played a pivotal role in certain important areas of the region. It was central to the industrial citadel of Birmingham and the manufacturing area in Gadsden, both in Alabama, and played a major role in certain border states, most notably Maryland (with its enormous Bethlehem Sparrows Point facility, located near Baltimore), West Virginia (with key steel centers in Weirton and Wheeling), Missouri, Tennessee, and Kentucky, and had a small presence in a number of other southern states.[1] Like coal, wood, and longshore in the South, the steel industry had a large percentage of African-American workers, a not insignificant factor in understanding the dynamics of unionism in the industry. Further, the steel industry had important ramifications in other industries. It sought to control large parts of the coal industry, iron ore mining, transportation, especially shipping and rail, as well as many smaller industries, including limestone quarries. Horace Davis argues that, in 1933, "the Steel industry is not only a basic industry—it is the key industry of the nation . . . dominated by a single firm which in turn is controlled by the leading financial interests in the country" (1933:9). From a different analytical perspective, Frederick Harbison states, "Steel is the veritable keystone of American industry" (1940:1). Thus, the nature of unions in the country as a whole, as well as in the South, was not unrelated to the character of unionism in steel.

The Economics of the Steel Industry

To understand labor–management relations in the steel industry, one must begin with the economics of the industry. Like that of coal, the growth of both iron and steel production was tied to the railroad industry. Until 1880, practically all

---

[1] Note, however, that tens of thousands of steelworkers organized under Operation Dixie after World War II; many mainstream CIO leaders harbored hopes that steelworkers would supplant coal miners as key supporters of unionism in the South.

The Southern Key. Michael Goldfield, Oxford University Press (2020) © Michael Goldfield
DOI: 10.1093/oso/9780190079321.001.0001

steel (as well as iron) was used in the production of rails (Davis 1972:446). The railroads enabled local and regional industries to become large national industries, as delivery times and shipping rates fell substantially. The development of steel rails (along with powerful locomotives) allowed for the carrying of heavy loads at higher speeds, both lowering the costs and decreasing the time of transportation. Steel rails were far more durable than iron ones; they thus required less frequent replacement, which meant less downtime for the railways. By the time the price of steel rails dropped to that of iron rails in the late nineteenth century, iron rails had disappeared completely. The techniques for making stronger, cheaper, and longer-lasting steel advanced rapidly during the nineteenth century, beginning with the Bessemer process (invented in 1854 and commercially introduced in 1866; Temin 1964:127), the open hearth in the 1860s (although it was not used extensively until the late 1870s and the 1880s), and the basic process of Thomas and Gilchrist in 1875 (widely in use as a liner for furnaces by the 1880s). The qualities and efficiencies of steel production were continually improved in the later part of the nineteenth and the early twentieth centuries, in part through control of the amount of carbon and the addition of various alloys, and also by the use of higher temperatures and more extensive heat (see the useful summary of Ahmed White 2016). Other uses for steel, in addition to rails, developed quickly. In 1882, for example, 90% of steel went into rails, while the percentage was less than half by 1890 (Brody 1960:4). Steel revolutionized ocean transportation through the production of steel hulls for ships and the development of more powerful engines that relied on the stronger and harder qualities of steel castings. By the end of the 1800s and the beginning of the 1900s, steel was also becoming important in the construction of skyscrapers and the emerging automobile industry, as well as widely used for wire nails, armor plate, iron rods, iron and steel pipes, galvanized steel, cans, structural steel for bridges, and a variety of other applications (Magdoff 1968:12–18; H. Davis 1933:441–46; Warren 1973:55).[2]

Before the Civil War, most iron, including that used for rails, was imported from the United Kingdom. In 1850, production in the United States was one-fifth that of Britain; three-quarters of the iron rails used in this country during the 1850s were supplied by British rail manufacturers (Temin 1964:21). The rise of the Republicans, the inauguration of President Abraham Lincoln, and Republican control of Congress in 1861 led to the enactment of the Morrill Tariff, the first of many restrictive tariffs, which protected the nascent iron and steel industry, allowing U.S. producers to gain control of the domestic market for themselves. By 1895, U.S. iron and steel production had already surpassed that of the UK. In 1900, the

---

[2] Aside from sources cited, I have relied heavily for the early growth of the steel industry on Temin (1964), Warren (1973), and William Thomas Hogan's (1971) comprehensive five volumes, as well as raw data from the Census Bureau, the Bureau of Labor Statistics, and the American Iron and Steel Institute.

tremendous efficiencies of U.S. steel producers, their easy access to raw materials, and the unmatched national transportation system led the leaders of the industry to consider tariffs no longer necessary (Temin 1964:213).

By 1906, U.S. steel production was four times as great as that of the UK. At its peak in 1945, 62% of the world's steel was produced in the United States. By 1968, the figure was down to 22%, and in 1971, the former USSR surpassed the United States in production (Warren 1973:10–11), the first time a foreign producer had outproduced the United States since the UK in the late nineteenth century. The demise of the steel industry in the 1980s and 1990s is traced in a wide and varied literature, although contrary to popular legends, U.S. steel production has hardly disappeared. Still, during the 1930s and 1940s, steel was indeed a premier industry, central to the U.S. economy.

Unlike that of wood and coal, however, the production of steel required enormous capital investment (Warren 1973:96). It was only large economies of scale and well-integrated operations that allowed one to produce steel in an efficient manner. As Alfred Chandler notes, "Modern factory management was first fully worked out in the metal-making and metal-working industries. In metal-making, it came in response to the need to integrate (that is internalize) within a single

Table 4.1 **Raw Steel Production, 1895–2000, Selected Years (Tons)**

Year	% of Capability Utilization	Total	Open Hearth	Bessemer	Basic Oxygen Process	Crucible	Electric
1895	—	6,784,734	1,218,841	5,493,500		72,393	
1916	93.4	46,792,802	34,278,265	12,233,806		135,180	145,551
1918	84.6	49,010,095	38,065,348	10,335,270		127,796	481,681
1921	34.5	21,638,719	17,065,498	4,460,759		7,975	104,487
1929	88.5	61,741,962	53,152,445	7,945,496		6,453	637,568
1932	19.5	15,123,477	13,242,665	1,712,248		270	168,294
1937	72.5	56,636,945	51,824,979	3,863,918		1,046	947,002
1938	39.6	31,751,990	29,080,016	2,106,340		7	565,627
1941	97.3	82,839,259	74,389,619	5,578,071		2,313	2,869,256
1950	96.9	96,836,075	86,262,509	4,534,558			6,039,008
1955	93.0	117,036,085	105,359,417	3,319,517	307,279		8,049,872
1969		141,261,662	60,894,041	—	60,235,671		20,131,950
1982	48.4	74,577,000	6,110,000	—	45,309,000		23,158,000
2000	86.1	112,242,000			59,485,000		52,757,000

Source: American Iron and Steel Institute, Washington, DC.

works several major processes of production previously carried on in different locations" (1977:258). Steel manufacturers, led by the entrepreneur Andrew Carnegie were driven in a number of directions. First, they designed and established enormous, highly coordinated industrial facilities, taking advantage not only of large economies of scale but capital-intensive technical innovations. Second, they attempted to control their costs—including labor costs, which were substantial—by the careful accounting and squeezing of all factors of production. Third, they attempted to control uncertainty in supply and cost of raw materials by controlling them directly, striving for the vertical integration of the industry by owning their own coal and ore mines, limestone quarries, and transportation networks, including ships and railroads. Finally, they attempted to control the price of their products by collusion in the setting of prices, and ultimately by mergers and the acquisition of competitors.[3] An understanding of these factors is essential to comprehending both the possibilities for labor organization and militancy and the differences between labor management struggles in steel and many other industries. Contrary to that employed in most discussions of the strike propensities of various workers, the methodology for evaluating militancy in different industries is complex, especially, for example, when one is comparing an industry comprising thousands of relatively small workplaces (like coal) with the steel industry. This point cannot be overemphasized.

Capitalists also searched for the best locations to place their mammoth operations. Bessemer, Alabama (near Birmingham), uniquely located in a region that had large quantities of both coal and iron ore, went from a forest-covered tract with no residents in 1887 to a town in 1891 with more than forty-five hundred people and seven railway connections (Warren 1973:71). In 1890, however, almost 60% of the iron and steel production was still located in Pennsylvania, largely in the Pittsburgh area, because of the large, rich deposits of coal there. At least initially, coal was more difficult to transport than iron ore, especially after it was made into coke, which deteriorated quickly in a way that iron ore did not. After the formation of U.S. Steel (USS) in 1901, which became the dominant firm in the industry, the benefits of the Great Lakes shore—with its direct water access to iron ore from the northern Mesabi range—particularly in the Calumet region (the southeast Chicago and northwest Indiana areas), but also in Ohio and Buffalo, New York, and even Michigan, led to an increased concentration of the industry there (Warren 1973:106–107). East Coast mills, most notably Bethlehem plants, tended to import their iron ore from abroad, since it was priced competitively and often had a richer iron content than even that from the Mesabi range.

The development of iron and steel in the South was concentrated in several areas. Of special importance for our purposes here were the plants in Alabama, particularly

---

[3] David Brody notes the unique concern of US steelmakers for efficiency and costs (1960:2).

around Birmingham, whose TCI (Tennessee Iron and Coal Corporation) operations had been bought in 1907 by U.S. Steel. Despite the close access of large quantities of both iron ore and coal, and the company's far lower wage structure, the steel industry in Alabama never took off to the degree many expected (for comparative wages by steel district in 1933, see Table 4.2). While the South as a whole had between 9 and 14% of the nation's steelworkers between 1910 and 1960, the Birmingham area—which had the largest concentration of the South's steelworkers—never turned into the rival of Pittsburgh that its boosters predicted. There were several reasons for this. First, the South in general, because of its immense relative poverty and largely agricultural economy, had few natural markets compared with the North and West. Although proximity to markets was not the only factor, extreme remoteness often meant out of sight, out of mind. Second, while U.S. Steel wanted to control production in Birmingham (especially to eliminate the possibility that one of its competitors might produce steel more cheaply there), its policies, including pricing formulas, disadvantaged its southern operations in favor of those in the North. Finally, coal in Alabama had more impurities

Table 4.2 **Wage Differentials Between Different Districts, August 1933**

	District	*Minimum Rates of Pay for Common Labor, Cents per Hour*
1	Eastern District	35
2	Johnstown District	37
3	Pittsburgh District	40
4	Youngstown Valley District	40
5	North Ohio river District	40
6	Canton, Massillon, and Mansfield District	37
7	Cleveland District	40
8	Buffalo District	38
9	Detroit-Toledo District	40
10	South Ohio River District	37
11	Indiana-Illinois-St. Louis District	37
12	Chicago District	40
13	Southern District	25
14	Birmingham District	27

Source: Code of Fair Compensation of the Iron and Steel Industry, Schedule E, reproduced from Horace B. Davis, *Labor and Steel* (New York: International, 1933), 284–85.

than much of that from the North and West Virginia, and the iron ore was inferior to the rich deposits from the Mesabi range in Minnesota, as well as in northern Michigan and Wisconsin. Despite these disadvantages, however, the World War II economic expansion gave an enormous boost to southern steel production.

The steel industry was distinguished from other industries by a number of factors. The first, of course, was the large size of its plants and the sizable amount of capital invested in each location, something by which virtually every commentator has been struck. As Horace Davis notes, "American steel makers have astonished the world not only by the size of their furnaces and mills but by the way they scrapped an old plant before it was worn out, in order to build a bigger one" (1933:173). In addition, the industry, especially compared with wood, coal, and textiles, was distinguished by the concentration of ownership, which can be seen from Table 4.3 (Davis (1933:293, 181). The top ten producers accounted for 84% of the steel capacity in the United States (1933:180). While U.S. Steel was clearly the dominant firm in the industry, its sway was most important in western Pennsylvania and the Midwest. On the East Coast, it was Bethlehem that had the largest share of production.[4]

This horizontal combination was not based exclusively on the technical requirements of the industry. As Davis notes, even relatively smaller producers were sufficiently large and well capitalized to be at the vanguard of technical innovation and productivity in their plants (1933:175). Rather, it was the need to control the market, prices, and ultimately profits that led to the increased concentration of ownership. The push for this concentration came from the banks and financiers who quite literally controlled the industry. Because of the need for large amounts of investment capital, Morgan financial interests not only controlled U.S. Steel, but had important interests in Bethlehem and other companies. Mellon interests had a major influence on many independents, while Mark Hanna's banking empire had important control over Republic Steel; also in evidence were the fingerprints of financier Cyrus Eaton, who by 1927 had become the major shareholder in the newly reorganized Republic Steel (Kollros 1998:6).

There was also little worry that the federal government would find any of these relations a violation of federal anti-trust laws. Some have suggested that capitalist influence on governments in capitalist societies is indirect, a result of societal "logic," not direct or, as they would say pejoratively, "instrumental." Such criticisms are mostly unfounded when one looks at the influence of the steel bourgeoisie: much of the federal government does indeed appear to be, in Marx's words, their "executive committee." Davis examines these ties in detail and they are indeed rather lurid. Philander C. Knox, the U.S. attorney general when U.S. Steel was formed in 1901,

---

[4] The top seven firms by market share were USS 38.4%, Bethlehem 13.2%, Republic 8.6%, Jones and Laughlin 5.2%, Youngstown 4.4%, American Rolling Mills 3.2%, and National 3.1% (Kollros 1998:7).

Table 4.3 **Number of Steelworkers Employed by Certain Leading Steel Firms, 1929–1930 and July 1, 1933**

Company	Actual Average Number of Employees, 1929 and 1930	Total Number of Employees Given Some Work on or Around July 1, 1933
U.S. Steel	139,622	115,466
Bethlehem Steel	43,679	33,848
Republic Steel	22,322	19,349
Jones & Laughlin Steel	16,753	14,439
Youngstown Sheet & Tube	15,931	13,873
American Rolling Mill	9,477	8,287
National Steel	13,158	14,689
Inland Steel	6,824	6,231
Wheeling Steel	11,043	12,633
Colorado Iron & Steel	6,246	2,696
Crucible Steel	8,022	5,358
Corrigan-McKinney Steel	3,223	3,187
Newton Steel	2,639	1,293
Otis Steel	3,685	4,034
Pittsburgh Steel	5,962	4,998
Gulf States Steel	2,157	2,152
Roebling's Steel	4,464	3,225
Spang-Chalfant	3,102	2,289
International Harvester	2,800	1,936
Granite City Steel	2,278	2,360
McKeesport Tin Plate	2,870	2,876
Sharon Steel Hoop	1,983	2,008
Newport Rolling Mill	1,403	1,009
Continental Steel	2,409	2,333
Acme Steel	1,627	1,488
Lukens Steel	2,000	1,534
Total	341,654*	288,945*

*Includes figures from unlisted minor employers.

Source: American Iron and Steel Institute, Statement of Employment Conditions and Rate of Operations in the Steel Industry, Submitted to the National Recovery Administration at Steel Code Hearings, July 1, 1933. Reproduced in Horace B. Davis, *Labor and Steel* (New York: International, 1933.), 293.

was the former chief council for Carnegie Steel Corporation and an intimate of Henry Clay Frick, a prominent USS director. When Knox was replaced (to become secretary of state), it was by George W. Wickersham, previously USS's attorney. Another former attorney for USS, Elihu Root, had preceded Knox as secretary of state. Secretary of the navy was a position also filled by several former USS officials (Davis 1933:201). When U.S. Steel received a tax rebate of 96 million dollars, it was Pittsburgh steel financier Andrew Mellon who was secretary of the treasury, who okayed the deal, supposedly guarding Americans' taxpayer dollars (Davis 1933:191). These connections are just a titillating sampler. Of course, it is perhaps arguable that these connections were really secondary, and the welfare of USS was just part of the accepted ethos of ruling class America. Such is a legitimate conclusion that one might have drawn when the Supreme Court, in what Davis calls a "coat of judicial whitewash," exonerated USS for anti-trust violations, the imprimatur being given by the highly liberal judge Oliver Wendell Holmes, whose bleeding heart went out to USS (1933:202).

The bigger employers controlled a large percentage of the raw material and related product industries. U.S. Steel, for example, dominated most of the Great Lakes ore in the 1930s and more than 10% of the coal resources in the entire country (Davis 1933:177). Certain major companies had their own steel mills, including International Harvester, which owned Wisconsin Steel in Chicago, and Ford in Dearborn, Michigan, which even recycled old automobile parts as scrap in making steel. Thus, the fate of literally millions of workers was controlled by decisions made by banking officials and top managers in steel and steel-related industries. These companies and officials had the ability to mobilize enormous resources against any challenges to the absolute control of their labor forces. As we shall see, the economics of the industry, the development of its technology, and its patterns of concentration and collusion had an enormous relevance to the development of labor–management relations.

Finally, it is important to mention the concentration of African-American steelworkers, who play a special role in our story. In 1910 only 5.5% of the nation's steelworkers (approximately fourteen thousand) were African-American, a majority in the South, mostly in Alabama. It is estimated that the steelmakers brought in up to forty thousand Black strikebreakers during the 1919 steel strike, most remaining in the industry after the strike. This enormous increase in Black steelworkers is reflected in the 1920 census, where we find almost a tripling of their number in the industry as a whole, almost 14% of the total. While 75–80% of Alabama steelworkers were African-American, both before and after the strike, large increases in numbers and percentages occurred in northern steel centers in Pennsylvania, Ohio, Illinois, and Indiana (see Tables 4.4 and 4.5). By 1930, Bethlehem's large Sparrows Point plant in Maryland was more than 50% Black. And by 1950, virtually every major steel-producing area had large percentages of African-American workers.

Table 4.4 **Workers in the Steel Industry by Race, 1900–1960, United States and South**

Year	Footnote	Region	White	% White	African American	% African American	Other	% Other	Total
1900	1, 2	U.S.	252,387	95.54	11,767	4.45	9	0.00	264,163
	3	South	19,541	70.65	8,119	29.35	0	0.00	27,660
1910	4, 5	U.S.	243,062	94.38	14,330	5.56	141	0.05	257,533
		South	11,508	59.84	7,722	40.15	1	0.01	19,231
1920	6, 7	U.S.	287,580	86.28	45,620	13.69	122	0.04	333,322
		South	18,647	57.06	14,027	42.92	5	0.02	32,679
1930	8, 9	U.S.	256,077	83.65	41,784	13.65	8,258	2.70	306,119
		South	12,672	66.23	6,461	33.77	0	0.00	19,133
1940	10, 11	U.S.	495,468	93.31	35,413	6.67	102	0.02	530,983
		South	39,514	81.41	9,019	18.58	2	0.00	48,535
1950	12, 13	U.S.	707,842	86.98	105,520	12.97	406	0.05	813,768
		South	81,886	74.38	28,173	25.59	33	0.03	110,092
1960	14, 15	U.S.	757,547	86.77	114,647	13.13	851	0.10	873,045
		South	88,348	77.94	24,966	22.02	43	0.04	113,357

[1] For each decade, the workers are given under a different name in the source and their composition also varies; 1900 is composed of "Iron and Steel Workers."

[2] *Source*: Special Reports; Occupations, Twelfth Census, Department of Commerce and Labor, Bureau of the Census (Washington, DC: U.S. Government Printing Office, 1904).

[3] The "South" comprises Alabama, Arkansas, Florida, Georgia, Kentucky, Louisiana, Mississippi, Missouri, North Carolina, Oklahoma, South Carolina, Tennessee, Texas, Virginia, and West Virginia.

[4] 1910 is composed of "laborers and semi-skilled operatives in blast furnaces and rolling mills."

[5] *Source*: Thirteenth Census of the United States, vol. 4: *Population, 1910*, Occupation Statistics,. Department of Commerce, Bureau of the Census (Washington, DC: U.S. Government Printing Office, 1914).

[6] 1920 is composed of "laborers and semi-skilled operatives in 'blast furnaces and steel rolling mills."

[7] *Source*: Fourteenth Census of the United States, vol. 4: *Occupation, 1920*. Department of Commerce; Bureau of the Census (Washington, DC: U.S. Government Printing Office, 1923).

[8] 1930 is composed of "laborers and operatives in blast furnaces and steel rolling mills."

[9] *Source*: Fifteenth Census of the United States, 1930, Department of Commerce, Bureau of the Census (Washington, DC: U.S. Government Printing Office, 193?).

[10] 1940 is composed of persons employed in "blast furnaces, steel works, and rolling mills."

[11] *Source*: Sixteenth Census of the United States, 1940, *Population*, vol. 3: *The Labor Force*, parts 2–50, Department of Commerce, Bureau of the Census, (Washington, DC: U.S. Government Printing Office, 1943).

[12] 1950 is composed of workers employed in "primary iron and steel industries." This includes blast furnaces, steelworks, rolling mills, and other primary iron and steel industries.

[13] *Source*: Seventeenth Decennial Census of the United States: 1950 Census of Population, vol. 2: *Characteristics of the Population*, parts 2–50, U.S. Department of Commerce, Bureau of the Census (Washington, DC: U.S. Government Printing Office, 1952).

[14] 1960 is composed of workers employed in "primary iron and steel industries."

[15] *Source*: Eighteenth Census of the United States, 1960 Census of Population, vol. 1: *Characteristics of the Population*, parts 2–50. U.S. Department of Commerce, Bureau of the Census (Washington, DC: U.S. Government Printing Office, 1961).

Table 4.5 **Steelworkers by State and Race, 1900–50**

1910 Leading States in Steel Employment

State	White	% White	African American	% African American	Other	Total
Pennsylvania	118,976	97.3	3,337	2.7	4	122,317
Ohio	41,502	97.8	927	2.2	0	42,429
New York	15,410	99.0	144	0.9	4	15,558
Illinois	20,993	97.9	446	2.1	0	21,439
Maryland	1,789	59.2	1,231	40.8	0	3,020
Massachusetts	5,619	99.7	16	0.3	0	5,635
New Jersey	10,455	99.3	69	0.7	0	10,524
Indiana	12,159	97.8	272	2.2	1	12,432
West Virginia	4,699	99.5	25	0.5	0	4,724
Alabama	2,042	27.6	5,365	72.4	1	7,408

1910: Number of "laborers and semi-skilled operatives in blast furnaces and rolling mills."
Source: Thirteenth Census of the United States, 1910, vol. 4: *Population*, Occupation Statistics, Department of Commerce, Bureau of Census (Washington, DC: U.S. Government Printing Office, 1914).

1920 Leading States in Steel Employment

State	White	% White	African American	% African American	Other	Total
Pennsylvania	135,598	89.2	16,444	10.8	19	152,061
Ohio	57,930	90.1	6,359	9.9	16	64,305
New York	16,003	95.0	833	4.9	7	16,843
Illinois	20,292	88.6	2,618	11.4	0	22,910
Maryland	2,301	57.0	1,733	43.0	0	4,034
Massachusetts	7,509	99.4	45	0.6	0	7,554
New Jersey	6,191	92.1	533	7.9	1	6,725
Indiana	15,707	85.7	2,605	14.2	8	18,320
Alabama	3,006	23.1	9,981	76.9	0	12,987
West Virginia	9,206	95.2	467	4.8	0	9,673

1920: Number of "laborers and semi-skilled operatives in blast furnaces and rolling mills."
Source: Fourteenth Census of the United States, 1920, vol. 4: *Occupation*, Department of Commerce, Bureau of the Census (Washington, DC: U.S. Government Printing Office, 1923).

1930 Leading States in Steel Employment (more than 5,000 employed)

State	White	% White	African American	% African American	Other	Total
Pennsylvania	113,899	89.9	11,851	9.4	881	126,631
Ohio	57,407	86.3	8,206	12.3	885	66,498
New York	13,406	88.2	1,533	10.1	260	15,199
Illinois	22,121	80.0	3,073	11.1	2,441	27,635
New Jersey	7,873	92.4	641	7.5	4	8,518
Maryland	4,349	49.0	4,519	50.9	2	8,870
Indiana	17,269	66.4	4,974	19.1	3,759	26,002
Alabama	2,814	32.6	5,805	67.4	0	8,619

1930: Number of "laborers and semi-skilled operatives in blast furnaces and rolling mills."
Source: Fifteenth Census of the United States, 1930, Department of Commerce, Bureau of Census (Washington, DC: U.S. Government Printing Office,)

1940 Leadings States in Steel Employment (more than 5,000 employed)

State	White	% White	African American	% African American	Other	Total
Pennsylvania	185,517	95.8	8,127	4.2	15	193,659
Ohio	111,522	95.6	5,100	4.4	13	116,635
New York	25,210	95.6	1,148	4.4	23	26,381
Illinois	42,378	94.5	2,461	5.5	14	44,853
New Jersey	7,360	96.5	265	3.5	1	7,626
Maryland	16,587	77.5	4,808	22.5	1	21,396
Indiana	39,891	90.9	3,978	9.1	13	43,882
Alabama	14,086	66.4	7,129	33.6	0	21,215
Kentucky	4,873	94.3	291	5.6	1	5,165
Michigan	12,833	96.6	444	3.3	9	13,286
California	9,612	99.4	46	0.5	11	9,669
West Virginia	12,767	97.7	305	2.3	0	13,072

1940: Number of "laborers and semi-skilled operatives in blast furnaces and rolling mills."
Source: Sixteenth Census of the United States, 1940, Population, vol. 3: The Labor Force, parts 2–50, United States Department of Commerce, Bureau of the Census (Washington, DC: U.S. Government Printing Office, 1943).

1950 Leading States in Steel Employment (more than 5,000 employed)

State	White	% White	African American	% African American	Other	Total
Pennsylvania	242,242	93.9	15,595	6.0	43	257,880
Ohio	147,292	87.7	20,535	12.2	36	167,863
New York	46,691	89.6	5,339	10.2	76	52,106
Illinois	72,454	83.7	14,063	16.2	83	86,600
New Jersey	17,860	87.6	2,513	12.3	10	20,383
Maryland	21,395	72.4	8,131	27.5	7	29,533
Massachusetts	14,142	98.2	257	1.8	3	14,402
Alabama	26,821	63.5	15,442	36.5	5	42,268
Kentucky	5,843	93.2	427	6.8	0	6,270
Michigan	38,678	82.0	8,448	17.9	47	47,173
California	25,202	90.9	2,466	8.9	68	27,736
West Virginia	17,055	97.7	397	2.3	0	17,452
Texas	8,113	75.3	2,657	24.7	1	10,771
Missouri	10,371	77.2	3,058	22.8	4	13,433
Tennessee	2,963	59.1	2,051	40.9	0	5,014

1950: Number of "workers employed in primary iron and steel industries" including blast furnaces, steel works, rolling mills, and other primary iron and steel industries.

Source: Seventeenth Decennial Census of the United States, 1950, Census of the Population: vol. 2: *Characteristics of the Population*, parts 2–50, U.S. Department of Commerce, Bureau of the Census (Washington, DC: U.S. Government Printing Office, 1952).

1960 Leading States in Steel Employment (more than 5,000 employed)

State	White	% White	African American	% African American	Other	Total
Pennsylvania	223,932	93.8	14,601	6.1	114	238,647
Ohio	135,920	87.7	18,967	12.2	54	154,941
New York	44,347	88.0	5,935	11.8	119	50,401
Illinois	61,955	84.2	11,561	15.7	88	73,604
Indiana	62,816	83.9	11,995	16.0	53	74,864
New Jersey	14,240	84.7	2,567	15.3	11	16,818
Maryland	25,928	72.5	9,827	27.5	30	35,785
Massachusetts	9,596	96.9	305	3.1	0	9,901
Alabama	28,262	69.4	12,468	30.6	4	40,734
Kentucky	7,954	97.3	218	2.7	0	8,172
Michigan	42,260	81.4	9,601	18.5	51	51,912
California	30,626	91.7	2,541	7.6	224	33,391
West Virginia	16,720	97.9	358	2.1	0	17,078
Texas	12,847	74.9	4,313	25.1	0	17,160
Missouri	7,929	77.9	2,238	22.0	15	10,182
Wisconsin	17,579	90.5	1,781	9.2	64	19,424

1960: Number of "workers employed in primary iron and steel industries," including blast furnaces, steel works, rolling mills, and other primary iron and steel industries.

Source: Eighteenth Census of the United States, 1960, Census of the Population, vol. 1: *Characteristics of the Population*, parts 2–50, U.S. Department of Commerce, Bureau of the Census (Washington, DC: U.S. Government Printing office, 1961).

Occupational Structure in Steel

As Katherine Stone's pathbreaking work has shown, after the defeat of the 1892 Homestead strike and the subsequent elimination of unions in steel, companies created a series of job hierarchies and promotional ladders. These job hierarchies provided lines of progression within which workers could slowly advance to higher job categories, often on the basis of their seniority within these lines, creating an "internal labor market" (Stone 1974:114). According to Stone, these jobs had very little to do with skill, since even those in the highest categories could usually be learned in six weeks or less (1974:136). While the systems were complicated and often varied somewhat by region and company, several generalizations can be made. The pay differentials and promotion ladders were designed for several purposes. First, they were intended to break the control that skilled workers previously had (Stone 1974:143). Second, their goal was to wed workers to their companies, and even departments over long periods of time, thus creating job stability and loyalty. Finally, they were meant to give workers in different lines of progressions, and even at different levels on those lines, distinct interests from other workers. Stone argues that little changed with the unionization of the steel industry in the 1930s and 1940s (1974:134).

When hired, workers were assigned not only to particular departments, but to particular jobs within well-defined lines of progression. They rarely moved outside these lines, much less their original departments. African-Americans were usually hired into and assigned to the dirtiest, hottest, and most dangerous departments, without job ladders similar to those in white departments. In addition, when they were in departments with such job ladders, they were generally confined to the lowest jobs, with no promotion to the top rungs, as in blast furnaces (Nelson 1996:167, 169). In some plants, in contrast to southern and eastern European immigrants, they were confined to janitorial jobs. Moreover, in those jobs that actually did require certain learned skills, especially in maintenance and machine operation, but also in the operation of cranes and much of transport, they were largely excluded (Nelson 1996:177; Cayton and Mitchell 1939:35). Hinshaw notes that companies had strong preferences for job, line of progression, and departmental seniority units (2002:77). In Bethlehem's Johnstown mill, for example, there were 130 job lines in eighteen different departments, all with their separate promotion chains. Despite an extensive literature that asserts that most white workers supported these arrangements, Hinshaw argues that, even in the 1950s, most workers had "preference for broad interpretations of seniority" (2002:126).

There were occasional departures from the general lack of opportunities (most of which disappeared after unionization) for African-American steelworkers; for example, some left-led locals fought for the rights of their Black members. As Dickerson documents for Pennsylvania, "Promotions of Black workers occurred rarely. Those holding semi-skilled jobs in the blast furnace and open hearth departments had little prospect of advancing beyond first or second helper." The modest numbers of skilled Black workers "were concentrated in small specialty shops where steel managers both hired and promoted Black employees. Some of them, like Lockhart Iron and Steel in McKees Rocks, had a tradition of employing skilled Blacks which began before World War I" (1986:122). Even in Birmingham, there were occasional deviations from Black exclusion from the more skilled jobs before the advent of unionism. As Norrell argues, between 1910 and 1930, TCI "assigned blacks to semiskilled jobs and sometimes to skilled jobs such as machinist . . . The elevation of some blacks reflected U.S. Steel's strategy for shopfloor control: Divisions among workers, in this instance competition between blacks and whites for good jobs, undermined a sense of unity and helped to prevent unionism" (1986:671–72; also Northrup: 1943). Hinshaw argues that the main cause of segregation in the steel industry was the "discriminatory and promotion policies" of the steel companies themselves (2002:76; also Nelson 1996:170). Confirming Stone's analysis, Hinshaw argues that hierarchies were designed for control purposes: "Technology plays only a minor role in this process" (2002:165)

Working Conditions

By all accounts, before unionization in the late 1930s, workers found conditions in the steel industry highly oppressive. Wages were relatively low, even compared with those in other non-union manufacturing industries (Interchurch 1920:45). Hours were quite long. In 1920, fully 50% of workers were still working twelve-hour shifts, and 25% were working more than sixty-hour weeks, an amount usually regarded as the maximum in most other industries (1920:44). Even in 1930, hours were longer than those in other industries, with ten- to twelve-hour shifts common and double shifts not unusual (H. Davis 1933:76). In 1936, U.S. Steel, the major supplier of armored plate to the U.S. military, faced a ban on its government contracts because its standard forty-eight-hour workweeks were in direct violation of the 1936 Walsh-Healy Act (Hinshaw 2002:5). The vaunted efficiencies and detailed control of the production process by the steel giants also resulted not only in greater profits but in a large amount of speedup and at times heavier workloads (H. Davis 1933:76; more generally Brody 1960:32–33, 37–39, 42–49).

The rates of accidents, industrial illnesses, and deaths were far above the abysmal averages in other non-union industries (H. Davis 1933:36). Death rates were especially high in blast furnace areas, irrespective of the technology. Blast furnaces had a tendency to explode, which companies invariably tried to blame on workers' carelessness, although that seemed most often not to be the case (H. Davis 1933:43;

Stone 1974:137 argues that company plant and equipment design were responsible for the overwhelming majority of accidents). In one notorious case in 1926, for example, a blast furnace at Woodward Iron Company in Alabama exploded and poured 400 tons of molten steel on its crew, killing twenty-one workers (for additional graphic cases, see Nelson 1996:149–50).

As with autoworkers and others, one of the biggest issues for steelworkers was the absolute rule of the foreman, which Robert Brooks describes as "feudal" (1940:193).[5] Finally, the extent of espionage and physical repression was extreme even for U.S. industry, perhaps matched only by that in Henry Ford's River Rouge plant or what occurred in some West Virginia coal districts (Interchurch 1920:26–29; La Follette Committee Hearings 1936–41; Auerbach 1966). All these conditions were worse in the South.

Steel Unionism

Steel was, by the 1930s, a mass production industry with hundreds of thousands of workers, and it was central to the U.S. economy, the development of the country into an industrial power, and U.S. world economic dominance.[6] Steel also had a polyglot, racially diverse labor force, which at times displayed heroic levels of militancy and solidarity. Yet in the end, when workers finally organized, despite episodic rank-and-file supported opposition, they remained under the control of an authoritarian business unionist leadership.[7] Our task is to understand why and to consider some of the implications for the development of the labor movement and the nature of American politics, especially in the South.

[5] In certain Alabama plants, it was not unusual for armed supervisors and thugs to hover over workers, which became a key issue in certain plants with the advent of unionism (Beddow to McDonald, February 19, 1941, District 36 1:4).

[6] Davis estimates that in 1930, steel companies directly employed 621,000 workers (520,000 of whom were wage earners), with another 300,000 employed in supporting, company-owned industries, exclusive of fabricating and finishing products. The largest geographical concentrations were in Pennsylvania, with 212,000 workers, and along the Great Lakes, in Illinois, Indiana, Ohio, and New York, with roughly 262,000 workers (1933:15–16). Slightly different figures were given by union president Philip Murray in a speech at the first Steel Workers Organizing Committee (SWOC) organizational meeting, in 1936. He claimed then that 48% of U.S. steel was being produced in the Pittsburgh District, 10% in Birmingham, and a larger amount in the Great Lakes region, especially the Chicago area (Minutes of SWOC Organizational Meeting, held at UMWA headquarters, June 17, 1936, Catholic University (CU), CIO, NIU, box 33, USWA, 1).

[7] The degree to which the Murray leadership has been completely and apologetically whitewashed by most commentators will be explored in detail.

Early Organizing

Organization in steel, as in a number of other industries where skilled workers were central to the production process (e.g., the farm equipment industry), began early.

Highly skilled iron puddlers used their leverage to organize and gain high wages and improvements in working conditions from the steel companies. Their first organization, the Sons of Vulcan, was established in 1858 in the Pittsburgh district. Other skilled steelworkers subsequently organized with varying degrees of success (Commons and Associates 1935:80). These unions were open only to skilled workers, virtually always white. In 1876 (Commons and Associates 1935:179; Brody 1960:50), or 1875, according to Commons and Associates (1935: 80), the Sons of Vulcan, the Associated Brotherhood of Iron and Steel Heaters (roughers, rollers, and catchers), and the Iron and Steel Hands merged to form the Amalgamated Association of Iron and Steel Workers of the United States ("known as 'AA' or 'Amalgamated'"); 85% of its initial members were puddlers. In 1873, the Knights of Labor established locals open to all workers in a large number of steel plants, eventually creating pressure for industrial unionism in the Amalgamated. The lodge at the Edgar Thompson Works, in North Braddock, Pennsylvania, just outside of Pittsburgh—according to Alfred Chandler, the most advanced steel facility in the world at the time (1977:260–62)—opened itself to all workers (H. Davis 1933:225), eventually affiliating with the Knights of Labor (Taft 1957:140). Although the AA took part in and led a number of strikes (e.g., Brody 1960:50), it was generally a narrow craft union, which sought to accommodate the steel companies. It also failed to adjust in the late nineteenth century when major technological changes undermined the leverage of skilled workers by displacing them with more efficient, automated industrial processes. Nevertheless, from 1867 to 1875 the Sons of Vulcan called eighty-seven authorized strikes. The Amalgamated, like its predecessor, "was not unwilling to engage in strikes," authorizing ninety-three between 1876 and 1885 (Taft 1964:137).

In 1892, the AA at Homestead, Pennsylvania, participated in what Philip Foner accurately calls "one of the bloodiest clashes between capital and labor in American history" (1955:206). There are literally dozens if not hundreds of accounts.[8] The Carnegie Works at Homestead was a large steel-producing facility. The management of the whole Carnegie Company had recently been taken over by the virulently anti-union H. C. Frick, whom Taft describes as "the personification of the ruthless business leader who would tolerate no opposition" (1964:138). What Frick recognized was the greatly diminished role of skilled workers in the production process and the decreased leverage of their unions. He was thus determined, using Coal and

---

[8] Here for brevity's sake, I follow the graphic and informative account of Foner (1955:206–18); for a more detailed version see Krause (1992).

Iron Police, Pinkerton guards, deputy sheriffs, and state militia, to "stamp out unionism." On June 29 and 30, 1892, before the contract with the AA had expired, the company locked out its workers. All thirty-eight hundred workers struck, including those in the other seven skilled trades lodges, skilled and unskilled workers, union and non-union, Black and white, native-born and immigrant. Mass picket lines were established, and union boats patrolled the Monongahela River, on whose banks the plant was located. The Committee of 50, made up of leaders elected from the eight unions to run the strike, essentially took over the town. On July 6, 1892, three hundred armed Pinkertons on barges (attempting to bring strikebreakers to the plant) shot it out with thousands of armed strikers and their supporters. At least nine steelworkers were killed, along with three Pinkertons. A memorial still exists in downtown Homestead, erected by the CIO's Steel Workers Organizing Committee (SWOC) in 1941 to commemorate the steelworkers who were killed there. The strike was in the headlines of virtually all major newspapers, as mass meetings of workers met around the country to denounce Carnegie and the Pinkertons. On June 10, the governor mobilized eight thousand National Guardsmen, who were eventually used to break the strike, destroying the unions. On July 23, New York anarchist Alexander Berkman, unrelated to the strike, shot and stabbed Frick, who survived the attack. Hundreds of strikers and their leaders were arrested and indicted. Foner asserts that no worker "was found guilty by a jury" (1955:215), although Taft notes that a cook in the mill was convicted for giving poison in their food to strikebreakers inside the plants (1964:145).

What Foner finds especially noteworthy is that despite the exclusionary policy of the AA (by both race and skill), not a single worker scabbed, a point that was even acknowledged by Frick in his correspondence with Andrew Carnegie (Foner 1955:218). The union seemed to learn nothing from this, refusing to open its membership to non-whites or the unskilled, even after the strike. The defeat at Homestead led to the steady decline and elimination of the AA in steel mills across the country. Yet as Brody notes, "The Amalgamated Association faced its decline in steel with a certain equanimity" (1960:60).

On June 1, 1909, U.S. Steel announced that all its installations (shipping, coal, coke, fabricating, as well as steel production) would henceforth be non-union. Finally, in 1910, the AA convention amended its constitution to open membership to everyone involved in the industry, belatedly admitting that its exclusionary policies had hurt its organizing efforts (Brody 1960:125–26). The formal change in its position, however, was barely registered in the way the union functioned.

Even during the period of union defeat, steelworkers took part in strikes. Immigrant workers especially had their own ways of developing solidarity, contrary to the prejudiced views expressed by AFL President Samuel Gompers and numerous other AFL leaders. The *Chicago Daily Socialist* (January 31, 1910) describes a strike meeting of immigrant steelworkers in Hammond, Indiana:

The lights of the hall were extinguished. A candle stuck into a bottle was placed on a platform. One by one the men came and kissed the ivory image on the cross, kneeling before it. They swore they would not scab. (Brody 1960:139)

As Brody notes, rather than educating white native-born workers on the importance of sympathizing with and joining with immigrant workers, Gompers and other AFL leaders saw their role as educating subhuman immigrants "without full mental development" into the virtues of trade unionism (1960:141).[9]

The 1919 Steel Strike

An important attempt to organize steelworkers came during the 1918–19 period, culminating in the 1919 steel strike, led by William Z. Foster. The 1919 steel strike is one of the most studied and analyzed events in U.S. labor history, with a book-length account by its leader, a detailed study by a respected research organization (the Commission of Inquiry of the Interchurch World Movement 1920), several sustained critiques of this latter study, and analyses by a wide range of labor historians.[10] Although I will give a brief account of the 1919 strike and some of the different analyses, one of the most important aspects of the strike for our purposes is that it became the benchmark for planning how to successfully organize the industry in the 1930s (the dramatic organizing successes leading up to the 1919 strike and the reasons for its ultimate failure were discussed at length by mainstream and radical activists during the 1930s). In addition, the "how to" pamphlet by Foster (1936), by this time one of the main leaders of the U.S. Communist Party, was a must-read for all the activists and leaders.

During World War I, membership in U.S. unions grew rapidly. A Democratic administration in Washington, in part beholden to organized labor, and the need to keep production going during the war imposed some restraints on the anti-labor propensities of major corporations.[11] Perhaps more important, however, huge wartime demands for steel, together with a tight labor market, made employers less

[9] These views were shared by John Commons (1903, 1920), who is still regarded as the premier U.S. labor historian.

[10] This vast literature comprises accounts by Taft (1957), Taft and Perlman (1935), Brody (1965), Foner (1955), Foster (1920, 1936), and Brown (1998), among many others. The 1919 strike is strangely minimized by Stone (1974:151); her lack of interest in labor struggles is perhaps reflected in the fact that she got the year of the 1937 Memorial Day Massacre wrong (1974:153)

[11] Many have questioned why the Wilson administration was so responsive to the relatively small American Federation of Labor. Elizabeth Sanders (1999), in a highly perceptive analysis, shows how the much larger and electorally more influential farmers' organizations, desirous of a long-term farmer–labor alliance, aggressively pushed union demands.

desirous of labor conflicts while record profits were pouring in. Union growth across industries throughout the South and in the country as a whole multiplied rapidly (Bureau of Labor Statistics 1946:154–60). World War I thus seemed the perfect time to finally organize the U.S. steel industry.

Virtually all the main leadership factions in the AFL recognized the incompetence of the AA leadership; if steel was to be organized, the AFL itself would have to play a major role. Little action was taken by these leaders, however, including those around AFL president Samuel Gompers. It is therefore not surprising that the impetus for organization came from the Chicago Federation of Labor (CFL), according to Taft the "largest and . . . the most important and vigorous of any of the Federation's city central labor unions" (1957:385). The CFL was headed by the leftist John Fitzpatrick, then a close colleague and supporter of William Z. Foster (and his small band of radical labor activists), who had just led the initially successful organization of the meat slaughterhouse industry centered in Chicago.[12]

Let us follow Foster's detailed account, then note some of the gray areas.[13] In 1918, Foster and his colleagues saw not only a tremendous opportunity for organizing steel but also the potential for transforming the whole U.S. labor movement. On April 7, 1918, Foster presented a resolution that was passed by the CFL requesting the AFL Executive Council to organize steel (1920:17). The resolution, which was then forwarded to the AFL, was meandering along, "with a loss of much precious time," when the resolution was readopted by the CFL and sent to the AFL national convention, to be held in St. Paul, Minnesota, on June 10–20, 1918, where Foster had been delegated to organize a meeting (1920:18). Foster was able to pull together a number of conferences, with the critical unions agreeing to have AFL president Samuel Gompers call another conference in Chicago in thirty days, thus, as Foster complains, involving "further waste of probably the most precious time for organizing work that Labor will ever have" (1920:19). President Gompers and the leaders of twenty-four unions with members in steel met in Chicago at the New Morrison Hotel, August 1–2, 1918, with Gompers presiding. They established the

[12] Harry Haywood notes that in this period Chicago was the most vibrant center of labor radicalism in the country, as well as a focal point of Black activism (1978:84, passim; Storch 2007:10–18). See oral history interview with David Saposs (SWOC Records, n.d., Penn State University, PSU) for extremely positive evaluations of the capabilities of both Fitzgerald and Foster.

[13] Foster was not merely a brilliant tactician and charismatic leader (as even his bitterest enemies in the labor movement readily acknowledge). He was also a penetrating analyst and writer. According to David Saposs, an anti-communist researcher, later a strong critic of Foster and the CP, and at times a government researcher, Foster's book on the 1919 steel strike was exceptional. In an oral history interview in the late 1960s, Saposs says, "Now, he wrote this book on the steel industry, which I think is a monumental book . . . Foster really had an academic mind" (SWOC Records, n.d., PSU, 2, 10)). The information, data, and general analysis by Foster are accepted, cited, and the basis for discussing the 1919 strike by virtually every serious analyst.

National Committee of the Iron and Steel Industry, with Gompers as chair, John Fitzpatrick as vice chair, and Foster as treasurer.

Foster proposed that the twenty-four unions contribute half a million dollars, putting up a quarter million immediately to hire hundreds of organizers, who would promptly be dispatched to all steel centers in the country at the same time. The plan, according to Foster, was "to make a hurricane drive simultaneously in all steel centers that would catch the workers' imagination and sweep them into the unions en masse . . . The essence of the plan was quick, energetic action." Three to four weeks later there would be huge mass meetings of steelworkers (Foster 1920:21). When it came time to commit themselves to the plan, the twenty-four unions "failed dismally," each agreeing to contribute only a hundred dollars and a few organizers.

Discouraged but undaunted, Foster and his friends called a conference in Chicago on August 16, 1918, with representatives from the CFL and the Chicago Building Trades Council, which decided (given the limited resources) to begin the campaign in the Calumet district, the steel corridor stretching along Lake Michigan from South Chicago to Gary, Indiana (Perlman and Taft 1935:462). According to Taft, the campaign and its subsequent spread to other districts "was an immediate success . . . it can be regarded as one of the great organizing feats in American labor history" (1957:386); Taft and Fink call it "a magnificent organizing achievement" (1981:97; see also Brody 1965:216–19). Harbison, on the other hand, with typical one-dimensional thinking, states that "the industry-wide strike of 1919 was a dismal failure" (1940:13).

The movement spread rapidly to many other steel centers, although not nearly as fast as it would have if the requested support had been given. Pittsburgh, the largest steel district, however, was proving difficult to organize because the repression was so intense, with firings, arrests, refusals to rent space, and violence against organizers the order of the day. Finally, with the rest of the steel districts almost completely organized, a "Flying Squadron" was formed to open the Pittsburgh-area steel mill towns to organizing. A meeting was announced for April 1, 1919, in Monessen, a steel town forty miles south of Pittsburgh on the Monagahela River. In keeping with my thesis that coal miners were the vanguard of the U.S. working class during the first four decades of the twentieth century, ten thousand armed union miners on April 1, 1919, led by uniformed former servicemen, marched into town, and the city was opened for the organizing of steelworkers. Speakers at the Monessen meeting included mine workers organizer Mother Jones (then eighty-nine); James Mauer, president of the Pennsylvania Federation of Labor; Philip Murray, president of United Mine Workers of America (UMWA) District 5; and Foster. The town of McKeesport was taken on May 18, with regular street meetings occurring after that. The whole district was soon opened up. When the town of Donora refused to yield, union coal miners boycotted the town's businesses, and the tide turned (Foster 1920:53–53; Brody 1965:231–33).

With the steel companies refusing to yield and perhaps hundreds of thousands of steelworkers joining the union movement, votes were taken on whether to strike, with near unanimity in favor. September 22, 1919, was set as the date. Hundreds of thousands of workers answered the call. With the ending of the war, a great deal of their leverage had disappeared. Public hysteria was created by the steel companies and the media, with the press seeing massive bloodshed and rioting where there was none (Brody 1965:246; Interchurch 1921; Rosenow 2003). False stories were spread about production resuming and the strike being broken elsewhere. All accounts agree, however, that the repression against the strikers was often savage, especially in the Pittsburgh district. Taft argues that "the ultimate failure of the strike was due not to lack of unity or support among the strikers or the officers of the union," but to violent repression (1957:390). Foster argues the steel manufacturers won "by carrying on a reign of terror that outraged every just conception of civil and human rights" (1920:1; on various atrocities, 110–39).

The degree of violence was staggering, as carefully documented by the 1920 report of the Interchurch World Movement. Twenty-two workers were shot or beaten to death by police or company gunmen. The first was Fannie Sellins, a UMWA organizer murdered by company thugs outside the Allegheny Steel Company in West Natona, Pennsylvania, on August 26, just before the strike officially began. When she begged company agents to stop beating an elderly worker, they knocked her down and dragged her by the heels from a truck, a deputy crushing her head with a cudgel in front of a large number of witnesses. Foster notes, "The guilty men were named in the newspapers and from a hundred platforms. Yet no one was ever punished for the crime." On August 26, 1938, on the anniversary of Sellins's murder, UMWA District 5 erected a monument to her near the spot where she died (for the quote and a full account, see Foner 1979:107–108; on her life, see Cassedy 1992).

Taft is perhaps too quick to absolve the AFL and its member unions for the failure of the strike. First, the foot dragging postponed the organizing until after the war had ended, and thus the critical time period when the steelworkers might have had the greatest market power leverage was lost. Part of this wasted time was due to the lack of financial support. Taft looks at the total amount of money raised (almost half a million dollars, meticulously documented by Foster) and calls the financing successful (1957:391). But this conclusion is disingenuous. Most of the money was raised during the course of the strike and went for relief. Virtually none of it came from the twenty-four most involved unions. In a lesson on the finances of business unionism, the AA, in fact, even came out ahead. According to Foster's careful records, almost half the money came from several industrial unions, including Local 33 in New York City of the Marine Engineers, the Fur Workers, the International Ladies' Garment Workers' Union (ILGWU) (which gave $60,000), and the Amalgamated Clothing workers (which gave $100,000), the latter two of which did not even belong to the AFL. Finally, another $150,000 was raised at the November 8, 1919, rally in Madison Square Garden in New York City, with some unions donating as much as half of their local treasuries for strike relief (Foster 1920:221).

Gompers gave only "lukewarm support," and there was disunity from the beginning among the craft unions (Foster 1955:152). Brody notes that the twenty-four unions barely ceded any authority or prerogatives to the National Committee (1965:216). Even Taft and Perlman (generally sympathetic to the AFL) note that AA president Mike Tighe continued to act as an independent operative, even attempting to negotiate separately with the steel companies (1935:463).

As if all this were not enough, the racial backwardness and anti-immigrant attitudes of the majority of AFL unions, including the Amalgamated, as well as many of the white, native-born skilled workers, helped doom the strike. Forming the backbone of the strike were the unskilled and semi-skilled immigrant workers, who supported the strike everywhere with great militancy and in overwhelming numbers. The skilled workers—largely native-born whites—once the bedrock of unionism in the industry, made a "poor showing. To begin with they organized slowly; then they struck reluctantly and scatteringly" (Foster 1920:197). Part of their problem was, of course, their privileged position in the plants; another was the long history of crushing defeats of their union, the Amalgamated. Foster also emphasizes their racism and ethnic chauvinism toward both Blacks and foreigners, tendencies exploited by the companies to a large degree (1920:198–99). Hence, there was a general lack of support among African-American steelworkers and a willingness by other African-Americans to be used as strikebreakers. Foster regards this as a factor contributing to the defeat of the strike, while the Interchurch Report sees it as the main reason (Whatley 1993:527 accepts the Interchurch Report explanation without exploring other factors.). John Fitzpatrick, however, head of the Chicago Federation of Labor and effective chair of the National Committee during the 1919 strike (and a left-wing ally of Foster), discounts the importation of Black strikebreakers as a reason for the failure of the strike. He argues that the strike was lost by the native-born skilled craftsmen, some of whom scabbed originally, many of the rest of whom were among the first to go back. Fitzpatrick asserts that these steelworkers could not have been replaced by new hires if they had held firm, and it was they who lost the strike (interview with Fitzpatrick given in Cayton and Mitchell 1939:79). Either way, racism among whites seems to have been a major cause for the defeat of the strike.

Before World War I, according to the 1910 census, less than 6% of U.S. steelworkers were African-American, and most of these were located in Alabama and Maryland. With the cutoff of immigration during World War I, combined with increased steel employment due to higher wartime production, steel companies began recruiting heavily among southern Black workers (Nelson 2001:164).

By the end of World War I, according to the 1920 census, Black steelworkers made up 13.7% of production workers; most of that increase came in the North. The increases by state were dramatic (especially those in Pennsylvania, Ohio,

Illinois, and Indiana). At U.S. Steel's mammoth Gary Works, there were 189 African-American steelworkers in 1915 and 1,295 in 1918 (Brody 1960:186). By the time of the 1919 strike, 1,737 of the 14, 687 employees at the Homestead Steel Works were African-American. When management and clerical employees were subtracted, the percentage of production workers who were Black may have been as high as 14%. During the initial organizing campaign, only eight Blacks at Homestead joined the union, and only one struck, although he stayed loyal to the end. In Duquesne, of 344 Blacks employed, none went on strike (Foster 1920:206). These trends existed more or less across the industry.

Several reasons for them are given. First, many of the African-Americans were new to the industry and had not had sufficient time to develop union consciousness (Cayton and Mitchell 1939:77; Spero and Harris 1931:258). More important, however, was the racially discriminatory nature of the unions involved, whose policies seemed to offer little to Black workers. As Cayton and Mitchell note about the AA, "In its fifty-three years of existence from 1880 to 1933, the Amalgamated Association had not made a single serious attempt to include Negroes in its ranks in a position of full equality with white union members" (1939:81). Although the AA was no longer officially discriminatory by 1919, some of its lodges still refused to admit Black members. Even worse were many of the other twenty-four unions (including the machinists and electrical workers) whose constitutions legally barred African-Americans from joining. Despite the urging of Foster and others, the National Committee refused to hire any Black organizers.

There were certain exceptions to the lack of interest in the union by Blacks, which suggest that there may have been greater possibilities for interracial solidarity. Foster notes that Cleveland and Wheeling, West Virginia, were the most notable places where such solidarity occurred (1920:206). Wheeling is of less significance because of the small number of African-Americans there. It may have benefited because of the strength of the interracial miners' union. Cleveland is of special interest because it had both a high percentage of Blacks and virtually 100% participation by them in the strike. In fact, solidarity was so strong that the companies found it difficult to recruit Black strikebreakers from within the city and had to import them from other areas, in contrast, for example, to the situation in Chicago, where strikebreakers were easily recruited locally (Brown 1998:121). There is no clear explanation for the degree of interracial unity in Cleveland. Foster seems to attribute it to a more successful organizing strategy among the leaders (1920:179), while Brown suggests that the strength and farsightedness of the Socialist and Communist Parties there, led by future CP head Charles Ruthenberg, may have been a factor, although he can find no direct connections in the various local accounts (Brown 1998:121–22). Spero and Harris found that 85% of the African-American steelworkers at U.S. Steel's South Works in Chicago initially struck, but soon went back to work, in part because the National Committee made no special attempts to organize them (1931:260). Needleman argues that press and scholarly accounts of interracial division and violence are inaccurate with respect to Gary, Indiana, although this is not the generally accepted view (2003:21). She reports regular recruiting meetings in the Black community by union organizers. Two of the most important leaders of the Lake County [Gary] Strike Council, Louis Caldwell and C. D. Elston, were Black, and "these two men helped turn the promise of interracial unity into a reality in Gary," at least during the strike (Needleman 2003:24).

The causes of the defeat of the 1919 steel strike are thus overdetermined. Foster thinks that the lost opportunities during the war were the main cause; striking when the iron was hot would have won the strike. He concludes that it was the procrastination and shortsightedness of the AFL unions that spent more time looking out for their jurisdictional concerns than in promoting the general drive. This procrastination was in part related to the lack of resources and the narrow,

> particularistic interests of many of the craft unions, who refused to contribute significant sums of money. Even if the unions had been more committed, the craft union nature of the organizing, with its multiple centers of leadership and authority, helped disorganize the campaign. When the moment of best opportunity had passed, the steel companies were less constrained to use the extreme measures of repression. (Foster 1920:110–39)

The resistance by the steel companies included not merely repression but an overwhelming propaganda offense, aided by virtually all major steel center newspapers. This offensive included racial and ethnic attacks on the strikers, the branding of them as un-American, unpatriotic revolutionaries, as well as the trumpeting of false information about the number of strikebreakers, the productivity of the mills, and the number of workers actually out on strike. Due to a lack of resources, the National Committee was unable to combat this barrage.

The lack of strong support for the strike by African-Americans and native-born white skilled workers was, of course, a glaring weakness. In the context of the false information published in newspapers and company publications about the lack of solidarity in other strike centers, the importation of large numbers of African-American strikebreakers was the ultimate demoralizing act by the companies, leading to the final collapse of the strike. With the defeat of the 1919 steel strike, unionism once again disappeared from the industry, until the 1930s.

The 1930s in Steel

The backdrop of the 1919 strike and its aftermath were to prove central to all interested parties in the next wave of organizing. There are, however, a large number of myths, which dominate the historiography, about how the steelworkers organized in the 1930s. The standard story has more than a grain of truth, but at its best that truth is only partial and incomplete, overall a distortion. Of particular interest for us is the rapidity with which the steelworker's union became a conservative, racially backward business union.

The official story goes like this: John L. Lewis made steel the CIO's top priority. A significant percentage of coal production in the country (11% of bituminous coal output in 1933) was in "captive" mines, those owned by major steel companies (Davis 1933:82). These steel companies were reluctant to recognize the UMWA or make significant contractual concessions in mines where they did deal with the union, since this might set a precedent that could be applied to their non-union workers in steel. Because Lewis and the UMWA felt that the security of their own union required the organization of steel, they were prepared to pour large amounts of money and energy into the task.

Lewis appointed Philip Murray, loyal lieutenant and UMWA vice president, to head the drive; Lewis also loaned the drive a large number of other paid union officials and organizers. Meanwhile the steel companies (in response to the passage of Section 7(a) in 1933 and the 1935 Wagner Act) began to strengthen their employee representation plans (ERPs). Those companies that already had company unions gave them more power and resources. Those that did not have them initiated plans with great fanfare. Breaking with the AFL tradition of denouncing company unions, Murray and his assistants developed a brilliant strategy of encouraging the ERPs, eventually incorporating them into SWOC (Galenson 1960:88). Myron Taylor, the president of U.S. Steel with a financial rather than an operational background—in a farsighted, statesman-like move—saw the handwriting on the wall and signed an agreement with John L. Lewis recognizing the union.

This story was told initially by Harbison (1940) and Robert Brooks (1940), soon after the fact by Clint Golden, later by Galenson (1960), by Bernstein (1969), in various SWOC documents, and more recently Zieger (1995)(there were many other accounts; see, e.g., Harbison 1940:chs. 3 and 4; Galenson 1960:75–122). Even as elite history, the story leaves out some of the most important actors. Missing from the narrative is not only the historic militancy of steelworkers (who are often described, quite inaccurately, as relatively passive), but the dramatic upsurge, beginning in 1933, of the militancy of this multiethnic, multiracial workforce, without whose actions nothing else would have been possible. First, the historic militancy of steelworkers is belittled in general. Second, false comparisons are made to the situations in coal, and even auto, with no recognition of the impact of plant size and concentration of ownership on strike characteristics. There were thousands of individual small owners in coal who could each be affected by a single strike at a single mine; militant actions initiated in one or more mines easily spread across a whole region. Even in the auto industry, organization often began in smaller companies—for example, White Motors in Cleveland, home of early autoworker leader Wyndham Mortimer and Briggs in Detroit, where Flint strike leader Robert

Travis began his career. During the 1930s, skilled trade venues were still far more important in the auto industry than in steel. Steel's enormous concentration of ownership, along with its more extensive deskilling, allowed for an unprecedented degree of control over its workforce, requiring huge momentum on the part of its workers to overcome. Failure to recognize these structural characteristics makes analysis of workers' militancy and strike propensities superficial. The amount of energy necessary for the takeoff of a campaign was far higher in steel than in other industries, but once the takeoff point had been reached, the solidarity and militancy were impressive. Thus, most comparisons of the militancy of different groups of workers tend to be of limited value.

The role played by left-wing activists, primarily the Communists, at virtually every level of this organizing, including their central role in the early organizing, the development of early joint opposition within the AA, and their key role in SWOC itself, is largely missing from the standard accounts.[14] There is an understandable collective amnesia about this role by the anti-communist officials who controlled the union, not only in their retrospective retelling but even at the time. But this is no excuse for the conscientious, diligent historians whose succumbing to the fantasies of the Cold War ideological consensus is largely inexcusable and intellectually dishonest.[15] Finally, it is only by specifying the central role of the CP that one can see the weakness of the Party's approach, which made it so easy both to minimize their influence and to clear the field for the early dominance of the bureaucratic, repressive, and white chauvinist Murray leadership.

It is most evident from contemporary documentary material that the Communist role was not somehow independent of the SWOC drive or the leadership strategy. Murray, Lewis, and others who attempted to learn the lessons of the 1919 strike's failure understood that they needed large numbers of experienced organizers and special targeted strategies to win African-American and ethnic workers to the campaign.[16] They therefore had meetings with top leaders of the CP to solicit their help and initially took on at least fifty full-time Communist organizers. While the CIO leaders had access to a large number of staffers from the mine workers' union, they had few contacts and organizers working in the steel mills and living in the steel mill towns. The CP was well rooted here. The efforts to organize African-American workers in steel, as in other industries, relied most heavily

---

[14] Even Bruce Nelson, who gets some of the story right but other parts wrong, incorrectly asserts that most of the initial staff came from the UMWA (2001:186).

[15] That these omissions and distortions by the vast majority of labor historians were unnecessary can be seen in the more balanced approaches of a few of the more careful liberal historians. See, e.g., Ray Marshall's *Labor and the South* (1981).

[16] This can be contrasted with the approach in post–World War II Operation Dixie, where appearances trumped substance and those in charge of the drive hired largely inexperienced, unrooted, often incompetent, southern-born white male veterans.

on the Communist-influenced National Negro Congress (NNC) (most standard commentators emphasize the NAACP and barely mention the NNC, but see Beth Bates 1997 and Streater 1981). The organizing of foreign-born and first-generation ethnic steelworkers was virtually given over to CPers tied to the International Workers Order (IWO).

Left out of the standard story is the tremendous upsurge of mass militant activity that accompanied the SWOC drive, in many places demonstrating a surprising degree of interracial solidarity, noted in many documents at the time and in certain historical accounts (e.g., Drake 1945, vol. 1:324–25). Finally, the Herculean efforts of the SWOC leadership to stifle mass participation, democratic activities, and local leadership and to remove and transfer leftists once things were relatively stable at the local level are barely mentioned. These activities by the leadership included not only eliminating Communists and other leftists as well as many African-American officials and organizers, but also kowtowing to the white supremacist policies of the companies and a segment of white steelworkers, especially in the South. The standard story also paradoxically (because it belittles and underestimates the CP's role in SWOC) does not allow us to analyze and understand the weaknesses of the Communists' approach in steel, an approach that made it easy for the Lewis and Murray leadership to eliminate them (and other militants and radicals as well) from positions of influence in the union, once the hard work of successful organizing had been completed. Thus, the standard story fails to explain adequately not only how the steelworkers organized, but how a union with such initial promise quickly devolved into a bureaucratic, anti-democratic, racially discriminatory, narrow-minded business union.

Steelworker Militancy

Unlike coal miners, steelworkers engaged in few militant struggles in the years before 1933. Although there were several small strikes in 1931 and 1932 in which the CP-led Steel and Metal Workers Industrial Union was involved, as Horace Davis notes, "expressions of militancy by rank and file steelworkers have been rare in the past decade (1933:265)."[17] The official membership of the AA in September 1932 comprised 4,944 workers in eighty-nine lodges (H. Davis 1933:254). The differences between the situations in coal and steel were complex. They, of course, included the large-scale power of the steel companies, their brutal repression, the ineffective stance and ineptitude of the AA leaders, and the virtual nonexistence of AA organization. In comparison, miners not only had strongholds of organization

[17] See also the table of industrial disputes in steel in Davis (1933:265).

that remained in the early 1930s but had active traditions of militancy and organization in virtually all the main coalfields.

Struggles in steel began to change dramatically in 1933. As with coal, the standard explanations attribute this rise to the passage of Section 7(a) of the National Industrial Recovery Act (NIRA). It is important to note the tremendous associative power that steelworkers had gained by 1933 from coal miners, whose newly organized unions were often in close proximity to the largest concentrations of steel mills, especially in western Pennsylvania and Alabama. In addition, powerful social movements, most important of which were the struggles of the unemployed, gained strength in virtually every steel center in the country (Kelley 1990; Hudson and Painter 1979). In certain industrial centers, simultaneous organizing campaigns in different industries were often mutually supportive.[18]

Like other groups of workers in 1933, steelworkers began to organize en masse, flowing into previously moribund AA locals and forming large numbers of new ones, resuscitating the putrid corpse of this virtually dead union. According to AA secretary Louis Leonard, more than 150,000 workers joined the AA in 1933, paying full initiation fees (Taft 1957:110).[19] As with much other industrial organizing at this time, the weakness of the leadership (read here timidity and bureaucratic small-mindedness) so alienated these new members that most of them soon quit. In the rather charitable description of AFL historian Philip Taft:

> The officers of the Amalgamated . . . feared every manifestation of protest . . . The leaders had tasted defeat many times . . . Unaware that drastic changes were in the making, they wanted to follow a policy of caution. On the other hand, thousands of workers who had joined the union looked upon it as a means of gaining relief from the difficulties facing labor. As a result, conflicts and losses of membership followed. (1959:110–11)

Even when times did not seem propitious for unionism, workers occasionally organized. This was true even in the South. Ruben Farr, later an official with SWOC

[18] E.g., Murray to Mitch, June 19, 1936, about the supportive role of the rubber workers' organizing in Gadsden, Alabama, and the strength of Mine Mill in the Birmingham area, as well the support of the latter for steel organizing there, District 36 files, 10:14, PSU.

[19] Exact figures are hard to come by. Clint Golden, later a leader of SWOC and the steelworkers' union, who was working as a federal mediator and had close contacts with the AA, including both dissidents and official union leaders, made some careful estimates in 1935. He suggested that while there were no more than 7,000 members whose dues were fully paid, "perhaps" as many as 150,000 had either signed pledge cards, applied for membership, or paid some sum of money as an application fee. He also noted that of the 122 AA lodges chartered by the union, 78 had sent representatives to the opposition rank-and-file conference of February 3, 1935 (Thomas Brooks 1978:141–42; for a different version, see Taft 1959:110–21).

in Alabama and later still the Alabama district director for United Steel Workers of America (USWA), describes an AA local in Birmingham in 1931: "We tried to form a union in the steel mills when I was working there at that time. We went ahead and set up a local and elected a president and vice president. The next day, when the president and vice president went to work, they found themselves fired. The president was Carey Haigler [later head of Operation Dixie for Alabama]." Farr notes that there was no AA organizer there, that the local formed on its own. He describes another spontaneously organized local in 1935 at Republic Steel's big blast furnace, also in Birmingham.[20]

Horace Davis notes that "a wave of struggle and organization swept through the mills of some of the more important companies" (1933:270). It was initially tied to the strike of miners at the H. C. Frick Company, the large captive mine of U.S. Steel (1933:270). In Homestead, organizing began in 1933. On June 16, 1933, the day the NIRA was passed, a meeting was announced via loudspeakers mounted on a truck that drove through Homestead's working-class neighborhoods. That night one thousand steelworkers showed up to found the "Spirit of 1892" lodge of the AA (Davin 2000:266). By early 1934, militant steelworkers had begun agitating for a strike to which the national officers of the union were adamantly opposed. As Brody notes, contrary to claims by many, there were as many strikes in steel as in the auto and rubber industries (1987:15). In 1934, in Aliquippa, state police helped open up the town, and on October 14, 1934, Cornelia Bryce Pinchot, the liberal wife of Republican governor Gifford Pinchot, spoke at a labor rally of four thousand there. On May 31, 1935, the Ft. Dukane Lodge of the Amalgamated (Duquesne) tried to strike in solidarity with strikers in Canton, Ohio. The lodge officers were then arrested for parading without a permit. Upon their release from jail, "a mass meeting of Duquesne steel workers called for a strike at all U.S. Steel facilities" (Davin 2000: 266).

Philip Murray at the time was quite clear in identifying the militancy and courage of these workers. Speaking at the 1935 AFL convention, Murray related how the Jones and Laughlin workers had organized themselves: "The workers employed in that plant, of their own volition, of their own motion, without an organizer attending the meeting in its initial stages, called meetings . . . without any assistance from the American Federation of Labor, at that time organized 6,500 of the 8,000 workers at the Aliquippa plant into an independent union" (Davin 2000:269).

The southern district exemplified the widespread nature of these national trends. In Birmingham's overwhelmingly African-American steel mills, a large-scale organizing campaign was making important gains in 1933. W. H. Crawford, AA's representative in Alabama, reported successes for both AA and Mine Mill in Alabama's iron and steel industry. At Sloss Local 109, for example, 301 out of 302 "colored

---

[20] Farr interview, March 27, 1968, Oral Histories Project, PSU. .

men" had joined the union and only three whites had failed to become members.[21] The next meeting of the Alabama Steel and Iron Council on January 6, 1934, reported numerous cases of new organizing and local strikes, including a large meeting of steelworkers in Gadsden, Alabama, which featured songs by the Colored Junior Quartet, including "Who Built the Ark," which suggests that such a worthy vessel could only have been built by union labor, since the "the Ark had stood the test." At the meeting of April 1, 1934, a report was presented on a representation election at the Republic Steel plant in Thomas, Alabama, where 282 out of 300 voted in favor of Mine Mill. In May 1934, Republic employees in Birmingham voted 282 to 8 for an AA local (Taft and Fink 1981:99). The sheer one-sidedness of these votes compared with much closer votes in later times should suggest to even the most cautious analysts that a movement with enormous momentum and support was already under way. The above tends to belie reports about the lack of militancy and unwillingness to organize by the nation's steelworkers once a critical mass was achieved. The special readiness of Alabama's African-American steelworkers should here be noted; the same was also true of the early organizing in Atlanta (Nelson 2001:241).

Such successful organizing and overwhelming support for unionism in the South took place in the face of vicious opposition and repression. Repression in Pennsylvania was, if anything, more intense than that in Alabama. One tactic in the Keystone State was to kidnap union activists and forcefully commit them to state insane asylums. A celebrated case was that of union organizer George Issoki, who was eventually examined by a state psychiatrist and found not to be insane.[22] Beatings, kidnappings, and even occasionally murder were regular occurrences, judging by the numerous letters of protest to the state government. One rank-and-file worker was even kidnaped by company officials and placed in an insane asylum when it was discovered by his supervisor that he had written a letter to President Franklin Delano Roosevelt. Despite such tactics used against the steelworkers, at the large Jones and Laughlin complex in Aliquippa thirty-six hundred out of five thousand workers at the main plant had already joined the union.[23]

As in auto, coal mining, and numerous other industries, Communists had been organizing workers in steel throughout the 1920s and early 1930s. From 1929

[21] Minutes of Alabama Steel and Iron Council, November 4, 1933, GSU Newspapers Collection, Carey Haigler Collection, 95:2121.

[22] *Pittsburgh Post Gazette*, October 25, 1934; *Pittsburgh Sun Telegraph*, October 24, 1934, October 25, 1934, Clinton S. Golden Papers, 3:2. A lengthy file with numerous affidavits on the Issoki case and Issoki's eventual release from the Torrance insane asylum under orders from Governor Gifford Pinchot can be found in Golden Papers, 5:28. Other cases are also documented there.

[23] Clinton S. Golden Papers; *Pittsburgh Register*, November 1, 1934; Wm. Green to Governor Gifford Pinchot, August 30, 1933; M. H. Tighe to Pinchot, August 31, 1933; Golden Papers, 5:25, 5:28; *Federated Press*, October 24, 1933, press release.

to 1933 they began organizing steelworkers into the Steel and Metal Workers Industrial Union (SMWIU), a revolutionary union that was part of the CP-led Trade Union Unity League (TUUL), which was itself affiliated with the Red International of Trade Unions, a sectarian creation of the Communist International during its so-called revolutionary Third Period (Tosstorff 2018). Although they led only two strikes before 1933, they had organizers and activities in virtually every steel center in the country, with activists leading job actions and calling meetings at the department, plant, and district levels (Cayton and Mitchell 1939:111–22). Their approach was often contradictory. They believed, at least until late 1933, that they could build a revolutionary union independent of the Amalgamated. They also operated within the Amalgamated and the employee representation plans, testifying before government bodies.[24] In addition, in virtually every steel center, they had strong CP and unemployed organizations; they also had active organizations of African-Americans and the foreign born.

After the triumph of the Nazis in Germany in early 1933, the Comintern began revising its orientation toward mainstream trade unions. And by late 1933, the CP had increased its opposition work within the Amalgamated.[25] By early 1934, the Party had disbanded the SMWIU and moved all its activities into the AA, helping lead the militant opposition to the virtually clueless leaders of the union.

The struggle within the AA was continuous from late 1933 to 1935. At a large meeting on February 4, 1935, involving dissident groups both in steel and among captive miners, workers denounced both Michael Tighe and John Lewis. The next day Tighe expelled seventy-eight lodges. Tighe was then summoned before the AFL Executive Council subcommittee, chaired by John L. Lewis, which examined the expulsions. A *Pittsburgh Press* article of November 27, 1934, had already described AFL plans to organize steel. That the Communists were not bystanders or intruders is clear, since one of the main AA opposition spokespersons and a member of the committee of twenty-five, chosen at the rank-and-file conference, was Al Martin, a Young Communist League leader from McKeesport, Pennsylvania.[26] An article in the *Pittsburgh Press* on February 18, 1935, also announced that the outlawed AA lodges planned to start a national steel drive themselves.

Staughton Lynd (1972) argues that the rank-and-file upsurge in steel from 1933 to 1935 was perhaps sufficient to have formed an industrial union independent of the AA and AFL. He traces the failure to the inability of the non-Communist opposition leaders in the AA and the SMWIU to work out a successful alliance. The

---

[24] On their work within the AA, see *Party Organizer* 5 (September–October 1932), 9–10; for their work within ERPs, see *Party Organizer* 6 (August–September 1933), 8–9; for the testimony of SMWIU president E. P. Cush on the failures of the NIRA steel codes, see Cayton and Mitchell (1939:112).

[25] *Daily Worker*, November 11, 1933.

[26] *Pittsburgh Press*, February 14, 1935, February 18, 1935; Golden papers (10:16).

former leaned too heavily on a group of four social democratic intellectuals who had little faith in the adequacy of worker self-activity, relied to an unreasonable degree on the Roosevelt administration, were too close to John L. Lewis, and were viscerally anti-communist. (Lynd 1972 argues that it was Heber Blankenhorn and Harold Ruttenberg who persuaded the rank-and-file leaders not to work with the SMWIU in 1934.) The Communists were not without blame, according to Lynd. Their sectarianism led them to demand too much credit for the SMWIU.[27] Whether such an alliance would have succeeded, especially given the limited financial resources of both groups and the steel companies' immense resources and readiness to use violence, is, of course, a matter of conjecture.

Because of the incompetence of the AA leadership, a rebellion began within the AA, led by the oppositionists, who had substantial support of AA members, not to mention numerous other steelworkers. This rebellion is important for understanding the dynamics of organization, both before and during the SWOC campaign. First, it is necessary to factor in the powerful movement among steelworkers to organize industrially and interracially, which carried over into SWOC. Second, the rebellion is key to understanding why the AA leadership eventually capitulated so completely to John L. Lewis and the CIO, virtually abandoning the union to them. Throughout 1934, the many opposition locals began campaigning for an organizing drive in the industry and a national strike. By 1935, however, the average yearly paid membership had dropped to less than 10,000 (Galenson 1960:75).

On February 4, 1935, a large number of local leaders at a rank-and-file meeting launched public attacks on the AA leadership. The next day, Tighe responded by expelling 22 locals outright and suspending 74 others, out of roughly 150. In a letter to AFL president William Green, Tighe not only announced the actions, but sought to justify them. On February 18, the outlawed locals met to plan their own drive to organize the industry. Despite the fact that it was common knowledge that many of the leading oppositionists were Communists, Green, John L. Lewis, and other AFL leaders were none too happy with the actions of the AA leadership and their squandering of such clear opportunities to establish a beachhead in the traditionally anti-union steel industry. After much negotiation and pressure (including a lawsuit against President Mike Tighe of AA by rank-and-file groups), on October 1, 1935, they forced the AA to reinstate the rebel locals and activists (Taft 1959:114).

Lewis from the beginning had made clear his desire to see the steel industry organized (this is one part the standard story gets right). When most coal mines were being organized with little opposition from owners, captive mines resisted. In 1934, the H. C. Frick coal company (a USS subsidiary) was forced to sign an agreement

---

[27] Lynd bases much of his information on a lengthy, rather extraordinary interview with Clarence Irwin, a key leader of the rank-and-file AA oppositionists (1972, esp. 43–40; see also Brooks 1940:46–74.

with the union, but still refused to formally recognize it. As Lewis argued at the 1935 AFL convention:

> We are anxious to have collective bargaining established in the steel industry, and our interest is . . . selfish . . . it would remove the incentive of the great captains of the steel industry to destroy and punish and harass our people who work in the captive mines. (*Proceedings of the 55th Annual Convention*, 1935, 539; see also Harbison 1940:25)

After the organization of coal, this became the UMWA's top priority. At Lewis's and others' instigation, both the 1934 and 1935 AFL conventions had drawn up resolutions authorizing the AFL to take charge of organizing the steel industry. William Green, AFL president, interpreted these resolutions as mandating the setting up of federal locals on an industrial basis (Galenson 1960:76). At the February 1935 AFL Executive Committee (EC) meeting, both Green and Lewis demanded that the AA give up its jurisdiction to the industry. Green argued, "I am satisfied in my own mind that the officers of the Amalgamated can not organize those workers with their own resources or with the set-up as it is." Lewis stated that if the AFL did not carry the struggle to steel, the steel companies would attempt to destroy the UMWA (Galenson 1960:76–77). Green attempted to rally support from other AFL unions but got little encouragement and no aid. Lewis and other industrial unionists became convinced that the AFL would do nothing.

Nevertheless, on February 21, 1936, the CIO (then still a committee within the AFL) offered the EC a half million dollars (of a proposed AFL $1.5 million fund) for an industrial organizing campaign. On March 2, William Green, in a circular letter, asked the other national unions to contribute to an AFL campaign, a proposal that was either rejected or ignored by the leaders of other AFL unions. On April 14, the machinists rejected the proposal outright. On April 18, the CIO offered its own proposal directly to the AA leadership. Both the AFL and the CIO formally presented their proposals to the 1936 AA convention held in May. The AFL proposal signed by Green offered no money, stipulated that the EC control everything, and affirmed that the jurisdictional rights of all craft unions would be respected. Lewis, on the other hand, offered "cooperation, money, and organizers" and respect for the industrial jurisdiction of the union, ominously stating that "a right to jurisdiction ceases to have weight unless it is put into effect."[28]

---

[28] See Green, "To the Officers and Delegates in Attendance at the Convention of the Amalgamated Association of Iron, Steel and Tin Workers, Canonsburg, Pennsylvania," May 8, 1936; Lewis to the Executive Board of the Amalgamated, May 21, 1936; Fact Sheet, "What Led to the C.I.O Steel Campaign"; and various memos by Katherine Pollak—all in CIO collection, National Industrial Unions, Catholic University, box 33, USWA, 1.

The leaders of the AA were reluctant to accept the CIO offer, but the strength of the opposition within their union forced them to capitulate.[29] A memorandum of agreement was signed on June 3, 1936, by Lewis, Brophy, Philip Murray, and Thomas Kennedy for the CIO (all incidentally mine union officials) and Thomas Gillis, Edward Miller, Josephy Gaither, vice presidents, and Louis Leonard, secretary-treasurer, of the AA. President M. H. Tighe was ill and did not attend the meeting but delegated his authority to the other officers. The agreement effectively dissolved the AA into the SWOC. The CIO named Murray the chair, and the committee chose two members from the AA and the rest from the CIO. Apart from the fact that he was not allowed to abrogate the rights and charters of existing AA lodges, the chair was all-powerful. The CIO also contributed all the money for the campaign and was given the authority "to grant dispensation from the payment of initiation fees." On June 17, 1936, the SWOC held its first meeting at UMWA headquarters, assigning twelve UMWA representatives to the various steel centers. The UMWA also provided thirty-five to forty fieldworkers from its payroll, without charging SWOC. Murray further announced in a policy statement that the goal of SWOC was "to avoid industrial strife and the calling of strikes, if we are met in a reasonable spirit by the employers."[30]

All this was fine and good, but SWOC and the UMWA had few contacts among steelworkers. Typical of the early SWOC staffers who came from the UMWA was Lewis loyalist James Robb, who was working in a mine as a local official when he got a telegram from Lewis assigning him to work with Van Bittner, himself a Lewis loyalist, formerly the district director for the UMWA in West Virginia. As Robb recalled, "I was the first director in the Steel-workers Union . . . I didn't know steel from nothing. In fact the only time I had been out of Terre Haute was at the conventions or maybe when Lewis called a policy committee. I didn't have contact with anybody in the industry."[31]

Despite having no roots in the industry, Lewis and his UMWA colleagues had studied the lessons of the 1919 steel strike carefully and knew the many reasons for its failure. Foster's work, both recent and earlier, were the key texts. Foster's fascinating 1936 pamphlet, "Organizing Methods in the Steel Industry," became a "blueprint for CIO policy" (Cohen 1990:341, 502). Lewis and Murray assiduously followed Foster's advice on recruiting Blacks, ethnic groups, and women, as well as on how to deal with company unions. Foster also stressed the importance of radio: "In an industry such as steel where the company maintains terrorism to

---

[29] For additional confirmation, see the *Pittsburgh Press* article by Vin Sweeney, June 5, 1936, describing the strength of the rebellion and how it factored into the decision, Golden papers, 10:17; see also *Pittsburgh Post Gazette*, June 6, 1936, Golden papers, 10:17, . as well as the account in the *Amalgamated Journal*, June 4, 1936.

[30] Memorandum of Agreement, June 3, 1936, CU, CIO, NIU, box 33, USWA, 1.

[31] Oral history interview, February 20, 1969, 28–29, PSU,

prevent workers from attending open meetings, the radio takes the union message directly into the workers' homes" (Cohen 1990:341). Lewis and Murray were cognizant of this advice and quickly followed it (Cohen 1990:341).[32]

They followed Foster in concluding that U.S. Steel, the industry leader, was key. Simultaneity, as William Z. Foster had argued, was also essential. They could not wage a series of autonomous, relatively uncoordinated campaigns, as had been done in coal. In order to mount such a campaign, a large amount of organization, support, and money, involving hundreds of organizers, would be needed (here would seem to be one weakness in Lynd's conjecture, since neither the Communist nor non-Communist oppositionists had such resources in 1935).

For the organizing to be successful, a determined effort would have to be made to address those key constituencies that the AA and AFL had ignored or slighted. Special attention would have to be paid to the circumstances and demands of African-American steelworkers, who had been abandoned and discriminated against. In addition, the foreign-born and their children, who had been the backbone of the 1919 strike, had been abandoned, downplayed, and even insulted by the AA and the AFL. These latter two constituencies were strongholds of the CP, which had large numbers of activists among the racial and ethnic groups of workers in the industry.

Although Lewis and the UMWA had the money and a lot of manpower, the support of the critical constituencies and the seasoned steel activists around the country depended on the CP and other activists who were outside Lewis's orbit. A series of meetings were held between members of the CP Politburo and Lewis and Hillman of the CIO, the two most influential CIO leaders. Foster described the situation in detail in his 1952 *History of the Communist Party*, but few people took this very seriously until recently.[33] The accounts of many of the principals years later tend to downplay the CP role. This situation and the role of the CP are critical to understanding how steel was organized. Without the central activities of the CP, the story is a mirage. Confirmation of Foster's account and greater detail are documented in contemporaneous reports of CP leaders to the Comintern, whose leaders were skeptical of the alliance and believed (correctly it turns out) that the Communist Party of the United States of America was being used. Some of the relevant documents are translated in Klehr et al. (1998). The documents also show the

---

[32] So carefully did they follow the Foster pamphlet that in an anti-union publication entitled "Join the CIO and Build a Soviet America," the documentation of the SWOC strategy duplicated Foster's work, line by line. The title is perhaps a play on the title of Foster's 1932 book, *Toward a Soviet America* (only briefly distributed), which he used in his 1932 CP presidential campaign. A lengthier version of the anti-CIO publication can be found in Henry Kraus Papers, Reuther Library Archives, Wayne State University, 16:16, 18.

[33] Even Kollros, in his otherwise penetrating account of the Calumet region, doubts this claim (1998:193–94).

Comintern's switch during 1934 from supporting the TUUL's revolutionary unions to urging the Party to disband these organizations and send its members back into the AFL unions (Klehr et al. 1998:54–70, passim; Williamson 1969:125–26, who, as the CP district organizer for Ohio, noted, "In Ohio our entire party and Young Communist League staffs in the steel area were incorporated into the staff of the committee. This included Gus Hall, in charge of Warren and Niles; John Steuben, in charge of Youngstown, and many others")."

Foster notes that by 1936 the CP had branches in all the main steel towns and mills, as well as many individual steelworkers among its members (1952:349). He also claims that the CP also had a large number of members in African-American and foreign-born working-class organizations, though he neglects to mention that the CP provided a good deal of the leadership in these groups. Clarence Hathaway, a member of the CP Politburo, mentions several meetings between Politburo members and Lewis and Hillman. Hathaway, in trying to convince Comintern leaders of the importance of their alliance with the CIO and Lewis, notes some of the immediate benefits of this relationship. He reports that at a meeting with Lewis, he raised the question of the CPers and other militants who had been expelled by AA president Mike Tighe from the union. Lewis "asked for a list of names . . . We provided him with it and immediately, all were reinstated." Hathaway then urged the employment of Communists as organizers, whereupon Lewis asked for "our recommendation." Forty-five to fifty were quickly made full-time SWOC organizers (Foster 1952:68). There were, of course, other avenues for CPers to become SWOC organizers. Many African-Americans in or close to the Party got their jobs through the National Negro Congress, a central vehicle for its contact with Black steelworkers.[34] Thus, Foster estimates that of the initial two hundred full-time SWOC organizers, at least

---

[34] Streater, in what is by far the most comprehensive study of the National Negro Congress, claims that its national secretary, John Davis, convinced SWOC to hire a dozen of its members as staffers (1981:200). Correspondence between Davis and leaders of SWOC suggests the figure may have been higher. See Davis to Murray, February 19, 1937, about the hiring of "three Negro organizers" (Papers of the National Negro Congress [NNC], New York Public Library, 11); Davis to Richard Moore, June 6, 1936 (NNC 6), mentioning seven, with the possibility of "10 or more"; correspondence between Davis and Murray, June 28, 1936, on the hiring of Clarence Irwin and MacPherson, two leaders of the National Emergency Committee of Lodges of the AA (NNC 6); Davis to Golden, October 12, 1936, on the hiring of B. D. Amis (NNC 5), a known CPer; Golden to Davis (NNC 5), August 19, 1936, confirming the hiring of Arthur Murray, an organizer from SMWIU; Bittner to Davis, n.d., confirming hiring of CPer Henry Johnson and Eleanor Rye of the NNC, the latter also a member of the CP-led Fur Workers Union Executive Board; George Kimbling, SWOC organizer and NNC leader to Davis, March 18, 1938, reporting on Gary (NNC 13); among much other correspondence. Kelley mentions a number of leading Black Communists on the SWOC payroll in Alabama, including Hosea Hudson, Edd Cox (also a local UMWA leader), C. Dave Smith, and Henry Mayfield, a "leading CIO organizer in both coal and steel" (1990:143). Ben Careathers was another Black CPer, sent by Murray and Clint Golden to Aliquippa via Ambridge in 1936 (Bonosky 1953:34).

sixty were CPers (1952:349; see also De Caux 1970:279), and these included the SWOC district leader in Pittsburgh, Bill Gebert, a Polish-born member of the CP's national committee and a national leader of the International Workers Order, a fraternal and benefit organization of foreign-born workers. Hathaway's report goes to great lengths to justify the relationship to the Comintern, arguing that the UMWA was becoming more democratic, the reinstatement of CPers who had been expelled from the union, and even the election of many Communists to local leadership positions in the UMWA, allegedly with Lewis's blessings. Whether or not the facts are true or as Hathaway describes them, this is clearly a total misreading of the dynamics of what was happening within the miners' union; and it was 180 degrees askew of what actually happened to the CP in the steel drive. Hathaway also notes that W. Gebert was the Party liaison with SWOC (Klehr et al. 1998:66–68).

At certain times the CP and the CIO leaders made a division of labor, operating with parallel strategies. This was especially the case in the struggle with the AFL. Lewis, Hillman, and other CIO leaders carried out their struggle at the top organizational levels, claiming that an appeal to the grass roots would "prejudice their case." At the same time, however, they encouraged the CP to appeal to local unions, central bodies, and state federations, introducing "resolutions . . . calling for the endorsement of the steel drive and of the general drive to organize the mass production industries and against the threats of a split" (Klehr et al. 1998:60–61).

SWOC Campaign to Organize Steel

The national campaign began almost immediately after the signing of the agreement between the CIO and the AA on June 3, 1936, unlike the delay and procrastination we have seen with the AFL and the 1919 organizing. The official launch of the steel campaign was on June 17, 1936. Headquarters was set up in a downtown Pittsburgh office building, and Philip Murray quickly appointed regional directors, including UMWA officials William Mitch for the South, Van Bittner for the Great Lakes region, and Clint Golden for Pennsylvania and the rest of the East. By late September, there were 35 subregional offices, 158 full-time fieldworkers, staff organizers, and office employees, 80 part-time organizers, and 5,000 volunteers.[35] Galenson estimates that in the first year, SWOC spent 2.5 million dollars, most of which came from the UMWA. By July 1937, it had 437 full-time staffers (1960:110).

Rank-and-file activity also began to accelerate, especially in the South. Southern regional director William Mitch reported to Murray about a meeting of 1,500 steelworkers in the steel town of Bessemer, just outside Birmingham, Alabama, although there were already some jurisdictional conflicts with Mine Mill regarding

---

[35] See Minutes of SWOC meeting, September 29, 1936, District 36, 10:20, PSU.

the coke plants. On Labor Day in 1936, there was a rally of more than 200,000 in Pittsburgh's South Park, many of whom were steelworkers.[36]

The formation of the SWOC also stimulated large-scale grassroots activity, which was uncoordinated from the top. Part of the story of western Pennsylvania is graphically told by Eric Davin (2000). The steel towns along the Mongongahela, Allegheny, and Ohio Rivers were tightly controlled by the steel companies, with many of the elected local government offices held by steel company officials. Police forces were an adjunct of the companies' private police forces and were rarely inhibited from deputizing private company police forces to attack strikers. In Aliquippa, the site of the enormous steel complex of Jones and Laughlin (J & L), there were over ten thousand registered Republicans in 1928 and only thirty-five registered Democrats (Davin 2000:262). Aliquippa was the town where J & L in 1933 organized a private group armed with submachine guns to cross the bridge into nearby Ambridge in order to crush a strike that the Ambridge burgess, Philip Caul (himself an AFL official), had refused to break (Davin 2000:263). A similar situation existed in Homestead: in 1933 the burgess denied Roosevelt's secretary of labor, Frances Perkins, the use of the city hall to address a group of pro-Roosevelt workers. Steelworkers in these and other western Pennsylvania towns were simultaneously organizing independent locals and AA lodges, as well as within the employee representation plans (Davin 2000:266–67). The trajectory of Elmer Maloy exemplifies these trends. While having a connection with the AA, he was elected in 1935 to head the Duquesne ERP, then to head the association of ERPs for all the Carnegie-Illinois plants of the Pittsburgh District. He later became president of the SWOC lodge and a full-time staffer. He, along with other militant steelworkers in western Pennsylvania, began organizing to run for local political offices. Taking over the local Democratic Party organizations from the regular Democrats, Maloy and others ran on a program of what Davin, perhaps overenthusiastically, calls "class war" (2000:250, 340). This organizing culminated in the election of steelworker mayors and city councils in seventeen steel towns. Maloy became the mayor of Duquesne. Davin argues that these victories were engineered not by SWOC or Labor's Non-Partisan League, but by local unions "acting on their own" (2000: 253). Maloy held the first meeting (after his election) of the SWOC local in the City Council chambers. He then revoked the gun permits from the company police and appointed his brother the new police chief. He strictly enforced the right to leaflet at company plant gates.[37]

---

[36] Regional Director to Murray, July 24, 1936, District 36, 10:14, PSU; "200,000 March on Labor Day, South Park Pittsburgh," report by Vincent D. Sweeney, publicity director, September 7, 1936, Golden papers, 10:18, SWOC, PSU.

[37] In 1939, Elmer J. Maloy was also listed as a SWOC international grievance officer negotiating on behalf of workers at Duquesne Works (District 36 16:1, December 12, 1939).

But the true test of democratic agendas in America always revolves around race. The new steelworker administrations aggressively claimed they stood for civil rights. In Pittsburgh, African-American teachers for the first time became part of the public school teaching staff. In Clairton, three thousand Black residents forced the desegregation of the city's all-white swimming facility. In Homestead, Black civil rights activists desegregated the area's major movie theater, restaurants, and department stores. In the 1940s, pickets at downtown Pittsburgh department stores forced the hiring of Black sales clerks, two decades before such jobs were opened up in most other northern cities. Davin argues:

> Perhaps the relative ease with which the public facilities of SWOC-controlled Steeltown were desegregated in 1937, 1938, 1939 and the 1940s—15 and more years before the Civil Rights Movement—has obscured the significance of the changes in attitudes and values which took place in Steeltown at this time. The belief that "all men are created equal" is an expansionist doctrine which, set in motion, doesn't stop at the color line. (2000:277)

While these stories are not definitive proof by themselves, the potential for building interracial and racially egalitarian unions seems to have existed to a significant degree. The degree to which the Murray leadership failed to take advantage of these possibilities should be emphasized, too.

The attempt to appeal to foreign-born steelworkers was a critical feature of SWOC's strategy, and here the CP was also central. During the 1930s there were millions of members of fraternal benefit societies, which were organized by nationality and religion (for a solid overview, see Keeran 1980:385). SWOC, according to Murray, saw working with fraternal organizations of the foreign-born as a major part of its strategy. Bronislav Konstantine ("Bill") Gebert, the central figure of the Polonia Society of the Communist-led International Workers Order, was named by Murray as the SWOC director of the Pittsburgh subdistrict.[38] Gebert was also responsible for building alliances with other ethnic and foreign-born organizations. He became head of the massive consortium of organizations called the Fraternal Orders Committee, whose organization had been spearheaded by Gebert and the IWO, and because of this "he was recognized by a great deal of Slavic America" (Walker 1982:184). The IWO thus became an important "base of operations" in steel towns in Pennsylvania, Ohio, Indiana, and Illinois (Walker 1982:50). At the time, Nick Fonocchio, a former mine union official (and Lewis loyalist) and the first SWOC director of the Calumet region, had the highest praise for the openly CP-led IWO: "The Steel Workers Organizing Committee considers the International

---

[38] For the best overview of the IWO, see Keeran (1980); Walker (1982).

Workers Order one of the outstanding organizations which is laboring for the social and economic welfare of the people" (Walker 1982:51).

After a preliminary conference on August 8, 1936, the full Fraternal Orders Conference (FOC) was held in Pittsburgh on October 25, 1936, the attendees coming from western Pennsylvania, northern West Virginia, and eastern Ohio. The conference was chaired by Gebert. The principal speaker was SWOC chair Philip Murray, with SWOC leader Clinton Golden also sharing the rostrum. The delegates, who came from seventeen national fraternal organizations, representing almost six hundred thousand members, decided to set up the permanent Fraternal Orders Committee, with Gebert as the chair. A subsequent conference was held in Chicago on November 29.[39] Keeran (1980) notes the degree to which SWOC helped build the IWO and FOC.

There was also a major thrust to appeal to Black steelworkers, both by hiring Black organizers and by working through major Black civil rights organizations, especially the left-wing National Negro Congress. Here too, the IWO was important; its vice president, Louise Patterson, was an African-American woman. In many steel areas, the only available halls and public meeting places that could be used were those of the IWO, which lent them willingly (Keeran 1980:399, passim).

Murray reported that SWOC had placed several Black organizers on staff and was cooperating with the National Negro Congress, Workers Councils of the National Urban League, and the NAACP. He also reported that there had been important inroads in Chicago, but so far "we have not made satisfactory progress in getting these workers enrolled." Despite much evidence to the contrary, he concluded, "*It is our conviction that the organization of the Negro steel workers will follow, rather than precede, the organization of the white mill workers* ... The mill owners keep up a constant barrage of propaganda directed to the negroes and designed to not only make them fearful of losing their jobs if they join the Union, but to also create distrust and suspicion of our motives. The fact that we have declared our policy to be one of absolute racial equality in Union membership has served to win the support of the most progressive and intelligent of the negro leaders of the nation, and a generally favorable attitude on the part of the negro press and organizations."[40]

The SWOC strategy for appealing to Black steelworkers was similar in many ways to that of organizing first- and second-generation ethnic workers. Black organizers, mostly leftists, were hired. In addition, Murray relied on the CP to organize a national conference of Black and civil rights organizations, held in Pittsburgh, February 6, 1937, to aid the steel drive. The chief visible spokesperson was Benjamin Careathers,

[39] Statement of Philip Murray, November 8, 1936, CU, CIO, NIU, box 33, USWA; Foster (1952:349–50); Walker (1982:50–51, 181, 183–84); Keeran (1980:390–91).

[40] District 36 files, 10:14, Murray Report to SWOC, Pittsburgh, Reports of September 29, 1936, and November 8, 1936; emphasis mine.

a Pittsburgh African-American Communist leader and a full-time SWOC organizer. Top SWOC officials, as well as CPers and others, spoke at the conference. Foster argues compellingly, "The intense activity of the Communists on the Negro question was a basic reason why the Negro workers joined all the CIO unions in such numbers ... why the CIO took its generally advanced position regarding the Negro people" (1952:350).

Despite renewed militancy among steelworkers and overwhelming support from African-American and ethnic leaders and organizations, the actual growth appeared to be going slowly, especially compared with the explosion of growth of the Amalgamated in 1934. In 1936, there were again only five thousand AA members initially and only fifteen thousand additional members over the course of the first few months of the campaign, not counting the thousands who had signed pledge cards, according to a report from Murray. Forty lodges were established by SWOC, twenty-eight in the Chicago district, ten in the Pittsburgh district, and two in the Birmingham district. Lots of application cards "have been signed by steel workers, although they have not yet seen fit to pay their dollar a month dues."[41]

There are differing ways to read the statistics and overall information on steelworker organizing. There were those who saw an enormous social movement beginning to erupt and those who were pessimistic about steelworkers ever doing anything. Perhaps the most pessimistic was David McDonald, formerly Murray's personal assistant in the mine workers' union, secretary-treasurer of the new steel union, and eventually president, in 1952, after Murray's death. His lack of confidence in workers and direct action was legendary within the labor movement, even compared with that of his cohort of former UMWA officials (Nelson 2001:223–24).

According to McDonald, "The biggest problems we had were with the workers themselves. Contrary to union propaganda, some of which I helped to write—the steelworkers did not fall all over themselves to sign a pledge card with the SWOC" (1969:94). Compared with the miners, who were "union oriented, they were angry and they eagerly sought a collective voice. The steelworkers were deeply infected with antiunion propaganda and were generally passive" (1969:94–95). "What we hoped would be a torrent turned out, instead, to be a trickle ... Oftentimes locals consisted of the half-dozen men daring enough to sign the chapter application" (1969:95). McDonald further stated:

> Towns began to look the same to me. There was Warren, Ohio, where the local charter signers had promised me a big audience and four people showed up in a hall that seated five hundred. In Birmingham, there were more people on the stage than in the audience. In Weirton, we promoted a "mass meeting" of twelve people. And I was never quite sure whether it was

---

[41] Minutes of SWOC, Pittsburgh, September 29, 1936, District 36, 10:20, PSU.

apathy or fear that kept them away . . . But the steelworkers continued to be dubious that we could improve their lot and fearful that, if we tried and lost, they would lose everything. We used every gambit we could imagine. The only one that achieved much success on a broad basis was a campaign of boring from within the company unions of U.S. Steel. (1969:96, 101)

Despite McDonald's lack of confidence, the signs of worker self-activity were there for others to see. In January 1937 there were two sit-down strikes by steelworkers in Alabama, first when workers at the American Casting Company struck, successfully winning a 20% wage increase, payment for the previously unpaid two hours of work, and time and a half for overtime. A second sit-down, at the Birmingham Stove and Range Company, lasted a month and ended when the company raised wages (Taft and Fink 1981:105). Similar reports came in from other steel centers.

When workers mobilized and gathered momentum, participation often snowballed. Such was certainly the case in the formerly union-resistant Jones and Laughlin mill in Aliquippa in the spring of 1937. Previously, Meyer Bernstein, a recent college graduate working on research and other matters in the SWOC headquarters, had written in letters to his friend "Nick:" "All the meetings you spoke of were failures," even Murray's talk at Aliquippa. "The men will not come out to meetings . . . We have the membership. Our problem is to get them to come out to the meetings."[42]

But when the Jones and Laughlin steelworkers in Aliquippa finally rose up (achieving what I have argued in Chapter 1 is the threshold required for takeoff, a threshold much higher in steel than other industries), passivity was no longer a topic of conversation. In spite of loyalists and company and city police, Aliquippa workers rose up and 100% of them struck. Bernstein wrote, "It was something of a revolution, too. Aliquippa rose up against a tyranny that had held them in bondage for years. For all practical purposes, the workers took over the functions of government. They were in complete control. Only for less than two hours were city police even in sight. The picket lines were absolutely effective. No one got through, not even the police who tried to force through an allegedly empty bus." He added, "The strike is a rank and file affair. SWOC may have called it, but it is in the hands of anybody who can lead." Bernstein estimated that there were five hundred to a thousand pickets, while thousands more (de facto pickets) looked on.

He continued, "The strike is doing wonders for the men. Remember Jefferson once said something about a revolution every twenty years or so being a blessing? The same is true of a strike. There is real solidarity now. And certainly no fear. In fact, workers go out of their way to thumb their noses at company police by whom they had been cowed for years . . . Thousands, yes thousands of men have joined the

---

[42] Meyer Bernstein to Nick, April 18, 1937, Meyer Bernstein, 1:3, PSU.

union during the last few days, and especially after the strike was called. *And they are eager to pay their dues and get their button.* We ran out [of them] "" He explained that "The burden of argument for the strike was carried by two Negroes from the South Side Workers." And the next day, he was exultant: "J.&L. has been brought to its knees. Think of it. The toughest corporation in America, the one Foster could not even come near has been forced to capitulate."[43]

Let me put this in perspective. I have argued that labor movements usually grow by leaps. This is especially true in an industry like steel where the threshold for successful action is extremely high. None of the so-called initial passivity was actually a reflection of the desire of workers to organize. Rather, it was a testament to the difficulties of gathering sufficient forces and creating momentum for takeoff. Once the dam burst, the momentum was virtually unstoppable. At the same time that SWOC leaders were complaining of worker apathy, they were trying to control worker militancy, with no apparent sense of irony. See, for example, the SWOC memo from Golden to Staff members, local officers, and members, Northeastern Region, March 31, 1937: "To make matters still more difficult, new members of some of our recently formed Lodges have begun issuing ultimatums to their employers as well as to this Committee saying that unless the contract is signed by a certain date, the men will go out on strike . . . If your Lodge officers and members indulge in these methods, it will result in the destruction of the Union . . . Self-restraint, control and discipline on the part of all officers and members will make possible a powerful industrial Union. Lack of it will destroy our new organization. Lack of self-restraint, control and discipline result in mob action, and this sets in motion the forces that bring about Fascism and Dictatorship" (Golden Papers, 20:10). A key question for us will be how to analyze the tremendous militancy, solidarity, and pro-union sentiment, given the perception of apathy by many union officials.

The Employee Representation Plan Strategy

The first employee representation plan (ERP) was set up at the Rockefeller-owned Colorado Fuel and Iron Company after the machine-gunning of a tent colony of striking workers by coal company–supported state militias at Ludlow, Colorado, on April 20, 1914. It is considered one of the deadliest incidents in U.S. labor history: mostly women and children were killed, thirteen of whom were found burned to death under a single tent. This slaughter, known as the Ludlow Massacre, created much negative publicity for John D. Rockefeller. In its aftermath, the corporation

---

[43] May 13 and 14, 1937, Meyer Bernstein, 1:2, emphasis mine.

hired Mackenzie King, future Canadian prime minister and labor relations specialist, to design its Employee Representation Organization (see Sweeney 1947, the initial publicity director of SWOC). The development of ERPs was uneven after that, but by the mid-1930s, virtually every major steel company had a plan (for more detail on King, see Eiden 2018).

Simultaneous with these activities was a strategy of working within the ERPs, a tactic that had been advocated by Foster during the 1919 steel strike and had been used by the CP and others. This was clearly an important arena of activity, yet some historians' exaggeration of its extent and impact is hardly based on careful research. It was most certainly not the invention of Murray and his team. Galenson, for example, argues, "The initial strategy of the SWOC was to invade the company unions for they were the only real centers of organization in the industry" (1960:88). Harbison describes some of the SWOC involvement with the ERPs in great, highly informative—even if gushing—detail. He concludes, "The capture of the Carnegie-Illinois representation plans might well be recorded among the most decisive victories for organized labor in the history of American trade unionism" (1940:49). In careful historical analysis, such hyperbole must be recognized as inflated cow manure. It was one important bump on the road. One must reemphasize, against the CIO Right and their academic hagiographers, that the strategy of working within existing ERPs was not the instant creation of Murray and his cohorts. Foster had, of course, recommended this tactic in his influential pamphlet. Communists, long active in International Harvester (IH) plants, had been secretly operating within that company's Works Councils during the mid-1930s. Joseph Webber, a Communist Party organizer, who, according to Max Kampelman, had received training in Moscow and was a key Chicago/Indiana-area SWOC organizer, was recruiting members of the Works Council of IH Tractor Works in 1936 (1957:68). By April 1937, he had recruited the majority of the leadership of the ERP at Tractor Works, as well as large numbers at other IH plants in Chicago. Among his biggest coups was the recruitment into the CP (perhaps as early as 1936) of Gerald Fielde, the formerly submissive leader of the McCormick Works Council in Chicago, the heart of the IH empire (Ozanne 1967:196–97).

David Saposs also notes that it was quite common for leaders of the ERPs in a variety of industries to come over to the CIO. When describing how Elmer Maloy, head of the company union at Duquesne, joined SWOC and was elected mayor of the town, Saposs remarks, "I found it in other industries as well. I found it in the rubber industry, that the fellows that I had interviewed at Goodyear and Goodrich, who were the heads of the company unions, immediately went over to the union just as soon as the decision was declared." It was thus hardly an accident that the largest number of early SWOC locals and the greatest activity of the ERPs were in the Chicago/Northwest Indiana Calumet region, where there was a heavy concentration of CP activists.[44] Communists were especially strong in the Chicago area, a long-term stronghold of left-wing labor activists (Foster 1952; Haywood 1978; Storch 2007).

In some areas, of course, militant employee representatives were active early, well before SWOC. In August 1935, employee representatives at U.S. Steel's large Chicago South Works facility voted to form an independent union, and in January 1936, thirteen out of twenty-five representatives at U.S. Steel's Gary Works formed the Rubicon Lodge of the AA. In the Chicago area, representatives from USS subsidiaries formed the Calumet Council. In November 1935, Clairton representatives had dinner together. And in January 1936, seven of the nine plants (with eighty delegates) met without the sanction of management to form an inter-plant committee (Harbison 1940: 21–22). All this activity was prior to SWOC's formation.[45] Thus, militant ERP activity was extensive well before SWOC.

In other areas, however, company representative plans were given new energy by the formation of SWOC. Van Bittner, regional director of the Chicago/Great Lakes SWOC district at the time, reported on August 1, 1936, an unauthorized meeting called by Roland Eckert, general secretary of employee representation, Carnegie-Illinois Steel Corp, Gary Works.[46] On August 19, 1936, Bittner reported again that at a meeting of all the employee representatives of the Chicago district under the ERP, sixty-five employee representatives were present, representing Illinois-Steel Company, Youngstown Sheet and Tube Company, Inland Steel Corporation, South Works, Carnegie-Illinois Corporation, Joliet Works Carnegie-Illinois Corporation, Gary Screw and Bolt Company, Gary Sheet Mill Company, Gary Tin Mill, American Bridge Company, and Universal Atlas Cement, and voted unanimously to endorse the drive of the SWOC and give their cooperation and support in organizing the steelworkers into the Amalgamated Association of Iron, Steel and Tin Workers of North America.[47] Philip Murray, taking note of these developments, urged staffers at a conference of Pittsburgh and Chicago SWOC delegates on September 9, 1936,

---

[44] Bert Cochran (1977:97) suggests that thirty-one or thirty-two of the thirty-three SWOC staffers in the Calumet region were attending the "Communist caucus." Kollros (1998:194) is highly dubious about this, but to me it seems reasonable, since the CP was where the action was, and clearly those inside the CIO who were working closely with the Communists were untainted by their association.

[45] Clint Golden also mentions a group of employee representatives from eleven mills of Carnegie-Illinois Steel Company in the Pittsburgh–Youngstown area, who presented demands to USS president Fairless in April 1935 (Golden to Blankenhorn, May 21, 1936, Golden papers, 3:2).

[46] A note at the bottom of the report says that "C-I refuses to allow the meeting to be held in the main office auditorium of Gary Works, so it will be held in the Moose auditorium" (statement by Van A. Bittner, Chicago–Great Lakes regional director, SWOC, August 1, 1936, District 36 10:19, PSU).

[47] Statement by Van A. Bittner, Chicago– Great Lakes regional director, SWOC, August 19, 1936, District 36 10:19, PSU.

to "establish a personal, and wherever possible, friendly contact. . . . I want names and contacts, as well as those of opponents of SWOC, etc. . . . I have assigned Harold J. Ruttenberg and John J. Mullen of our staff to concentrate on this work."[48] At the next meeting of the SWOC board in late September, Murray reported: "As part of our activities we have concentrated much of our energy upon the company union situation in the steel industry. We have found company union reps in a rebellious mood, and we have lent them encouragement. We have stimulated them to make wage and hour demands upon the management." The Carnegie-Illinois Steel Chicago-Pittsburgh Representatives Council was a SWOC split-off from the ERP council, originally "fostered by management," representing fifteen thousand workers, with those that did not split representing six thousand.[49]

Militant ERP organizing, however, was highly uneven, going on intensely in some companies and plants and hardly at all in many others. U.S. Steel and its Carnegie-Illinois division was a hotbed, providing at least part of the incentive for U.S. Steel to sign its contract with Lewis. Still, geographically, this activity seems to have been widespread. Reports from the South were particularly encouraging: as southern SWOC director William Mitch noted, "What I wanted to report to you particularly was the success we are making with substantial members of the company union representatives." He further reported that he would soon have a meeting in an auditorium that seated seven thousand, hardly the zero participation suggested by McDonald.[50]

---

[48] Two days later, on September 11, he sent out a memo, Philip Murray to All Sub-Regional Directors, on Employee (Company Union) Representatives, which underscores the "independent thinking and action among employee (company union) representatives of certain subsidiaries of U.S. Steel Corp., and particularly the Carnegie-Illinois Steel Co" (September 11, 1936, District 36, 10:14, PSU).

[49] Murray wrote: "Unlike the traditional A.F. of L. policy of calling company union representatives names, we have catered to them with a view to swinging them over. In a large number of cases we have enlisted as members of the Amalgamated Association most of the company union representatives in the mill, many times including the chairman of the Company union." He added parenthetically, "We have also had the fortunate support of numerous racial and fraternal organizations, and Negro organizations" (Minutes of SWOC, Pittsburgh, September 29, 1936, District 36 10:20, PSU).

[50] Murray wrote back to Mitch on February 2, 1937, about the "progress of our organizational campaign in the Birmingham area . . . Am delighted to note the substantial progress that you are making in converting certain of the leading company union representatives . . . And also your success in broadcasting" (Regional Director File, SWOC, Birmingham, District 36 10:14, PSU). Extremely positive reports also continued to come in from the Pittsburgh area, one of the historically most difficult places to organize. See Resolution, probably November 16, 1936, District 10:20, PSU, demanding more wage increases and rights, adopted by General Body, Duquesne Workers, Carnegie-Illinois Steel, ERP; also REPS News Letter, Pittsburgh District, Joint Representatives Council, November 12, 1936, which states that all the elected leaders in the area are "progressives . . . not one controlled by the company." There is a reference to "progressive, militant, pro-Lewis" men. Already seeking legal advice from Lee Pressman."

Yet the revisionist history of the centrality of the ERP campaign and who was responsible for its thrust and enactment begins early. Certainly, this is reflected in much contemporary correspondence. See, for example, Cornelia Bryce Pinchot's letter of March 22, 1937, to top Murray assistant Clinton Golden: "You are personally to be congratulated. Your strategy for the winning over of the company Unions and the intensive campaign you put over was a magnificent achievement. Mr. Lewis and I were talking it over last night."[51]

The attempts to deny that the Communists had played any role, much less a central role, began early. McDonald, in particular, went to great lengths to deny their role: "Trouble is brewing with the Communists. As usual they take all the credit for organizing steel . . . First result is an order to keep away from May Day celebration." He added, "The Communist Party of America [sic] was at its high-water mark about this time, and it unquestionably did manage to plant some organizers in the SWOC. We routed them out when we found them, but some were pretty smooth operators" (1969:97). He noted that CPer Gus Hall was an organizer for SWOC in Warren, Ohio (1969:98).

In 1942, SWOC was renamed the United Steelworkers of America (USWA). Once organized, the USWA became a highly conservative business union. It was also one of the most undemocratic, authoritarian of all U.S. unions. Despite the proclamation of its democratic character by Cold War liberals, the lack of commitment to substantive democracy of the USWA must be repeatedly underscored. The USWA leadership successfully purged Communists and other oppositionists, many of whom had played major roles in organizing the union, doing its best to stifle most of the grassroots democracy and militancy that had been so central to building the union. Finally, beginning quite early, it took a strong turn toward racism, defending white supremacist practices, especially inside the workplace and union. These three factors are, of course, closely related, but I will start with the last first.

Race and the USWA

As is invariably the case in the United States, the prism through which to fully understand the United Steel Workers of America and its longtime president Philip Murray is race. Almost across the board among labor historians and even many activists there is a tendency to describe Murray as someone who was strongly committed to fighting racial discrimination. He was held back, so the argument goes, by the racist attitudes of white workers in the union (Nelson 2001:187, 201). Without denying, of course, the often-strong racist attitudes of many of his white constituents, I want to suggest that this view is a whitewash of Murray and the USWA. The following

---

[51] Cornelia Bryce Pinchot, Milford, PA, to Clinton Golden, July 8, 1937, both in Golden papers, 7:7.

section is an attempt to provide balance and to correct this traditional assessment and, in doing so, to allow us to achieve a degree of understanding that traditional accounts do not.

Walter Galenson (1960) unequivocally evaluates Murray positively. Irving Bernstein describes Murray as the "good man of the labor movement," comparing him favorably to Lewis and asserting that Murray must have found Lewis's "methods hard to stomach" (1969:433). Melvyn Dubofsky (the coauthor of the definitive biography of John L. Lewis) also lauds him. "Murray was a trade union leader drawn directly from the ranks, never far from the rank and file in his style and behavior, and a perfect exemplar of the working-class leader who never forgot his roots" (in Laslett 1996:31). Robert Zieger summarizes him thus: "Steeped in the traditions of adversarial unionism . . . his modest lifestyle and mild public demeanor provided a sharp contrast with the glowering figure of his predecessor" (1995:333). None of the above writers, however, focus sharply on the issue of race. Perhaps the most extreme book dealing with race and the steelworkers is that of Judith Stein (1998), which Herbert Hill accurately describes as a "celebration of the white male bureaucracy that has controlled the union since its founding in 1942" and where "the black voice is silent" (2002:2). In other places Hill is not as kind in his assessment of Stein and her laudatory reviewers. Robert Norrell, who deals skillfully with the racially discriminatory employment practices in steel (1986:692), cites the racial liberalism of Philip Murray and Walter Reuther. He contrasts their attitudes with the racist attitudes of the workers (1986:681).[52] Even Bruce Nelson, such an astute critic of racial discrimination in the steel industry, and the union's role in maintaining it, largely gives a free pass to Murray and the national leadership, sympathizing with the insurmountable difficulties these "racial liberals" faced in dealing with a racist white rank and file (2001:201).

These views on Philip Murray and his cohort of leaders are mistaken. Although Murray and the UAW leaders were not the hooded members of the Ku Klux Klan depicted in certain pieces of Mine Mill propaganda during the 1949 secession battle, they were your typical racially insensitive, obtuse liberals, who largely turned a blind eye to racial prejudice and discrimination, placed a low priority on combating these practices, and tended in most cases to "blame the victim." In fleshing out this picture, I will start with seemingly minor issues, then move to the more hardcore ones.

[52] According to Norrell, "Philip Murray [was] . . . a man known to have strong opinions against racial discrimination" (1986:691); he referred to the UAW as "one of the most racially enlightened unions." For my cut on the racial attitudes of Walter Reuther, see my lengthy review and debates on Reuther in Goldfield (1997a).

"They Stick Like Concrete": Underestimating Black Workers

The initial stance of the union was to appeal to Blacks and whites alike on the basis of equality for Black steelworkers. This is confirmed by many detailed studies. SWOC also hired large numbers of Black organizers. From the beginning, the pessimism expressed by the national leaders about the union-consciousness and militancy of Black steelworkers, however, was disconnected from the reports on the ground.[53]

Their attitudes might be considered astounding, given that the reports on Black workers were quite consistent from virtually all parts of the country. Reports from the South were notable. Ruben Farr, southern regional director for SWOC and the USWA confirms this assessment: "After the other organization, the Steel Workers Organizing Committee, came in, the Negroes were very strong. They were one of the first to join and then they were the stickers." Although certain prominent Blacks opposed unions, there were a lot of activists who helped, including A. G. Gaston and John Moses.[54]

Ned Beddow, who preceded Farr as southern director, wrote to Murray in 1939 about various SWOC victories among Black workers. One took place at U.S. Pipe and Foundry Co. Plant in Bessemer, where there was a large majority of Black support. Another occurred at the majority– African-American Woodward Iron Company. Coal miners had been on strike for nine weeks; Mitch spoke to the strikers and asked if they wanted to give Woodward conditions that miners were not giving to other companies: "You should have heard the hillsides echo with their 'no's.'" As Noel Beddow, executive director of District 36, wrote to Philip Murray, SWOC chair, on June 7, 1939, *"Years ago I thought the colored man would be the hardest class on God's green earth to organize but in Alabama they stick like concrete* (emphasis mine)."[55] This theme was a consistent one throughout the 1930s, 1940s, and 1950s. On April 12, 1946, for example, the steelworkers lost an election at a small plant to the AFL. Farr wrote that "it was purely racial, 32–21. There were 21 colored in the plant," all of whom presumably voted for the CIO. "But since the election, at least two of the white men told me they had made a mistake and were ready to correct the mistake they made."[56]

Any notion that the union stood for civil rights was quickly dropped. Southern SWOC leaders made this clear in their statements in court in Gadsden, Alabama. Their subservience when challenged by authorities is noteworthy. For example,

---

[53] The views of the SWOC national leaders on race are seconded by Bernstein (1969:454).

[54] USWA Oral History Project, PSU, 9–10.

[55] I found this quote so striking, especially coming from a CIO conservative, that I initially wanted to entitle this chapter or even the book "They stick like concrete." District 36 16:1, PSU.

[56] Farr to McDonald, April 17, 1946, District 36 55:5, PSU.

SWOC leader Ned Beddow testified at the trial of a Mr. L. A. Yother in Gadsden, "We are not concerned with equality between whites and blacks. We are concerned only with the equality of wages, hours and working conditions."

Yeverton Cowherd, another SWOC leader, stated, "We have always proposed and our policy has been and is to respect the Jim Crow laws . . . As long as there are Jim Crow laws we are going to abide by the law."[57] These statements can be contrasted with those of CP activists, Wobblies, and even many racial liberals (Heideman 2018).

A symbolic issue faced by many interracial unions was how to manage the housing of their racially mixed delegations at conventions and whether to patronize discriminatory hotels. Firm stances were taken on these issues not only by virtually all the left-wing unions, including the Farm Equipment Workers Union, Mine Mill, and the United Packinghouse Workers, among others, but even at times by mixed delegations from more conservative unions. It is perhaps not unimportant that at the 1948 steelworkers' convention in Atlantic City, Philip Murray and David McDonald were staying at a hotel with a sign out front reading, "No Negroes, No Jews, and No Dogs." Eight to ten Black steelworkers threatened to picket the hotel if they did not leave, but they finally convinced the leaders to do so, "particularly the reluctant McDonald" (Dickerson 1986:225). In contrast to many other unions, the international office was helping locals obtain separate accommodations for their Black and white delegates. The national office wanted separate reservations for two whites and two Blacks, stating that it did not "have the names of any hotels in Washington, D.C. that takes [*sic*] care of the colored people."[58]

Within the union, little attempt was made by the leadership to portray the union as anything but a white organization. In local unions and district offices, in contrast to many more racially progressive unions, most officials refused to hire black secretaries (Hinshaw 2002:147). Black staff members were equally scarce even in areas with large numbers of Black steelworkers. As Hinshaw concludes, "Racial discrimination simply did not loom that large in the calculations of the national leaders of the CIO or SWOC. When pressed by black workers, Murray hired a single black 'troubleshooter' for the international USWA, who accomplished little more than serving as window dressing . . . USWA officials admitted that unlike the UE, Murray failed to recommend any African-Americans to serve on government boards or to force all districts with appreciable numbers of black members to hire a black representative" (Hinshaw 2002:76). These actions rather than the pious rhetoric of Murray and others about civil rights issues are more revealing of their real attitudes.

Many things indicate that the SWOC, at least symbolically, attempted to address some of these issues in the initial organizing period, but abandoned them as the

---

57 February 29, 1940, District 36 5:43, PSU.
58 May 10, 1949, District 36 55:7, PSU.

industry became organized. Cayton and Mitchell, writing in 1939, saw the USWA as racially progressive (1939:201). In the UMWA "the national officers have tried consistently to keep down any manifestation of racial prejudice on the part of the white union members... One of the most striking phases of the entire SWOC's campaign was the extent to which the union had been able to modify racial prejudice within the ranks of white laborers" (1939:212). Whether or not these statements were accurate or really wishful thinking, any pretenses that the steelworkers' union stood firmly for racial equality had largely been abandoned by the early 1940s. Or as Black Gary steelworkers activist Walter Mackerl told Ruth Needleman, "The union did little, however, to try to educate the white membership" (Needleman 2003:208).

Whites in steel, as elsewhere, often responded to Black organizers in the early organizing period. As Cayton and Mitchell note, "Because of their ability and courage, most of the Negro organizers were as effective *in organizing whites as Negroes and did much to forestall and allay racial strife*" (1939:206, emphasis mine). Hinshaw argues that many early rank-and-file activists, even before SWOC, were committed to interracial unity: despite the prejudices of its national leadership, many rank-and-file activists in the Amalgamated saw interracial unity as the precondition for success. The president of Duquesne's local, William Spand, for example, was particularly concerned about racism: "My sole idea in going into the movement . . . was to get white and colored people together whom capitalists had tried to keep apart" (Hinshaw 2002:53). In this local Blacks were elected to numerous offices, including vice president. Black workers responded enthusiastically, with 90% of all workers enrolled in the union (Hinshaw 2002:53). In Homestead, where Blacks were largely excluded from offices, only 30% of workers were in the union. Hinshaw concludes, "*Unionists willing to recruit black workers apparently proved more successful in organizing all kinds of workers*" (2002:53, emphasis mine). These observations about organizing in the early and middle 1930s suggest a fluidity that could have been used to push anti-discrimination issues if the leadership had been so inclined.

Even on questions of staffing, SWOC was, to say the least, crass in its treatment of African-American organizers. Pictures of the 1937 southern SWOC staff suggest to this observer that approximately one-third of the seventy or so members were African-American. By 1940, it appeared that there were at most three.[59] After the initial organizing, especially at U.S. Steel's TCI installations in Birmingham, most African-American staffers were released. These facts are underscored by a poignant

---

[59] Ruben Farr Collection, Birmingham Public Library, at the time unsorted. Although I have examined these photographs with a magnifying glass, precision is, of course, impossible, since it is not always easy to distinguish between light-skinned African-Americans and darker whites. Thus, one is bound to either make errors or at least be unable to make a definitive determination in a small number of cases. Nevertheless, the changes in racial composition are so stark as to leave little ambiguity regarding the trends. A similar observation can be made about the pictures of delegates to the southern SWOC conventions (the latter pictures are in Mitch files, District 16, no. 2653, PSU).

letter from the editor of Birmingham's Black newspaper, which is worth quoting at length: "We are all big supporters of CIO. If the CIO is to be successful in organizing this district, it must also be accomplished with the aid of colored organizers ... News of treatment received by colored organizers of this district has trickled into labor ranks and to leaders alike for several months. Information reliable in every respect, that intelligent and competent organizers have no place in the organization here, that colored men are continually insulted by C.I.O. officials themselves will eventually cause a break that all of us will hate to see ... Workers are resentful ... it is talked that some plan to stop the payment of their dues until organizers are re-employed and that others hesitate to join when they are informed by company officials and the remnants of company unions that the two-faced program in existence here is just what 'I told you so.' We have known colored organizers and the officials of the CIO since its beginning. We have been on the side of the C.I.O. as its policy is nationally carried out since our first information about it ... We feel that the employment of colored organizers in proportion to the number engaged in the industries whose plants are being invaded by the C.I.O. is essential."

The editor goes on, "Of the three and one half colored men now engaged in the organization here two are slated to be dropped for the 'lack of funds' by October first. During the past three months and as late as Monday, September 20, others have been employed ... Investigate the local set-up and let us again be able to tell the workers in good faith that prejudice, narrowness, inefficiency have no place in the C.I.O."[60]

When in 1943 the national office proposed the addition of a Black loyalist to the organizing staff in a Birmingham district where the majority of steelworkers were African-American, Farr refused. Writing to Secretary-Treasurer David McDonald on May 31, 1943, Farr said he already had "two colored organizers and, as you probably know, in my District here in the South I can't use these organizers for anything except organizational work among the colored people; therefore, I feel that my staff needs white staff members, at the present time, in order to assist in negotiations and 4th step grievances. For this reason and this reason only, I would prefer white men on the Staff in preference to Morgan Goodson." Although the president had absolute authority to appoint district staff members, there is no indication that he did not defer to Farr's wishes. On other issues, of course, they paid no attention to rank-and-file or district-level preferences. The stance of the Murray regime was in sharp contrast not only to most Left unions, but also to the Alabama UMWA.

A further indication of the lack of commitment to fighting discrimination at the workplace was Murray's establishment of the union's Civil Rights Committee (CRC) and the appointment of Boyd Wilson as special assistant to the president for

---

[60] H. D. Coke, Managing Editor, *Birmingham World*, President Birmingham Negro Chamber of Commerce, to Mr. John Brophy, SWOC, October 1, 1937, District 36 2:30, PSU.

civil rights, first under Murray, then under McDonald.[61] After further pressure from Black steelworkers, in 1948 the union established a Civil Rights Committee, allegedly to help the fight against discrimination against Black steelworkers. The committee was entirely white and was chaired by Thomas Shane, with his brother Francis Shane as executive director (Hinshaw 2002:139). The union paid the Shanes, but provided them with no staff to investigate grievances and only a minimal budget. The committee's main function was to make recommendations to the USWA president. It had no enforcement powers. Its main activity, as evidenced by the minutes of its meetings in the archives, was to pass resolutions and put the union on record as favoring certain types of federal legislation, including a national Fair Employment Practices Commission. As Hinshaw remarks, "In terms of confronting racism in steel, the CRC was designed to fail . . . even committed black unionists referred to [it as a] farce" (2002:140). One white union official called the union's support for civil rights legislation, along with a complete failure to challenge racial discrimination in steel or the union, as "Schizophrenia." Yet as Hinshaw notes, this was less a result of mental illness than of Cold War liberalism, which viewed symbols, rather than substance, as the key in the fight against Communism, suggesting that it was racial dissension, rather than racial discrimination, that was the problem. Those who tried to mobilize the union against company discrimination were labeled Communists. When the *Pittsburgh Courier*, a major African-American newspaper, criticized the union for expelling Communists as opponents of democracy while allowing white supremacists and KKK members to remain in the union, the union was defended by Boyd Wilson, Murray's African-American special assistant on civil rights. When Black unionists claimed that their seniority rights had been violated in deference to less senior white workers, neither the CRC nor the executive board ever took any action (Hinshaw 2002:142).

Boyd Wilson, appointed to his position in 1942, investigated Black grievances. Yet he was forbidden to examine such complaints without Murray's or McDonald's permission (Dickerson 1986:195). He was not even appointed to the union's Civil Rights Department until 1958. His main role was to provide window dressing for the union as a member of the national board of the Urban League or as the USWA's representative to various events, including to Ghana's independence celebration. He thus helped promote the unions' totally unwarranted reputation as a champion of Black rights (Dickerson 1986:195). (The type of role Boyd played is immortalized in the book *The Spook Who Sat by the Door*, Greenlee 1969). The union's lack of commitment to fighting the company's discrimination and failure to educate its white members put it in an extremely weak position to combat discrimination within the union itself.

---

[61] Farr to McDonald, April 17, 1946, District 30, 55:5.

By 1950, it had become something of an embarrassment for an allegedly liberal union like the USWA to have segregated facilities in its local and district offices, especially in the South. A directive was issued on April 24, 1950, by Arthur J. Goldberg, CIO general council (also chief lawyer for the USWA), saying that the CIO was opposed to any segregated facilities. "Therefore, no segregation in the use of facilities in buildings or office space under the control of CIO Industrial Union Councils should be permitted, and there should be no signs indicating such segregation. It is also our position that any provision requiring segregation in leases or other agreements under which property is rented or occupied are unenforceable in the courts."[62]

When there were protests against eliminating segregation in USWA offices, district and national leaders capitulated immediately. Shane wrote to Murray stating that the letter of Murray and Goldberg to all state and city councils in the South caused "a very unfavorable reaction, especially in Basic Steel companies, among our Local Union officers, grievance committeemen and rank-and-file as a whole; virtually all employees are signing decertification petitions. So, postpone conference . . . There is no doubt in my mind that if District 50 or some of the AFL Organizations learns [sic] of the dissatisfaction among our members here, that they will take over 'lock, stock and barrel.' " So rather than use this as an opportunity to take a firm stand, the union canceled its civil rights conference to be held in Birmingham. [63] A further letter was sent on June 13, 1950, by seven local presidents to Murray on ending the importation of outside union leaders to work in the South.[64]

Even in the North, USWA leaders seemed clueless about issues of race. The eastern Pennsylvania district did not even have, as did Alabama, a token African-American staffer out of its seventeen or eighteen members. The regional director was attacked for this lack of diversity, in an article in the *Pittsburgh Courier*, December 9, 1950. Charles Ford, regional director from Philadelphia, enclosed the clipping and wrote to Francis C. Shane, secretary of the USWA Civil Rights Committee, "I have no idea as to why this attack on me was made." At the first sign of significant resistance from white steelworkers and local leaders, the national leadership caved. It is useful to contrast this with the actions of those unions that were actually committed to fighting racial discrimination.

One stark contrast, involving less openly racist behavior, is to be found in a comparison of the racial practice of the left-led Farm Equipment (FE) Union with that of the United Auto Workers at the Louisville, Kentucky, International Harvester

---

[62] Arthur J. Goldberg, General Council, CIO, "Segregated Facilities in CIO Offices and Halls," to all CIO Regional Directors and CIO Industrial Union Councils, April 24, 1950, United Steelworkers of America [USWA], Civil Rights Department, 5:26.

[63] Shane to Murray, on postponing Civil Rights Conference in Birmingham, May 23, 1950, USWA, Civil Rights Department, 5:26.

[64] R. E. Farr to Murray, May 19, 1950, USWA, Civil Rights Department, 3:13.

(IHC) plant in the late 1940s and early 1950s. The story is told in great detail by Toni Gilpin (1992). FE Local 236 represented all production and maintenance workers except for those in the foundry. The plant, which opened in 1946, was represented by the FE from the beginning, having by 1949 more than six thousand employees, approximately 14% of whom were African-American. Local 236 was characterized by a large steward system, frequent meetings, an active militant membership, and many work stoppages. From the beginning, its leaders and members, white as well as Black, displayed an unusual aggressiveness around issues of racial equality, both within the plant and in the community at large. These activities were acknowledged even by many sources not especially friendly to the union. The local was unusual, especially for the South. It was a largely white local with many African-American leaders as local officers and even as stewards in overwhelmingly white departments. In addition to its aggressive stance in defending the rights of Black plant workers and refusing to countenance segregated locker room, washroom, and cafeteria facilities, Local 236 mobilized its white and Black members to fight for the integration of parks and hotels in Louisville. Finally, there was a great deal of socializing, often involving wives and families, of Black and white workers outside the plant, something unheard of elsewhere in Louisville in the late 1940s and early 1950s. The context was, of course, important. The Harvester management had a rhetorical commitment to nondiscrimination; Louisville was not the Deep South, although its segregated bus lines and across-the-board Jim Crow policies distinguished it from much of the North. The FE leadership, however, was the central ingredient. This can be seen by its contrast with the United Auto Workers (UAW) leadership at the same plant. In 1949, IHC began production in its new foundry. The large facility, which would eventually employ more than fifteen hundred workers, was a separate bargaining unit, won by the UAW in that year. Unlike the overwhelmingly white plant, the foundry was one-half Black. One would think that there would have been an even greater base for civil rights activities in the foundry than in the main plant. There is, however, no evidence that civil rights was an important issue for the UAW local. In fact, as of a 1953 study by the National Planning Association, the foundry had racially separate locker rooms designated "White" and "Colored," which as yet had received no protest from the UAW local; the same report indicated there were no vestiges of the original racial separation in the comparable production areas of the main plant, represented by the FE. This contrast is a highly revealing commentary on the differing priorities on racial issues of the two unions, and especially of the Reuther leadership.

A further spotlight on the practices of the Murray leadership is evident from an examination of the approach of the United Packinghouse Workers of America (UPWA) to fighting for racial equality. Racist white workers were not the sole provenance of the steelworkers. A survey taken by the UPWA after its 1948 strike indicated that 30% of white members did not want to work with a Black in the same job classification and that 90% of southern whites favored segregated eating facilities. The union nevertheless fought for the upgrading of Black workers and their entry into formerly all-white job classifications. Not only in Chicago, where Black packinghouse workers were often a majority, but in whiter Kansas City, packinghouse workers fought to end segregation in swimming pools, municipal parks, schools, and public accommodations. This occurred during the late 1940s and throughout the 1950s (Horowitz 1997:220–24). As Horowitz argues with respect to the UPWA, aggressive action by the union often had long-term results, as in cases where whites who initially opposed integration of their departments ended up electing Black stewards, a phenomenon I personally witnessed at International Harvester in Chicago, when the electrical department was forced to hire qualified Black apprentices against the opposition of virtually all the white electricians. A year later, when their white steward took a job as a foreman, they elected a young Black electrician as their steward. When the company attempted to fire him sometime later while he was confronting management over a department grievance, these same white electricians led a plantwide wildcat strike, claiming that nobody was going to fire "their steward." These incidents suggest the occasional malleability of racial attitudes on the part of whites when aggressive union leadership is provided.[65]

A dramatic confrontation over racial issues took place in Fort Worth, Texas, where a large group of racist white workers attempted to reimpose segregated cafeterias and washrooms against the wishes of the UPWA national leadership (Horowitz 1997:231). The 1952 contract negotiated with Armour mandated the desegregation of all in-plant facilities. On November 11, 1952, management took down all the "White" and "Colored" signs. Later in the day two hundred white workers stormed the union hall, demanding that the polices be rescinded. The next day the plant was leafleted. The international officers flew to Fort Worth, where a meeting did not go well. "There were knives and guns all over . . . screaming and hollering," UPWA national President Ralph Helstein noted. A former president of the local and a fundamentalist minister assembled members and blamed Communists in Chicago. The international union responded on several levels. First, it pressured a hesitant Armour to stand by the contract, threatening strikes at other plants in the chain if they did not. The union also sent in additional staff and restrained the reluctant district leadership, giving strong support to local Black and Latino leaders. Even though a number of southern locals disaffiliated, the union stuck to its guns (Halpern 1991:172–74).

The struggle in the UPWA was no less seamless than that in the steelworkers' union. As Horowitz argues, "White workers initiated disaffiliation efforts in southern packing unions, sugar processing units in the New Orleans area, and all-white stockyard locals"

---

[65] See the in-plant newspaper, *Workers' Voice*, n.d., circa 1977, in possession of author.

(1997:233). Black workers and UPWA officials tried to highlight the enormous economic gains that the union had brought them, but they never tried to backtrack on civil rights issues. Such commitments stand in stark contrast to the Murray leadership, which tended to side on the ground with the racists.

The Murray leadership's tolerance and even encouragement of racism and racist practices was consolidated in the 1940s, limiting its ability to challenge the racist attitudes of white workers, as well as the discriminatory practices of the company. Perhaps the defining moment came during its confrontation with the Black-majority, civil rights–oriented Mine Mill locals in the Birmingham area in 1948 and 1949.

The International Union of Mine, Mill and Smelter Workers of America (Mine Mill) had its roots in the left-wing Western Federation of Miners, a mainstay of the Industrial Workers of the World (IWW) at the time of the IWW's founding in 1905. Such a tradition, it should be noted, did not necessarily lead to egalitarian practice, or even to a commitment to the organization of African-American workers. One organization that had IWW roots, the Seafarers International Union-Sailors Union of the Pacific (SIU-SUP), is a case in point. SIU-SUP's syndicalism, while rooted in IWW tradition, developed an all-white, eventually racist job-control orientation. The right wing of the International Woodworkers of America in the Northwest also had its roots in the IWW, but its syndicalism emphasized local control, turning it toward provincialism, anti-communism, and abandonment of the South and that region's largely African-American woodworkers.[66] Mine Mill's tradition was less provincial. At the time of the union's revitalization, an active minority of Communists was committed to interracial unionism and the vigorous organization of African-American workers. This influence was particularly strong among the overwhelmingly Black metal miners in the Birmingham area. The Communists, a distinct minority of the national union in 1934 and highly critical of both the local and international Mine Mill leadership, gained dominant influence in the union after Reid Robinson was elected president in 1936; elected as a non-Communist, he quickly gravitated toward Communist politics after his election. Metal mining in the Birmingham, Alabama, area, like coal mining there, was done by a workforce whose pay and occupation classifications were not highly differentiated. In the early 1930s, 80% of this workforce was Black. Pay lines, mine cars, and work areas were integrated and had both Black and white foremen, although integrated crews and whites working for Black foremen were eliminated by the companies after Mine Mill became established (Huntley 1977:20–26). From the beginning of organizing

---

[66] It should be noted that racial obtuseness was not solely the province of liberals. The racist SUP was being supported and extolled by the Third Camp, former Trotskyist Workers Party (against the racially progressive, CP-allied NMU), for many years. Even in the 1960s and later, Stan Weir (1972, 1974, 1996), one of its former leaders, praised the job control militancy of this racist union.

in 1933, Mine Mill had far greater support from Black workers than from whites, although at certain times, such as in 1938, when Mine Mill won reinstatement of all 160 workers fired in a 1936 strike (many of whom were white), there was also significant white support. In part because of the preponderance of Black workers, but also because of the growing role of Communists (many of whom were Black), Mine Mill from the outset had "an air of civil rights activism" (Kelley 1990:66, 145).

Mine Mill not only fought in the workplace for better working conditions and racial egalitarianism, but campaigned actively in the community. Along with Alabama miners and steelworkers, Mine Mill members engaged extensively in voter registration and in campaigns against the poll tax and lynching, giving these unions the character of broad-based social movements as well as workplace organizations. Robin D. G. Kelley claims that "more blacks were elected to leadership positions within Mine Mill than any other CIO union, and its policy of racial egalitarianism remained unmatched," although he gives no figures or comparative measures (1990:145).[67] Asbury Howard, a non-Communist African-American leader of Mine Mill (and later of the steelworkers' union and eventual key ally of Martin Luther King, Jr. in Alabama), said that the union in the 1930s, 1940s, and 1950s was highly revered in the Black community: "To the Negro people in the deep south, Mine Mill was as Moses to the children of Israel. . . I don't think Mr. Murray was for it."[68] Asbury also notes that in a union that was never more than 20% African-American at the national level, he never had any problems being elected to national and regional offices, including national vice president of the union.

Mine Mill's original jurisdiction in the AFL, confirmed in the CIO, was to represent industrially all non-coal miners (Jensen 1954). Even after Mine Mill had failed to organize iron ore miners on the Mesabi range, and they were subsequently successfully organized by SWOC, there was an understanding that these miners would eventually be transferred to Mine Mill. From the beginning of Mine Mill organizing in the Birmingham area, there was a KKK element among white miners that was supported by sympathizers in the community, who attacked Mine Mill. Many of these whites had been leaders in the original company union, and later in the company-supported Brotherhood of Captive Miners.[69] Robinson asserts, however, that in the beginning there was not much hostility on the part of most white workers to "being organized in the same locals as blacks . . . No, not that much at that early date. Things were so damn tough that their misery was joined, . . . although we had Negroes sitting on one side and whites on another." Yet Robinson indicates that

[67] It is important to note in this context that Mine Mill's record with regard to Chicano workers in the Southwest was equally egalitarian, despite the difficulties that it had in facing recalcitrant employers there (Garcia 1990).

[68] Oral history interview, March 27, 1968, PSU.

[69] Huntley (1977: 129); Oral History interview, Reid Robinson, SWOC records, Penn State University, December 1969.

racial tensions clearly existed: "I used to be told by some of the white workers down
there that I shouldn't shake hands with the Negro members and I shouldn't call
them Mister and so on."

By 1948, due to more than a decade of preferential white hiring policies at
TCI, only 52% of the workforce remained Black, while 48% were now white.
Steelworkers' leaders claimed that they received numerous letters from Alabama
iron ore miners who were dissatisfied with the Mine Mill leadership and wanted
to join the steelworkers union. They also claimed that there was much support
among Blacks for doing this and that they were not appealing to white workers
on a racial basis. This claim is seconded by Judith Stein, who presents the
steelworkers, including their fight with Mine Mill, as exemplary. Stein's account
is highly distorted. She states, "Although intimidation was employed by both
sides, the steelworkers probably used it more than Mine Mill did. And, although
the leaders of the secession were not racists, some of their supporters certainly
were" (1993:60). Her statement on the issue of violence and intimidation is not
supported by the facts.

The racism of the leaders of the secession and their support from the top ranks of
the CIO leadership are described by Vernon Jensen, an ardent supporter of the CIO
right wing and a vehement, unequivocal anti-communist. Jensen describes the case
of Homer Wilson, a right-winger in Mine Mill, who was defeated for the vice presidency in that union in 1947. After his defeat, Wilson conferred with CIO President
Philip Murray, organization director Alan Haywood, and Operation Dixie head Van
Bittner. Wilson was hired and eventually sent to Alabama to urge iron ore miners to
leave Mine Mill and join the steelworkers. According to Jensen, "When he arrived in
Bessemer, only whites were in attendance at the meeting that had been called. The
most conservative and reactionary union men in the district were leading the movement, with no intention of including the Negroes as they had long been included
in the Mine Mill locals. Wilson then told them they had to have the Negroes if they
were going to win for the Steelworkers and advised bringing them in and explaining
to them that the Communists were not the only effective grievance machinery, that
the Steelworkers would be very effective along these lines. The local conservative
leaders would not listen. They did not wish to have Wilson around, and so informed
Haywood, whereupon Haywood promptly telephoned Wilson and discharged him.
Instead, Van Jones was hired and the white men among the iron-ore miners were
approached on the ground that they were going to have a white union" (1954:234).

Just before the 1949 TCI NLRB election between the steelworkers and Mine
Mill, the KKK staged a large rally in support of the steelworkers. Despite the early
anti-racism of the SWOC, the leadership of the union, led by CIO president Philip
Murray, barely complained. In demagogic fashion, the steelworkers attempted to
hide their activities by accusing Mine Mill of fomenting racism and further claiming
that this overwhelmingly Black local union with its Black leadership was itself allied with the KKK (Huntley 1977:110, 162, 189). The steelworkers, in tactics

reminiscent of the those of the KKK during Reconstruction and those in the coun-terattack on the Populist movement, attempted to isolate Black workers by physi-cally attacking the small number of whites who remained loyal to Mine Mill. In at least one instance, at the Muscoda Local 123 in Bessemer, Alabama, Black Mine Mill members rallied armed contingents from the Black community to success-fully defend their white union brothers from steelworker-led assaults (Huntley 1977:208–209). These racist activities and assaults by the steelworkers were among many events that moved the CIO as a whole from an incipient anti-racism to acqui-escence to, if not open support for, discrimination against Black workers.

This impression is confirmed by issues of the *Red Mountain Emancipator*, the highly professional and polished publication of the secessionists. Some pictures of the meetings and rallies show hundreds of workers, 99–100% of whom appear to be white.[70] Nevertheless, both at the time and in later oral history interviews, various steel union leaders deny that the local secessionists were overwhelmingly white or that there was any attempt by the steelworkers to make racial appeals to whites. In fact, they continually claimed that it was Mine Mill that was stirring up these is-sues. Even when hundreds of hooded Klansmen marched on Mine Mill headquar-ters in Birmingham in support of the steelworkers, the USWA not only refused to disassociate themselves from the march (reminiscent of—but in this case decidedly worse than—Donald Trump's 2016 ambivalence about disavowing the support of former KKK leader David Duke and of neo-Nazis in Charlottesville, Virginia, in 2017), but blamed Mine Mill for the incident.[71] Why would we expect this situa-tion to be otherwise? When anti-communism trumped racism, and a union relied

---

[70] See issues of February 2 and April 14, 1949, University of Colorado, Mine Mill papers, box 46:5.

[71] See, e.g., letter of March 16, 1949, from USWA Secretary-Treasurer David McDonald to Mine Mill President Clark, claiming that it is Mine Mill which is "doing all in its power" to stir up "racial conflict" in Alabama. Even in later oral history interviews, the key national and district leaders of the se-cession made the same accusations and disclaimers. When USWA district leader Ruben Farr was asked whether "there [was] an issue as far as Mine, Mill siding with Negroes and the Steelworkers siding with whites, mostly? Did you notice this?," Farr responded, "No, sir, I didn't. Now Mine, Mill tried to bring that question up, but it didn't stick because we had Negroes who were in the ore mines at that time who worked very hard to get into the Steelworkers union" (March 27, 1968, Ruben Farr Collection, 30). Nick Zonarich, sent by Murray to oversee the secession struggle, made even more emphatic claims: "I cannot emphasize too strongly that we from the Steelworkers Union and the steelworkers certainly did not do anything to create a racial issue. This matter was magnified on the part of the Mine Mill and Smelter Workers leadership . . . They made Phil Murray a Klansman. They tried everything they could to make this a racial issue" (May 5, 1967, Reuben Farr Collection, :27). Yet these gentlemen perhaps protest too much. The detailed records of the national CIO office are housed in Catholic University, Washington, DC. There are comprehensive records by year for CIO strongholds. The records for 1949 and 1950 for Alabama and Birmingham are missing. When I asked what happened to them, the original archivists told me that they were not included among the documents that had originally been donated. I leave it to readers to draw their own conclusions.

on racist white members to oppose a Black-supported civil rights–oriented union in a Deep South center of KKK strength, even without the damning facts, logic dictates that this would be the case. We should also not be surprised that the re-action of the Black community in Birmingham, even that of NAACP activists, was a long-lasting revulsion toward not only the steelworkers' union, but the CIO it-self. For the African-American community, unlike the white liberal racists among the steelworkers' leadership, could hardly be oblivious to the stench of racism by Murray and the USWA.

This is made abundantly clear in the confidential report by NAACP labor re-lations assistant Herbert Hill to Walter White, NAACP president, dated May 3–17, 1953. Hill was sent to Alabama by White to investigate why the state's NAACP chapters had no relations with the USWA or even with much of the other CIO unions. Hill held extensive meetings with CIO officials across Alabama, as well as meetings with NAACP branch leaders and activists. He found that there was "abso-lutely no organizational contact between NAACP and CIO unions." The "decisive factor" was "the action of the Bessemer NAACP branch in refusing to support the United Steelworkers of America against the Communist-controlled Mine, Mill and Smelter Workers Union." Hill, a virulent anti-communist, a former Socialist Workers Party activist, and later an FBI informant, unconvincingly blames the Bessemer branch and asserts that they were acting "in violation of official NAACP policy." "Many Negro workers indicated a sense of despair and futility because the one im-portant institution operating in the South that they hoped would provide a bridge across the divide of color was not doing so." Hill believed (erroneously as I have al-ready suggested) that the USWA had "vigorously defended the job rights of Negro workers." Yet in other cities around the state, including Mobile and Montgomery, NAACP branches also refused to support the CIO.[72]

Even after the defeat of Mine Mill in workplace representation elections in the Birmingham area in 1949 and 1950, the union continued to be heavily involved in civil rights activities. In Bessemer, large numbers of Mine Mill members joined the NAACP chapter, taking it over and carrying out an aggressive set of civil rights ac-tivities throughout the early 1950s (Huntley 1977:215–18).

Mine Mill made a strategic mistake in not attempting to challenge more vigor-ously the change in hiring policy of Tennessee Coal, Iron and Railroad (TCI, the largest mine and steel company in the Birmingham area). After Mine Mill's 1938

[72] USWA, Civil Rights Department, Box 5:25. All quotes are from a confidential report by NAACP labor relations assistant Herbert Hill to Walter White, NAACP president, dated May 3–17, 1953. While some anti-racist academics were shocked, it should have been no small surprise that Hill also turned out to be an FBI informant, given his support of the USWA against Mine Mill and his un-yielding anti-Communism. For the definitive exposé, see Phelps (2012). For further discussion, see Griffey (2013); Phelps (2013).

National Labor Relations Board victory, white workers joined the union in large numbers. TCI then attempted to divide the workforce. Whereas it had previously hired mostly Black workers, after 1938 it began predominantly hiring whites. The company also gave better jobs to those workers who did not join Mine Mill.[73] One could argue, of course, that the structure of metal-mining employment and the high percentage of African-American workers in the Birmingham area led Mine Mill initially to interracial, egalitarian unionism and that the reaction of the increasing percentage of white workers to union policies was also inevitable. Such an analysis, however, while containing an important grain of truth, would ignore two important factors. First, the alternative leadership group made conscious choices. Communist-led Mine Mill chose to emphasize demands for racial equality, appealing directly to the interests of African-American workers. The conservative Murray leadership was willing to make racist appeals to white workers and abandon the interests of Black workers to defeat the Communists. Second, the victory of the Murray leadership against Mine Mill was not preordained either. They won only during the high point of Cold War anti-communism with support from local and regional white supremacists in the South, "Dixiecrat" politicians, the CIO national office, the might of the federal government, and USWA violence against Mine Mill members and officials. And even then, the critical elections were close. The significance of structural factors and the racial attitudes of white workers cannot be assessed without taking account of these decisive components.

The USWA and Democracy

It is one of the seeming ironies of U.S. labor history and industrial relations literature that the steelworkers' union—perhaps the most undemocratic and repressive of the CIO industrial unions—has been lauded as democratic, while the far more democratic and generally less repressive Communist-led unions were branded as authoritarian. I shall begin with the lack of democracy in steel. First, the steelworkers' union, unlike the UMWA, lacked democracy from its founding. Len De Caux, who was in charge of publicity and editor of the union's paper (as he was for the CIO as a whole and was "lent" to Murray by Lewis in 1936), describes the situation in detail: "SWOC was something new—a union planned and started from on top, with a half million bucks in the kitty to make it big business from scratch" (1970:276).

---

[73] The new hiring policy was "the subject of a heated debate in 1941 at the Wenonah local. The issue was raised by a rank and filer, who expressed the concerns of other Black miners that so few Blacks were being hired. One proposal was that the union demand that the company hire equal numbers of Blacks and whites. The Black vice president of the local opposed this suggestion, much to the pleasure of the white newcomers and the chagrin of Black miners. Although the vice president was subsequently voted out of office, attempts to get the company to change its hiring policies failed" (Huntley 1977:96–98).

"From the top down, SWOC was as totalitarian as any big business. The 'Committee' was a purely nominal board of directors. The Mine Workers supplied most money and so dominated . . . After a little rubber-stamping, it faded away. Murray was SWOC, even more than Lewis was UMW" (1970: 280).

The mineworkers, as we have seen, began as a highly fractious union with independent, often rebellions districts whose locals and districts were mostly tamed by the brutally repressive Lewis machine. Among his key hatchet men were Philip Murray, Van Bittner, and David McDonald, who were to become the key leaders of the SWOC, then USWA. The Murray machine was determined to tolerate no opposition from the beginning. Stepan-Norris and Zeitlin argue that those unions established by organizing committees (in contrast to those that began as rebellions within AFL unions or as insurgencies from strong locals) tended to be less democratic (2002:42–43). This was even more the case when the organizing committees had a large amount of money. Among the features of the steelworkers' union was the exclusive power of the president to appoint all staff people, all of whom were voting participants at national conventions. Lloyd Ulman estimates that at the 1958 convention, 700–1,500 of the 3,523 delegates were staff people, and comments that "their influence cannot be measured in numbers alone . . . [there was] disciplined and articulate floor leadership . . . derogatory background noise, or even the occasional application of muscle" (1962: 109–10). Further, "a rollcall vote has never been held at a Steelworker convention," even though some delegates from large locals had as many as ten votes (1962:111, 126). Nick Zonarich, already noted as a trusted assistant, recalled, "You must remember that the USW has always opposed opposition . . . Phil Murray believed that personal loyalty to the leadership was essential." Yet such lack of democracy was apparent from the beginning of the organization.[74]

There is considerable debate about what union democracy actually means, and even whether democracy is necessary for a "proper" union. It is clear that branding the USWA as a "democratic" union involves much hypocrisy. William Leiserson, for example, argues that the steelworkers' union at its founding in 1942 was a "mature" union: "Continuing factional struggles and bitter election contests in other unions were often pointed to as evidence of their democracy; in the Steelworkers' convention democracy was identified with its unity" (1959:159). While nominally the steelworkers were dependent on the CIO, they were "actually controlled by its appointed officers and administrators . . . There was no disunity at the convention" (1959:160). When the question of approving the new constitution arose, one delegate moved for a recess, so that the attendees could have time to read it, since it had just been handed out. This was defeated (1959:164). When another delegate asked if they could accept or reject each section as read, Murray replied, "Well, that

[74] Nick Zonarich, May 19, 1966, Ruben Farr Collection, 28.

is a form of totalitarianism" (1959:166)! There was, of course, only one slate of officers, and that was the one submitted by the Murray leadership. When another delegate suggested that a bit more democracy was needed since he thought that the members should have more input than they had had in the AFL, he was accused of not having confidence in the national leadership (1959:269). Later, Bittner, who was never known for his democratic inclinations, cautioned the delegates about wanting too much democracy and urged them to trust their leaders (1959:172). Leiserson concludes, "Much that happened at the convention suggests that the plan was to give the steelworkers a government considered good for them, rather than to permit their representatives to frame one more to their liking" (1959:177). Leiserson, a sympathizer, concludes that the USWA was not one of "the more democratic unions" (1959:177).

The steelworkers were considered democratic by a strange perversion of the English language. The rationale was given theoretical justification in a rambling, often contradictory book, *The Dynamics of Industrial Democracy*, by Clinton Golden, northeastern director of SWOC, later a vice president of USWA, and Harold Ruttenberg, the union's research director. Democracy for them did not involve membership control or even participation, but the elimination of conflict, industrial peace based on worker–management collaboration (1942:91). As Thomas Brooks writes in his biography of Golden, *Clint*, he was a "highly sophisticated proponent of an industrial democracy based on a worker-management partnership" (1978:x). Of course, as Kollros argues persuasively, the assumption by the union of union–management cooperation was "delusional," especially at the local level (1998:403). Golden and Ruttenberg also make the claim, with no empirical basis, that "the more problems the management is willing to share with its workers, the more interested the workers become ... the bigger do the union meetings grow" (1942:xvii). In fact, just the opposite was nearly always the case.

In perhaps one of the most controversial parts of their book, Golden and Ruttenberg defend the expulsion of union pioneer Stanley Orlovsky from the union (1942:60–61). They argue that the "belligerent type of union officer in the early stages of collective bargaining" was necessary but that eventually he had to be gotten rid of to sustain cooperative "industrial democracy." Orlovksy was expelled from the union for agitating too much against the internationally supported local officers. He had been chair of the grievance committee at his local (previously, he had been president of the National Recovery Administration [NRA] local union but was fired in 1933); Orlovsky was removed from office in 1940 by the SWOC district director for violating the contract (1942:61). "Stanley's leadership was essential to the establishment of the union against bitter resistance, but after it had been fully accepted by management such leadership was a handicap to the development of cooperative union-management relations. His expulsion was sustained by the SWOC national officers." Kollros says that this rationale looked on the surface like a plan to get rid of the thousands of rank-and-file unionists who "hated" management and wanted to carry on the "class struggle" against a management that was far from cooperative. Although Kollros backs off in the end, his initial evaluation is closer to the truth (1998:404; Nelson 2001:267). This patronizing definition of union democracy and the goals of the union in general justified the most egregious violations of democracy. Some representative cases will be given here.

In 1942, Joe Germano, the director of District 31 (Calumet region), had become distinctly unpopular. He was not only an import from the outside, but more anti-communist and conservative than many others in the district, as well as an alcoholic. Union pioneer and Left sympathizer (although hardly a Communist), George Patterson was convinced to run against Germano for the directorship. Both Bittner and Murray threatened him, the latter telling him he was destroying the unity of the union (Kollros 1998:413). In his autobiography, *Union Man*, McDonald brags about his role in fixing the election. At the 1942 convention, McDonald saw red because "our candidate, Joseph Germano, was in trouble. He was being challenged by a man who had consistently followed a Marxist line and whom we believed to be a Communist. The challenger had lost an eye in the Memorial Day Massacre and was looked on as a hero by a good many union members." After getting the okay from Murray, McDonald got the District 31 delegates to stall for time. He then rounded up delegates from outside the district, including members of his own auditing staff to enter the meeting and vote for Germano. "When we had enough to swing the election, I nodded," and a vote was called. "Germano won by a whisper" (McDonald 1969:158).

In 1945, Patterson was again convinced to run. By this time Germano had consolidated most of the staff around him, and his position seemed quite strong. Nevertheless, his thugs broke up meetings supporting Patterson, threatened to kill some of his supporters, and in the end got the draft board to induct Patterson into the army, six weeks before the election. Germano won easily, although McDonald claims that he had helped fix the election by sending thousands of blank ballots to "Germano's people" (Kollros 1998:416–18).

Violence against oppositionists was a common feature of the Murray regime, not exceptional as some apologists have claimed. At the 1948 convention, Nick Migas, an open Communist official and former president of Local 1010 of Inland Steel, handed out a signed leaflet critical of the Murray leadership's role in the previous strike. When Migas rose to speak, pro-Murray staffers "drowned him out." He was then taken outside by Murray's personal bodyguard, where thugs beat him, injuring him severely (Kollros 1998:440). But such violence, bad as it was, was not reserved for the left. Germano thug and staffer Norman Harris commonly went around beating up and threatening to kill those who were not full supporters. The numerous complaints against Harris to the district and to Murray disappeared or ended up vindicating Harris. When Harris tried to interfere with the elected tellers in a 1950 local election, Harris beat one of the complainants, knocking him out, breaking his jaw in two places, breaking three ribs, and causing a concussion. Charges were filed against Harris, but he was vindicated by the district (Kollros 1998:438).

Such violence against dissenters continued in the union long after most of the Communists had been driven out, not only under Murray but after Murray died and McDonald had taken over as president, even against those who were not ostensibly on the left. In 1956, a Dues Protest Committee was officially organized in Pennsylvania, a move spearheaded by three presidents of some of the largest locals there. When the dues protestors decided to run candidates for national union office, their meetings were frequently broken up violently by gangs of staffers, at times led by their district directors (Ulman 1962:140–43). After the McDonald slate won in 1958, retribution was in order (1962:147). Nicolas Mamula, a leader of the dues protest movement and president of the Aliquippa local, was removed from office, fined, and forbidden to run for office for five years. Anthony Tomko, president of a five-thousand-member local in McKeesport, Pennsylvania, was beaten by four "ushers" after he refused to stop circulating anti-McDonald literature on the convention floor. Donald C. Rarick, also president of a large local, claimed to have been beaten by a group of thugs led by staffers. Secretary of Labor Mitchell said it was "very unfortunate that in a democratic union such as this acts of violence take place." McDonald poo-pooed the charges, saying that any fighting that had taken place was initiated by the dissidents (Ulman 1962:148).

Some have argued that the high salaries of officers in many American unions both gave them a vested interest in holding onto their positions at all costs and put them in a different social class, far removed from and with little sympathy for the plight of their constituents. Officials in the USWA were among the highest-paid in any industrial unions. Ulman reports that in 1956, the president made $50,000 per year, other national officers $35,000, and district directors $16,000 (1962:151). Steelworkers, according to Jack Stieber, in 1956, made between $1.82 and $3.71 an hour; only the most skilled, an extremely tiny portion of the workforce, were paid the latter amount, which roughly translates into a yearly income of between $3,500 and $7,000, assuming fifty-two weeks of pay (1959:243).

Of course, not all commentators have been taken in by the veneer of democracy and liberalism projected by the USWA and its academic and government supporters. Stanley Aronowitz writes:

> For five years after the formation of SWOC, it was difficult for the membership to achieve a real voice in the affairs of the union, since most of the funds for the organizing drives came from the CIO . . . The Steelworkers were to become almost unique among the CIO unions in the absolutism of its bureaucratic methods of operation, its lack of social vision, and its fervent anxiety to please the corporate heads of the industry. (1991:235)

The early Socialist and trade union leader Eugene V. Debs (1905) said more graphically that "the role of AFL leaders was to chloroform the working class while the ruling class went through its pockets"—a judgment the reader may or may not feel applied to the Murray leadership. An interesting book entitled *Misleaders of Labor*, written by Foster in 1927 and published by the Trade Union Education League, which Foster led, contains lengthy astute insights into the transformation of the underpaid and harassed union pioneers into representatives "seeking first of all to protect [the union's] fat sinecures [and having] distinct group, if not class, interests in conflict with those of the workers . . . Naturally the well-paid trade union leaders exert every effort to retain their positions, against the strivings of other hungry office seekers and in the face of rank and file revolts." According to Foster, "Michels explains in great detail the many devices used by Social Democratic bureaucrats to maintain themselves in office, such as, making themselves technically indispensable[,] . . . playing themselves up in the organizational press and playing down their opponents[, and] . . . developing a rigid centralism, overstepping the mandates of the rank and file" (1927: 273). "But American trade union leaders use not only most of the tricks, but many more of which he never dreamed. To hang on to their jobs they appeal to the gun and knife, they make open alliances with the employers and state against the workers, and they ruthlessly suppress democracy in the organizations" (Foster 1927:273–74; also Stepan-Norris and Zeitlin 2002:57).

I have tried to show in this chapter that the common view of Philip Murray as a democratic, pro–civil rights trade union leader is wrong, an ideological distortion of history. First, I wish to stress the implications for the South, then address whether it could have been otherwise. The promise of the early SWOC was destroyed, even more than that of the UMWA. While Mine Mill and the coal miners' union at times advanced the cause of interracial solidarity and the struggle for civil rights, which was so crucial to the southern labor movement, the steelworkers, as I have documented, actively undermined it. Their de facto alliance with the KKK, their refusal to press civil rights and anti-discrimination issues, and even the support of some of their officials in Alabama for the openly racist Bull Conner constituted a break from this project. Their refusal to confront the white supremacist South and the white chauvinist attitudes of many white workers made labor support for civil rights near impossible. The white chauvinism of the Murray leadership and its continuing support for the white supremacist discriminatory policies of the steel companies accentuated the divisions among steelworkers, weakened the union, and emboldened white supremacists throughout the South, especially in Alabama.

Further, the activities of the leadership made the steelworkers, unlike the mineworkers, less able and willing to support the struggles of other workers. If they had been more democratic, more willing to engage in struggles, more civil rights–oriented, they might have pushed the woodworkers to be more committed to organizing in the South. If they had allied with Mine Mill, the National Maritime Union (NMU), and the Food, Tobacco, Agricultural, and Allied Workers (FTA), they might have acted more like the Farm Equipment Workers (FE) and the UPWA in the South, and because of the far greater numbers of steelworkers in the South, they might have had a bigger impact. In the end, it was the unwillingness of the Communists to challenge these developments that made the outcome that much more probable.

The question naturally arises as to why Foster and other leading Communists during the 1930s did not recognize the Murray machine for what it was and act accordingly. I will take a look at these and other related questions more fully in the chapter on the Communist Party. But I wish to give one caveat in advance: it was not just the liberal anti-communists who facilitated the whitewashing of Philip Murray and the steelworkers' union; the Communists played at least as important a role, especially during the 1936–49 period.

The national leadership of the Communist Party accepted without challenge the removal of Communist and African-American leaders from important posts and their loss of influence in the union. Communists had been the major and most successful organizers in virtually every major steel center, Chicago/Calumet, Pittsburgh, Alabama, and a good many other places. Their acquiescence without a struggle was a direct result of the desire of the Communist national leadership to maintain the popular front "center–left" coalition in which they played a subservient role. Even worse, their glorification of Murray's leadership was more dishonest than even that of his liberal hagiographers. They thus paved the way for the dominance of right-wing, racially insensitive business unionists in union after union, destroying the possibilities for southern organizing, as well as a national, independent union movement. These themes will be explored in more detail in my chapter on the Communist Party.

5

Paul Bunyan and the "Frozen Logger"

The Mystery of Woodworker Unionism in the South

"We Social Democrats always miss our opportunities."
Told to the author in 1986 by a leader of the West German Social
Democratic Party

"The Frozen Logger"

As I sat down one evening,
'Twas in a small café,
A forty year old waitress
To me these words did say:

I see that you're a logger,
And not a common bum,
For no one but a logger
Stirs coffee with his thumb.

I once had a logger lover,
There's none like him today.
If you poured whisky on it,
He'd eat a bale of hay.

He never shaved his whiskers,
from off of his horny hide,
He'd just drive them in with a hammer,
and bite them off inside.

My logger came to see me,
'Twas on a winter's day;
He held me in a fond embrace
That broke three vertebrae.

The weather tried to freeze him,
It did its very best;
At a hundred degrees below zero,
He buttoned up his vest.

It froze clear down to China,
It froze to the stars above;
At a thousand degrees below zero,
It froze my logger love.

And so I lost my logger,
And to this cafe I've come,
And it's here I wait for someone
To stir coffee with his thumb.

By James Stevens

Introduction

In the United States, workers in many industries have had their songs and mythical figures. The work songs of cotton plantation slaves have garnered much attention. Railroads, the first national industry, had songs about Casey Jones, an engineer who

The Southern Key. Michael Goldfield, Oxford University Press (2020) © Michael Goldfield
DOI: 10.1093/oso/9780190079321.001.0001

"steel driving man" who died drilling dynamite holes for the railroad faster than a new state-of-the-art steam drill. John Lee Hooker, the blues legend who spent much of his adult life in Detroit, sang about the automobile assembly lines. Some of the more heroic figures, however, worked in the extractive industries, including the coal miner who hand-loaded "16 Tons" of number 9 coal. Woodworkers, too, had their legendary heroes. The most famous was Paul Bunyan, the mythical giant logger (featured on a 1996 postage stamp), who allegedly dug the Great Lakes so his Blue Ox, Babe, would be able to drink water. Not as well known, but equally indicative, is the song "Frozen Logger."

Southern woodworkers are at the center of our story, and it will be my goal, while honoring the grains of truth in the myths, to separate fact from fiction. The woodworking industry was the second most important industry in the South during the 1930s and 1940s, and if we include related industries, it was perhaps as significant as the textile industry, which was generally regarded as the premier southern industry for much of the twentieth century.[1] Unlike textile employees, who were overwhelmingly white, logging and sawmill workers in the South were as likely to be Black. Also, in contrast to textile workers, woodworkers tended to be more easily organized. Further, the International Woodworkers of America (IWA) was the first CIO union where a concerted attack by forces outside the union itself dislodged a popular, democratically elected Communist leadership that was committed to organizing the South. Finally, as with the textile industry, but not mining, steel, and tobacco, the CIO completely failed to organize the majority of southern woodworkers. The question is why? For as Robert Dinwiddie observed many decades ago, the failure of the CIO to unionize southern woodworkers during the 1930s and 1940s not only suffers from a "lack of scholarly scrutiny" but is one of the "great unsolved mysteries of U.S. labor history" (1980:3). I should add that it is a mystery with enormous consequences for American society.

The Lumber Industry: By the Numbers

In the country as a whole, between 1910 and 1960, the number of workers employed in the core of the wood industry varied between a half million and 600,000 workers, overwhelmingly male (Table 5.1). The largest concentration of these

---

[1] Adolph Germer, a central national CIO operative, claims that at the time Operation Dixie (OD) was launched in 1946, Alan Haywood, director of organization for the CIO, had no idea how large the wood industry was in the South. Germer claims that he proved with figures to Haywood that it was the largest, even bigger than the textile industry. Germer to Brown, March 4, 1946, OD collection, reel 10:491. None of this is to belie the worldwide significance of the cotton industry, as argued eloquently and in exquisite detail by Sven Beckert (2014).

Table 5.1 **Logging and Sawmill Workers, United States and Canada, 1910–60 (Thousands)**

	U.S.	South	South	Northwest	Northwest	Canada
Year	Total	Total	% of U.S. Total	Total	% of U.S. Total	Total
1910	576	272	47.3			
1920	586	264	45.1	108	18.4	144
1930	566	260	46.0	126	22.3	157
1940	512	327	63.8	131	25.6	150
1950	599	338	56.4	178	29.7	
1960	432	331	76.6			

Sources: Historical Statistics of the United States: Colonial Times to Present, part 1, series D, 233–682, pp. 140–45.
Canada Year Book, 1925–1945.

workers was in the South, with approximately 260,000 workers in 1930 and 338,000 workers by 1950. This compares with the concentration in the Northwest, the unionized center of the industry, with 125,000 in 1930 and 178,000 by 1950, although the number of board-feet produced and profits were similar in the two regions. Even adding the important Canadian woodworkers in British Columbia to the Northwest figures does not make the number of employees higher than that of the South. In 1930, a majority of southern woodworkers were African-American, with some states (including Mississippi, Louisiana, Florida, Georgia, and South Carolina) having even higher percentages. The total number of employees is comparable to that in the southern textile industry during this period. If we include the broader industry beyond logging and sawmills, including finished lumber, plywood, shingles, barrels and pallets, pulpwood and paper, and wood byproducts, most important of which were resins and turpentine, and extend it even further to include wood furniture, with its roughly 200,000 workers nationwide, it could be argued that the woodworking industry was just as important in the South as the textile industry during this period (see Tables 5.2 and 5.3). For figures on comparative wages across industries and differences between the Northwest and the South, see Tatum (1970:15–16).[2]

---

[2] It is worth noting, of course, the distinctions between the generally more stable lives of sawmill workers and the more nomadic lifestyles of lumberjacks, who many writers have described as a "distinctive breed" (Jensen 1945:3; see the somewhat romantic account of lumberjacks in an earlier period in New England in Pike 1967). Tattam also notes the sharp distinctions between lumberjacks and sawmill workers (1970:2).

Table 5.2 **Lumber Production by Region, 1869–54 (Millions of Board Feet)**

Year	Total U.S. Production	South Production	% of Total	Northeast Production	% of Total	Midwest Production	% of Total	Far West Production	% of Total
1869	12,756	1,898	14.9	4,443	34.8	5,795	45.4	620	4.9
1879	18,125	3,448	19	4,511	24.9	9,319	51.4	847	4.7
1889	27,039	6,496	24	5,271	19.5	12,811	47.4	2,461	9.1
1899	35,078	13,839	39.5	5,490	15.7	12,259	34.9	3,490	9.9
1909	44,510	23,854	53.6	4,874	11	7,543	16.9	8,239	18.5
1919	34,552	18,287	52.9	2,443	7.1	3,662	10.6	10,160	29.4
1929	38,745	18,415	47.5	1,577	4.1	2,700	7	16,053	41.4
1939	28,755	13,164	45.8	1,706	5.9	1,814	6.3	12,071	42
1947	35,404	14,749	41.7	2,136	6	2,182	6.2	16,337	46.1
1954	36,356	12,815	35.2	1,873	5.2	1,688	4.6	19,980	55

Source: John C. Howard, "The Negro in the Lumber Industry," in *Negro Employment in Southern Industry*, 4:10–11, , ed. Herbert R. Northrup and Richard L. Rowan (1970), Philadelphia: Wharton School of Finance and Commerce, Industrial Research Unit.

Table 5.3 **Broader Wood-Related Industry Workers, 1910–50**

Year	Number (Thousands)
1910	749
1920	827
1930	839
1940	925
1950	1,113

The following categories are included: furniture and fixtures, laborers; furniture and fixtures, operatives; inspectors, scalers, and graders, log and lumber; lumbermen, raftsmen, and woodchoppers; misc. paper and pulp products, laborers; misc. paper and pulp products, operatives; misc. wood products, laborers; misc. wood products, operatives; paperboard containers and boxes, laborers; paperboard containers and boxes, o-peratives; pulp, paper, and paperboard mills, laborers; pulp, paper, and paperboard mills, operatives; sawmills, planing mills, and millwork, laborers; sawmills, planing mills, and millwork, operatives; and sawyers.

Source: *Historical Statistics of the United States: Colonial Times to 1970*, part 1, Bureau of the Census. U.S. Department of Commerce, 1975. series D, 233–682.

In eleven states in 1930—Washington, Oregon, California, Idaho, as well as the southern states of Mississippi, Arkansas, Louisiana, Florida, Virginia, Alabama, and Texas—woodworking employed more workers than any other industry. One-half of the wages in Washington and Oregon came from lumber; three-fourths in Mississippi, two-fifths in Louisiana, one-third in Florida, and one-quarter in Alabama were in timber and wood products (see Todes 1931:22).[3] In 1930, one-half of the world's lumber came from the country's 13,000 sawmills (Todes 1931:21; on methods of counting, see James 1946:120). Thus, it is a bit surprising that so much attention has been lavished by historians and other researchers on the textile industry and so little on the lumber industry. Even more surprising is that while there have been hundreds of books on the largely unsuccessful southern textile organizing, there have been barely a handful on the area's woodworking union drives. Woodworking unionism remains, as Jerry Lembcke noted as far back as 1978, "surprisingly under-researched" (1978:2).[4]

Background of Industry and Organization: The Demand for Wood Products

Wood and wood products have been an important part of the North American economy since the very beginning of colonial settlement. The early North American colonists found extensive strands of trees all along the Atlantic coast. Some of this wood was used locally, for homes, fences, and other necessities. The tallest trees, however, at times found a spot on the world market, where they provided masts for the largest ships of the world, including British Men of War. Eventually North American wood would be worked and sold by colonial craftsmen, not only as masts, but as hulls for boats, casks, barrels, and furniture. With extensive economic development in the United States in the nineteenth century, lumber was widely used for railroad ties, mine timbers, furniture, housing, and commercial construction. Profits were to be made from the sale of raw logs, as well as wooden furniture, paper, and various wood byproducts.[5]

[3] Exact numbers of employees differ in various sources, in good part because of different schemes for totaling the large variety of occupational and product categories and supporting types of work. For a slightly different but comparable set of figures, see John Howard (1970:15).

[4] Among the few more recent works are those by Jones (2000, 2005) and Goings (2005, forthcoming).

[5] I have relied heavily on the economic analysis of the industry provided in Zaremba (1963), which I have supplemented with a host of government publications and other works cited. For an informative discussion of the development of the industry from one oriented primarily toward local production to one geared toward regional, national, and even international markets, see James (1946).

By the 1930s, the uses for wood had changed a bit, but it was still as Todes argues,

> one of the basic raw materials of industrial society. Millions live in wooden houses, sleep in wooden beds, eat at wooden tables, write with wooden pencils, use wooden matches and toothpicks, read books and newspapers made from pulpwood, are intimidated by policemen with wooden clubs and are finally buried in wooden coffins. (1931:22)

Wood was also used extensively during the 1930s for building construction, railways, mines, airplanes, and automobiles; wooden poles, then as now, were used for telephone wires. Yet as a product, it often led a beleaguered existence, for even in 1930 there was no major commercial or industrial use for lumber for which there was not a satisfactory substitute (Todes 1931:22–24; James 1946:119; for 1929, Lembcke and Tattam 1984:18).

To understand the industry in the South, it is important to briefly look at the industry as a whole and its unique patterns of development. There are several reasons for this. First, its nature, patterns of industrial organization, labor intensity, organization of work, and attitudes toward unions were common structural features of the industry everywhere and set patterns of industrial relations that endured, both throughout American history and across regions. Second, the owners of timber and lumber companies often migrated with the supply of raw forestland, giving an unusual degree of continuity compared with certain other, more indigenously developed industries like textiles. Third, the actions of the unions centered in the Northwest had important effects on the trajectory of union organization in the South.

The Nature of the Industry

As the industry matured, it suffered from both intense competition and large-scale overproduction, the latter being typical of many natural resource industries without regulation, including coal, oil, and various types of metal mining (e.g., copper). Yet it also had its own problems. Even more than other extractive industries, wood required enormous tracts of virgin land. The primitive way the capital accumulation of timberlands took place in this country is central to the story of political and economic development in the United States. If the wood industry were the only example we had, Balzac's conjecture that "behind every great fortune lies a crime" would be an iron law of science.[6] Already by 1880, half of the almost one billion acres of public land were owned by several hundred individuals and corporations, a good portion acquired by fraud and corruption. Originally much of this land was earmarked for homesteaders. Yet Congress and state legislatures often accepted bribes in order to

---

[6] The quote, variously translated, can be found, among other places, in Balzac's *Père Goriot* (1917:142).

let corporations acquire extensive acreage at prices well below market. One company obtained thousands of acres of pine timber in the Great Lake states allotted for homesteaders by filing names obtained from the Chicago and St. Paul city directories (Todes 1931:12). Trainloads of individuals were often brought in to claim homesteads, which were then turned over by the thousands to timber companies. Sometimes companies illegally set up sawmills on public lands and proceeded to cut the timber, actions that were usually overlooked by public officials. A resolution introduced in the House of Representatives in 1910 denouncing Weyerhauser for fraud and for intimidating large numbers of settlers into giving up their lands was killed in committee. The Supreme Court in a series of decisions reversed attempts to prosecute those who had stolen public lands (Todes 1931:13). Railroad land grants were also used to appropriate (often illegally) huge tracts of valuable timberland. In 1910, for example, the Southern Pacific Railroad controlled 682 miles of valuable forests from Sacramento to Portland, 50 miles on each side of the track (Todes 1931:15). Ruth Allen similarly documents large-scale theft of timber on school lands in Texas, as well as undervaluation and fraud in the sale of public lands to timber interests (1961:20). Similar stories can be told many times over, in all parts of the country where valuable forests have existed. Drobney tells a parallel story about lands in Florida (1997:63–72). For the South in general, see Woodward (1951:111–15).

Thus, much of the wealth of the lumber industry came minimally from unethical dealings with government officials, and often from outright illegal activity. Given the existence of the industry in largely rural, often frontier areas outside of the easy reach of legal authorities and the watchful eye and outrage of urban working-class populations, the wood industry has always had something of a rogue attitude, particularly toward its workers. (In Texas, no major city reported as many as five hundred employees in the industry; no town with a population of ten thousand or more reported a thousand or more wood employees; Allen 1961:30.) Unlike more modern industries based on technology, innovation, and expanding markets, the lumber industry has always tried to make money the old-fashioned way, by under-paying and overworking its labor force, with little change in the production process.

Although no small number of major companies controlled the industry, several larger companies had an extensive degree of influence. Weyerhauser, for example, during the 1930s, owned 50% of all the timber in the state of Idaho, 37% in Western Washington, and 15% in Oregon (Todes 1931:16). Despite the importance and influence of the big producers, however, including Weyerhauser and Kirby, the industry was more competitive than other large industries, contrary to the claims of certain more populist writers. As Zaremba argues, "The lumber industry is one of the few large American industries which approximates the classical conception of competition" (1963:7) Despite the existence of some very large companies, the concentration of ownership was among the lowest in any industry in the country. According to a congressional study, in 1954 sawmills and planing mills ranked 435th out of 448 industries in terms of the share of the value of shipments of the top four, eight, and twenty largest producers (Zaremba 1963:19). This contrasts with the arguments of Todes (1931:54–69) and Lembcke (1978:37), both of whom suggest a high degree of concentration of capital in the industry. In addition, the lumber industry had more establishments than any other industry, with both a higher rate of entry and higher mortality than any other industry examined at the time (Zaremba 1963:20). The reasons for this will be examined shortly, but the bottom line is the existence of a great deal of competition, which was particularly difficult to control given the continual entry and exit of numerous producers (James 1946:121).

Prices in the industry, like those in most raw material industries, were volatile. Almost half of the lumber produced went to new construction and maintenance, with another 7 or 8% going to furniture, industries whose demands varied greatly (Zaremba 1963:36–37, figs.; 95–96, appendixes; ch. 7 generally). Although the largest producers invested in and developed modern technologies, making them far more efficient (faster, less wasteful, and less labor-intensive) than smaller producers, the specific characteristics of their raw materials often made it difficult for them to consistently use the technology to competitive advantage. In contrast to coal and oil, even in the best of circumstances trees are widely dispersed geographically. With the wanton destruction of most of the available old-growth forests, trees had become smaller (bigger strands/stumps being more efficiently utilized), more remote, and less concentrated, making their harvesting a more time-consuming and less efficient operation. Further, the most efficient way to process timber is to have a mill as close as possible to where the trees are cut, thus minimizing the cost of transporting unprocessed logs. Thus, despite the improved technological efficiency of large installations, the increased overhead (including the building of temporary rail spurs) often made small producers, particularly in a time of upward demand, highly competitive (Todes 1931:29–30; Zaremba 1963:21, 26).

Because of these problems, from 1899 to 1954 productivity in the wood industry increased to a lesser degree than that in virtually any other major industry (Kendrick, Lee, and Lomask 1976; Kendrick and Grossman 1980). Productivity increased on average during this period only 1.1% per year, compared with an average of 2.2% per year for eighty industries surveyed. Thus, despite the enormous technological advances and the fact that the smaller mills had both lower productivity and more waste than the larger mills, the increases in the distance between mill and timber largely offset the productivity advantages of the larger installations (Todes 1931; Zaremba 1961; Kendrick et al. 1976).

These characteristics, making for a high degree of competition in an unstable market, quite naturally led to the classic problems of capitalist overproduction. Additional industry-specific problems, however, were exacerbating overproduction. There was strong pressure on many producers to liquidate their holdings as quickly as possible. In many places, for example, owners of large tracts paid high taxes on uncut land. Further, a significant percentage of land was rented or on contract, and time limits were set on how long the renter might cut timber. Thus, companies were under pressure to cut the maximum number of trees before their rights expired. Together, these factors accentuated the boom-or-bust quality of the industry.

Finally, the wood industry is one of the most labor-intensive in the whole country. By some methods of calculation, wages constituted as much as 60% of the final cost of producing lumber. By a different method of calculation, the 1939 Census of Manufacturers rated labor costs in the wood industry the highest of major industries, with 5.1% for tobacco, 5.9% for oil refining, 9.5% for chemicals (to take some other important southern industries), and 27.6% for timber. Given the stagnant growth in productivity, the intense competition, and the high percentage of costs that went into labor, it is no wonder that the opposition of employers to unions has always been extremely intense. As Todes notes:

> Union organization in all these regions has been marked by some of the most bitter struggles in labor history and has been fought with bloodshed and murder. Neither the Industrial Workers of the World nor the American Federation of Labor has been successful in organizing unions able to cope with the powerful opposition and attacks of the employers, who have used all the traditional means of strike breaking— espionage, injunction, terrorism, and frame-up. (1931:152)

Horror stories of employer-led murder and brutality abound in every part of the country, yet the South was in many respects the worst. For as Industrial Workers of the World (IWW) leader, Vincent St. John noted, "extending the organization of lumber workers in the southern lumber districts involves a contest with the employing class in a section of the country where the employers have held undisputed sway since the American continent was first settled" (Todes 1931:171). When the workers were African-American, almost any degree of violence against them was deemed acceptable, as when more than a hundred striking Black Louisiana sugarworkers were massacred in 1887 by state militia and white vigilantes (Foner 1988:573, 595).

Geographic Movements

The geographic movement of the industry, both within regions of North America and from one region to the other, is one of the industry's defining characteristics, contrasting with that of virtually every other type of enterprise, particularly in its rapidity of migration. Production figures by region tell a part of the story. They fail, however, to show the degree of devastation within regions, and the natural waste and human dismemberment left behind. Lumbering moved first through the Northeast (primarily Maine, New York, and Pennsylvania), the main sites from early colonial times through the Civil War. In the late nineteenth century, railroads enabled timber barons to level the Great Lakes region (primarily Michigan, Wisconsin, and Minnesota, roughly in that order), practically denuding it by the turn of the century what seemed initially to be unlimited strands of trees, leaving barren land, abandoned towns, and jobless workers in their wake. The industry then moved South, where the rapid growth of pine made timber a bit more of a renewable resource, and later moved to the Northwest, including British Columbia, Canada. These two areas were the main site of the industry during our period of concern and continue to be so to this day.

Conditions of Work

In the sawmills, planing mills, and byproduct plants, the division of labor reduced most tasks to unskilled labor, with less than 10% of workers (mostly sawyers) being classified as skilled. In these mills, as well as in the logging operations, the work required great strength, the jobs being mostly unskilled and hard. Todes describes conditions in the sawmills as follows:

> Workers must have physical strength, steady nerves, and alertness to endure the exhaustive speedup, the terrific noise of the machines, the screech of the saw and repetition of the same dull motions in the monotonous daily grind . . . Since the mills require strong physique, endurance and energy, a majority of the young workers range from 16 to 21 years of age. These young workers are given the jobs of older men at lower wages and are driven at greater speed. (1931:80)

Art Shields describes the speedup of African-American workers in the Great Southern Lumber Company, Bogalusa, Louisiana:

> What speed! I saw a flat car loaded in about 12 minutes, a pair of Negroes singing together as they dragged on the chains that steadied the logs swinging through the air . . .
> "Watch those black boys step," grinned Supt. Carter as the steel gang laid track for a logging railroad line across the highway where our car was halted . . . I saw husky Negroes swing 200-pound ties to their shoulders, a man to a tie and rush at a trot to the track line. Then the gang would seize a rail, all together, and toss it into place with a song.

The task is to lay 30 rails a day. Only the strongest and young ones can stand the pace of a logging track-laying gang. (Shields, in Todes 1931:128–29)

Safety

As Lembcke and Tattam argue, "Woodworkers have traditionally suffered the most dangerous and degrading working conditions in North American industry; death and dismemberment routinely visited the woods" (1984:vii). Figures compiled by the Department of Labor confirm this statement. Logging and sawmills had the highest rate of disabling injuries of all industries in the United States. Injury rates in other wood-related industries, including furniture, plywood, and planing, was also near the top.

Writers have often attempted to sidestep the dangers by writing about the romantic lives of loggers. Falling trees and limbs, rolling logs, broken lines and cables, explosives, and powerful saws, as the accident figures indicate, clearly took their toll. Numerous impressions gave substance to these data. As Todes noted, "One rarely meets a shingle worker who has not lost one or more fingers, some having lost hands and arms. 'It's our trade mark,' a shingle worker cynically remarked" (1931:137).

Wages

For this hard, dangerous work there was scant compensation. Lumberworkers had among the lowest hourly and weekly wages of workers in any industry. The regional differentiation was also greater than in any other industry, with southern lumberworkers making barely 60% of the hourly wage paid in the West. Their 1937 hourly wages of just under 33 cents an hour and their average weekly wages of $15.62 were the lowest of any non-agricultural industry in the South (Table 5.4).

Living Conditions

Finally, the competitive pressures of the industry combined with the transient nature of production meant that employers, especially in the logging camps, attempted to scrimp heavily on the costs of living conditions for their workers. While no hard data exist, virtually all observers seem to agree that the situation was abominable. Henry David Thoreau, in a generalization that could suffice for the industry as a whole, aptly sums up the company-provided living conditions for lumberworkers in Maine: "There were the camps and the hovel for the cattle, hardly distinguishable,

Table 5.4 **Regional Wage Differentials by Industry, September 1937**

Industry	Region	Average Hourly Earnings	Average Weekly Earnings	Average Hours Worked/Week
Cotton	East	$0.527	$20.34	38.6
Cotton	South	$0.424	$15.52	36.6
Foundries and machine shops	East	$0.745	$30.36	40.7
Foundries and machine shops	South	$0.640	$25.13	39.3
Foundries and machine shops	Middle West	$0.750	$30.60	40.8
Foundries and machine shops	Far West	$0.752	$29.93	39.8
Furniture	East	$0.569	$23.91	42.1
Furniture	South	$0.422	$19.28	45.7
Furniture	Middle West	$0.552	$23.80	43.1
Furniture	Far West	$0.637	$25.61	40.2
Lumber	East	$0.457	$20.96	45.9
Lumber	South	$0.327	$15.62	47.8
Lumber	Middle West	$0.485	$20.44	42.1
Lumber	Far West	$0.749	$30.03	40.1
Electricity	East	$0.893	$37.63	42.1
Electricity	South	$0.643	$28.22	43.9
Electricity	Middle West	$0.882	$37.12	42.1
Electricity	Far West	$0.844	$35.30	41.8
Gas	East	$0.738	$30.26	41.0
Gas	South	$0.506	$20.82	41.2
Gas	Middle West	$0.685	$29.02	42.4
Gas	Far West	$0.675	$29.01	43.0
Paper and pulp	East	$0.619	***	***
Paper and pulp	South	$0.555	***	***

(*continued*)

Table 5.4 **Continued**

Industry	Region	Average Hourly Earnings	Average Weekly Earnings	Average Hours Worked/Week
Paper and pulp	Middle West	$0.618	***	***
Paper and pulp	Far West	$0.723	***	***

Survey included 1,675 companies with 741,025 workers.

Source: M. Ada Beney, *Differentials in Industrial Wages and Hours in the United States*, National Industrial Conference Board Studies no. 238 (1938).

except that the latter had no chimneys" (1972:19). The romantic songs and stories about loggers tended to obscure the desperate situation of woodworkers in the popular imagination.

Peculiarities of the Southern Wood Industry

While the living and working conditions of woodworkers across North America had much in common, the situations of southern woodworkers had certain distinct characteristics. I have already noted the low pay and interracial nature of the labor force. It is also important to note the existence of peonage.

Peonage and closely related convict labor were both widespread in the South. Although convict leasing was mostly gone by the early 1920s, peonage, both in agriculture and in certain extractive industries, of which wood was the most prominent, existed through the 1960s.[7]

Peonage, also called debt slavery or debt servitude, is a system whereby an employer compels a worker to pay off a debt with work. Legally, peonage was outlawed by the U.S. Congress when it passed an anti-peonage law on March 2, 1867, based on the Thirteenth Amendment. However, after Reconstruction, many southern Black men were swept into peonage by different methods, and the system was not eradicated until the 1960s.

---

[7] The definitive general work on peonage is Daniel (1972; see his 1970a thesis for additional information). The definitive work on convict labor is Lichtenstein (1996). For Alabama convicts, Curtin (2000) is equally penetrating. See also Blackmon (2008). There are numerous articles on both. These include Shaprio (1964); Goodnow (1915); Drobney (1995); Shofner (1981); Coles and Hughes (1969), Huff (1944); P. Daniel (1970b); and Holmes (1893). In addition, the literature on the wood industry in the South at times discusses instances and general information on peonage. I have drawn on much of this material for the above summary.

Table 5.5 **Percentage of African-American Woodworkers by State**

	1910	1920	1930	1940*	1950	1960
Alabama	47.4	56.7	52.1	43.6	50.0	46.1
Arkansas	43.3	43.1	40.3	32.9	36.2	30.8
Florida	67.7	66.9	71.0	51.8	58.3	46.3
Georgia	67.2	69.2	70.1	54.3	57.9	55.1
Kentucky	10.2	11.1	7.6	5.1	4.8	4.1
Louisiana	57.1	59.9	58.0	52.6	62.7	53.9
Mississippi	61.7	58.8	60.2	56.4	61.2	54.6
North Carolina	52.5	44.5	50.5	44.9	49.2	44.1
South Carolina	76.2	60.0	71.5	64.8	71.6	64.0
Tennessee	22.2	25.4	22.4	17.6	16.5	16.8
Texas	41.8	42.5	45.6	33.5	44.4	35.3
Virginia	56.0	50.2	51.4	46.6	53.9	47.3

* Census data for this year do not disaggregate African-Americans from other non-whites, so the percentages are skewed upward slightly. All other indications show that non-whites who were not African-American made up less than 1% of southern woodworkers.

Sources: *Thirteenth Census of the United States Taken in the Year 1910*, vol. 4: *Population, 1910*, Occupation Statistics, table 7, Bureau of the Census, U.S. Department of Commerce, 1910.

Fourteenth Census of the United States Taken in the Year 1920, vol. 4: *Population, 1920, Occupations*, Bureau of the Census, U.S. Department. of Commerce.

Fifteenth Census of the United States: 1930, vol. 4: *Occupations, By States*, table 11, Bureau of the Census, U.S. Department of Commerce.

Sixteenth Census of the United States: 1940, vol. 3: *Population, The Labor Force*, table 20, Bureau of the Census, U.S. Department of Commerce, 1943.

Census of Population: 1950, vol. 2: *Characteristics of the Population*, table 77, Bureau of the Census, U.S. Department of Commerce, 1953.

Census of Population: 1960, vol. 1: *Characteristics of the Population*, table 129, Bureau of the Census, U.S. Department of Commerce, 1961.

The methods of entrapment were varied. Blackmon summarizes:

> In some cases, employers advanced workers some pay or initial transportation costs, and workers willingly agreed to work without pay in order to pay it off. Sometimes those debts were quickly paid off, and a fair wage worker/employer relationship established . . . In many more cases, however, workers became indebted to planters (through sharecropping loans), merchants (through credit), or company stores (through living expenses). Workers were often unable to re-pay the debt and found

themselves in a continuous work-without-pay cycle . . . But the most
corrupt and abusive peonage occurred in concert with southern state
and county government. In the South, many black men were picked
up for minor crimes or on trumped-up charges, and, when faced with
staggering fines and court fees, forced to work for a local employer who
would pay their fines for them. Southern states also leased their convicts
en mass to local industrialists. The paperwork and debt record of individual prisoners was often lost, and these men found themselves trapped.
(Public Broadcasting System 2012)

Peonage was especially prevalent in those wood and wood-related industries that
few free laborers were willing to work in, especially the turpentine industry (where
the fumes were often toxic) and certain logging operations, for example logging of cy-
press trees, which mainly grew in muddy, snake-infested swamps. Daniel claims that
the overwhelming majority of employees in the turpentine and logging industries in
Georgia around 1905 were indebted Blacks, that is, peons. As late as 1951, an attorney
testified in court that peonage was quite common in the Georgia wood industry; he
had contacted the FBI and Justice Department concerning a dozen or so cases, but
they had done nothing about it (Daniel 1972:186–87). Left-wing journalist Stetson
Kennedy claimed that there were still millions of peons in the South in the early
1950s (1952:3). An IWA organizer in North Carolina in 1952 found an arrangement
whereby a judge with stock in a lumber company released prisoners to a company
manager (Dinwiddie 1980:8). Harry Shapiro examined data on peonage in the South
and its lack of prosecution by the Justice Department into the 1960s (1964). From
1961 to 1963, according to Shapiro, 104 complaints were lodged with the Justice
Department (which clearly represented only a tiny percentage of actual instances).
Ninety-two were dropped immediately, with only two prosecutions. Shapiro lists
the worst states in order as California, Florida, Georgia, Alabama, Mississippi, and
Arkansas (1964:85). Daniel concludes, "At the height of the civil rights movement
the Justice Department remained remarkably insensitive to peonage and slavery
complaints" (1972:187).

The most extensive documentation of peonage and convict labor in the
lumber industry is that for Florida. Drobney argues, "It wasn't until the late 1920s
that convict leasing was outlawed in the state of Florida, and it wasn't until a
decade later that peonage began to disappear in the piney woods" (1995:198);
"at its worst the convict lease system in Florida's turpentine camps was lethal"
(1995:225). Convict labor was at times even worse than slavery, since employers
had no financial stake in keeping prisoners alive (1995:226). "Whipping was the
most common form of punishment" (1995:227). Other types of punishment included hanging prisoners by the thumbs and what we now call "waterboarding";
in Florida, the latter led to the death of many convicts (1995:229). The system

of torture and forced labor is strikingly similar to that under slavery (for vivid descriptions of how various forms of torture, including dismemberment and murder, were used to increase productivity under slavery, see Baptist 2014:138–42; Drobney 1997).[8]

Under pressure from their constituents, Louisiana officials ended the practice in 1901, Mississippi in 1906, Oklahoma in 1907, and Texas in 1910 (Drobney 1995:230; Woodward 1951:424). In 1913, convict leasing was still legal only in Alabama, Florida, and Georgia (1995:238). It was finally ended in Florida in 1923 after a prominent white South Dakota man was arrested for vagrancy and sent to work as a leased convict, where he was whipped to death. For additional horrors, including cases in which workers were murdered for allegedly not working fast enough, see Blackmon (2008:151–54; 242–43, 334, 354–55). Rather than viewing debt peonage as the dominant form of labor in southern industry (which it was not), it is best to see it as reflective of the sense of entitlement southern employers had toward their Black employees.[9] Debt peonage in industry, as opposed to agriculture, where it remained for decades a dominant form of labor relations in the South, was often a way station to the proletarianization of Black labor (Jensen 1945:84 mistakenly doubts that it was ever a factor in the southern lumber industry).

During the very early part of the twentieth century, Black (as well as white) woodworkers often moved back and forth between industrial work and agriculture (even sharecropper Nate Shaw, made famous first by Rosen 1969, then by Rosengarten 1974, worked periodically in the wood industry). As agriculture became less lucrative (or rather less able to sustain a minimal existence) during the 1910s, and the lumber industry expanded greatly by buying up much potential farmland, opportunities proved greater for workers in industrial work. As William Jones has noted, during 1870–1910, lumber grew faster than any other southern industry and by 1900 employed more workers, producing twice the value of the southern textile industry, three times that of coal (2005:1). Jones demonstrates in a careful analysis that by 1930 Black sawmill workers, and southern Black workers in general, were no longer single male nomads (or Black Ulysseses, as the literature describes

---

[8] Of course, in neither of these cases was torture scientifically administered under the aegis of psychological professionals, including leaders of the American Psychological Association, as it was under the George W. Bush administration, whose practice of inflicting torture on alleged terrorists certainly deserves severe punishment, not merely apologies (*New York Times,* July 11, 2015).

[9] What Harry Haywood calls the "shadow of the plantation" in the North (1948:66) was reflected in the attitudes of many white woodworkers there. When southern management from Weyerhauser took over the Willapa Harbor Lumber Mills in Raymond, Washington, in 1931, white workers there referred to the plant manager, J. W. Lewis from Louisiana, as a "slavedriver" who did not know how to deal with "white men." In contrast to the South, only 29 of Washington's 51,683 loggers and millworkers were Black (Egolf 1985:204). For an insightful discussion of the racial restrictions on Black lumberworkers in the South, see Sumpter (2011).

them), but stable proletarians settled in industrial settings, who were more likely to have families than be single (2005:21). By 1930, only a third of Black men remained in agriculture (2005:21). By 1934, only 4% of Black lumberworkers owned or rented a farm (2005:50). There were one million Black women at the time in personal and domestic service, and a significant number in sawmill towns. By 1930 in the South, 170,000 Black men worked in railroads and railroad repair, with 75,000 in mining. Black men held 60% of sawmill and planing jobs in the South between 1890 and 1930 (U.S. 1935:310–22; Jones 2005:21.) Black sawmill workers were in many cases both more stable and more skilled than their white counterparts, including those in the Northwest (Jones 2005:42). In certain cases, wood employers, in their efforts to recruit indebted sharecroppers and retain stable Black workforces, often opposed attempts to enforce peonage, occasionally bringing federal anti-peonage charges against employers who tried to "steal" back their former employees by force, based on their alleged unpaid debts (2005:166–67). As we have seen with Alabama coal companies, lumber companies often opposed the KKK harassment of their Black workers, since they could not afford to let racist terrorists deprive them of Black labor (2005:27).

William Jones innovatively traces the transition of laborers from single migrant woodworkers who often returned to agriculture periodically to stable proletarians, by an analysis of sawmill town cultural activities. When sawmills drew on migrant single men for their workforce, employers promoted "barrelhouses" for their employees' leisure activities. Barrelhouses were raucous, often bawdy, sometimes violent. Blues legend Robert Johnson was a regular performer in Mississippi barrelhouses (Jones 2005:62–70). When the workforce came to include more stable, married workers, employers curtailed barrelhouses and supported more family-friendly activities, including socials, churchgoing, Negro League baseball, and performances by less bawdy groups like the Rhythm Aces. Jones also makes clear in a critique of a large number of writers who have searched for and extolled a separate Black culture that employers were always involved, and much of the activities, even in the Deep South, were in various ways surprisingly interracial (2005:70–87), including trading of music and skills by Black and white musicians, even under the harshest of Jim Crow.

History of Unionism and Struggle

Compared with those in many other large industries, the labor struggles of woodworkers have been largely ignored by virtually all mainstream labor historians, especially in the South. Ray Marshall (superb in so many other respects) deals with the World War I era struggles, but has virtually nothing to say about, and has no data for, southern woodworkers during the 1930s and 1940s (1967:268, 303; see also Galenson 1983:22). This is baffling, given the importance of the industry to the region and nationally, although perhaps understandable. The much-studied coal miners, in contrast, provide an example of successful early unionism and militant struggle. Though the textile industry, organized in the North, was less successful in the South than wood, it was still considered the premier southern industry, touted as the key to the region's economic success and development. Because woodworkers in the South have been so understudied, general statements about them by many labor historians are often uninformed. For one thing, there is the popular romanticization of woodworkers, their supposed rugged, macho individualism, made popular in "Frozen Logger," sung by Ronnie Gilbert first with the Pete Seeger–led Almanac Singers (placed by the U.S. attorney general on the subversive activities list) and later with the Weavers. It is hard to imagine Paul Bunyan as an underpaid, overworked logger suffering a disabling industrial injury, with missing fingers and body parts, sleeping in a crowded flea-ridden bunk room, eating inedible food, who desperately wanted and needed a union.

Many labor historians have considered lumberworkers in general, and southern ones in particular, too individualistic to form stable unions. Vernon Jensen, who wrote one of the few in-depth early studies of woodworkers, is typical in this respect (1945:5). He reflects the prevailing consensus of labor historians that woodworkers were unable to form unions (Galenson 1983; Taft 1964; Marshall 1967). Robert Zieger's more recent, seemingly comprehensive treatment of the CIO hardly mentions woodworkers or the IWA, except in passing, nor do his two collections on southern labor (1990, 1995, 1996). Jensen asserts, "In the Lake States, during the 'boom era' of the eighties, there was a growth of unionism but it was sporadic because individualistically minded workers, immigrants, and part-time agriculturalists could not be successfully organized. On the other hand, intense opposition from employers, schooled in individualism, was one of the greatest obstacles to unionism" (1945:5). With respect to the Northeast: "The men cursed and grumbled about their lot and treatment, but they seldom, if ever thought of an organization. They were too individualistic to believe they could stand on their own feet and fight their own battles" (1945:41). And Galenseon notes, "The South, while a significant producer in the nineteen-thirties, was virtually devoid of lumber unionism, and plays no role in our story" (1983:380; see also Cary 1968).

As I have argued previously, such descriptions of unorganized workers have a long history among allegedly knowledgeable observers. Socialist Party leader Morris Hillquit, for example, describes the perception of Jewish cloak workers by Socialist and union organizers in 1910:

> Practically all were recent immigrants, prevalently Jews from Russia, Austria, and Romania with a sprinkling of Italians and other nationalities.

Their pay was miserable, their work hours were long, and their general
conditions of work and life were almost intolerable. Like most Jewish
workers they were long-suffering, meek, and submissive. But every once
in a while, they would flare up in an outburst of despair and revolt, and go
on strike. The strikes were spontaneous and without preparation or organization. The cloak workers were long the despair of professional and union
organizers, including my own circle of young Socialist propagandists. They
seemed hopelessly unorganizable on a permanent basis.

The change came in 1910. (1934:130–31)

The Jewish cloak workers eventually became the staunchest, most disciplined
of union supporters and a bastion of support for Socialist and Communist politics.
The descriptions of their docility, individualism, and resistance to unionization,
however, are not unlike those of woodworkers. Jews were not the only immigrants
thought to be unorganizable. Similar claims were later made about eastern European
immigrants during the Great Steel Strike of 1919, although these workers acquitted
themselves more admirably than most at the time.

Casting the net a bit wider, it may be instructive to look at the convincing, sometimes eloquent arguments given by scholars before 1960 as to why government
employees could not be organized into unions. They were white-collar, too professionally minded; their strikes were illegal and harshly punished; they had job
security unavailable to private sector workers; strikes against the government had
no public sympathy; and so on (Burton and Thomason 1988:14–15; Goldfield
1989:404–20). Government employees are today among the most militant, highly
organized of U.S. workers and are still approximately 30–40% unionized. Thus, it
should be clear that explanations about why a group is unlikely to form unions,
based largely on the fact that the group is not at the time organized, as government
employees were not prior to 1960, should be treated with some caution. Similarly,
before the 1960s, many scholars believed that women were less likely to join unions.
A typical remark from the industrial relations literature is that of Jack Barbash, who
writes, "Women workers, with notable exceptions, are not the material out of which
strong unions are typically built" (1964:105). In retrospect it is easy to see that such
assessments were based on stereotypes and prejudice, as events such as the militant
struggles of women schoolteachers (among the highpoints of labor struggles in the
2010s) and female factory workers, including those at the Watsonville Cannery in
California in the 1980s have shown (Barbash 1964:105; O'Connor 1950).[10]

The above are typical assessments that one encounters over and over again
throughout labor history. When one digs just a little below the surface, one often
finds both a general inclination and an overwhelming propensity to organize in the

[10] For further discussion and references, see Goldfield (1987:135–37).

face of tremendous obstacles by a wide variety of workers. Even in the Northeast, in the early days of the woodworking industry, where most operations were small and hardly conducive to worker organization, there is evidence of major struggles. One cannot easily read the desires and future actions of most workers from their lack of organization or unwillingness to struggle at a particular point in time.

One of the few alternative assessments of southern woodworkers is offered by McLaurin (1971), who argues that low pay, harsh and dangerous working conditions, bad living situations, abusive treatment, and the intransigence of employers often led to militant, radical behavior by early industrial workers. Even Jensen notes some of these initial struggles. In the Northeast, there were many early furtive attempts at unionism. Most notable of these was the so-called Williamsport (Pennsylvania) riot of 1872, which was quashed only after troops were called in and all the leaders arrested. The latter aroused so much public sympathy that the participants were eventually pardoned by the Pennsylvania governor (Jensen 1945:41–42). As the industry spread to the Great Lakes states in the 1880s and large-scale operations became more common, numerous worker struggles took place. Much of the union organization there was continuous, not just episodic, particularly during the heyday of the wood industry in the 1880s. Organizing for higher wages and improved conditions began in earnest in Michigan in 1879, with strikes recorded in 1881 (Michigan) and 1884 (Michigan and Wisconsin), and a general strike in the Saginaw, Michigan, area in 1885 (Jensen 1945:59).

During this same period, there was also a high degree of labor organizing activity among woodworkers in the South. Records indicate an 1890 strike in Ray, Alabama (Douty 1946:150). In 1899, the Knights of Labor organized a major woodworkers' strike in Pensacola, Florida (Jensen 1945:86–87). Strikes also took place in Louisiana in 1902 (1945:87). A large strike in 1907 over wages spread across East Texas and Louisiana (Douty 1946:151).

According to McLaurin, "Although labor unions experience difficulty in establishing permanent footholds in the region, it does not mean that they failed because of the docility or lack of interest shown by southern laborers. Rather, they failed because of unyielding managerial opposition, the racial issue . . . [and] the weakness of the unions involved" (1971:5). In his comprehensive study of the Knights of Labor in the late nineteenth century, he concludes, "The willingness of the rank and file to challenge management with a strike was not limited by geography, occupation, or race. In every industry in which the Knights achieved a foothold, strikes occurred. Industrial laborers, miners, artisans, and even agricultural laborers sought to improve their economic condition . . . through direct action. Blacks, whites, and integrated work forces struck, as did laborers in both the upper and lower South. The Knights' strike activity alone provides ample evidence that southern laborers, like their northern brethren, found their economic status unacceptable and, given some organizational support, would fight to improve it" (1971:55). He notes that, in 1887, southern lumberworkers were especially militant: "The lumber industry experienced a rash of strikes, some of which resulted in temporary gains for the workers. Most of the strike activity occurred along the Gulf Coast in northwestern Florida, Alabama, and Mississippi.[11] In this region, large firms, many of them backed by northern and foreign capital, were becoming increasingly dominant within the industry. Like miners, loggers and millworkers followed a rugged and dangerous trade. And like miners, they were inclined to strike in order to settle grievances" (McLaurin 1971:60). So we need to take the claims of their individualism and unwillingness to organize with a grain of salt.

In Ruth Allen's study of East Texas lumberworkers, she concludes, "Industrial relations in the lumber industry of Texas have never been marked by peace" (1961:165). In August 1877, for example, the *Galveston Daily News* reported that 250 millworkers in Harrisburg were reportedly armed and "threatening to burn down the town." In the mid-1880s, stoppages took place with or without ties to unions. In May 1886, for example, all seventy workers at the Eylan sawmill struck without any connection to a broader organization. They won their demands after seven days. During a walkout of all the mills in Orange (near Port Arthur), workers demanded a reduction in the workweek; they struck again in 1893 and again for three months in 1894. More strikes occurred in 1902 and 1903, as the Texas Lumbermen's Association met to deal with unions (Allen 1961:167). During the 1900s, there were many organized actions in the Sabine County lumber camps. In 1907, in response to the low prices for lumber, operators in East Texas and western Louisiana restricted output and reduced wages. Workers in Texas and Louisiana walked out in protest in a spontaneous general strike, which was short and unsuccessful. In 1908, there were again numerous strikes (Allen 1961:171).

In Jacksonville, Florida, in 1873, the Labor League of Duval County organized a strike involving hundreds of mostly Black lumberworkers (Drobney 1997:171), idling seventeen of twenty mills, the other three being operated by white men, most of whom were recruited from rural areas. In the 1880s and 1890s, stimulated by the Knights, woodworkers struck frequently, often making gains. In 1886, all approximately fifteen hundred lumberworkers in Pensacola, Florida, were organized into segregated assemblies. Records also show strikes in the 1890s and in 1908 (Drobney 1997:172, passim).

The period between 1910 and 1913 was an especially active one for woodworkers, both in the South and in the rest of the country. Much of the organizing and the strikes took place under IWW auspices. One of the most intriguing campaigns of this period was that of the southern Brotherhood of Timber Workers

---

[11] In 1887, the Knights of Labor waged strikes at mills in the Moss Point-Pascagoula, Mississippi, area and won reduction of the working day from fourteen to twelve hours. In 1888, Knights in the Handsboro, Mississippi, area struck and got a reduction from fourteen to ten hours in a ten-week strike. Later, there was an Alabama strike at the Ray and Lillian Lumber mills (McLaurin 1971:61).

(BTW), an interracial union centered in Louisiana and East Texas.[12] Low wages, brutal and dangerous work, payment in scrip, and substandard living conditions were among the grievances. The tens of thousands of workers, more than half of whom were African-Americans, many with a history of militant struggle, joined together beginning in 1911. With strong community support from farmers and the middle class in lumber towns, the BTW, according to Southern Lumber Operators head John Henry Kirby, was "covering the country like a blanket" (Green 1973:175). Disguised as insurance solicitors and card sharps, the two main organizers enrolled hundreds of Black and white workers in early 1911. After some initial successes, major setbacks in 1912 led the BTW to affiliate with the IWW, which gave renewed vigor to the union. During a strike in July in the DeRidder area of western Louisiana, company gunmen in Graybow, Louisiana, opened fire on a peaceful demonstration of strikers and their families. Naturally, it was sixty-four unionists, not the company gunmen, who were indicted. In a major victory for the union, however, with strong community support for the defendants, the union men were acquitted.

The BTW was able to hold out against both repression and attempts at racial division. Eventually, however, the companies managed to undermine much of their support among townspeople (although not farmers) by means of economic pressure. This, combined with draconian repression, finally undid the union. As Green sardonically notes: "The participation of the 'best citizens' in the law and order leagues of the pine region, as well as in the Councils of Defense and the Ku Klux Klan which followed later, demonstrated that the middle classes of the region had a greater propensity for authoritarian activity than the workers" (1973:175). David Saposs describes the struggle against the union as "one of the most violent in the annals of the American Labour movement" (1967:168; see also Green 1973:197; Reed 1969:61–69).

As it turned out, however, the repression against the BTW pales in comparison to the wave of repression faced by woodworkers in the wake of World War I. One famous southern incident took place in 1919 in Bogalusa, Louisiana, which claimed to be the largest lumber center in the world at the time. It was run by the Great Southern Lumber Company, whose vice president and general manager, W. H. Sullivan, was also mayor of the town, an office he held until his death (Jensen

---

[12] A detailed account is given in Green (1973). The racial dimensions of the struggle are discussed by Roediger (see his introduction to the writings of strike leader Covington Hall in Roediger 1999. The BTW is discussed or mentioned in Todes (1931:171–74); Dubofsky (1969:209–20); Marshall (1967:94–99); Allen (1961:173–83); P. Foner 1965:233–57), and numerous informative contemporary articles in the *International Socialist Review*, including those by Covington Hall (1912a, b, c) and William D. Haywood (1912); An almost 800-page dissertation looks at the organization of employers and the background of the strike, providing many supporting details (Ferrell 1982). For a lengthy analysis, including a discussion of the racial aspects of the BTW, as well as a critique of Roediger, see Reich (1998:ch. 6).

1945:91). During World War I, partially protected by federal regulation of wartime labor–management relations but mostly buoyed by the tight labor market, workers around the country, including across the South, organized and struck. Southern lumberworkers were no exception.[13]

Although wartime conditions stimulated organizing, the AFL, exhibiting a lethargy parallel to that displayed by steel, did not seriously begin approaching lumberworkers until after the 1918 armistice, when conditions became considerably less favorable for organizing (Norwood 1997:610). Great Southern recruited literally hundreds of gunmen in response. When African-American workers began to organize, initially in a separate segregated local of the carpenters' union, Great Southern management brazenly announced that the planned June 14, 1919, union meeting would be broken up by its gunmen. Nearly a hundred armed white unionists, led by fifteen veterans in full uniform, entered the Bogalusa Negro Quarter that night to defend Blacks against violent attacks (Norwood 1997:615). On November 21, vigilantes made an attempt to lynch Sol Dacus, leader of the Black lumberworkers. Although his home was destroyed, he escaped into the swamps. The next day, escorted by two armed white union carpenters, Dacus and his comrades marched down the center of Bogalusa to the garage of the carpenters' president, Lem Williams. One hundred and fifty company gunmen surrounded the garage and opened fire; Lem Williams and three other unionists were killed, although Dacus escaped.[14]

Attorney General A. Mitchell Palmer turned down the request of the national AFL to investigate the case (Norwood 1997:620). Succeeding Louisiana governors likewise declined to open it. The Louisiana State Federation of Labor supported civil suits filed by Dacus and on behalf of the widows of the men killed. All suits eventually failed. The final court reversal took place in 1928, when the U.S. Supreme Court reversed a district court award of $30,000 in damages to Lena Williams, Lem Williams's widow. They ruled that the vigilantes were a "posse of voluntary police," conveniently ignoring the fact that Dacus would almost certainly have been lynched. The murder of its leaders ended this installment of the drive to organize southern lumberworkers, but by the next year organizing had resumed anew in key lumber centers in Mississippi (Norwood 1997:620–24).

---

[13] Woodworkers, especially those in the Northwest, were constrained during World War I and into the 1920s, when the U.S. military set up a company- and government-controlled organization, supposedly to maintain war production and break the disruptive power of the IWW. This organization, the Loyal Legion of Lumbermen and Loggers (4L), was swept away by the worker militancy of the 1930s and proved largely ineffective in stemming it. Though it is an important episode in the history of the wood industry, it plays only a minor part in the story here during the period on which I am focusing. There are a number of accounts of the 4L (for a detailed history, see Hyman 2012; also Nichols 1959; Egolf 1985:197–98).

[14] For further background on Bogalusa, the labor organizing there, and the leader of the carpenters' union, L. E. Williams, see Wyche 1999; Ovington (1920).

Repression of unionists, however, was not limited to the South. In Everett, Washington, during a 1916 lumber strike, a sheriff and vigilantes opened fire on 250 striking workers and Wobblies, who were on a boat attempting to dock. Seventeen workers died and more than fifty were injured. No one was ever arrested for these acts. Throughout the Northwest, there was a "wave of hysterical mob violence" against the IWW and union supporters. In the lumber town of Klamath Falls, Oregon, a mob ruled (Todes 1931:167).

In 1918, the union hall in Centralia, Washington, was destroyed by a mob led by F. B. Hubbard, the president of the East Railway and Lumber Company. The unionists did not defend themselves and were brutally beaten and driven out of town. In 1919, vigilantes, once more led by Hubbard, decided to again level the rebuilt hall during an American Legion Armistice Day March. This time, the unionists defended themselves, killing four of their assailants. All the men in the hall were arrested and placed in jail. One, who had shot Hubbard's nephew in self-defense, was taken from the jail in the middle of the night, castrated, and hung from a bridge. No one, of course, was ever tried for this lynching. While a picture may be worth a thousand words, the written words of the coroner are graphic enough: "Wesley Everest had broken out of jail, gone to the Chehalis River bridge and jumped off with a rope around his neck. Finding the rope too short he climbed back and fastened a longer one, jumped off again, broke his neck and then shot himself full of holes." Hundreds of pro-union and IWW suspects were arrested (Lembcke and Tattam 1984:15; Chaplin 1924:66).

How the Union Was Organized

For woodworkers in the United States and Canada, the 1920s were a difficult period, as they were for workers in most industries. The onset of the Great Depression in 1929, however, threw large numbers of people out of work and provided fertile soil for Communist-led organizing among the unemployed. This was true in many cities of the Pacific Northwest, both in the United States and Canada, where there were centers for lumberworkers; among these were Vancouver, British Columbia, Portland, Oregon, and the Seattle, Tacoma, area in Washington around the Puget Sound deepwater harbor, as well as Bellingham, Everett, and Aberdeen (for details, see Lembcke and Tattam 1984:26–30; for centers even in conservative Portland, 1984:32; Tattam 1970:12, 17–23; 28, 29; Egolf 1985:203).[15]

---

[15] As we saw in steel, virtually every lumber center in the Northwest had a militant, extensive unemployed movement, most often led by Communists. Among numerous sources, Egolf notes that "Seattle and timber towns including Bellingham, Mt. Vernon, Tacoma, Everett, and Aberdeen had flourishing unemployed movements by 1932" (1985:203).

The Communist Party also launched separate unions in both the United States and Canada. The U.S. union was the National Lumber Workers Union (NLWU), affiliated with the Communist Party's Trade Union Unity League. The NLWU led a few successful strikes, participated in unemployed worker demonstrations, and represented approximately three thousands workers at its first national convention, held in Seattle in 1933 (making itself a minor presence in the Pacific Northwest). The Canadian Lumber Workers Industrial Union (LWIU) had more outreach. Its first major victory was at the Fraser Mills, the largest lumber complex in the British Empire, the second largest in the world, employing eighteen hundred workers. The strike was led by twenty-seven-year-old Harold Pritchett, whose family had emigrated from Great Britain in 1912 when he was eight. Pritchett had also been the president of a Shingle Weavers Union local but had been expelled from office when his employer prevailed upon AFL president William Green to intervene. Pritchett, who worked at Fraser Mills, led the workers there to victory, establishing a reputation among woodworkers in both the United States and Canada. The strikers also challenged the inferior pay and working conditions of Asian workers—Hindus (the generic name given to all people from the Indian subcontinent), Japanese, and Chinese—who made up 15% of the industry's workforce. In 1934, the LWIU led a large strike against the operations of the Bloedel Lumber Company, using a variety of tactics that were to become a staple of later woodworker organizing: big rallies and fundraising in the major cities, flying squadrons (with groups that diverted the attention of company guards, while other organizers snuck into the camps to talk to the workers), visits to remote logging camps and sawmills, and the "logger's navy," a series of boats used to contact woodworkers in remote areas on the islands and along the coast (the above account generally follows Lembcke and Tattam 1984:18–46, esp. 18, 23, 25–26).

Despite the success of their activities among both the unemployed and woodworkers in the U.S. Northwest and British Columbia during the early 1930s, most woodworkers were not affected by the CP-led organizing or involved to a large degree. The event that brought new life to and energized a majority of woodworkers in the Northwest and British Columbia was the 1934 West Coast longshore strike, credited by a large number of observers as one of the three semi-revolutionary strikes that year that launched the industrial union movement (Bernstein 1969:252–98; Preis 1964:30–33; Nelson 1990:127–55 for an enthusiastic description of the longshore strike). Longshoreman struck the whole West Coast from May 9 to July 31, 1934, demanding higher pay, a thirty-hour week, union recognition, and a union-controlled hiring hall. Despite the large-scale layoffs of lumberworkers caused by the strike, the NLWU raised money and persuaded woodworkers to support the strike and not scab. Unemployed organizations successfully rallied the unemployed, convincing them not to cross the picket lines. In June, the big sawmills in Longview, Washington, struck in support. When the San Francisco labor movement launched a full-scale three-day general strike on July 19 in protest of the murder by police of two longshoremen and the wounding of dozens more, workers throughout the country, not least of whom were nearby Northwest woodworkers, were electrified (Lembcke and Tattam 1984:28–30; Tattam 1970:36–42, 48–50; Jensen 1945:160).

Following the victory of the longshoremen in 1934, tens of thousands of woodworkers poured into the AFL Sawmill and Timber Workers Union (STWU), which in 1935 was placed under the jurisdiction of the United Brotherhood of Carpenters and Joiners (UBCJ). Communists disbanded their radical unions in both the United States and Canada, joining the STWU with their followers. By May 1935, as many as thirty thousand lumberworkers were out on strike (Lembcke and Tattam 1984:32).

Jensen describes the strike as "spectacular" and as "the outstanding landmark of industrial relations in the lumber industry" (1945:164). The woodworkers received strong support from UBCJ carpenters, as well as longshoremen. The UBCJ headquarters, however, immediately sent Abe Muir to take control of the strike and end it as soon as possible. As militant workers began to attack Muir for trying to "sell out" the strike, Communists and other oppositionists on July 1, 1935, formed the Northwest Joint Strike Committee to gain rank-and-file control of the strike and oppose UBCJ attempts to compromise their demands. James Murphy—a Communist, former Wobbly, and former president of the NLWU—played a key role in the committee. Karly Larsen, a Danish immigrant, radical, and leader of the Sawmill and Timber Workers Union from Washington, was also a leader of the Joint Strike Committee. Longshoreman refused to load lumber, while thousands of demonstrators clashed with police and National Guardsmen in logging centers from California to British Columbia. The support among woodworkers, however, was not unanimous. Opposition to the strike and support for Muir was centered in the Portland area, the longtime traditional center for union conservatism (Lembcke and Tattam 1984:37; 34–42, passim; contrary to Jones 2005:167, 180).[16] Despite the eventual collapse of the strike, by the spring of 1936 seventy thousand lumberworkers belonged to the union. Meanwhile in Canada, in April 1936, the Communist-led LWIU merged with the UBCJ and became the Lumber and Sawmill Workers Union of British Columbia, based in Vancouver. In September 1936, still wanting to work within the UBCJ, 625 delegates from both countries met in Portland to form the Federation of Woodworkers. Representing seventy-two thousand workers, they elected the charismatic Harold Pritchett as their president. Woodworkers in Minnesota and Ironwood, in Michigan's Upper Peninsula,

---

[16] Egolf notes that political lines were often complex, with conservatism and IWW roots often combined with early support of the "red bloc," support for the CIO, and opposition to Muir, as he documents with respect to the Raymond, Washington, local, which contained activists in both later factions (1985:225–28). Lembcke and Tattam argue that the Raymond local was geographically between the more conservative and more radical woodworker centers, hardly making it "typical" (1984:33).

led by Finnish Communists, brought woodworkers into the new union. In 1937, the woodworkers joined the newly formed CIO. Harold Pritchett was again overwhelmingly elected president of the new union, the International Woodworkers of America–CIO (Lembcke and Tattam 1984:43–46; Tattam 1970:66–70; Jackson 1953:14–20).

The IWA was largely based in the Pacific Northwest and British Columbia, yet half the industry was located in the South. Thus, it is important to look at its prospects there. The question posed is whether southern woodworkers were organizable. Could they have been organized during the 1930s and 1940s? I want to first suggest that the reason woodworkers were first organized in the Northwest rather than the South had less to do with their organizability than with the impact of the 1934 longshore strike and the immediate support they got from the International Longshoremen's and Warehousemen's Union (ILWU).

Could Southern Woodworkers Be Unionized?

There was, to be sure, a large variation in the size and nature of firms in the wood industry in the South, with many small, technologically primitive, poorly capitalized, isolated operations. By the 1930s, however, a substantial proportion of the southern industry was located in large industrial centers (Memphis, Tennessee; Bogalusa, Louisiana; Vicksburg and Laurel, Mississippi; Pensacola and Jacksonville, Florida; and East Texas; among other places) or in company towns near huge tracts of timber (hundreds of thousands of acres of which were owned by large lumber companies) with state-of-the-art industrial equipment and often with their own railroads (Drobney 1997). In all these arenas, woodworkers had proved to be highly organizable.

One need not look merely at the early history of organizing to make this claim. During the 1930s, for example, woodworkers showed a strong propensity to organize in the heavily unionized coal counties in the South. In September 1937, the director of District 31 (West Virginia) of the United Mine Workers of America (UMWA) reported to IWA headquarters that at least five thousand woodworkers in his district wanted IWA membership (*Timber Worker*, September 25, 1937; Dinwiddie 1980:32). In Walker County, Alabama, the state's second-largest coal-producing county, with a history of militant unionism, 37% of workers were in the coal industry and had been completely organized by 1935 (Dinwiddie 1980:35). By 1937, virtually all other workers, including those in wood, were organized. The same was true in coal-rich Jefferson County, which included the Birmingham area (U.S. Department of Labor 1945:291; Dinwiddie 1980:38). As a result of the propensity of woodworkers to organize, the UMWA in Alabama in 1938 called for the unionization of the state's twenty-five thousand woodworkers, pledging assistance and asking for organizers from the IWA (*Timber Worker*, February 19, March 5,

1938; Dinwiddie 1980:33). Many individual coal mining locals pledged their support. And with little help from the IWA, in 1938 the CIO transferred nine thousand southern woodworkers in twenty-five local industrial unions to the IWA (*Timber Worker*, March 12, 1938). So it would seem that southern woodworkers were no less prone to unionizing, given some support, than their northwestern counterparts.

Woodworkers often showed a propensity to organize even when coal miners were not in the vicinity and even after the Depression ended. Memphis, for example, was the center of the southern hardwood industry; in 1937, one out of seven industrial workers there were in lumber. Their organizing victories were often overwhelming. This was the case at the Anderson-Tully Lumber Company, which employed more than a thousand workers: on February 5, 1943, the union won its National Labor Relations Board (NLRB) certification election by a vote of 526 to 101. The union also organized a thousand furniture workers in Memphis in early 1944 at U.S. Bedding and the Memphis Furniture Co. (*Tennessee CIO News*, July 31, 1944). Even in Mississippi, the IWA won by overwhelming margins, as in Vicksburg at the large Waltersville plant, where the IWA won certification 572 to 42; at two other Anderson-Tully plants in Vicksburg, the vote was 160 to19 and 93 to 6 in favor of the union (Dinwiddie 1980:86).

After World War II, woodworkers continued to be organizable. Operation Dixie officials found that woodworker organizing was highly successful, in contrast to the failures in the southern textile industry. Reports from Tennessee were equally enthusiastic, according to state director Paul Christopher when he reported on the CIO election victory at Miller Bros, 85 to 8, in late 1946. Similar results were reported from the North Carolina Lumber and Veneer Co, in Hallsboro, where the vote in favor of the union was 175 to 35 in June 1947.[17]

Thus, by all accounts, southern woodworkers could have been organized during the 1930s and 1940s, even by the less audacious methods supported by the right-wing leaders of the CIO and Operation Dixie—in contrast to textile workers, whose organizing during this period would have required, at minimum, a different approach. What would have been required to organize southern woodworkers was a commitment of resources and energy, comparable to that devoted to textiles and steel. Such resources were not forthcoming in the wood industry. If they had been—and the industry with its hundreds of thousands of workers in the South had been organized—the outcome of Operation Dixie as a whole might have been different.

[17] Van Bittner to IWA President James Fadling, July 31, 1946, OD collection, box 129, reel 25:276; Christopher to Bittner, December 30, 1946, OD collection, box 85; reel 11, frame 465.

The Peculiarities of the IWA: Cutting Off One's Nose to Spite One's Face

Most CIO unions, upon securing an organized base in their industry (especially when they had begun in the North), went on to attempt to organize the rest of their jurisdiction. This approach made perfect sense and was followed by unions, whatever their political orientation. The coal miners, of course, saw organizing the South as central to the vitality of their union and incorporated many principles into their organization that were specifically relevant to the South. The early union strongholds in Illinois and Pennsylvania were virtually all white. Nevertheless, the union was ever mindful of building solidarity in West Virginia and Alabama, two coal-producing centers that had high percentages of Black coal miners. They not only emphasized the importance of Black and white solidarity, but fought the KKK, appointed Black officials and organizers at the district level, and attempted to register Black coal miners to vote in the Deep South (Goldfield 1993:7–10; for the best in-depth study, see Lewis 1987). When the opportunity came in 1933 to organize the whole industry, the South received as much emphasis as the rest of the country. The United Rubber Workers, soon after organizing the main rubber centers in the North (notably Akron, Ohio), sent some of their best organizers to the secondary rubber centers in the South, including Gadsden, Alabama, and Memphis, Tennessee.[18] Any major unorganized center posed a threat to the life of the union. The more left-wing United Packinghouse Workers did not stop when they organized the major slaughterhouses in the Midwest, but proceeded to organize in Fort Worth, Texas. The Steel Workers Organizing Committee (SWOC) hired large numbers of Communist Party organizers to ensure that all jurisdictions had viable organizations. In Memphis, Tennessee, and Louisville, Kentucky, the large International Harvester complexes were the prize targets of the United Auto Workers (UAW) and Farm Equipment Workers (FE) respectively. Even in the textile industry, the CIO continued to pour money into losing campaigns in the South, just as the AFL had done decades before (C. Daniel 2001:chs. 7, 8, passim; Minchin 1997, esp. chs. 3–5). In contrast, the IWA underfunded and ignored the South, to the consternation not merely of its left critics but of its right-wing allies as well.

---

[18] The organizational drive at the large Memphis Firestone plant is told in Honey (1993:150–51, 154–55, 164, 184–86). In Gadsden even United Rubber Workers president Sherman Dalrymple was directly involved there (Nelson 1988:234–45). The rubberworkers continued to be successful at new southern plants into the 1970s (Post, forthcoming; Jeszeck 1982:ch. 5, passim).

Why the Woodworkers Were Not Organized in the South

The key question is why no concerted effort was made by the national union to organize southern woodworkers during the 1930s and 1940s. On the surface, the answer is simple: it was because of the provincialism and incompetence of the right-wing IWA national leaders, who were an obstructionist opposition from the 1937 founding until 1941, when they took over leadership of the union. While most activists, including all the leftists in the IWA, considered the right-wing, anti-communist IWA leadership incompetent, perhaps the most telling criticisms were those from their right-wing factional allies in the South and elsewhere. In 1942, for example, the servicing of many southern IWA locals was so bad that officials in the southern district of the steelworkers were afraid that they were ripe for bolting to the UMWA's District 50. A right-wing steelworkers' staffer even suggested that he would support the move by the CP-led but loyal CIO-affiliated United Cannery, Agricultural, Packing and Allied Workers of America (UCAPAWA), "to get them straightened out" and take them over from the IWA in order to avoid letting them go to Lewis's UMWA District 50. Even ultra-conservative CIO bureaucrat Van Bittner wrote to James Fadling, IWA president, on July 31, 1946: "In the past, several local unions, of the Woodworkers, have been organized [by the CIO] then died because of no one rendering any service to them. I know you agree with me that we just can't allow this to happen again." On May 31, 1949, one of Bittner's assistants, right-winger Ernest Pugh, writes, "At Lane Cedar Chest Company, Altavista, VA, 1000 employees, the organizing is going very well," but Pugh is "disturbed" about the service they get from the IWA and feels he is "getting the runaround from top IWA officials in Portland." The right-wing IWA leaders in Portland were not very good at running organizing campaigns, not very responsible about following through on things, and relatively lackadaisical about servicing and supporting newly organized locals, especially in the South.[19]

They also suffered from provincialism. To the extent that they paid attention and devoted resources, it tended to be in their own bailiwicks. Despite the fact that the South had the largest number of woodworkers and the lowest wages, thus creating competitive pressures on the organized woodworkers in the Northwest, the right-wing leaders showed little interest in the South, in contrast to their left-wing factional opponents. As I will show, they often argued against allocating any resources to the South. They tended to give two arguments. First, they asserted that there was

---

[19] Ned Beddow to McDonald, July 11, 1942, McDonald papers, 18:1, Penn State University (PSU); Will Watts to Beddow, July 10, 1942, McDonald papers, 18:1; Pugh to Bittner, July 12, 1942, OD collection: Bittner file, 229.

plenty of work to do in the Northwest, that it would be wrong to dissipate their resources and personnel in areas of union weakness, when the already partially organized areas needed more work. Second, they disagreed with the left, which wanted
more resources placed in the hands of the national office, so that some of it could
be allocated to the South. The right-wingers argued, in a debate that harked back
to the IWW in the teens, that it was undemocratic for the national office to usurp
power from the locals, that locals and districts should keep their resources and hire
their own organizers—ensuring, as critics pointed out, that key areas like the South
would never get much help.

In the first purge of a majority-supported left-wing/Communist leadership, the
CIO national office backed the right-wingers, playing a major role in allowing them
to take control of the union. This took place at a time when the CIO national office
was controlled by John L. Lewis of the United Mine Workers and his allies, who
were usually strongly supportive of efforts to organize southern industry. An additional question to ask is why any CIO national officers supported people whom
they viewed as incompetent, and who were unlikely to organize their industry in the
South, at a time when they were cooperating with CPers and other leftists in a large
number of other unions.[20]

By asking these questions, we begin a journey into various pieces of seemingly
left arcana and other hidden factors, deep below the surface, whose investigation
can be justified only if they shed light on the class politics of the era and on those
structural features that provide the real, rather than surface, explanations of how the
world turns. Our reward will be a better understanding of the actual politics and
the central dynamics of the CIO, as opposed to the way they are commonly characterized. Just as beauty is sometimes only skin deep, things are not always what they
seem to be.[21]

I shall try to unravel our mystery one layer at a time. As an advance map, the
IWA's failure to support southern organizing, the obstinance of the right-wing opposition (the so-called White Bloc), and its eventual success in taking over the
union can be found in a number of interwoven factors.

First, the factional struggle in the IWA cannot be understood without a focus
on the IWW background and identification of the leading activists on all sides
of the factional struggle. Second, the fact that the national office was deprived of
funds to carry on organizing work in the South was in part a consequence of this

---

[20] George Breitman, a Trotskyist leader (ergo, in principle opposed to the Communists), in an
astute analysis writes of the "Lewis-Stalinist bloc" (which he sees as a strong supporter of industrial
unionism) being defeated within the New Jersey CIO by the Hillman camp, who Breitman sees as prepared to capitulate to the government and to the AFL (1940:1, 4).

[21] There are many who see the attacks on leftists in the CIO only beginning in the post–World War
II period (Prickett 1975; Emspak 1972).

background. Third, the structure of the industry provided a material basis for the strong proclivities toward provincialism and conservatism, on the one hand, and radicalism, on the other. Fourth, there was the intensity of the battle of the IWA with the AFL in the Northwest. Fifth, the governments of Canada and the United States played a role, both in attacking radicalism in general and, more specifically, in regulating the crossing of the border by left-wing officials of this binational union, actions that eventually barred Harold Pritchett, the Canadian head of the IWA, from entering the United States and thus made it impossible for him to continue to function as president, forcing him to resign. Sixth, the desperate situation in which these factors placed the IWA, especially its left-wing leadership, led the IWA in early 1940 to turn to the national CIO for assistance. Seventh, the leftists made this decision while seemingly unaware of the treacherous waters they were about to enter, especially the changing balance of forces within the national CIO. Eighth, there was the overall impact of the changed political environment that existed in 1940, including the increased opposition to leftists and Communists within the government and the national CIO. With this slight inkling of things to come, let us try to put flesh on them thar' bones.

I begin by looking at the IWW heritage of the woodworkers in the Pacific Northwest. This heritage existed in many unions in the 1930s. These included maritime, longshore, specifically in a number of ports on the East Coast (especially Philadelphia and Baltimore; Kimeldorf 1985, 1999), packinghouse (most notably in the Hormel plant in Austin, Minnesota), and the Mine, Mill, and Smelter Workers, successor to the Western Federation of Miners, whose best-known son was "Big Bill" Haywood, the most prominent leader of the IWW, and even in a number of auto plants, including the militant Briggs plant in Detroit and the Toledo Autolite plant, site of the famous 1934 strike. In no other union, however, was this heritage as central as in the woodworkers. Their influence was especially strong in the Northwest, for as Tyler shows, "the I.W.W. in the Pacific Northwest was most active in the lumber industry" (1967:5).

Many of the prominent early leaders of the woodworkers had connections to the IWW. On the left, the list is extensive and includes James Murphy, prominent Northwest CP leader, president of the CP-initiated Lumber Workers Industrial Union, and a leader in the 1935 Northwest Joint Strike Committee, which provided the initial impetus to the formation of the IWA in 1937 (Tattam 1970:30, 56). Harold Pritchett, the first president of the union, also had connections to the more pro-Soviet IWW leaders. Almost all the early Scandinavian left-wing leaders had similar backgrounds. Many of the lumberjack activists also had IWW roots (Tyler 1967). On the right, leaders Al Hartung, Carl Wynn, and Worth Lowery had been Wobblies. Particularly noteworthy, Portland-area IWWers had constituted a center of opposition to the national IWW leadership from as early as 1907 through the 1920s. This heritage played a key role in the IWA (Egolf 1985). As Dinwiddie summarizes, "Virtually all the CRDC [Columbia River District Council] and IWA leaders had been members of the IWW, and they brought to the IWA the differences that had been present in the IWW" (1980:20).

The most important ideological divide in the IWW was over centralization. Paul Brissenden says, "This issue is perhaps the most fundamental one ever given wide discussion by the IWW membership" (1919:304). The IWW was never a very centralized organization. Its national office had at best a shoestring budget, an underfunded newspaper, and at most several paid staffers (one can, of course, compare this with many medium-sized unions today with hundreds of paid staff). Characterized by localists and decentralists as the "Headquarters," the national office was continually under attack. The suspicions of the national office began early. The first General Executive Board, elected at the 1905 founding convention, did not reflect the dominant tone of the meeting, having only two leftists— William Trautman and Vincent St. John—out of seven members. Its president was Charles O. Sherman, general secretary of the United Metal Workers Union, a conservative who squandered most of the treasury on travel and incidentals for himself. He was also discovered to be overcharging the organization for union buttons, from which he himself gained financially. At the 1906 convention, the office of president was abolished, and most of the right-wing leaders were forced out. Nevertheless, suspicions about the national office continued. They came up again in 1910. The center of decentralism was the Pacific Northwest, assuming an organized form at a Portland conference of West Coast IWW locals held in February 1911 at which the Pacific Coast District Organization was established (Brissenden 1919:312). The reduction of the per capita tax to be paid to the national office was always a flashpoint.

In 1912, however, there was a move to restrict the power of the national office. The convention gave the General Executive Board responsibility for centralizing support and control. Local chapters, however, were given free rein to mobilize for free-speech fights (Brissenden 1919:297). The issue was fought over even more forcefully at the 1913 convention. Those decentralizers who wanted to completely abolish the national office were mostly from the West. Brissenden characterizes the fight as "a struggle between the western membership, individualistic and tainted with anarchism," and those from the East, who were more stable industrial workers in large-scale industries, like textiles, longshore, and manufacturing (1919:306). According to one delegate, "Decentralization deals essentially with the right of locals to control themselves and through their combined wills to run the general organization" (C. Hall 1999:307). Of course, not all supporters were from the West. Even the Rebel Girl, Elizabeth Gurley Flynn, a hero of the 1912 Lawrence, Massachusetts, textile strike, later to be a leading Communist, was caught up in the decentralist fervor and advocated abolition of the national convention. The decentralist resolutions were defeated by 3 to 1 margins, but the issue never fully went away (Brissenden 1919:310). In his report on the 1913 convention, Ewald Koeltgen writes:

Decentralization in reality means localism, and it is reactionary in as much as it ignores capitalist development in industry . . . Each locality shall be independent of all other localities, thus preventing the various localities from acting together and utterly destroying the solidarity so necessary to working-class emancipation . . . Mass action requires close, centralized organization, because the larger the mass the surer the victory. (1913:275)

The issues and the heritage were unique neither to the United States nor to the particular time period in which they arose. The extreme localism, ultra-democracy, anti-authority stances have resonated throughout history, providing examples not only of impressive courage and militancy, but of great political backwardness. During the Russian Revolution, for example, the Bolshevik Party initially wanted to establish a mixed economy in order to retain the role of factory managers and technical people so as to be better able to maintain production. Local worker organizations were not supposed to seize their workplaces unless the managers were guilty of treason. Regarding every slight as treasonous, within the first year workers had seized virtually every workplace in the country, even extending to all the former empire's functioning one-person windmills, accelerating the radical development of the social movement (Nove 1969:69–70). Syndicalist railroad workers, on the other hand, who wanted the right to set their own timetables locally, clearly could not coexist with the rational, national running of an economy (1969:50). Sailors in Kronstadt who wanted to control military decisions themselves were deemed guilty of treason and repressed. The impressive militancy of sailors in the Seafarers International Union-Sailors Union of the Pacific (with a heritage of IWW activism), who upheld the right to take any action they deemed necessary to control their jobs, reached its nadir when the union engaged in successful work stoppages on ships to prevent the hiring of African-Americans (Nelson 1990: 48–50, 246–48). The decentralist themes have echoed through the years, finding a home in the 1960s New Left, in the anti-leadership, consensual decision-making traditions that plagued the early Student Nonviolent Coordinating Committee (SNCC) and Students for a Democratic Society (SDS), as well as some of the early radical women's organizations.

This localist, decentralist, ultra-democratic ideology was embraced by the Portland-centered right-wing leadership of the IWA in its plan to limit the power and finances of the national office, and thus to prevent it from engaging in nationally coordinated organizing campaigns, especially in the South. Those who suggest that IWW roots always meant radicalism are therefore mistaken here (Egolf 1985; Jones 2005).

Yet even those who opposed the decentralists in the IWW were often antipolitical, advocating a form of pure and simple syndicalism. Koeltgen, who so castigates the decentralizers, urges "that the organizers and speakers confine themselves strictly to teaching industrial unionism and organizing the workers; that the spokesmen of the I.W.W. should not waste their time in attacking politics and political parties, religion or any other outside issues" (1913:275–76). Here, too, was one of the basic charges of the IWA right-wingers against the left-wing leadership of the union, namely that they devoted pages of the IWA newspaper to political issues, including support for the Republicans in Spain. Finally, with the success of the Bolshevik Revolution, many IWWers, including important members of the executive board, gave their support to the Communist International, some even joining the fledgling Communist Party (the list is impressive; see Goldfield 1980:44, 59 n. 5). The center of opposition against the pro-Bolshevik tendencies in the IWW was once again Portland, where in 1919 Paul Rowan and the Portland IWW began organizing a movement opposing the executive board on this issue. One of the key leaders of this faction was the brother of Carl Winn, who would become a leader of the IWA (Lembcke and Tattam 1984:81).

Jerry Lembcke and William Tatam argue in their seminal 1984 work on the woodworkers that the right wing's ideology had its roots in certain types of industrial work situations, while the more left-wing perspective was rooted in very different environments. The right wing was almost exclusively based in the Portland area, especially in the many small, long-standing sawmills along the western Columbia River, east of Portland, and the Willamette River Valley, extending south. Many of these workers had roots in and often continuing ties to the rich agricultural economy in the surrounding area. Workers in such situations have historically had more craft union mentalities; like construction workers, they have more concern for local market conditions and less sympathy for workers in other places and industries. In contrast, workers in the newer, larger mills and forests in British Columbia, western Washington, and the Puget Sound area, where production was targeted at a national, and often world, market, were by necessity far more attuned than other workers to the importance of national coordination and the happenings of workers in other parts of the world. While not fixed in stone, these tendencies can be found throughout history, around the world, for example in Russian metalworkers during the 1905 Revolution and Cuban sugar mill operatives (Lembcke and Tattam 1984:ch. 2). As Godzilla allegedly said, size does matter (as does the relation to the world economy).

The history of the Portland area sawmill workers was reasonably consistent. In 1935, they were the strongest supporters of the AFL. They were the most hesitant to break with the UBCJ and the least enthusiastic about joining with the CIO. In the struggle over control of the 1935 strike, the Portland local of the Saw Mill and Timber Workers local was controlled by supporters of Abe Muir (Tattam 1970:59). These tendencies form an important background to the struggles and evolution of the IWA.

Conflict with AFL

When the sawmill workers and loggers broke from the UBCJ in 1937 to form the IWA–CIO, the struggle with the AFL was intense throughout the whole Northwest, but more so in Portland than anywhere else. First, the UBCJ was among the strongest unions in the AFL. Led by Bill Hutcheson, the new CIO organization was seen as a personal affront to the UBCJ leader, who in his debate with John L. Lewis at the 1935 AFL convention had been on the receiving end of Lewis's famous punch. Second, while many new CIO unions had minimal contacts with the AFL (the auto, rubber, steel, textile, coal mining, metal mining unions, among others), the IWA was in their midst. UBCJ locals picketed IWA sawmills. AFL teamsters refused to move IWA lumber, while UBCJ carpenters refused to handle CIO wood. AFL gangsters engaged in arson and violence against the new union, hardly giving it any opportunity to go about its work. As Walter Galenson remarks, "Thus was ushered in one of the most bitter rival union conflicts in the history of American labor" (1983:387; also Bernstein 1969:629; Jackson 1953:20–30). Violent conflicts existed in the Northwest, while AFL and CIO unions in other parts of the country were still cooperating in joint state and local labor councils.[22] The intensity of this conflict was of concern to the national CIO as a whole. The beleaguered IWA leadership simultaneously faced opposition from its right-wing opponents, some of whom were rumored to be secretly negotiating a return to the AFL, and powerful unions within the AFL itself.

A devastating blow was dealt to the union and its left-wing leadership by the loss of Harold Pritchett as president of the union. Lembcke and Tattam call him "a powerful speaker, an experienced and respected organizer and a hard worker" (1984:79). Others have described him as charismatic. Levenstein is more circumspect (1981:266). Pritchett early on had impressed even moderates and AFL types with his leadership abilities and was a central figure for the leftists in the union.

Pritchett had first entered the United States in 1933, from that time receiving twenty-two ninety-day visitor permits and nine extensions (the account here largely follows Lembcke and Tattam 1984:75–80). While he was affiliated with the AFL, the UBCJ and the Seattle central labor council had strongly supported these visas. Beginning in early 1937, after his election as IWA president, Pritchett, although a Canadian citizen, lived in Seattle, making occasional trips back to British Columbia to visit his family or to fulfill the terms of his permits. In February 1938, immigration officials turned down his request for a permanent visa, claiming they had secret information that he was a Communist Party member. From then on, the U.S. government increasingly made it more and more difficult for him to obtain even temporary

---

[22] Among numerous places, note Barberton, Ohio (Borsos 1996:258–73, passim), Memphis (Honey 1993), and Birmingham.

visitor's visas. On August 22, 1940, Pritchett's final appeal to obtain just a temporary visa was denied. His inability to visit the United States forced him to resign as president of the union. Not only the lumber operators but the AFL and the CRDC opposition were delighted, all having helped it to varying degrees (Lembcke and Tattam 1984:75–79). Even before his resignation, restrictions on his border crossings in 1938 and 1939 had made it increasingly difficult for Pritchett to function as president.

Organizing the South

The left-wing leadership of the union was committed to organizing southern woodworkers. After a tour of the South in March and April 1938, President Pritchett wrote:

> Organizing the South would double our membership and offset the employers' contentions that our living standards on the West Coast should be reduced to meet the unfair competition of the unorganized states of the South. Organization of the great Southern lumber industry is crucial, if only for protection of the Northern wage scale and working conditions. (*Timber Worker*, June 4, 1938; also cited in Dinwiddie 1980: 16)

Thus, by the time of the 1939 convention the leaders of the IWA felt nothing if not desperate. The referendum election after the convention had, to be sure, returned Pritchett and the left-wingers to office. The Portland-centered Columbia River District Council, however, disputed the election, claiming that it had been conducted improperly, even though the procedures followed had been approved by CRDC leader Al Hartung and the conservative regional CIO directors of Oregon and Washington beforehand. Michael Widman, an assistant to John L. Lewis, was sent to investigate the election and declared it legitimate. Nevertheless, the CRDC advised its locals to withhold their per capita taxes from the international, effectively starving the organizing program (Lembcke and Tattam 1984).

The IWA leaders, desirous of intensifying the union organizing campaign in the South and in British Columbia, turned to the CIO national office for financial help in early 1940. This was to prove an inopportune time: their request for aid would backfire on them with disastrous results. To understand why this was the case, we must look at changes that took place in the CIO in late 1939.

The Mini-Purge of the CIO, 1939–40

Although the shake-up of the CIO in 1939–40 has hardly been discussed in the literature and goes against the commonly cited wisdom that the CPers operated relatively freely within the CIO until 1948, the signs of this mini-purge were un-mistakable (Zieger 1995:82).[23] At the October 14, 1939, meeting of the CIO ex-ecutive board and regional directors, CIO president John L. Lewis denounced his erstwhile allies, the Communists, saying that no known Communist would be em-ployed by the CIO in any capacity (for an account of these and related matters, see Dubofsky and Van Tine 1977:319–22). He also announced a number of organiza-tional changes that restricted the Left. First, he abolished the office of West Coast director, demoting ILWU leader Harry Bridges, who had held that position since 1937, to California director. He appointed former UMWA assistants and CIO rightists, named William Dalrymple as regional director of Oregon, and made per-manent what had been the temporary appointment of Richard Francis as regional director of Washington State. He removed John Brophy as the organizing director of the CIO and placed him in charge of a department that until then had been nonexistent. Brophy was at this time considered a sympathizer of the left and had secured Bridges's original appointment as West Coast director. In the positions of real power, he appointed rightists Alan Haywood as director of organization, and former UMWA official Michael Widman as assistant director of organiza-tion.[24] These changes paralleled purges taking place in other venues. For example, in the Packinghouse Workers Organizing Committee (PWOC), director Van Bittner, an old UMWA right-wing apparatchik, used the signing of the German-Soviet Nonaggression Pact on August 23, 1939, as an occasion to remove key leftists throughout the PWOC. Those removed included national director Donald Harris, Chicago director Herb March, and regional organizers Tony Stephens and Kermit Fry. Van Bittner also removed Trotskyist Joe Ollman, who, unlike the Communists, had not defended the pact (Horowitz 1990:438–50, 1997:126–29; Halpern 1989:423–25). In SWOC and the UMWA, the squeeze on leftists also increased. And, in the UAW, as the CIO national office finally intervened to help remove the highly disruptive and organizationally ineffectual Homer Martin, they supported the relatively inexperienced (and, in the view of some, not very compe-tent) but non-leftist R. J. Thomas rather than the more popular and experienced leftists around Wyndham Mortimer.

[23] James Prickett, in a rich, fascinating analysis of the "communist issue" in the CIO, by focusing on auto, maritime, and electrical, sees the conflict taking place almost exclusively in the post–World War II period, missing, like Zieger, the early purges. He writes, "A firm guarantee of autonomy for each affiliate and a definite coolness toward anti-communism characterized the CIO until the post-war period" (Prickett 1975:377). Emspak notes, "The CIO functioned on a nonexclusionary basis . . . be-tween the years 1936 and 1947" 1972:18), and adds, "Between 1945 and 1949, the CIO changed from a progressive antiwar force to an anti-communist organization dedicated to maintaining the status quo" (1972:13).

[24] CIO Executive Board Minutes, Archives of Labor and Urban Affairs (ALUA), collection 751, box 1, October 1939.

The reasons for this mini-purge are not hard to find. The CIO—along with the New Deal and FDR himself—had been the subject of increasing attacks on many fronts in 1938 and 1939. These came from the AFL, Congress—especially the House Un-American Activities Committee headed by Martin Dies—formerly sympathetic journalists, employers, and others. Although conflicts between the CIO and the AFL were often intense in 1937 (witness, of course, that between the IWA and the UBCJ), the public attacks, particularly at the national level, did not begin in earnest until 1938.

During 1937, charters of individual CIO unions were suspended by the AFL. On February 24, 1937, AFL president William Green ordered all state federations and city central bodies to rebuff the CIO. In many areas, including Pennsylvania, New York City, Georgia, and West Virginia, as well as Alabama (where the bulk of the state AFL newspaper subscriptions were paid for by the coal miners and their locals), there was much resistance from AFL unions. All throughout 1937 there were also unity negotiations, which did not finally break down until the end of the year. It was not until the December 1937 AFL convention that the break was made official, and John Frey, AFL Metal Trade president, publicly denounced the CIO as Communist-controlled. After the AFL Executive Committee formally revoked the charters of the UMWA and other renegade unions in January 1938, the war of words saw few holds barred (Galenson 1983:29–44). Formerly sympathetic journalists, including Benjamin Stolberg and Louis Stark of the New York Times, the latter considered the dean of labor reporters, launched public attacks (for details, especially on Stolberg, see Zieger 1995:82–83, 96, 400; for an even more scurrilous attack on the CIO, see Harris 1940:132–39).

There were increased attacks by the Catholic Church hierarchy, which had initially been quiet as its more radical priests gave strong support to the early CIO efforts. With the establishment of the anti-communist Association of Catholic Trade Unionists (ACTU), led by Father Charles Owen Rice, "red-baiting of the CIO became a pastime for many Church patriarchs in the late 1930s" (Fraser 1991:424; for an overview of the ACTU, see Rosswurm 1992; for a largely epigenetic, uncritical account of Rice, see the commentary on his collected writings, Fighter with a Heart, 1996, esp. xviii, 80–88, 96–106; the latter includes his later public apology for his activities; Rice 1989; Remarkable, but certainly too little, too late).

The biggest public barrage against the CIO seemed to come from Congress. In May 1938, by a lopsided vote of 191 to 41, the U.S. House of Representatives approved the formation of the House Committee on Un-American Activities, chaired by right-wing Democrat Martin Dies of Texas. The bill was backed by Vice President Garner and House Majority Leader Sam Rayburn. Dies, with huge amounts of publicity, paraded witnesses before the committee, many of whom leveled highly inflammatory, unsubstantiated charges, especially against the CIO. Frey used it as a forum to denounce the CIO as a Communist front. Dies and his book, *The Trojan Horse*, proved popular, and his appropriations increased each year (Goldstein 1978:247). Anti-CIO or "Little Dies" committees were set up in twenty-two states. The Dies committee became a forum for calling for the deportation of Harry Bridges (ultimately unsuccessful) and of Harold Pritchett (successful) (Lembcke and Tattam 1984:75). Congress passed further anti-radical legislation, including the Smith Act, on June 28, 1940, and the Nationality Act, on October 14, 1940 (Goldstein 1978:245–46).

Yet rhetoric alone rarely carries the day.[25] What emboldened critics and made CIO leaders hesitant—especially the more moderate ones—was the complete stalling of the advance of the CIO in 1938 and 1939. The year 1937 had begun with the victory over General Motors (GM) and the signing of a contract with U.S. Steel and a wave of subsequent sit-downs around the country. By August 1937, however, the country was entering a major recession within the Depression (the "Roosevelt recession"), with production and employment dropping dramatically. The major advance of the CIO into the South, which was supposedly the site of the next great wave of organizing, was the establishment of the Sidney Hillman–led Textile Workers Organizing Committee, begun in earnest in the wake of the GM victory. Started with high hopes, it failed so miserably to organize the South that it degenerated, in the words of sympathetic Hillman biographer Steven Fraser, into a "bureaucratic mirage," which sustained "the illusion of its existence" (1991:420). All organizing ground to a halt. Galenson states succinctly, "The year 1938 was not a good one for trade unions" (1983:44).

The continuing attacks and the retreat by the previously unstoppable CIO caused consternation among the CIO business unionist/rightists. Those in the Hillman wing of the CIO, along with Philip Murray, were, of course, especially sensitive to the public attacks. They were also far more disposed in general than Lewis and the leftists to depend on the good offices of the Roosevelt administration. In a time of public attack and union stagnation, this tendency was heightened. Philip Murray believed that "we are living in a wave and an age of reaction" (Fraser 1991:441; see also CIO Executive Board, June 3–5, 1940). Hillman, often to the annoyance of Lewis, had developed a relationship with FDR as the president's foremost contact with labor unions, often doing Roosevelt's bidding within the CIO (Fraser 1991:435; Josephson 1952:468–69). Although he was not viscerally anticommunist like many of the other rightists, once the CP broke from the administration with the signing of the 1939 German-Soviet Nonaggression Pact, the CP became a major impediment for him.

Other conflicts were brewing as well. After the pact, the New York Labor Party split in two, in part because many Jews and others from Europe did not want to abandon their anti-Nazi stance. The state committee of the party came

---

[25] Or as Zieger notes, at least initially, "Lewis paid little attention" (1995:82).

under the control of the president of the International Ladies' Garment Workers' Union (ILGWU), David Dubinsky, now back in the AFL, while CP sympathizer Vito Marcantonio and his allies gained control of the New York City committee (Josephson 1952:473; Waltzer 1977:223–33). "Hints were dropped" by Hillman lieutenants, according to Fraser, "that the Amalgamated might leave if the party's activities were not curtailed" (1991:434). Pressure began to build on Lewis to distance himself from his left-wing allies. By January 6, 1940, Hillman had announced that he and the Amalgamated would support FDR for a third term, while Lewis and the CP opposed such a stance (Josephson 1952:474–75). Thus, the squeeze by the rightists was put on Lewis indirectly by going after the CP (contrary to Zieger 1995:82).

The question of special interest, however, is why the CIO national office would want to throw its lot in with the right-wing forces in the IWA in 1940, which showed wavering support for the CIO, had little interest in the South (a major point of concern for the CIO as a whole), and displayed a far higher level of incompetence than other right-wing CIO union leaders. This point is especially in need of examination since the CIO national leadership at this time had enthusiastically thrown its support to other CP-led groups, including the UCAPAWA, FE, Mine Mill, and the United Electrical Workers (UE), and Lewis continued to increasingly rely on the CIO general council, CPer Lee Pressman (Zieger 1995:83). Even in 1941, Murray had given the reins of the Oil Workers International Union (OWIU) drive to the leftist (and likely CPer) former head of the National Labor Relations Board, Edwin Smith, who went on to hire and work with many CPers during the successful oil workers campaign. On the other side of the ledger, the CIO rightists were quite concerned with the growing power and ambitions of leftist Harry Bridges, the powerful head of the ILWU and its nominal West Coast director, who was in a close alliance with the IWA Left-led leadership (Zieger 1995:82).

John L. Lewis, one of the more contradictory figures in U.S. labor history, was willing at times to work with and ally closely with Communists, other leftists, and former oppositionists. Sometimes he argued it was merely a matter of expediency ("Who gets the bird, the hunter or the dog?"). At other times he seemed to relish the role not merely of all-powerful, charismatic labor leader, but also of left-wing internationalist. To explore this further, we need to look carefully into the nature of trade unions under capitalism and how their contradictory functions affected major CIO unions, a discussion broached in Chapter 1.

John L. Lewis was primarily a trade unionist who saw political involvement as mainly expedient. Hillman and Murray, on the other hand, were corporatists, who by 1937 had hitched their wagons to FDR and the New Deal Democratic Party (Dubofsky and Van Tine 1977:320). Pressure to rein in the Communists intensified after the signing of the Molotov-Ribbentrop (also called the Hitler-Stalin) Pact on August 23, 1939. There was even some fear that the Amalgamated Clothing

Workers of America (ACWA) would follow the path that the ILGWU had taken in 1938, back to the AFL (Dubofsky and Van Tine 1977:322).

Thus, the IWA left-wing leadership, under the gun in fierce, often violent jurisdictional fights with the carpenters' union (UBCJ) and other AFL unions, undermined and starved financially by its own right-wing minority oppositionists, had picked a rather inopportune time to turn to the CIO national office for help (Levenstein 1981:80, 266).

The CIO insisted as a condition of its helping the union financially that the CIO national office appoint the director of organization and have complete control of the union's organizing campaign, including the hiring of organizing staff members. As director of organizing, Lewis picked the skilled and experienced Adolph Germer, a sectarian anti-communist bureaucrat with few scruples about doing whatever he could to get his way. Len De Caux, CIO publicity director and editor of the national CIO News, described him as "once socialist, rigidly factional red-hating" (1970: 412) and "rigidly sectarian anti-leftist" (1970:462). With respect to the 1937 Flint sit-down strike, De Caux wrote, "Germer, long a rightwing socialist fighting the left, got gloomy when the masses were on the move" (1970:255).

Although Germer was not a freelancer, an independent operator, or someone who determined policy on his own—he operated freely so long as he supported the interests of the CIO rights in the national CIO office—it is still important to understand the personal and ideological proclivities that motivated him. It is also important to understand how the earlier, more radical, presumptively democratic Adolph Germer had been transformed into a narrow-minded, authoritarian, bureaucratic operative; for Germer was in many ways typical of an emerging layer of professional union bureaucrats whose ideology would eventually characterize virtually all of U.S. union officialdom.[26]

Adolph Germer's father was a Socialist miner from northern Germany. Germer came to the United States as a young child with his family in 1888. As a sixteen-year-old coal miner, he took part in 1897 in a strike in Mt. Olive, Illinois. He was also impressed by the strike in nearby Virden, which was defeated when coal mine operators brought in African-American strikebreakers protected by armed guards (Cary 1968:1–6). His early racial attitudes paralleled those of other right-wing Socialist Party leaders, especially the overtly racist Victor Berger. In 1901, he joined the SP at its founding. He was an active proponent of rank-and-file democracy in unions, an opponent of the two major parties, as well as an anti-capitalist advocate of the class struggle. He opposed the "pure and simple" trade unionism of Samuel Gompers, urged support for strikes by other unions, and advocated industrial

---

[26] For Germer, I have leaned heavily on Cary's outstanding 1968 dissertation, as well as a careful reading of Germer's own papers at the Wisconsin State Historical Society archives.

unionism, at first supporting the IWW—even initially attending its founding convention in 1905—before turning against it for its refusal to honor signed contracts. In the next decade he gradually became a right-wing Socialist, his racial proclivities hardening and his interests focusing more on trade unions than party politics. Nevertheless, while working for the UMWA in Colorado (late 1912 to early 1914), he saw no conflict between his work organizing miners and his work agitating on behalf of the SP. During World War I, like most U.S. Socialists, including others on the right, he strongly opposed the war, the sale of liberty bonds, and the draft.

Like virtually all Socialist Party members, Germer initially supported the 1917 Bolshevik Revolution in Russia. In 1919, however, as the left wing of the Party gained a clear majority, the right wing, with Germer as a leader, voided the left wing's massive gains in the election of Party leaders and began expelling left-wing chapters, including most of the foreign-language federations as well as the left-wing state chapters in Michigan, Ohio, and Massachusetts. This was a defining moment for Germer and other right-wing Socialists, as they abandoned any semblance of commitment to democratic principles in order to maintain control of the Party machinery. It also accentuated a vitriolic anti-communism (which Germer had earlier denounced as scurrilous), as Germer publicly claimed—without evidence and as a way of defending such a blatant violation of democratic principles—that the Left was supported by Wall Street (Cary 1968:46). He continued to move to the right during the 1920s and by 1934 had even dropped his membership in the SP. In 1935, he approached both William Green, by then president of the AFL, and his old enemy John L. Lewis, hat in hand, looking for work. By the time Lewis offered him a job with the new Committee of Industrial Organizations in November 1935, he had long given up his belief in the class struggle, working-class democracy, Socialist agitation, and independent political action. He merely had a verbal commitment to making the collective bargaining process work (Cary 1968:85).

With the CIO, Germer had stints working with the autoworkers, then with the rubberworkers. With the latter, he was continually at odds with rank-and-file militancy. Trying to push a U.S. Labor Department–engineered settlement on striking Goodyear workers, he was overwhelmed by angry rank-and-file opposition. When workers began further sit-downs, "Germer had no sympathy for them" (Cary 1968:97). With his primary concerns being to assert the authority of the international, curb worker militancy, and preserve the sanctity of contracts, Germer "would repeatedly misread rank and file tendencies" (1968:98). In 1937, Germer played a major role in ending the sit-down at Chrysler against much opposition. He tended to see antagonism to his views as Communist, for he no longer understood the basis for much worker militancy with which he had previously sympathized. He had the same problem with the oilworkers' union, seeing Communists behind the factional struggle there, although there were virtually no Party members or sympathizers in the union at the time. Yet Germer's attitudes reflected not merely the degree to which his own thinking had dramatically changed, but also the degree to which the CIO (in contrast to the AFL) wished to tightly control its new affiliates (Cary 1968:116). When Alan Haywood was promoted to the position of director of organization in 1939, Germer was moved to Haywood's old position as New York regional director. After the IWA and the CIO signed their agreement, Germer, in June 1940, was made director of organizing for the IWA.

Germer had other characteristics that made him an especially vitriolic factionalist. He was a highly sectarian, combative individual. During the battles with the AFL, for example, Germer took the time to write a large number of poison pen letters to his old acquaintance and former mineworker official, then AFL President William Green, many of them in 1938. Even as late as January 19, 1940, he belligerently wrote Green that medical science had "discovered a process by which the backbone can be stiffened. Naturally, my thought was that you would want to take advantage" of it. By November 19, 1940, he was writing Green letters comparing him to Hitler and Stalin. As the CIO battled the mineworkers' District 50 in organizing drives during World War II, he talked about his former benefactor John L. Lewis in the same vein, comparing him to Hitler.[27]

It has been argued by some that Germer's anti-communism was principled, but the facts do not bear this out. Unlike Lewis or even Hillman, Germer thought the CP only hindered organizing, never recognizing, as many other rightists did, that CP organizers and leaders were often among the most successful organizers (on Lewis's views, see Zieger 1995:83). Despite the successes of the CPers in organizing woodworkers in British Columbia (acknowledged by virtually everyone, including Germer himself at times), he asserted, "While our people are out trying to organize, settle grievances, and conduct negotiations, the 'Comrades' are injecting their poison into the rank and file."[28]

He tended to view them solely as conspirators, "a hive of plotters and spies . . . Almost daily a new spy appears on the scene and confesses . . . the conspiracy to capture the labor movement or destroy it." He put great stock in the scurrilous and decidedly dubious account of Benjamin Gitlow in *I Confess* (1940). He was characteristically more than willing to distort the facts to make his point. He railed to C. E. Orton, then the left-wing president of the IWA, in a letter on March 26, 1941, "Don't you know that when the rank and file 'cleaned house' and kicked

---

[27] Germer to Haywood, June 21, 1945, Germer papers, reel 9. This proneness to exaggeration is reflected in the reaction of other CIO liberals. Joe Cannon, the CIO regional director for eastern Pennsylvania, for example, accused a congressman who supported the anti-communist, anti-union Dies committee's appropriation in 1940 of "going over to Hitler." He characterized supporters of the Walter-Logan Bill, which would allow the findings of agencies (including the NLRB) to be reviewed for factual determinations by the courts, of doing the same. Cannon to all eastern Pennsylvania affiliates, February 7, 1940, Germer papers, reel 4, frame 644.

[28] Germer to Haywood, April 10, 1941, Germer papers, reel 5.

Homer Martin and his Communist pals out, the United Auto Workers grew from an almost wrecked organization to more than 400,000 members? You are still young and obviously there [is] much for you to learn." Martin's "Communist pals" were actually the anti-communist followers of Jay Lovestone, while CP autoworkers, including their leaders, Windham Mortimer and Bob Travis, played a major role in building the organization and opposing Martin.[29]

Finally, Germer was decidedly insensitive to racial issues (a generous understatement), something he shared with many right-wing Socialists, although his views contrasted greatly with those of a small number of more left-wing Socialists like Highlander founder Myles Horton and even CIO operative Paul Christopher. He displays none of the sensitivity of most CPers, for example, when he writes to CIO director John Brophy that an operative of UAW president Homer Martin is "a nigger in the woodpile." In 1942, Germer was refused entry into Canada as an "alien enemy." Immigration officials asked him if he belonged to the German race. Germer replied, "I belong to the white race." He never disputes Theodore Debs (Eugene's brother) in their frequent correspondence, who writes that the machinists union (notoriously racially discriminatory) "was among the most progressive, aggressive, advanced labor organizations in the country. There is no questioning the fact." Unlike even right-wing coal and steel officials, who were often (as we have seen) impressed by the militancy and union solidarity shown by southern Black workers, Germer and his associates almost always saw them as backward. Germer defends the IWA in not wanting to mention race or questions of racial equality in the South, even though the constituency there was often majority–African-American. "The International Woodworkers are carrying out the CIO policy in the broadest sense in the South, but we are not making much fuss about it publicly. We carry it out in action and say very little about it." He thus opposed the "liberal" position on race taken by the CIO-supported National Religion and Labor Foundation, even after right-wing CIO secretary-treasurer James Carey (himself not noted for his aggressiveness on racial issues) had rebuked him: "Although I appreciate your reservations concerning the reaction in the South on the statement issued by the National Religion and Labor Foundation, I don't think any progress would come from retreating from the liberal position that the foundation is taking." When the left won an election in (southern) District 10 of the IWA (because of the overwhelming support of Black woodworkers), one of Germer's supporters wrote to President Lowery to say that the results of the election were "a severe blow to the white folks in this territory."[30]

[29] Germer to Ralph Korngold, January 17, 1940, Germer papers, reels 4 and 5.
[30] October 28, 1937, Germer papers, reel 4. See also Germer to Haywood, March 12, 1942, reel 6; Debs to Germer, September 22, 1937, reel 4; George Brown to Germer, July 19, 1944, reel 8; Germer to James Carey, February 11, 1944, reel 7; Carey to Germer, February 5, 1944, reel 7; February 8, 1942, reel 6.

Germer noted when he stopped at a Mine Mill hall in Idaho that the hall was located "where in 1899 the miners were bull-penned by colored troops sent to the area by President William McKinley." He opposed a "colored speaker" at the Cincinnati Industrial Union Council (IUC) meeting.[31]

Such attitudes on the part of Adolph Germer made it unlikely that he would have appreciated not merely the importance of organizing the South, but the tremendous potential that a majority Black workforce of hundreds of thousands of workers would have.

Germer Takes Over as IWA Organizing Director

On June 19, 1940, IWA president Harold Pritchett sent out a circular to all district councils and local unions announcing the arrival of Adolph Germer as the new CIO-appointed IWA director of organization. Germer had a close personal and political relationship with Alan Haywood, the new CIO director of organization.[32] Certain of Germer's attitudes and preconceptions dovetailed neatly with those of leaders of the IWA White Bloc. Upon his arrival, Germer immediately developed a close working relationship with the oppositionist leaders of the Columbia River District Council, especially its president, Al Hartung.

With the influx of money from the national CIO and the passage of the dues surtax for new organizing, the question of who were to be the new organizers and where they would be organizing came to the fore. Germer's approach was to gain adherents in small sawmills who would be more likely to support the oppositionists and to avoid organizing more radical loggers, workers in larger sawmills, and those in the South or British Columbia who might be more predisposed to supporting the left. Germer also wanted to make sure that the bulk of the newly hired organizers were right-wingers and had no relation to the CP. When President Pritchett gave Germer a list of nine proposed organizers, Germer wrote Haywood, "I went over the list with Director Dalrymple and one of the other boys in the Columbia River District and they said that with about two exceptions out of the nine names they were all 'labeled,' [meaning connected to the Party]." At the same time Germer continually claimed that he would not discriminate politically.[33] He often went to great lengths, using his extensive contacts, to ferret out those who were not 100% in his corner politically. His friend August Scholle, Germer's successor as the Michigan regional CIO director, reported that a Clifford Baker, recommended by

[31] Memorandum, September 17, 1940, Germer papers, reel 5; Germer to Haywood, September 18, 1945, reel 10.

[32] E.g., letters beginning "Dear Bud" and signed "Your buddy, Alan," including one on November 19, 1946, Germer papers, reel 10.

[33] Germer to Haywood, July 13, 1940, Germer papers, reel 4.

a UAW representative, was "a very qualified and competent fellow" but was a "pal of Matt Savola" (a leftist) and should not be hired. He also vetoed as an IWA organizer William H. Riley, an IWA delegate from Bessemer, Alabama, who had been recommended by conservative southern CIO leaders, because Riley did not toe the line at the convention. Thus, in contrast to the early organizers in steel and many other key industries, the organizing staffers that Germer hired were both personally loyal to him and committed to doing battle with the elected left-wing leadership of the union; in addition, few on his staff were known (or ever displayed any competence) for their organizing skills. In these and other activities Germer had the complete support of the CIO national office. Haywood, for example, wrote him, "I think your position in the matter is absolutely correct . . . Keep up the good work—I know you will." Germer simultaneously began a concerted attack on the IWA newspaper The *Timber Worker*, which Germer accused of injecting outside politics into trade union issues. He claimed to Haywood that there had been much opposition to these policies from the rank and file.[34]

The first big showdown between the Left and the Germer organized rightists came at the Washington State Industrial Union Council meeting on September 20, 1940. The IUC was an organization set up to coordinate CIO activities throughout the state of Washington and was decidedly leftist in its orientation. Before the convention, both Germer and state CIO director Richard Francis had spoken at IWA meetings urging members to oppose the current leaders of the IUC. They also wanted to exclude the counting of delegates from the radical IWA and Cannery local unions, whose seasonal work allowed workers to remain members without paying dues. When these tactics failed, it was clear that the Left had a large majority at the meeting. On September 22, 1940, when the convention was officially opened, Germer announced that the convention was illegal since the call had been "illegally issued" (Lembcke and Tattam 1985:84). On September 26, John L. Lewis appointed a committee of conservatives, including Germer and Richard Francis, to administer the Washington State Council. Harry Tucker, an extreme anti-communist, was selected to be secretary-treasurer of the committee.[35] So much for democracy.

The next blow was struck at the IWA constitutional convention in Aberdeen, Washington, on October 7–12, 1940. Although they were observers in the gallery, Germer, along with Francis and Dalrymple, quite visibly directed the opposition forces.[36] On the first day of the convention, Worth Lowery, the IWA vice president and

[34] Scholle to Germer, July 15, 1942, Germer papers, reel 6; Haywood to Germer, August 27, 1940, reel 4:1061; Germer to Haywood, September 4, 1940, reel 4:9–10.

[35] Telegram to Germer from Lewis, September 26, 1940, Germer papers, reel 5; Records of the International Woodworkers of America (henceforth, IWA), reel 5:87; Lembcke and Tattam (1984:84–85).

[36] Nigel Morgan, Executive Board member from BC District One to Orton, October 31, 1940, Germer files, reel 5.

a White Bloc leader, attacked the *Timber Worker* for creating "dissension and dissatisfaction within our ranks by lending its columns to the furthering of causes and issues
divorced from our problems as workers in the lumber industry."[37] A resolution to exclude all Communists and fascists from the IWA was ultimately defeated 134 to 124
(Lembcke and Tattam 1984:86). While the Left had barely won out at the meeting, the
Right had been energized and gained the full support of the CIO national apparatus.

Immediately after the convention, oppositionists held a meeting of one hundred
delegates led by CRDC head Al Hartung. They demanded that John L. Lewis investigate the strife within the union, which they blamed on the left-wing union leaders.
On October 17, five days after the convention had ended, the union executive board
met to discuss getting rid of Adolph Germer, whom they accused of being responsible for most of the trouble. They sent Orton to Washington, DC, to meet with
Lewis, who paid little attention to him (Lembcke and Tattam 1984:87).

Other incidents reflected the escalating struggle. The large Longview Local 36
had been a left-wing stronghold. In August Germer had appointed two rightists to
be organizers for the local and the surrounding area. The local immediately objected
to the appointment of George Brown and Chet Dustin, "given the friction with international and district officers." They elected a committee of five men to meet them
upon their arrival and to "escort them out of town."[38] On December 20, 1940, Brown
and a number of other Germer's associates appeared at a Local 36 executive board
meeting and demanded admittance. Upon being refused, they waited outside, yelling
and making threats. When the meeting ended, the group attacked members of the
executive board, with Germer-paid thug Freddy Thompson attacking business agent
Bob Williams. In a letter of protest that Orton sent to Philip Murray, dated December
24, 1940, he wrote, "More recently, two organizers under the direction of Germer,
and who are paid by the CIO, namely Gola Whitlow and Fred Thompson, led a gang
of some 15 or 18 men in an attempted beating of the president, business agent, and
three other members of our Local Union in Longview, Washington."[39]

In the left-wing Northern Washington District, the IWA was battling the AFL in
a number of workplaces. In a move considered by many workers in the union to be
barely short of treason, the CRDC joined forces with the AFL to defeat the IWA.
The large, left-wing Aberdeen-Raymond local became so annoyed by this treachery
that it decided to withdraw from the union, weakening the Left within the IWA
(Lembcke and Tattam 1984:89).[40]

---

[37] "Report to the Fourth Constitutional Convention," October 7, 1940, Germer files, reel 5.

[38] Don Latvala, Recording Secretary, Local 36, IWA to Germer, August 24, 1940, reel 4.

[39] Orton to Murray, December 24, 1940, Germer files, reel 5; Lembcke and Tattam (1984:88).

[40] Note the distorted analysis of the Socialist Workers Party (SWP), which saw the unity of the AFL
and the CRDC as "progressive," combating the CIO sectarianism of the CP-led IWA. See "AFL-CIO
Unite in Big Lumber Strike," *Socialist Appeal*, December 14, 1940, and "AFL-CIO Lumber Workers
Win Gains Despite Stalinist Treachery," *Socialist Appeal*, Dec. 21, 1940.

In the midst of these events, the IWA executive board voted to fire Adolph Germer, informing him by letter. IWA president Orton then wrote a letter to Philip Murray explaining the decision:

> First, when President Lewis and Director Haywood selected Adolph Germer for the all-important and responsible position of Director of Organization for the IWA, we naturally believed in his ability and impartiality to work with and cooperate with the elected International officers in effectively organizing the unorganized woodworkers and creating the highest degree of harmony within out union as a whole.
>
> In assuming his duties, he immediately made contact with the self-appointed leaders of the so-called "opposition bloc" some members of which were then, or have since become, identified with reactionary officials of the AFL and particularly that of the Carpenters and Joiners, who have spent several hundred thousands of dollars in continued attempts to destroy the IWA ever since it was first established as part of the CIO.
>
> His direction of our organizational campaign has resulted in no increase in membership to any appreciable extent in proportion to the amount of money that has been spent.[41]

Orton quotes a press statement of Germer's in the *Seattle Post-Intelligencer*, December, 7, 1940: "Under the present administration of the IWA the organization was all but wrecked. The CIO was asked for help and the IWA received it. The rank and file of the woodworkers want none of the Communist Party interference, influence or control. The CIO wants none of it. Deny it as they may, the fact remains that the Communist Party representatives have definitely meddled in the affairs of the IWA as well as with other unions of every description."[42]

Subsequently, Philip Murray appointed an investigating committee consisting of conservatives Sherman Dalrymple, president of the rubberworkers' union, and J. C. Lewis, a conservative mineworkers' official and the CIO-appointed administrator of the Washington CIO Industrial Union Council, and Reid Robinson, the left-wing leader of the Mine, Mill, and Smelter Workers Union, to look into the charges against Germer. With the acquiescence of the two non-radical members of the committee, Germer succeeded in turning his trial into a witch hunt against Communists in the union. Germer's testimony was taken up in part by reading material from Communist Party turncoat Benjamin Gitlow's diatribe, *I Confess*. The response to Germer was made by IWA vice-president Ilmar Koisvunen, a Finnish logger from Michigan. Koisvunen argued incisively that Germer's testimony itself showed that he had come to the IWA intent on a

---

[41] Bertel McCarty, IWA Secretary-Treasurer to Germer, December 6, 1940, Germer files, reel 5.
[42] To Murray from Orton, December 18, 1940, IWA 5:431–36.

witch hunt rather than with the intention of rising above factional disputes and helping to organize woodworkers (Lembcke and Tattam 1984:96). The results were preordained, and the committee found the charges against Germer to be "not supported."[43]

The results of the trial accelerated the factional activity of the White Bloc. On February 20, Worth Lowery announced the formation of a "CIO Organizing Committee," based in the CRDC and funded by the CIO, with its own newspaper. The committee then set about organizing the small sawmills along the Willamette River, running south from Portland, workplaces that might be more predisposed to support the White Bloc—largely avoiding loggers and workers in the larger sawmills, especially in the Puget Sound area near Seattle, and the more desperate workers in the South.

The split between the two factions grew more intense. Alan Haywood stepped in as mediator, allegedly attempting to adjudicate between the two groups. He proposed a change to the IWA constitution that would alter the voting formula at conventions, effectively giving control of the union to the rightists. Why, then, did the leadership agree to these changes? Much speculation exists that the left merely conceded control, as Soviet foreign policy changed after the German invasion that began on June 22, 1941 (Galenson 1983:405). Lembcke and Tattam suggest this speculation is not accurate. They argue that the CP did not lose rank-and-file support after its line change, but in fact gained support (for unrelated reasons). Further, they note that Orton refused to agree to Haywood's proposals before the convention. They argue that it was the CIO's politicking of wavering locals, particularly those in the South, that gave the White Bloc a majority at the convention (Lembcke and Tattam 1984:100–101). The truth, however, is probably more complicated than either perspective suggests. Why did the union leadership, which controlled the union apparatus, not politic harder, winning over more locals? Though we have no hard evidence, we can see parallels in other unions. In 1936, for example, the leftist Unity Caucus, led by popular founding leader Windham Mortimer, was poised to take over the leadership of the UAW. National CIO officials prevailed upon Communist leaders, led by Earl Browder, to pressure left-wing delegates to support a non-leftist candidate. The national Communist Party leaders, forever amenable and wanting a cozy relationship with the CIO top leaders, obliged (some would say mistakenly, since they got very little in return). Rank-and-file leftists were dismayed, many of them still voting for the Unity slate. They did not want to see the union that they had played a major role in building taken from them by undemocratic, bureaucratic fiats, no matter the source. Similarly, we can speculate that a Party decision to fight to maintain control of the IWA might have yielded different results. Therefore,

---

[43] Murray to Germer, January 21, 1941, Germer papers, reel 4; statement of committee, February 13, 1941, reel 5.

it is quite likely that a national decision of the Party to sacrifice all else to the defense of the Soviet Union while maintaining its so-called center–left alliance in the CIO meant a withdrawal of resources from the battle, leaving Orton and others fighting alone for the union. Here, the CP helped lay the basis for the defeat of the Left and the domination of right-wing leaders, as they did in many other unions. When the 1941 convention met, the White Bloc had the votes to pass a resolution banning Communists from membership in the union. The post-convention election of union officers resulted in a clean sweep by the rightists, with Worth Lowery voted in as president, James Fadling and Carl Winn as vice-presidents, and Ed Benedict as secretary-treasurer.

The White Bloc Victory: Evaluation and its Legacy

The legacy of the White Bloc victory was manifold. It is not, however, unrelated to an analysis of why the Right was able to take control of the top union leadership positions. Vernon Jenson argues that it was a democratic rank-and-file victory over the CP, which had been trying to infiltrate and seize control of the union; that the election of Worth Lowery as president helped to unify the union; and that the IWA ended up far stronger than it had been:

> Culminating a struggle lasting more than five years, the rank-and-file action changed the leadership of the I.W.A. by using democratic procedures. There is no doubt, however, that it was fortunate that such a person as Worth Lowery was available as the leader because he commanded respect from timber workers everywhere. It was fortunate too that he could rise above the bitterness which had developed during the long struggle and the bitter convention arguments. Under his leadership the organization achieved a unity that it never experienced before. The strength and importance of the I.W.A. in the industry has been noticeably increased. (1945:270)

This analysis is seconded and even extended in the official histories of the union. In a 1973 history, for example, the Left is accused of rigging votes and of undemocratic tactics. The CP is blamed for almost all the previous problems of the union, including the inability to organize workers. It argues that at the 1937 convention, the "nomination of Harold Pritchett and a slate of pro-Communist officers touched off an internal factional dispute which in the next four years all but wrecked the IWA" and that even prior to the convention, "the Communist Party had made abortive attempts to impose Communist leadership on the organized woodworkers." Within a year after the CP was disposed of, according to this history, "membership in local unions increased 30 to 300 per cent."[44] Germer's analysis, not surprisingly, is quite similar to the official version and to Jensen's.

The Trotskyist Socialist Workers Party saw the Columbia River District Council and the White Bloc as a progressive "anti-Stalinist" force within the IWA. It argued that the actions of Lewis against the CP leadership of the IWA were a result of a rank-and-file revolt against them, in which Lewis's hand was forced. There is little evidence to support any of these claims; it represents at best wishful thinking on the SWP's part.[45]

When one examines the history of the IWA, what is most striking about the above analysis is its surreal character, the distance from the facts, including facts clearly known by all involved. We can begin with Harold Pritchett's early leadership. Pritchett was supported by overwhelming majorities of woodworkers and was not a controversial figure—certainly in the early years—among militant trade unionists. As David Stone notes, in 1936, when the Federation of Woodworkers was first formed as an AFL affiliate (with Pritchett as its leader), even the highly conservative Portland Central Labor Council unanimously adopted a resolution demanding a permanent visa for Pritchett (Stone 1973; Tattam 1970). The council did not reverse this position until 1937, after the woodworkers had broken with the AFL to join the CIO. At the First General Convention of the Federation of Woodworkers, held at the Portland Labor Temple on September 18–20, 1936, Pritchett was hardly a divisive figure. Quite the contrary. He was nominated by all district councils to be the chairman of the convention. Al Hartung, president of the Columbia River District Council, who was the initial convener, was enthusiastic about turning the chair over to Pritchett, remarking that he was "very much pleased to turn the chair over to such a capable man as Brother Pritchett."[46] His selection as president of the Federation of Woodworkers was equally uncontroversial. When the new union joined the CIO in 1937, a referendum was held for the election of officers. Hartung ran against Pritchett.

Pritchett and his ticket won by a margin of 2 to 1, winning overwhelmingly in every district except for the Columbia River, Hartung's home base. Nevertheless, the factional conflict did not begin in earnest until 1938. David Stone (1973), in a detailed analysis of the factional struggle, concludes that at no time were the rank

---

[44] "History of the International Woodworkers of America (1973)," IWA, University of Oregon (UO), 275, folder 1, history.

[45] See "Rank and File Workers," *Socialist Appeal*, October 27, 1939, 1, 3. *Socialist Appeal* was the official SWP paper, changing its name to the *Militant* after the Trotskyists left the Socialist Party. I am indebted to the staff of the Prometheus Research Library for helping me locate articles in the SWP papers on the struggle in the IWA.

[46] Proceedings, UO, IWA, box 35.

and file of the union against the leftist leadership in a majority. Further, they were never the main opponents of the leadership. Rather, it was the Columbia River District Council leaders who opposed the leftists. The CRDC leaders, however, could never make serious inroads until they had the aid of the national CIO office, the U.S. and Canadian governments, governmental and non-governmental anti-communist organizations, as well as the AFL and employers. Lembcke and Tattam (1984) tend to concur with this analysis, as do I. The factionalism in the union was largely instigated by the Right. Their victory was not a result of rank-and-file displeasure with the leftists, nor was it particularly democratic.

Another seemingly bizarre argument of Germer and the rightists was that they were the most capable organizers, that Communists tended to be not merely disruptive but incapable of or uninterested in building the union. Certainly, neither John L. Lewis nor Philip Murray was of this opinion, as they both made extensive use of Communist organizers. Zieger also highlights "Communists' impressive talents as organizers and activists in the cause of industrial unionism" (1995:83, 400n.).

Germer and the rightists disagreed with this assessment, not only with respect to the woodworkers but in general, much as climate change deniers, birthers, and anti-evolutionists today let their right-wing anti-communist ideology get in the way of their acknowledgment of clear facts. Germer writes, "While our people are out trying to organize, settle grievances, and conduct negotiations, the 'Comrades' are injecting their poison into the rank and file." He uses the presence of CPers as an excuse for the IWA's lack of success in 1944 in the Inland Empire: "The organization in the Inland Empire would have made far more progress and would be in a far better position if those, who are too small to build a movement, would refrain from undermining others who take the IWA, the CIO and the labor movement seriously." A supporter of his argues that getting rid of the CP, even involving Taft-Hartley, was necessary to build unionism:[47]

> You know Adolph dear how determined I was to dump the Commie from the bay area, well I finally succeeded. How did I do it well I really hate to admit that the vicious law know[n] as the Taft Hartley was a help . . . But honestly Adolph we could not build a Union with that element doing everything in their power to divide the workers.[48]

Germer and his friends had the view that the CPers, left to themselves, were incapable or unwilling to build a union. These extreme right-wingers argued that it

---

[47] Germer to Haywood, April 10, 1941, 5:895; Germer to Brown, July 20, 1944, Germer papers, reel 8:274.

[48] Marie DeMartini, Telephraph Traffic Employees' Organization, San Francisco, General Chairman, to Germer, May 27, 1948, Germer papers, reel 11:16.

was the leftists, not Germer and the rightists, who were incapable of organizing.[49] They believed that the left-led Mine Mill and Smelter Workers (once the rightists left the union in 1948) would soon fall apart.[50] They even claimed that the whole labor movement would fall apart if the CP got control. Adolph Germer's friend from Spokane, John M. Glenn writes: "And Adolph unless we rid our entire CIO of these nefarious groups, the whole movement will decay and collapse"[51] And gaining control was indeed their goal: "The 'Commies' will try to capture the whole American labor movement, not only the CIO, but the AFL." This control was for the purpose of using the CIO as a transmission belt, not to build the organization as a trade union to benefit its members.

Germer wrote, "The convention records when published will reveal that there is an organized block that uses the name of the CIO to carry on its anti-CIO propaganda. It is the group that glorifies Bridges. One of them in a committee meeting I attended made the statement that Harry Bridges is the greatest labor leader in the country. This group disputes everything as false that Dalrymple, Francis, and I say and accept as absolute truth everything that is said by Bridges, Orton and McCarty."[52] He said in another letter, "The group is repeating everything that is printed in the *Daily Worker*, the *People's World*, both Communist publications and in the "Voice of the Federation" with respect to the internal affairs of the IWA and the Washington State Industrial Union Council . . . It is clear that to them the CIO is nothing more than a cloak to conceal their real purpose which is, namely, to carry out the often changed line of the Communist Party."[53]

Yet the immediate facts, which stood right in front of Germer and the White Bloc, belied their basic assessments. With control of the union apparatus, funds from increased assessments in addition to extra money from the national CIO, and more paid organizers, the IWA—controlled by Germer and the White Bloc during World War II—grew little (unlike virtually every other CIO union during this period, including that of the textile workers), not merely in the South but even in the union stronghold of the Northwest. In contrast, when Harold Pritchett's final visa application was turned down and he returned to British Columbia, he was elected president of the British Columbia district. With no support or funds from the IWA international office, and quite a bit of hassle and interference from Germer, Brown, and their cohorts, the Left in British Columbia succeeded in organizing virtually all of the British Columbia woodworkers in the face of intense employer opposition. The growth is well documented by union membership data. Jack Greenall, an IWA

---

[49] H. Y. Tucker, Secretary-Treasurer of the Washington State IUC to J. C. Lewis, Administrator, Washington IUC, December 17, 1940, 5:426.

[50] Michael Livoda, Regional Director, Denver, to Germer, June 2, 1948, 12:14–15.

[51] Germer papers, reel 11:498.

[52] Germer to Stanley Earl, July 2, 1946, Germer papers, reel 9:705.

[53] Germer to Haywood, October 10, 1940, Germer papers, reel 5:169.

left-wing leader, attributed this "phenomenal" growth largely to Pritchett's "organizational talents."[54]

Germer and the rightists were not only knowledgeable about the tremendous success of the Left in British Columbia, which had now become, according to Germer, "one of the largest districts in the IWA, if not THE largest district." In fact, the Left had become so strong that even under the new representation rules, they stood a good chance of regaining leadership in the union. Because of this, Germer now tried to restrain his right-wing allies and preached unity with the Left.[55]

Rather than revise their views about the capabilities of the Left as organizers, White Bloc leaders loudly trumpeted even more absurd views. George Brown, Germer's assistant organizing director, for example, claimed that the majority of the British Columbia membership was opposed to the "activities in the political field" of the officers of the District Council, including President Harold Pritchett, Nigel Morgan, member of the District 1 International Board, and Jack Greenall, secretary of British Columbia District Council 1. Brown refused to send organizers recommended by the district officials into the interior.[56] Yet as even George Brown knew quite well, in British Columbia, support for the White Bloc had been minuscule. In 1948, as David Stone notes, the Left defeated White Bloc candidates for every office in British Columbia by margins ranging from 4 to 1 to 80 to 1 (1973:34).

The narrow-minded approach of Germer, Brown, and the White Bloc leaders was to eschew the use of highly successful and competent left-wing organizers and elevate many incompetents, whose main redeeming characteristic was their political loyalty. This, of course, was the accusation of the left. When George Brown refused to appoint the organizers recommended by British Columbia District 1 officials, the district opposed his substitute appointments "on the grounds that these men had demonstrated no organizational ability."[57] Yet incompetence is not merely a value judgment; it has a way of asserting itself objectively.

Even Germer himself became frustrated at times by the ineptness of his own protégés: "I pleaded with the spokesmen for both sides to be extremely careful about getting into another fight and one of the spokesmen for the left-wing forces told me they were desirous of getting along with the International. On the other hand, a few of the administration spokesmen insisted on 'taking them on.'" After detailing the sins of the Left, he says, "At the same time, I am obliged to admit that

[54] Jack Greenall, "The I.W.A. Fiasco: A Political Analysis of a Strange Event," published by the Progressive Workers Movement, Vancouver, n.d., UO, IWA, box 275, History.

[55] Germer to Haywood, July 31, 1944, Germer papers, reel 8.

[56] George Brown, Director of Organization, to Alan Haywood, Vice President and Director of Organization, July 21, 1945, IWA 9:684.

[57] Minutes of Special Executive Meeting, District 1, April 25, 1945, IWA 9:109.

certain individuals on the other side have gone out of their way to antagonize the officials of the Washington District Council."[58]

The incompetence and factionalism of Germer's own protégés and supporters are continually apparent in his increasingly frustrated correspondence. Adolph Germer writes to Alan Haywood about a special meeting of the Bellingham, Washington, IWA local to discuss suspensions; the local invited the international officers, who refused to attend. The Right-controlled international executive board first illegally suspended two locals. Germer then met with his assistant organizing director George Brown, District 1 president Karly Larson, and IWA international president Ballard. A stipulation was worked out by lawyers for both sides, which Ballard refused to sign. Extensive correspondence from Germer shows increasing frustration with his own allies, including President Ballard and Secretary Benedict, both of whom he describes as "idiots and unnecessary factionalists." Germer adds, "I observed that they are certainly not spending their money intelligently to send delegates to a convention and never utter a word." He continues, "Well, we may not send delegates to any more conventions." In reference to a period that presumably includes the Pritchett and Orton years, when Germer first took over as organizational director, he exclaims, "The organization has never been so leaderless in the five years that I have been associated with it as it is now . . . My feelings are voiced by others in the IWA, others of the so-called "white group" . . . P.S. I might add that George Brown gave me no help when I suggested that Claude Ballard sign the stipulation, so that there might be at least a temporary lull in conflict between the two factions. In his failure to do so, of course, I was disappointed." So in those rare moments of openness, the truth, according to Adolph Germer himself, is that his own supporters, and the leadership he promoted, not the Communists, are incompetent organizers and unrelenting factionalists.

These problems even extended to regional CIO officials appointed by Germer and Alan Haywood, many of whom were meant to replace leftists: "I recently received complaints to the effect that in general a number of regional directors in the Western Area were giving too much time to a lot of administrative work and that organizing was not going on . . . I wish you would take up this matter with them and impress upon them the necessity for increasing their organizing activities. It is very important that we do that."[59]

On the other side of the ledger, successful left-wing organizers were rejected. Germer removed Carl Hoessler from the international payroll because he was allegedly a "CP factionalist": "Carl I realize has a lot of ability, but I certainly could not recommend him, especially in a situation such as you have in the Wood

---

[58] Germer to Haywood, July 31, 1944, Germer papers, reel 8:324.
[59] Haywood to Germer, April 17, 1945, IWA 9:63.

Workers, where I am quite sure he would not uphold the prestige of Lowry [sic], the president."[60]

The South

Nowhere was the legacy of Germer and the White Bloc leadership more disastrous than in the South. Aside from the factional reasons for not concentrating on the South and his own racist attitudes, Germer tended to show a real ambivalence that was marked by fatalism (in many ways paralleling the economic determinism of right-wing social democrats like Eduard Bernstein). He often assumed that the South would, perhaps automatically, be organized once its level of economic development increased, a view he tended toward even before he came to the IWA: "As the South becomes more industrialized, it will also become unionized, and all that these run-away chislers [sic] are doing is to aid their own ruin."[61]

In Mississippi, his assistant director of organizing complained about company anti-unionism, protesting against, for example, the huge fund raised by the Southern Pine Operators Association to fight the CIO.[62] The cause of the operators was echoed by the Mississippi *Jackson Daily News*, which stated that the "formation of CIO labor unions of any kind, even if limited to white people, would be a calamity to industry in Jackson." Meanwhile, Brown complained to the government about the continual arrest of organizers in the state. As Germer writes to Brown, "It is clear beyond question that we have come to a show down in the South and I hope that enough force will be developed to successfully accept the challenge."[63]

In a subsequent letter to Brown, he writes, "Sooner or later the futile [sic] lords of the South must be compelled to become a part of the United States and recognize it's [sic] laws and obey them. Unless that is done the sacrifice made during the Civil War will have been in vain." But for all his whining and complaining, little was done by the Germer team in the IWA.[64] The proof of the pudding, as they say, is in the eating. Germer's actions indicate how low a priority he placed on attempting to organize the South. On October 1, 1940, Germer wrote a letter to Alan Haywood, giving a long list of new organizers whom he had appointed. It is perhaps noteworthy that none were in the South. It took very little to convince Germer to avoid the

---

[60] R. J. Thomas to Germer, December 10, 1942, IWA 6:977.

[61] Germer to W. W. Swift, May 23, 1936, Germer papers, reel 4:352.

[62] For similar complaints, see Germer to Haywood, March 25, 1943, Germer papers, reel 7:195, and N. I. Callowick, Regional Labor Representative, to Wm F. Rafsky, Assistant to Deputy Vice Chairman, Office of Labor Production, War Production Board, March 10, 1944, Germer papers, reel 7.

[63] George Brown to Mr. Hall, U.S. Attorney in Jackson, March 15, 1944, IWA 7:830.

[64] Germer to Brown, April 10, 1944, Germer papers, reel 7:926.

South. As he wrote to Haywood, "At a previous conference we discussed placing an organizer in West Virginia and Alabama. I had some correspondence with Regional Director Cowherd and State CIO President William Mitch . . . I asked him if he was willing to delay activities in the South and he said yes. So that's the way the matter stands now."[65]

As other CIO unions organized woodworker locals as a side effect of their own organizing, the IWA received thousands of new members without having to organize them themselves. Yet they did precious little to maintain or service these locals. After the split of the UMWA from the CIO, CIO officials were worried that the IWA locals might bolt to District 50 of the UMWA.[66] Again in 1942, mainstream CIO officials in the South were complaining that the IWA had hardly any organizational presence in the South; they claimed that Harry Koger of the left-wing UCAPAWA had been servicing IWA locals in Arkansas.[67] The situation hardly seemed changed in 1943. Germer wrote to Hayward, "I am enclosing a copy of a letter by President Lowery of the International Woodworkers of America to Donald Henderson of UCAPAWA. I discussed these matters with Henderson in Boston, and his explanation was that the IWA had no representative down there and that if these things were true, it was because we had no one on the spot . . . I explained to him that the CIO had somebody in that section of the country [who] would [represent the] interests of the IWA temporarily—until such time we get someone in the South."[68]

The prospects for organizing southern woodworkers looked good even to the White Bloc:

> From our experience in the South, we find it has not been difficult to obtain the bargaining agency, but it is not always so easy to obtain signed contracts. After the contract has been signed comes the problem of administration of the Local Unions, and the development of competent local leadership to administer the agreement and the general affairs of the organization. Some time ago, the IWA placed Bro Wm. Botkin in the South for administrative work, and he has had outstanding success in negotiating contracts where none previously existed, and improving those contracts. already in force.[69]

---

[65] Germer to Haywood, September 25, 1940, Germer papers, reel 5:84.

[66] See, e.g., Yelverton Cowherd to Germer, March 14, 1941, Birmingham CIO director, Germer papers, reel 5:763–64.

[67] Wm. Henderson to Haywood, April 30, 1942, IWA 6:438.

[68] Germer to Haywood, January 9, 1943, IWA 7:29.

[69] Worth Lowery to Murray, June 26, 1943, IWA 7:395.

From this we might conclude that no stable locals were built because no one tried.

> George Brown writes to Germer:
> We are still having fair success in organizing and have recently estab-
> lished some very good contracts in the South ... Anderson-Tully will come
> in as soon as their contract is finished, and I believe it will only be a period
> of time until we have them all in one group. We have discussed this matter
> several times and it is simply a question of getting started and forcing the
> issue in spite of the opposition of a few of the colored officials of the var-
> ious local unions.[70]

On paper, they occasionally seemed to have a plan:

> President Murray and I met with President Worth Lowery when he was
> here last week and we discussed the problem of organization in the lumber
> industry in the South and the financial situation and it was agreed that the
> approximately $30,000 which the IWA owes CIO in per capita tax, would,
> when paid to us, be refunded for this organizing drive.[71]

They even claimed to national CIO officials that they were about to launch a
southern campaign:

> In conjunction with Brother Germer, we have worked out an organizational
> plan for the South, involving the placement of twelve to fourteen organizers
> in the lumber belts of Eastern Texas, Louisiana, Arkansas, Tennessee,
> Alabama, and Mississippi. The $28k owed by the IWA to the National CIO
> will maintain this drive for approximately six months ... Brother George
> Brown, Assistant Director of Organization to Brother Germer, is the unan-
> imous choice for Southern Drive Director.[72]

But all this was smoke and mirrors. The refunded money was never used to begin
a major campaign in the South. When the IWA did finally hire just a few organizers,
they were again incompetent loyalists, with whom even Germer was disgusted.
CIO right-wing officials in other unions continually complained about the incompetence of IWA staffers in the South.[73] At the 1944 Arkansas state CIO convention,
Germer was furious with Henderson when he claimed that "all of the organizers and

---

[70] George Brown to Germer, July 19, 1944, IWA 8:262.

[71] Haywood to Germer, November 23, 1942, 6:945.

[72] Worth Lowery to Murray, June 26, 1943, IWA 7:395.

[73] See, e.g., Wm R. Henderson, Subregional Director for Arkansas, to Haywood, October 6, 1944,
IWA 8:986.

business agents in the State were present with the exception of the IWA representatives, and that one of them was opposed to Political Action Committee [PAC] and the other was a new man and would not come to any meetings ... [Germer] did not appreciate the remark regarding lack of co-operation from IWA, but regardless of this, it is a fact that the two largest IWA locals in the state are not affiliated with the State Council." William E. Runton, the anti-PACer, was finally removed. "We now have one IWA representative left in the state, and he is Robert Hill of West Helenaa [sic]; a man who never belonged to a union until this spring." In his private correspondence, Germer fully acknowledged the truth of these accusations: "It is unfortunate that both Chrisman and King were not fired when you were down South, but that is 'water over the dam.' You will recall that for some months I had been uneasy about both of them."[74]

Or take the note from SWOC representatives indicating that District 50 had been organizing in the lumber industry since the UMWA–CIO split had become more pronounced: "I am sending Carey Haigler to Jasper today to try to keep the five locals we have in Jasper from swinging to District 50."[75]

But the most egregious sin of Germer and the White Bloc was their obtuseness and backwardness on questions of race, which kept them from realizing the enormous potential of an industry that was majority-Black in the South, an insight that was quickly realized by conservative, yet less obtuse steelworker officials there. The woodworking industry posed a number of thorny problems for CIO conservatives. Most central were those of Black–white unity and making open appeals to Black workers who were invariably the readiest to organize. An approach like that used by other more civil rights–oriented unions in the South surely was necessary (Zieger 1990). The result of bringing large numbers of Black workers into the IWA would have been on one level quite predictable. They would have become battering rams in the fight against white supremacy, a continuation and extension of the labor-based civil rights movement that one saw in Winston-Salem with the Food, Tobacco, Agricultural and Allied Workers, Louisville with the Farm Equipment Workers (FE), Birmingham with Mine Mill, as well as United Auto Workers Local 600 in Detroit and the United Packinghouse Workers in Chicago. Some hint of this possibility is suggested by William Jones (2000, 2005) in his research on North Carolina.

Summary and Conclusion

The bottom line is that woodworkers in the South appeared to have been imminently organizable. The unionization of 300,000-plus woodworkers, over half African-American, could have potentially created a "Folsom effect" in politics across

---

[74] Germer to Brown, March 17, 1944, IWA 7:840.
[75] Beddow to McDonald, July 11, 1942, McDonald papers, 18:1.

the South. Unionized woodworkers could also have been an aid in organizing other workers, including those in the textile industry.

Despite the verbal support of these aims by the CIO rightists who controlled the national office, as well as by the Left, it was the CIO right-wingers and their incompetent right-wing allies in the Columbia River district who were immediately responsible for the failure to organize the woodworkers. There were also, however, other culprits. John L. Lewis empowered the rightists by sending in right-wingers to the Pacific Northwest, appointing Hayward and demoting Bridges.

The Communists, starting with those in the wood industry, also bear a major responsibility. Rather than surrender to the CIO rightists in the national office, they might have formed an alliance with the Bridges-led ILWU. Such a relationship would have been natural, given the close connection between woodworkers and longshoremen throughout the Northwest. In the battle for control of the union, given their effectiveness as organizers, it is more than a little surprising that they did not spend more time winning the support of wavering locals.

All of these possibilities, however, never materialized. Many were sabotaged by the Stalinized CP, which felt that the maintenance of the Popular Front and the "center–left" alliance with the CIO rightists was more important than advancing the class struggle, even if it meant sacrificing the political influence of their own working-class leaders.

6

Textile—Where the Fabric Meets the Road

The Perils of Cultural Analysis

During the 1930s and 1940s, the textile industry was the largest industry in the country (as measured by both dollars in sales and number of employees). By the 1930s, the bulk of production, especially that of cotton textiles—the largest component of the industry—was overwhelmingly concentrated in the South, especially the southern Piedmont region of North Carolina, South Carolina, Alabama, and Georgia. For many analysts of U.S. labor, the question of why unions have been less successful in the South than in other areas revolves almost completely around the textile industry.

As Nolan and Jonas have accurately argued, "Eventually, every serious student of Southern labor grapples with a most difficult question: Why has unionism made so few inroads? In the case of the textile industry, the question can be put more forcefully: Why have the textile unions failed so completely to form stable local organizations and to negotiate improvements in wages and working conditions" (1977: 48). Or as Emil Rieve, former president of the Textile Workers Union of America (TWUA) and then head of the CIO's Operation Dixie, said at a meeting of his southern staff in 1949, in Birmingham, Alabama: "Unless Textile is organized in the South, you have no labor movement in the South. You may have a labor movement in Alabama because you have a Steel Industry and Coal Industry, but not in the entire South" (Emil Rieve, 1949:9).

Why Have Southern Textile Workers Proved So Difficult to Organize? Some Working Hypotheses

The hypotheses advanced by leading investigators to explain the difficulty of organizing southern textile workers have covered a wide range; while many of these

The Southern Key. Michael Goldfield, Oxford University Press (2020) © Michael Goldfield
DOI: 10.1093/oso/9780190079321.001.0001

hypotheses are interwoven into most analyses, it is useful to separate them initially for analytic purposes, as follows:

1. The economic character of the South, especially its relatively low level of economic development compared with that in the rest of the country, and its large, low-paid, underemployed agricultural labor force.
2. Union-resistant attitudes of southern workers and the grip of southern culture generally that has buttressed these attitudes, attitudes that have been reinforced in the textile industry by the paternalistic relations in southern textile mill towns.
3. The violent opposition of southern employers (especially those in textiles), aided by an interlocking network of southern law enforcement officials, politicians, state militias, churches, newspaper editors, and others.
4. White supremacy in the South and the white chauvinist attitudes of southern white workers in general that allegedly made them reluctant to join with Black workers. In the textile industry, it was the overwhelmingly white character of the labor force that supposedly reinforced their racial privileges and kept them from joining unions (especially the CIO), which were seen as champions of racial equality.
5. The weakness (or, in the views of some commentators, the utter incompetence and timidity) of textile union leaders.

I will discuss these hypotheses a bit in the course of this chapter, yet the context in which they are generally examined is, I believe, too narrow. While some of them have partial merit, the overriding answers to the question posed at the beginning of this chapter, I will argue, must be found elsewhere. Thus, I believe it is best to step back and look at the industry as a whole on a worldwide basis, and to examine how textile unions and struggles developed, before tackling the specific conditions of the U.S. South.

Economics of the Textile Industry

I have argued that the activities of workers in particular industries, and the development of distinct working-class organizations within those industries, cannot be fully understood unless they are examined within the broadest structural, political economic, and historical context. Thus, despite the many insights and much fascinating material presented by numerous social historians, their overall perspective is generally too limited to provide a full understanding of the underlying features of most labor struggles. For textile workers this means starting with the development of the world textile industry from its very beginning. Studies that do otherwise will almost certainly make provincial and misleading statements. Although this may seem initially far removed from the South, it is difficult to understand textile labor struggles without this context.

The World Textile Industry

An Old World textile industry and trade existed thousands of years ago. Some say that the production of textiles (derived from the Latin word *textere*, meaning "to weave") dates from prehistoric times. Many ancient cultures, including Persia, Turkey, China, Japan, Kashmir, and India, had well-established methods for producing textile handicrafts. The *Rigveda* (many thousands of years old) refers to a vibrant weaving culture in India. In the Middle Ages, there was both elaborate textile production (including Italian velvets used by royalty) and a worldwide trade.

The Takeoff of British Industrial Textile Production

Yet the development of a massive, commercially viable textile industry dates only from the mid-eighteenth century. The modern industry, based on factory production, was first developed in England. It was the cotton textile industry that was the basis for the Industrial Revolution, or as Eric Hobsbawm asserts, "Whoever says Industrial Revolution says cotton" (1987:56).[1]

The industry grew quickly in the eighteenth century with the rapid introduction of a series of technical innovations that made cloth cheaper and more efficient to produce. These techniques were best applied by bringing a large number of workers together in a single factory, under the same roof. Originally, both the spinning of raw cotton into thread and the weaving of the thread into cloth were slow, time-consuming, labor-intensive processes. Spinning was generally less productive than the use of handlooms and became more so when the latter process was speeded up by the flying shuttle, which was invented in the 1730s and in general use in Great Britain by the 1760s. Spinning in turn became faster with the invention of the spinning jenny in the 1760s, allowing one spinner to make multiple threads simultaneously. The water frame of 1768 combined rollers and spindles to increase the efficiency of spinning again. The process was given a tremendous boost in the 1780s with the 1779 invention of the spinning mule by Samuel Crompton, to which steam power was soon applied. This device was highly successful and was patented by Richard Arkwright, who though not the original inventor nevertheless soon became rich. As spinning became rapid and efficient, old-fashioned handloom weavers proliferated. Although it was invented during the 1780s, the power loom (which would eventually drive the handloom operatives to ruin) did not become widespread until after the Napoleonic Wars (which had essentially ended with the defeat of Napoleon at Waterloo in 1815), although the effect of the power loom on

---

[1] I have largely followed Eric Hobsbawm's account in this section, supplemented with additional information as indicated by the references.

weavers had been severe enough in previous years to lead to the Luddite upheavals of 1811–12.[2] When the power loom was finally fully utilized, weavers (who had been mostly male) were replaced by women and children, so that by 1838 only 23% of textile workers in Great Britain were men (Hobsbawm 1987:68). This sexual composition of the workforce has remained the same in textile factories around the world, with certain exceptions, as will be noted.

Finally, cotton itself was a fiber that was difficult to clean and use. It was only in 1793, with the invention of the cotton gin (patented by Eli Whitney in the United States), that it could be easily cleaned and made available for large-scale use. While exact figures are difficult to come by due to the tremendous diversity of textile products, the cotton industry very early became primarily an export industry, and cotton quickly became England's major export. England, however, captured foreign markets not merely by outcompeting domestic producers in their home markets, but by capturing colonies and destroying domestic competition, even though British producers had ironically won domestic protection against Indian imports by 1700 (Hobsbawm 1987:48–49). So much for free trade. By 1790, most British cotton textiles were produced for export; by 1885 more than 80% were (1987:58–59). Cotton textile manufacture was thus the basis for capitalist takeoff in England, the first country to embark on this journey.

The British industry dominated the world market from the beginning of the Industrial Revolution until the end of World War I. At its heyday, the British industry supplied most of western Europe, North and South America, as well as other countries and colonies around the world. Centered in Lancashire, it was later to become technically conservative, by the late nineteenth century losing its markets in Europe, the Americas, and other independent countries (Hobsbawm 1987:58–59). As Hobsbawm argues:

> The British cotton industry was certainly, in its time, the best in the world, but it ended as it had begun by relying not on its competitive superiority but on a monopoly of the colonial and underdeveloped markets which the British Empire, the British Navy and British commercial supremacy gave it. Its days were numbered after the First World War, when the Indians, Chinese, and Japanese manufactured or even exported their own cotton goods and could no longer be prevented from doing so by British political interference. (1987:58)

---

[2] The Webbs describe the "Luddites" of 1811–12 as "riotous mobs of manual workers . . . destroying textile machinery and sometimes wrecking factories," whose cheaper methods of production had driven hand weavers to impoverishment (Webb and Webb 1920:87–89).

Cotton production itself, however, was initially based on one of the seemingly most economically primitive pre-capitalist forms of production, slave labor. The demand for raw cotton, supplied after 1790 almost exclusively by southern U.S. slave plantation labor, led to the enormous growth of the U.S. population and the accumulation of most of its initial fortunes.[3] Hence, as Marx argues, modern slavery, far from being merely a pre-capitalist form of labor, was at the center of the development of world industry and capitalism, making African slavery a central component (not at all a peripheral feature) of world capitalist development.

Marx argues that the "production relations of every society form a whole."

> Direct slavery is just as much a pivot of bourgeois society as machinery, credits, etc. Without slavery you have no cotton; without cotton you have no modern industry. It is slavery that gave the colonies their value; it is the colonies that created world trade, and it is world trade that is the pre-condition of large-scale industry . . . Without slavery North America, the most progressive of countries, would be transformed into a patriarchal country. Wipe North America off the map of the world, and you will have . . . the complete decay of modern commerce and civilization . . . Cause slavery to disappear and you will have wiped America off the map of nations. ([1847] 1976:167)

The Development of British Industrial Textile Unions

British dominance would appear to have been ideal for the growth of successful unions, giving workers tremendous marketplace leverage. It is often claimed that unions in monopoly industries or in ones that are technological pacesetters find it relatively easy to organize. Although textile workers in Great Britain would eventually organize, their path was far from smooth. It was an arduous battle, with the early history of textile unions showing major struggles and massive defeats. Further, there were numerous statutes, including the Anti-combination laws, admittedly unevenly enforced, that branded unions, and particularly their strikes, as illegal conspiracies.[4] The first textile workers to organize, as early as the 1760s in Lancashire,

---

[3] Cotton exports between 1815 and 1860 accounted for over half the value of all domestic U.S. exports. Investment capital for railroads and major port development were derived from cotton profits. The economic importance of the South was reflected in the region's political dominance (even though its population represented only a fraction of that of the North and West by the time of the Civil War in 1861; Goldfield 1997:84, 86–7; for the most careful treatment of the overall importance of cotton, see Beckert 2015).

[4] The Anti-combination laws, originally passed in 1799–1800, had a tortured history in the UK; they were repealed in 1824 but reinstated in the 1830s (Webb and Webb [1894] 1920: 64–73, 137, 143, passim).

were skilled (Fraser 1991:13). Cotton spinners and calico printers had continuous traditions of organization after the 1790s. By the early nineteenth century, the mule spinners were among the best organized workers in the country (Fraser 1991:13–14). Nevertheless, throughout the 1820s and 1830s, there were massive strikes, occasionally involving tens of thousands of workers, most ending in the defeat and destruction of worker organizations. Textile unions also played an important role in the Chartist movement, contributing to their influence in national politics.[5] Strikes continued to reemerge, growing more militant and stronger, despite prior defeats. The 1853–54 strikes, for example, involved twenty-five thousand Preston weavers who held out for seven months against a 10% pay cut (Fraser 1991:55).

Employers used all the standard tactics to keep their employees from developing strong organizations, including mass firings, arrests, and violence. These tactics worked for a while, but in the end the employers found it impossible to dislodge and replace the highly skilled mule spinners, who saw themselves, from an early time, as the nucleus of a general textile movement. It was the mule spinners who helped the vast majority of unskilled textile workers unionize; their stance was based on a variety of factors, among which were that the unskilled workers often included their wives and children (Hobsbawm 1987:65).

Once organized, however, British textile workers stayed organized and remained highly political. One indication of this is the central role they played in the anti-slavery campaign during the U.S. Civil War (1861–65). The advent of the Civil War in the United States drove down the supply of cotton on the world market, choking it off to a large extent. With no raw material for production, British textile factories faced short workweeks, eventually laying off large numbers of workers. Manufacturers and the government agitated from the beginning for intervention on the side of the South, attempting to whip up enthusiasm among the British public. As Marx and Engels noted, "English interference" was posed as a "bread-and-butter question for the working class" (1937:140). Nevertheless, English textile workers mobilized massive demonstrations in support of the U.S. North and in opposition to intervention on the side of the Confederacy by their government, which, in the opinion of some, checked this likely move by the British government (e.g., Marx and Engels, *The Civil War in the United States*, 1969).

Finally, it is sometimes argued that the acceptance of unions by employers was eventually encouraged because the employers came to see unions as a means of helping them improve labor discipline (Fraser 1991:64). Here one might add parenthetically that the monopolistic nature of the technological innovators allowed

[5] The Chartist movement was an attempt by English workers to extend the franchise to British working-class males. Following its formation in the 1820s, it formulated the People's Charter in 1837 and lasted roughly until the late 1840s (Webb and Webb [1894] 1920:174–78).

them the freedom to consider such an advantage once the workers' movement placed their backs against the wall.

Although British supremacy in the world textile trade lasted until after World War I, by the mid-1850s textile manufacturing began to spread to potential competitors in lower-wage countries. Each of the major players had hundreds of thousands of textile workers. While it would take us far afield to adequately survey each of these countries or even to present a sketch of the development of textile unionism in each of them, some general comments are appropriate.

The Spread of Textile Production to Other Countries

While the British were dominating the world textile market, a number of other countries entered the arena. These included India, China, Japan, Brazil, Germany, the Soviet Union (before 1918, Russia), and, of course, the United States, later South Korea, and more recently Vietnam, Thailand, Indonesia, and Bangladesh. The start-up of production in other countries was relatively easy. Once the technology became readily available, the low capital requirements and minimal skill levels necessary for most textile jobs made barriers to entry for new participants quite low, a situation that continues to define textile production in today's world economy.[6] The changing access to technology and the low capital and labor requirements had a major effect on the types of struggles in which textile workers engaged and the types of organizations they were able to build. While I have examined the development of the textile industry in all of the above (and several other countries as well), a few remarks on the development of the industry in several of these countries will illustrate a few important points.

India

India has many typical as well as unique features that provide insights into textile worker organizing possibilities. The center of the Indian textile industry for almost a century was Bombay (now Mumbai), where the British set up the first automated mills in the 1850s. Although almost all the mills quickly became owned by Indian capital, machinery continued to be imported from Lancashire.[7] The industry grew rapidly.

---

[6] On the other hand, for the possibility of automated textile mills returning to the United States in the future, devoid of workers, see Clifford (2013).

[7] Amartya Sen notes the tremendous pressure Great Britain placed on British investors not to put money into industries that would compete with home industry (2005:335).

Indian textile products tended to dominate the East Asian Market until the end of World War I, when their Japanese and Chinese competitors began to take over larger shares of the market. World War II gave the industry a renewed burst, given the worldwide restrictions on trade involving China and Japan. The destruction of Japanese industry—by then India's main competitor—in the aftermath of World War II gave Indian cotton textile manufacturers another reprieve in the world textile market. By this time, the Indian textile industry had already begun a substantial movement to Calcutta (now Kolkata) and Madras (now Chennai). By 1947, however, the Japanese textile industry was quickly being rebuilt. By the 1950s, Japanese apparel dominated the world market, flooding developed countries. Japan came to symbolize the manufacture of consumer goods by cheap foreign labor (as did, formerly, China, and now Bangladesh, Indonesia, Thailand, Vietnam, and other parts of East Asia today).

From the late nineteenth century until well past independence in 1947, the largest concentration of textile workers in India was in the Girangaon district of Bombay.[8] Even in the 1970s, well after textile production had substantially moved to other parts of the country, the Girangaon district remained a "working class belt" with well over a million inhabitants (Menon and Akarkar 1994:4)

The textile workers in Bombay were overwhelmingly male (unlike in virtually every other country, where female workers predominated), in part because the city was one of largely male immigrants (one study suggests that 84% of the city's population in 1921 were migrants). Their work situation was one of long hours and low pay, compounded by the uncertainly of daily work, which was based on a shape-up system whereby workers were hired by the day each morning at the factory gate. Repression at the workplace was intense, not only by mill owners but by the British colonial state, which arrested, and even sometimes beheaded, those it saw as organizers.

Consequently, there was little room for traditional organizing or collective bargaining. The presentation of grievances to management by groups of workers quickly led to the discharge of all involved. Thus, workers were forced to organize secretly and act swiftly in order to spread their strikes to as many workplaces as possible and gather all the allies they could in the community and beyond (i.e., develop broad associative power, along with structural leverage).

---

[8] I rely heavily for the account of Girangaon on the excellent, lengthy introduction by Rajnarayan Chandavarkar in Meena Menon and Neera Akarkar's One Hundred Years, One Hundred Voices (2004). As late as 1953, when textile production had already begun to diffuse to other parts of the country, according to figures from the India Textile Association, the majority of spindles and looms, as well as the majority of textile workers, still resided in Bombay (Mehta 1954:239–44, 266).

Those best able to lead such struggles were the Communists (or Communist Party, India, CPI), the best, most fearless, and most uncompromising of organizers[9] From the late 1920s until the late 1940s, the leaders of the textile workers and of others throughout Girangaon area were Communists. The labor movement in general, and that of the textile workers in particular, played a key role in the independence struggle against the British and had broad support within that movement, in spite of the stereotypical view, which focuses almost exclusively on Gandhi and the Congress Party (whose importance, of course, is undeniable). Textile workers were engaged in frequent strikes beginning in the 1880s, leading a massive general strike in Bombay in 1908.

Between 1918 and 1940, there were eight general strikes in Girangaon, all lasting at least a month, one for more than a year. Some of these struggles met with success. The Communists continued to lead strikes, and even had major electoral influence in Bombay, into the 1970s; by the late 1940s, however, their leading role was diminishing (Chandrvarkar 2004:11–12).

The Communists and other radicals and labor groups maintained the social and political cohesion of Girangaon, aided in part by a dense network of cultural and community activities. There were dozens of theater groups, many of which performed in the streets, although some had permanent theaters. There were also hundreds of poets, singers, bards, and artists (including sculptors) who mixed community art and entertainment with politics and class struggle. There was a constant stream of marches, festivals, and rallies, still a characteristic of politics in certain parts of India today. This widespread activity is described in fascinating detail by Menon and Adarkar (2004). It was this rich cultural heritage that laid the basis for Bollywood to emerge in Bombay. Communist-led *tamasha*s (an India folk form combining acting, singing, and dancing) were transformed into the Bollywood cinema, as leading Communist writers, dancers, poets, singers, and actors played a central role in its development (Menon and Adarkar 2004:25–26)

The textile workers lost their ability to win victories and many of their Communist leaders with the coming of independence. The 1946 Industrial Relations Act legitimized unions. It also attempted to certify only one union to represent workers within an industry. To be recognized, the union had to renounce the willingness to strike until all other "options" were exhausted. To compete with and supplant the CP-led textile workers union, the Congress Party, moving rapidly to the right as it attempted to solidify its alliance with Indian capitalists, formed its own union, the

---

[9] Chandrvarkar explains, "It became clear that the most effective method of developing a base within industry, in the face of employer hostility and state repression, was to intervene relentlessly in every dispute and to seek to generalize it beyond the individual mill and department. This energetic intervention was wholly compatible with the larger political strategy to which the communists were committed" (2004:33).

RMMS (Rashtriya Mill Mazdoor Sangh) in 1945. Without a vote by textile workers, the RMMS was certified as the official union with access to the workplace, official grievance procedures, and a company dues collection agency. As a clientist union of the Congress Party, it was often accused of being a company union rather than an organization that represented its workers (Chibber 2003, 2008).

Communists and other militants (including other leftist groups) continued to lead textile worker struggles, including general strikes in 1950 and 1974. The last gasp of the Bombay textile workers was the general strike of 1982. All these strikes, although they often had important community support, were opposed by the Congress and RMMS (in contrast to the pre-independence strikes). Unlike the earlier strikes, having now lost their associative power from the independence movement, they were all defeated (Chibber 2003, 2008; Sukomal Sen 1977; for Kanpur, UT, see Joshi 2003; for Bengal, see Mitra and Parry et al. 1999).

Russia

The Russian textile industry was massive, although it mostly produced for consumers within the vast czarist empire before the 1917 Bolshevik Revolution and for the Soviet Union thereafter. In 1914, on the eve of World War I, it was the fourth-largest producer after the United Kingdom, the United States, and Germany (Ward 1990:9; for an overview, see Dobb 1960). As in other early industrializers, it was a dominant industry, accounting for 15% of the industrial production of the empire by 1897 (Ward 1990:10). It not only was a key component of the economy, but was heavily concentrated both geographically and in extremely large workplaces. Its 480,000 workers in 1913 were almost exclusively in Russia, with the overwhelming majority in the guberniyas of Moscow and Ivanovo. Near Moscow, for example, one large textile manufacturer had four plants employing 54,000 workers, while the industrial textile town of Ivano-Voznesensk had 150,000 workers, virtually all of whom were in the textile industry (Ward 1990).

By far the most penetrating and nuanced discussions—not merely of strike propensities but of the character of the strikes and the role they played in overall working-class mobilizations—are those of V. I. Lenin in his many articles on the strikes that took place during the 1905 Russian revolution. During this time, textile workers showed a great readiness to strike. Yet according to Lenin, their strikes were not nearly as advanced as those of the metalworkers. The criteria for this were as follows: (1) While the metalworkers carried out a preponderance of political strikes throughout the year, the textile workers largely engaged in economic strikes, until the very end of 1905. (2) During strike waves it was invariably the metalworkers who struck first, arousing textile workers and other sectors of the labor force, who soon followed. Lenin argues that, although the textile workers were two and a half times as numerous as the Russian metalworkers in 1905, they were more narrow-minded and politically backward. They were also—in a pattern we find in many other places, including the U.S. South—the worst-paid group of workers in the country. Further, compared with the metalworkers and certain other groups of workers, they had not fully severed their connections with their peasant relatives in the villages (Lenin [1917] 1964:23:236–42). Finally, Lenin concludes from Russian strike statistics that those workers with the broadest demands and who fought with the greatest tenacity were invariably those from the largest mills and factories, and in the bigger cities. Textile mills in Russia at this time, while quite large, tended to be not nearly as large as metalworking factories ([1917] 1964:236–42).

South Korea

During the late 1960s and early 1970s, textile production expanded swiftly in South Korea. This growth was encouraged by the country's government and greatly aided by Japanese textile manufacturers, who began seeking lower-wage production sites once the Japanese economy had expanded into more capital-intensive industries and wages in Japan had begun rising. (Interestingly, Toyota began as a manufacturer of textile machinery, but off-loaded this production as it placed more emphasis on transportation equipment).

In South Korea during the 1970s, hundreds of thousands of textile workers struck against oppressive working conditions. Most were young women, who often worked sixteen hours a day and sometimes, during the peak season, worked two or three days without sleep, with employers forcing them to take pills or receive injections to keep from falling asleep on the job (Harrod 1987:186). Deyo notes that South Korean textile workers, despite extremely high levels of militancy in the late 1970s and 1980s, were far less successful than workers in the "capital-intensive, male-dominated, heavy industries" (1989:79–80)—a pattern he finds in other industrializing Asian countries during this same period. Choi (1989) documents the tremendous militancy of South Korea's female textile workers and their dramatic break from traditional restraints on female behavior. In Dong-il in 1977, for example, women textile workers engaged in sit-ins, hunger strikes, a Labor Day demonstration, and a fast at a cathedral. During one strike, seventy women textile workers stood nude, "forming a human wall in front of riot police" (Choi 1989:136–40). Yet it was not until the early 1980s, when in alliance with workers from the rapidly expanding metal industries (especially the auto and steel industries) gaining important associative power, that textile workers were to prove successful.

The Development of Textile Unionism Worldwide

Textile workers around the world have been almost universally militant, prone to strike, and almost everywhere generally unsuccessful, with the exceptions, in part noted above, tending to prove the rule. Textile workers were the first large-scale industrialized workers. They have at all times, in all places, almost always showed a great tendency to engage in strikes. Kerr and Siegel, looking at seventeen industries, found them to be among the mostly likely to engage in strikes (only after mining and maritime and longshore workers), rating their propensity to strike as "medium high" (1954:190, 206–107). They suggested this was especially true of workers in isolated company towns, where they formed "a race apart" (1954:191), although this speculation is highly disputed by many analysts. Beverly Silver, looking at a long-term, worldwide data base, likewise observed that "wherever textile capital went, labor-capital conflict emerged" (2003:81). Yet she noted that in contrast to autoworkers, "the world's textile workers, while extremely militant, faced almost universal defeat." She found only two types of exceptions to this outcome. The first was in Great Britain, the innovator of large-scale textile production, where capitalists making windfall profits had a greater incentive to reach stable relations with their unionized workforces. The other was in situations where textile workers were able to ally with anti-colonial movements (Silver 2003:83).

With this gloss on the broader context, we are better prepared to look at the development of the U.S. textile industry and the trials and tribulations of textile workers and their attempts at organization. I will build on the above to draw out a deeper analysis.

The Growth of the U.S. Textile Industry

Clothes and textiles in the United States, as in much of the rest of the world in the late eighteenth century, either came from Great Britain or were home-produced by laborious methods. In the period leading up to the Declaration of Independence of 1776, one highly public issue in the colonies was the boycotting of English goods, especially British textile products. Elite women in New England, for example, publicly turned to spinning and weaving products (abandoning their customary fine imported British clothing). Wearing homespun (something about which the lower classes never had a choice) became a badge of honor among many North American commercial and plantation elites (although there were numerous scandals and rumors about those who broke the boycotts).

Modern British technology came to the United States in the person of Samuel Slater, a high-level British textile manager/engineer, who immigrated to America in 1789. By 1790, Slater, with several partners, had introduced the first spinning mule and other state-of-the-art equipment into the country in Pawtucket, Rhode Island, which was to become an early center of the industry (Davis et al. 1972:419; for more detail, see Tucker 1984). U.S. textile growth took place quickly, much earlier than in most other countries outside the UK.

By the 1820s, U.S. cotton textile production, centered in New England, had taken off, and by the 1840s its expansion was "phenomenal" (Rostow 1978:49, 141). Tariffs played a major role in protecting the nascent U.S. industry, but its impact before the Civil War was both patchy and mixed (Davis et al. 1972:424).

Textile production was central to U.S. industrial development. Among other things, it stimulated the growth of a textile machine industry that relied heavily on skilled machine builders. In addition, along with other products, it stimulated the growth of a large-scale transportation system (Davis et al. 1972:424). Despite the fact that cotton was a major component of the price of textile production, textile manufacturing remained primarily a northern industry throughout the nineteenth century.[10] In the 1850s, for example, the U.S. South supplied two-thirds of the world market in raw cotton, yet there was little movement of textile production to the South until the 1890s (Davis et al. 1972:330). Eventually, however, it did move to the South.[11]

Finally, it should be noted that, despite the emergence in the early twentieth century of the United States as the world's leading economic power, with immense industries in steel, auto, coal, shipbuilding, and many other industries, it was the textile industry during the 1930s that still was the largest in the country. By 1930, the United States had 4.5 million growers, millworkers, and others associated with textiles. One-eighth of all U.S. manufacturing workers (1.1 million) were textile workers, almost 470,000 in cotton textiles, 155,000 in woolen and worsted. The value added was greater than that for any other industry (Dunn and Hardy 1931:37).

Movement of the U.S. Textile Industry to the South

Between 1900 and 1930, the center of gravity of the textile industry in the United States shifted from New England to the South. In 1900, New England had 13 million spindles, while the South had 4.4 million; by 1930 there were 12.5 million spindles in New England, while the number in the South had risen to 18.5 million (Dunn and Hardy 1931:44). The value of output in the South, which had been 13 million dollars in 1880 and 85 million in 1900 had reached over 800 million dollars by 1930, more than twice the 370 million of northern output (Silver 2003:87). The time of greatest crisis for northern textile was in the 1920s as the number of

---

[10] Even in 1795, expenses for raw cotton constituted two-thirds of the costs of operating Samuel Slater's Pawtucket mill (Tucker 1984:53).

[11] There is, to be sure, some dispute (minor for our purposes) over when exactly southern textile production "took off." Oates says 1880 (1969:5), while Gavin Wright says 1875 (1986b:124, passim). Figures suggest to me that it was not until 1890 that the movement really accelerated.

Table 6.1 **Core Textile Workers, 1910–50**

Year	Number of Workers (Thousands)
1910	421
1920	559
1930	556
1940	694
1950	679

Note: Core textile workers include the following: knitting mills, operatives and kindred workers; yarn, thread, and fabric mills, operatives and kindred workers; knitting mills, laborers; and yarn, thread, and fabric mills, laborers.

Source: *Historical Statistics of the United States: Colonial Times to 1970*, part 1, Bureau of the Census, U.S. Department of Commerce, 1975, series D, 233–682.

Table 6.2 **Broader Textile-Related Workers, 1910–50**

Year	Number of Workers (Thousands)
1910	885
1920	1,059
1930	1,108
1940	1,598
1950	1,678

Note: Broader textile-related workers include the following: knitting mills, laborers; dyeing and finishing textiles, except knit goods, laborers; carpets, rugs, and other floor coverings, laborers; yarn, thread, and fabric mills, laborers; miscellaneous textile mill products, laborers; apparel and accessories, laborers; miscellaneous fabricated textile products, laborers; synthetic fibers, laborers; knitting mills, operatives; dyeing and finishing textiles, except knit goods, operatives; carpets, rugs, and other floor coverings, operatives; yarn, thread, and fabric mills, operatives; miscellaneous textile mill products, operatives; apparel and accessories, operatives; miscellaneous fabricated textile products, operatives; and, synthetic Fibers, operatives.

Source: *Historical Statistics of the United States: Colonial Times to 1970*, part 1, Bureau of the Census, U.S. Department of Commerce, 1975, series D, 233–682.

northern millworkers declined while those in southern mills went from 190,000 in 1919 to 290,000 in 1929 (Wright 1986b: 147).[12]

[12] Yet Oates points to a problem. Unlike the North, the South saw little movement toward fine, finished products or the production of textile machinery between 1910 and 1940 (1969:45). In 1900, there was even a reduction in demand for skilled workers (1969:6–8; see also Wright 1986b:124–55; Galenson 1960; Kane 1988).

Table 6.3 **Number of Textile Workers in the South by State, 1925–54**

State	1925	1933	1937	1947	1954	1958
Alabama	11, 486	33,030	41,401	49,913	44,288	37,141
Arkansas	376	452	819	*	*	*
Georgia	53,940	63,924	81,595	98,255	96,767	87,966
Kentucky	2,787	1,336	1673	3,354	3,390	2,417
Mississippi	2,350	3,448	4467	5,081	4,915	4,579
North Carolina	98,698	126,892	154,005	200,880	209,929	195,992
South Carolina	66,991	76,220	89,091	119,345	122,004	118,533
Tennessee	22,641	26,875	29,868	33,891	30,926	27,197
Texas	4,713	4,996	5,538	7,745	8,006	6,868
Virginia	11,486	14,977	21,392	3,1451	33,562	31,341
West Virginia	678	759	1,032	3,554	1,997	1,669

Note: Textile employment encompasses the following industrial/occupational codes: 1925: Cotton Goods, Knit Goods, and Woolen Goods; 1933: Cotton Goods, Knit Goods, Silk & Rayon Goods, Woolen & Worsted Goods; 1937: Cotton Manufactures, Knit Goods, Rayon & Silk, Wool and Hair; 1954: Textile Mill Products; 1958: Textile Mill Products.

Sources: Biennial Census of Manufactures, 1925, 1933, 1937, and 1947, Bureau of the Census, U.S. Department of Commerce; United States Census of Manufactures, 1954 and 1958, Bureau of the Census, U.S. Department of Commerce.

Technology of Industry

The textile industry, unlike that of steel or autos, for example, was not monolithic. On the one hand, its inputs consisted of four distinct natural fibers, as well as a number of synthetics, the latter generically called rayon, during the 1930s. The natural fibers—cotton, wool, linen, and silk—had different methods of production. In addition, even cotton (the largest segment) had numerous subdivisions, usually produced in different workplaces, including threads, braids, twine, cordage, yarns, sheetings, tire fabrics, print cloth, shirtings, ginghams, cotton flannel, denims, towels, and hundreds of other types of cloth (Truchil 1988:2). Because of the differing circumstances in each of these areas, it is difficult to talk not only about the development of one industry, but even more so about the development of worker organization in the industry as a whole. Numerous reports by union organizers and officials note significant disparities in the organizing of different branches of the industry. I will mention two well-known examples. First, workers in men's fine hosiery were always more organized than workers in the rest of the industry, in part because the production and quality control required more skilled workers who were not easy to replace. Second, rayon workers were also more likely to be organized, in part because they had more workplace leverage. Rayon production required greater investment and more complex machinery. In addition, rayon required a continuous production process. If the machines were abandoned at the wrong time, the raw materials could gum up, even destroy, the machinery. Thus, rayon workers' strikes were not so easily defeated or crushed as those of cotton textile workers.

Still, textile cycles of production and growth have a number of common features. In general, textiles are , among other things, low-level consumer goods that find markets in virtually all countries. The start-up of textile manufacturing in all nations has usually been extremely rapid. With its low start-up costs and efficiencies of technology and scale, it has had the ability to swiftly displace home and artisan production. This was certainly the case in the United Kingdom, but also in the United States in the early and middle nineteenth century, as textile manufacturing easily drove out home-produced products. Yet these same factors meant that the industry often faced intense competitive pressures, both at home and abroad.

The low level of capitalization necessary to efficiently produce textile products, however—along with the low levels of skill necessary for the labor force—had several consequences. First, there were fairly low barriers to the entry of new competitors. In times of market expansion, large numbers of low-cost producers entered into competition with established manufacturers, creating both cutthroat competition and massive overproduction, especially when the market demand receded. The textile industry was one of the earliest to display global tendencies of competition, dramatically decreasing exports from the early producers in more developed countries like the United Kingdom and the United States.[13]

As a consequence of these pressures, U.S. textile goods from the South arrived on the scene too late to find a dominant niche in the world market. Therefore, the market for southern textiles by the 1930s was limited to that at home in the United States, as most attempts to penetrate the world market were unsuccessful (Carlton and Coclanis 2003). The home market could be protected by tariffs from outside competitive pressures, but not from internal competition. Still, in times of rapidly increasing demand, as during World War I, there could be huge profits accruing to established, efficient producers, as market prices tended to be set by the costs of the least efficient producers. Hence, the low barriers to entry meant that it was almost inevitable that overexpansion of production facilities would lead to busts, once the boom receded.

---

[13] U.S. Department of Commerce figures indicate that the textile industry is among the least capital-intensive of industries, surpassing only apparel and leather. In 1950, capital stock per hour worked was almost one-tenth that of petroleum and transportation equipment (the most capital-intensive), one-sixth that of mining, and even one-fifth that of tobacco, the last two being other important southern industries (for additional data, see Truchil 1988:3; on the low barriers to entry, see Lahne 1944:21).

These characteristics of the industry put an enormous amount of pressure on the companies, but especially on the labor force. In addition, other characteristics of the southern textile industry and of the southern labor market in general put further pressure on southern textile workers. Earlier, I mentioned the large surplus agricultural population. By the 1930s, cotton agriculture in the United States was declining, in part due to the competition from other, even lower-wage producers in less developed countries, including India and Egypt. This competition in raw cotton (along with the Great Depression itself) led to sharp declines in the world market price of cotton, which began well before the Depression.

Even without the decline in the demand for cotton-growing labor, a tenant family could make far more money per year working in a textile mill. As Marjorie Potwin explains, early-twentieth-century textile workers came from "three streams": tenant farmers, mountaineers, and those already living around the mills. A tenant family might earn on average $375 per year in 1909 and a mountain family still less. Even with the meager wages paid by southern textile mills compared with those in the North, a family of three workers could expect to receive "on the lowest earning basis, $900 per year" (1927:48). Thus, as Marshall concludes, "the southern farmer or mountaineer found that his lot improved considerably when he moved into a mill village" (1967:80). While southern workers lived poorly, worked longer hours, and were paid considerably less than their northern counterparts, they were supposedly more satisfied and less likely to want a union to represent them, since they were doing quite well by the rural, agrarian standards with which they were familiar. The poor agrarian economy that was the experience of most workers in the South made southern workers allegedly less attracted to unions. The existence of an almost inexhaustible supply of rural labor meant that the glut of unskilled workers on the labor market kept wages at rock bottom. Even in the 1920s, well before the Great Depression, surplus labor was so high in the South that most southern industrialists were forced to acquiesce to the abolition of child labor (Wright 1986b:152).

Cotton textile production was subject to large boom and bust cycles. During a boom, when the market greatly expanded, when profits were high, and when experienced workers were in demand, workers engaged in successful strikes and often achieved union organization. During a bust, however, when the industry had a glut of producers and goods, market prices and profits fell, making workers expendable and giving them little leverage. Even during these times, however, textile workers often struck. Large manufacturers prepared themselves for the periods of large profits and the onslaught of competition by installing more and more efficient labor-saving technology, "ever-more-advanced high-speed automatic machinery, operated by ever-smaller numbers of workers" (Wright 1986b:154). By 1930, "industry's role as a dynamic source of regional employment growth was essentially over. (1986b:155).

U.S. Textile Strikes and Organization

Despite the remarks of many commentators to the contrary, we will find that U.S. textile workers in the South as well as the North, like textile workers around the world, were both extremely militant and equally likely to suffer crushing defeats. Strike figures for the United States show a higher incidence of strikes among U.S. textile workers than among workers in other industries, in all periods from 1916 to 1940; from 1927 to 1940, textile workers and coal miners waged a comparable number of strikes (Edwards 1981:274–75; see Table 6.4).

In the United States, as in England, militancy among craft textile workers accompanied the early stages of the industrial revolution. As in England, more efficient technology, especially power looms, began to displace handloom workers and dramatically lower their wages.

Table 6.4 **Strikes by Industry, 1916–26**

Industry	% of All Strikes Accounted for by Each Industry	Number of Strikes per Million Employees	
	1916–26	1919–22	1923–26
Building	15.0	401	172
Clothing	12.3	592	547
Coal and other mining	7.7	124	115
Metals: iron and steel	1.3	47	8
Metals other	11.4	N/A	N/A
Printing and publishing	3.2	610	43
Slaughtering and meatpacking	1.2	314	64
Ships	1.7	636	32
Stone	1.1	367	118
Textiles	6.9	163	99
Tobacco	1.2	211	85
Transport	5.1	37	4
Lumber and wood	3.4	63	51
Leather	0.8	81	29
Paper	1.1	177	43
All above industries	73.5	161	81
All industries	100.0	102	45

Source: P. K. Edwards, *Strikes in the United States, 1881-1974* (New York: St. Martin's Press, 1981), 275.

Handloom workers in New England in the 1840s, like their British Luddite compatriots, went about violently trying to destroy the new textile factories as they appeared in their towns. In 1842, hand weavers in several Pennsylvania towns struck over the reduction of their piecework prices. There were also numerous riots and strikes, with "the strikers entering the homes of the 'scab' weavers and cutting the chains from the looms and burning them." An attempt was made to burn down Kemptons Mill in Manaynk, Pennsylvania, but the fire was extinguished by volunteers. Weavers threatened to tear a house down if the tenant allowed manufacturers to hold a meeting there. One arrested leader was freed from a jail by his coworkers. As in the United Kingdom, there were numerous threats to destroy factories. Between 1843 and 1846, earnings for handloom workers for sixteen-hour days, six days a week, were reduced by almost half, to as low as $2.50 per week, not nearly enough on which to live (Ware 1924:62, 63).

Before the Civil War, the textile industry expanded rapidly in New York, New England, and Pennsylvania, the early centers of the U.S. industry. Like capitalists everywhere, New England mill owners, despite their high-minded claims, treated their employees as mere factors of production. One Fall River, Massachusetts, manager stated for the record, "I regard my work-people just as I regard my machinery. So long as they can do my work... I keep them, getting out of them all I can... When my machines get old and useless, I reject them and get new ones, and these people are part of my machinery" (Ware 1924:77). One Holyoke, Massachusetts, manager decided his workers were sluggish in the morning because they had had breakfast. He found that if he worked them without breakfast, he could get more work out of them (Ware 1924:77). These conditions quite naturally led to revolts. By 1878, the national Cotton Mill Spinners union had formed (Commons et al. 1918:313). Female textile workers were at the forefront of the strikes demanding a ten-hour day in New England and Pennsylvania (Foner 1947:207–11). In Pennsylvania, when corporations attempted in early July 1848 to re-extend the workday to 10 hours, angry workers struck. When a Pittsburgh employer attempted to open his mill with scabs, female strikers, armed with axes, stormed the plant, defeated a group of Allegheny police, captured the factory, and forced the strikebreakers to leave and march out with the strikers. The strikers first won the ten-hour day back, eventually winning their former twelve hours' pay for the new day-hours of work (Foner 1947: 212–13).

As the textile industry moved South, there were many similar stories. Commons saw major obstacles to unionism in the South, with its huge "untouched cheap labor reservoir" (Commons et al. 1918:266). Yet there is little evidence that textile workers' militancy or desire to form unions was any less intense in the South than in the North. Milton McLaurin makes this point well in his study of the Knights of Labor in the South (1978:55). Some of the more spectacular southern strikes during this period were those mounted by textile workers, among them a three-month-long 1886 strike at a large mill in Augusta, Georgia. Douty likewise found that during the 1880s, cotton textile unions formed across the Piedmont region, including Alabama, Greenville, South Carolina, Maryville, Tennessee, and Roswell, Georgia (1946:556).

The AFL paid a great deal of attention to these militant organizing efforts of southern textile workers, at least in part for opportunist reasons (McLaurin 1978:128–31). In 1897, a large group of striking textile workers in Atlanta, Georgia, successfully appealed to the AFL convention for aid (Taft 1957:131). At the turn of century, Douty reports major strikes and organizing in Augusta, Georgia, in various places in North Carolina, and in Danville, Virginia (1946:558). Yet the major response of the AFL was typified by the tours of the South to meet with southern manufacturers by AFL president Samuel Gompers, beginning in 1895. Gompers got warm receptions and favorable newspaper coverage, as he preached the virtues of cooperation to southern elites (McLaurin 1978:108–109). Still, even in this early period, the militancy and organizing efforts of southern textile workers matched that of textile workers in the North. The National Union of Textile Workers (NUTW) was led by southerners and held its national convention in 1900 in Augusta (McLaurin 1978:149, 206).

My point in mentioning in passing these many accounts (which are themselves merely a small sampling) is to suggest that both the struggles and organizational successes of southern textile workers (and also their difficulties and failures) were in many ways similar to those of textile workers in the North and in other parts of the world. In fact, the largely cultural and southern-specific explanations given by hundreds (perhaps thousands) of commentators are generally misleading. Their erroneous conclusions are the result of both biases and a myopic approach to historical analysis.

Spectacular Textile Strikes: Lawrence, Massachusetts

The history of textile workers in the United States is replete with numerous spectacular strikes, many led by radicals and revolutionaries. Perhaps the most famous of these was the 1912 strike in Lawrence, Massachusetts, led by the Industrial Workers of the World (IWW). Twenty miles north of Boston, Lawrence was known as the "worsted center of the world," with three of the largest mills owned by the J. P Morgan–controlled American Woolen Company, the most powerful textile company in the United States.[14]

The textile mills in Lawrence had recorded huge profits, but still paid extremely low wages. The conditions were considered oppressive, the housing "sub-human"; the tenements had unsanitary toilets, which were considered by the town council "to be good enough for 'Hunkeys, Poles, and WOPs'" (Foner 1965:311). Infant

---

[14] I follow Philip Foner (1965:307–50), supplemented as noted.

mortality was high, and the slums were among the most congested in the country. There was widespread cheating of workers on wages, while tyrannical foremen often insisted that women workers have sex with them. The workers represented more than two dozen nationalities, the largest ethnic group being Italian, and over fifty languages.

IWW organizing began in 1911. When a fifty-four-hour maximum workweek was passed by the Massachusetts state legislature, the mills prepared to implement it with a reduction in wages. Italian workers, among the lowest-paid, led the first walkouts, taking flying squadrons from plant to plant. A common slogan was "Better to starve fighting than to starve working" (Foner 1965:316). There were daily marches of strikers singing revolutionary songs, often twenty thousand strikers a day on moving picket lines, and a large number of translators at every mass event. Leading the strike were top IWW leaders, including Joseph Ettor, a native Italian, Big Bill Haywood, and Elizabeth Gurley Flynn, then only sixteen years old. Flynn organized an exodus of children from Lawrence, who marched in New York City, emaciated and ill-clothed, creating widespread anger against the mill owners. On March 18, 1913, the companies settled with the IWW, which by September claimed sixteen thousand members in Lawrence.

The success of the Lawrence strike encouraged strikes across New England and in other major textile centers, including Little Falls, New York, and among twenty-five thousand silk workers in Patterson, New Jersey. Detailed accounts of these and other strikes appear in numerous articles, books, and dissertations (Brooks 1935).

WWI Organizing, Especially in the South

The South continued to be the site of intense organizing and numerous strikes. After the Knights of Labor activity in the late 1880s, there was a "vigorous" amount of union activity in cotton textiles in the South during the period from 1898 to 1902 (Douty 1946:557). Yet the World War I and immediate postwar periods saw an increase in union activity across the nation, including the South. The economic environment was especially conducive to such activity. Structural power—both labor market and workplace—gave leverage to all workers. A general nationwide increase in economic activity, mostly a result of war production for Europe, raised prices and created labor shortages. These shortages were especially severe because naval conflicts in the Atlantic eliminated what had been a continuous, massive stream of immigrants from central and southern Europe. Textile production and profits rose. National union membership more than doubled. During the war and the postwar period, textile unionism spread across the South. By 1919, unions existed in all the main southern textile states (Douty 1946:563). Many strikes in 1919 were over a reduction of hours, most being successful. The North Carolina State Federation of Labor claimed to have chartered forty-three new textile locals with thirty thousand new members by the middle of 1919, spurred in part by a dramatic victory in Charlotte (Douty 1946:563). The nationwide depression, especially in the southern textile industry during 1920 and 1921, reduced their leverage, providing, according to Douty, "the occasion for the virtual disappearance of union strength" (1946:158; see also Mitchell 1921:51–52). But the unions did not give up without a fight. A 1921 conference of forty North Carolina locals, on April 20 in Concord, North Carolina, issued a strike call to restore wage cuts. On June 1, workers across North Carolina struck, but with few orders, textile companies were under little pressure. Troops sent by the governor broke the strike (Douty 1946:564).

For most of the 1920s, the textile industry was depressed. There was too much capacity, a large decrease in demand after World War I, and a loss of international markets to cheaper producers. Larger manufactures pursued a multiprong strategy: They accelerated the trend to move many of their operations, especially those that involved low skills and little capital, to the South in search of cheaper labor. They also raised the efficiency of production while increasing workloads, known colloquially as the "stretchout," sometimes doubling, even tripling, workloads, often beyond the limits of what was physically possible. By the late 1920s, the increase in the stretchout and the decline in piece rates had led to deep cuts in wages. Finally, the agricultural collapse in the South, particularly of cotton, by the late 1920s led to an exodus of agricultural workers from the land, leading to a further increase in the abundance of cheap labor.

In this context, the 1920s were a relatively quiescent period, both for textile workers and labor in general. Yet even in the textile industry, the worsening conditions occasionally led to militant, labor struggles.

Particularly prominent were two Communist-led strikes in the North: one in Passaic, New Jersey, in 1926, and the other in New Bedford, Massachusetts, in 1928.[15] The remaining nuclei of these two strikes were to be the basis for the formation of the CP-led National Union of Textile Workers, formed in 1929. In the South, the only major strike took place in 1927, in Henderson, North Carolina, led by the Hosiery Workers Union (Mitchell 1930:61).

The 1929–30 Textile Strike Wave in the South

From early 1929 to 1930, a large strike wave swept the southern Piedmont area, primarily in North Carolina, South Carolina, and Tennessee, although also extending into Virginia. Very little is known about these strikes, aside from the four or five most important ones. Salmond finds records for eighty-one separate strikes in South Carolina

---

[15] There are numerous short descriptions of these two strikes, e.g., Dunn and Hardy (1931:220–27) and Brooks (1935:260–69). I discuss the Passaic strike in greater detail in the chapter on the Communist Party. A book in progress by Jacob Zumoff promises to be definitive.

involving more than seventy-nine thousand workers and claims that in North Carolina, "even more workers were involved" (2002:9). Tindall asserts that most of the local strikes in which no unions were involved were settled successfully (1967:350) but gives no evidence for this claim (suggesting that this may be an anti-union urban legend spread by employers). Dunn and Hardy suggest that in those strikes where employers made some small concessions, conditions usually worsened once workers returned to work (1931). The mostly "spontaneous" strikes in South Carolina seem to have begun within days of the first organized strike at Elizabethton, Tennessee. Some details on a few of these are given in Mitchell (1930:78–81).

The four most prominent and lengthy strikes are well documented and will be discussed briefly.[16] But the scope and range of the strikes illustrate a number of important points. While the strike waves and successful unionism of southern textile workers during World War I and its aftermath showed that southern workers, when they had leverage, especially favorable labor market conditions, and an industry making record profits, would readily strike and organize, the 1929–30 strikes illustrated that southern workers, even in a sick, overinvested industry, with an unfavorable labor market, would strike in large numbers as their working conditions and wages deteriorated, even though their chances of success were minimal.

I begin with the scope of the strikes. Of the major strikes, the first began on March 12, 1929, in one section of the large, German-owned Bemberg and Glantzoff rayon plant complex in Elizabethton, Tennessee; by March 18, the strike involved all five thousand workers at both plants. It was led by young female workers. The two Elizabethton rayon plants were highly capitalized and manufactured a product that was relatively new; they did not operate in a saturated market and were highly profitable.[17] Initially no union was involved, and it was only after the company refused to discuss their grievances that the leaders began to look for assistance from the AFL and the United Textile Workers (UTW). A verbal settlement was reached on March 22, which the company quickly repudiated. In the meantime, the UTW organizer and Edward McGrady, AFL president William Green's personal representative, were kidnaped and driven out of town. On April 15, five thousand rayon workers struck again en masse. The AFL provided little relief to the strikers and

---

[16] These are the strikes in Elizabethton, Tennessee; Marion and Gastonia, North Carolina; and Danville, Virginia. There are scores of sources. The best accounts of them are those of Tippett (1931), Mitchell (1930), Dunn and Hardy (1931), and Brooks (1935). Gastonia has been written about in dozens of books (including at least six historical novels) and in numerous articles and pamphlets, most important of which have been those by Theodore Draper (1972) and William Dunne (1929). Salmond's recent work provides much valuable new information (2002). Gilmore provides both important new information on Gastonia and perhaps the most balanced synthetic account (2008).

[17] Except where otherwise noted, I rely on Tippett (1931), a contemporary observer, who still seems to give the fullest and most accurate overall account.

spent much of its time appealing to owners and the government for sympathy. On May 25, the AFL settled the strike on the company's terms. The union convinced the workers at Elizabethton to return to work and let the issues be settled by a so-called impartial arbitrator, the mill's new personnel director, E. T. Wilson, who had been imported from Passaic, New Jersey, where he had won a well-deserved reputa- tion as an anti-union villain. He moved quickly to solidify this reputation in his new venue by immediately firing all known union activists. In the meantime, however, workers all across the Piedmont textile region faced similar issues of long hours, de- clining wages, and, above all, the "stretchout."

Workers at Marion, North Carolina, were undoubtedly encouraged by the devel- oping strike wave to organize a union and strike. They sought out AFL organizers and eventually organized a UTW local. On July 11, 1929, six to seven hundred workers at the East Marion Manufacturing Company struck, joined for a time by as many as fifteen hundred other workers from the Clinchfield Manufacturing company. Although the workers belonged to, and were led by local officials of, the UTW, the national union provided no leadership, active support, or financial aid for the strike, citing a constitutional provision that it would not support strikes of locals that had been in existence for less than six months. The active outside support came from members of the Brookwood Labor College, affiliated with A. J. Muste's Conference for Progressive Labor Action (CPLA). Their main leader in Marion was Alfred Hoffman from both Brookwood and the CPLA. While the demands and activities were similar to those in other 1929 strikes, the Marion strike was distin- guished by the high level of violence. Police opened fire on hundreds of unarmed picketers, killing six and wounding twenty-five, one shot while handcuffed, others shot in the back. Neither the sheriff nor any of his deputies were charged, although Hoffman and a number of strikers were indicted. Most of the money to finance the strike came from outside the official labor unions, including groups affiliated with Brookwood and a variety of religious organizations. AFL president William Green, however, did find time to serve on a fundraising committee for the Citizens Military Training Camps; the latter trained state militias, which were at the same time helping to crush two other AFL strikes, the Ware Shoals textile strike in South Carolina and the New Orleans streetcar strike (Tippett 1931:123–24). After the strike was over, Green, in a speech on January 30, 1930, in Richmond, Virginia, repudiated the strike and "the very martyrs who had been killed" (Dunn and Hardy 1931:230).

The last major strike took place in 1930, in Danville, Virginia, at the Dan River and Riverside Cotton Mills. The plant was modern. The wages were low by northern standards; they were not the lowest in the South, but were not higher than those at other large mills there (wage data in Smith 1960:297–98). The struggle began when the company union rejected a 10% wage cut, and the company instituted it anyway. Workers quit the company union en masse to join the AFL-affiliated United Textile Workers. They then began a many months' campaign of meetings, marches, and membership drives to solidify their union and to gain broad sympathy. Eventually they were forced to strike and were defeated.

The most important of the 1929 strikes, that in Gastonia, North Carolina, quickly achieved legendary status, despite its similarities to the other strikes and the fact that it was not at all the largest. The reasons for this are severalfold. Most important, it was openly led by Communists. The CP, then just beginning its left-sectarian Third Period, was hardly shy about trumpeting its revolutionary view. The CP was predicting revolutionary upsurges against capitalism, but it had yet to openly lead other major struggles in the United States—that is, before the unemployed rallies and marches, farmers' revolts, and CP-led miners' strikes.

Furthermore, the strike was put forward as the centerpiece for extending mass workers' struggles throughout the South. It revolved around the same issues (wages, hours, the stretchout) as the other strikes and faced a similar level of repression.[18] It was the first major struggle in the South where the CP pushed its newly minted revolutionary civil rights/integrationist program.[19] The strike had its unique drama, including the trial of both CP and non-CP major leaders for the killing of the police chief O. F. Aderholt and the cold-blooded murder of strike organizer and acclaimed balladeer Ella May Wiggins, whose well-publicized killers were never indicted. For our purposes, however, the strike provides another portal into our examination of the differing strategic perspectives on organizing in the South.

The events of the strike are relatively straightforward. Gastonia was the county seat and industrial and textile center of Gaston County, by the mid-1930s having the most textile spindles of any county in North Carolina, the South, and the U.S. Gastonia, with a population of thirty-three thousand, had fifty-two cotton mills (Draper 1972). The Loray Mill was not only the largest in the county, having been incorporated into the Manville-Jenckes empire in 1923, but as a manufacturer of yarn and automobile tire fabric, it was the largest of its kind in America. It also had "some of the worst conditions in North Carolina" (Tippett 1931:77). Although the mill was highly profitable and its machinery was state-of-the-art, the stretchout, beginning in 1928, had reduced the workforce from thirty-five hundred to twenty-two hundred and lowered wages at the same time. In January 1929, Fred Beal, a Communist and newly appointed southern organizer for the CP-led United Textile

---

[18] Its demands, however, were even criticized within the CP as being unrealistic and providing no basis for compromise in order to end the strike. These demands included a forty-hour workweek (when the standard workweek tended to be between sixty and seventy-two hours), a $20 a week minimum wage (when workers often considered themselves lucky to get $13), and equal pay for women and children (in an industry in the South in which they formed the majority). See Gilmore (2008:85) and Tippett (1931:80) for a full list of demands.

[19] This program was based on the Communist International's position, put forth and approved at the 1928 6th World Congress, that there existed a potentially revolutionary "Negro Nation" in the southern Black Belt cotton-growing areas. For an extended discussion of this position, see Goldfield (1979).

Workers arrived in Charlotte looking for a place to begin textile organizing. He began at the Loray Mill, where several union activists were eventually fired at the end of March. On April 1, 1929, a mass rally was called, and the overwhelming majority of the Loray Mill workers walked out.

Unlike the AFL, which abandoned the contemporary strikes that took place in its name, the CP poured organizers and support into the area, with some commentators estimating that as many as twenty-three party-affiliated personnel worked at one time or another in Gastonia, setting up both a union headquarters and a relief building in two different buildings on the main business street of Gastonia (Draper 1972:15; Pope 1942:244). Tippett notes the special steadfastness of the strikers (hardly the southern individualists mentioned in much of the literature):

> The court issued sweeping injunctions, which the strikers consistently violated, forbidding all union activity. The strikers were clubbed and beaten in the streets and carted off to jail en masse. Their reaction to this unwarranted brutality is one of the most outstanding phases of the struggle. Their parades were broken up by force every day, and just as consistently the strikers would form again the following day to march, with full knowledge of what they were doing, into the clubs and rifles . . . I saw a woman striker knocked down and stuck with a bayonet until she bled profusely. She struggled to her feet and marched on. (1931, 86–87)

Theodore Draper, hardly sympathetic to the CP, gives the workers his grudging admiration: "Another union might well have decided to cut its losses and get out of Gastonia . . . Isolated and alone, the N.T.W., together with the Gastonia workers, were no match for the Manville-Jenckes Company, the local press, state and city government, courts, National Guardsmen, deputy sheriffs and vigilante bands" (1972:15). Despite the CPers facing "hopeless odds," they won the confidence of large numbers of workers and displayed "extraordinary reserves of courage, discipline, and determination," qualities hardly ever associated with AFL functionaries (1972:16). It is hard not to hear echoes of the CP-led struggles in Girangaon.

The Communists made explicit their anti-capitalist politics. Some have speculated that this led to greater repression against them and their union, but careful observers have found no evidence of this. Conservative AFL unions fared no better. Also, most astute observers have found that the explicit revolutionary politics of the UTW did little to dampen the allegiance of the strikers to the union and the Communists. One anecdote from Tippett has been widely quoted:

> I asked a middle-aged woman elected to speak for the strikers if she was a Communist. She answered, "Sure I am. I joined the minute I heard of it in my section and came right out on strike with the others."

> At this point I interrupted to differentiate between the strike per se and Communism, and to clear up my point I quoted from the Gastonia Gazette which had that day published its regular vitriolic attack on the union and its leaders—"Negro lovers, against America, free love, northern agitators, Russian reds." "Do you mean to say you are lined up with a bunch like that?" I asked the group that had crowded around.
>
> The woman trembling with anger, shaking her long finger in my face answered: "Say you! Listen to me. These people are helping us. They are feeding us. That paper is a liar, and so are you, if you say things like that." (1931:83–84)

Most commentators attribute such remarks to dismal ignorance and desperation on the part of the strikers, who were willing to work with anyone who would support them (Tippett 1931:83–84; Draper 1972:12). There are, of course, other possible interpretations that less explicitly anti-communist observers might find plausible. Perhaps what most differentiated the CP strategy, however, was its trumpeting of equality for African-Americans. Most observers at the time, including virtually all others on the left, viewed the Party's uncompromising commitment to racial equality as totally crazed.

What the Communist Party Did with Respect to Race

The Loray Mill employed hardly any Black workers, while the town of Gastonia itself was 15% African-American. There were ten Blacks (out of the twenty-two hundred at the time of the strike) who actually worked in the plant. Yet, as with many textile mills in the South, there were quite a few more who worked outside the plant preparing cotton for production, a job that was still crucial for the production of textile products and is usually ignored by most analysts of textile labor. In nearby Bessemer City, the composition of the workforce was dramatically different. In American Mill Number One, the two hundred–person workforce was roughly divided equally between Blacks and whites. In American Mill Number Two, a totally African-American labor force of one hundred "was used to recover the post-production cotton remnants" (Gilmore 2008:78).

The CP program to pursue the issue of full equality for the "Negro" in all places and at all costs began in 1929. This was, of course, no easy task, especially in the Deep South. As Black central committee member Cyril Briggs wrote during the strike, the situation "brought our Party for the first time in its history squarely up against the Negro question in its most acute form" (Briggs 1929:324). The Party openly proclaimed its views on racial equality and tried, at times with great difficulty, to bring Black and white workers into the union together. It managed to lead a strike during this period at the American Mills (where the balladeer and strike leader Ella May Wiggins worked and lived). To the utter scandal of the CP, they initially allowed Jim Crow separation at a union meeting, for which they were vociferously attacked by the Party, with Briggs calling this "a shameful capitulation" (1929:325–26). Yet the organizers persisted, eventually convincing many of the key activists among the textile workers of the importance of the issue, despite the self-described resistance of Beal (Draper 1972:23; Beal 1937:140). Slowly, as many top CP leaders paid visits and reviewed the scene, they gained an appreciation of the circumstances, so that by September 1929, Briggs, in his critical review of CP work among Blacks, said that compared with other arenas, "the Gastonia fraction [was] an honorable exception, with all its mistakes and wobblings" (1929:428).

While the CP stance and activities regarding race and interracial equality are beyond dispute, there is wide disagreement about the Party's impact. Salmond, for example, says that pushing the race question so aggressively fatally weakened the Loray local and caused many of the original strikers to become antagonistic towards the NTWU (1995:67). In this respect, he follows Liston Pope but also relies far too heavily on the autobiographies and oral history material of two former Communists, Fred Beal and Vera Buch Weisborg, whose antagonism toward the CP should have led him to question their accounts. He argues that "the race issue was always divisive." Clearly, as Draper (1972) notes in great detail, pursuing an aggressive program of racial egalitarianism in the South in 1929 had (to say the least) its complications. Yet several contemporary observers did not see insurmountable obstacles to pushing racial issues. George Mitchell, a critic of the CP, states:

> The most arresting element in the whole disturbance is the ready acceptance by large numbers of the Gastonia workers of the Communist leadership, . . . [who] preached from the first the whole Communist doctrine—revolution, racial equality, syndicalist operation of the mill, and internationalism. The Gastonia mill people . . . entered enthusiastically into the program of the leaders." (1930:71)

Specifically on the race question, he writes, "It is noteworthy, however, that in Gastonia . . . attempts to destroy the agitation by discrediting the Communists' advocacy of racial equality had no success" (1930:74). Mitchell concludes by arguing that racial issues are not ultimately impediments to organizing southern textile workers (1930:87). Tippett (1931), a political opponent of the CP, seems to concur; his assessment of their stand on racial issues is quite laudatory.

Despite the ultimate loss of the strike, the CP achieved some notable successes. It recruited a number of the strike's white leaders, who became strong exponents of full equality for African-American workers (Gilmore 2008:88). After the killing of the police chief outside the union headquarters, vigilantes began searching for strike leaders to lynch and murder. A group of white strikers came across Black CP organizer Otto Hall (brother of Harry Haywood), put him in the trunk of their car, helping him to escape, thus saving him—at the risk of their own lives—from almost certain lynching (Gilmore 2008:89–90). At the American Mill plant in nearby Bessemer, whose workforce was half African-American, Hall and Wiggins patiently created an important interracial union (2008:86–89). If nothing else, these pre–New Deal, even in some cases pre-Depression, southern textile strikes should put the lie to the myth that southern workers, especially textile workers, were somehow less militant, less ready to strike and unionize over grievances, and more intractably racist than those elsewhere.

Textile General Strike of 1934

The 1934 textile general strike has until recently been largely ignored by most labor historians. But it is a signal event for understanding southern workers, the nature of textile worker struggles, and the problems of various organizing strategies offered by both mainstream labor leaders and the Left. In addition, as is almost always the case in the United States, a careful reading will give us many insights into questions of race.[20]

It turns out that the 1929 and 1930 struggles were only the opening salvo for textile workers in the South. The 1934 textile strike was the largest industrial strike in the United States up to that point. Its course confirms many of the general points made so far: U.S. textile workers, like their cohorts in the northern United States and in other parts of the world were not averse to striking and forming unions in large numbers, even when their leverage in the labor market was problematic. The strike suggests good reasons to question the notion that southern textile workers were

[20] There are hundreds of mentions and discussions of the 1934 strike, as well as a fair amount of archival material. I rely here mainly on Janet Irons's (2000) superb work, which focuses on the South, Salmond's (2002) book, which gives a rich, detailed account of the strike nationally, as well as various data and insights from James Hodges's (1986) work. In addition, I use some details from other studies, as well as my own archival research. As to older material, Philip Taft, in his exhaustive, somewhat in-house study of the AFL, has three pages on the 1929 strikes (1957:9–12) but no mention of the 1934 strike, although he does look at some of the post-1929 organizing in the South. George Tindall, in his classic study of the South during this period, has a section on the 1929 textile strikes (1956:342–53), which relies on Tippett (1931) and Pope (1942), but only a phrase mentioning "a major textile strike" in 1934. Marshall, in his classic *Labor in the South*, does have a few pages on the 1934 strike (1967:167–69) but leaves most of his discussion for the 1929 strikes, to which he devotes a whole chapter (1967:101–20). Galenson, in his standard, much-quoted history of the CIO, finds the 1934 strike barely worthy of a mention; seemingly misunderstanding the issues and result; he mistakenly states: "420,000 textile workers went on strike to protest against the failure of the NRA codes to guarantee them the right to bargain collectively. The strike ended inconclusively" (1960:325). A Russian book published in 1977 does give it equal billing with the other 1934 strikes (Mikhailov et al. 1977:238–40). And so it goes.

too culturally backward, too submissive to revolt against their paternalistic masters, lacking the discipline and wherewithal to develop any class solidarity. Their relatively limited workplace leverage (i.e., structural power) meant that they were most successful when they had significant allies, especially among organized workers in other industries. Where they did not have such allies, or where they did not cultivate alliances with them, they tended to be less successful. The strike also suggests the incompetence of the union leadership, something to which many commentators have pointed. In addition, however, it highlights the self-defeating ideological stance of both the union leadership and the AFL, given the realities of the industry and the obstacles that would have to be overcome if the workers and the union were to be successful. This perspective was shared by many future CIO leaders.

The Strike

Although low wages, unsafe conditions, and supervisor harassment were key elements of textile labor struggles, it was the stretchout that was the focal point and galvanizing issue for the 1934 textile strike, as it was for the strikes in 1929 and 1930. Textile manufacturers, union leaders, and liberal "friends of labor" denied that there was such a thing as the stretchout. The AFL and UTWA leaders claimed that strikes and incidents were based on misunderstandings between well-meaning manufacturers and their workers. More rational mediators could settle the problems to the satisfaction of both sides. In response to workers' grievances and subsequent work stoppages, they often would send their own technology and time study experts to straighten out the problems. This interpretation was shared by Robert Wagner and his liberal friend Louis Brandeis, both of whom believed that time studies based on Taylorism were a boon to both workers and management (Irons 2000:43, 51).[21] Thus, few union leaders, much less politicians, took textile workers' grievances seriously. As Irons states, "Until the spring of 1934, UTW leaders like McMahon and Gorman had been so eager to win the favor of government officials that they had squelched rather than encouraged workers' expression of dissatisfaction." Somewhat more attuned to his constituents than AFL leaders, South Carolina

---

[21] This view was shared by AFL head Phillip Green as well as Amalgamated Clothing union head and future CIO leader Sidney Hillman, who thought that talk about the stretchout was "nonsense" (Irons 2000:146). So, not surprisingly, liberals less sympathetic to labor concurred. "Roosevelt simply could not take seriously that southern mill owners were as heartless as the strikers were portraying them to be . . . southern mill owners were among Roosevelt's acquaintances in Warm Springs, Georgia, where he often spent his holidays" (2000:143). This situation certainly provides more grist for the argument of those like William Domhoff and C. Wright Mills who document the process by which political elites and union leaders assimilate ruling-class ideology.

Congressman John C. Taylor in 1933 introduced a bill in Congress to abolish the stretchout in southern mills (2000:97).

Barely a year or two after the initial 1929–30 strikes, textile workers in the South, largely ignoring their national union, began organizing, launching unauthorized local strikes. This activity received a decisive boost where workers in other industries were effectively organizing. This was especially true in Alabama, where the state's twenty-three thousand coal miners provided a powerful example, as well as steadfast support—that is, associative power. Alabama was to be the vanguard of textile union organizing in the South, the leading edge of the general strike. In the coal centers of Walker County and around Huntsville, Alabama, union organizing among textile workers was particularly successful (Irons 2000:69). Such support from the coal miners was not unique to the South. In Hazelton, Pennsylvania, for example, a regional textile center, striking workers were initially attacked by police and special deputies. The response by the area's unions, including fourteen thousand coal miners from thirty-four United Mine Workers of America (UMWA) locals, who marched in solidarity, quickly turned the tide.

At the same time, however, activity at the national level was undermining union organizing. The 1933 passage of the National Industrial Recovery Act, setting up the National Recovery Administration (NRA), was a boon for textile manufacturers. They gained complete control of the textile code apparatus, completely ignored Section 7(a), and passed regulations that reflected their interests, not the concerns of the workers. UTW officials continually urged their workers not to strike and to work through the NRA machinery. Code officials invariably dismissed workers' complaints, allowed employers to fire whistle-blowers, enraging many workers. The Textile Code Authority in the spring of 1934 announced that it was ordering a cut in textile output by 25% with an associated drop in pay; the UTW then threatened a general strike (echoing a long history of conservative union leaders making such threats, from Gompers to Green to Kirkland; Irons 2000:86). President Thomas McMahon called off the general strike in May for a seat on the pro-company NRA textile labor board.

Meanwhile, walkouts escalated in all four of the main southern textile states. Despite the opposition of top union leaders, the strike unofficially began in earnest in July 1934. At a meeting of Alabama UTW locals on July 15, forty-two out of forty-four voted to join already striking workers in Gadsden, Alabama, beginning July 17. And so the general strike began (Irons 2000:114). Here is Janet Irons's take on the reason for the vanguard role of Alabama textile workers:

> Culturally, too, Alabama's textile workers were in a better position than workers in any other southern textile state to welcome organized labor into its mills. Since the turn of the century, Alabama had witnessed the development of an industrial union culture based on heavy industry

in Birmingham and surrounding mines and mill in the mountain to the north. *Union presence was strong enough that Alabama governor Bibb Graves actively sought the support of organized labor in his 1928 campaign.* (Irons 2000:32, emphasis added)

Here I would make a slight correction to Irons's insightful analysis. While culture played a role to be sure, that role was decidedly secondary. It was the material support of Alabama's coal miners that allowed the state's textile workers to play the role they did. Associative power was key, the basis for the "Alabama exceptionalism" discussed in the introduction.

This pattern was not unique to Alabama. Textile workers gained strength in many other areas where unions in general were strong. They were able to maintain their organizations when they were near major cities, including Charlotte, North Carolina, and Columbus, Georgia (Irons 2000:87). In Gaston County, North Carolina, all 104 mills were eventually closed, as many hundreds of workers from nearby mills, in Gaston County, as well as in Charlotte and nearby Shelby, surrounded initially non-striking textile facilities with mass picketing (2000:130). Thus, there was power in numbers and concentrated workers. Isolated mills were often harder to organize.

Despite strong rank-and-file support, the national union leadership displayed its typical incompetence. Having been pressured by members and convention delegates to call the strike, they began with no organized cadre in charge of strike preparations. There was no public relations department and no organizing of resources, whether in the form of soup kitchens, strike benefits, or otherwise. No requests were made for manpower or support from other unions or outside organizations. This was true even in New England, the most fully organized region. Years later, Solomon Barkin, a participant in the strike, long-term research director, as well as general theorist and strategist for the union, argued that this "overall lack of preparation and organization" was the main reason for the strike's failure (Salmond 2002:83). Or as Clete Daniel aptly remarks, it was "always a union in which conspicuously talented leaders were in short supply" (2001:46).

Given all these problems, it is not surprising that the strike displayed unevenness. It is thus extraordinary how broad and successful the strike action became. Many commentators note the large number of women involved as militants and local leaders (Salmond 2002:151). Violence was widespread. When six picketers were murdered at the Chiquola Mill in Honea Path, South Carolina, ten thousand people attended their funerals. Janet Irons argues that the strike initially gained momentum in the first few weeks, then largely held firm in the face of strong violence against it (2000:149–50). Meanwhile, top union leaders were looking for a way to escape and end the strike. Francis Gorman, the national strike leader, argued in 1941, "We went as far as we could, short of starting a revolution" (Hodges 1986:11; see also *Textile Worker*, December 1941).

Nevertheless, with no agreement or concessions, merely a plea from FDR, on September 21,1934 the UTW Executive Committee unanimously voted to end the strike, declaring victory, to the utter amazement of many. In the aftermath of the strike, most of the locals were destroyed and tens of thousands of workers were fired and blacklisted (Irons 2000:155). It was not just the defeat of the strike that demoralized textile workers, but the false declaration of victory and the complete abandonment of textile workers by their union.

An interesting gloss on the strike concerns a much-discussed issue: the alleged racism of white textile workers. There has been much debate about who were the moving forces for racial discrimination and the exclusion of African-American workers from the textile workforce. As I noted in the discussion of the 1929 strikes in Gastonia, Black workers often played a larger role than was recognized. Irons also has discovered the records of a least a dozen "colored" locals during the textile strike, suggesting that there were perhaps many others (2000:71). Salmond notes that it was mill supervisors, not regular workers, who made up the KKK chapter in Greensville, North Carolina (2002:165). Telling, perhaps, was the political activity of textile workers. In the aftermath of the strike, textile workers became "vigorous proponents" of an independent labor party that did not rely on the two capitalist-dominated parties. Irons finds some fragmentary evidence of local labor party activity among textile workers (2000:164, 167). Even more telling was the election of Olin Johnson, a former millworker, as the governor of North Carolina in 1934. He was defeated in 1938 by notorious racist "Cotton Ed" Smith, who said that Johnson's support for the New Deal was a threat to white supremacy. Many who had formerly supported Johnson now abandoned him. Yet "whatever fears southern mill workers might have had about black southerners, the textile labor vote for Johnson remained solid" (Irons 2000:169). Many have suggested, on the basis of oral history interviews that took place years later, that the 1934 strike cast a pall on future textile organizing in the South for years, perhaps decades, afterward (Hall et al. 1987). On the contrary, I wish to suggest that the response of workers to the 1937–38 organizing campaign belies such a conclusion, rendering it at best presumptuous.

The TWOC Campaign of 1937–38

The 1937–38 campaign to organize the textile industry, particularly in the South, sheds much light on the fundamental problems of the CIO from its inception. It is a useful lens through which to gain a sharpened focus on the fight for the soul of the CIO. Its defeat, in an important sense, marks the beginning of the decline of organized labor in the United States, of which the failure of Operation Dixie was just a coda.

In early 1937, the time seemed propitious for the CIO to organize the textile industry, especially the formerly resistant mills in the South. Southern coal mines had been organized for several years. Much of the auto and steel industries had fallen to the CIO in dramatic victories, including the southern components of these. Great progress had been made in other industries as well. The CIO's cachet was cresting, and perhaps had reached its zenith. As Clete Daniel notes:

> The momentum created by the triumphs in steel and autos and by the lesser but still important victories it had won in rubber, electrical manufacturing, and other mass-production industries over the preceding six months, invested the CIO, during the late winter and early spring of 1937, with a mythic power and presence it would never again enjoy. (2001:69)

Fraser suggests that in early 1937, "for a moment anything seemed possible" (1991:375).

The leader of the campaign to organize textile workers was Sidney Hillman, the second most important leader of the CIO, after John Lewis. Lewis had argued for making the organization of steel its top priority, based on the vulnerability that an unorganized steel industry non-union "captive" coal mines posed for the UMWA. Similarly, Hillman argued that an unorganized textile industry presented similar problems for his Amalgamated Clothing Workers. Whether this was really true is another question, since it could be argued that the ownership of captive coal mines by major steel companies was a far more direct threat to the coal miners than any indirect influence textile manufacturers had on the apparel industry. Nevertheless, the stated argument was the same. Most important, Hillman's clothing workers were prepared to mobilize a similar level of resources as the mine workers did for the Steel Workers Organizing Committee (SWOC) campaign.

Other CIO unions were supportive. Major CIO leaders believed (as had many other unionists since before the turn of the century) that unionism in the United States could not be secure as long as the South was unorganized. The key to the South, in the eyes of most of the CIO leadership—whether on the left or right—was the textile industry.[22] Zeiger, echoing the thoughts of certain CIO leaders, makes the following additional argument for giving the textile industry in the South top billing: that the industry was overwhelmingly white would supposedly make organizing easier. Zieger argues:

---

[22] This point has been echoed by numerous more recent commentators. For example, "Without textiles, any industrial union initiatives in the South would be marginal, but a vigorous textile workers' union could spur the subsequent organization of metal miner, and food, chemical, furniture, paper, and other industrial workers" (Zieger 1995:74–5). For a slightly less enthusiastic perspective, see Hodges's account of Hillman's views (1986:149,151).

> *Thus one of the most difficult obstacles to organizing southern workers—the seemingly irreducible barrier of racial antagonism—was not a factor in textiles ... But bringing industrial unionism to the South would be a far less daunting prospect with the region's leading industry largely unburdened by the racial issue.* (1995:75; emphasis added)

As I will argue, such contorted logic is based on a misunderstanding of the dynamics of race in America.

The Campaign

For the textile industry, craft unionism was a non-starter, and the leaders of the UTW had long been painfully aware of this. They also knew their own resources were insufficient to launch a viable campaign to organize the U.S. textile industry, especially in the South (Daniel 2001:55–63; Richards 1978:31). Having little chance of receiving support from the AFL craft union leadership, the UTW was one of the founding members in 1935 of the Committee for Industrial Organization. The UTW leadership began making overtures to the CIO for help and in 1936 was engaged in discussions with Sidney Hillman and the Amalgamated Clothing Workers for financial aid to launch a national drive. Hillman and Lewis, however, had other ideas. Taking their cue from the SWOC, they decided to take over the UTW and make it part of a new Textile Workers Organizing Committee (TWOC). Power in the new organization would rest at the top, completely in the hands of Hillman, just as the SWOC had been controlled by Phillip Murray.[23]

On March 9, 1937, the TWOC was established, with Lewis appointing Hillman as chair and Thomas Kennedy of the mineworkers as secretary-treasurer. Of the other five members, Emil Rieve (head of the UTW's largely autonomous hosiery workers) and Frances Gorman, recently anointed president of the UTW, were the only two from the UTW. All decisions were in fact in the hands of Hillman and his assistants. Eight regions were initially set up (the number eventually expanding to twelve), with anywhere from ninety to ninety-nine subdistricts. Five of the six regions in the North were headed by officials of the Amalgamated Clothing Workers

---

[23] As former CIO publicity director Len De Caux said: "The Textile Workers Organizing Committee, launched shortly after SWOC got its U.S. Steel agreement, was conceived as a twin to SWOC. Sidney Hillman was the Murray of the TWOC (also its Lewis). Lewis loaned me to Hillman to help get things started. In drafting statements, I found it hard to avoid echoes of those I had done for SWOC. In planning, financing, direction, Hillman deliberately followed the SWOC pattern. The TWOC, like the SWOC, was to be run from the top—by Hillman. His ACW—like UMWA in the SWOC—would supply most of the money, leaders, key organizers" (1970:284). For a fuller account of the organization of the TWOC, see Richards (1978:37–48).

of America (ACWA). Of the two in the South, John Peel (the ACWA southern representative) was in charge of the upper South, while Steve Nance (more on him
later), a rather cautious, conservative CIO leader, was in charge of the lower South.

What was new in this campaign was the amount of money and number of
organizers that the TWOC possessed. Beginning with $500,000 in seed money, it
eventually raised over $2 million from 1937 to 1939, of which as much as $800,000
came from the Amalgamated, and another several hundred thousand each came
from the Mine Workers and the International Ladies' Garment Workers' Union
(ILGWU). The TWOC at its peak had almost five hundred staff people (mostly
organizers)and six hundred totally under its control, counting those loaned from
other unions (many from the ACWA). It is interesting to note that the scope of
money and people dwarfs that of the entire, far more famous CIO 1946 southern
organizing campaign, which was focused on other industries in addition to
textiles.[24]

Analysts have rightly tended to emphasize the similarities between the TWOC
campaign and that of the SWOC.[25] There were, to be sure, certain clear similarities
between the two campaigns. Both featured the takeover by a CIO organizing committee of a long-standing but moribund and problematic former AFL union. Each
had totally centralized control under the direction of mainstream CIO officials.
Both mobilized enormous resources, in terms of money and number of full-time
organizers and staff members. *Both waived dues and initiation fees* in order to overcome workers' reluctance and suspicions about previous union drives, especially
their past major defeats. Each began with enormous publicity, fanfare, and initial
claims of success.

[24] Information on the figures and the campaign in general is taken from numerous reports in the
TWUA archives and elsewhere. Figures, even the number of regions, were constantly changing, and
differ in various reports. In addition, stated amounts of money often vary since some of the money
was donated in the way of services or support for staff. For example, while it is usually stated that the
ACWA contributed $800,000, one report suggests only $500,000 in cash was given, while another
$330,000 was supplied in services. In any case, the scope, scale, and ballpark figures (whatever their
variations) are quite informative. Among the most useful of these reports are the "Chronology of the
Textile Workers Union of America, 1934–1976" (undated) in TWUA, history file; "A Summary of
Textile Campaign" (undated, but going through mid-July 1937); a detailed (untitled, unsigned) re-
port dated September 2, 1937 (seemingly written by Solomon Barkin); the lengthy "Resolutions
and Determinations of T.W.O.C., September 3, 1937," with its attached tables; "Report on TWOC
Progress, October 9, 1937 (including appendixes A–G); "Textile Workers Organizing Committee,
Southern Locals, July 8, 1938; and "Report Presented to the Second Meeting of the T.W.O.C. Advisory
Council," by Solomon Barkin, January 4, 1939 (TWOC file 596 and partially duplicated in box 7A, file
20) all included in Textile Workers of America Papers, Wisconsin Historical Society. For further details
and information, see numerous other accounts, especially Hodges (1986:148–55).

[25] Daniel (2001:69–70); Richards (1978:37); Stepan-Norris and Zeitlin (2002:75–6); De Caux
(1970).

There were also numerous differences, both in the industries and in the campaigns. Textiles was a far more competitive, diffusely controlled industry than steel. The economics and structure of the textile industry made it especially difficult, historically and internationally, to organize without outside support, barring unique circumstances. Further, while the Amalgamated had little strength in the steel industry by the time of the SWOC, the textile union had a historical base in New England and some solid strengths in particular subindustries, including hosiery and synthetic fibers. There were also, however, important strategic differences that played a role in the different outcomes of the two campaigns. The strategy in textiles was closely associated with Sidney Hillman, who dictated the approach of the TWOC, so it is with Hillman's approach that I begin.

In order to understand the strategy of the TWOC, one must cut through the hagiography surrounding Hillman, which focuses on his personal characteristics, including organizational skills, leadership abilities, charisma, and negotiating abilities. The evaluation of him as a sort of labor superstar, in many ways superior to Lewis, is virtually universal. For example, Clete Daniel suggests:

> The TWOC's prospects for success were further enhanced by the exceptional leadership qualities of the man at its helm. In Sidney Hillman, president of the Amalgamated Clothing Workers and John L. Lewis' chief collaborator in the formation of the CIO, the TWOC had a leader as able and resourceful as any who has served the labor movement in the United States. (2001:11)

Hillman's several biographers are even more effusive. An early biographer, George Soule, describes him as an industrial relations magician, charming and outwitting recalcitrant employers in negotiations. According to Soule, Hillman was also able to settle intractable disputes within the labor movement, as he allegedly did during a major autoworkers faction fight. Soule even describes Hillman's illness during the abortive 1937 AFL–CIO disputes as the reason for the failure of the negotiations (Soule 1939:192–99). Liberal muckraker Matthew Josephson's chapter on the TWOC in his later biography of Hillman (1952) is one long celebratory cadence. Hillman is portrayed as a statesman who could have unified labor and created a stronger movement if not for the divisive and egotistical Lewis (Josephson 1952:415–30). Not surprisingly, his own union's biography is even more embarrassingly laudatory (Hardman and Giovannitti 1948). Current writers have been no less kind. Further accolades are presented in Steven Fraser's thorough, richly researched, and highly informative contemporary biography:

Hillman's strategy was grand indeed. It was simultaneously industrial and political, alert to the cultural sensibilities of both Northern and Southern workers, sensitive to the structural peculiarities and vulnerabilities of the industry, inviting to dissident elements within the business community, choreographed to elicit the sympathies of liberal opinion, and coordinated with the actions of friendly federal agencies. Hillman brought to bear all his talents at mass organizing, his elite business connections, his political acumen, and his bureaucratic finesse. And his planning was meticulous. (1991:386)

One would hardly know from the above that the TWOC campaign led and conceived by Hillman ended in total disaster.

Hillman's Approach

Usually emphasized by commentators is the meticulous planning of Hillman and his aides. This was undoubtedly true, as the planning and research, under the indubitable direction of Solomon Barkin, were indeed more thorough than they ever had been in the textile industry. The headquarters of the TWOC were in New York City, as Hodges notes, "far removed from the Piedmont mills" (1986:150). This was not unreasonable, given that Hillman's main goal was *not* to organize textile workers for struggle, but to convince mill owners and local elites of the reasonableness of the TWOC. To supplement his argument, the TWOC would help mobilize the support of the federal government, especially the CIO-friendly National Labor Relations Board. Hodges argues that Hillman more or less abandoned any attempt to organize the South, particularly southern cotton mills (1986:151; for a slight counterposition, see Zieger 1995:76). Of the more than six hundred organizers, barely a hundred were concentrated in the two southern regions. The forty-two in the upper South were largely deployed in organizing rayon workers. The campaign in the South was itself run out of Atlanta, far from the bulk of southern textile workers. The southern operation was directed by Hillman's assistant for the South, Steve Nance, charitably described as having "innate caution" and sharing Hillman's "strong conviction that enduring success was best achieved by educating southern mill owners and the local power elite" (Daniel 2001:79). Nance explained to a journalist that "he wanted contracts, not conflicts" (Hodges 1986:152). Despite his abysmal failures, he gets a gold star from most commentators. Irving Bernstein, whose pathbreaking work at the time it was written played a major role in bringing workers themselves back into American history as active participants, nevertheless frequently fails to understand the big picture. He sees Nance as "an attractive, popular, and effective leader" whose death was "a blow to TWOC" (1969: 619).

Because of this strategy, Hillman, unlike the SWOC, had no need for Communists or other radical or militant organizers.[26] Even fellow socialist Paul Christopher was "yanked from place to place with no fixed long-range target" (Hodges 1986:165; Garrison 1977). If the organizing was secondary, this had a certain convoluted logic. In the South, organizers were in some sense selected for show, not effectiveness. Hillman chose native southerners only (whatever their skills and experience), so as to blunt the idea (quite unsuccessfully, it turns out) that the TWOC was what mill owners and many southern newspapers described as a plot by the "Jewish, Bolshevik" Hillman to invade the South. Some see this choice as a plus. Daniel, for example, notes an "impressive spectrum" of backgrounds for the activists Hillman recruited, displaying "Hillman's faith in the presumably unique capacity of native southerners both to persuade and reassure their kinsmen" (2001:11–12, 74). "The more than one hundred organiz[ers] assigned in the Lower South were as committed and resourceful as any who had served the cause of textile unionism in the Piedmont" (2001:89). Fraser also attests to the largely southern-born organizers, but none of the commentators note how many (in this high-percentage female workforce) were women (1991:387).[27]

Given their cautious, non-aggressive approach to organizing, "TWOC's initial results were nothing short of spectacular" (Daniel 2001:78). TWOC organizers quickly concluded "that past failures in the region did not preclude future successes. Indeed, in some cases, TWOC organizers reported, they found it harder to restrain southern millhands than to incite them (2001:79).[28] The results of worker enthusiasm and "responsible" collaborative union leadership were failure. If one wanted to use hyperbole, one might be apt to say that Hillman was like Nero, fiddling while Rome burned. All commentators seem to agree that opposition to the TWOC by mill owners, especially in the South, was universal and unrelenting. Cooperators were a species that had not evolved. Richards notes, "The chief barrier to TWUA-CIO success was still southern mill owner opposition to unions within their mills" (1978:6). In Georgia, the response to the union olive branch was violence and beatings at the hands of company thugs (Richards 1978:107–10). Even Irving Bernstein, with his penchant for melodrama, states, "The union was now confronting the fortress of southern cotton. With a handful of exceptions, employers here ignored the Wagner Act and invoked the tested methods of smashing the

[26] Galenson notes approvingly, "There was virtually no communist infiltration of the TWOC, despite a long-standing communist interest in the low wage textile industry," a parallel he erroneously attributes to the SWOC (1960:329–30). Zieger correctly draws the contrast (1995:76).

[27] My perusal of organizers' reports and mentions of the names of organizers suggests that the organizers were, with only a few exceptions, white males.

[28] This would seem to belie Zieger's claim that "from the beginning the campaign faltered" (1995:76) and to more or less discredit the claims of numerous commentators, taken from oral histories recorded thirty to forty years later, that the 1934 strike cast a pall over future organizing.

union—discharge of members, eviction from company housing, denial of credit at company stores, mobilizing the community including local authorities, the press, the preachers, and the Ku Klux Klan, against the TWOC, and, on occasion, outright violence" (1969:621), although it should be noted that Bernstein never gives documentation for the alleged "handful" of exceptions!. Hodges, the more careful researcher, notes that industry's "answer" to the TWOC would be "to battle it in every mill in the South" (1986:153). As one journalist noted, "The CIO may yet discover that compared with southern textiles, steel was a playful kitten" (*Christian Century*; see Hodges 1986:153–54). Such employer reactions were not merely obvious but predictable, even before day one.[29] Or as Dunn and Hardy argued, several years earlier:

> All these struggles . . . indicate that the workers must organize into a union that will be ready and able to fight. No one who has read our description of the mill owners' organization and tactics can still be so innocent as to believe that the corporations will concede demands without the most vigorous struggle. Gentle offers of class collaboration will not organize these workers. (1931:234)

Hope springs eternal. Despite the reality on the ground, "Hillman constantly preached the virtues of moderation, professing to believe that 'management will cooperate with the workers' when the real TWOC-CIO program got a full hearing" (Zieger 1995:77). The TWOC sent CIO patrician organizer Lucy Randolph Mason to woo South Carolina governor Olin Johnson, who was born to tenant farmers, all to no avail (Hodges 1986:162). In the face of harsh opposition, Steve Nance continued to preach to his organizers, saying that "cooperation with industry to stabilize it was to be the prevailing motif" (Fraser 1991:388). Hillman saw better uses of his time than mobilizing his enthusiastic textile worker army. "As he had throughout his career in the clothing industry, Hillman vigorously cultivated allies and potential allies within the business community" (Fraser 1991:389). He was, for example, friends with Robert Johnson, president of Johnson & Johnson and owner of the Chicopee Mills (a captive mill). Even Fraser, the Hillman enthusiast, however, admits that his long list of close friends in the textile industry in the end proved to be a "a weak reed" (Fraser 1991:390).

Hence, as Fraser notes, when Hillman finally became convinced "that the textile conundrum could not be cracked from within by mobilizing the angers and esprit of the mill workers, he turned to Washington . . . But even more than his friends in high places, it was the second leg of the strategic tripod—the legislative campaign for a

---

[29] They were predictable from past events, present attitudes, and not least, as I have tried to argue, the structural imperatives based on the economics of the industry.

national wages and hours bill—on which Hillman counted to crack the solid South" (1991:390–91). The NLRB and the national government, however, also proved to be no substitute for mass mobilization of the textile workers and their allies. All this to the surprise and shock of Hillman and his colleagues. Richards notes the

> ironic fact that even with NLRB election victories and pro-union major-
> ities among southern workers—as in Covington [Virginia]—southern
> hostility to unions could prevail to prevent consolidation of these
> sentiments into functioning local unions with contracts. In the South, pro-
> union majorities among textile workers proved insufficient in themselves
> to guarantee success for the union drive (1978:55).[30]

He adds, "Again and again, mill hands voted in favor of the TWOC only to be suppressed by mill owners and by local governments" (Richards 1978:57).

This was true even in places where victories were overwhelming, as in South Carolina's Kendall Mills' Mollahan plant (where the union won the NLRB election 447 to 13 in March, 1938, the type of victory that textile unions could not even dream of several years later). The result was the same in Merrimack Mills, in Alabama, in November, 1938, where the vote was 670 to 100 in favor of the union (Richards 1978:106, 112). Thus, not just attempting to sweet-talk the employers but also relying on the federal government proved to be a total failure.

Hillman and his cohorts were as well connected in Washington as anyone in the labor movement. As Richards (1978) notes, they went to extraordinary lengths to ensure the company compliance that led to the union's decision to concentrate on Washington, DC, influence in order to strengthen NLRB and federal minimum wage legislation. None of this worked. Hodges wrote that labor's "friends" in Washington were themselves helpless in the face of textile owner intransigence.

> J. Warren Madden, chair of the NLRB, said in 1936 that employers in the
> textile industry were resisting all efforts of the board to enforce the NLRA
> and that orders were not followed by the manufacturers. Representative
> Kent Keller (Democrat from Illinois), who conducted the hearings at
> which Madden testified, reported that southern mill owners were more ad-
> amant in their opposition to collective bargaining than employers in other
> parts of the country. (1986: 145)

The problems with relying on the NLRB are shown in numerous individual cases. In the Gaffney case, where there were egregious violations of the law at Hamrick Mills, the company appealed in every possible venue within the NLRB, eventually

---

[30] It might be noted that this was not merely a southern phenomenon.

going to court; though it lost in every instance, it still refused to obey government orders. According to Hodges, "The TWOC campaign in southern cotton textiles in 1937 and after and its use of the Wagner Act dramatically demonstrated that federal legislation was not a substitute for union power and that the legislation by itself did nothing to create union power" (1986:168). This is a telling conclusion and should give pause to those who are convinced that it was labor legislation that allowed or facilitated union organizing during the 1930s. To state the matter more emphatically, this point underscores the shallowness of those who have argued that it was the New Deal that was responsible for union organizing successes during the 1930s, rather than the workers themselves and their organizations. The cautious approach of Hillman, with its time-consuming reliance on lengthy government procedures, did more than fail to organize textile workers. Its timing fortuitously led to disaster, setting back perhaps the best possibility of finally organizing all of the southern textile industry, creating a cynicism among textile workers that even the incompetent handling of the 1934 general strike had failed to do. In the fall of 1937, there was an economic collapse (the "Roosevelt recession" within the Depression), which hit textiles especially hard. According to Fraser, "The impact in textiles was practically instantaneous. The TWOC simply crumbled like a sandcastle in the rain" (1991:400). This was perhaps only a slight exaggeration, given the overwhelming NLRB victories noted above. It was his unwillingness to seize the moment and take advantage of the opportunities that actually existed that resulted in Hillman's approach being a complete disaster for textile workers and organized labor in general.

Thus, the conclusions drawn by otherwise intelligent commentators are, to say the least, confounding. Fraser concludes his discussion of the TWOC by asserting that "the TWOC revealed Hillman's mastery of the mass movement qua political-bureaucratic institution" (1991:395). Astoundingly, he lays the blame for the TWOC's failure on the old saw of the provincialism and backwardness of southern workers (1991:398–89).

So how, we might ask, could there have been such a huge discrepancy between Hillman's and others' perceptions and what was in fact the reality of the situation? The answer is simple: it was merely a question of ideology. Robert Zieger, of course, notes correctly that top moderate CIO leaders were very much like the more conservative AFL leaders in certain respects, namely they "stood for stable contractual relations and [were] committed to taking labor disputes off the streets and into courtrooms and negotiating chambers" (1995:70). Other moderate CIO leaders did not always act quite so slavishly as Hillman. Rather, Hillman's approach had its roots in the most conservative traditions of the AFL. We can see the parallels in his approach to former AFL President Samuel Gompers's tour of the South, mentioned earlier, where he met not with union members and locals but with corporate and civic leaders, often under the auspices of the National Civic Federation. This scenario was repeated by Gompers's successor as AFL head, William Green. In response to the aforementioned 1929 strikes in the southern textile industry, the

AFL executive board decided that—rather than give material support to southern textile workers' demands and struggles—"Bill Green should talk the region's mill owners into submission . . . Green retained the ardent faith of a missionary despite his dismal record in persuading employers of the doctrine's redemptive powers" (Daniel 2001:35).[31]

One of the more devastating critiques of the TWOC was that of former UTW president Francis Gorman, who undoubtedly had his own ax to grind, given the dismantling of his union by the CIO. He argued convincingly, however, that the attempt to organize manufacturers, rather than workers for militant struggle, especially in southern cotton, was doomed to failure. In his report, Gorman quoted a North Carolina textile worker saying that the TWOC is "the AFL with a CIO face" (for a fuller discussion of Gorman's stance, see Daniel 2001:114–20).

SWOC versus TWOC

One of the reasons for the failure of the TWOC compared with the relative success of the SWOC had to do with a crucial difference in approach. This difference was especially critical for the textile industry, whose successes in unionization, as I have argued, would depend, at least in part, on its ability to mobilize external allies within the working class—*associative power*. The SWOC, as Murray's assistants, Golden and Reuthenberger make clear, believed in the importance of radicalism and class struggle for organizing the union. The SWOC cultivated allies, especially in mining, but in other industries as well. It recruited CP organizers en masse, even appointing them to important positions in the SWOC organization. The SWOC also worked closely with CP-dominated groups, including organizations of the foreign-born (specifically the International Workers Order) and Black civil rights organizations (especially the National Negro Congress), to effectively mobilize a broad range of workers. The steelworkers then spent the next decade both working with and restricting the influence of the CP and other left-wing allies (including the overwhelming majority of their Black staff), until they finally purged them from the apparatus.

They then attempted to drive them out of local positions as well, with mixed success. The TWOC made none of these initial overtures, thus limiting the degree to which it could effectively mobilize its core constituencies.

---

[31] For additional discussion of the AFL campaign, see Tippet (1931:179–81); Bernstein (1960:35); see also Daniel (2001).

The Aftermath

In the face of its total defeat, the TWOC's funding was cut, and the organizing committee grew even more cautious. As Hodges notes, "Battered by the forces against it—worker and industry history, the recession, unfair labor practices, the more subtle refusal to bargain, and a resurgent modernized paternalism—by early 1939 TWOC more resembled the UTW in 1935 than a militant union on the march" (1986:173). In May 1939, at a special convention in Philadelphia, the TWOC was disbanded, transformed into the Textile Workers Union of America (TWUA; Richards 1978:81). A main goal of this new organization was financial solvency (i.e., narrow business unionism), which led to an abandonment of the South and a turn to building the organization exclusively in the North. "TWUA was more cautious than TWOC, and its organizers tried to avoid conflict with management" (Hodges 1986:178).

With the start of the Roosevelt recession in late 1937 until the revival of the economy in early 1941, based in good part on a surge of World War II orders, union growth and successful organizing campaigns in virtually all industries markedly slowed. This was especially true in the textile industry.[32] As Richards notes, from the end of 1937 "until 1941, southern organizing patterns remained relatively constant. In virtually every southern state the union's gains were hard-won and difficult to maintain" (1978:91). The union's position in the industry remained precarious: in 1938, the number of TWUA dues-paying members was below 200,000, though the industry had 937,000 operatives. In the South, union contracts covered 27,000 workers, with 408,000 operatives. By1940, more than 75% of the industry's almost 356,000 cotton operatives were in the South (Richards 1978:124).

As the economy picked up, however, many unions began to aggressively organize at those companies that had remained intransigent during the 1936–37 union upsurge. These included Ford, Little Steel, Allis-Chalmers, International Harvester, and Montgomery Ward; 1941 saw a long list of lengthy, often successful campaigns in industries other than textiles (Lichtenstein 1982:46). The situation for unions again changed substantially after the bombing of Pearl Harbor on December 7, 1941, and the U.S. entry into the World War II. On December 17, 1941, President Roosevelt held a top-level meeting of labor and industry leaders, which laid the groundwork for the National War Labor Board (NWLB). FDR elicited an agreement to ban lockouts and strikes. In return, union leaders wanted union security and maintenance of living wages. The tripartite board was officially formed on January 12, 1942, with twelve members, four each from business and labor, and

---

[32] One bright spot, unsurprisingly, was Alabama. As Lucy Randolph Mason told John Lewis, "It is significant that with one exception every Alabama textile company with which TWUA won an [NLRB] election now has a contract with the union" (Daniel 2001:130,140–41).

four "public" members (Gross 1981:243; Lichtenstein 1982:70–71). It was only in June 1942 that the board announced its "maintenance of membership" policy, which would be applicable to those unions whose leaders agreed to the no-strike clause (Lichtenstein 1982:79).

For many unions, this government support allowed them to solidify their hold, and even dominance, in important industries, including autos, electrical, and steel. As Lichtenstein notes:

> The practical impact of this government policy dramatically increased the size and financial stability of wartime industrial unions. Lee Pressman later described the NWLB decision as the single most important reason for CIO growth during the war. (1982:80)

The impact on textile organizing was, at best, mixed. While membership grew in the North beginning in 1941, as the economy began to expand gains in the South were still difficult to come by. Even when the union won NLRB certification elections handily, these results meant little for the vast majority of millhands, whose intransigent employers refused to negotiate a first contract (Daniel 2001:132–33, 139, 140, 141). The growth of the textile union and the improvement of its finances also allowed a significant increase in the organizing staff, but almost none of the staffers were women, and very few were in the South (Daniel 2001:132).

The union's most important success in the South was the organizing of the immense Dan River and Riverside Mills in Danville, Virginia. In June, 1942, the 13,000 employees voted 7,204 to 4,716 for the TWUA in a certification election (Richards 1978:168).This success was based on the extreme structural leverage the union had, due to wartime labor shortages, and the immense profits it was making. Eventually, in 1943, the company was forced to sign a contract with the union, leading to further organizational gains in the state. Still, in the three major textile states of Alabama, Georgia, and South Carolina, with more than 350,000 textile workers, the union was able to bring only 12,000 new workers into the union (Richards 1978:170).

The TWUA held representation rights in forty-two new mills employing 42,500 workers. Virtually all of these contracts were a result of NWLB orders. By 1944 and 1945, the textile industry in the South had "virtually repudiated the board" (Lichtenstein 1982:210). By January 1945, fully 44 mills in the South were openly ignoring board directives. They represented by far the largest compliance problem of the NWLB. Yet little was done to enforce these orders, due to the great power exerted by the southern Democratic congressional delegation (Lichtenstein 1982:210). As Richards notes:

> The Gaffney and Mary Leila firms expressed their ultimate rejection of the union's stabilization program, preferring government seizure of their property to government regulation of their property rights. They also led the

general, heightening resistance to unionization all over the south in 1944 and 1945. By the end of the war almost every organized mill in Georgia was operating in open defiance of NLRB orders and many South Carolina owners whose mills had been organized had forced their workers into defensive strikes. (1978:175)

By the war's end, a widespread anti-union offensive was under way. When the war finally ended, the industry, now unconstrained by government regulations, stepped up its resistance (1978:207).

Concluding Remarks

I have argued and attempted to show that the economic structure of the textile industry provided special challenges that union leaders failed to address in the South. Stated simply: Coalworkers in Alabama and other southern states faced many of the same problems with respect to southern culture and interlocking resistance from southern elites as textile workers did. Nevertheless, southern coal miners, like their compatriots in the North and in most other parts of the world, successfully organized. Textile workers surely needed to mobilize their ranks for struggle, and contrary to much misinformation and in spite of the reluctance of their leaders, they often did. They also needed broad support to be successful—associative power— as Alabama textile workers received at times from coal miners and others. Their leaders, often incompetent, failed to realize this. This was also true of their more competent liberal leaders, like Sidney Hillman and the rest of the CIO establishment. Thus, we must conclude that the economic structure of the textile industry and the unwillingness of union leaders to engage in broad forms of struggle doomed textile organizing in the South. The culture of southern workers played hardly any role at all, while the failure to recognize and confront employer and government opposition can be traced to the ideology of union leaders, not to barriers that could not be overcome.

Here I must underscore the important differences in the strategies of Lewis / Murray in steel and Hillman in textiles. All three, of course, proclaimed a desire for harmonious and collaborative relations with employers. In steel, however, this was not the end of the story. SWOC leaders knew they needed to mobilize their full, diverse workforce. They did not rely on sweet-talking the steel barons. They also knew their own limitations and relied on Communist organizers well rooted in steel towns. They often used CP-led civil rights and ethnic organizations to deepen their appeal to specific groups of workers. And in addition to getting outside support from these groups, they broadened their associative power by allying with the power of already organized coal miners and other workers, as well as militant unemployed organizations. They worked with the rebellious employee representation plans. The TWOC did none of this, failing ignominiously.

Finally, while I have argued that white supremacy and racial divisions were indeed barriers, they were barriers to be challenged and overcome. The failure and unwillingness of mainstream union leaders to address them doomed their organizing efforts. This failure was on full display during the post–World War II attempt to organize the South, Operation Dixie.

7

The Failure of Operation Dixie

The Poverty of Liberalism

> Hegel remarks somewhere that all facts and personages of great impor-
> tance in world history occur, as it were, twice. He forgot to add: the first
> time as tragedy, the second as farce.
>
> Marx ([1852] 1979:103)

Operation Dixie

Operation Dixie (an unofficial name), begun in 1946, is viewed by many
commentators as the most serious attempt by U.S. unions to extend the unionization of the 1930s and 1940s to the South. This is a view that I once publicly shared,
but no longer believe is true (Goldfield 1993, 1997). I now regard Operation Dixie
as at best a coda, the end of major union growth in the United States, at least in
the private sector. To be blunt, it was also a bureaucratic nightmare, characterized
by gross incompetence, one of the most racist (by which I mean unaware, insensitive, and discriminatory) of all major CIO campaigns to date, and clueless with
respect to women on numerous levels. Operation Dixie is a primer on how not to
organize, even compared with campaigns that I have critically viewed so far, perhaps
a tragedy, certainly a farce.

Background: The Labor Upsurge in the South

It is, of course, true that the North (which includes the Northeast, upper Midwest,
and West Coast), with the bulk of the nation's manufacturing, was the scene of
the largest amount of union organizing during the 1930s and 1940s. It is also true
that some of the most significant defeats of the union organizing drive had taken
place in the South, most notably the 1934 textile general strike. But the assumption that southern workers were anti-union or that the South was largely bypassed
by the 1930s upsurge would be a mischaracterization. While the defeat of union

The Southern Key. Michael Goldfield, Oxford University Press (2020) © Michael Goldfield
DOI: 10.1093/oso/9780190079321.001.0001

organizing in the textile industry should not be underestimated, there were also important victories. A preliminary review is in order.

First, those primarily northern industries that successfully organized were generally able to organize their southern constituencies. This proved to be the case in the auto, electrical, meatpacking, and eventually rubber industries, where intransigent resistance put off successful organizing until the early 1940s.

Second, there were major national industries whose southern components were central to the industry as a whole. In steel, the large Birmingham, Alabama, district was organized along with the rest of the industry. In coal, the heavily African-American Alabama mines, the racially heterogeneous West Virginian fields, and the important Tennessee and Kentucky operations were organized during the 1930s along with coal mines nationwide. Metal miners, especially in the important Alabama mines but also elsewhere in the South, successfully organized. Longshore and maritime workers in the main ocean ports and along the Mississippi River built stable organizations. The tobacco industry, centered in North Carolina and Virginia, became substantially unionized. And oilworkers, largely southern-based, with heavy concentrations in Louisiana and Texas (then as today), succeeded in organizing their industry during the early 1940s.

Third, important industrial cities across the South became unionized. These included not only cities like Atlanta, Georgia, Tampa, Florida, and New Orleans, Louisiana, places with long histories of unionization, but also violently anti-union, virulently racist strongholds in the Deep South—Memphis, Tennessee, Gadsden, Alabama, and Laurel, Mississippi. Thus, southern workers—white as well as Black, female as well as male—when they had sufficient structural and associative power, were often as ready and able to unionize as their compatriots in the North.

In 1946, labor unions, their allies, and partners—which included civil rights and African-American organizations, broad, left-wing, Popular Front organizations, organized students and intellectuals, organizations of the foreign-born, armed service veterans, retirees, less affluent farmers and farmworkers, among others—seemed on the verge of increasing their political strength and the number of their workers who were organized, exerting a decisive influence on American politics. Labor unions alone had grown from less than three million members in 1933 (barely 10% of the non-agricultural labor force) to fourteen million members in 1945 (more than 35% of the non-agricultural labor force). In the private sector, I estimate that roughly 43% of workers were organized, with higher percentages in most major manufacturing industries. On the economic front, unions were also pressing forward, substantially raising the wages of their members (Goldfield 1987:xiii–xiv). With this increased membership and organizational strength came greater resources. Finally, while resistance to unions in most of the South was still strong, much of the violence and extralegal opposition, as we shall see, had largely disappeared.

Idea of Organizing the South: Precursor
Statements and Activities

The idea of organizing the South—and of its critical importance both for the national strength of unions and for their long-term survival in other parts of the country—was not a new one. Contrary to popular conceptions, unions had shown a great deal of interest in organizing the South for many decades before 1946. This interest was not merely reflected in numerous rhetorical statements by leaders (of which there were plenty), convention resolutions, and announced campaigns. The South had also been the target of extensive organizing by national unions and the scene of heroic, indigenous, and massive struggles by laborers and other common people.

Despite widespread misconceptions, especially prevalent in the North but also promulgated by southern elites (who, from the late nineteenth century onward, attempted to tout the region as a premier investment site in good part due to its supposedly loyal, patriotic, hardworking, and docile labor force), extensive struggles by southern folk against southern ruling elites began early. Scholarship especially documents intense labor struggles in the South during early colonial times, particularly in Virginia from roughly 1660 to 1682.[1]

The modern labor movement begins in the South in the early 1880s with large-scale and geographically widespread labor organization under the auspices of the Knights of Labor (McLaurin 1978). According to Garlock, the Knights had local assemblies in 1878 in every major coal mining district, including those in Alabama, Virginia, West Virginia, Kentucky, and Tennessee (1974:86, 88). They had strong locals in major industrial cities, among which were Jacksonville, Florida (then the state's largest city), Atlanta, Georgia, Birmingham, Alabama, Newport News, Virginia, and hundreds of others. They could be found representing lumberworkers, textile workers, tobacco employees, and even sugarworkers. The center of their strike activity in the wood industry was Mississippi (McLaurin 1978:60–74). After the successful Knights-led national railroad strike in 1885, the order's organizing snowballed (1978:47). By 1886, Richmond, Virginia, alone had forty local assemblies (1978:89). The importance of southern labor was underscored when the Knights chose Richmond as the site of their 1886 national convention (for a detailed account, see Rachleff 1989).

In 1890 the United Mine Workers of America (UMWA) was formed with heavy concentrations of members in Alabama, where they engaged in numerous statewide strikes. By 1902, fully 65% of Alabama miners were organized (Douty 1946:558).

---

[1] For a short summary, see Goldfield (1997:40–42); for more detailed accounts, see Morgan (1975:246, 250–76; Allen 2012:148, 151–62, 203–22, the latter especially for an alternative account of Bacon's Rebellion).

As McLaurin notes, the AFL had begun devoting major attention to the South by the late nineteenth century, in part for opportunistic reasons (1978:128–31). AFL president Samuel Gompers toured the South in 1895 (McLaurin 1978:108–109). The newly formed National Union of Textile Workers (NUTW) was initially led by southerners, holding its 1900 convention in Augusta, Georgia (McLaurin 1978:149, 206).

With the expansion of textile and coal production in the South, the region was regarded with a combination of alarm and urgency because its rapidly growing, lower-paid, largely non-union workforce served as a threat to better-paid workers in the North. Rhetorically, the organization of the South became a priority of the AFL.

The drumbeat for organizing the South continued after the turn of the century. A careful survey of AFL convention reports and minutes highlights this heightened interest. Attention was given to the South by the leadership and in on-floor plenary discussions at the 1912 AFL national convention in Atlanta. The AFL's Southern Labor Congress (SLC) held special meetings in 1912 (October, Atlanta), 1913 (September, Nashville), 1914 (September, Birmingham), and 1915 (September, Chattanooga) on how to organize the South. At the 35th Annual Convention of the AFL, held in San Francisco on November 8–22 (Convention Proceedings 1915:231), Colonel Jerome Jones, representing the SLC, gave a special plenary report. At the 39th Annual Convention of the AFL, held in Atlantic City on June 9–23, 1919, amid optimistic reports of southern organizing, John Golden of the United Textile Workers of America (UTWA), speaking in support of an official resolution to condemn violence against the UTWA the previous month, which ended in the killing of seven workers, describes the rapid unionization of the South and states, "Our greatest battle now is in the Southern States" (Convention Proceedings 1919:31).

The World War I boom, with its ensuing tight labor markets and more favorable federal labor policies under Woodrow Wilson's administration, provided fertile grounds for union organization throughout the country, and the South was no exception. As H. M. Douty notes, "Aside from lumber and furniture, which remained relatively untouched, union activity penetrated deeply into the industrial life of the South during the First World War. Organization was extensive in tobacco, textiles, iron and steel, coal mining, and other industries" (1946:561). Douty details "a fairly extensive labor movement existing in the South during this period" (1946:566). But with the collapse of the World War I boom in 1921 and 1922, unions across the country were beaten back and those in the South were no exception.

Although local union activity in the South did not completely disappear after World War I, national attention on the labor movement mostly did. By 1925, however, the American Federation of Hosiery Workers (AFHW) increased its focus on the South. The hosiery industry, previously almost exclusively located in the North, had early on been substantially organized. The union's concern increased as the industry began to grow in the South. The AFHW sent organizers south, following the new hosiery mills (Lahne 1944:216). By 1927, hosiery leader Alfred Hoffman had formed the Piedmont Organizing Committee, which conducted union propaganda throughout the southern textile industry (Douty 1946:567). The AFL convention in Los Angeles in October 1927 called for support for southern textile organizing, proclaiming, "The southern textile workers are now ready for organization" (Convention Proceedings 1927:210).

Southern union activity led the AFL again to direct its attention there. Symbolic was the holding of the 48th Annual Convention of the AFL in New Orleans on November 19–28, 1928. Southern delegates met in caucuses and "laid plans for a union drive" (Douty 1946:567). Matilda Lindsay of the National Women's Trade Union League summarized much of the renewed interest and the argument that the industrial makeup of the South was changing. She stated that it was no accident that

> in the last two or three years our attention has been directed toward the South . . . Practically one-half of the cotton mills in the United States are situated south of the Mason and Dixon line and practically two-thirds of the output of cotton manufacturing in the United States in this country is done in the South. North Carolina and Virginia are the big tobacco centers of the country . . . These two industries are employing women in large numbers, which is an additional reason for our interest in this subject. (Convention Proceedings 1928:197)

The 1929 textile strikes that took place across the Piedmont region of the South captured national attention. Even the AFL became optimistic. At the 1929 annual convention, held in Toronto on October 7–18, the official organization report stated:

> An outstanding labor development of the year is the awakening of the South . . . We urge all organizations to include in their organizing plans for the coming year definite provisions for work in the South . . . Organizing work in the South cannot stop until all industries are thoroughly organized. (Convention Proceedings 1929:59–60)

The AFL stated: "Resolved, That the officers of the American Federation of Labor be instructed by this convention to call together for conference the officers of all National and International unions for the purpose of devising a policy that will be acceptable to all interested parties in the proposed campaign of organization among Southern workers regardless of craft or calling" (1929:266). As Douty noted, "Tremendous enthusiasm for a southern organizing campaign was displayed at the 1929 convention of the American Federation of Labor" (1946:270; see also Convention Proceedings 1929:225–83). The drive got under way on January 6, 1930, at a large conference in Charlotte, North Carolina (Douty 1946:570).

A headquarters was set up in Birmingham and more than fifty organizers worked directly for the federation. A good part of the strategy was the time-honored AFL one of attempting to convince southern employers of the benefits of having unions in their plants. There is, of course, no evidence that either southern employers or southern workers were at all attracted to the idea. But ideology trumped reality.

The southern organizing campaign was discussed, analyzed, and extolled again extensively at the 1930 AFL convention. During the whole period from 1927 to 1934, organizing and labor militancy proceeded at a rapid pace, largely separate from official national organizing. During the early 1930s, especially, numerous local struggles, strikes, and organizing campaigns took place, particularly in textiles and coal. Most of the walkouts in 1931 and 1932 were localized and often spontaneous, most ending in defeat. These struggles laid the basis for more massive campaigns, from 1933 on in coal and the 1934 general strike in textiles. Strikes and organizing campaigns gained widespread support in other southern industries as well, including tobacco, longshore, metal mining, maritime, and steel. By the late 1930s, southern workers were largely organized in coal, metal mining, basic steel, longshore, and maritime, and unevenly in tobacco. While inroads had been made in southern textiles, the bulk of the industry was still unorganized.

In 1940, the AFL announced with great fanfare another new southern organizing drive. As President William Green stated in an editorial in the *American Federationist* in March 1949, "The Southern Labor Conference, to be held in Atlanta beginning March 4, will herald a new organizing campaign in the South . . . The Atlanta Labor Conference will constitute a new milestone in Southern union progress under the American Federation of Labor." In a lengthy article in the *American Federationist*, March 1941, George Googe (1941:20–22) summarized the tremendous gains made by the AFL across the South, highlighting the victory of the AFL longshoremen against the CIO along the Gulf and southeastern Atlantic coasts.

The CIO, at the 1st Constitutional Convention, in Pittsburgh, on November 14–18, 1938, also recognized the importance of the South. In March 1937, it had already established the Textile Workers Organizing Committee (TWOC), giving some attention to the South. The many successes of the TWOC were regularly trumpeted in the *CIO News*.[2] After a lengthy discussion, the convention unanimously passed a resolution calling for a southern organizing campaign, mandating the executive officers to call a conference of all organizations for a joint campaign (Convention Proceedings 1938:169–80).The December 18, 1939, issue of the *CIO News* reported on a conference of southern union leaders called by Allan S. Haywood, CIO director of organization. An organizing committee of top CIO

---

[2] See, e.g., "TWOC Organizes the South; CIO Campaign Brings Hope to Workers," *CIO News*, March 26, 1938; *CIO News*, July 9, 1938; and the editorial entitled "The CIO in the South," *CIO News*, July 16, 1938.The November 21, 1938, issue reports on the convention decision to speed up the organization of the whole South.

leaders was set up to coordinate the drive. A great deal of optimism was expressed. As William Mitch, leader of the mineworkers and southern regional director for the steelworkers stated: "The South is the hardest nut we have to crack in this country. We're cracking it" (1939:3).

The 4th Constitutional Convention of the CIO, held on November 17–22, 1941, in Detroit, Michigan, unanimously passed the following resolution:

> Whereas, It having been recognized by this convention that *the organiza-tion of the workers in the South is the No. 1 task before the CIO* . . . Resolved, That the officials of the CIO are urged immediately to formulate and put into effect plans in conjunction with all interested national and interna-tional unions designed to bring about the organization of all Southern workers into unions of the CIO. (Convention Proceedings. 1941:306, emphasis added)

Paul Christopher, a CIO official from Tennessee, said: "Mr. Chairmen and fellow delegates, the American Federation of Labor in days gone by as frequently as the years rolled around used to say, 'We are going to organize the South.' Bill Green used to come down and say it, and it never was done" (1941:314).

There were lengthy testimonials by southern labor leaders (1941:306–14). The special pre-convention issue of the *CIO News* had a full-page article by Lucy Randolph Mason, CIO southern public relations director, on the growing strength of CIO unions in the South. She argued that "the CIO is accepted as part of the com-munity" (1941:14). There were fewer strikes, more settlements, and more business people, and the politicians were friendlier. In a post-convention issue, a headline rang out, "CIO Convention Backs Drives in South and Oil Industry" (*CIO News*, December 1, 1941). The article quotes from CIO president Philip Murray's speech to CIO delegates at the convention: "'I don't mind telling you,' Murray declared, 'that in so far as the CIO is concerned nothing is going to stand in our way of orga-nizing the South during the current year. We have to do it; we are going to do it. Let us pledge ourselves to see that this job is done before your convention meets next year'" (*CIO News*, December 1, 1941). And, in fact, in a whirlwind campaign, the oil industry, in a drive led by former chair of the National Labor Relations Board (NLRB) and leftist Murray appointee, Edwin Smith, was fully unionized.

At the CIO's 7th Constitutional Convention, held on November 21–24, 1944, in Chicago, vice president of the CIO and director of organization Alan Haywood, commenting on a resolution exhorting the organizing of the unorganized after World War II, urged, "We must organize the South. We must oust the reactionary Southern Democrats and Northern reactionaries who are in our Congress" (Convention Proceedings 1944:154). A delegate of the oilworkers, whose union had just finished a whirlwind campaign of organizing oilworkers across the country, an industry overwhelmingly concentrated in the South, argued that the defeat of ultra-reactionary and racist Texas Congressman Martin Dies by the oilworkers suggested that they were more advanced than autoworkers and others in the North. As soon to be appointed director of Operation Dixie, Van Bittner, stated, "Certainly we should organize the South. I spent a lot of time in the South myself. I understand something about the conditions in the South. You know in the United Mine Workers of America we were able to organize every old miner there is working in the South and in the South, in so far as that industry is concerned, every worker is organized" (1944:156).

As I have perhaps tediously shown, the idea and the impetus for finally fully organizing the South were not new. But with the promise of greater resources and commitments, many were led to expect a dynamic and effective campaign.

Launching Operation Dixie

A. G. Mezerik, the unofficial journalistic cheerleader for the right wing of the CIO, proclaimed, "The consequences of C.I.O. success will benefit the whole country politically." He continued:

> On the day that the South is finally organized, the death knell will sound for the elective restrictions which deprive the poor white and the Negro of their votes. More information and better education will follow in the wake of unionization. The combination spells the beginning of the end of the long domination by prejudice— it means a happy goodbye to the Bilbos and the Rankins. (1947a:)

Initial Announcement

In early February 1946, the CIO executive Board launched Operation Dixie, an attempt to unionize all southern industry. Philip Murray, the CIO president, later told the board, on March 15, that the southern organizing drive was "the most important drive of its kind ever undertaken by any labor union in the history of this country" (Minutes of the Executive Board of the Congress of Industrial Organizations 1946). Such sentiments, along with reports of initial successes, were echoed in virtually every issue of the weekly *CIO News* beginning in early March 1946 and continuing for at least a year.[3] The AFL), the former parent, now rival of the CIO, began its own campaign to organize the South at its May 11 and 12, 1946, Southern

---

[3] In an article titled "SOC Organizes the South; CIO Campaign Brings Hope to Workers," March 3, 1946, the *CIO News* described it as "one of the greatest organizing drives in labor history." See also the April–May 1946 issue of *Labor and Nation* focusing on the South, especially the article by Allan

Labor Conference held in Ashville, North Carolina. The AFL paper, the *American Federationist*, described the AFL effort as "the most intensive Southern organizing drive ever undertaken by the trade union movement" ().

Resources Committed

Along with the braggadocio and high-flown rhetoric, both labor federations seemed ready to commit major resources, including organizers and money to the task of organizing the South. The AFL promised a drive that would be "an operation primarily by Southerners for Southerners (*American Federationist*, May 1946:7).[4] To this end, the federation set up a board of forty-five southern AFL leaders, who met in Atlanta on June 3–5, 1946. Long-term AFL southern leader George Googe was placed at the head. How the AFL southern drive mobilized its resources—especially its organizational structure and the number of additional organizers—is still a bit obscure, since the policy board largely intended to use existing resources, including organizers from individual unions in the South and personnel already attached to southern state federations. The AFL executive council initially transferred $200,000 to the southern campaign from a defense fund for local unions directly attached to the federation, rather than to an existing national union (Marshall 1967:250). By the spring of 1947 (less than a year after announcing its campaign and after spending just a little over $350,000), the AFL decided to terminate its southern drive, largely because of the unexpected resistance it encountered from southern employers (Marshall 1967:252–53). Thus, the AFL promises proved once again to be little more than empty rhetoric.

The CIO's southern drive was more highly organized, better funded, and longer-lasting than the AFL's. The CIO Executive Board established the Southern Organizing Committee (SOC) to oversee its campaign. The SOC was chaired by CIO vice president and director of organizing Allan Haywood, with the steelworkers' David McDonald as secretary and Lee Pressman as general counsel. Other members included George Addes of the United Auto Workers (UAW), Julius Emspak of the electrical workers, George Baldanzi of the textile workers, J. B. Carey of the steelworkers, Charles Lanning, William Pollock, Jacob Potofsky of the clothing workers, and Joe Curran from the maritime union. Van Bittner—then a vice president of the steelworkers, originally a coal miner and long-time aide to John L. Lewis and then to Murray—was made director of the drive. Bittner was given autonomous and largely unrestricted control of the SOC by CIO President Philip Murray. The SOC established an extensive structure, which included six full-time

S. Haywood, CIO vice president and director of organizing, "We Propose to Unionize Labor in the South" (1946).

[4] The account here of AFL plans relies heavily on Marshall (1967:247–48).

assistant directors and twelve state directors, each of whom had regional and area directors working for them, as well as organizers and administrative personnel, who reported to them. Alan Swim, a conservative CIO official from Memphis, Tennessee, was made publicity director; John Ramsey of the steelworkers served as a liaison to the churches; and white, blue-blood southerner Lucy Randolph Mason contacted newspapers and local elites in places where the CIO was organizing. One million dollars was initially pledged to launch the drive, with Murray telling the Executive Board that the new campaign, informally christened Operation Dixie, would require 1.8 million dollars a year. CIO unions gave a little more than 3/4 of a million dollars to launch the campaign. Besides using organizers working directly for individual unions, the SOC hired over two hundred additional organizers who worked directly for and were paid for by the SOC. While these numbers have seemed impressive to most previous analysts, they were, as I will show later, hardly commensurate with the amount of money and number of personnel committed to two single industry drives in the mid-1930s, that of the Steelworkers Organizing Committee SWOC and that of the Textile Workers Organizing Committee (TWOC).

Initial Successes

Operation Dixie did begin with some impressive early successes. The first major campaign took place in Oak Ridge, Tennessee, home of the production facilities for the atomic bomb. Oak Ridge was a town that was built from scratch during World War II; in 1946, the government facilities employed between thirty and forty thousand production workers. Unions had agreed to hold off their organizing campaigns until after the war because of the secrecy involved. In early 1946, the AFL successfully petitioned the government and the NLRB to hold certification elections at three Oak Ridge plants, run—on government contract—by the Tennessee Eastman Corporation, Monsanto Chemical Company, and the Carbide and Carbide Corporation. Together these three units employed almost twelve thousand workers, 45% of whom were women.[5]

The AFL had a significant head start in the organizing at Oak Ridge. Thousands of AFL construction workers had been used in building the project. The government had worked with the AFL in recruiting the workers, then placed them under closed shop agreements. These workers included many organizers, since the AFL was expecting to organize the production units after the war. Many construction workers eventually were placed on production jobs. Before the campaign for the three production facilities, the AFL had already organized the laundry workers and

[5] Christopher to Bittner, May 29, 1946, Southern Organizing Committee files; henceforth SOC files, box 28.

won a closed shop agreement for the six hundred bus drivers at Oak Ridge who voted in a 90% majority for the AFL.

Nevertheless, the CIO decided to enter the fray and contest the elections. On May 1, 1946, Paul Christopher, the SOC director of Tennessee, and C. W. Danenburg, the southern director of the left-leaning United Gas, Coke and Chemical Workers of America (UGC&CWA), wrote a lengthy analysis and proposal to Van Bittner, head of Operation Dixie. They proposed a modest investment of fifty thousand dollars and twenty organizers to match the one million dollars committed by AFL unions and their many dozens of organizers. The CIO News announced the campaign as the first major concentration point in the CIO's organizing campaign (May 20, 1946), while Paul Christopher called the Oak Ridge organizing "the most important single drive in the South."[6]

The battle between the AFL and the CIO unions during the organizing campaign was intense. According to James Barrett, the director of the AFL drive, "More money has probably been spent by both unions here than in any other place in the South." The AFL set up an "Atomic Council" of almost a dozen craft unions and waived initiation fees for new members. The AFL also mentioned many shop issues important to workers in their numerous leaflets and frequent newspaper advertisements. By far the biggest emphasis of the AFL campaign, however, was the "Communism" of the CIO and its own unimpeachable patriotic credentials. The election was scheduled for August 20, 21, and 22, 1946. As the dates approached, the AFL red-baiting became more strident and dominated its leaflets and advertisements. As one AFL ad in the August 12, 1946, Knoxville Journal stated, "The real operators of the CIO communist drive to stop the American Federation of Labor at Oak Ridge and in the South are devoted followers of the Party Line." The AFL's ad in the August 19, 1946, Knoxville Journal focused exclusively on the ongoing struggle in the left-wing United Furniture Workers Union. It was entitled "Another Ten Thousand CIO Members Cast Off the 'Yoke of Communism.'" The red-baiting got so intense that Danenburg was attacked by more conservative CIO officials for having Communist sympathies. The AFL, according to James Barrett, was so confident of victory in the week before the election that union representatives had been working with plant delegates on a contract to present to the companies "as soon as possible after we have won and the workers tell us what they want."[7]

---

[6] Christopher and Danenburg to Bittner, May 1, 1946, Operation Dixie (henceforth OD) 128, reel 25; Knoxville News Sentinel, May 1, 1946, AFL-CIO Region 8 Papers, box 1886, folder 2.

[7] Knoxville Journal, August 20, 1946, AFL-CIO Region 8 Papers, box 1886, folder 2. See, e.g., the lengthy ads in the June 2, 1946, Knoxville News Sentinel and the June 3, 1946, Knoxville Journal, AFL Region 8 Papers, box 1855, folder 11; box 1886, folder 2. See also Danenburg's extensive reply to charges, in Danenburg to Christopher, July 4, 1946, AFL Region 8 Papers, box 2589, folder 1; Knoxville Journal, August 20, 1946, AFL Region 8 Papers, box, 1886, folder 2.

The August elections did not result in outright certification for either union. The runoff elections on September 12, 1946, represented an important victory for the CIO. While the AFL won the Monsanto plant with 565 workers, the CIO gained a majority at the Carbide and Carbide 5100 worker installation. The six thousand–employee unit at Tennessee Eastman chose "no union" over the AFL in the runoff. The CIO's major foothold at Oak Ridge would lead them eventually to organize the majority of production workers there.[8]

Two large International Harvester (IH) plants were also won overwhelmingly by the CIO. In March 1948, the Memphis plant voted 861 to 4 to join the United Auto Workers (UAW).[9] The Louisville plant, newly acquired by IHC after World War II (eventually to employ more than six thousand workers by 1949) joined the Communist Party–led Farm Equipment Workers (FE) when workers there in July 1947 voted 1,276 for the FE-CIO, 380 for UAW-CIO, and 207 for UAW-AFL (Gilpin 1992:429; contrary to Zieger 1995).

The Food, Tobacco, and Allied Workers (FTA) had a high degree of success, especially among tobacco workers in Virginia and North Carolina. As one reporter stated, "So far the CIO hasn't lost a single election among the tobacco workers" (Martin 1947), a statement that was not quite true, but makes the point nevertheless. The CIO also met with a great deal of success in southern woodworking, the second-largest industry in the South, after the textile industry. Much of this initial success, however, was dissipated by the provincial, Northwest-based International Woodworkers of America (IWA), which failed to service many of its newly formed locals. Even sharper complaints by other fellow conservative CIO officials were voiced later.[10] Numerous victories were won in woodworking between 1946 and 1947. The *CIO Round-up* for North Carolina reports in its June 1947 issue on three overwhelming victories by the IWA, the biggest of which was at North Carolina Lumber and Veneer Company in Hallsboro, North Carolina, under the direction of Elijah Jackson. The Communication Workers of America (CWA) won an election in the Burlington and Winston-Salem, North Carolina, plants of Western Electric, 871 to 541 for the International Brotherhood of Electrical Workers-AFL.[11] The CIO also had success in organizing taxi and bus drivers in major southern cities.

The CIO consolidated and extended its gains in a number of important southern industrial centers, including Gadsden, Alabama, Memphis, New Orleans, Atlanta, and in Laurel, Jackson, and Natchez, Mississippi. In Laurel, Mississippi, a town of thirty-thousand inhabitants, the CIO had more than six thousand members. In late 1948, the Textile Workers Union of America (TWUA) won an election at the Laurel

---

[8] Alan Swim, CIO Organizing Committee Public Relations Director to State Directors, CIO Organizing Committee, September 16, 1946, OD 128, reel 25.

[9] Christopher to Bittner, March 8, 1948, OD, reel 25; OD, box 108, Bittner file.

[10] See, e.g., Pugh to Bittner, May 31, 1949, OD 229, Bittner file.

[11] Smith to Baldanzi, February 14, 1949; OD 53, Bittner file, reel 2.

Textile Mill, the last major non-union plant in town. This victory came despite the fact that openly white supremacist Senator Theodore Bilbo and Representative John Rankin came to town specifically to campaign against the CIO, which (unlike the UAW defeat at Volkswagen in Chattanooga in 2014) did not stop the majority-white workers there from voting overwhelmingly for the CIO.

The CIO even won some important victories in the textile industry. TWUA won the Roanoke Mill No. 1 in Roanoke Rapids, North Carolina, on March 12, 1948, by a vote of 428 to 309 for no union. As a result, the union began to rapidly sign up other workers in the town working for the same company.[12] In 1949, TWUA won the big Celanese plant with its more than twelve hundred workers. In 1946, it had won the Glendale Mill 388 to 271, but over a year later was not able to start negotiations. At the Sophie Manufacturing Co. in Rockingham, North Carolina, with more than a thousand workers, the management refused to meet with a committee of workers about holding an NLRB election. The workers then struck for three days, until management agreed to an election, which the union then won, although as Minchin (1997) documents it was never able to gain a contract there.[13] At Industrial Mill, a plant owned by J. P. Stevens, the local voted 690 to 18 for a union security clause.[14] In good part, however, these initial victories were low-hanging fruit, which did not foreshadow future, broader successes.

Initial Claims of Success

These initial successes were publicized by CIO and SOC leaders. For public consumption, Van Bittner told the *Charlotte Observer* in July 1946, "The campaign has been amazingly successful to date. It has been so successful that we are planning to accelerate it." Operation Dixie officials often said similar things in private correspondence and staff memos. Bittner, in a letter to South Carolina director Franz Daniel dated April 9, 1947, wrote, "It is indeed heartening to myself and the entire CIO to know of the splendid job you and your staff are doing under most difficult conditions in South Carolina." Daniel in correspondence to Milton MacKaye on July 18, 1946, wrote, "For the first time in all my experience in the South, I am really optimistic about the possibilities. We are definitely making headway, even in South Carolina." And on December 11, 1946, James Gallagher of the Gas, Coke, and Chemical workers wrote to Paul Christopher, "According to all reports, the Southern Drive is rolling along at top speed."[15] In writing to Bittner, November 10,

---

[12] Smith to Bittner, March 17, 1948; OD 53, Bittner file, reel 23.

[13] Bittner to All State Directors and Staff Members, CIO Organizing Committee, March 24, 1947, OD 128, reel 25.

[14] Article submitted to *CIO News and Textile Labor*, June 17, 1948; OD 102.

[15] AFL Region 8 Papers, box 2589, folder 1.

1947, Daniel related: "George Baldanzi will undoubtedly report to you the general feeling of optimism that is prevailing in South Carolina. I just want to add this word. In my opinion the prospects are better now for organization than at any other time since I have been here. The staff is enthusiastic, response is very good, and there is a general feeling of excitement in the air that always marks successful organizational work . . . I think we're on the verge of really big things." In a memo to Operation Dixie staff, dated December 14, 1948 and entitled "We Are On The March," Bittner stated, "Things never looked brighter for the Southern Drive." And at a press conference during the same period in Atlanta, December 8, 1948, Bittner stated that all-time records were about to be set for organizing and that "1949 will be a great year in Dixie."[16]

In announcing its claims, the CIO was not above inflating its own figures, not merely in public, but in private too. At a CIO Executive Board Meeting on August 30–31, 1948, held in Washington, DC, it was claimed, "When the Southern Organizing Drive began two years ago the CIO membership in the South was about 400,000. Today, it exceeds 800,000." These figures are belied by the organization's own tally sheets, membership lists, and occasionally franker, highly pessimistic assessments.

The Reality Is Failure

Despite the contribution of substantial resources by unions, optimistic prognoses from many quarters, and some initial successes, Operation Dixie failed abysmally.[17] Not only did unions gain few new members and hardly any new stably organized locals, but most of the gains made during World War II were subsequently lost.

The key to the Operation Dixie strategy was the organization of the southern textile industry. The main foci were the largest textile firms usually located in rural mill towns. It was there where the majority of CIO organizers and resources were directed. And it was there where Operation Dixie quickly ground to a halt. The largest concentration point was the Cannon textile chain, located primarily in Kannapolis and Concord, North Carolina. The two major plants in Kannapolis were Plant No. 1 with nineteen thousand workers and Plant No. 4 with five thousand workers. The drive to organize Cannon, which at times involved several dozen organizers in these two towns, was officially launched on June 28, 1946. The southern area director for North Carolina, D. D. Wood, who reported to North Carolina director William Smith, stated in a letter dated July 29, 1946: "The general picture in Concord and Kannapolis area is very bright . . . the staff are working day and night and their work

---

[16] AFL Region 8 Papers, box 1885, folder 11.

[17] In its October 1948 issue, *Fortune* magazine observed that "the C.I.O. southern drive . . . [was] now grinding to a halt."

is satisfactory." He announced that at one mill in Concord, "our first distribution of leaflets was amazing in this plant." Smith dutifully reported to Bittner that at Cannon "the Drive is progressing splendidly. All of our carefully thought out plans are being carried out to the letter and the organizers assigned to Cannon are working in perfect harmony and teamwork . . . There is a spirit of victory over there and our drive, without question, is cracking."[18]

All of this talk was either delusional or self-serving puffery. No mill at Cannon was ever brought to an NLRB election for good reason. Initiation fee and membership records show the meagerness of results. Out of 41,000 workers at Cannon, only 839 ever became members of the union, barely 2%, compared with the 50 or 60% that unions required before elections. Most mills had no members; Cannon No. 1 had only 485 out of 19,000.[19] Despite the paucity of results, the Cannon campaign moved forward in an otherworldly manner, moving to open meetings and big rallies because of the supposed high degree of support. Dean Culver, the head organizer for Cannon, spurred along by the spirit, even put out a leaflet in September 1946, which said in part: "Dear Fellow Worker: You will be pleased to know that the organizing campaign in Cannon Mill is running ahead of schedule . . . We are winning." It would be interesting to know what the schedule was and how Operation Dixie leaders would have defined defeat. The correspondence and public statements suggest that the organizers of the campaign were indeed clueless.

Many of the large mills, like Cannon, were never brought to election. Even in the more favorable environment of Alabama, organizing in textiles largely stagnated. At the Avondale Mills in Alabama, the TWUA director for the state, unlike the Operation Dixie officials, did not give an optimistic account. The 3,600-worker plant in Sylacauga was abandoned because of lack of staff, even though 350 workers were signed up. At the Avondale plant in Pell City, Alabama, the state TWUA director wrote, "we have discontinued our activities . . . because after a long campaign we were only successful in getting 83 people signed out of 700 in the mill." In the Avondale plant in Birmingham, Alabama, "34 people out of 700 signed with the union. Practically every one of them have been run off, fired, or demoted, and there is no semblance of Union activities in this plant."[20] So it went across the southern textile industry, with hardly any exceptions. Those mills brought to election generally suffered overwhelming defeat (unlike the mills brought to election in the 1937 TWOC campaigns). Even in mills where victory seemed certain, the election was usually lost. In an unusually candid note, dated October 10, 1946, William Smith shared his frustrations with Van Bittner:

---

[18] Smith to Bittner, August 8, 1946, OD 53.

[19] Initiation and Membership Record for Concord and Kannapolis, since the beginning of the drive, with no date, but presumably early 1947, OD 53, reel 3.

[20] Alabama TWUA director Edmund Ryan, Jr. to George Baldanzi, January 6, 1947, OD 53.

We seem to be able to win elections in every other industry except in textile and I frankly, am worried and heartsick about the loss of these two textile elections this week as I realize only too well that unless we crack some
of the major textile mills in the state, the rest will not mean too much.
I never wanted to do anything more in my life than to do a real job in the
textile industry. . . .

The lethargy and disinterest of the textile workers is enough to frustrate
anyone and, frankly, while I have some ideas, I do not know the answer
at all . . . At the Southern Webbing Company, Incorporated, there were
52 eligible workers, 42 signed up and paid one dollar. The workers themselves had approached us with a committee for organization and did the
job of signing up the workers . . . Shortly before the election, the employer
appointed a workers' committee and signed a contract with the workers,
granting them almost everything that union contracts have. The committee
disintegrated and we couldn't get any action from them. Up to a day before
the election our organizers felt sure we would win this election . . . In the
Handleman Mills, Incorporated, of 208 eligible voters, 154 had signed up
with us on a $1.00 basis. The organizer there did a good job and worked
hard. The workers at the outset had several issues which bothered them.
They, therefore wanted the union. However, the employer granted them
their requests and there was no longer any interest in the Union. . . .

*While both companies fought us and put out literature of the type enclosed,
we did not get any violent opposition.*[21]

In an article in the *Greensboro Daily News* on February 2, 1947, Bittner admits
that textile organizing has been "pretty tough" and that not too many gains have
been made, but expresses optimism, saying that the industry will eventually be organized. The top leaders of the SOC invariably blamed southern textile workers,
not themselves. In a letter by South Carolina director Franz Daniel to Bittner dated
October 9, 1948, he writes, in discussing the loss of the Winnsboro election, 707 for
UTW-AFL to 588 for UTW-CIO:

Essentially, the textile workers in South Carolina are very timid people.
The constant barrage of strike propaganda put out by the AFL was, in my
opinion, the determining factor. We were simply unable to convince the
people that we could get a contract without the necessity of a strike. In addition to that fact, the UTW turned loose a large amount of money at the
last minute. A good many influential people in the mill who had supported
us in the first election, switched as a result of this money.[22]

[21] OD 53, reel 10 (emphasis added).
[22] OD 102, reel 16, file 577.

Curtailment

In spite of the problems faced by the SOC and the clear need for more resources and a larger number of staffers, the Operation Dixie budget and staff were drastically cut in late 1946, the grandiose promises by CIO leaders at the beginning of the year notwithstanding. Most unions in the CIO were not prepared to fund major organizing drives and money could not be raised.[23] With this curtailment, what little hope the mainstream CIO leadership and their minions who were running Operation Dixie had for broad success was for all practical purposes lost.

Strategy of Operation Dixie

All of the CIO unions had supposedly recognized the importance of organizing the South. Although a number of left-wing unions were highly active in the South, including Mine Mill, the National Maritime Union (NMU), and the FTA, and left-wingers had played central roles in the organization of southern workers in steel, coal, and oil, Operation Dixie (OD) was to be organized as a strictly right-wing show (Levenstein 1981:292). Specifically, the leadership of OD, including the director, assistant directors, and state directors were all CIO right-wingers. In addition, CPers and, by and large, even non-CP organizers from left-wing unions, with a few initial (soon to be rectified) exceptions, were excluded from OD staff. The main industry chosen for a focal point was one in which the Left had by 1946 little influence (textiles) and in which there were seemingly few Black workers.

The CIO leaders were confident that OD could be successful as a right-wing affair without help or hindrance, as they saw it, from the left. They also believed (incorrectly, as it turned out) that such an orientation would undermine anti-communist

---

[23] See, e.g., "Personal and Confidential Memo to All District Directors, CIO Organizing Committee" from Van A. Bittner, November 21, 1946, OD 229, announcing that appropriations have been cut in half. See also Confidential Memo to All Organizing Directors, CIO Organizing Committee, from Bittner, November 21, 1946, as well as a letter stating that appropriation has been cut in half and that 130 men will be off the payroll by January 1, 1947, with a budget held to $93,000 per month (Copeland to Christopher, November 26, 1946), all in AFL Region 8 Papers, box 2589, folder 1. One laid-off organizer, Jesse Smith, wrote to Baldanzi: "Mr. Daniel informed us that the entire CIO staff in Spartansburg, S.C., were being laid off, and that also applied to the entire South, which means as the workers at the Brandon mill will phrase it, that the whole CIO campaign is a flop, and many of them express their regret that they had ever confided in the CIO." December 11, 1946, OD 101, reel 12. Baldanzi replies: "This action should by no means be interpreted as meaning that the CIO campaign in the South is being called off or discontinued." December 13, 1946, OD 101, reel 12. South Carolina director Franz Daniel wrote to TWUA's Gladys Dickason on December 5, 1946, "As you know, I have been forced to terminate the employment of eight of my CIO staff." OD 106, reel 1 (where "Dickason" is misspelled as "Dickenson").

attacks from the AFL and southern elites. They thought they could get broader support in the South, not only from allegedly socially conservative white workers, but also from southern leaders, particularly newspaper editors and religious leaders. They believed that they could also appeal more successfully to imagined forward-thinking capitalists, who would take their desires for cooperation more seriously.

Finally, they saw the successful organization of the South as a chance to increase their own power and influence within the CIO and to minimize, if not eliminate, the power of the left. I have suggested that such expectations were delusional and that in spite of historical and recent experience to the contrary, hope springs eternal.

Operation Dixie Director Van Bittner

The choice of Van Amberg Bittner to be the head of Operation Dixie was an odd one, destined to make the campaign a stodgy, dull affair, diminishing its chances of success. Bittner was not only a conservative, virulent anti-communist, but authoritarian, racially insensitive, unimaginative, dull and boring, and, to say the least, hardly charismatic. One might contrast his appointment with Murray's appointment of Edwin Smith—the dynamic, former head of the NLRB, a left-winger, and most likely a member of the Communist Party—to the Oil Workers Organizing Committee (OWIU) in November 1941. Smith was exceedingly popular with CIO members and unions for the aggressive and supportive positions he took on industrial unionism as NLRB chair. When OWIU representatives tried to avoid the left- wing NMU (which previously represented workers on Standard Oil tanker ships), Smith made sure they were central allies in the campaign. Smith involved NMU vice president Frederick (Blackie) Myers, a CPer, in the campaign. The NMU provided important support and manpower, especially in the huge seaside Texas Company refinery in Port Arthur, Texas, a breakthrough victory. While oil workers had important structural power, the additional associational power proved crucial (Johnson 1977).

Bittner was not to be confused with Edwin Smith. As the *West Virginia Encyclopedia* states, Bittner "was one of the United Mine Workers of America's most durable infighters for nearly 40 years starting in 1911." Along with Philip Murray, he was a key enforcer and Lewis supporter, beginning with the January 1920 UMWA convention where Lewis was first elected. Aside from his authoritarianism, which he shared with other top Lewis supporters, he was bureaucratically cautious and unimaginative except when it came to fighting factional opponents. In 1921, he was sent to Kansas to take over the district from the popular, radical Lewis oppositionist Alex Howat (Dubofsky and Van Tine 1977:118). At the 1924 UMWA convention— although Bittner had originally played a role in inserting a ban on KKK members into the union constitution—he was the main spokesperson for a constitutional amendment to undermine this original position. "The convention delegates would have none of this truckling to the Klan, however ... white delegates immediately jumped to their feet to reject the committee's report in sharp language." It was defeated by "an overwhelming majority" (Lewis 1987:109). In 1931, in West Virginia, Bittner played the leading role in destroying the militant leadership of former district director Frank Keeney. Although Keeney was vaguely a socialist (he had briefly been a member of the Socialist Party in 1912), Bittner traveled the coalfields, red-baiting him as a "Bolshevik" and outsider (Corbin 1976:147, 151).[24]

In 1937, Bittner was appointed head of the Packinghouse Workers Organizing Committee (PWOC), riding herd over a collection of preexisting militant locals. He appointed regional directors, most of whom were from outside industries. "The autocratic style of PWOC national chair Van A. Bittner . . . particularly clashed with the democratic sensibilities of packinghouse unionists. The complaints of Mason City, Iowa, activists were typical. They accused Bittner of being a 'dictator'" (Horowitz 1997:125). In the fall of 1939, Bittner decided to purge all the CP activists (many of whom had been central to organizing the industry). He also fired Joe Ollman, a Trotskyist (Horowitz 1997:127). In 1941, Bittner fired then–assistant national director Hank Johnson and his two closest allies, prominent Black organizers Arthell Shelton and Frank Alsop, who were subsequently hired by Lewis's District 50. The CIO was forced to rely on Herb March and other CP activists to keep the pro-Johnson forces from taking the union into District 50. As a consequence, CP packinghouse leaders were brought back into key positions in the union (Horowitz 1997:129, 132). Bittner had succeeded in uniting every fractious group within the PWOC against him. Opposition to Bittner began to assume the same tactics that had been used against the companies, including pickets, sit-downs, and mass gatherings at his office and speaking locations (Halpern 1997:191–92). By May 1941, Bittner was "reassigned" (Horowitz 1997:134). As Hennen (2017) states, during Operation Dixie, "his refusal to form alliances with integrationist groups and his rigid antiradicalism undermined the CIO's organizational unity, probably doing mortal damage to the southern campaign."

Exclusion of Left

As I have already suggested, organization in the textile industry always required the broadest possible outside support—associational power. Such was not the

---

[24] In attacking the CP, Bittner continually claimed in Trump-like fashion that he had never been a "red-baiter." In dozens of documents, Bittner continually made this claim. See, e.g., his letter to Donald Henderson, CP president of the FTA: "It seems this situation is getting serious. Everyone who knows me knows I am not out 'red baiting.'" Bittner to Henderson, October 18, 1946, OD 128, reel 25, 185. Bittner to Henderson, October 18, 1946, OD 128, reel 25, 185. Of course, everyone who knew his history, knew him as a consummate red-baiter.

approach taken, however, by SOC director Van Bittner. On April 18, 1946, he called a press conference to repudiate all "outside" organizations (*New York Times,* April 19, 1946). "No crowd, whether Communists, Socialists, or anybody else, is going to mix in this organizing drive," he said. "That goes for the Southern Conference for Human Welfare [SCHW] and any other organization living off the CIO" (SCHW being a group that was even supported by first lady Eleanor Roosevelt). Then he singled out a New York group called "Help Organize the South," whose chairman was Harlem Congressman Adam C. Powell, Jr. It had invited Alan S. Haywood, CIO organizing director, to a rally in Harlem on May 5 and he, declining, had asked Bittner to reply. In replying to the group's coordinator, Bittner wrote, "Your so-called organization has no connection with the CIO. We do not need any money. We will tolerate no interference from organizations outside the CIO."

Fellow conservative Ernest B. Pugh, Virginia CIO regional director, wrote approvingly to Bittner on April 23, 1946: "I am so glad you came out boldly and so forthrightly on the issue that the organizing drive will be a simon pure CIO effort with no other group or groups forming the tail on the CIO kite . . . Already I have been approached by some of the fellow-travelers, working for some internationals, wanting me to recommend them for use in the drive. I put them off without any committal." Such a stance was not new to Pugh, who had expressed concerns to Allan Haywood about CP organizers earlier. Taking a further cue from Bittner and Pugh, the Richmond, Virginia, Industrial Union Council passed a resolution echoing these sentiments. The Virginia CIO State Convention held in Norfolk the previous week also passed a resolution "barring Communists, Nazis, and Fascists from holding office."[25]

But it was not just leftist allies who were shunned. Bittner also had a policy of forbidding any of the Organizing Committee staff to have anything to do with the CIO's own Political Action Committee (PAC).[26] Bittner's broad horizons led him to write the following to Franz Daniel on July 3, 1946: "I think the PAC in South Carolina is about as useful as [AFL president] Bill Green as a CIO organizer. We have instructed all our leaders to drop out of all other activities and devote their entire time to organizing. If I had my way about it, as vice-chairman of PAC, I would simply dissolve PAC in South Carolina and I expect to work toward that end. I know I will have your support."

Bittner also wanted to exclude Communists from any organization the CIO had anything to do with. He was upset enough about the existence of two Mine Mill officials on the Executive Council of the Highlander Folk School to write his Tennessee director, Paul Christopher: "I am sure that Lawrence is an out and out

[25] See, e.g., Pugh to Haywood, May 13, 1944; OD 236; *Richmond Times-Dispatch,* Friday, May 10, 1946, AFL Region 8 Papers, box 1886, folder 2; Pugh to Bittner, May 14, 1947, OD 229.
[26] Bittner to William Smith, September 30, 1947, OD, 53, reel 10.

communist and recent developments demonstrate that Charles Wilson is a fellow traveler."[27]

Bittner's tunnel vision even extended to his own right-wing assistants. As Paul Christopher wrote to Fred C. Pieper, Louisiana and Mississippi regional director, on May 12, 1946: "Brother Van A. Bittner informed me in no uncertain terms that I would hereafter confine my activities exclusively to the southern organizing drive in Tennessee. I am given to understand by him that all my other activities, for the sake of the success of the organizing campaign, are at an end for the duration of the drive. Also, that no state director will leave the borders of the state without his express authority. Maybe time will make these rather rigid instructions more flexible; I don't know." Yet Bittner was to reiterate his "rigid instructions" continuously, stating them even more emphatically over time as if they were new instructions: "From now on, it shall be our purpose to devote our entire time to organizing—no politics or any other side issues—just organizing the unorganized."[28]

Mezerik, always an enthusiastic proponent of whatever the CIO rightists proposed, approved of this approach: "The C.I.O.'s policy of political aloofness has given rise to more violent criticism than that aroused by its failure to make strong statements on the Negro question. The Southern organizing drive, through its directors, has ignored the entire left, including the constructive Southern Conference for Human Welfare. It has not even gone along with the P.A.C. which is hard to take. But the drive is designed to unionize." (1947). Thus, as I have already suggested in the preceding chapter, Bittner's stance was doomed to ensure that organizing in the textile industry failed.

The One-Dollar Initiation Fee

Perhaps no other issue symbolizes both the rigidity of Bittner and his lack of attunement to the organizing of southern workers than the demand for a one-dollar initiation fee. Bittner and others correctly thought that the Organizing Committee should move toward financial self-sufficiency as quickly as possible. To this end, Bittner instituted a policy of forcing all members signed up by his staff to pay a one-dollar initiation fee. The problem with this approach was that many southern workers were rightly skeptical of unions. In some cases, these workers had paid initiation fees and dues to AFL or CIO unions in the past—sometimes even both— then been abandoned. Examples of this were common and even occurred during Operation Dixie. Lewis Haynie, an organizer in Virginia, writes to E .B. Pugh, his state director about the Frank Ix plant: "The Frank Ix workers that I have talked with

[27] Bittner to Christopher, November 12, 1947, AFL Region 8 Papers, box 2589, folder 3.

[28] Memo from Bittner, "To Each State Director and Staff Member of the CIO Organizing Committee," December 13, 1948, OD 102; reel 15, 581.

all want a Union, but due to the fact that both the U.T.W.–A.F.of L. and T.W.U.A.–C.I.O. have both started campaigns here before and would only stay from six weeks to two months then pull out and leave them, the biggest job that Vic and I have to do is convincing the workers that we won't pull out on them also. As you know Vic has been pulled out of here three times since he started this campaign last March."[29] Asking for money in situations like this was often deadly. The policy of most serious organizers, especially in the South, in the past, including the earlier TWOC campaign, the successful drive at Oak Ridge, and the approach of both the UAW and FE at International Harvester, thus had been to waive such fees initially, at least until a local was organized and functioning. In fact, this had been an approach Bittner himself had once taken both with PWOC and as the Midwest director of the SWOC. (Note also that in attempting to win over workers from a company union in a refinery in South Norfolk, Virginia, the CIO representative Robert Johnson urged that monthly dues be waived until a contract was signed).[30] Bittner's inflexibility on this issue led him into frequent conflicts not only with organizers, but even with his state directors and the leaders of conservative unions.[31]

Bittner sent strict instructions on this issue to all state directors.[32] He stressed that initiation fees were to be waived for veterans, but for no one else: "Any deviation from the above set policy must have the approval of Van A. Bittner, National Director of the CIO Organizing Committee." Because many locals needed to gain the confidence of workers who were already skeptical of unions, Bittner received a number of such requests. Two weeks later, he replied, "I have received entirely too many requests from State Directors asking that the $1.00 initiation fee not be collected. My honest opinion is that the worker who can't pay $1.00 to belong to the union is not of much benefit to our organization." Still, there continued to be numerous letters requesting exceptions and clarifications.[33]

Bittner's policy brought him into conflict with the conservative hosiery workers, the autoworkers, and the brewery workers, to whom Christopher wrote, "We have a

[29] Haynie to Pugh, August 30, 1947, OD 236.

[30] Johnson to E. C. Conarty, Secretary Treasurer of OWIU, March 6, 1944, OD.

[31] AFHW representative Floyd Buckner told Paul Christopher that "he did not know if Hosiery Workers would be part of the southern drive." The AFHW demanded that the dollar initiation fees be refunded to workers in the Van Raalte Hosiery Mill in Athens, Tennessee, since it was not the union's policy to charge such fees. Christopher to Bittner, July 5, 1946, OD 128; reel 25, 77.

[32] See letter of June 3, 1946, in files of Franz Daniels, South Carolina, box 102, Paul Christopher of Tennessee, box 128, and E. Pugh, Virginia, box 229, all in OD.

[33] Assistant Secretary-Treasurer Richard Bauer to Franz Daniel, September 19, 1946, OD, box 101; Wm. Smith to Bittner, September 11, 1946, and Bittner to Smith, September 12, 1946, box 53, 10; Christopher to Bittner, May 29, 1947, OD, reel 25, folder 49; Bittner to Christopher, June 22, 1948, OD, reel 25, folder 49

rather rigid policy" and with the TWUA, which initially refused to follow it, at least in Virginia.[34]

State directors were themselves brought into conflict with their own staff, and even at times with in-plant organizers. A letter from W. A. Swofford, a member of the in-plant organizing committee at the Peerless Woolen Mill, to assistant Operation Dixie director George Baldanzi, dated September 17, 1946, succinctly states the problem: "In regards to the dollar initiation fee you have demanded, the people won't pay it . . . Surely Mr. Baldanzi you realize that a union can't be organized on lies and broken promises. We've had too much of that treatment already." Swofford adds, "We want a union and intend to have one. We also want your cooperation . . . I have written this at the request of our committee."[35] Lloyd Chapman's organizer report of April 19, 1947, notes considerable opposition among workers in Elizabethtown, Tennessee, which elicits an immediate reply from regional director Paul Christopher. Another organizer, J. H. Fullerton of the Joint TWUA Board in Charlotte, writes to TWUA president Emil Rieve that the failure to organize an important mill is due directly to the demand that the workers pay the initiation fee.[36]

Throughout all this, including numerous setbacks, Bittner's position remained inflexible and unchanged.[37] Pugh requests an exception in Bittner's absence from Operation Dixie secretary-treasurer, Sherman Dalrymple. Pugh notes, "The past history of AFL organizing in Pulaski is one of collecting initiation fees from a great number of workers then running out on them and coming back after a few years and starting the cycle anew."[38] Dalrymple replies that he does not have the authority to make such a momentous decision.[39]

After Bittner died and Baldanzi had become national director, the policy was dropped. "I have had on many occasions, referred to me by directors and organizers, the theory that the collection of initiation fees has been a hindrance to our organizing campaign. My own personal feeling is that it makes very little material difference whether you do or do not collect initiation fees, but in order to eliminate as many excuses as possible, imaginary or otherwise, that the organizers say they have, impeding their progress, we have decided that we will proceed on the basis of no initiation fee."[40] Enough has been said perhaps about Bittner, whose stubbornness

---

[34] Baldanzi to John McCoy, Second Vice President of the American Federation of Hosiery Workers, June 26, 1946, OD 53; Christopher to Bittner, August 13, 1946, Tennessee series, reel 25, Baldanzi file, Bittner folder; October 15, 1946, OD 133; report of Ernest Pugh, August 39, 1946, OD 229, reel 2; and with the United Electrical Workers; Christopher to Bittner, October 17, 1946, OD 128, reel 25,179.

[35] OD 53, reel 18, Baldanzi file.

[36] January 6, 1947, Baldanzi file, box 53.

[37] Bittner to Ernest Pugh, Virginia SOC director, January 29, 1947, OD, box 229, Bittner file.

[38] January 18, 1947, OD, Bittner files.

[39] January 23, 1947, OD, Bittner files.

[40] Baldanzi to Christopher, September 16, 1949, OD, reel 25, file 44.

and incompetency are easily documented. Yet in most of the secondary literature, he is given a pass as an efficient, competent, effective leader.

Choice of Organizers

Because of his desire to appear "simon pure," Bittner wanted an organizing staff that the southern press and southern elites considered irreproachable. Thus, he and his assistants excluded not merely known leftists but even experienced organizers from left-wing unions. (This can be seen not merely from the letters, but from lists of union affiliations of OD staffers.) Baldanzi claimed that "almost all the leaders and organizers of the CIO drive 'are born-and-bred Southerners' and '95% of them are veterans.'" Later, he claimed that "over 75 per cent of the CIO drive leaders and organizers are native Southerners."[41] A CIO Organizing Committee press release claimed that "about 85 per cent of the new organizers are war veterans who were born and reared in the South and are familiar with its economic and social problems." Such was also the conclusion of a reporter for the *Knoxville News-Sentinel*, October 29, 1946, after visiting some textile organizing campaigns in Alabama. Because of their priorities (conservative identity over substance), it is not surprising that Operation Dixie hired apolitical and inexperienced, ergo basically ineffective, organizers. Other remarks indicate the inexperienced character of organizers. Ernest Pugh, for example, writing to Allan Haywood, describes "six new organizers, all good fellows but inexperienced." CIO officials explained that "when their drive first began their organizers were inexperienced and required training. Now, however, they claim everything is running smoothly." The detailed accounts emphatically contradict the latter statement.[42]

George Baldanzi gives a similar cheery message in his comments on the overall staff: "I am gratified with the staff we have been putting together and feel we will have as about as fine an organizing crew as any place in the South."[43] Ralph Martin, writing in the *New Republic*, seems to agree: "Most of their labor organizers were green at the job and had to be trained. Some worked out, some didn't" (January 13, 1947). The sycophantic Mezerik concurs, justifying this as follows: "The South is still predominantly rural, and its traditional back-country aversion to unions can be overcome only by proof that the C.I.O. is indigenous and working in the interest of the entire community" (1947). Let me suggest that this is self-justifying hokum, as one finds little aversion to unions when the situation is ripe.

---

[41] Baldanzi to Wingate, n.d. [1946]; OD 86, reel 11, Baldanzi file.

[42] Press Release from Allan Swim, CIO Organizing Committee, public relations director, June 4, 1946, OD 128, reel 25, folder 49; AFL Region 8 Papers, box 1886, folder 2; CIO officials cited in *Nashville Tennessean*, October 13, 1946, AFL Region 8 Papers, box 1886, folder 2.

[43] Baldanzi to Bittner, July 1, 1946, OD 53, reel 1, folder 18.

Virtually all the leaders of Operation Dixie were complicitous in hiring inexperienced organizers (a mistake one should note that Lewis never considered making in steel). One organizer hired by OD was Sal Tuzzeo, who had a master's in physical education from the University of Chicago, was a major in the army air corps, and had personal reference letters from Governor Olin Johnson of South Carolina and Fred McCullough, the mayor of Greenville, South Carolina. He is recommended by Ben Manney, business agent for the Passaic Joint Board of the TWUA, to George Baldanzi.[44] Baldanzi recommends him to Franz Daniel, who feels "that you will be a definite asset to our campaign in this state."[45] Daniel gets approval from Bittner and appoints him at the highest full-time salary level for organizers.[46] There were, of course, some experienced organizers. Paul Christopher describes one Garland Defriese, who seems to have organized plants and locals wherever he worked, as well as in the surrounding areas,[47] although I was unable to find any evidence that this person was ever actually hired.

There were several problems with such a hiring policy. First, many people do not have the temperament or skill set to be good organizers. Second, even those who do require a learning curve. Operation Dixie would have done far better to have hired experienced organizers with a proven track record, whatever their regional roots or military experience. Paul Christopher, for example, writes to three inexperienced organizers who want to file for an election when they have only 40% of the workers organized in a plant. There are many complaints about the irresponsibility of a number of individual organizers. Amazingly, in the midst of perhaps the most important campaign of all of Operation Dixie—the Cannon Drive—the whole staff refused to work weekends. As North Carolina director William Smith (who, as noted previously, lauded his staff without reservation) complains:

> As you know, I have been spending considerable time in Concord the past week or two and have come across one thing that bothers me very much . . . Despite my instructions to the contrary, the Cannon Drive closes up on Saturday afternoon and does not start again until Monday morning with the majority of organizers going home. This must cease immediately . . . This is a seven day job and the campaign is to operate seven days and at least 50% of the staff must be on the job over the weekend. There are hundreds of things that they can do and under no circumstances is Saturday afternoon and Sunday to be wasted . . . I do not want to have to

---

[44] Manney to Bladanzi, October 10, 1946, OD 120, reel 19.
[45] Daniel to Tuzzeo, October 31, 1946, OD 120, reel 19.
[46] Daniel to Tuzzeo, November 6, 1946; OD 120:51, reel 19.
[47] Christopher to Bittner, April 29, 1946, reel 25, folder 51.

repeat these instructions again and I insist that they be carried out to the letter."[48]

Of all the things that CP organizers were accused of, no one ever accused them of not being willing to work on the weekends. Further comment would be superfluous.

Edmund Ryan, state TWUA director for Alabama, comments on the problem of the incompetency of organizers to Baldanzi on October 26, 1946: "In my opinion three or four of the people out of the nine assigned to textile will not make competent material and should be replaced." Later he notes, "There seems to be quite a problem of eliminating incompetent personnel in this state. There are some reluctant to get rid of organizers who are not measuring up mainly in the fear that they will not be replaced." And there is no reason to assume that these problems were peculiar to Alabama. As Bittner himself notes: "In many instances our directors report to me that one of the reasons we are losing National Labor Relations Board Elections is due to the fact that we are not fully prepared for these elections."[49]

Relation to Southern Politicians

While Van Bittner was discouraging his state officials from having anything to do with the CIO's PAC, whose avowed purpose in the South was to defeat racist, anti-labor, politicians, I have found no evidence that he ever questioned or voiced disapproval of any of his directors' relations with racist, Dixiecrat, often anti-labor southern politicians. William Smith, Southern Organizing Committee director in North Carolina, for example, was pleased to receive an invitation to a dinner hosted by the North Carolina governor Robert Cherry at which several other even less "progressive" southern governors would attend. In a letter to Van Bittner, he commented, "I believe that this is a sign of recognition in this state."[50] South Carolina director Franz Daniel considered himself an intimate of South Carolina governor Strom Thurmond, even after Thurmond had run as the 1948 presidential candidate for the racist States Rights Democratic (Dixiecrat) Party. Thurmond appointed Daniel as his personal representative to a national labor conference. Daniel not only accepted, but congratulated Thurmond on his recent marriage.[51] Right-winger and southern CIO director, Carey Haigler, was an ardent campaigner for the racist Bull Connor's campaign for mayor of Birmingham, Alabama. The

[48] Smith to D. D. Wood, area director for the Cannon campaign, August 12, 1946, OD 85, reel 11, folder 516.

[49] Bittner to All State Directors, June 17, 1947, OD 229.

[50] See Smith to Bittner, October 17, 1947, OD 53, reel 10.

[51] Thurmond to Maurice Tobin, Secretary of Labor, November 8, 1948; Daniel to Thurmond, November 19, 1948; both in OD 120:18.

Birmingham Legislative and Political Action Committee of the Birmingham IUC had voted 14 to 12 to endorse Bull Connor. Haigler had played a key role in getting the committee to narrowly support Connor. He subsequently campaigned "vigorously" for Connor and was attacked publicly by Homer Wilson of Mine Mill for having sold out.[52] None of these activities seemed to bother Bittner or Christopher. There are many other examples.

Concentration Policy

As already noted, the textile industry was to be the major focus of Operation Dixie. The most resources—the allocation of money and staff—were in the major textile states, especially North and South Carolina, and in those states it was the largest mills that were targeted.[53] Or as the press release from Wm. Smith, July 21, 1946, stated, "Of all the campaigns under progress, we consider the campaigns in the Cannon chain and in the combed yard industry in Gaston County our major projects. Textile is the major industry of North Carolina, and the wage and working conditions in this industry determine the welfare of the entire state. It has long been a recognized fact in the industry that the pattern set by the union mills is always duplicated by the Cannon chain. The Cannon interests are the employer of the largest single group of textile workers in the industry, and we feel that it is important that these workers assume their natural position of union leadership, thereby furthering the progress towards better wages and working conditions. We have our largest concentration of organizers in this situation." The campaign in the Cannon chain, under the leadership of Dean Culver, was officially launched on Friday, June 28, 1946.[54]

As assistant director George Baldanzi reported to Van Bittner about North and South Carolina: "We are making it a policy to go after the large concentrations first and not dissipate ourselves on anything small. The drive is being carried on primarily in textiles, furniture, tobacco and clothing. We shall naturally pick up other stuff as we proceed with the campaign."[55] When the staff and financial cutbacks took place in December 1946, many organizers from other industries were transferred to textile. Bittner claimed that the policy was being revamped and put forward as an innovation, but in reality it was the same strategy. Later, as Virginia director Ernest Pugh dutifully reported to his staff, on January 28, 1949, in "Doings of the Doers": "Concentration is now the object."

---

[52] Haigler to Christopher, marked confidential, September 24, 1945, AFL Region 8 Papers, box 2588, folder 7.

[53] Wm. Smith to all staff members, September 12, 1946, OD 85, reel 11, 381.

[54] OD 86, reel 11, 562.

[55] Baldanzi to Bittner, July 1, 1946, OD 53, reel 1, Pugh folder 18.

An alternative strategy was proposed by another CIO conservative, Georgia regional director Charles Gillman. Gillman proposed that the key to organizing Georgia was to concentrate on the four largest cities, which would then influence the rest of the state. Gillman argued that there were a number of organizations already established in each of the big cities and lots of contacts in unorganized workplaces. Implicitly the city provided more social space to organize, a greater concentrated mass of potential union members, and a large amount of support for any one particular struggle. Gillman also felt that the successful organization of these urban areas would lead to successful political attempts to oust the congressional representatives in each of these areas. Such a strategy was an alternative to the Baldanzi/Bittner one of concentrating on large textile mills in isolated rural towns.[56] Gilman's suggestions began to address the necessity for associative power in textile, but there is no indication that they were ever taken seriously.

Where Were Unions Strong in the South?

To fully understand the problems with the Operation Dixie strategy, it is useful to step back and examine where unions tended to be successful in the South. Although there is at times considerable overlap, it is useful to categorize the areas of strength.

First, in some industries, workers had great or substantial structural power. These included industries that became fully organized during the 1930s and early 1940s, starting with coal. They also included metal mining, longshore, shipping, and oil, all industries that were locationally specific and could not be moved without considerable difficulty. Other industries where unions were successful throughout the 1930s, 1940s, and 1950s were lumber, woodcutting, and tobacco. Finally, workers in furniture and cotton processes, industries that were largely located in the South, often near other union/urban strong holds, had structural power.

Second, unions were extremely strong and successful in those industries that were primarily located in the North and had already become unionized. The unionized northern workers in these industries often tended to have substantially higher wages than their southern counterparts. To begin with, in steel, between 1946 and 1953, the United Steel Workers of America (USWA) won hundreds of elections in the South, winning more than one hundred thousand workers, while losing twenty-four elections and roughly thirty-five hundred workers. All of these election results for which records are available seem to indicate victories by substantial majorities.[57]

[56] Gillman to Allan Haywood, February 13, 1946, with a copy to Paul Christopher, AFL Region 8 Papers, box 2589, folder 2.

[57] See McDonald Papers, SWOC Records, 142:12, March 27, 1953, John Riffe, National Director of CIO Organizing Committee, Atlanta to David McDonald, President of USWA, with an eleven-page enclosure of elections won and lost by the USWA in the South since 1946.

As previously mentioned, two large International Harvester plants were won over-whelmingly by the CIO, while all southern auto plants, including the large GM facility in Atlanta, were won handily.

In meatpacking and related processing and storage industries, the United Packinghouse Workers of America (UPWA) not only organized all the large southern plants (including the Armour facility in Ft. Worth, Texas, which they won by a 6 to 1 margin in 1942), but consistently won substantial victories in small facilities all across the South, even in areas where textile workers suffered defeats.[58] For example, in North Carolina, they won small units (largely located in urban areas), including the following: Armour unit, Wilmington, NC 3-11-53 10-0; Hormell, Winston-Salem, UPWA 40-2, Oct 22, 1952; Swift plant 28-7 Rocky Mount, 10-8-52; Swift April 16, 1953 33-1, NLRB report, Wilmington, NC. In electrical, the CWA likewise won numerous small workplaces, in addition to the large Western Electric plants in Burlington and Winston Salem.[59] The United Rubber Workers of America (URWA) not only won all the major plants in the South during the 1940s but continued to unionize large plants built in the South through 1976, all within two years of their opening.

Third, certain cities in the South had become union strongholds, where usually difficult to organize workplaces were unionized and at times had strong local aid and support. Memphis, Tennessee, described in great detail by Michael Honey, had become a solid CIO town by the end of World War II. Subsequent victories there often were landslides. The UPWA, for example, won election victories in 1947 at Railway ICE Co., 77-1 and at Article Ice, 47-0. Even in textiles, they won clear-cut victories. TWUA won an important victory on August 13, 1948, at the Kimberly-Clark Corporation, makers of Kleenex and Lotex, over the AFL papermakers and a second AFL union, 340 to 172, with no votes against the union. It similarly won convincingly in Nashville, Chattanooga, and Union City, Tennessee. In Knoxville, also a center of union strength, the TWUA won an election at the Brookside plant, 1308 to 420.[60]

Birmingham, Alabama, the southern center of the steel industry and the hub of area-wide metal and coal mining districts in Jefferson and surrounding counties, had become a labor organization stronghold. Huntsville and Gadsden, Alabama, were likewise centers of CIO strength. In Gadsden, it was estimated that in a population of 60,000, at least 10,000 were CIO members, which included 3,000 women in steel, rubber, and textile. Textile unionism was unusually strong in Gadsden. Membership figures for textile companies under contract in the greater Gadsden area were substantial, including those of Dwight: 2,200 out of 2,600; Sauquoit: 418

    [58] Christopher to Grover Hathaway, southern director, UPWA, March 25 1943, also documenting the overwhelming victories in many Tennessee cities, OD 212.

    [59] Smith to Baldanzi, February 14, 1949, OD 53, reel 2.

    [60] Christopher to Joel Leighton, July 30, 1942, OD reel 196, 6.

out of 463 (Standard-Coosa-Thatcher); Kahn: 500 out of 550; Albertsville: 350 out of 400; and Guntersville: 345 out of 390. In 1947, when workers at Star Laundry struck and the company fired 60% of the union members, then hired scabs, union support was quick to mobilize. Textile workers, steelworkers, and rubberworkers placed a mass picket in front of the workplace, forcing the company to capitulate, a clear case of associative power carrying the day.[61]

Even in Mississippi, important industrial centers became organized. These included the capital, Jackson, as well as Natchez, the latter the site of a large Armstrong tire and rubber plant. Laurel, Mississippi, had also become a CIO town by the late 1940s, with six thousand members in a town of thirty thousand. Laurel was a center for plywood manufacturing.[62] In 1948, the TWUA handily won the election at the Laurel Textile Mill, the last major non-union plant in town. In line with my argument about the centrality of associative power for certain industries, one should note that in those places where AFL or railway brotherhood unions were especially strong and concentrated they too did well, even in industries that were dominated by CIO unions. In Elizabethton, Tennessee, an industrial part of the state, for example, the TWOC lost an election at North American Rayon Corporation covering four thousand workers in July 1938. In 1940, it lost again, but this time to the UTW-AFL. AFL trades were strong and well organized in the area. As Richards summarizes, "Where AFL Building trades or railway brotherhoods exercised influence, as in Charlotte or Durham, NC, or in Rock Hill, SC, the AFL could concentrate its effort to win textile workers and provide them with some services through local central bodies" (1978:97).

One also sees a phenomenon in urban areas of the South that most analysts did not expect and that, even today, hardly any historians or other analysts mention. In certain southern cities, public sector workers and transportation workers successfully organized. Some examples in reports from Virginia are certainly intriguing. In the capital of Richmond, city employees signed up in large numbers for the State, County, and Municipal Workers of America (SCMWA), a left-wing union.[63] The organization of University of Virginia hospital employees is mentioned in a letter from SCMWA President Abram Flaxer to DuCuennois, May 19, 1944. SCMWA Local 550-P won an "overwhelming majority of members" (81 out of 139) in a municipal unit in Charlottesville, Virginia (hometown of the University of Virginia).[64]

[61] Report of James Wilson, Manager of Joint Board, Gadsden Textile Workers, October 14, 1946, to Emil Rieve, President, TWUA, October 14, 1946, OD 245, SCMWA file.

[62] See, e.g., "CIO Cracks Solid South," *Business Week*, December 18, 1948; see also May 3, 1947, *CIO News*, Mississippi Products, Jackson, Mississippi; and OD 113, reel 2.

[63] T. D. DuCuennois to J. B. Beasley, October 19, 1943, OD 245, SCMWA file; Joseph R. Adamson, SCMWA representative, to T. D. du Cuennois, October 6, 1945, concerning the meeting of city employees in Richmond.

[64] Randolph White to Ernest Pugh, July 10, 1944, OD 245, Pugh file.

The organization of taxi drivers and public transportation workers was also widespread. In Lynchburg, Virginia, 53 out of 63 paid initiation fees. Organization in Florida, Roanoke, and Charleston is discussed in other letters. Employees of the Roanoke Railway and Electric Company and the Safety Transit Corp, 130 in all, organized with the assistance of a large TWUA local of 2,400 members.[65]

While there were certain unusual, sometimes atypical circumstances that led textile workers to be successful in building strong unions, it was in general their associative power that proved crucial. Organizing in Alabama during the 1930s underscores this point, as do successes in Memphis and Laurel, strong CIO towns. The successful organizing of Dan River Mills in 1942 was perhaps an exception, although workers there had unusual structural power during World War II. Associative power was weakened in 1937–38 to some extent with the split between the AFL and the CIO, although in many parts of the South the two federations tended (by necessity for several years afterward) to continue collaborative arrangements. In some parts of the South, however, the 1941–42 split between the CIO and the UMWA had devastating effects, since the type of support and mobilizations the miners had been willing to offer other workers greatly diminished. Thus, textile unions were weakened in Alabama during World War II.

There was a hope that the void left by the mineworkers would be taken up by the increasingly successful steelworkers, but that was not to be the case.[66] The meeting was chaired by the steelworkers' Noel R. Beddow, who reported that the split was inevitable. Further, "Labor in the South had been a group of step children to other organizations in the CIO, except steel and coal. It was stated that steel was putting forth a great effort in the South now and is going to do more in the South than has been done in the past to organize."

Although Lewis and the mineworkers used anti-communism when it was opportune, he was not shy about trying to convince the Communist-led Mine Mill and Smelter Workers to join District 50.[67] Aside from their expressions of solidarity with other workers (which, as noted, was considerable), the loss of the miners in Alabama caused many organizational difficulties. For example, it was reported that the CIO Alabama News Digest, published by the Alabama Industrial Council, was supported by UMWA subscriptions and was in danger of failing without additional

[65] Michael Quill to Pugh, August 11, 1944, OD 245; Pugh to Quill, August 4, 1944, OD 245; Walter Case to Pugh, January 13, 1944, OD 245; Pugh to Quill, January 4, 1944, OD 245.

[66] Minutes of Meeting of CIO Directors and Representatives in the South, June 14, 1942, Birmingham, Alabama, Haigler Papers, 952/9.

[67] Beddow stated that "Lewis branded Murray as a supporter of communism because he had to have some reason to throw Mr. Murray out of his job as vice president of the Mine Workers." William Mitch and Yelverton Cowherd, long-term Lewis associates, then left their positions in the CIO for the miners. Mitch, after defending Murray at the CIO convention, signed the UMWA resolution one week later saying that Murray was a Communist. At the same meeting in 1942, Mike Ross of the Communist-led Mine Mill reported being approached to join District 50.

support. As Paul Christopher reported to Van Bittner on March 16, 1948, the CIO was fighting District 50 in a number of textile mills in Kingsport, Tennessee, an area near UMWA strongholds.

A More Coherent Strategy for the South

Given the problems with textile organizing, its choice as the prime focus was certainly a mistake. Given the weak structural leverage of most textile workers, it would have behooved Operation Dixie to organize them in areas where they could obtain the broadest possible support, both from unions and from other community and political groups. This approach was antithetical to Van Bittner and his fellow right-wingers in the CIO leadership. And needless to say, the Gompers/Hillman approach of attempting to befriend textile owners and southern politicians should have been recognized as the non-starter that it was. As is evident from Minchin's (1997) detailed work, the TWUA in the post–World War II period was cognizant of the intransigence of non-union textile owners and the importance of welcoming outside support, to a degree not found in Operation Dixie.

While there is never any surety of success, even in the most promising situations, a more coherent strategy might have consisted of the following: concentrating first on the more easily organizable woodworking industries before concentrating on the textile industry. Unions should have insisted on the careful follow-up, servicing, and maintenance of organized woodworkers after they had become unionized. This would have been more likely to happen if the right-wing CIO leaders had not driven the left-wing leaders in the IWA out of positions of control in the union in 1939 and 1940, and again after 1946. When they did attempt to organize the textile workers, they should clearly have focused on organizing textile mills (as well as other industries) near big cities or already organized centers. Given the limited structural leverage of textile workers, the leaders of Operation Dixie should have used broad associative power strategies, without cutting themselves off from the Left and civil rights organizations. Whether the intensity of the splits from first the AFL and then the miners was inevitable is a more complicated issue.

The Situation in the Southern Textile Industry After World War II

The leaders of Operation Dixie in general had a poor grasp of the situation that they faced in the textile industry. Conservative business unionists, ideological liberals, are frequently under the illusion that their own cautious, collaborationist reliance on government and pro-business stances, as well as their personal skills, play a major role in much successful organizing. Bittner certainly believed this about himself, whereas in coal and steel, he had merely been along for the ride. In wood, the ousting of a left-wing leadership group—which had played such a central role in organizing woodworkers in the Canadian and U.S. Northwest—by the CIO national office led to a moribund union in the South, whose failures to take advantage of favorable opportunities chagrined even their right-wing allies. Unions during World War II had organized under rather unique circumstances. Due to large war orders from the government, industry in general made enormous profits. The combination of increased production and millions of young men leaving the labor force to join the armed forces led to severe labor shortages, affecting textiles particularly acutely since textile workers' wages had started out among the lowest of those in any industry. Unions that acted moderately and obeyed the no-strike pledge received a certain amount of support from the National War Labor Board (NWLB) and the federal government. In many cases, unions had used these circumstances to solidify their organization throughout an industry or, in the case of oil, to engage in a whirlwind campaign that organized the whole industry. Yet this is not what happened in textiles. During the war, more than 80% of cotton production was for the military. By 1945, it was almost 98%, leading to soaring profits for the whole industry (Minchin 1997:8–9). Labor shortages were especially severe in textiles. The NWLB, as already indicated, had forced a small number of reluctant textile manufacturers to accept unions. By the end of World War II, 80% of textile production was by then in the South (Minchin 1997:1). These favorable circumstances had helped the TWUA organize almost all of the northern mills but only roughly 20% of southern mills. Although some southern mills were solidly organized into militant locals, others were not. As Minchin (1997) explains, in by far the most careful investigation of textile workers in the decade after World War II, this put the TWUA in a rather tenuous position.

The strategy of Operation Dixie was not designed to deal with the actual situation in southern textiles after World War II. Its leaders did not recognize the degree to which what little success they had during the war was a result of very special circumstances. They thus expressed an unwarranted optimism about the ease with which southern textile workers might be organized. As Minchin underscores, these special circumstances had substantially raised the wages of southern textile workers by 1946. Textile workers (whose wage gains were greater than those of workers in any other industry), by the end of the war had sufficient money to buy automobiles, to purchase formerly company owned houses (or move farther away from their workplaces), and to buy modern appliances, but not enough money, of course, to buy them without weekly installment plans. These new purchases came at the cost of being shackled with enormous debts.

Because of the high profits that continued after the war, unions were often able to convince large unionized employers in the South to give substantial wage increases. Major employers in the non-union mills, also making large profits, tended to match union pay scales and conditions as part of their strategy of union avoidance. This tended to undercut the ability of the TWUA to organize these non-union mills. The TWUA thus faced a massive free-rider problem. As Minchin (1997) argues, Operation Dixie and the approach of TWUA were not designed to deal with the fragility of union organization in the southern textile industry or the strategy of employers to avoid further unionization.

Textile Union Avoidance Strategies

Non-union employers in textiles had a severalfold strategy to avoid unions. As Minchin argues, textile manufacturers, especially in the larger non-union chains, after World War II until the 1951 strike, which effectively destroyed southern textile unionism, matched or even in some cases exceeded union wages, thus creating de facto pattern bargaining (1997:102–103). When union organizing campaigns did take place at their factories, they pioneered a series of tactics that became prevalent in other parts of the country from the 1970s on (Goldfield 1987). They used the cumbersome NLRB apparatus to challenge rules and delay the holding of elections as long as possible, often demoralizing workers in the process. When the NLRB finally ruled against them, they increased the delays by appealing their decisions in the courts. They hired anti-union "consulting" and "law" firms to aid them in their struggles. They also consciously violated the National Labor Relations Act, including the firing of in-plant union supporters and activists, preferring to take the relatively minor financial penalties rather than permit organizing drives to proceed. If unions won NLRB certification elections, they refused to bargain, often aided by their legal advisers, in ways that courts would not penalize (for a detailed analysis of these tactics in the country as a whole, especially in the 1970s and 1980s, see Goldfield 1987). And in those cases where these measures failed, they were not above provoking strikes in order to break unions. At times, as Minchin (1997) documents, they worked with the Ku Klux Klan and relied heavily on racist and anti-communist appeals. They also engaged in anti-Semitic attacks on Jewish union organizers, even when the plants themselves had Jewish owners.

In an industry in which workers' structural power was limited, intransigent anti-union employers were often able to defeat unions and their organizing drives with these tactics even when the militancy and strength and solidarity of the workers were exceptional. The goal of Operation Dixie was to attempt to win NLRB certification elections in a workplace. If an election was won, the workplace was turned over to the appropriate union. But even when elections were won in textiles, this was often only the beginning of a long struggle for the TWUA, even when the union had the staunch support of the vast majority of the workers. A clear illustration of this problem can be seen in Gaffney, South Carolina. In 1944, the Gaffney Manufacturing Company refused to implement a contract ordered by the NWLB, because it objected to a dues checkoff and a maintenance of membership provision, both of which the Roosevelt administration had ordered, when unions accepted the no-strike pledge. In May 1945, the government seized the plant and ran it for several months. When the government returned the plant to the owners, they still refused to recognize the union, whereupon the union struck. The Gaffney workers stayed out for twenty-two months; even after this length of time, almost none of the workers had returned to work (Minchin 1997:71). The company recruited outside scabs and eventually got two shifts up and running. In numerous other strikes across the South, textile workers struck against recalcitrant employers, refusing to break ranks (Minchin 1997:74). As Minchin concludes, "Very few strikes actually failed because of a large-scale defection of workers" (1997:75), which among other things seems to strongly undermine the notion that southern workers in general, and textile workers in particular, were not interested in unions or were unwilling to struggle.

Minchin suggests that employers often adeptly used the leverage of higher wages, mortgage payments, and installment debts to inhibit workers from striking. Though this was not an unimportant factor, Minchin relies on it too heavily. Steelworkers and rubberworkers, for example, had similar issues. Yet steelworkers successfully organized their southern constituency during this same period. Rubberworkers, whose initial organization, especially in the South, was resisted so violently by companies during the 1940s, had fully unionized all tire plants in the country by 1950. As tire companies began to move many of their production facilities south in the 1950s, 1960s, and 1970s, the URWA successfully unionized all the new facilities in a relatively short time after they became operational (Jeszeck 1982:331). The success of unions in wood, tobacco, and meatpacking during this same period is also suggestive of possibilities for successful organizing.

1951 Strike

Finally, the tenuous hold that the TWUA had on the southern textile industry was destroyed by the debacle of the defeated 1951 strike, in which the union, especially its flagship locals, were decimated (for the best account of the strike, see Minchin 1997).

Other Problems with Operation Dixie

The Operation Dixie drive was deficient and shortsighted in numerous other ways. Here I wish to sketch briefly two of the most important.

The Woman Question

Women were numerous in several of the key southern industries, including textiles. They also suffered a variety of forms of gender-rooted discrimination and harassment (including sexual), as is documented in hundreds of complaints and examples. They were excluded from virtually all skilled work and supervisory positions. Even when they did the same work, their pay was invariably lower than that of men, even in government-run facilities. For example, at Milan Arsenal, in Milan, Tennessee, in 1952, female employees were paid considerably less than their male counterparts, starting at 97.5 cents per hour, while men started at 112.5; women were also less likely to get their step raises.[68]

Yet, unlike two left-wing unions with a high percentage of women, Operation Dixie did little to recruit female organizers or, when it did, to treat them fairly. At various times CIO officials recognized the need for more female organizers.[69] At the beginning of the campaign at Oak Ridge, Paul Christopher wrote to Van Bittner on May 29, 1946, about "the need for some first-rate women organizers, especially at Oak Ridge, Tennessee, where approximately 45% of the production and maintenance employees of the three operating units are women." Despite this clear need, it is striking the degree to which the organizing staffs in the key textile states were virtually all male.

Of the roughly 65 members of NC staff (as of September 20, 1946) there were four women, not counting secretaries and one woman in publicity. Two of the women organizers worked for the TWUA and two for the FTA; none were hired by the SOC, which paid forty organizers. The situation in South Carolina was perhaps even worse. According to the TWUA Research Department, 45% of the capital in the state was invested in textiles. The industry had 110,000 workers, 72% of all wage earners in the state in 1945. In 1946, there were 117,000 workers in textiles, 97,000 of whom were in cotton. Of these, 51.8% were white males, 43.1% white females, 5% Black males, and 0.4% Black females.[70] Of the many dozens of Operation Dixie organizers listed as staff, none seem to have been women. As Operation Dixie proceeded through the year, if anything the gender composition got worse. In reports to Bittner, listing the names of organizers in Tennessee, hired either by CIO unions or Operation Dixie, out of many dozens only four were women, two of whom were on loan from TWUA.[71]

While I have noted the great lengths Operation Dixie went to in order pay the highest salaries and full expense accounts of inexperienced male organizers, in

[68] Maurice Allen, United Gas, Coke, and Chemical Workers, Milan director to Paul Christopher, October 3, 1952, OD 125.

[69] C. B. Baldwin to George Mitchell, May 16, 1944, AFL Region 8, box 1878, folder 3.

[70] TWUA Research Department, May 28, 1946, AFL Region 8 Papers, box 120, folder 3.

[71] Christopher to Bittner, September 11, 1946, and December 16, 1946, OD box 53.

many instances female as well as African-American organizers for OD were paid far less than their white male counterparts, and often without expenses. Consider, for example, the cases of Lucille Savoie and Marjorie Geier, two experienced and highly successful textile organizers. They went on staff full time with the southern drive in New Orleans, and "they are now being paid by the Joint Board and we can only afford to pay $45 and $35 respectively. Yet they are required to do the same work and put in as much time each week as the CIO Southern Drive workers who are getting $63 a week plus expenses (these girls do not get any expenses) . . . They are both competent people who have proven their worth to the union and it is only because of our lack of funds that we have been paying them as little as we are."[72] In a snub that is hard to conceive of today, the OD office decided to remove the pictures of female office staff members and the two office secretaries from the tribute album made up for Van Bittner in 1948.[73]

Race

As I have argued, the question of race is fundamental, not merely for U.S. labor but for American society. While there were undoubtedly complications and difficulties in dealing with racial issues, some peculiar to an overwhelming white industry in the South, a disturbing current runs through much of Operation Dixie. Given that an avowed purpose of the drive was to remove racist, Dixiecrat, anti-labor politicians from office, some of the actions taken by southern CIO officials were mind-boggling, even to many sympathizers at the time.

From the beginning, Van Bittner claimed that Operation Dixie was color-blind. The following statement, which in one form or another was repeated many dozens of times, appeared in numerous press releases in 1946: "There is no question of race or national origin in our campaign of organization. We are organizing all workers in industry because they are God's human beings. This Christian precept of mankind is fundamental with the C.I.O."[74]

But like Bittner's professions of opposition to red-baiting, even this mild statement rang hollow and was contradicted by his own actions and those he condoned. While Bittner was quick to criticize all types of petty transgressions, I find no evidence that he ever criticized South Carolina director Franz Daniel for his close relation to South Carolina governor Strom Thurmond. Daniel wrote two letters, for example, on May 7, 1947, to J. King Gordon, managing editor of the *Nation* magazine, asking him to run a special article praising Strom Thurmond (I find no

[72] Paul Schuler, director of New Orleans Joint Board of the TWUA, to George Baldanzi, July 29, 1946, OD 53; reel 18, 390.

[73] Baldanzi to Pugh, October 26, 1948.

[74] Van A. Bittner, National Director of CIO Organizing Committee, OD, box 107, Bittner folder; box 53.

evidence that the magazine ever did so). In the first letter, he brags, "I am a state's rights man,"[75] In the second letter of the same date, he makes the following case for Thurmond, already recognized by most observers as a virulent racist:

> Back of the whole story is the new governor of South Carolina, J. Strom Thurmond. Potentially he is a great man. If nothing else happens to Ellis Arnall, his name will go down in history as the man who guided a new set of Southern politicians. Arnall has convinced the intelligent Southerners that the day of Bleases, Talmadges, Rankins and Bilbos is over. You can no longer be a successful politician by rabble-grazzing, wool hat, bloody shirt yelling . . . Thurmond should be encouraged and known. It would be worth the Nation's interest to do a story on him. In my opinion he is a coming man. As a by-product, it would be to the Nation's interest to do a job on Olin Johnson. Johnson represents the interim politician. I was glad when he beat Cotton Ed Smith; I will be just as glad when somebody else, I hope better, beats Olin D. Johnson. As of this writing, I think Thurmond is the man.[76]

One might object and say that this merely represented bad judgment on Daniel's part. Yet in 1949, a year after Thurmond ran an openly racist campaign as the presidential candidate of the States' Rights (Dixiecrat) Party, Daniel was still writing him letters, saying that he wanted "to play ball with you, good buddy."[77]

If nothing else, Daniel's stance was consistent. Upon receiving a letter from Nelle Morton of the Fellowship of Southern Churchmen to protest against an upcoming march by the Ku Klux Klan, he replied, "Will you write, telephone or wire today?" Daniel considered such an action too audacious: "I think it a big mistake for labor groups in a state like South Carolina to get in front of a fight against a vicious thing like the Klan."[78] Nor was Daniel particularly concerned when the *Industrial Leader*, a CIO paper coming out of Winston-Salem, reprinted an article from the *Wall Street Journal* telling Blacks to count their blessings and supporting the southern governors who opposed President Truman's civil rights program. He also came out against the anti-lynching bill. CIO churchman David Burgess (who began work for the CIO in the South in good part because of its civil rights stance) protested both to the paper and to Daniel, seemingly to no avail.[79] While Daniel was quite sympathetic to hiring inexperienced white males, he was rather uninterested in hiring

[75] OD 106; reel 18, 103.
[76] OD:106; reel 18, 104.
[77] Franz Daniel to Strom Thurmond, September 7, 1949, OD 120, reel 18.
[78] February 16, 1949, OD 107, reel 18, folder 56.
[79] Burgess to Daniel, April 5, 1948, OD 102, reel 16, folder 18; Burgess to Wm. Bradford, March 21, 1948, OD 102, reel 16, folder 18.

three Black college students who wanted to make a career of labor organizing in the South.[80] The file on Daniel could be expanded greatly.

Daniel, however, was not an aberration among those running Operation Dixie, but the norm. For a little diversity, one might note the very public, racist anti–Native American speech by conservative CIO official Carey Haigler at the May 28–30, 1948, Tennessee Industrial Union Council (IUC) Convention in Chattanooga, Tennessee. Haigler's attitude toward Native Americans could be juxtaposed to that of West Virginia miners' leader Frank Keeney, who identified with Native Americans, saying that the capitalists wanted to do the same thing to the miners that they had already done to the Indians, namely exterminate them (Corbin 1977:146–47).

The examples of bigotry among southern CIO officials in Operation Dixie are legion. They were certainly not color-blind. In hiring and pay, they were as discriminatory as the factory owners whose workplaces they were trying to organize. In innumerable ways, big and small, OD policy and the attitudes of a number of more conservative CIO officials and staffers indicated their lack of commitment to fighting racial discrimination in the South. Joe Donovan, an area director in South Carolina, for example, wrote a letter complaining to then–state director Lloyd P. Vaughan.

Donovan informs Vaughan that he has taken all the copies of the "Southern Edition of the CIO News" out of the state CIO office and put them in the "mimeographing room on the floor." The reason for this action was that "on page 3 in that picture of the last CIO Convention, it has pictures of Negroes sitting next to white women and all around the Convention floor . . . I don't think it would help us at all to put it out at all."[81]

Because of the attitudes of right-wing CIO officials and the failure to address problems of discrimination effectively, Operation Dixie and southern mainstream CIO leaders did not always have the full support of Black workers, even though all available evidence shows that they were among the most supportive constituencies of the CIO. The Southern Organizing Committee officials, for example, distributed a public opinion poll by the American Leadership Panel that asked questions of southerners about the AFL and CIO drives to organize the South. Fully 73% of southern workers approved of the CIO drive and 71% the AFL drive. When it came to African-Americans in general, however, the figures were 95% for the CIO and 90% for the AFL. Even conservative CIO officials at times recognized that southern Black workers were more easily organized, but most often seemed to view this as a liability.[82]

---

[80] Alvin Rose to Daniel, November 26, 1951, OD 54, reel 15; Daniel to Rose, November 27, 1951, OD 54, reel 15.

[81] December 27, 1950, OD 106, reel 18, folder 48.

[82] See, e.g., Christopher to Carl Albrecht, southern director of the Amalgamated Clothing Workers of America (ACWA), describing racially conservative W. A. Copeland's position, June 2, 1944, OD

In Virginia, T. D. du Cuennois wrote about the desire to organize whites first, before Blacks, at the Mutual Ice Co.:

> John we are going to win the election as Earl Davis has been working with the negros [*sic*] but we want white leadership in that Union and it is up to you, as Earl can't approach the other white workers in that plant. You should see the white truck drivers and if they don't want to join the Union now to make sure they vote for the union and then join right away after the election so that we can have that white leadership.[83]

As a consequence, contrary to the experience of more progressive unions, where Black workers were almost always the most supportive, Operation Dixie often had trouble gaining the support and confidence of Black workers. The key White Oak Mill in Greensboro, North Carolina, the site of a major organizing drive, had 2,200 workers. Unlike many other southern textile mills, a significant proportion (600) was Black. "The negroes are our weakest spot and can either win or lose the election for us."[84] In contrast, Franz Daniel reported on an FTA local with solid support from Black workers that was now gaining added support from white workers.[85] Operation Dixie lost the White Oak election, in good part because it had alienated Black workers there and lost their support.

It is of interest to contrast the situation at White Oaks with the racial dynamics of a stable TWUA local with a substantial percentage of African-Americans, that of Dan River Mills in Danville, Virginia. The story begins during World War II, when southern textile companies began to make immense profits after suffering large losses during the 1930s. As the war proceeded, they began to lose many white employees, who began to take higher-paying jobs in other industries, sometimes in the South, often in the North. Yet even in the face of labor shortages, the inability to meet orders, thus a loss of profits, many southern textile companies refused to hire readily available Black workers. Dan River, however, was not among them. By the end of the war, as many as 15% of the anywhere from 11,000 to 14,000 workers there were African-American. From a loss of one million dollars in 1938, Dan River averaged profits of a million dollars a year during the war, and more than fifteen million in 1948 (Minchin 1997:9). On June 26, 1942, the TWUA won an NLRB certification election 7,204 to 4,716, out of 11,920 valid votes (13,000 eligible employees). George Baldanzi, vice president of the TWUA (soon to be assistant director of Operation Dixie, later director), personally led the campaign. The company, at first

125, reel 23, folder 6; see also Franz Daniel, South Carolina Director, to Gladys Dickason, of ACWA, September 28, 1946, OD 101, reel 16, folder 1. Copeland was actually an outright racist.

[83] T. D. du Cuennois, CIO Area Director, to John W. Goforth, October 14, 1947, OD 234.

[84] Wm. Smith to Bittner, December 12, 1947, OD 53; reel 1, folder 23.

[85] Daniel to Bittner, December 16, 1947, OD 102; reel 16, folder 14.

reluctantly, accepted the decision, recognized the local, and began collective bargaining.[86] On June 25, 1943, a contract was signed with vacation time, additional benefits, and a modest wage increase. The official union position was to treat all workers equally and in one inclusive local. As was common with CIO unions in the South, poll tax forms were distributed by the local in 1943 and 1944 to both Black and white union members to try to get them to vote, along with notes saying they were being collected at the union office.[87]

The early days of the local were not devoid of racial conflict, however. On May 22, 1944, there was a wildcat strike of four hundred white spinners over the introduction of "Negro operatives" into the spinning room. The company at first agreed to desist, the white spinners eventually going back to work. The company then said it had government orders and a shortage of workers; they then put the Black spinners in a separate room, conforming to state law. The white spinners struck again; after two weeks, the union was still unsuccessful at persuading the spinners to go back. Originally, the two white locals had agreed to merge with the "colored" local and form one Danville TWUA local. The white locals later rescinded that decision, and as a result one white local and a separate Black local were formed (*Danville Register*, September 28, 1944).

As Minchin notes and as other commentators have at times seen in other workplaces in the South, many Black workers supported the separate local. At Dan River, it gave them far greater influence than if they had been a minority in a single mixed local. With their own local, they had a Black business agent, convention delegates, and representation on committees that they might not have otherwise had. According to all reports, "The leadership among the Negroes in the union is aggressive and capable." Because of this, as Minchin notes, white unionists on the joint council often gave their votes to Black leaders (for a detailed analysis of these council votes, see Minchin 1997:137). All delegates that the Danville TWUA sent to national meetings were interracial. As white and Black unionists began working with one another, eventually white delegates refused to eat, sleep, or ride in public transportation where their Black cohorts were excluded. Thus, despite the white chauvinistic beginnings, a certain degree of interracial comity developed in the locals, with all union activities, including social events, being integrated. Some of these same results accrued in AFL textile locals in the South as well (Minchin 1997:140). Yet Minchin's claim that "on the whole, black workers rarely gained equality, fair treatment, or recognition in mixed CIO unions" in the South is too general. In the mixed mineworkers' locals in the South and in numerous southern left-wing unions (including the FTA, Mine Mill, UPWA, FE, and the NMU, but

---

[86] TWUA Danville files, box 10A; *Danville Register*, June 27, 1942.

[87] Report of Pat Knight, TWUA international education staff, on the Danville local, February 25, 1944, TWUA files, 8a:2/5.

decidedly not the UAW under Walter Reuther or the USWA under Philip Murray), great efforts were often made to promote Black leadership, to fight against discrimination, and to mobilize white as well as Black workers in the broader struggle for civil rights (Minchin 1997:141; Goldfield 1993, 1994).

The loyalty of Black workers to the union was on full display in the 1951 textile strike. When the TWUA suffered a massive defeat in the 1951 strike at Danville, it is estimated that once the strike was finally called off, only 35% of the white workers were still out, compared with 95% of the Black workers (Minchin 1997:134). This support of Black workers for their unions in the South across every industry was almost universal. Thus, the loss of Black support in certain Operation Dixie campaigns, as in White Oaks, must be regarded as especially damning.[88]

Summary of Operation Dixie

To make a long, many-faceted story short, let me summarize my conclusions about Operation Dixie. Despite overblown rhetoric about its importance for and commitment to organized labor, and the promise of large-scale resources (which most commentators, including myself until recently, believed), Operation Dixie was none of the above. In terms of (real) money and numbers of staff and organizers, Operation Dixie did not compare favorably with two single-industry campaigns in

---

[88] It is interesting to note that Minchin essentially whitewashes reporter A. G. Mezerik's support for the relatively racist position of Operation Dixie. Mezerik's initial position echoing the CIO's right-wing leadership was as follows: In a sycophantic article in the *Nation* on January 11, 1947, Mezerik writes, "It has made no daring pronouncements on the place of the Negro in its organization and for that reason has been soundly condemned by some Northerners. Yet in practice the C.I.O. recruits without reference to color, and it goes to bat on color issues, major and minor, when they arise"—a bunch of fluff, which I have suggested is patently false. Minchin quotes Mezerik from a 1950 *Nation* article (which he finds in the TWUA file with no date) in which Mezerik sings a different tune: "He argues that every recent primary in the South 'has been fought exclusively on the race issue.' 'Talmadge in Georgia rode to glory and the governorship shouting, "Nigger, Nigger!"' 'Senator Claude Pepper was defeated largely on that issue. Senator Frank Graham was forced into a runoff and subsequent defeat in North Carolina, the most emancipated state in the South. And this happened despite the lamentable fact that the hitherto valiant Dr. Graham and Senator Pepper, along with all the other candidates on the side of the angels, did a heap of compromising of principles while campaigning . . . The issue of equality for the Negro is still the big one, and he who says he stands for that equality, but talks out of the other side of his mouth during campaigns, will get just as badly beaten as he who carries through on his principles. Would Senator Pepper have gone down to a worse defeat if he had not equivocated? Many here say not, and point out that, by running backward so hard, Pepper demoralized the very forces who must go forward to carry on the fight. . . . The truth is that the old reactionary Southern leaders had won a psychological victory before they won their victories at the polls." I mention this at great length only because the overwhelming tendency in the literature is to give a free pass to liberals like Bittner and their journalistic fellow travelers.

1936 and 1937, each funded largely by the treasuries of a single union (steel by the UMWA; textiles by the ACWA).

The choice of staff (even if there had been more resources and a far better strategy) would have doomed it in any case. The top leadership, with perhaps one or two exceptions, was populated by conservative, cautious bureaucrats, led by the narrow-minded, unimaginative, rigid director Van Bittner. The decision to hire largely inexperienced and untested organizers (identity over substance), almost exclusively male, in a high-percentage female industry undermined the work in many ways.

Above all, its strategic choice of concentrating on the textile industry, particularly large mills located in isolated rural areas, and its failure to understand the type of associative power that would be needed to mobilize workers in an industry with limited structural power—and intransigent, deep-pocketed capitalists—were fatal. Thus, Operation Dixie's narrow approach of rejecting rather than soliciting the broadest range of allies was arrogant, ill-informed, and shortsighted.

Given that Operation Dixie's ideological stance and caution, as well as its insensitivity and obtuseness toward African-Americans and women—one must say, its white and male chauvinism—was deeply rooted in its leaders' personal prejudices and their ideology, it is not at all surprising that it backfired. Their ideological stance did not lead them to see the necessity of a broad, egalitarian, solidaristic labor movement, both as a goal in itself and as the best means of organizing. Operation Dixie must, therefore, be seen as a primer on how not to organize.

8

Dr. Jekyll and Mr. Hyde

The Pluses and Minuses of the Communist Party

One must start by acknowledging that this is a complex subject, with a long history of contentious historiographies.[1] The original Cold War historiography—despite having some occasionally interesting information that portrayed the U.S. Communist Party (CPUSA) ("CP") as primarily a nest of spies, a treasonous fifth column controlled by the Soviet Union—has been largely discredited owing to its factual errors and ideological prejudices, although there are still echoes of this view in certain more contemporary works (Klehr 1984; Klehr, Haynes, and Anderson 1998). A more subtle, compelling version of this view is put forth in the seminal works of Theodore Draper, whose careful research and analysis provide an initial benchmark for subsequent scholarship. The essential problem with this view is that it denies the central role that Communists played in building the mass movements of the 1930s in the United States: mobilizing the unemployed, students, farmers, the elderly/retirees, immigrants, and ethnic groups and, above all, leading the fight for racial equality and the rights of African-Americans. This historiography makes the untenable claim that Communists played no major role in the building of industrial unions and completely denies that Communists were generally far more democratic, more aggressive in pursuing trade union goals, more militant, and less thuggish in certain respects than their right-wing, liberal, Socialist, often racist anticommunist opponents (for extended arguments about the positive features of CP work, see Prickett 1975; Stepan-Norris and Zeitlin 2002). The often-egregious flaws of the anti-communists are usually overlooked, while their dubious behavior and undemocratic organizational practices often receive praise.[2]

---

[1] My own analysis begins with Goldfield (1980, 1985) and continues in several subsequent articles and encyclopedia entries. See also Zumoff (2014:1–20); Palmer (2007); Devinatz (2007).

[2] Schlesinger (1949:134–46, passim). The work of the much-lauded historian Arthur Schlesinger displays ideological biases and distortions in numerous instances, as when he describes the Communists as "a clique of dreary fanatics and seedy functionaries, talking to themselves in an unintelligible idiom, ignored by the working class, dedicating their main efforts to witch hunts against liberals

The Southern Key. Michael Goldfield, Oxford University Press (2020) © Michael Goldfield
DOI: 10.1093/oso/9780190079321.001.0001

Needless to say, historiography has evolved since the 1960s, although as I argue explicitly in my 1985 essay, there were a few earlier authors who seem to have struck many of the right notes, especially James Cannon, on whom Draper often relies for certain of his most interesting analyses. Rather than address the issues of historiography again here, I wish to underscore two related, although seemingly contradictory points. First, the Communist Party played an even more central role in building the 1930s and 1940s labor movement in the South and nationwide than even its most strident defenders assert. CPers did not merely "gain influence" in the CIO, but were often both the original, actual builders of the movement and the most dedicated, talented, militant activists.[3] They, of course, often gained leadership in these situations. What is most surprising, however, is that, rather than taking over unions either openly or by stealth, they often backed away from leadership positions in the name of unity with more mainstream, conservative leaders, even when they had majority support and could legitimately win office democratically. In addition, as certain recent authors have documented, their role in keeping the fight for racial equality in the forefront was mostly laudatory.[4]

Second, the Communist Party ended up playing a central role in demoralizing and ultimately destroying the left wing of both movements, undermining the radical thrust that could have potentially led to the formation of a mass-based revolutionary party in the United States. It could not have accomplished this second task if it had not been for the former. Neither of these claims are uncontroversial, especially the second one. The crux of this apparent dichotomy lay with the CP's international ties to the Soviet Union, which initially aided the Party's effectiveness in the labor movement and oriented it to make the fight against racial oppression central to its activities, especially during the 1920s and early 1930s. Changes in the Communist International (Comintern or CI) that began in the mid-1920s ultimately became the albatross that destroyed the Party. Its ties to the Soviet Union as the Stalinist leadership gained a stranglehold on international Communism proved to be fatal. The dating of these contradictory trends is complex and varied. I begin, however, with why American Communists were so central to the upsurge of the 1930s and 1940s, a story that must start at least as early as 1917.

and Socialists" (1957:222). Even an impressive scholar like Fischer seems to get the balance wrong when he accuses the CP of "attempting to subvert mainstream unions," a distortion of the historical record (2016:180).

[3] Note the pathbreaking research of William Regensburger (1987).

[4] Among the more impressive of this genre is Glenda Gilmore's *Defying Dixie: The Radical Roots of Civil Rights* (2008).

The Communist Party's Indigenous Roots as the Inheritor of the Mantle of U.S. Radicalism

The Communist Party of the United States originated in 1919 when the right-wing leadership of the Socialist Party (SP) undemocratically refused to allow the over-whelming left-wing majority to take control of the organization.[5] The main issues dividing the two groups were the left wing's support for the Russian Revolution and the consistency of its opposition to World War I, especially after the United States entered the war (Zumoff 2014:26–29, 35). The Left had won twelve of the fifteen seats on the SP's National Executive Board (NEB) in the March 1919 elections. Even after this period, more local bodies began to support the left. SP executive secretary Adolph Germer—who later played such an important role in the International Woodworkers of America (IWA)—along with NEB member Morris Hillquit, worked to expel individuals and groups of left-wing supporters, thus overturning the elections. In less than six months, Germer and Hillquit had expelled two-thirds of the SP's members. At the September 1919 convention in Chicago, Adolph Germer and his brother called the Chicago police to eject the left-wing delegates. Eugene Debs, the nominal leader of the SP, claimed to agree with the left wing, but refused to get involved in the internal party struggle.[6] SP member-ship, almost 110,000 in January 1919 but less than 40,000 in July, had dropped to perhaps 10,000 by 1923.[7] By its violations of any elementary notions of democracy and the exit of the more dynamic left wing, the Socialist Party effectively declared its moral and political bankruptcy, moving closer to the AFL craft union leaders, whom they had previously despised (Zumoff 2014:35–36; Draper 1957:156–58).

The largest number of potential Communists came from the seven suspended language federations (Russian, Lettish, Lithuanian, Ukrainian, Hungarian, South Slav, and Polish) and the Jewish/Yiddish and Finnish language groupings. At the time of the expulsion, together they made up a majority of the left wing and the entire Socialist Party, Finns being by far the most numerous (Buhle 1987:112; for figures, see Zumoff 2014:45; on left support, see Zumoff 2014:35).

From its inception and throughout the 1920s and early 1930s, the CP recruited many of the most dynamic radicals from a wide swath of the U.S. population. Despite factionalism, conflicts, and numerous mistakes (which are the exclusive focus of many commentators), either with significant direct Soviet help or because of

---

[5] For a description of the name changes and organizational evolution, see Goldfield (1980:59).

[6] In 1919, Debs had publicly declared, "From the crown of my head to the soles of my feet, I am a Bolshevik, and proud of it" (Draper, 1957:110). He also—like a number of left-wingers in both the SP and the Industrial Workers of the World (IWW)—served time in jail for his determined opposition to World War I (Devinatz 2015).

[7] For one set of figures, see "Social Democratic Party Annual Membership Figures," http://www.marxisthistory.org/subject/usa/eam/spamembership.html.

Bolshevik élan and their affiliation with the Russian Revolution, the Party recruited heavily from every strand of American radicalism. In addition to the SP leftists, large numbers of Wobblies and former Wobblies joined the Communist Party. Initially, Bill Haywood (the best-known and titular leader of the Industrial Workers of the World, IWW), James Cannon (the future leader of American Trotskyism), Vern Smith, and Bill Dunne joined, as did many more, including others imprisoned for their opposition to World War I. Former IWW general secretary George Hardy joined, as did prominent leader Harrison George, who was in jail for his opposition to the war. Like many other Wobblies, Elizabeth Gurley Flynn eventually drew close to the Party as a result of her involvement with the International Labor Defense (ILD), which played an important role in the U.S. defense movement for Sacco and Vanzetti (1926 and 1927). Large numbers of Finnish IWWers joined (estimated between several hundred and one thousand), often bringing their Finnish-language newspapers with them. By 1932, as many as two thousand former Wobblies had joined the CP (Zumoff 2014:96).[8] While two thousand is not an inconsiderable number, Cannon notes the difficulties of further recruiting IWW members after the initial wave, calling it a "historic miscarriage" that more did not join the Party (Zumoff 2014:94).

The other radical wing of the labor movement was represented by William Z. Foster's Trade Union Education League (TUEL). Foster, along with his hundreds of cohorts (it is estimated that the TUEL had at least five hundred "hardcore activists"; Barrett 1999:122, 126), had led the 1918 packinghouse workers' strike and the 1919 national steel strike. After discussions in Moscow in 1921 with Lenin and Trotsky, Foster was recruited to the leadership of the Party, with his whole grouping and the TUEL joining en masse. As a result, the Communists gained a decisive hold on the left wing of the labor movement (Barrett 1999:118–47; Johanningsmeier 1994:150–74).

The CP's ethnic organizations continued to provide an important base for its activities. The Russian Federation had been the largest in 1919 but declined substantially as thousands of its members returned to the new Soviet Union. The largest foreign-language groups in the mid-1920s were Jews and Finns, each with daily newspapers. The Jewish Socialist Federation's *Morgen Freiheit* had the "most impressive array of poets and fiction writers of any Yiddish newspaper" (Buhle 1987:129–30). It is estimated that, in 1924, the 6,500 Finns were the largest ethnic group of the CP's roughly 16,300 members. In Superior, Wisconsin, "the local Finnish branch with one hundred fifty members [had] an orchestra, dramatic club, male choir, brass band and athletic club, along with a newspaper. Its buildings, papers and

---

[8] See also the testament of former IWWer and Northwest lumberworker Tom Scribner (1996), who joined the CP and the TUUL National Lumber Workers Union in 1928 and found that many of the activists were IWW "fellow workers."

agricultural coops were worth millions" (Zumoff 2014:173–77). In 1925, Finns still made up one-third of Party members (Johanningsmeier 1994:222).

Black radicals were slower to join. The split between the right and left Socialists also took place among the small number of African-American Socialists, including its most prominent group around the *Messenger* magazine in New York City. The left wing, led by Cyril Briggs and Richard Moore, formed the African Blood Brotherhood, whose main leaders were close to, if not already members of, the CP by 1921 (Haywood 1978:121–31; see also Taylor 1981; Makalani 2004). By the early 1930s, however, CP leadership in the unemployed workers movement in inner-city African-American communities, their militant fight for racial equality even in the Deep South, and especially their lead in the Scottsboro defense paved the way for their recruitment of thousands of Black radicals into the Party. Virtually every author, even the most anti-communist, describes the recruitment of previously unsympathetic or antagonistic African-American activists to the CP. Even at the height of sectarianism between 1928 and 1933, the CP in Harlem recruited former leaders of Marcus Garvey's United Negro Improvement Association (UNIA), despite bitter CP attacks on the UNIA. Harold Cruse's 1967 *The Crisis of the Negro Intellectual* is one long complaint about the virtually total domination of Black artistic and intellectual life by the CP (Goldfield 1980:59, 1985:322; Naison 1983). Solomon provides additional insight on how the CP gained respect in the Black community during the early Depression, including how future CP leader Claude Lightfoot, a Chicago Garveyite in 1930, joined the CP after participating in an "eviction riot" (1998:156, passim).

The Communist Party recruited activists from every venue in the country. By the mid-1930s, it was again recruiting many SP members. An indication of the degree to which the CP was regarded as the only show in town was its recruitment of Meta Berger. Berger was a maverick leader of the SP in her own right, but as the widow of Victor Berger, former Wisconsin congressman and leader of the SP right wing, she was the grand old lady of the Party (Goldfield 1980:59). The South was also not immune. Radical preacher Don West, a leader of the Southern Tenant Farmers Union, switched from the SP to the CP in 1934 (Kelley 1990:124).

Right-wing author Harvey Klehr describes the flood of intellectuals joining the Party during the Third Period, but none joining the SP: "Homeless and confused intellectuals barely favored [SP left-wing leader] Thomas with a glance. 'Becoming a Socialist right now,' famous author and CP follower John Dos Passos explained in 1932, 'would have just about the same effect on anybody as drinking a bottle of near beer'" (1984:78).

Zumoff argues that the various strands of American radicals recruited by the CP were complementary and made the "movement more vital" (2014:97). The CP had powers of attraction based on its identification with the Bolshevik Revolution and was the most serious, dedicated, revolutionary group in the country. Those who merely look at the declining membership before the 1930s, or the Party's small electoral support compared with that for the SP in 1932 and 1936, totally miss what contemporaries understood. James Cannon, one of its most trenchant critics, states: "The CP entered the thirties—the period of the great radical revival—as the dominating center of American radicalism. It had no serious contenders" (1979:93). Or as James Weinstein, a bitter detractor who caustically declares that the CP was neither revolutionary nor socialist after 1935, concedes: "From the early 1930s until 1956 or so, the Communist Party was not only the largest and best organized party on the left, but for all practical purposes it was the socialist left" (1975:60; for complete references, see Goldfield 1980:60).

As I have indicated in other writings, many commentators on the CP belittle the importance of Communist work in the 1920s and early 1930s in contributing to later growth. Both the Cold War historians and the Popular Front enthusiasts tend to focus on the factional fights and maneuvering by Party leaders, incorrectly concluding that little practical work was accomplished. While these factional struggles are not unimportant, especially for understanding the trajectory of the Party (central to our story), such obsession or exclusive focus on them often leads to a misreading of the historical evidence.[9]

During the 1920s, as trade union membership declined, worker militancy waned, and working conditions became even more brutal, Communists continued to organize and recruit, largely under the auspices of the Foster-led TUEL, even when company-organized repression involved threat of discharge, no less violence and murder. The TUEL was enriched and its activities multiplied as a result of the CP affiliation of former SP activists, hundreds of former Wobblies, large numbers of ethnic CPers, and the emerging African-American cadre. But Foster was key. This patient and often dangerous opposition work during the dreary 1920s proceeded along with the factionalism and disunity among Party leaders. Yet in spite of these sometimes disruptive and contradictory activities , the work went on. The CP's militant activists in virtually every coalfield in the United States and Canada allied themselves with radical opposition groups, especially the expelled leaderships in Kansas led by Alex Howat, those in British Columbia, and radical miners in Nova Scotia (Foner 1991:221, 259–61; on Nova Scotia, 1991:239). The work took place under the guidance and enormous range of contacts that Foster had built in his many years of work, the dramatic leadership in packinghouse and steel industries, and numerous other venues. The CP's deep roots in the labor movement were primarily a direct result of recruitment by William Z. Foster and his followers.[10] One

[9] Bert Cochran, former head of the Social Workers Party auto fraction and later academic historian, describes the 1920s as a "Decade of Failure" for the CP (the title of the second chapter of his 1977 book). Manley (2005) seems to concur with this assessment, which I suggest is a myopic reading of the historical record.

[10] James Cannon, who was in as good a position to know as anyone, argues that Foster originally had very few fully committed followers, barely a handful of whom actually joined the CP, which made Foster's accomplishments all the more extraordinary, because they were largely due to his personal

must note that Foster was a highly contradictory figure for a radical. First, his immense skills, energy, and organizing talents were recognized by virtually everyone, although they were often simultaneously belittled. Zumoff describes him as "a hero of radical labour militants, and arguably the period's greatest labour leader" (2014:98). Taft calls the 1919 campaign he led in steel "one of the great organizing feats in American labor history" (1957:386). Cochran gives him similar, although more backhanded, compliments (1977:92–93). James Cannon's evaluation is perhaps the most incisive:

> Foster's astounding success in organizing the packinghouse worker (1917–1918) in an AFL craft union set-up almost designed and guaranteed to make such a thing impossible, and his repeat performance in the steel strike (1919) under still more difficult conditions were extraordinary personal accomplishments . . .
>
> In the year 1919—before the depression and before the rise of the CIO—no one but Foster with his executive and organizing skill, his craftiness, his patience and driving energy, could have organized the steel workers on such a scale and led them in a great strike . . .
>
> Foster's work and achievements in the early days of the Trade Union Educational League (TUEL) under the Communist Party were no less remarkable than his stockyard and steel campaigns. His rapid-fire organization of a network of effective left-progressive groups in a dozen or more different unions demonstrated convincingly that his previous successes in the AFL were no fluke . . . Foster was a trade union organizer without a peer. (1962:111–13; emphasis in original)

Foster's skills and ability were appreciated by a wide range of people. Both Eugene Debs and Sidney Hillman were enthusiastic supporters of Foster and the TUEL (Barrett 1999:127). In 1920, Foster's speech at the SP convention was greeted with a tremendous round of applause (Johanningsmeier 1994:154). Conservative labor historian John Commons invited him to speak to his class at the University of Wisconsin (Johanningsmeier 1994:177). Charlie Chaplin held a reception for him at his home in Hollywood (1994:178). Theodore Dreiser stated that he admired Foster "more than any man alive" (1994:265). Foster's drive and dedication were immense, even at the risk of his health and life. During the winter of 1912, he hoboed across the country, traveling many thousands of miles on open freight trains, giving hundreds of talks to small groups of radicals. He nearly froze to death riding in "open freights in subzero temperatures," averaging "one meal a day."

---

skills (1962:109–11). Despite the contrasting assessments about his followers, no one disputes his role.

Barrett notes, "That he regularly subjected himself to such extreme deprivation" shows both "dedication and toughness," as well as the "discipline . . . which characterized his political life" (1999: 54). Even when his health was failing between 1948 and 1957 and he could not cross a street or walk upstairs by himself, he wrote numerous books and hundreds of articles and pamphlets, often working for an hour, then lying down for an hour, before getting back to work (1999: 246–47).

Foster was clearly a giant of American labor as well as the Communist Party, and it is worth examining those aspects of his character and orientation that put his particular stamp on Party work. He was a principled, anti-capitalist labor activist, believing firmly that the satisfaction of the basic needs of working people demanded the overthrow of capitalism. Like most U.S. socialists, prior to the CIO he believed that industrial unions were inherently radical. This was also clearly the view of Eugene Debs, beginning with his founding of the American Railway Union, and by 1900 it was certainly that of early socialist leader Daniel DeLeon (Barrett 1999:54; Buhle et al. 1990:711–16). Although profession of this belief was not uncommon, Foster's was certainly as hard-nosed as anyone's, and he held it consistently throughout his lengthy career.[11] He also shared this idea with the IWW, to which he belonged until 1912.

Foster posited that there was a militant minority of left-wing revolutionary activists who could influence the direction of the labor movement. The IWW, on the other hand, believed that these activists should set up independent revolutionary unions. Foster had rejected this view by 1912, claiming that revolutionary trade unionists should stay within the conservative unions (both the AFL and the railway organizations), build their internal, left-wing oppositions, and win over members to the revolutionary position rather than build separate organizations. He was and remained an absolutist in his rejection of "dual unions," a position from which he rarely wavered and which at times cost radicals dearly.

Since Foster believed that building mass industrial unions was the key to everything else, he often took positions and engaged in activity that led to a chorus of left-wing criticism. One of his harshest critics was former IWW and then Communist leader William "Big Bill" Haywood, who thought the Foster-led 1919 steel strike was a "dismal failure" because Foster had renounced the opportunity for "revolutionary propaganda" and put himself forward as a "patriot" (Zumoff 2014:102).[12]

---

[11] One can see this view expressed in the coauthored 1913 pamphlet "Syndicalism" and again in the 1915 pamphlet "Trade Unionism: The Road to Freedom," where he argues for the spontaneous revolutionary character of industrial unions, as well as his 1922 epic piece, "The Bankruptcy of the American Trade Union Movement" (all in the author's possession). See also Foster (1937:74). According to one longtime party colleague, Foster held this view to the end (Barrett 1999:192); see also Johanningsmeier (1994:88–89); Devinatz (1996:5).

[12] Cannon reprints some of Foster's 1920 Senate testimony, in which Foster states his complete agreement with conservative AFL leader Samuel Gompers, his renunciation of his published radical

Haywood also wrote critiques of the TUEL and its obtuseness on questions of race, which circulated throughout the highest levels of the Comintern and the CP (Johanningsmeier 1994:194). As Johanningsmeier notes, "The irony of his situation at the steel strike hearings was that, at the point of his very highest visibility in American life, as a radical with a political identity he came closest to disappearing. 'I have no teachings or principles, . . . I apply the principles of the American Federation of Labor as best I understand them'" (1994:143).[13] As discussed in detail in the chapter on steel, Foster subordinated his politics to building a massive industrial union in steel, thinking it would automatically lead to the revolutionizing of U.S. labor. However, when it came to making alliances with John L. Lewis or subordinating the views of the Communist Party to support for President Roosevelt, his radical instincts led him to be the most skeptical of CP leaders. So, in summary, Foster was intensely interested in those issues that affected industrial labor, but far less attuned to the importance of international issues, the nature of the Soviet Union, or sticking to broader working-class principles. The Trade Union Education League was initially formed by Foster and his associates in November 1920. Foster and the TUEL received strong support from leftist union forces, including the Chicago Federation of Labor (CFL) and the Amalgamated Clothing Workers (ACWA). The ACWA Socialist president Sidney Hillman was an outspoken early supporter of the Bolshevik Revolution; its education director and Foster's longtime close friend David Saposs sponsored him on a paid speaking tour organized through ACWA locals (Foner 1991:103, 106, passim). Foster's former syndicalist follower Earl Browder convinced him to come to Moscow as an observer at the founding Congress of the Red International of Labour Unions (RILU) in July 1921. Impressed by the revolution and the workers' government, and intellectually attracted to Lenin's incisive tactical pamphlet "Left-wing Communism, an Infantile Disorder," Foster was easily recruited to the top leadership of the U.S. Party by the CI, without consultation with U.S. Party leaders (Barrett 1999:109). On February 27, 1922, the TUEL was officially launched through a series of local meetings around the country (Foner 1991:123).[14]

Even before joining the Communist Party, Foster and the TUEL made no pretense of being loyal supporters of Gompers and the AFL, insisting that the TUEL was merely an educational body within the AFL rather than a dual union (collecting no dues). Contrary to those who sometimes claim that it was merely a body pushing

views, and his loyal support of World War I, for which he sold war bonds (Cannon 1962:105–8; Johanningsmeier 1994:143).

[13] Leon Trotsky, who knew Foster well and was involved in his original recruitment, has an interesting lengthy assessment, regarding him as "astute" in an empirical way but centrist, i.e., devoid of strong principles ([1929] 1975:131).

[14] The most comprehensive account is that of Foner (1991). Further information is available from the well-researched theses and biographies of Foster by Johanningsmeier (1994) and Barrett (1999).

for rank-and-file democracy, the TUEL had a ten-point program: "1) rejection of dual unionism; 2) rejection of the AFL's class-collaboration policies and adoption of the principle of class struggle; 3) industrial unionism through amalgamation of existing unions; 4) organization of the unorganized; 5) unemployment insurance; 6) a labor party; 7) the shop delegate system; 8) affiliation of the American labor movement with the RILU; 9) support for the Russian Revolution; 10) Abolition of the capitalist system and the establishment of a workers' republic" (Foner 1991:130–31). Foster later argued that three of these demands were central: amalgamation, a labor party, and recognition of Soviet Russia (1952:205). As a practical matter, most accounts suggest that militant workers were attracted to TUEL activists for their honesty, their dedication and commitment, and their unrelenting desire to carry out the class struggle.

Long after he left the Communist Party, J.B.S. Hardman (Jacob Salutsky), a top official in the ACWA, claimed that the early 1920s had been "the heyday of American Communism" due to the immense influence of the TUEL in the labor movement (Zumoff 2014:108, 111). James Barrett also notes, "By the middle of 1923, the TUEL had sunk deep roots in the labor movement and was active throughout the country" (1999:131).[15]

The TUEL led active opposition movements in virtually every union and labor venue in the country. The *New York Times* as well as the TUEL notes that its resolutions in support of industrial unionism/amalgamation were passed in local unions, central labor bodies, and state federations representing a majority of AFL members (Foner 1991:156–57). While these resolutions might be considered mere paper votes, there was hardly a union or industry in which they were not at least major components of the opposition, if not the leaders. This was true in coal, railroads, the building trades, electrical, packinghouse, metal mining, longshore and seamen, and more. In the machinists union, their opposition slate against the entrenched leadership garnered strong support. Despite its stated opposition to dual unions, their members were active throughout the 1920s in a united front with Socialists in organizing the independent Auto Workers Union (AWU).[16]

The CP had substantial influence in the needle trades. On the basis of its capable organizing and militant strike leadership, it gained overwhelming majority support among fur workers, eventually setting up the CP-led Fur and Leather Workers Union (Foner 1950). It had majority support in the International Ladies' Garment Workers' Union (ILGWU), including a large majority in the industry's center in

---

[15] See a similar assessment in Johanningsmeier (1994:184–86). The most detailed secondary account of TUEL activities is that of Foner (1991, 1994), whose material I draw on for much of the analysis here. It should also be noted that the fiasco of the Farmer-Labor Party led to a major decrease in CP influence and to a break with many of its allies, including Fitzpatrick and the Chicago Federation of Labor (Zumoff 2014:112–51; Palmer 2007:177–88; Draper 1960:29–51, 75–79, 96–126.).

[16] As I have discussed in previous publications, Keeran's (1980) work here is key.

New York City. It was ultimately defeated by the SP leaders' bureaucratic and anti-democratic methods (a replay of their earlier expulsion of the left from the SP) and the ILGWU leaders' reliance on gangsters to brutalize oppositionists.[17]

Perhaps the CP's greatest struggle during the 1920s, and the strike that more or less "put Party on the map" for CPers abilities as labor leaders and organizers in the 1920s, took place outside the TUEL, and largely in opposition to the AFL. The Passaic textile strike began in January 1926, lasted a whole year, and at its peak involved well over twenty thousand workers.[18] Passaic, New Jersey, was a major textile center just outside New York City; two-thirds of the workers were foreign born and spoke at least thirty different languages. Conditions were oppressive, yet each ethnic community seemed quite insular, suspicious of outside organizers. Several times previously, the IWW had tried without success to organize the Passaic workers. The AFL was nonexistent and had never had a presence. The 1926 strike was led by Albert Weisbord, a young, dynamic Communist graduate of New York City College and Harvard Law School (Zumoff 2014:196). As a concession to the Party line of "boring from within" (what some were already calling "AFL fetishism"), Weisbord called his organization the United Front Committee (UFC); however, in reality it was an independent union that issued membership cards and collected dues. The UFC regularly had large meetings and massive picket lines. It was actively and publicly supported by Elizabeth Gurley Flynn. Its popular newspaper was professionally edited by the well-known radical labor journalist Mary Heaton Vorse, whom Flynn had recruited. The UFC had broad, disciplined support for the duration of the strike in opposition to a company demand to reduce wages. Weisbord had plans to extend the strike to nearby Patterson, New Jersey, then to other textile centers. Despite the heavy involvement of large numbers of the Communist cadre, the strike had lukewarm support from the Foster wing of the Party leadership in New York

[17] One of the best accounts is by Prickett (1975:50–108), who estimates that the Left had the support of two-thirds of the members but a minority of "rotten borough" delegates (1975:78). Levenstein argues that the CP's (and especially Foster's) sometimes maniacal opposition to "dual unionism" and dogged persistence at staying in moribund AFL unions, even when the CP had overwhelming support from the workers, cost it dearly. He argues that support for CP leaders in the ILGWU (especially during the 1924–26 period) was demonstrated not merely in elections but in CP-led strikes and rallies often involving tens of thousands of workers; this support would in all probability have enabled them to set up an alternative union to replace the ILGWU (for a largely unsympathetic confirmation of CP strength, see Epstein 1953:133–49). Levenstein further blames the CP for helping destroy a potentially successful 1928 secession movement in the United Mine Workers of America, by which time most CPers and other oppositionists had already been expelled from the union by Lewis (1984:10–12). His argument is compelling, but his conclusion is overly broad, failing to take into account the CP's many successes, alongside the Comintern's undermining of important parts of the CP trade union work.

[18] A short summary of the Passaic strike can be found in Buhle et al. (1990:558–60). Book-length accounts are Siegel (1952) and Murphy et al. (1974). Important informative analyses can be found in Cannon (1962:140–44) and Zumoff (2014:189–204). Foner (1994) also discusses it in detail. See also Zumoff (2015); Zumoff (forthcoming).

City, who saw it as a violation of their "boring from within" tactic (contrary to Foner's 1994 account, which portrays it incorrectly as a TUEL-sponsored campaign; Foster 1937:212). In Cannon's analysis, the UFC was formed, and the strike took place because of the skill and energy of Weisbord, "a powerful mass orator and a human dynamo if there ever was one." The strike featured many "violent clashes" with the police and was the major labor news story in the national and metropolitan press for a long period of time. As Cannon claims:

> The Passaic strike really put the party on the labor map . . . It revealed the Communists as the dynamic force in the radical labor movement and the organizing center of the unorganized workers disregarded by the AFL unions—displacing the IWW in this field . . . The Passaic strike was well organized and expertly led, and under all ordinary circumstances should have resulted in a resounding victory. (1962:142)

The failure of the Party to fully support the strike was the basis for the later famous criticism by the Comintern and Profintern head Abraham Lozovsky that the Party had been "dancing quadrilles" around the AFL (1928). Nevertheless, as Cannon notes, the Passaic strike raised the stature of the Party in the eyes of militant and radical workers.

International Labor Defense

The CP gained wider support with the formation of the International Labor Defense (ILD) in 1925, beginning with the defense of the Passaic strikers. The CP had previously been engaged in legal defense work of its own members, notably Foster. Foster had been arrested for his attendance at the 1922 Bridgeman, Michigan, CP meeting.[19] The support for his legal defense was extensive: he had a pro bono support team led by the American Civil Liberties Union's (ACLU) Roger Baldwin that included the then–radical preacher Norman Thomas, Eugene Debs, Scott Nearing, Jeannette Rankin (parenthetically, the first female member of Congress and a leading labor party activist), Oswald Garrison Villard (great-grandson of abolitionist William Lloyd Garrison), and James Mauer (president of the Pennsylvania Federation of Labor). Chicago Federation of Labor head Fitzpatrick arranged for prominent defense attorney Frank Walsh to be Foster's lead attorney; his allies in the CFL mobilized support, while Foster joined the ACLU, serving briefly on its

---

[19] The meeting was not illegal and may actually have been organized by an FBI agent provocateur. The raid itself was led by the anti-labor agent Jacob Spolansky, praised by the *New York Times* (forever conservative, despite its undeserved liberal reputation; Fischer 2016:132–33). Spolansky was also a major adviser to employers during the 1926–27 Passaic strike (2016:134–35).

board. Foster was eventually released after a hung jury refused to indict him on April 6, 1923 (Foner 1991:141–43; Barrett 1999:133).

In August 1922, while on a speaking tour to support the national railroad shopmen's strike, Foster was kidnaped by Colorado state rangers, dumped on the open range near the Nebraska state line, and threatened with murder if he returned. With the help of the ACLU, the kidnaping became a central issue in Colorado politics, contributing to the gubernatorial victory of William Sweet, a liberal Democrat from Denver, over the incumbent, who had apparently ordered the kidnapping. Foster was subsequently invited back to Denver and spoke to a large crowd at the Printers' Union Hall, with support from the Colorado State Federation of Labor. Foster had many other run-ins which only added to his fame and notoriety. On August 27, 1923, for example, three gunmen attempted to assassinate Foster while he addressed two thousand garment workers in Chicago; he refused to stop talking during the attempt (Barrett 1999:132; Foner 1991:150–52). The idea for the ILD seems to have originated with Big Bill Haywood, who apparently convinced Cannon to form a broad united front defense organization led by the CP to defend all who were threatened by the capitalist state apparatus. Under Cannon's leadership, the ILD mobilized wide support for both Communists and non-Communists, including Sacco and Vanzetti and Tom Mooney, among others. Many regard the 1920s Cannon-led ILD as a compelling example of how a radical party should engage in united front activity.[20]

The Third Period in the United States

In 1928, the Sixth World Congress of the Comintern declared the existence of a third period in the growing crisis of world capitalism. A first period had occurred after World War I, when the Bolshevik Revolution ushered in a time of revolutionary struggles. A second period was characterized by capitalist stabilization, supposedly beginning sometime after 1923 with the defeat of the last German workers' uprising. The Comintern declared a third period beginning in 1928, which would witness the final capitalist crisis, the rapid growth of Communist organizations, the disintegration of reformist workers' groups, and the revolutionary overthrow of capitalism. To understand what all this meant for the U.S. Party, one must view what this meant internationally, especially for Germany.[21]

---

[20] A short summary is available in Buhle et al. (1990:366–67). Zumoff (2014:197–204) and Palmer (2007:260–279) provide incisive analyses, especially of Cannon's role. The Sacco and Vanzetti case is discussed adequately in Wikipedia, although the role of the ILD is not emphasized, nor is it even mentioned by D'Attilio in Buhle et al. (1990:667–70). This role is discussed in more detail in Palmer (2007:274–79). For additional documents, see Davis (2004).

[21] The best guides to these issues include E. H. Carr's *Twilight of the Comintern* (1982) and Trotsky's writings, collected in *The Struggle against Fascism in Germany* (1971). Another useful source is Claudin

The policies following from this analysis nowhere had a more disastrous impact than in Germany. The German Communist Party and the CI vastly exaggerated their own influence, minimized the threat of the Nazis (even arguing that if the Nazis took power it would pave the way for a Communist-led workers' revolution), and continued to focus their attack on the "social fascist" Social Democrats as the main enemy, even after the Nazis had seized power.[22] In addition, the schemata of the CI with respect to Germany had no empirical basis in reality. The Social Democrats were not disintegrating. Despite some electoral losses, they continued to dominate the trade unions, shop groups, and other working-class organizations. The KDP (German Communist Party), on the other hand, could not make inroads due to its highly sectarian and divisive policies, especially that of forming revolutionary unions outside the established organizations. Despite a huge growth in Nazi membership and votes and the growing murderous violence of its storm troopers, the CP continually underestimated Nazi strength. While the slogan "After Hitler, Us" (Nach Hitler, Kommen Wir) can actually be traced to the SPD (German Social Democratic Party) it was clearly also the KDP's assessment. Trotsky analyzed the pitfalls of this approach and offered alternative tactics in a series of prophetic pieces beginning in 1930. In addition (and especially relevant to the United States), Trotsky showed that KDP policies in Germany were not consistently ultra-left but zigzagged between sectarian adventurism (including the calling of numerous general strikes to which nobody responded) and making appeals to the SPD leaders while ignoring Social Democratic workers, even repeating the nationalist demands of the Nazis. These flip-flops and inconsistencies came to characterize the CPUSA, but with less fatal consequences.[23]

In general, past commentators on the Third Period activities of the CPUSA have described it both as highly sectarian and detrimental to Communist mass work

(1975, Part One). Trotsky analyzed the theoretical problems of the program of the Sixth Congress in *The Third International After Lenin* (1957). He specifically focused on the discordance between the Third Period turn and tactics with the defeats in Britain (1926) and China (1927), and the decline in CI membership around the world in the previous years, in "The Turn in the Communist International and the Situation in Germany" ([1930] 1971).

[22] In 1933, Hitler took power in Germany. The largest Communist Party outside the Soviet Union was destroyed during the next two years, with virtually all its cadre murdered or thrown into concentration camps. The CI began, at first gingerly, to reassess the question of fascism, including how best to unite with Social Democratic workers. The public line of the CP, however, showed barely any change, even after the Thirteenth Plenum of the Executive Committee in December 1933. A new official position was declared at the Seventh World Congress in 1935. Thus, the end of the Third Period lies ambiguously anywhere between 1933 and 1935. Few of the many writers who take strong positions against the Third Period take into account the 1933–35 transition period or the various inconsistencies discussed below.

[23] Here I concur with Manley, who sees "no significant degree of autonomy or initiative from below" (2005:49).

and organizational growth. Although the present generation of New Left historians tend to concur with this assessment (preferring the Popular Front period), many of them describe highly important gains during these years. Even Klehr's book is full of interesting details about Third Period Party activities. He describes, for example, a funeral attended by fifty thousand people in January 1930 for Steve Katoris, a Party activist killed by New York City police at a demonstration (Klehr 1984:32–33; see also Folsom 1991:243–44). A similar funeral in Detroit in 1932 for four Party activists killed by police in a protest march on Ford's River Rouge plant was attended by "20,000 to 40,000 people." "Above the coffin was a large red banner with Lenin's picture" (Klehr 1984:59). At the initiative of the Comintern, the CP took the lead with unemployed workers by organizing demonstrations on International Unemployment Day, March 6, 1930, attended by over one million.

Characteristically, Klehr belittles these activities as ephemeral. Membership increased from seven thousand to twenty-six thousand from 1929 and 1933 (an almost fourfold increase).[24] Most occurred in 1932 and 1933, as the recruitment of workers was especially low during 1929 and 1930. (Keeran 1980:65 says that no workers were recruited to the CP in-plant auto nuclei during these earlier years.) Recruitment among unemployed workers was uneven. Perhaps the high point was achieved in Chicago. Klehr describes one incident in 1931 in which five hundred people in a Chicago South Side Black neighborhood returned furniture to the home of a recently evicted widow. The police returned, opened fire, killing three people. The coffins were viewed, again under an enormous portrait of Lenin. The funeral procession of sixty thousand participants and fifty thousand cheering onlookers was led by workers carrying Communist banners. "Within days, 2,500 applications for the Unemployed Councils and 500 for the Party were filled out" (Klehr 1984:332–33). Sectarian and militant—admittedly; ineffective—hardly.[25]

The CP and the Black Question

The Third Period commitment to fighting against Black oppression made the CP unique among radical groups. Consequentially, the CP's work reaped many positive

---

[24] Some of this was undoubtedly due to the Depression. In contrast, however, SP membership increased roughly from 9,500 to 18,500, a little less than doubling during this same period. Thus, CP membership increased twice as much as the more moderate SP membership (see http://www.marxisthistory.org/subject/usa/eam/spamembership.html).

[25] The struggles of unemployed workers are discussed in more detail elsewhere. Let me merely note that CP-led organizations and struggles existed in hundreds if not thousands of large cities and industrial venues throughout the country. Large-scale protests and continuing activity in Birmingham, Alabama, aided rapid Party growth there (e.g., Kelley 1990). The CP's unemployed worker organizations played a major role in recruiting members to the Party and giving support to labor struggles in those industries.

results, in contrast to CP work in many other countries. The CP was the first largely white U.S. radical group to focus attention on the plight of Blacks. The IWW organized Black workers, since it stood for the militant unity of all workers in one big revolutionary union but had no program for fighting discrimination. The SP policy ranged from the benign neglect of Debs, who said, "We have nothing special to offer the Negro and we cannot make separate appeals to all races," to the undisguised white chauvinism of SP leader Victor Berger (Spero and Harris 1931; Heideman 2018; both have useful summaries of left groups' racial programs). What the SP line permitted in practice is seen in the publication of racist jokes in the Auto Workers Union newspaper when the union was under SP leadership (Keeran 1974:54).[26]

Even during the early 1920s, the CP was rhetorically outspoken in its opposition to racial discrimination and in its demands for Black equality. The 1928 Sixth Congress of the CI, however, placed the "Negro Question" at the center of the CPUSA's strategy. The CI resolution argued that Blacks were an oppressed nation with a territory in the Black Belt region of the South, so-called because of its dark soil in which cotton flourished. Blacks were entitled to the democratic right of territorial secession if they so desired. The Negro question was revolutionary in two other senses. First, the demands against Black oppression were viewed as posing a fundamental challenge to the whole capitalist system. Second, winning whites to the fight for these demands was seen as a prerequisite for attracting them to revolutionary positions in general, and hence for the revolutionary unification of the working class. The CP began to change fundamentally on the basis of the 1928 and subsequent 1930 resolutions. Its largely successful efforts—not without a great deal of prodding by Black CP leaders and activists—to involve white members in fighting discrimination duly impressed a wide range of people in the Black community. The Party's efforts even penetrated to its extensive immigrant membership. As Naison notes, "Not only Jews felt moved by the Party's position: Finnish, Polish, Hungarian, Irish, Italian, and Slavic Communists became passionate exponents of the Party's position on the Negro question" (1983:49). Another key result was to put special emphasis on organizing Blacks in the South, giving an impetus to Party activities among Black workers centered in Birmingham, Alabama. The new CP orientation also led to the highly dangerous organization of Black sharecroppers. This effort, potentially a lever for the future unionization of the whole South, was liquidated by the CP in 1936 (Goldfield 1980; Klehr 1984:335; Kelley 1990:122).

The Party's position on the South also led it to publicize and fight against the lynching of Blacks. In 1931, the heart of the Third Period, the CP took an initiative that was to bring it major political leadership among Blacks throughout the country.

---

[26] A small, radical grouping within the Socialist Party, centered in the South at the Highlander Folk School, believed in fighting for racial egalitarianism, working with Communists, and sympathy for the Soviet Union. It had little influence within the SP (Kelley 1990:120).

This was the case of the Scottsboro boys, nine Black youths seized on a freight train in rural Alabama and accused of raping two white girls who had been riding with them. The Scottsboro defense laid the basis for large-scale influence and the recruitment of Blacks of every stratum throughout the United States. Defense activities involving significant numbers of whites as well as many Blacks were numerous, widely attended, broadly supported, and well publicized. Naison comments:

> The campaign to free the Scottsboro boys, more than any single event, marked the Communist Party's emergence as a force in Harlem's life. The Party's role in the case, and its conflicts with the NAACP, were front-page news for years, and its protest rallies gave it entry to churches, fraternal organizations, and political clubs that were previously closed to it. (1983:57)

In the South, the Scottsboro defense played a major role in the recruitment of African-Americans to the CP (Kelley 1990:23). The diverse and highly successful work of the CP among Blacks during the early 1930s underscores the need to move beyond most writers' limited stereotypical view of the Third Period in the United States as invariably sectarian, isolated, and quite limited. These writers attribute the gains made solely to the Depression. Nonetheless, the CP's audacity and radical approach, sectarian as it might have been, won it numerous supporters, not only among a wide range of political moderates but, *more important*, among thousands of potentially revolutionary working-class people. The moderates respected the CP and allied with it, whether in Harlem or in the CIO, because they recognized the value of its committed cadre and its ability to mobilize support. These abilities were based on the CP's growing strength among new layers of emerging militants throughout the population.

The Third Period did indeed mark a sea change in the activities of the CP, but like the pre-1928 period, it had many complexities and contradictions. Most commentators make glib, unsupported remarks about the rigidity of the CI's directives, thereby concluding that the deviations from this alleged template were a mark of CP independence from Moscow.[27] While the Third Period line was indeed often divisive, sectarian, and sometimes self-defeating, it was not the end of the story. One must first note that independent unions were a feature of CP work before the Third Period, at certain times and in certain venues, despite rigid Party positions, especially those of the Fosterites. Work within the independent AWU and the 1926–27 Passaic strike certainly fit this description and were not criticized by the CI for this "deviance."

---

[27] One extreme example is that of leftist critic James Prickett, who denies the existence of separate periods and, by implication, the importance of CI line changes for the CPUSA's activities (1975:x), or as a sign of independence from the CI in the broad united front work during the Third Period (1975:117).

As other researchers have noted, the expulsions of TUEL and CP members from a large number of AFL unions throughout the 1920s made it increasingly difficult for TUEL activists to "bore from within" (Johanningsmeier 1994:161; Devinatz 2007:37). Several independent unions had already been established before the founding of the TUUL in August 1929, including the National Miners' Union (NMU) and National Textile Workers Union (NTWU) in September 1928 and the Needle Trades Workers Industrial Union in January 1929.

The TUUL conference outlined three strategies. The first, although far from exclusive, was the formation of independent "red" trade unions in coal, textiles, steel, and wood. This strategy was the main focus of discussion and reporting in public Party documents (Devinatz 2007:37). Where there was not enough support for such unions, the TUUL was to group local unions and shop committees into "industrial leagues." Finally, throughout the Third Period it organized left-wing opposition in existing AFL unions when the opportunity presented itself, contrary to the claims of many commentators (Devinatz 2007:36, 37). This three-prong strategy was also the officially stated policy of Abraham Lozovsky, head of the Profintern. TUUL unions led strikes in coal, wood, and textile throughout the Third Period. In addition to Gastonia, starting in February 1930, the CP led a strike of twelve thousand textile workers in Lawrence, Massachusetts, in which they won most of their demands (Devinatz 2007:37). Until the nation's coal miners fully organized, the Lawrence strike and virtually all other strikes in the period from 1929 to early 1933 went down in defeat. Nevertheless, this organizing should not be underestimated. Thousands of TUUL and CP activists not only gained experience, but also earned the respect of their co-workers, often planting the initial seeds of organization that became the basis for the later industrial union upsurge.[28]

Problems and Inconsistencies of the Third Period

In many ways the work was contradictory, zigzagging between cooperation with other groups and sectarianism, destructive attacks, a refusal to work with them, and labeling them as stool pigeons and fascists. More than consistent sectarianism, these zigzags, as Bryan Palmer has argued, were a defining feature of the Third Period and a feature of the CI approach internationally (Palmer, forthcoming). They hardly exhibited the independence posited by those who glorify the Popular Front or those who wish the CP had been a consistent revolutionary group.

The CP-controlled Auto Workers Union, for example, led a strike in the summer of 1930 at the Fisher Body plant in Flint, Michigan. Communists had nothing to do with the initial work stoppage or the spread of the strike to the rest of the factory.

[28] Barrett notes that the CP had as many as fifteen thousand AFL members between 1934 and 1936 (1999:199).

At a mass meeting, workers voted to work with the AWU and elected a strike committee of over one hundred members. The AWU supported the strike committee, in which it was a small minority, and allied with the local unemployed organization. From these actions, Prickett concludes, "At the height of the 'third period,' when most accounts picture Communists as intensely sectarian and isolated, the AWU actively worked to create coalitions with elected strike committees in which AWU adherents were in a distinct minority" (1973:190–91; 1975:114–17). However, at the Briggs auto parts plant in Detroit in 1932, the AWU characterized everyone opposed to its leadership as "stool pigeons." At the Mack Avenue Chrysler plant in Detroit, the AWU refused to work with the elected strike committee, calling a separate rally at which all the main speakers were outside Communist leaders, including AWU national leaders, Detroit CP district organizer Bill Gebert, the Chicago CP leader, and national party secretary Earl Browder. IWW and AFL activists in the plant were excluded (Prickett 1973:205–206; 1975:123, 130–31). In October 1931, a new strike broke out in the textile town of Lawrence, Massachusetts. The CP refused to cooperate with the AFL's UTW and followers of A. J. Muste, both of whom had support among the strikers. There were competing mass meetings and separate picket lines, leading to an early collapse and defeat of the strike (Barrett 1999:173). In other places, however, the CP and TUUL worked within the AFL as oppositionists. In Alabama, activists abandoned the National Miners Union in 1932 to work within the AFL coal and steel unions, providing them with an important base of operations as industrial unionism accelerated (Ottanelli 1991:26; Kelley 1990:60–65, passim). CPers carefully built up their committees inside the longshoremen's union on the West Coast and eventually gained full control of the organization in ports on the West Coast; the 1934 longshore strike was led by Harry Bridges and his CP cohort (for general material on the strike, see Ottanelli 1991:51).[29] The instability of the Party line and the zigzagging on practical work characterized many Communist parties around the world; they were certainly not proof of CP independence from Moscow. Such inconsistency, of course, as we shall see, would not be tolerated when it came to international issues, or even certain domestic issues, after 1935.

At its worst during the Third Period, the CPUSA poisoned the well and made enemies forever. On February 16, 1934, five thousand CP supporters led by *Daily Worker* editor Clarence Hathaway and politburo member Robert Minor physically assaulted and broke up an SP rally at Madison Square Garden that had been called to protest the murder of Austrian SP workers by the fascist chancellor Dollfuss. The CP was publicly criticized by many of its supporters, including John Dos Passos.

---

[29] On the development of the West Coast longshore union, see Selvin (1996); Buchanan (1975); Kimeldorf (1988); Larrowe (1972); Nelson (1988); Wellman (1995). For a more theoretical long-term discussion of the union, see Ahlquist and Levi (2013).

SP executive board members of the American League Against War and Fascism, a united front organization, all resigned. The Party's action was publicly defended by CPUSA chair Earl Browder. In steel, as we have seen, CP sectarianism toward independent radicals was a factor in keeping the oppositionists from either taking over the AA or forming an independent steelworkers' union in 1934 (Klehr 1984:114–16). CP attacks and thuggishness toward Trotskyists and those who criticized the Moscow trials continued long after the Third Period ended.

Contrary to Prickett, such sectarian stupidity and the destruction of important mass movements and organizations were repeated ad nauseum. The back and forth on the question of forming broad united fronts was a feature of the Stalinized Comintern as well as of the CPUSA. This schizophrenic feature is analyzed in detail by Bryan Palmer, from the beginning of the Third Period in 1928 up to and including the "half turn" toward the united front in 1932.[30] The CP's contradictory stance on united fronts helped destroy one of the most important defense movements of the 1930s, the case of Tom Mooney, previous leader of the left wing of the California labor movement. Mooney and Warren Billings were convicted of bombing a 1916 Preparedness Day Parade in San Francisco. It soon became clear that the conviction was based on perjured evidence, a conclusion drawn by both President Woodrow Wilson and a conservative federal commission. Mooney's case became an international cause supported by a broad spectrum of groups and individuals from the ACLU to conservative AFL unions to radicals. In 1932, still imprisoned, Mooney issued a call for a wide defense coalition to free him and Billings, specifically including the CP, its many followers and allies. A united front conference of more than a thousand delegates took place in May 1933 in Chicago, although the actual control of the conference executive committee was in the hands of the CP. James Cannon, leader of U.S. Trotskyism, played a major role serving on the National Council of the developing organization. Many called for broader actions and a national day of action to free the prisoners. All this was too much unity for the Third Period CP, which moved quickly to sandbag the developing broad organization and actions, quickly deciding it wanted no relations with other organizations, only a "united front from below." Finally, even Mooney, who had originally invited the CP's participation, grew tired of its stalling and sabotage, and repudiated the new organization.[31]

Nonetheless, despite much of the self-destructive sectarian behavior of the Communists between 1928 and 1934, the Party made huge gains in support and membership. Thus, one must draw several conclusions from the above representative facts. First, the harsh stances of the Communists appealed to millions of angry, destitute people across the country, be they the unemployed, workers, farmers,

---

[30] I have benefited greatly from and used extensively in this analysis ideas and information from Bryan Palmer's forthcoming second volume of his biography of James Cannon.

[31] A general summary and references can be found in Buhle et al. (1992:485–86). My analysis of the conference generally follows Palmer (forthcoming).

students, or African-Americans, among many others. They also focused people's attention on both immediate demands and a powerful indictment of the whole capitalist system. Len De Caux summarizes this well. With respect to the unemployed movement,

> the communists made immediate demands. More relief, in cash and jobs. Public workers at union wages. Hot lunches for school children. An end to evictions. They exposed and fought racist discriminations . . . they fought . . . by raising hell to force concessions from the rulers. . . . The communists didn't fail to emphasize that capitalism was proving a losing system, and should be replaced . . .
>
> If the communists were as nasty, cantankerous, conspiratorial and subversive as charged, that scared the ruling class . . . all the more and forced more concessions. Somehow the communists didn't scare the unemployed. In hundreds of jobless meetings, I heard no objections to the points the communists made, and much applause for them. Sometimes I'd hear a communist speaker say something so bitter and extreme I'd feel embarrassed. Then I'd look around at the unemployed audience—shabby clothes, expressions worried and sour. Faces would start to glow, heads to nod, hands to clap. They liked that stuff best of all. (1970:163)

Second, the Communists proved to be the hardest-working, most reliable, and courageous of activists in daily struggles in the workplace or elsewhere. These attributes won the trust of millions of the most militant and radical in the population during the Depression. Third, the CP's potential was far greater than even its dramatic, large-scale gains during the Third Period would suggest. Thus, one can easily speculate that a less sectarian Communist Party that was more balanced in its united front work would have had far more influence and support, perhaps even many times its size and outreach.

Membership Growth

All this being said, it is important to look at the membership figures for the CP to comprehend what led to its growth (Table 8.1). In the past I have argued extensively that membership figures of trade unions can be only a rough guide to the growth and influence of labor organizations.[32] There are usually lengthy lag times in actual membership growth of many organizations; the activities that create élan

---

[32] Goldfield (1989, 1990); Goldfield and Bromsen (2013). It should also be noted that there are times when unpopular positions (like early opposition to a war) will lead to initial declines but later raise a party's moral stature.

Table 8.1 **U.S. Communist Party Membership, 1919–94**

Year	Membership	Source
1919	34,000 (25,000–40000)	Draper 1957:189–90
1923	10,000	Fourth National Convention 1925:40
1924	13,500	Fourth National Convention 1925:40
1925	16,000	Glazer 1961:39
1929	9,300	Glazer 1961:40
1930	7,500	Glazer 1961:92; Eighth National Convention: 80–81
1931	8,000–9,000	Glazer 1961: 92
1932	12,000–14,000	Glazer 1961: 92
1933	16,000–20,000	Glazer 1961: 92
1934	24,500	Glazer 1961: 92
1935	31,000	Glazer 1961: 92
1936	42,000	Glazer 1961: 92
1937	40,000–48,000	Klehr 1984,:366, 380
1938	55,000	Glazer 1961:92
1942	50,000	Glazer 1961:92
1945	65,000–76,000	Glazer 1961:92
1946	52,500	Glazer 1961:92
1956	12,000	Klehr 1998:353
1958	3,000	Klehr 1998:353
1994	1,000	Klehr 1998:353

and attractiveness for mass workers' and social movement organizations often take time to register. Nevertheless, the figures of CP membership tend to cast doubt on the generally accepted view that the CP's main periods of growth were due to a shift to Popular Front policies.

The Communist Party grew fourfold from 1930 to 1935 and between five- and sixfold from 1930 to 1936. In no other period was growth nearly so rapid. If one considers 1936 lagged growth time from the Third Period, the most spectacular growth was not likely a result of the Popular Front, when the Party grew by much smaller percentages. I would also argue that the careful, patient work during the 1920s helped lay the groundwork for this later growth in the depths of the Depression. So I humbly submit that the arguments of those who glorify the

Popular Front as responsible for the way the Party grew are likely incorrect and undoubtedly ideologically driven. This also goes for the right-wingers like Klehr. Between 1935 and 1937, Communist parties in most countries, the United States included, changed dramatically. This change was signaled by the 1935 Seventh World Congress of the Comintern, led by Georgi Dimitrov.[33] The change had been partly prefigured by the "half turn" of the Tenth Plenum of the CI Executive Committee in 1932 and the Thirteenth Plenum in 1933. Even so, the 1935 break was dramatic. In order to evaluate this change, first toward a redefinition of the united front, then to the Popular Front, and at times to a people's front (which included so-called progressive segments of the capitalist class), it is helpful to begin with the overall goals of Communist parties, which have been espoused forcefully over many decades, at least in the abstract. In philosophy, one might call this "immanent critique," a strategy used by Hegel in his *Philosophie des Rechts*, but also often used in general to draw out the implications and (in)consistencies of various theoretical systems.

An Evaluation of the Communist Party

From the time of Marx and Engels, Communists had two interrelated, sometimes seemingly contradictory goals. The first was to build mass movements for reform in the broadest possible fashion, especially among workers. For V. I. Lenin, this meant being "a tribune of the people" ([1915] 1961:423). For the revolutionary IWW in the United States, this translated into "fan the flames of discontent" (Industrial Workers of the World 1916; (1923) 2014:1). For Marx, it was necessary for workers to resist every instance in which capitalists continuously and invariably tried to worsen their conditions. If they should abandon such resistance, "they would be degraded to one level mass of broken wretches past salvation." And if they should "cowardly" give up "in their everyday conflict with capital, they would certainly disqualify themselves for the initiating of any larger movement" (Marx and Engels 1968:228). The CPUSA, as we have seen so far, often excelled at this aspect of the struggle. But this was not enough. According to Marx, these struggles were only temporary "palliatives, not curing the malady." At the top of

---

[33] Georgi Dimitrov was a leader of the Bulgarian Communist Party and the head of the Western European Bureau of the CI in Berlin. He was accused by the Hitler government of being complicit in the burning of the German Reichstag in February 1933 and was arrested in March. He became an international sensation when he was eventually declared innocent after out-dueling Nazi prosecutors in a closely followed public trial in Leipzig. Named to head the CI by Josef Stalin after his 1934 release to the Soviet Union, he was, according to Carr, an early proponent of abandoning the Third Period for a new united front and eventually adopting a popular front policy (1982:88–155, passim). Dimitrov's speeches at the Leipzig trial are in Dimitrov (1968). The progression of his views can be studied in Dimitrov (1972). His speeches and writings from the 1935 Seventh Congress of the Communist International through 1937 are available in numerous places, including Dimitrov (1975).

their banners must be, not reform demands, but the revolutionary watchword "abolition of the wages system" (1968:229). The IWW also claimed to adhere to this goal. The preamble to its constitution stated, "The working class and the employing class have nothing in common. . . . Between these two classes a struggle must go on until the workers of the world organize as a class, take possession of the means of production, abolish the wages system, and live in harmony with the earth" (Industrial Workers of the World 1916). For Communists, this meant continuously engaging in education and propaganda to convince working people of the need to reconstruct society on a socialist basis. The failure to put forward this goal was a major component of IWW leader Big Bill Haywood's critique of Foster's leadership in the 1919 steel strike. During the 1920s and first half of the 1930s, Communists ostensibly adhered to this goal.

The view that both the capitalist class and the working class were international is derived from this second goal. Workers should not fight against fellow workers of other countries in wars for the gains of their own national capitalist class; their allegiance was to their fellow workers, not their country. This involved support for struggles around the world. The IWW, with its flare for the dramatic, often burned American flags at the beginning of their meetings to underscore this point. Along with support for the Bolshevik Revolution, these three shared values attracted and recruited the more radical Wobblies to the CP, the reason Communist parties around the world originally made strong overtures and recruiting efforts toward revolutionary syndicalists like the IWW. Socialist parties, especially after 1919, split with the Communists, generally rejecting at least two of the revolutionary goals. First, they equivocated on the goal of doing away with the capitalist system; they tended to see the development of social welfare and pro-labor policies as a way to reform capitalism (the classic statement being that of the German SPD leader Eduard Bernstein's *Evolutionary Socialism*, 1909). Second, they were less staunch in their internationalism, tending to support their own capitalist classes in foreign wars.

The Communists, however, adhered to two other important principles, which distinguished them from revolutionary syndicalists like the IWW. The first was a commitment to a disciplined party of professional revolutionaries with a unified program, a division of labor, and the rooting CP members in shops and other groups, wherever oppression and mass protest existed.[34] A second key difference from the revolutionary syndicalists was the CP's strategy of winning the masses of workers and other segments of the population to their long-term goals. This strategy was dubbed the "united front," elaborated in various writings of Lenin and the proceedings of the first four congresses of the Communist International. Briefly, it had

---

[34] Dozens of articles in the internal CP publication, the *Party Organizer*, from 1927 (when it was founded) into the early 1930s, discuss the proper organization and functioning of CP shop nuclei (in possession of the author).

two major components. On the one hand, Communists were to work within conservative organizations, including AFL trade unions that had the allegiance of large numbers of workers, presenting demands and programs to transform these organizations into militant, fighting units. They were also to participate in electoral politics, not in order to win executive positions in the "bourgeois state," but to gain a greater platform for espousing their views. They took as a model the activities of the Russian Bolsheviks in the czarist Duma. As the pre–World War I German Social Democrats, who had substantial representation in the German parliament, used to say, their role was not merely to exert pressure for more far-reaching reforms, but to talk "auf dem Fenster" (literally, out the window), using their positions as a larger platform for their views. On the other hand, Communists were to form "united fronts" with other Left and working-class parties in order to broaden the radical and popular movements, while at the same time maintaining their own independence to propagate their long-term goals. Submerging themselves in reform coalitions without this independence constituted abandonment of their revolutionary goals.

I have already given some indication of the inconsistencies and problems in applying united front principles that the CPUSA had during the Third Period. However, with these principles in mind, it is instructive to look at the period of the Popular Front to see the extent to which they adhered to, deviated from, or abandoned their principles. It is especially interesting to us, since this is the period in which their trade union influence, including that in the South, seemed to be at its height.

The Popular Front Period

The Popular Front period (roughly 1935–39 and during World War II, beginning after the June 22, 1941, invasion of the Soviet Union by Nazi Germany until the end of the war in 1945) was one in which the Communists were barely recognizable from the Third Period Communists. Critic Harvey Klehr (1984) labels it the "Heyday of American Communism." Failing to recognize the roots the Party had established in American life during the 1920s and first few years of the 1930s, he argues that it was only by submerging itself in the liberal mainstream that the CP was able to grow after 1935. Hundreds of others subscribe to this same belief, many of them with more favorable evaluations than Klehr (for a sampling, see Naison 1983; Dennis 1977; Healey and Isserman 1990; Richmond 1972.) Many have described the influence of the CP on life in the United States during the Popular Front period. The Party and its allies were the leaders of the National Negro Congress, a large consortium of civil rights groups that set the tone and stage for virtually all such struggles; it allied itself closely with the CIO, receiving strong support from many of its leaders, including John L. Lewis. Party members were the leaders of the main left-wing student group, the American Student Union, and its more inclusive successor, the American Youth

Congress. They led coalitions of anti-war and anti-fascist organizations and were key activists and leaders in farm organizations. Within the labor movement, Party activists controlled or had influence in a large part of the CIO.

According to Bert Cochran, former leader of the labor work carried out by the Trotskyist Social Workers Party (SWP), the CP controlled organizationally as much as 40% of the CIO's membership:

> They had decisive influence over half of the auto union, hegemony in the electrical union, the mine mill and smelter workers, the office and governmental workers, a voice in the rubber and steel union. They were in effective control of the most important central labor bodies, including New York, Cleveland, Detroit, Chicago, Los Angeles. (*Fourth International*, March 1949; also quoted in Cannon 1973a:9)

One might add control of the National Maritime Union (NMU), International Fur and Leather Workers Union, United Furniture Workers of America, United Cannery, Agricultural, Packing, and Allied Workers of America (UCAPAWA) (later the Food and Tobacco Workers of America, FTA), International Longshore and Warehouse Union (ILWU), marine cooks, Farm Equipment Workers (FE), among others, and important influence and acceptance in many other unions, including the United Packinghouse Workers of America (UPWA).

The shift from the united front and later to the Popular Front proceeded fitfully. The united front involved coalitions with other left and working-class groups. The Popular Front, in addition, involved coalitions with important capitalists. I have mentioned the "half turn" announced by the CI in April 1932 (Kling 1983:188, 291), the evaluations of the failures of the German Communist Party by the CI, and the Thirteenth Plenum of the Communist International Executive Committee, on December 1933, which began to elaborate both a united front line that involved coalitions with other leftist groups and extreme sectarianism (Klehr 1984:98–99). After massive pro-fascist demonstrations in France on February 6, 1934, the CI sent the French Communist Party a telegram on June 24 demanding unity with Socialists "at any price"(Klehr 1984:167).

At the 1935 Seventh CI Congress, led by anti-Nazi hero Georgi Dimitrov, as Klehr sarcastically states, "the Third Period itself was unceremoniously laid to rest" (1984:170). After the Seventh Congress, one begins to see cooperation and joint actions by the CP and SP in the United States, evident in the auto union and elsewhere, including at autoworkers' conventions (Prickett 1975:173).[35]

---

[35] In his tortured attempt to search for party independence from Moscow (thus hypothesizing that the CP could have chosen to maintain a more revolutionary stance), Prickett states that the changes in tactics within the trade unions did not emanate from Moscow (1975:162–64).

So to what degree did the Popular Front period mark merely a change in revolutionary tactics and to what degree was it an abandonment of the Communists' proclaimed revolutionary role?

The Popular Front period(s) saw a complete reversal of the Communist Party's previous stances. The CP dropped its revolutionary slogans and criticism, allied with moderate leaders and groups, and not only failed to distinguish itself from its allies but in most cases even failed to criticize them. The CP's attitude toward President Roosevelt evolved substantially. During the Third Period, he had been criticized for virtually every policy, even being called a "fascist." During 1936, the Party uneasily moved from advocating farmer-labor party to tacit support for FDR's reelection. The so-called people's front or anti-Fascist coalition was eventually extended to include the Democratic Party. In 1936, it had criticized FDR for failing to lend aid to the embattled Loyalists in Spain. By 1937, it republished and lauded his speeches in the *Daily Worker*. In late 1937, it described him as "the most outstanding anti-fascist spokesman within the capitalist democracies." At the May 1938 tenth Party convention, the hall was decorated with American flags and delegates sang the "Star-Spangled Banner" and a sanitized version of the "International." As Ontanelli convincingly argues, "The CPUSA became the political force which possibly supported the New Deal most consistently even when Roosevelt wavered from its ideas" (1991:117). The Party became Roosevelt's abject apologist. When the president refused to support anti-lynching legislation, it blamed reactionaries in Congress and refused to criticize him directly. It blamed his policy on Spain on members of his cabinet. It even claimed at times to be the most consistent of New Dealers.[36] Ottanelli notes, "By 1938 Communist national and state leaders had contacts and sometimes meetings with senators, congressmen, local and state officials, and even White House intermediaries. Tolerance for Communist activities was such that when the New York State legislature passed a law banning the Party, Governor Lehman vetoed it" (1991:120). Thus was the CP's slavishness rewarded.[37]

It not only abandoned its revolutionary aims. In many spheres, rather than fan the flames of discontent, the CP retreated, quietly dropping many of its more radical forms of organization. Among the first to go in 1935 was the League of Struggle for Negro Rights, which agitated against lynching and gave the full Party analysis of the roots of Black oppression; its publication, the *Liberator*, was discontinued. In 1936, the militant Sharecroppers' Union was dismantled. Overwhelmingly Black, attacking some of the most heinous forms of white supremacy, it was considered an embarrassment to the CP as it undertook less radical work in largely white farmers' organizations (Haywood 1979:402–403; Kelley 1990:122). Mark Naison argues that the CP had gained strength in Harlem in the early 1930s on the basis of mass

---

[36] For a detailed examination of these policies, see Ottanelli (1991:107–20; quote on 114).
[37] Emspak sees only their "rightward ideological drift during the early forties" (1972:47).

mobilizations and militant tactics. The Party ended this approach, relying more on institutional power in politics, "wheeling and dealing like Tammany stalwarts" (1983:172).

Within the trade union movement, Party work was mixed. Often its members remained the most militant, dedicated, rank-and-file unionists. Yet the Party itself often abandoned its members in order to preserve harmonious relations with national CIO leaders, bending the stick far to the right. In steel, the CP supported Philip Murray unequivocally, even as he was eliminating, purging, and transferring key CP activists who had been the major organizers of the union. This uncritical support continued at least through 1945 (Emspak 1972:39). The CP did much to create the myth of the steelworkers and CIO leader Philip Murray by continuously describing him as "progressive" and democratic, although he ruled a labor organization as racially backward and authoritarian as any. The Communists had abandoned any real conception of their birthright.

In the auto industry, their slavishness seemed to know no bounds. The second convention of the United Auto Workers (UAW) was held in April 1936, in South Bend, Indiana. The convention was dominated by the Unity Caucus and its popular leader and early organizer, CPer Wyndham Mortimer. All commentators suggest he would have easily been elected president. Party leaders did not want to alarm national CIO leaders and demanded that Communist delegates support Homer Martin (who it later turned out was being advised by former Communist right-winger Jay Lovestone).[38] Mortimer withdrew his candidacy and became the union's first vice president (Ottanelli 1991:148–49). A similar scene was repeated in 1939. The Unity Caucus again dominated the convention. Mortimer, the most prominent member of the Caucus, was forced by national CP leaders to withdraw his candidacy even for an executive board position. When Murray and Hillman objected to Unity Caucus leader and CP ally George Addes running for president, he settled for secretary-treasurer. In a union where the CP and its allies had majority support, no CPer ran for the executive board. Prickett and Levenstein regard this as the fatal decision that cost the Party its influence within the union, paving the way for the ascendancy of Walter Reuther and the purge of the left in 1949. Both argue that it would have been difficult for CIO right-wingers to destroy the CP if the Party had still controlled the UAW.[39]

---

[38] For more on Lovestone, see Le Blanc and Davenport (2018).

[39] Levenstein's argument is that the CI destroyed much of the CP's trade union work and that the Party was least successful in gaining leadership in those unions in which the top CP leadership intervened directly (1981:17, 49). With respect to the 1939 UAW convention, he argues, "If any single event could be said to have contributed most to this crucial defeat of the Communists in postwar America, it was Browder's intervention" (1981:84). Some of the complexities of the shifting politics of the UAW caucuses are described in Halpern (1988:19–28).

The national CP leadership was often willing to sandbag its own members when they were "fanning the flames." After the 1936–37 Flint strike, the UAW demanded Chrysler recognize the union. When the company refused, workers seized all its plants. The strikers voted to stay in the plants after an injunction was issued, while an estimated forty thousand sympathetic workers picketed outside. Lewis, supported by the CP, agreed to have the plants evacuated. Subsequently, Earl Browder criticized rank-and-file Communists who had supported those who refused to evacuate for jeopardizing the relationship of the national CP and the leaders of the CIO (Prickett 1975:205). In the 1941 California North American Aviation strike, ultimately broken on orders from the CIO, the Party sided with the more conservative UAW leaders and the national CIO, refusing to defend Wyndham Mortimer, the main national organizer of the strike. Mortimer was fired and never had a responsible position in the union again (for a compelling account, see Prickett 1975:262–66, 1981; see also Riesel 1941; for the standard, now-discredited anti-communist account, see Cochran 1977:176–81).

By 1939, the Communists had disbanded their shop units (which were allegedly the vehicles both for deciding tactics within the workplace and for articulating their independent anti-capitalism and, according to Lenin, the root of party identity) (Goldfield 1985:332–33; see the meandering rationalization by CP labor chief Roy Hudson 1939).

It was not just individual members, however, that the Party left out to dry. In organization after organization, it supported anti-communist resolutions that attacked its own legitimacy. The American Youth Congress (AYC) was a broad organization supported by a wide range of liberals, including First Lady Eleanor Roosevelt, in good part based on a coalition between Socialists and Communists. At the July 1939 convention, a resolution was passed denouncing "all forms of dictatorship . . . Communist, Fascist, Nazi or any other type." Young Communists made up a large proportion of the delegates and could have defeated the resolution, but chose not to do so in order not to jeopardize their coalition (Ottanelli 1991:171). Such self-effacing behavior also took place within the labor movement. At the 1940 CIO convention in Atlantic City, rather than defend themselves politically, the Communists supported a unanimously adopted resolution) stating that "totalitarianism . . . such as Nazism, Communism and Fascism . . . [has] no place in this great modern labor movement" (Convention Proceedings 1940:114). The resolution was in fact introduced by CP supporter and CIO corporate counsel Lee Pressman. The Communists supported a similar resolution at the 1946 convention. At this convention, the resolution to rein in the CP-led city and state CIO councils was introduced by Reid Robinson, CP president of Mine Mill. As Bert Cochran argues, this was a public, "unedifying spectacle of Communists voting to denounce themselves" (1977:267). While these decisions were defended as "smart moves" to save the Party, as Cochran notes, "it was an accumulation of such 'smart moves' that helped in time to bury the Communists" (1977:145). This was hardly the way Communists were supposed to engage in united front work!

Though willing to compromise on virtually all their sacred principles on do-mestic issues as avowed Communists, the CPers brooked no quarter in their defense of Soviet domestic or foreign policy. This was especially true of their vituperative attacks against those who questioned one of Stalin's greatest crimes—the prepos-terously staged 1936–38 Moscow show trials and the execution of numerous Party members, including virtually all the old Bolshevik leaders.[40]

Interpreting the Role of the Communist Party in the United States

So how can we summarize the Communist Party and its role and influence in the U.S. labor movement? During the 1920s through the early 1950s, the Party com-bined several characteristics that seemed utterly incompatible. Most interpretative approaches fail because they deny one or another of these.

1. On the one hand, with some noted exceptions, from the 1920s until the mid-1950s, Communists were generally the most committed, militant, and fear-less activists and organizers for the civil rights of African-Americans and other minorities, doing and accomplishing what no other group (especially majority-white) had done. Yes, they made errors and were overly sectarian at times, but their commitment to the cause was head and shoulders above that of others, a fact recognized both by conservative African-American newspapers and organi-zations and, even at times, by their bitterest critics.[41] Even after the expulsion of CP-led unions from the CIO in 1949, they continued to fight to open up hiring of Blacks and other minorities, especially in the South. Much of this activity was under the rubric of the National Negro Labor Council (NNLC) (disbanded in 1956), which was particularly active in the UE stronghold of St. Louis and, in Louisville, bolstered by the FE at the International Harvester plant (for a

---

[40] Those who harbor doubts can usefully consult Roy Medvedev's *Let History Judge* (1971) and Robert Conquest's *The Great Terror* (1973). On their unrelenting attacks on the questioners, see Palmer (forthcoming), esp. ch. 6.

[41] Thus, one sign of disloyalty and of Communist sympathies during the McCarthy period was a commitment to civil rights and participation in interracial activities (Goldfield 1987:270–71). The most notable exceptions include the Communists' support for the internment of Japanese citizens during World War II. They also include the Party's backing off from certain militant activities during the popular front period, as well as downplaying the fight against racial discrimination in the name of war production during World War II. However, even in Alabama in 1937, the Party leaders "began to compromise its militant anti-racism for the sake of political expedience." They even supported Lister Hill for Alabama senator, despite his refusal to support anti-lynching legislation (Kelley 1990:124).

summary of the NNLC, see Thompson 1978, as well as hundreds of leaflets and press clippings in possession of the author).

2. As I have documented and has been acknowledged by many, Communists were among the most militant and dedicated of trade unionists, often successful in the most difficult and dangerous situations.[42]

3. In general, the trade unions that the Party led were far more democratic than those led by their Socialist, liberal, and right-wing competitors, a fact denied by their earlier critics but proved unequivocally by the best modern scholarship (a compelling argument is that of Stepan-Norris and Zeilin 2002).

4. However, their own organization was far from democratic. By 1928, not only was the top leadership of the CPUSA beholden to Moscow, but its policies were subject to change with little or no input or debate from rank-and-file members, or even from the top CPUSA leadership. This was in sharp contrast to the large-scale open debates in Lenin's Bolshevik Party, as well as the situation in the early and middle 1920s, where the CI leaders in Moscow struggled at length to get the U.S. Party factions to unify, to emerge from the underground, to work within AFL unions, and over a lengthy period of time to place the struggle against white supremacy at the center of the Party's activities. CPUSA leaders' about-faces and changes in leadership often made them appear to be "trained seals," in the words of James Cannon. Moscow at times exercised control over the U.S. Party's general policy; at other times it changed the leadership of the Party by fiat, and at still other times micro-managed daily activities. This control and "interference" increased after the mid-1920s, contrary to the assertions of the Popular Font enthusiasts, who assert the opposite, contrary to clear evidence.

5. By the late 1920s, the CPUSA had failed abysmally, with occasional exceptions that were never the rule, to engage in effective united front activities. From its Third Period sectarianism to the Popular Front activities, the Party abandoned all semblance of the radical project. This abandonment was stark in the South, where more than one thousand Communists in Birmingham alone subordinated themselves to CIO organizing, losing any special identity as Communists (Kelley 1990:144).

6. Finally, until the 1956 Twentieth Congress of the Communist Party of the USSR (CPUSSR) and Khrushchev's speech,[43] the U.S. Party defended not just the seemingly positive social policies of the Soviet Union (full employment, national health care, free education, and a rhetorical, if not actual, commitment

---

[42] This is contrary to the evolving view of the Trotskyist Socialist Workers Party and its leader, James Cannon, who by the post–World War II period saw them as no better than the conservative AFL trade union bureaucrats (Cannon [1947] 1977).

[43] For Nikita Khrushchev's speech at the Twentieth Congress of the CPUSSR, February 26, 1956, and assorted other documents, see the Russian Institute's 1956 *The Anti-Stalin Campaign and International Communism*.

to equality for women) and the elimination of capitalism, but the most horrific policies of the terror and the gulags.

Any theories that cannot account for all six of the above characteristics miss the mark. Any theories that see members of the CPUSA merely as foreign agents and spies cannot account for 1 through 3. Some theories deny 4 and 5. Those who glorify the Popular Front period and sympathize with so-called progressive movements have little sympathy for the Party's revolutionary goals and inaccurately see the Party's subordination to Moscow as a freely chosen. Likewise, those who see the Party as having abandoned its revolutionary goals deny that it was based on directives from Moscow and see it as a choice made by the U.S. leadership. The above interpretations all fail to make sense of *all* the facts and are engaged in various forms of denial.

The Comintern, Stalinism, and the Roots of Communist Schizophrenia

In 1919, the Comintern was established on the basis of a set of principles called the "Twenty-One Points." Its goal was to coordinate and assist Communist parties around the world to build revolutionary movements in order to eliminate capitalism and to begin building new societies. Between 1924 (after the death of the leader of the Bolshevik Party and Bolshevik Revolution, V. I. Lenin) and 1928 (under the leadership of the Soviet Party general secretary, Joseph Stalin), the goals of the Soviet Union and the CI changed. No longer oriented primarily toward world revolution, the goal was now to build "socialism in one country." The role of the Communist parties in developed countries changed from building revolutionary movements to overthrowing capitalism and to helping protect the USSR while it developed. The Soviet government was buying time, attempting to secure "peaceful coexistence" with capitalist countries and governments, particularly in developed countries. Communist parties in these countries eventually oriented themselves toward building broad reform coalitions.

The most penetrating theoretical analysis of these changes is that of Leon Trotsky, most fully developed in *The Revolution Betrayed* (1937), which examines the domestic dynamics of Soviet society, and the *The Third International After Lenin* (1957), which focuses on a critique of the new program of the Third International at its 1928 Sixth World Congress. Trotsky analyzes the changes in the CI line that have reduced Communist parties to instruments of Soviet foreign policy, superimposed on their role as the leaders of militant, popular movements. Despite variations between parties and a certain amount of domestic flexibility, the Communist parties outside the Soviet Union were treated largely as tools of Soviet policy by the late

1920s. Contrary to wishful thinking by Isserman and others, the situation grew worse, not better.

A clear understanding of the evolution of the U.S. Communist Party must be based on a recognition of its gradual evolution from a revolutionary working-class party to mainly a guardian of the Soviet state. By the late 1920s, with Stalin at the helm, the bureaucratic degeneration of the Soviet Communist Party and state was far advanced. With the failure of the British general strike in 1926 and the bloody defeat of the Chinese uprising in 1927, Soviet leaders no longer saw the possibilities of their own country's survival being linked to revolutionary success abroad. Rather, they saw that their best defense now had to be located in diplomatic maneuvering, supported by the CPs in capitalist countries. This was to be their strategy for buying time for the economic and military development of Soviet society.[44]

Trotsky argued that the Soviet leadership during the late 1920s and the 1930s squandered many revolutionary opportunities. According to Trotsky, Stalin engineered crushing defeats, most dramatically in Germany in 1933 and in Spain in 1936–39. Thus, the traditional Communist goals of organizing the working class and its allies for the revolutionary struggle for socialism became subordinated to supporting and complementing Soviet foreign policy and to the unqualified defense of crimes against the population in the Soviet Union. Despite its policies at home and its debilitating effect on foreign Communist parties, the Soviet Union remained a contradictory social formation, a society in which capitalism remained overthrown but that had stalled in its attempt to build socialism.[45]

The traditional Marxist view, of course, was that socialism could not be built in one country, certainly not a less developed one. The successful transition required the joint efforts of at least several economically developed countries. Thus, stimulating and aiding revolutions were high priorities. If, however, socialism could be successfully built in the Soviet Union alone, facilitating the ultimate triumph of socialism on a world scale, further revolutions would not be necessary. Foreign Communist parties could be reduced to the role of active supporters. That this role often required the organization of broad liberal pressure groups or occasional self-effacement was part of the bargain. The contradictory nature of the CPUSA arose from the fact that it was not merely a foreign policy office or an unregistered lobbyist. Its supportive role was superimposed on its historical and continuing role as a mass-based militant working-class party. The two roles often were in conflict, occasionally in diametric opposition. In such cases, it never was in doubt which was master. And in the end, the one played a large role in destroying the other.

---

[44] For the more benign, "realistic" assessment of this change, see Carr (1982); for harsher criticism, see Trotsky (1971).

[45] For my own analysis of the nature of the Soviet economy and society, see Goldfield and Rothenberg (1980). I tend to agree with the criticisms of Trotsky's views internationally, as described by Perry Anderson (in Ali 1984:125–26).

Why the Communist Party Failed and Why It Declined So Drastically

The immense influence that the Communists had in the labor movement and in other spheres of U.S. society (an influence I argue could have been far greater) was virtually all lost by 1950. The question remains: what led to the decline of the CP? As James Cannon asks, "Why did it collapse so miserably in the 1950s?" (1971:93). Most writers in this country accept that subordination to Moscow was primary. Not only Klehr, Jaffe, and traditional anti-communists, but most liberals and Left reformists also take this to be the key. I have argued, however, that this is at best only part of the answer. Thus, I will look at some of the alternative explanations before drawing out a fuller explanation from the discussion so far.

Objective Conditions

Roger Keeran lucidly puts forward the traditional explanation of those who defend the general policies of the CP. The explanation hinges on at least five factors: the backwardness of U.S. workers, the tenuousness of the CP leaders among them, postwar affluence, the intensity of the Cold War, and the extent of the repression faced by the Party. These objective conditions need little elaboration. Any radical movement in the post–World War II period would have been on the defensive and facing a difficult situation (among the most compelling, well-documented accounts are Schrecker 1998; Goldstein 1978:285–368; Fischer 2016). Were it not for the conjunction of all these unfavorable conditions, the CP might well have maintained its strong toehold in U.S. politics. An analysis of the role played by these conditions is usually absent from the explanations of more conservative writers. It is also clear to some students of the CP, including myself, that the Party had done much to prepare its own grave. The CP hung on and hardened itself during the lengthy boom of the 1920s, under often fierce repression (Fischer 2016:26–70; Goldstein 1978:137–91). However, starting with a larger cadre and more resources in 1945, it reached a state of collapse and total isolation little more than a decade later. What were the reasons?

Browderism

Isserman (1982), echoing earlier claims by Gates (1958), Dennis (1977), and Starobin (1972), argues that the CP could have been successful if it not only had been more independent from Moscow but had continued its stance of progressivism as the left wing of the New Deal. In the eyes of these critics, which oddly enough sometimes include the anti-communist Jaffe (1975), it was the break with

"Browderism" and the return in 1945 to sectarian, "un-American" politics that hurt the CP fatally. This argument, however, has many weaknesses. It refuses to recognize the policies of the CP during the 1920s and early 1930s from which it developed strength, attracted militants, gained moral authority, and came to be the dominant force on the left. Its ties to the Soviet Union, its militant position on the "Negro question," and its general program of class struggle played no small part in this. Isserman and other writers make the unwarranted assumption that only Popular Front coalitions attract people. But sometimes, even if only sometimes, the more radical positions attract; they particularly attract, at such times, the most militant members of the working class.

Contrary to certain claims that the CP had greater independence under Browder, its support for Roosevelt as well as support for the Moscow trials, and its patriotism as well as its hiding of its socialist views under liberal democratic "American" traditions, were all dictated by Moscow. To the extent that the CPUSA had any independence, it was during the earlier, revolutionary period of the 1920s so disliked by the pro-Browder authors. Further, the CP's general acceptance during World War II was not merely based on its political subordination to the New Deal coalition. It was also due to the coincidence of the CP's pro-Soviet orientation with the wartime aims of U.S. capitalism and its politicians. When the wartime alliance broke down, either the CP's relation to the liberal Democrats or its relation to the Soviet Union had to go.[46] The only way this alliance with the politicians and moderate CIO officials could have continued after the onset of the Cold War would have been for the CP to have abandoned its support of the Soviet Union. To have done so would have been to reject everything that the CP stood for; few of the pro-Browder supporters have gone this far.

The idea that Browderism was a phenomenon somehow different, more "American" than the role of border guards demanded of all Stalinists parties is a myth. To hold this view is to fail to understand the nature of the political relations between the CI and Soviet Union and its subordinate parties. A similar error, of course, is made by those leftist critics of the CP who see its problems as based on its failure to break sufficiently with Browderism.

The view I find most plausible about the Communist Party's demise is put forward in the writings of James Cannon, founder and leader of the SWP: the fundamental cause of the CP's demise, according to Cannon, was its moral bankruptcy, a characteristic that became more and more apparent to militant workers as well as to liberal and leftist critics. The accumulation of perfidy, unprincipled behavior, and outright treachery from the 1930s on eventually caught up with the Communist

---

[46] Even in the more conservative International Brotherhood of Teamsters, where the union aided in the indictment of Trotskyists teamsters in Minneapolis, the leadership was reluctant to go after Communists until after World War II (Haverty-Stacke 2016:151– 52).

Party. Much of the moral corruption of the CP is exposed in its 1940 support for the federal government's prosecution of the SWP Trotskyist leadership under the Smith Act, later to be used against the CP itself in the late 1940s. But in 1940, as Jaffe demonstrates, the CP supplied briefs on the SWP to the government. It branded the SWP as enemy agents, sometimes as imperialist agents (during the pact period), at other times as Nazi agents (1975:50–52). Some of the CP "exposures" were used by the national teamster leadership when it broke the militant SWP-led Minneapolis truckers' local (Glaberman 1980:140; Cannon 1973a:128).[47]

The culmination of these activities may well have been the summary way the CP, on orders from Moscow in 1945, first attacked Earl Browder, its longtime general secretary, then removed him from the leadership, and finally expelled him. In 1944, Browder, who had been called the world's greatest English-speaking Marxist and "the American Stalin," had overseen the dissolution of the CP and the formation of the Communist Political Association. In this activity in May 1944, he had the unanimous public support of the whole CP leadership.[48] In July 1945, after indirect criticism from the Soviets (in the form of a public letter from French CP leader Jacques Duclos), Browder was denounced as a "revisionist," getting not a single vote from his former supporters. Cannon refers to such behavior by the entire CP leadership as degrading, exposing to all that the Party leaders were no more than the "trained seals of the Communist apparatus" (1977:119).

While moral bankruptcy was the underlying cause of the Party's rapid demise, the immediate cause was its policies in the labor movement during World War II: the CP, unlike the leftist groups and labor leaders who opposed the no-strike pledge, lost leadership of the increasingly militant workers in the CIO. This was reflected in day-to-day shop activities, in many local union elections, and in some convention meetings. The Party leaders shared this growing isolation from rank-and-file workers with other top labor leaders. The resulting bureaucratization of the labor movement during World War II is described in detail by Nelson Lichtenstein (1982). The CP's activities also placed it in opposition to all other forces on the left, many of which were gaining support based on their association with the anti-no-strike-pledge. The CP came more and more to depend on its bureaucratic relations with other union officials to maintain its position.

When the tide had turned and the Cold War began, moderate labor leaders whose alliance with the CP had only been based upon a coincidence of wartime interests

---

[47] Levenstein argues that the initial stance of Minnesota Communists was to oppose the prosecution, a view that eventually changed when the *Daily Worker* finally supported it (1981:132; see also Haverty-Stacke 2016:78–79).

[48] Foster had, in fact, written a critique of Browder at the time, which was circulated to members of the CP Central Committee and, of course, their contacts in Moscow, but it was not made public at the time; he garnered little support with the exception of that of Sam Darcy, his closest ally (Ottanelli 1991:210–12; Johanningsmeier 1994:295–307; Barrett 1999:218–22).

turned on the Party. These labor leaders had corporate and government support in their attacks. What the CP lacked was the backing of militants, in whose eyes they had become discredited, and other left-wing forces, whom they had denounced and betrayed to the government during the war. With few friends, unable to generate much credibility, the CP, unlike previous radical groupings under attack, was easily blown away with nary a trace.

Was the CP Decline Inevitable?

I have suggested that the CP did not establish its most important roots by subordinating itself to liberal politicians and moderate labor leaders. There is some evidence that the CP gained its most reliable support when it followed left-wing policies based on a class struggle approach, taking strong stands in struggling against Black oppression and engaging in uncompromising exposure of liberal politicians and reformist labor leaders. It often gained the most credibility when it put forward and defended its own views. Such an argument in no way condones the sectarian idiocy of the Third Period or the Stalinist treachery that pervades much of the Party's history. But this framework not only takes issue with those commentators who extol the 1935–45 period; it also suggests why their analysis of the first decade of party history (1919–29) and the Third Period is so wanting. The reason most commentators give short shrift to this early period is that they "prefer" the later, less radical periods. If the CP gained strength and successfully prepared itself in its revolutionary periods, then perhaps its more moderate periods were not the key to its later growth. The New Left historians and present CP defenders are advocates of these later periods. They achieve an uneasy marriage with conservative interpreters, whose preference is to show that the United States is inhospitable to radicals; according to these analysts, the CP grew only when it rejected radicalism. It should be clear that all the CP's capitulations and conciliations, from hiding its politics, failing to defend its own views at conventions, and disbanding its shop groups, to refraining from criticism of Roosevelt or CIO leaders, all did the CP little good in the end. Moreover, there is evidence that when the CP's organizing efforts were actually based on the building of solid political support, that support did not desert them when the Cold War began. One example, among many, is the Party's base in the fur and leather workers' unions, formed not only by building a militant union, but by winning people to the CP's revolutionary politics in the 1920s (Foner 1950). This political support did not readily elude them when the Cold War began. This was also true in the FE, where even the weakest locals were fairly immune to attacks from the UAW.

The Tragedy of the Communist Party Demise

In what lies the tragedy of the demise and isolation of the Communist Party in the United States? Its elimination as a political force in the labor movement and in the political life of this country meant a crippling of the Left; neither the SWP or other left-wing groups were spared. Cannon argues that the Communists themselves, having sown the seeds of their own destruction, are neither tragic nor worthy of tears. Rather, he argues that the CP was

> directly responsible for the demoralization and disorientation of the richly promising movement. The Roosevelt social program was the decisive factor in heading off the mass movement and diverting it into reformist channels, but the Stalinists, who supported Roosevelt for reasons of Kremlin foreign policy, miseducated, betrayed, corrupted, and demoralized the vanguard of this movement—a vanguard which numbered tens of thousands of the best and most courageous young militants—and thus destroyed the first great prospect to build a genuine revolutionary party in America on a mass basis. (1973a:127)

The tragedy of the Party is what the CP did to its victims and the possibilities that it destroyed:

> The chief victim of Stalinism in this country was the magnificent left-wing movement, which arose on the yeast of the economic crisis in the early Thirties and eventually took form in the CIO through a series of veritable labor uprisings. Such a movement, instinctively aimed at American capital, was bound to find political leadership. Conditioned by their frightful experiences, the workers in the vanguard of the great mass movement were ready for the most radical solutions. The Stalinists, who appeared to represent the Russian Revolution and the Soviet Union, almost automatically gained the dominating position in the movement; while thousands of young militants—not the worst, but in many cases the very best—were recruited into the Communist Party. (Cannon 1973b:295)

The tragedy, according to Cannon, lies ultimately in how the CP betrayed the confidence of the tens of thousands of militants it attracted:

> By their whole policy and conduct; by their unprincipled opportunism, their unscrupulous demagoguery, systematic lying and calculated treachery—the Stalinists demoralized the left-wing labor movement. They squandered its militancy and robbed it of the moral resources to resist the

reactionary witch-hunt instituted in the unions with the beginning of the "cold war." Murray and Reuther only appear to be the conquerors of the left-wing workers. It was really the Stalinists who beat them. (Cannon 1973b:296)

This view of the demise of the Communist Party of the United States, a view that I believe most fits the facts reported by all other investigators, finds little echo in their writings. It helps explain the differences among various authors, and why each has such difficulties explaining certain facts that are incompatible with their political perspectives. The perspective presented here also suggests not only that the exceptional character of U.S. politics is not inevitable, but that broad class alternatives to labor reformism and Popular Front politics are not, at certain conjunctures, incongruous with U.S. society.

Conclusion

The Historical Balance Sheet

I now return to the counterfactual questions raised at the beginning of this book. Could southern workers have been organized during the 1930s and 1940s? What difference would this have made? And what can the failures tell us about the trajectory of American politics up to the present? In the preceding chapters, two types of failures have been discussed: first, the failure to organize the biggest industries in the South; and second, the degeneration of certain organized unions where some of the initial promise was gutted, especially with respect to issues of race.

I start with the inability of the CIO to organize the more than three hundred thousand southern woodworkers, half of whom were African-American. By all accounts, including those of CIO right-wingers, southern woodworkers were ripe for unionization. The failure to organize them was a result of the narrow-mindedness and incompetence of the national leadership of the woodworkers. These leaders had been installed and supported by the mainstream/conservative CIO leaders, undermining and replacing a more dynamic and competent left-wing/Communist leadership that was committed to organizing southern woodworkers. National Communist Party leaders were themselves not without blame. They refused to aggressively support the left-wing leaders when they controlled the union, sacrificing them in order to maintain their "center–Left" alliance with the right-wing CIO leadership. The successful organizing of the woodworkers, I argue, had the potential to radically transform the 1950s to 1970s civil rights movement in the South by providing immense organizational support and increased numbers of white as well as Black working-class participants, while shaping its economic agenda. What allowed the white backlash to be so dominant was the limited (white) working-class opposition to it.

The other large group of workers in the South that could potentially have been organized were textile workers, also several hundred thousand strong. I have suggested that a more militant strategy by the Textile Workers Organizing Committee (TWOC) during its 1936–37 drive (given the overwhelming National

The Southern Key. Michael Goldfield, Oxford University Press (2020). © Michael Goldfield
DOI: 10.1093/oso/9780190079321.001.0001

Labor Relations Board election victories among textile workers) might have been far more effective than the more submissive, class-collaborationist approach of Hillman. This strategy, combined with that of organizing broad support from other unions and groups—associative power—an approach used in the coal, auto, oil, and steel industries, could have been potentially successful. The textile campaigns of 1946–47, seemingly more difficult than the earlier TWOC organizing, were perhaps doomed (especially given the go-it-alone approach of the right-wing leadership), leading to embarrassing defeats. Textiles, to be sure, was a more difficult venue than wood, but definitely within the realm of possibility, as my analysis of the TWOC campaign suggests. And promising starts among public sector workers, tobacco, and public transportation could certainly have been more successful.

These counterfactual possibilities are, I argue, not at all fanciful, given that coal miners, steelworkers, longshoremen, maritime workers, oilworkers, and to a large extent furniture workers successfully unionized, along with workers in industries that had secondary production sites in the South, including the auto, rubber, farm equipment, electrical, animal slaughtering, and trucking industries. By comparing those industries and places where organizing was successful with those where it failed, one is able to make reasonable assessments of what might have been possible in those areas that were unsuccessful. Let me therefore suggest that the decline of organized labor in the United States (which can be identified statistically from its highpoints in 1945 and 1953) can arguably be traced to its roots in Hillman's 1937 TWOC strategy of attempting to collaborate with unwilling capitalists and relying on an ineffective and unwilling federal government to enforce labor rights. A parallel failure, although not focused in the South, was the defeat of the 1937 Little Steel strike, which can in part be attributed to the unwillingness of the Murray leadership of the steelworkers' union to pull out all stops, as well as attempt to mobilize the broadest range of allies, in the face of militarized, murderous opposition from the companies (White 2016).

The early glimmers of alternative possibilities can be seen in a large variety of arenas during the 1930s and 1940s. Many such activities have been discussed in previous chapters, including the impact of the coal miners' and Mine Mill's successful support of workers in other industries in Alabama, among whom were those in the textile and wood industries. There were also the activities of the Farm Equipment Workers (FE) in Louisville (Gilpin 1992), the United Packinghouse Workers of America (UPWA) in Ft. Worth, Texas (Horowitz 1997: 231–32), and the union and civil rights activists of the large Food and Tobacco Workers of American (FTA) local in Winston-Salem, North Carolina (Korstad 2003; Korstad and Lichtenstein 1988). Even the activities of certain more conservative CIO unions are suggestive. When the Oil Workers International Union (OWIU) organized the thousands of oil refinery workers in Port Arthur, Texas, in 1942, they not only successfully negotiated a union contract, but also began to register their members to vote and took a strong stand against the poll tax (Johnson 1976; Priest and Boston 2012).

Port Arthur was in the congressional district of the racist, reactionary Martin Dies, chair of the House Committee on Un-American Activities, which was virulently anti-labor and anti-communist. The local announced that its first task was to mobilize the district for the defeat of Dies. The mobilization was so successful that Dies withdrew from running for reelection in 1944 (Priest and Boston 2012: 106; also documented in the OCAWU archives). The United Electrical Workers Union (UE) in St. Louis, in a secondary production area, not only mobilized its own members throughout the 1930s and 1940s, but also gathered a broad range of allies to provide important associative power to its struggles (Feurer 2006).

I have argued and tried to document that the calcification of the industrial union movement began far earlier than is generally claimed by most analysts. The reasons can be found in two disparate developments. The first was the degeneration of so-called liberal trade unionists and the ascendancy of the most conservative factions within the CIO. The people who were responsible for this were authoritarian and anti-democratic, racially backward, unwilling at most times to mobilize their followers for any sustained struggle against corporations, and anti-radical (a stance that extended not merely to Communists but to Trotskyists, militant Socialists, and all insurgent workers' movements and leaders). The second was the enabling of these conservative trade unionists by the Communist Party leadership, beginning in the popular front period. The Communist leaders often lauded these conservatives, especially the authoritarian, racist head of the CIO and steelworkers' union, Philip Murray. They did this in the name of consolidating an alleged "center–Left" coalition, in which they played a subordinate and sycophantic role. As the Cold War gathered steam and the more conservative CIO leaders turned on them, the alleged coalition evaporated, and the main CP-led unions were expelled from the CIO, the majority severely weakened or decimated.

The failures of southern labor organizing in the 1930s and 1940s determined the character of the civil rights movement in the 1950s and 1960s, as well as the strength of the white backlash in the South (and the North and West). The contours of these two activities provide the backdrop for the Republican Party southern strategy (which begins in 1964 with Barry Goldwater's presidential run) and Democratic Party complicity. The labor-based civil rights movement that existed in the 1930s and 1940s, and its weakened remnants that survived into the 1950s, can be sketched. It is from these glimmers of activity, too limited to affect more than certain local areas, that it is possible to project what might have been possible. Let me mention briefly here some of the differences between a labor-based civil rights movement and the strictly "rights"-based movement that dominated the struggle in the 1950s through the 1970s. The modern civil rights movement fought for equal rights, the recognition that all human beings regardless of race, gender, and other characteristics should be treated equally in the social and political spheres. Socially, this meant equal access to public venues, be they schools, libraries, universities, parks, or swimming pools. It also included access to public-private facilities, including restaurants, motels and hotels, and shopping areas, as well as political rights, most paramount of which was voting, but also jury selection and law enforcement. These rights are the rights of civil society, what Hegel calls "bourgeois rights," with no pejorative implications. These goals were addressed and partially achieved in good part by mass mobilizations rooted in communities and schools, both North and South, as well as winning over public opinion in the North.

The labor-based civil rights movement also mobilized around these goals, but in addition around economic issues, including hiring, upgrading, and training. It primarily mobilized its members, white as well as non-white, and drew on the organizational and financial resources of its unions. Mainstream unions, many purportedly liberal and in favor of civil rights, generally abandoned both sets of goals and mobilization methods, despite occasional lip service.

The largest coordinator of the labor-based civil rights strategy during the early 1950s was the National Negro Labor Council (NNLC), a coalition of largely CP-led or -influenced national unions and locals, and numerous local labor and community activists. The NNLC began with the June 1950 Conference for Negro Rights in Chicago, whose stated goals were anti-discrimination clauses in all union contracts, an end to lily-white employment in all industries and job categories, admission of African-American workers to all apprenticeship courses, and full job opportunities for Black women, the last being a central thrust of virtually all the campaigns. The conference claimed to have set up twenty-three local Negro Labor Councils by the time of the NNLC founding conference in Cincinnati, on October 27–28, 1951. The NNLC had a rhetorical commitment to organizing the South, with numerous activities and chapters there.[1]

As other commentators note, the NNLC was hounded by government bodies, including the House Un-American Activities Committee (HUAC), and by employers, and was attacked by putatively liberal organizations, including the NAACP, National Urban League (NUL), and mainstream unions. The NNLC thus also engaged in defense work against government and racist attacks. Typical was its support for Harold Ward, financial secretary of FE Local 108 at McCormick Works at International Harvester (IHC) in Chicago, who was framed for the murder of a scab on October 3, 1952. The signature model for defense against mob violence was the 1949 trade union mobilization in Peekskill, New York, to provide protection at a concert by Paul Robeson, which had been previously canceled due to attacks by racist mobs (Horne 2016: 121–24; Robeson 1978).

The NNLC drew its primary support from a number of leftist unions and locals, including the UE, FE (later UE-FE), FTA (later part of Distributive Processing and Office Workers of America), Mine Mill, Fur and Leather Workers Union, International Longshore and Warehouse Union (ILWU; especially SF Local 10),

---

[1] For more details, see the convention proceedings of the NNLC founding meeting, *Get on Board the Freedom Train*, Ernest Thompson papers, 1:1.

certain important locals in the United Auto Workers (UAW; especially Local 600), and UPWA (especially District 1 in Chicago). The NNLC played a crucial role in coordinating several national campaigns and also gave substantial support to key local activities. A short summary of both NNLC and certain non-NNLC activities follows. The NNLC, as early as 1951, emphasized the importance of runaway shops to the South. General Electric (GE) opened up a major manufacturing facility in Louisville, Kentucky, planning to expand to as many as thirty-thousand employees. Half of the workers were women, and besides a token number of Blacks, the initial five thousand hires were all white (Thompson 1978: 68). With its base in FE Local 236 at IHC, the NNLC began pressuring for the hiring of more Black workers, especially Black women. It also forced the Louisville City Council to provide training for non-white workers for jobs in the plant. The NNLC's New York branch led large demonstrations at New York's GE headquarters, while UE locals at GE plants around the country made demands and led demonstrations in support. This coordinated campaign resulted in the increased hiring of Black workers, especially Black women (Thompson 1978: 70).

The Chicago Negro Labor Council (with strong bases of support in the three FE-organized Chicago International Harvester plants and in District 1 of the UPWA) targeted downtown Chicago department stores, groceries, and lunch counters, many of whose customers were African-American, but refused to hire Blacks, except as janitors or maids (Horowitz 1997:224). With large demonstrations and boycotts, many local stores quickly capitulated. Horowitz claims that by the mid-1950s, most of Chicago's South Side businesses had been integrated (1997:224). Sears and Woolworths were more recalcitrant and became the subjects of national campaigns, both eventually agreeing to hire Blacks on their sales floors (Thompson 1978:36, 42–43). Another campaign that was less successful was the hiring of Black pilots, office personnel, and flight attendants by American Airlines, culminating in a large demonstration at its Cleveland headquarters coincident with the 1952 annual NNLC meeting. A picket line of two thousand persons (police estimated fifteen hundred) carried signs, including "Negro Pilots Fly in Korea—Why Not in America?" (*Cleveland Plain Dealer*, November 13, 1952). District 1 also served as a voice for civil rights inside the UPWA's national organization, pressing the centrist leadership of the 1950s and 1960s to include anti-discrimination clauses in master contracts (Horowitz 1997:207, 222, 225). Let me suggest that these were not inconsequential victories, especially for a small, beleaguered group. Despite claims to the contrary, the much larger NAACP and NUL failed to match these achievements.

The NNLC gave wide publicity and support to a strike of nine thousand Black fishermen in the coastal waters of North Carolina, Virginia, and Florida, organized by the Fur and Leather Workers Union. Left-wing UAW Local 600, representing workers at the largest auto plant in the country, Ford's River Rouge plant (whose recording secretary was NNLC leader William Hood), organized and won a citywide vote in the town of River Rouge for a local Fair Employment Practices Committee

(FEPC). The vote passed 4,175 to 3,180. Since it is estimated that there were at most only a thousand Black voters, the total suggests that a majority of whites supported the FEPC.[2] The River Rouge FEPC stipulated "up to 60 days in jail and a $200 dollar fine for persons who discriminate in employment because of race, color, religion, sex, national origin or ancestry" (Thompson 1978:49). This success is particularly impressive given the UAW national leadership's opposition to both militant civil rights activity and left-wing influence generally. This and other activities suggest that the labor/civil rights approach had the potential for gaining the support of significant numbers of white workers. The tradition of civil rights militancy in Local 600 ran deep: earlier, in 1943, it had mobilized thousands of Black and white workers to integrate and defend Black residency in the Sojourner Truth Homes, a federally funded project in the "housing-starved black community" of Detroit (Korstad and Lichtenstein 1988:797).

The civil rights activities in San Francisco were equally impressive. Supported by the NNLC, they were led by Local 10 of the ILWU. The ILWU's Local 10 engaged in, perhaps, the most radical internal program dedicated to the racial equality of any American union, transforming a workforce that included less than a dozen African-Americans before the "Big Strike" of 1934 to a majority-Black workforce by 1970, in a city composed of less than 14% Blacks. Black workers were elected to leadership positions in Local 10 almost immediately upon its creation, and initiatives to increase the number of Blacks in the local, as well as in other locals (e.g., the integration of the highly skilled longshore clerks' Local 34), received overwhelming (white) rank-and-file support. Indeed, when longtime ILWU president Harry Bridges suggested seniority-based layoffs following the decrease in workload at the conclusion of World War II, rank-and-file whites unanimously rejected the proposal, recognizing that the layoffs would disproportionately affect Blacks. Bridges recollected, "When I marched in with the idea of laying off a thousand men, I am telling you not one single person voted for me. They still preferred to go on and work 26, 28 hours a week." As Peter Cole puts it, "Local 10, with its large white majority, voted to retain a significant Black minority even though doing so, at least in the short run, reduced the earnings of the more senior, mostly White members." This episode further confirms Mosimann and Pontusson's (2017) contention that not only do unions help workers pursue their material interests, but they also, at times, inculcate in workers solidaristic norms that lead them to pursue actions that are in the interest of the working class as a whole, even if those actions actually harm their own material interests in the short run.

Besides the internally progressive policies of Local 10, San Francisco longshoremen pursued racial equality in the Bay Area as a whole. For instance, in the mid-1940s, Local 10 forced the San Francisco Municipal Railway System to hire its

[2] See report of Coleman Young, executive secretary, November 21, 1952, at the annual convention, 1–2; Ernest Thompson papers 1:1.

first Black driver. Racist whites beat and whipped the driver on his first run; Local 10 activists reacted by riding with the driver, four or five at a time. As one of the participants later related, "He didn't have any more trouble [after that]." Local 10 also integrated, through boycotts, pickets, and/or financial pressure, the Bay Area's building trade unions, department stores, local government, and Kaiser Hospital. In 1960, the local funded (through its pension fund) the construction of the St. Francis Square Housing Cooperative, the first integrated housing development in San Francisco, its first manager being a Black leftist from Local 10. Local 10 organized a solidarity march with the Birmingham campaign of 1963 (the largest civil rights march in the Bay Area), contributed to the Sheraton-Palace Hotel protests of 1964 (leading to increased hiring of Blacks in the city's hotel industry), and transported food and supplies to and from Alcatraz Island during the island's occupation by Native American activists in 1969. San Francisco longshoremen also used their profound levels of structural power to exert pressure internationally and to help organize other industries. In 1962, Local 10 refused to unload the Dutch ship *Raki* in protest against the South African apartheid regime (it would do so again in 1984 to much fanfare) (Cole and Limb 2017:313–14). From the late 1970s to the early 1980s, Local 10 refused to load or unload a number of ships bound to or from military dictatorships; in 1978, for example, it refused to load a ship with U.S.–manufactured weapons headed to the military government in Chile (2017:314). Local 10 also refused to handle DiGiorgio grapes during the United Farm Workers' strike of 1965, adding much-needed structural support to the organization of an industry with almost no structural power (Melcher and Goldfield 2018; Ahlquist and Levi 2013).

Civil rights unionism was not limited to the CP-led unions, however. Teamsters Local 688's leader, Harold Gibbons (who was white), and his assistant, Ernest Calloway (who was Black), were vehemently anti-communist, cutting their teeth in the labor movement by red-baiting CPers in the United Retail, Wholesale, and Department Store Employees of America (URWDSEA) and the FTA (Bussel 2003:51). However, both were self-proclaimed socialists and were dedicated to racial equality (2003:51). Using the tactics of the labor movement, beginning in 1951 Gibbons and Calloway implemented a community steward program that solicited grievances related to quality-of-life issues (e.g., "garbage pickup, street repair, police protection, recreation facilities") and enjoyed some "significant successes" (2003: 52). In 1966, they formed the Tandy Area Council (TAC) (Tandy being a poor Black neighborhood in St. Louis), with the Black members of Local 688 as an "indigenous base" for a "trade union oriented war on the slums" (2003:55). They used TAC to lead pickets of local supermarkets to achieve price reductions, won higher payments of state welfare with sit-ins, lowered food stamp prices, lobbied for the hiring of Black firefighters, pressed for the inclusion of African-American history in the schools, and challenged police brutality. TAC also organized tenants, forcing landlords to repair buildings and the city to punish delinquent landlords

(Bussel 2003:57). To increase white rank-and-file support within Local 688 (some whites in the local were openly racist; a majority of whites, for example, supported George Wallace in 1964; 2003: 63), Gibbons developed a parallel organization, the Carondolet Area Council (Carondolet being a white working-class neighborhood), to pursue similar goals for poor white workers (2003: 64). In 1969, Gibbons brokered an end to the St. Louis rent strike, ultimately decreasing rents and shifting the administration of St. Louis's public housing to the Civic Alliance for Housing, a front for Local 688, until 1972 (2003: 60–62). Clarence Lang (2009a) adds greatly to our understanding of non-Communist labor-based civil rights activity in St. Louis in the 1950s and 1960s. St. Louis was perhaps unique in its broad array of civil rights groups with a class agenda, although unlike the CP, they tended to be almost exclusively male-oriented and less sensitive to the plight of African-American women.

These activities, especially those of the NNLC, were attacked by all ostensibly liberal organizations, including the UAW, United Steelworkers of America (USWA), NAACP, and NUL, with Gibbons being attacked by the International Brotherhood of Teamsters, eventually being removed from office for his outspoken opposition to the Vietnam War (Bussel 2003: 65). None of these organizations took up the mantle themselves, demonstrating that their anti-communist attacks were indeed hypocritical, and their rhetorical commitment to NNLC demands largely phony. Indeed, the contrast between the UAW national leadership's position on civil rights—and its actions locally—and the left-led NNLC affiliates is especially telling. In part due to the hagiography that passes for scholarship on Walter Reuther's life, the UAW, particularly during Reuther's reign, has been characterized as a democratic, civil rights–oriented alternative to the outwardly racist right wing of the labor movement and the "authoritarian," Communist-led left wing. It was, according to Nelson Lichtenstein, the best of the possible (1995:442–43; for a critique, see Goldfield 1997b). Besides limited successes, however—including donating large sums of money to the NAACP and, through the Reuther-backed National Committee for Fair Play in Bowling, forcing the American Bowling Congress to open up its membership to Blacks—the UAW under Reuther was largely backward on questions of race, stifling rank-and-file civil rights militancy when it arose (particularly in Left-led locals, like Local 600) and catering to white supremacy where it dominated (Wigderson 1989:349–50). Instead, the Reuther forces put their attentions elsewhere, sending hundreds of organizers to raid FE locals. On one afternoon in 1949, for instance, close to a hundred UAW organizers, including three executive board members, participated in leafleting the FE-represented East Moline International Harvester plant (Gilpin 1992:240).

While the civil rights activism of the left-led unions was limited, it still illustrates how effective a union-backed civil rights campaign can be, as well as how effective a broader labor/civil rights movement could have been. Even when unions were isolated, their structural power was often sufficient to allow them to proceed unimpeded, even in the deepest South. The potential importance of their activities can be seen in contrast to the fate of white liberals in the South during the early civil rights movement. Those few liberals who supported the movement were easily crushed and isolated, fired, ruined financially, threatened, even victimized by violence. Workers at large industrial plants were not so easily intimidated. Such was the case with the FE in Louisville, Mine Mill in Birmingham, and unions in many other areas. This was also the case in the North in combating racist violence. The activities of UAW Local 6 at International Harvester's Melrose Park, Illinois, plant in the 1970s provide an example. C. B. Dennis, a Black worker in the plant, had moved into a formerly all-white neighborhood in the racist white Chicago suburb of Melrose Park, only a few miles from the factory. Dennis's house was firebombed several times. The Local 6 UAW Fair Practices Committee, under the control of left-wing militants, mobilized a defense picket seven days a week around the house. Hostilities ended abruptly. Though there were certainly some workers in the plant who were not enthusiastic about the defense, it was clear that an attack on the defense line would have provoked outrage among the more than three thousand workers at the factory.

The unwillingness of virtually all industrial unions in the South to participate in the civil rights movement, in any way other than giving verbal support (especially true of the USWA and the UAW, two powerful, ostensibly pro–civil rights unions), undercut the possibilities of support from white workers, effectively isolating the civil rights movement from potential coalitions with interracial organizations. In general, the only unions that effectively mobilized their members in support of civil rights were Local 1199 (originally a small union of several hundred left-wing Jewish druggists) and the UPWA, both of which bused in their members to both civil rights and anti-war demonstrations in the 1960s. The American Federation of State, County and Municipal Employees, as suggested by its union organizing in 1968 of Memphis sanitation workers, also at times merged its campaigns with those of the civil rights movement.

By 1954, the CP had abandoned its labor/civil rights activities, a pursuit it had initiated as part of a broader social movement in the 1930s. Writing retrospectively in 1958, Harry Haywood, the Party's foremost theoretician of the Black Nation thesis, claimed that the CP's adherence to the self-determination line was a proxy for the Party's actual commitment to the pursuit of civil rights. While this is probably a stretch, at least in the postwar period, it provides a useful heuristic. While the period from 1947 to 1953 saw a number of trade union line changes—ultimately culminating in an extreme version of "boring from within," where the Left-led unions were instructed to self-liquidate and join the "true base" of the U.S. labor movement: not merely the CIO industrial unions, but even the right-wing unions of the AFL (leading to the merger of the Fur and Leather Workers Union with the Amalgamated Meat Cutters and to dozens of UE locals, with a membership of around fifty thousand, disassociating from the UE and joining the International Union of Electrical Workers, International Brotherhood of Electrical Workers, International

Association of Machinists, or United Auto Workers)—the line on race changed little during this period (Stepan-Norris and Zeitlin 2002:321). The first rumbling that a change was imminent came in a 1953 pamphlet by Charles T. Mann, entitled "Stalin's Thought Illuminates Problems of Negro Freedom," which Haywood summarized as accusing the CP's Black cadre and trade unionists as "left-sectarian" because "they did not accept bourgeois leadership" (Haywood [1958] 1959:47). In 1954, CP leader James Allen submitted a memo to the National Committee arguing that the self-determination line was obsolete, given the postwar integration of Blacks into "all aspects of American life" (Haywood 1959:8). Eugene Dennis declared in 1956 that the line had been dropped in 1954, rejected explicitly by Foster in 1955, and refuted theoretically in 1956 (Haywood 1959:4). The new line—besides rejecting self-determination theoretically on the grounds that the economic basis of racial inequality (southern sharecropper feudalism) had been eliminated, thus initiating its inevitable abolition—necessitated the dissolution of all independent, CP-led civil rights groups (including the NNLC) and uncritically following the NAACP (Haywood 1959:44–45). According to Haywood, "The thinking behind the policy of liquidating ALL left centers in the Negro field was the idea that the NAACP adequately covered the whole field of Negro freedom struggle—that any other movement would be a splitting movement, comparable to 'dual unionism'" (1959:45). Belatedly, then, the trade union policy of self-liquidation and "boring from within" the right-wing organizations found its way to the left-led civil rights struggle.

The CP's shift in party line on the "race question," while informative, seems to have trailed actual shifts in the Party's behavior toward the left-led civil rights groups. Nelson Peery (2007), Black Communist and NNLC leader, contends that the CP first ordered its members to leave or disband the local Negro Labor Councils and the National Negro Labor Council in early 1953. Those who refused, like Bert Washington, "the best-known and most respected African-American Communist in Ohio," were accordingly expelled from the CP (Peery 2007:153). Peery relates that some Black party loyalists heeded the CP's demand and dissolved their branches of the NNLC, as happened in Cleveland (2007:152). Loyalists who remained in the CP—when not expelled—rationalized the sudden shift in party line by chalking it up to "the communist way of inner Party struggle" and urged NNLC members to abide by the Party's decision while "struggle[ing] to change it" (2007:152). Peery himself, seemingly conceding to Party discipline, was expelled on March 5, 1953, the same day as Stalin's death (2007:154). The NNLC, no longer a CP affiliate and led by (now) former Communists, finally collapsed under the weight of HUAC investigations in 1955.

One can speculate on the ultimate cause(s) of this abrupt shift in CP practice and theory; like the other abrupt shifts in party line, it is likely attributable to the ever-changing exigencies of Soviet foreign policy. The CP's newest trade union line, first consequentially promulgated in 1949, demanded that the left-led unions do anything to stay in the "mainstream" of the labor movement (Stepan-Norris and Zeitlin 2002:301). First defined as maintaining affiliation with the CIO, and by early 1955 as liquidation and joining the AFL, the reintensification of "boring from within" can be attributed to the Soviet Union's post–World War II foreign policy demand of "peaceful coexistence" (2002:299). Hoping to defuse Cold War hostilities, the USSR defanged the Communist movement in the United States, effectively abandoning its involvement in the labor movement. For the most part (with major exceptions in the UE, FE, and Mine Mill unions), U.S. Communists obsequiously abided by Moscow's directives (2002:316). The shift in party line on race in 1953–54 can largely be attributed to the same dynamic, with the gap between their implementation owing to the USSR's courting of newly independent African countries in the early 1950s. By 1953, Soviet leaders had apparently decided that they could do the latter without independent civil rights groups in the United States.

In the end, the civil rights movement, for all its heroic struggles and important successes (not least of which were gaining voting rights in the Deep South for African-Americans and ending police and KKK terror in the Black Belt counties of the Deep South, including Mississippi), was not able to confront the economic roots of white supremacy. Class-based racial issues that had the potential to unite white and Black workers never got off the ground.

These failures led almost inexorably to the success of white backlash in the South and the mobilization of whites in opposition to civil rights. Massive resistance in the South began shortly after the 1954 *Brown vs. Board of Education* decision by the U.S. Supreme Court, which declared school segregation unconstitutional. As with previous racist movements in the South, it was led and organized by economic and political white elites, starting in the Mississippi Delta, majority– African-American cotton plantation areas (Bartley 1969:104). For a variety of reasons, however, it also drew support from working-class and poor whites. The vehicle for massive resistance was the White Citizens' Council. With little resistance from organized labor, opposition was effectively crushed. Despite the White Citizens' Council's rhetoric of eschewing violence, terror was widespread, with the KKK making open raids on Black communities throughout the South, injuring and killing many. In Birmingham, Klansmen castrated a Black handyman as part of a ceremony. In Camden, South Carolina, they flogged a white schoolteacher who had supported desegregation. In Gaffney, South Carolina, they dynamited the home of a white physician. Bombed houses and burning crosses were there for all who deviated from the racial order; Blacks were beaten for no reason at all. Murders that went unpunished were ubiquitous, the most notorious case being that of fourteen-year-old Emmett Till, kidnapped, beaten, and killed for allegedly whistling at a white woman (Tyson 2017). Economic repression was even more widespread: for those who challenged white supremacy, being fired, denied credit, loans, or mortgages, or being prevented from running a business, was the order of the day.

The Republican Party set out to win racist whites in the South in order to expand its base. Klinkner argues that this began as early as 1957 (1992:8). This approach was pushed strongly in 1961 by Barry Goldwater, head of the Republican Senatorial Campaign Committee for the 1962 elections (Phillips 1970:203). This strategy was aptly named "Operation Dixie." Goldwater's 1964 presidential campaign, according to commentator Richard Rovere, was a barely veiled attempt to appeal to racial hatred. His all-white rallies, especially in the South, "made it possible for . . . una-pologetic white supremacists to hold great carnivals of white supremacy" (Rovere 1965:140). Parallel to Goldwater and the Republican's strategy were the 1964 and 1968 racist populist campaigns of Alabama governor George Wallace. While Wallace had tremendous support among whites in the South, in the 1964 Democratic pres-idential primaries he got 34% of the vote in Wisconsin, 30% in Indiana, and 43% in Maryland, including a majority of the white vote in the latter (Black and Black 1992:161). Democrats and Republicans both took notice. Nixon in 1968 attempted to appropriate the racist Wallace message in more veiled forms. Wallace, running on the racist platform of his American Independence Party, seemed, according to polls, to at times have strong support across the country. Yet by election time, his support had evaporated, except in the South, where his votes doubled those of the 1948 Dixiecrats. Nixon strategist Kevin Phillips, in his pathbreaking 1970 book, *The New Republican Majority*, laid out the strategy for Nixon and future Republicans to win the racist white vote from Democrats. This strategy was faithfully followed by Nixon in 1972 and by future Republican candidates. Ronald Reagan campaigned against Black crime, "welfare queens," and "forced busing," even kicking off his 1984 reelection campaign in Philadelphia, Mississippi, the site of the 1964 kidnapping and murder of three civil rights martyrs, James Cheney, Michael Schwerner, and Andrew Goodman. From George H. W. Bush's racist Willie Horton ad (the senior Bush being currently extolled as the humanitarian Republican alternative to Donald Trump), tying the case of a Black rapist to Democratic presidential candidate Massachusetts governor Michael Dukakis, to North Carolina senator Jesse Helms's anti-affirmative action ads, to the 1990 Louisiana Republican senatorial campaign of KKK and Nazi leader David Duke, to the 2016 presidential election of the racist, xenophobic Donald Trump, the GOP message and strategy have been consistent.

Democrats, of course, were themselves not blameless, although their strategy was more complex given their need to maintain minority support. Yet the signs were there as well, from presidential candidate Jimmy Carter's calls for racial pu-rity to the Chicago Democratic machine's racist attacks on 1983 Black mayoral can-didate Harold Washington. President William Clinton's campaign and presidency reached new lows, from his attacks on Sister Soulja to his ordering, as governor of Arkansas, the execution a Black, mentally deficient, death row prisoner. His support for the gutting of welfare programs, and his successful push for an omnibus crime bill whose draconian penalties fell disproportionately on Black youth, hardly distin-guished his policies from the racist ones of the Republicans.

The failures (and successes) of southern labor organizing in the 1930s and 1940s remain the golden key to understanding the trajectory of not just American politics, but much of contemporary U.S. society as well. The failures, I have argued, were not inevitable. Greater success could have led to a broader, more effective labor/civil rights movement during the 1950s and 1960s, one that might have won the support of large numbers of white as well as Black workers, thus creating the possibilities for transforming not merely the South but the United States as a whole. That this did not happen is the legacy of right-wing business unionism and a Stalinized CP, which were willing to be the hand servants of a neutered, racially deficient liberalism unwilling to mobilize workers for democratic struggle.

ACKNOWLEDGMENTS

As with any lengthy research and writing project, I have incurred many debts. This book, on which I have worked, off and on, for many decades has a lengthy list, some of which I am sure have been inadvertently forgotten.

First and foremost are my former students, at both Cornell University and Wayne State. My two most recent graduate research assistants, Amy Bromsen and Cody R. Melcher, have helped with virtually all aspects of the project, including clarification, editing, literature searches and much more. Although I take full responsibility for the final project, they have been so involved, that I am tempted to blame any lapses and errors on them. At Cornell, Jonathan Plotkin, and Sherrie Wallace helped with some of the initial work. At Wayne State University, my many student research assistants included David Parrish, Brad Markell, Rob Gordon, Glenn Bessemer, Joe Torino, Sudheer Bonala, Anthony Daniels, Matthew Cross, and Nicholas Budimir.

All or parts of the current manuscript were read by the following colleagues, to whom I am immeasurably grateful: Edward Cliffle, Bryan Palmer, Frances Fox Piven, Rosemary Feuer, David Roediger, Jim Pope, Michael Brown, Bill Fletcher, Judith Stepan-Norris, Victor Devinatz, Paul Buhle, Michael Honey, Jacob Zumoff, Marcel van der Linden, Will Jones, Paul LeBlanc, Richard Boyd, Jim Barrett, Tim Minchin, and Robert Brenner. Early phases of the work were discussed with Robert Zieger, Robin Kelley, Ted Allen, Ira Katznelson, Ken Casebeer, and Ahmed White. And, I have been discussing my work for decades with two of my closest friends (now departed), General Baker and Mike Hamlin.

While I have not been the recipient of any major grants or fellowships during my academic career, I have received many small grants and stipends that have greatly facilitated the work, and a good bit of institutional support. These include while at Cornell, money from the Jonathan Meigs fund in the government department (allowing for the primitive accumulation of relevant dissertations, as well as archival copying), and a small ACLS travel grant aiding in several early archival visits. While at Wayne State, I have received 2 small Humanity Center grants. Most importantly, I had an at large appointment as a Professor of Urban and Labor Studies at Wayne's

College of Urban, Labor, and Metropolitan Affairs, from 1992 to 2007 (when the college was abolished) which paid for research assistance and travel. More recently, I have been a research fellow at the Fraser Center for the Study of Workplace Issues, part of Labor@Wayne, whose director Marick Masters has generously supported several graduate students who have assisted my research.

My family has been a source of support and joy, throughout. My parents, Roslyn and Joseph Goldfield (now deceased), themselves lifelong political activists, were a constant source of support. My wife Evi, my lifetime partner for numerous decades, has supported and encouraged me throughout, and put up with me, despite her own illustrious career. Finally, numerous political organizations and activities, as well as my lengthy stints as a machinist, teamster, steelworker, and assembly-line worker, have all informed my work.

REFERENCES

"CIO Convention Backs Drives in South and Oil Industry." 1941. *CIO News*, December 1.

"Rank and File Loggers Revolt against Stalinist Misrule." 1939. *Socialist Appeal* 3 (82).

"Social Democratic Party Annual Membership Figures." 2014. Socialist Party of America.

"The CIO in the South." 1938. *CIO News*, July 16.

"TWOC Organizes the South; CIO Campaign Brings Hope to Workers." 1946. *CIO News*, March 26.

Ahlquist, John S. 2017. "Labor Unions, Political Representation, and Economic Inequality." *Annual Review of Political Science* 20: 409–32.

Ahlquist, John S. and Margaret Levi. 2013. *In the Interest of Others: Organizations and Social Activism.* Princeton, NJ: Princeton University Press.

Alexander, Michelle. 2010. *The New Jim Crow: Mass Incarceration in the Age of Colorblindness.* New York: New Press.

Ali, Tariq. 1984. *The Stalinist Legacy.* New York: Penguin Books.

Allen, Frederick Lewis. 1939. *Since Yesterday: The 1930's in America, September 3, 1929–September 3, 1939.* New York: Harper & Row.

Allen, Ruth Alice. 1941. *Chapters in the History of Organized Labor in Texas*, vol. 4143, November 15. Austin: University of Texas, Bureau of Research in the Social Sciences.

Allen, Ruth Alice. 1961. *East Texas Lumber Workers: An Economic and Social Picture, 1870–1950.* Austin: University of Texas Press.

Allen, Theodore. 2012. *The Invention of the White Race*, vol. 2: *The Origin of Racial Oppression in Anglo America.* London: Verso.

Amenta, Edwin. 2006. *When Movements Matter: The Townsend Plan and the Rise of Social Security.* Princeton, NJ: Princeton University Press.

American Coal Foundation. 2014. "Types of Coal." http://www.ket.org/trips/coal/agsmm/agsmmtypes.html. Accessed January 15, 2014.

Anderson, Kristi. 1979. *The Creation of a Democratic Majority, 1928–1936.* Chicago: University of Chicago Press.

Aouragh, Miriyam and Anne Alexander. 2011. "The Egyptian Experience: Sense and Nonsense of the Internet Revolution." *International Journal of Communication* 5: 1344–58.

Apted, Michael, dir. 1980. *Coal Miner's Daughter.* Film. Universal Pictures.

Aronowitz, Stanley. 1992. *False Promises: The Shaping of American Working Class Consciousness.* Durham, NC: Duke University Press.

Auerbach, Jerold S. 1966. *Labor and Liberty: The La Follette Committee and the New Deal.* Indianapolis: Bobbs-Merrill.

Aurand, Harold W. 1971. *From the Molly Maguires to the United Mine Workers: The Social Ecology of an Industrial Union, 1869–1897.* Philadelphia: Temple University Press.

Balzac, Honoré de. 1917. *Le Père Goriot.* Boston: Little, Brown.

Baptist, Edward. 2014. *The Half Has Never Been Told: Slavery and the Making of American Capitalism*. New York: Basic Books.

Barbash, Jack. 1964. "The Elements of Industrial Relations." *British Journal of Industrial Relations* 2 (1, March): 66–78.

Barkey, Frederick A. 2012. *Working Class Radicals: The Socialist Party in West Virginia, 1898–1920*. Morgantown: West Virginia University Press.

Barnett, Jessica C. and Marina S. Vornovitsky. 2016. *Health Insurance Coverage in the United States: 2015*. Current Population Reports, P60-257(RV). Washington, DC: U.S. Government Printing Office.

Barrett, James R. 1999. *William Z. Foster and the Tragedy of American Radicalism*. Urbana: University of Illinois.

Bartley, Numan. 1969. *The Rise of Massive Resistance:Race and Politics in the South During the 1950s*. Baton Rouge, LA: LSU Press.

Bartley, Numan V. 1995. *The New South, 1945–1980*. Baton Rouge: Louisiana State University Press.

Baskin, Alex. 2001. "The Ford Hunger March—1932." *Labor History* 13: 3.

Bates, Beth Tompkins. 1997. "A New Crowd Challenges the Agenda of the Old Guard in the NAACP, 1933–1941." *American Historical Review* 102 (2, April): 340–77.

Bates, Beth Tompkins. 2001. *Pullman Porters and the Rise of Protest Politics in Black America, 1925–1945*. Chapel Hill: University of North Carolina Press.

Bates, Beth Tompkins. 2012. *The Making of Black Detroit in the Age of Henry Ford*. Chapel Hill: University of North Carolina Press.

Beal, Fred. 1937. *Proletarian Journey*. New York: Da Capo Press.

Beckert, Sven. 2014. *Empire of Cotton: A Global History*. New York: Vintage Books.

Bernstein, Eduard. 1909. *Evolutionary Socialism*. Trans. Edith C. Harvey. London: Independent Labour Party.

Bernstein, Eduard. 1961. *Evolutionary Socialism: A Criticism and Affirmation*. New York: Schocken Books.

Bernstein, Irving 1950. *The New Deal Collective Bargaining Policy*. Berkeley: University of California Press.

Bernstein, Irving. 1960. *The Lean Years: A History of the American Worker, 1920–1933*. Boston: Houghton Mifflin.

Bernstein, Irving. 1969. *Turbulent Years: A History of the American Worker, 1933–1941*. Boston: Houghton Mifflin.

Bimba, Anthony. 1932. *The Molly Maguires*. New York: International.

Bingham, Clara and Laura Leedy Gansler. 2002. *Class Action: The Landmark Case That Changed Sexual Harassment Law*. New York: Anchor Books.

Black, Earl and Merle Black. 1992. *The Vital South*. Cambridge, MA: Harvard University Press.

Blackmon, Douglas S. 2008. *Slavery by Another Name: The Re-Enslavement of Black Americans from the Civil War to World War II*. New York: Doubleday.

Blizzard, William C. 2004. *When Miners March: The Story of Coal Miners in West Virginia*. Gay, WV: Appalachian Community Services.

Bonosky, Philip. 1953. "The Story of Ben Careathers." *Masses and Mainstream* 6: 33–44.

Borsos, John. 1996. "We Make You This Appeal in the Name of Every Union Man and Woman in Barbeton: Solidarity Unionism in Barberton, Ohio, 1933–41." In *"We Are All leaders": The Alternative Unionism of the Early 1930s*, ed. Staughton Lynd. Urbana: University of Illinois Press.

Boyd, Lawrence William. 1993. "The Economics of the Coal Company Town: Institutional Relationships, Monopsony, and Distributional Conflicts in American Coal Towns." PhD diss. 9410200, West Virginia University.

Brattain, Michelle. 2001. *The Politics of Whiteness: Race, Workers, and Culture in the Modern South*. Princeton, NJ: Princeton University Press.

Breitman, George. 1940. "Hillman Win in Jersey CIO Body." *Socialist Appeal* 5 (51):

Brinkley, Alan. 1982. *Voices of Protest: Huey Long, Father Coughlin, and the Great Depression.*

Brissenden, Paul. 1919. *The I.W.W.: A Study of American Syndicalism.* New York: Columbia University Press.

Brody, David. 1960. *Steelworkers in America: The Nonunion Era.* Cambridge, MA: Harvard University Press.

Brody, David. 1965. *Labor in Crisis: The Steel Strike of 1919.* Philadelphia: Lippincott.

Brody, David. 1987. "The Origins of Modern Steel Unionism: The SWOC Era." In *Forging a Union of Steel*, ed. Paul Clark et al. (p. 15). Ithaca, NY: ILR Press.

Brody, David. 1993. *In Labor's Cause: Main Themes on the History of the American Worker.* New York: Oxford University Press.

Bromsen, Amy. 2011. "They All Sort of Disappeared: The Early Cohort of UAW Women Leaders." *Michigan Historical Review* 37 (1): 5–29.

Bromsen, Amy. 2018. "The Messenger, Not the Message: Union Substitution as Union Avoidance." PhD diss., Wayne State University.

Brooks, Robert R. R. 1935. "The United Textile Workers of America." PhD diss., Yale University.

Brooks, Robert R. R. 1940. *As Steel Goes: . . . Unionism in a Basic Industry.* New Haven, CT: Yale University Press.

Brooks, Thomas R. 1978. *Clint: A Biography of a Labor Intellectual, Clinton S. Golden.* New York: Atheneum.

Brophy, John. 1964. *A Miner's Life, an Autobiography.* Madison: University of Wisconsin Press.

Brown, Benjamin Clifford. 1998. *Racial Conflict and Violence in the Labor Market: Roots in the 1919 Steel Strike.* New York: Garland.

Buchanan, Roger. 1975. *Dock Strike: History of the 1934 Waterfront Strike in Portland, Oregon.* Everett, WA: Working Press.

Buhle, Mari Jo, Paul Buhle, and Dan Georgakis. 1992. *Encyclopedia of the American left.* Oxford: Oxford University Press.

Buhle, Paul. 1987. *Marxism in the United States: Remapping the History of the American Left.* London: Verso.

Bureau of Labor Statistics, U.S. Department of Labor. 1946. "Labor in the South." Bulletin no. 898.

Burton, John F., Jr. and Terry Thomason. 1988. "The Extent of Collective Bargaining in the Public Sector." In *Public Sector Bargaining*, ed. Benjamin Aaron, Joyce M. Najita, and James L. Stern. Washington, DC: Bureau of National Affairs.

Bussel, Robert. 2003. "'A Trade Union Oriented War on the Slums': Harold Gibbons, Ernest Calloway, and the St. Louis Teamsters in the 1960s." *Labor History* 44 (1): 49–67.

Bynam, Victoria E. 2016. *The Free State of Jones, Movie Edition: Mississippi's Longest Civil War.* Chapel Hill: University of North Carolina Press.

Calhoun, John C. 1837. "Slavery, a Positive Good." Speech to the U.S. Senate, delivered February 6. https://en.wikisource.org/wiki/Slavery_a_Positive_Good.

Cannon, James P. (1944) 1972. *The History of American Trotskyism from Its Origins (1928) to the Founding of the Socialist Workers Party (1938): Report of a Participant.* New York: Pathfinder Press.

Cannon, James P. (1947) 1977. "American Stalinism and Anti-Stalinism." Reprinted in *The Struggle for Socialism in the American Century.* New York: Pathfinder Press.

Cannon, James P. 1962. *The First Ten Years of American Communism.* New York: Pathfinder Press.

Cannon, James P. 1971. *Speeches for Socialism.* New York: Pathfinder Press.

Cannon, James P. 1973a. "Factional Struggle and Party Leadership." In *Speeches to the Party: The Revolutionary Perspective and the Revolutionary Party.* New York: Pathfinder Press.

Cannon, James P. 1973b. "Trade Unionists and Revolutionists." In *Speeches to the Party: The Revolutionary Perspective and the Revolutionary Party.* New York: Pathfinder Press.

Cannon, James P. 1973c. *Speeches to the Party.* New York: Pathfinder Press.

Cannon, James P. 1973d. *Notebook of an Agitator.* New York: Pathfinder Press.

Cannon, James P. 1977. *The Struggle for Socialism in the "American Century."* New York: Pathfinder Press.

Cannon, James P. 1979. *The History of American Trotskyism*. New York: Pathfinder Press.

Carlton, David L. and Peter A Coclanis. 2003. *The South, the Nation, and the World: Perspectives on Southern Economic Development*. Charlottesville: University of Virginia Press.

Caro, Niki, dir. 2005. *North Country*. Film. Warner Bros. Pictures.

Carr, E. H. 1982. *The Twilight of the Comintern, 1930–1935*. New York: Pantheon.

Carter, Dan T. 1969. *Scottsboro: A Tragedy of the American South*. Baton Rouge: Louisiana State University Press.

Carter, Dan. 1995. *The Politics of Rage: George Wallace, the Origins of the New Conservatism, and the Transformation of American Politics*. New York: Simon & Schuster.

Cary, Lorin Lee. 1968. "Adolph Germer: From Labor Agitator to Labor Professional." PhD diss., University of Wisconsin–Madison.

Cash, W. J. 1941. *The Mind of the South*. New York: A. A. Knopf.

Cassedy, J. 1992. "A Bond of Sympathy: The Life and Tragic Death of Fannie Sellins." *Labor's Heritage* 4 (4): 34–47.

Cayton, Horace R., and George Sinclair Mitchell. 1939. *Black Workers and the New Unions*. Chapel Hill: University of North Carolina Press.

Chandavarkar, Rajnarayan. 1994. *The Bombay Cotton Textile Industry, 1900–1940*. Cambridge: Cambridge University Press.

Chandavarkar, Rajnarayan. 2004. Introduction to *One Hundred Years, One Hundred Voices*, ed. Meena Menon and Neera Akarkar. Calcutta: Seagull Books.

Chandler, Alfred D. 1977. *The Visible Hand: The Managerial Revolution in American Business*. Chapel Hill: University of North Carolina Press.

Chaplin, Ralph. 1924. *The Centralia Conspiracy: The Truth About the Armistice Day Tragedy*. Chicago: General Defense Committee.

Chibber, Vivek. 2003. *Locked in Place: State-Building and Late Industrialization in India*. Chicago: University of Chicago Press.

Chibber, Vivek. 2008. "Into the Fold: The Legacy of Labour's Subordination in Post-Colonial India," In *Labour, Globalization and the State: Workers, Women and Migrants Confront Neoliberalism*, ed. Debdas Banerjee & Michael Goldfield. London: Routledge.

Choi, Jang Jip. 1989. *Labor and the Authoritarian State: Labor Unions in South Korean Manufacturing Industries, 1961–1980*. Seoul: Korea University Press.

Chumley, Cheryl K. 2013. "It's Official: Mississippi Finally Ratifies 13th Amendment Outlawing Slavery." *Washington Times*. https://www.washingtontimes.com/news/2013/feb/18/its-official-mississippi-finally-ratifies-13th-ame/. Accessed September 30, 2019.

Church, Roy and Quentin Outram. 1998. *Strikes and Solidarity: Coalfield Conflict in Britain, 1889–1966*. Cambridge: Cambridge University Press.

CIO News IV:46 November. 17, 1941.

CIO News. 1:31. July 9, 1938. 1:32:1–3.

CIO News. 1939. November 21, 1938, 1:50:2

CIO News. December 18, 1939, II:51:1,3

Claudin, Fernando. 1975. *The Communist Movement, Parts One and Two*. New York: Monthly Review Press.

Clifford, Stephanie. 2013. "U.S. Textile Plants Return, with Floors Largely Empty of People." *New York Times*, September 20.

Cochran, Bert. 1977. *Labor and Communism*. Princeton, NJ: Princeton University Press.

Cohen, Lizabeth. 1990. *Making a New Deal: Industrial Workers in Chicago, 1919–1939*. New York: Cambridge University Press.

Cohen, Robert Paul. 1987. "Revolt of the Depression Generation: America's First Mass Student Protest Movement, 1929–1940." PhD diss., University of California, Berkeley.

Cohen, Robert. 1992. "Student Movements—1930s." In *Encyclopedia of the American Left*, ed. Mari Jo Buhle, Paul Buhle, and Dan Georgakas. Urbana: University of Illinois Press.

Cohen, Robert. 1993. *When the Old Left Was Young: Student Radicals and America's First Mass Student Movement, 1929–1941*. New York: Oxford University Press.

Cole, Peter. 2018. *Dockworker Power: Race and Activism in Durban and the San Francisco Bay Area*. Urbana: University of Illinois Press.

Cole, Peter and Peter Limb. 2017. "Hooks Down! Anti-Apartheid Activism and Solidarity among Maritime Unions in Australia and the United States." *Labor History* 58 (3): 303–26.

Coles, Robert, and Harry Hughes. 1969. "Peonage in Florida." *New Republic*, July 26, 17–21.

Commons, John A. and Associates. 1935. *History of Labour in the United States*, vol. 3. New York: Macmillan.

Commons, John R. 1903. "Racial Composition of the American People: Race and Democracy." *Chautauquan* 38: 33–42.

Commons, John R. (1907) 1920. *Races and Immigrants in America*. New York: Macmillan.

Commons, John R., David J. Saposs, Helen L. Sumner, E. B. Mittelman, Henry E. Hoagland, John B. Andrews, Selig Perlman, Don D. Lescohier, Elizabeth Brandeis Raushenbush, and Philip Taft. 1918. *History of Labour in the United States*, vol. 2. New York: Macmillan.

Conquest, Robert. 1973. *The Great Terror*. New York: Collier.

Convention Proceedings. 1919. American Federation of Labor 39th Annual Convention, June 9–23, Atlantic City, NJ.

Convention Proceedings. 1927. American Federation of Labor 47th Annual Convention, October, Los Angeles.

Convention Proceedings. 1928. American Federation of Labor 48th Annual Convention, New Orleans, November 19–28

Convention Proceedings. 1929. American Federation of Labor 49th Annual Convention, October 7–18, Toronto, Canada.

Convention Proceedings. 1938. American Federation of Labor 47th Annual Convention.

Convention Proceedings. 1938. Congress of Industrial Organizations, 1st Constitutional Convention, November 14–18, Pittsburgh.

Convention Proceedings. 1940. Congress of Industrial Organizations, 3rd Constitutional Convention.

Convention Proceedings. 1941. Congress of Industrial Organizations, 4th Constitutional Convention, November 17–22, Detroit, MI.

Convention Proceedings. 1944. Congress of Industrial Organizations, 7th Constitutional Convention, November 21–24, Chicago.

Corbin, David A. 1976."'Frank Keeney Is Our Leader, and We Shall Not Be Moved': Rank-and-File Leadership in the West Virginia Coal Fields." In *Essays in Southern Labor History: Selected Papers, Southern Labor History Conference*, ed. Gary M. Fink and Merl E. Reed. Westport, CT: Greenwood Press.

Corbin, David. 1981. *Life, Work, and Rebellion in the Coal Field: The Southern West Virginia Miners, 1880–1922*. Urbana: University of Illinois Press.

Corbin, David. 2011. *Gun Thugs, Rednecks, and Radicals: A Documentary History of the West Virginia Mine Wars*. Oakland: PM Press.

Cruse, Harold. 1967. *The Crisis of the Negro Intellectual*. New York: Morrow.

Curtin, Mary Ellen. 2000. *Black Prisoners and Their World: Alabama, 1865–1900*. Charlottesville: University Press of Virginia.

Dahl, Robert and Charles Lindblom. (1953) 2017. *Politics, Economics, and Welfare*. London: Routledge.

Daniel, Cletus E. 2001. *Culture of Misfortune: An Interpretive History of Textile Unionism in the United States*. Ithaca, NY: ILR Press.

Daniel, Pete. 1970a. "Peonage in the New South." PhD diss., University of Maryland.

Daniel, Pete. 1970b. "Up from Slavery and Down to Peonage: The Alonzo Bailey Case." *Journal of American History* 57 (3): 654–70.

Daniel, Pete. 1972. *The Shadow of Slavery: Peonage in the South, 1901–1969*. Urbana: University of Illinois Press.

Darby, Michael R. 1976. "Three-and-a-Half Million Unemployed Employees Have Been Mislaid: Or, an Explanation of Unemployment, 1933–1941." *Journal of Political Economy* 84: 1.

D'Attilio, Robert. 1990. "The Sacco and Vanzetti Case." In *Encyclopedia of the American Left*, ed. Mari Jo Buhle, Paul Buhle, and Dan Georgakas. New York: Garland.

Davin, Eric Leif. 2000. "Blue Collar Democracy: Class War and Political Revolution in Western Pennsylvania, 1932–1937." *Pennsylvania History* 67 (2, Spring): 241–97.

Davin, Eric Leif. 2010. *Crucible of Freedom: Workers' Democracy in the Industrial Heartland, 1914–1960*. Lanham, MD: Lexington Books.

Davin, Eric Leif and Staughton Lynd. 1979–80. "Picket Line and Ballot Box: The Forgotten Legacy of the Local Labor Party Movement, 1932–1936." *Radical History Review* 22 (Winter): 43–63.

Davis, Horace B. 1933. *Labor and Steel*. New York: International.

Davis, John, ed. 2004. *Sacco and Vanzetti*. Melbourne: Ocean Press.

Davis, Lance E. 1972. *American Economic Growth: An Economist's History of the United States*. New York: Harper & Row.

Davis, Lance E., Richard A. Easterlin, William N. Parker, Dorothy S. Brady, Albert Fishlow, Robert E. Gallman, Stanley Lebergott, Robert E. Lipsey, Douglass C. North, Nathan Rosenberg, et al. 1972. *American Economic Growth: An Economist's History of the United States*. New York: Harper & Row.

Dawley, Alan. 1991. *Struggles for Justice: Social Responsibility and the Liberal State*. Cambridge, MA: Belknap Press of Harvard University Press.

Death Penalty Information Center. 2017. "Facts About the Death Penalty." https://deathpenaltyinfo.org/documents/FactSheet.pdf.

Debs, Eugene V. 1905. "Speech at the Founding of the IWW." Founding Convention of the Industrial Workers of the World.

Debs, Eugene V. 1921. *Industrial Unionism*. New York: New York Labor News Co.

De Caux, Len. 1970. *Labor Radical: From the Wobblies to CIO—A Personal History*. Boston: Beacon Press.

De Leon, Daniel. 1921. *Industrial Unionism*. New York: New York Labor News Co.

Derickson, Alan. 1996. "The Role of the United Mine Workers in the Prevention of Work-Related Respiratory Disease, 1890–1968." In *The United Mine Workers of America: A Model of Industrial Solidarity?*, ed. John H. M. Laslett, 224–38. University Park: Penn State University Press.

Derickson, Alan. 1998. *Black Lung: Anatomy of a Public Health Disaster*. Ithaca, NY: Cornell University Press.

Devinatz, Victor G. 2007. "A Reevaluation of the Trade Union Unity League, 1929–1934." *Science & Society* 71 (1): 33–58.

Devinatz, Victor G. 2015. "Right-to-Work Laws, the Southernization of U.S. Labor Relations and the U.S. Trade Union Movement's Decline." *Labor Studies Journal* 40 (4): 297–318.

Deyo, Frederic C. 1989. *"Beneath the Miracle": Labor Subordination in the New Asian Industrialism*. Berkeley: University of California Press.

Dickerson, C. Dennis. 1986. *Out of the Crucible*. Albany, NY: SUNY Press.

Dimitrov, Georgi. 1968. *Leipzig, 1933*. Sofia: Sofia Press.

Dimitrov, Georgi. 1972. *Selected Works in Three Volumes*. Sofia: Sofia Press.

Dimitrov, Georgi. 1975. *The United Front*. San Francisco: Proletarian.

Dinwiddie, Robert Carlton. 1980. "The International Woodworkers of America and Southern Laborers, 1937–1945." MA thesis, Georgia State University.

Dobb, Maurice. 1960. *Soviet Economic Development Since 1917*. London: Routledge.

Dobbs, Farrel. 2004. *Teamster Rebellion*. New York: Pathfinder.

Douty, H. M. 1946. "Development of Trade Unionism in the South." *Monthly Labor Review* 63 (October): 560–66.

Drake, St. Clair. 1945. *Black Metropolis: A Study of Negro Life in a Northern City*. 2 vols. New York: Harcourt.

Draper, Hal. 1967. "The Student Movement of the Thirties: A Political History." In *As We Saw the Thirties: Essays on Social and Political Movements of a Decade*, ed. Rita James Simon. Urbana: University of Illinois Press.

Draper, Theodore. 1957. *The Roots of American Communism*. New York: Viking.

Draper, Theodore. 1963. *American Communism and Soviet Russia*. New York: Viking.

Draper, Theodore. 1972. "Communists and Miners, 1928–1933." *Dissent* 19: 371–92.

Dreiser, Theodore and National Committee for the Defense of Political Prisoners. 1932. *Harlan Miners Speak: Report on Terrorism in the Kentucky Coal Fields*. New York: Harcourt.

Drobney, Jeffrey A. 1995. "Lumbermen and Log Sawyers: The Transformation of Life and Labor in the North Florida Timber Industry, 1830–1920." PhD diss., West Virginia University.

Drobney, Jeffrey A. 1997. *Lumbermen and Log Sawyers: Life, Labor, and Culture in the North Florida Timber Industry, 1830–1930*. Macon, GA: Mercer University Press.

Dubofsky, Melvyn. 1969. *We Shall Be All: A History of the Industrial Workers of the World*. Chicago: Quadrangle Books.

Dubofsky, Melvyn. 1979. "Not So Turbulent Years: Another Look at the American 1930's." *Amerikastudien* 24: 1–20.

Dubofsky, Melvyn and Warren R. Van Tine. 1977. *John L. Lewis: A Biography*. New York: Quadrangle.

Du Bois, W.E.B. (1935) 1998. *Black Reconstruction in America, 1860–1880*. New York: Free Press.

Dunbar, Anthony P. 1981. *Against the Grain: Southern Radicals and Prophets, 1929–1959*. Charlottesville: University Press of Virginia.

Dunlop, John. 1982. Interview in *Fortune*, September 20, 98–108.

Dunn, Robert W. and Jack Hardy. 1931. *Labor and Textiles: A Study of Cotton and Wool Manufacturing*. New York: International.

Dunne, William F. 1929. *Gastonia, Citadel of the Class Struggle in the New South*. New York: National Textile Workers Union, Workers Library Publishers.

Dyson, Lowell K. 1982. *Red Harvest: The Communist Party and American Farmers*. Lincoln: University of Nebraska Press.

Edwards, P. K. 1981. *Strikes in the United States, 1881–1974*. New York: St. Martin's Press.

Egolf, Jeremy R. 1985. "The Limits of Shop Floor Struggle: Workers vs. the Bedaux System at Willapa Harbor Mills, 1933–1935." *Labor History* 26 (2): 195–229.

Emspak, Frank. 1972. "The Break-up of the Congress of Industrial Organizations (CIO), 1945–1950." Ph.D. diss., University of Wisconsin.

Engels, Friedrich. (1845) 2009. *The Condition of the Working Class in England*. Oxford: Oxford University Press.

Epstein, Melech. 1953. *Jewish Labor in U.S.A., 1914–1952*, vol. 2. New York: Trade Union Sponsoring Committee.

Farhang, Sean and Ira Katznelson. 2005. "The Southern Imposition: Congress and Labor in the New Deal and Fair Deal." *Studies in American Political Development* 19: 1–30.

Faue, Elizabeth. 1991. *Community of Suffering and Struggle: Women, Men, and the Labor Movement in Minneapolis, 1915–1945*. Chapel Hill: University of North Carolina Press.

Federal Bureau of Investigation. 1995. "Membership of the Communist Party USA, 1919–1954." https://ia902709.us.archive.org/24/items/foia_FBI_Monograph-Membership_of_CP USA_1919-1954/FBI_Monograph-Membership_of_CPUSA_1919-1954.pdf.

Feeley, Dianne. 1983. "In Unity There Is Strength: The Struggle of the Unemployed Throughout the 1930s." Unpublished paper in possession of the author.

Ferrell, Geoffrey. 1982. "The Brotherhood of Timber Workers and the Southern Labor Trust, 1910–1914." PhD diss., University of Texas at Austin.

Feurer, Rosemary. 1996. "The Nutpickers' Union, 1933–34: Crossing the Boundaries of Community and Workplace." In *"We Are All leaders": The Alternative Unionism of the Early 1930s*, ed. Staughton Lynd. Urbana: University of Illinois Press.

Feurer, Rosemary. 2006. *Radical Unionism in the Midwest, 1900–1950*. Urbana: University of Illinois Press.

Filippelli, Ronald L. and Mark D. McColloch. 1995. *Cold War in the Working Class: The Rise and Decline of the United Electrical Workers*. Albany, NY: SUNY Press.

Fink, Leon. 1985. *Workingmen's Democracy: The Knights of Labor and American Politics*. Urbana: University of Illinois Press.

Finley, Joseph E. 1972. *The Corrupt Kingdom: The Rise and Fall of the United Mine Workers*. New York: Simon & Schuster.

Fischer, Nick. 2016. *Spider Web: The Birth of American Anticommunism*. Urbana: University of Illinois Press.

Fishback, Price V. 1996. "The Miner's Work Environment: Safety and Company Towns in the Early 1900s." In *The United Mine Workers of America: A Model of Industrial Solidarity?*, ed. John H. M. Laslett, 201–23. University Park, Penn State University Press.

Fitch, Robert. 2006. *Solidarity for Sale: How Corruption Destroyed the Labor Movement and Undermined America's Promise*. New York: PublicAffairs.

Fogel, Robert William and Stanley L. Engerman. 1974. *Time on the Cross: The Economics of American Negro Slavery*. Boston: Little, Brown.

Folsom, Franklin. 1991. *Impatient Armies of the Poor: The Story of Collective Action of the Unemployed, 1808–1942*. Niwot: University of Colorado Press.

Foner, Eric. 1988. *Reconstruction: America's Unfinished Revolution, 1863–1877*. New York: Harper & Row.

Foner, Philip S. 1947. *History of the Labor Movement in the United States*, vol. 1: *From Colonial Times to the Founding of the American Federation of Labor*. New York: International.

Foner, Philip. 1950. *The Fur and Leather Workers Union: A Story of Dramatic Struggles and Achievements*. Newark, NJ: Nordan Press.

Foner, Philip S. 1955. *History of the Labor Movement in the United States*, vol. 2: *From the Founding of the American Federation of Labor to the Emergence of American Imperialism*. New York: International.

Foner, Philip S. 1965. *History of the Labor Movement in the United States*, vol. 4: *Industrial Workers of the World*. New York: International.

Foner, Philip S. 1979. *Women and the American Labor Movement: From World War I to the Present*, vol. 2. New York: Free Press.

Foner, Philip S. 1991. *History of the Labor Movement in the United States*, vol. 9: *The T.U.E.L. to the End of the Gompers Era*. New York: International.

Foner, Philip S. 1994. *History of the Labor Movement in the United States*, vol. 10: *The T.U.E.L., 1925–1929*. New York: International.

Foster, William Z. 1920. *The Great Steel Strike and Its Lessons*. New York: B. W. Huebsch.

Foster, William Z. 1927. *Misleaders of Labor*. New York: Trade Union Education League.

Foster, William Z. 1932. *Toward Soviet America*. New York: Coward-McCann.

Foster, William Z. 1936. *Organizing Methods in the Steel Industry*. New York: Workers Library.

Foster, William Z. 1937. *From Bryan to Stalin*. New York: International.

Foster, William Z. 1952. *History of the Communist Party of the United States*. New York: International.

Fraser, Steven. 1991. *Labor Will Rule: Sidney Hillman and the Rise of American Labor*. New York: Free Press.

Freeman, Richard B. and James L. Medoff. 1984. *What Do Unions Do?* New York: Basic Books.

Fry, Richard. 2010. "Fighting for Survival: Coal Miners and the Struggle Over Health and Safety in the United States, 1968–1988." PhD diss., Wayne State University.

Gabin, Nancy F. 1990. *Feminism in the Labor Movement: Women and the United Auto Workers, 1935–1975*. Ithaca, NY: Cornell University Press.

Galbraith, John Kenneth. 1988. *The Great Crash*. Boston: Houghton Mifflin.

Galenson, Walter. 1960. *The CIO Challenge to the AFL: A History of the American Labor Movement, 1935–1941*. Cambridge, MA: Harvard University Press.

Galenson, Walter. 1983. *The United Brotherhood of Carpenters: The First Hundred Years.* Cambridge: Harvard University Press.

Gallup. 2012. "State of the States: Religion." http://www.gallup.com/poll/125066/State- States. aspx?ref=interactive. Accessed January 12, 2014.

Ganzel, Bill. 2003. "Farming in the 1930s." Wessels Living History Farm. Lincoln, NE: Ganzel Group Communications. http://www.livinghistoryfarm.org/farminginthe30s/money_ 05.html. Accessed October 31, 2016.

Garcia, Mario T. 1990. "Border Proletarians: Mexican-Americans and the International Union of Mine, Mill, and Smelter Workers, 1939–1946." In *Labor Divided: Race and Ethnicity in United States Labor Struggles, 1835–1960,* ed. Robert Asher and Charles Stephenson. Albany, NY: SUNY Press.

Garlock, Jonathan. 1974. "A Structural Analysis of the Knights of Labor." PhD diss., University of Rochester.

Garrison, Joseph Yates. 1977. "Paul Revere Christopher: Southern Labor Leader, 1910–1974." PhD diss., Georgia State University.

Gates, John. 1958. *The Story of an American Communist.* New York: Thomas Nelson.

Gellman, Erik S. 2012. *Death Blow to Jim Crow: The National Negro Congress and the Rise of Militant Civil Rights.* Chapel Hill: The University of North Carolina Press.

Giardina, Denise. 1987. *Storming Heaven: A Novel.* New York: Norton.

Gilmore, Glenda Elizabeth. 2008. *Defying Dixie: The Radical Roots of Civil Rights, 1919–1950.* New York: W. W. Norton.

Gilpin, Toni. 1992. "Left by Themselves: A History of the United Farm Equipment and Metal Workers Union, 1938–1955." 2 vols. PhD diss., Yale University.

Gitlow, Benjamin. 1940. *I Confess: The Truth About American Communism.* New York: E. P. Dutton.

Glaberman, Martin. 1980. *Wartime Strikes: The Struggle against the No-Strike Pledge in the UAW During World War II.* Detroit, MI: Bewick Editions.

Glazer, Nathan. 1961. *The Social Basis of American Communism.* New York: Harcourt.

Golden, Clinton S. and Harold J. Ruttenberg. 1942. *The Dynamics of Industrial Democracy.* Harper and Brothers.

Goldfield, Michael. 1980. "The Decline of the Communist Party and the Black Question in the US: Harry Haywood's Black Bolshevik." *Review of Radical Political Economics* 12 (1): 44–63.

Goldfield, Michael. 1985. "Recent Historiography of the Communist Party U.S.A." In *The Year Left: An American Socialist Yearbook,* ed. Mike Davis, F. Pfeil, and Michael Sprinker. London: Verso/New Left Books.

Goldfield, Michael. 1987. *The Decline of Organized Labor in the United States.* Chicago: University of Chicago Press.

Goldfield, Michael. 1989a. "Public Sector Union Growth and Public Policy." *Policy Studies Journal* 18: 404–20.

Goldfield, Michael. 1989b. "Worker Insurgency, Radical Organization, and New Deal Labor Legislation." *American Political Science Review* 83 (4): 1257–82.

Goldfield, Michael. 1990a. "Reply to Critics." In "Explaining New Deal Labor Policy," by Theda Skocpol, Kenneth Finegold, and Michael Goldfield. *American Political Science Review* 84 (4): 1297–1315.

Goldfield, Michael. 1990b. "Public Sector Union Growth, Do the Laws Matter?" Unpublished manuscript.

Goldfield, Michael. 1993. "Race and the CIO: The Possibilities for Racial Egalitarianism During the 1930s and 1940s." *International Labor and Working-Class History* (44): 1–32.

Goldfield, Michael. 1994. "Race and the CIO: Reply to Critics." *International Labor and Working-Class History* 46: 142–60.

Goldfield, Michael. 1997a. "On Walter Reuther: Legends and Lessons." *Against the Current* 67.

Goldfield, Michael. 1997b. *The Color Politics: Race and the Mainsprings of American Politics.* New York: New Press.

Goldfield, Michael. 1998. "Lipset's Union Democracy After 40 Years." *Extensions* (Spring): 22–26.

Goldfield, Michael. 2001. "Class, Race, and Labor Organization in the United States of America." In *Race in 21st Century America*, ed. Curtis Stokes, Theresa Melendez, and Genice Rhodes-Reed. East Lansing: Michigan State University Press.

Goldfield, Michael. 2008. "The Impact of Globalization and Neoliberalism on the Decline of Organized Labour in the United States." In *Labour, Globalization, and the State: Workers, Women and Migrants Confront Neoliberalism*, ed. Debdas Banerjee and Michael Goldfield. London: Routledge.

Goldfield, Michael. 2009. "Communist Party of the United States of America (CPUSA)." In *International Encyclopedia of Revolution and Protest*, ed. Immanuel Ness. Oxford: Blackwell Reference Online.

Goldfield, Michael and Amy Bromsen. 2013. "The Changing Landscape of US Unions in Historical and Theoretical Perspective." *Annual Review of Political Science* 16: 231–57.

Goldfield, Michael and Alan Gilbert. 1995. "The Limits of Rational Choice Theory." In *Rational Choice Marxism*, ed. Terrell Carver and Paul Thomas. London: Macmillan Press.

Goldfield, Michael and Cody R. Melcher. 2019. "The Myth of Section 7(a): Worker Militancy, Progressive Labor Legislation, and the Coal Miners." *Labor: Studies in Working-Class History* 16 (4): 49–65.

Goldfield, Michael, and Melvin Rothenberg. 1980. *The Myth of Capitalism Reborn*. San Francisco: Soviet Union Study Project.

Goldstein, Robert Justin. 1978. "Political Repression in Modern America, 1870 to Present." PhD diss., University of Chicago.

Goodnow, Marc N. 1915. "Turpentine: Impression of Convicts' Camps of Florida." *International Socialist Review* 15: 721–34.

Googe, George. 1928. *American Federationist* 35 (November): 13–26.

Googe, George. 1941. *American Federationist* 48 (3, March): 20–22.

Gowaskie, Joe. 1976. "From Conflict to Cooperation: John Mitchell and Bituminous Coal Operators, 1898–1908." *Historian: A Journal of History* 39 (4): 669–88.

Graham, Richard. 1981. "Slavery and Economic Development: Brazil and the United States South in the Nineteenth Century." *Comparative Studies in Society and History* 23 (4): 620–55.

Gramsci, Antonio. 1977. *Selections from Political Writings, 1910–1920*. Trans. J. Matthews, ed. Q. Hoare. London: Lawrence and Wishart.

Green, James R. 1973. "The Brotherhood of Timber Workers, 1910–1913: A Radical Response to Industrial Capitalism in the Southern U.S.A." *Past and Present* 60 (August): 161–200.

Green, James. 2015. *The Devil Is Here in These Hills: West Virginia's Coal Miners and Their Battle for Freedom*. New York: Atlantic Monthly Press.

Green, William. 1940. *American Federationist* 47 (3, March).

Greenall, Jack. n.d. "The I.W.A. Fiasco: A Political Analysis of a Strange Event." Vancouver, BC: Progressive Workers Movement, University of Oregon, International Woodworkers of America, box 275, History.

Greenlee, Sam. 1969. *The Spook Who Sat by the Door*. New York: Richard W. Baron Publishing.

Griffey, Trevor. 2013. "Was Herbert Hill, NAACP's Labor Secretary, an FBI Informer?" January 25. LAWCHA, Labor Online. http://lawcha.org/wordpress/2013/01/25/was-herbert-hill-naacps-labor-secretary-an-fbi-inf ormer/#comment-376. Accessed May 10, 2019.

Gross, James A. 1981. *The Reshaping of the National labor Relations Board*. Albany, NU: SUNY Press.

Hall, Covington. 1912a. "Negroes against Whites." *International Socialist Review* 13 (4, October).

Hall, Covington. 1912b. "Revolt of the Timber Workers." *International Socialist Review* 13 (1, July).

Hall, Covington. 1912c. "The Victory of the Lumberjacks." *International Socialist Review* 13 (6, December).

Hall, Covington. 1999. *Labor Struggles in the Deep South and Other Writings*. Chicago: Charles H. Kerr.

Hall, Jacquelyn Dowd. 1987. *Like a Family: The Making of a Southern Cotton Mill World*. Chapel Hill: University of North Carolina Press.

Halpern, Martin. 1988. *UAW Politics in the Cold War Era*. Albany, NY: SUNY Press.

Halpern, Rick. 1989. "'Black and White, Unite and Fight': Race and Labor in Meatpacking, 1904–1948." PhD diss., University of Pennsylvania.

Halpern, Rick. 1991. "Interracial Unions in the Southwest: Fort Worth's Packinghouse Workers, 1936–1941." In *Organized Labor in the Twentieth Century South*, ed. Robert H. Zieger, 158–82. Knoxville: University of Tennessee Press.

Halpern, Rick. 1997. *Down on the Killing Floor: Black and White Workers in Chicago's Packinghouse, 1904–1954*. Urbana: University of Illinois Press.

Harbison, Frederick H. 1940. "Labor Relations in the Iron and Steel Industry, 1936 to 1939." PhD diss., Princeton University.

Hardman, J. B. S. and Len Giovannitti. 1948. *Sidney Hillman: Labor Statesman, a Story in Pictures and Text of the Man and the Amalgamated*. Intro. by J.B.S. Harman. New York: Amalgamated Clothing Workers of America.

Harris, Herbert. 1940. *Labor's Civil War*. New York: Knopf.

Harris, Wess. 2012. *Dead Ringers: Why Miners March*. Gay, WV: Appalachian Community Services.

Harris, William Hamilton. 1977. *Keeping the Faith: A. Philip Randolph, Milton P. Webster, and the Brotherhood of Sleeping Car Porters, 1925–37*. Urbana: University of Illinois Press.

Harrod, Jeffrey. 1987. *Power, Production, and the Unprotected Worker*. New York: Columbia University Press.

Haverty-Stacke, Donna T. 2016. *Trotskyists on Trial: Free Speech and Political Persecution Since the Age of FDR*. New York: New York University Press.

Hawthorn, Geoffrey. 1991. *Plausible Worlds: Possibility and Understanding in History and the Social Sciences*. Cambridge: Cambridge University Press.

Haywood, Allan S. 1946. "We Propose to Unionize Labor in the South." *Labor and Nation* (April–May): 35.

Haywood, Harry. 1948. *Negro Liberation*. New York: International.

Haywood, Harry. (1958) 1959. "For a Revolutionary Position on the Negro Question." https://www.marxists.org/history/erol/1956-1960/haywood02.htm.

Haywood, Harry. 1978. *Black Bolshevik*. Chicago: Liberator Press.

Haywood, William D. 1912. "Timber Workers and Timber Wolves." *International Socialist Review* 13 (2, August).

Healey, Dorothy and Maurice Isserman. 1990. *Dorothy Healey Remembers: A Life in the American Communist Party*. New York: Oxford University Press.

Hegel, Georg Friedrich Wilhelm. (1819) 1983. *Philosophie des Rechts*. Frankfurt: Suhrkamp.

Heideman, Paul M. 2018. *Class Struggle and the Color Line: American Socialism and the Race Question, 1900–1930*. Chicago: Haymarket.

Hennen, John. 2017. "Van Bittner." *West Virginia Encyclopedia*. https://www.wvencyclopedia.org/print/Article/503.

Herndon, Angelo. 1969. *Let Me Live*. New York: Arno Press.

Hevener, John W. 1978. *Which Side Are You On? The Harlan County Coal Miners, 1931–39*.

Hill, Herbert. 2002. "Race and the Steelworkers Union: White Privilege and Black Struggle, Review Essay of Judith Stein's, Running Steel, Running America." *New Politics* 8 (4): 174–207.

Hillquit, Morris. 1934. *Loose Leaves from a Busy Life*. New York: Rand School Press.

Hinshaw, John. 2002. *Steel and Steelworkers*. Albany, NY: SUNY Press.

Hirschman. Albert O. 1970. *Exit, Voice, and Loyalty: Responses to Decline in Firms, Organizations, and States*. Cambridge, MA: Harvard University Press.

Hobsbawm, Eric J. 1964. *Labouring Men*. Garden City, NY: Doubleday.

Hobsbawm, Eric J. 1987. *Age of Empire, 1875–1914*. New York: Pantheon Books.

Hodges, James. 1986. *New Deal Labor Policy and the Southern Cotton Textile Industry, 1933–1941*. Knoxville: University of Tennessee Press.

Hogan, William Thomas. 1971. *Economic History of the Iron and Steel Industry in the United States*. 5 vols. Lexington, MA: Heath.

Holiday, Billie with William Duffy. 1956. *Lady Sings the Blues: The Searing Autobiography of an American Musical Legend*. New York: Penguin Books.

Holmes, George K. 1893. "The Peons of the South." *Annals of the American Academy of Political and Social Science* 4: 65–74.

Honey, Michael K. 1993. *Southern Labor and Black Civil Rights: Organizing Memphis Workers*. Urbana: University of Illinois Press.

Honey, Michael K. 2013. *Sharecropper's Troubadour: John L. Handcox, the Southern Tenant Farmers' Union, and the African American Song Tradition*. New York: Palgrave Macmillan.

Horne, Gerald. 2016. *Paul Robeson: The Artist as Revolutionary*. London: Pluto Press.

Horowitz, Roger. 1990. "The Path Not Taken: A Social History of Industrial Unionism in Meatpacking, 1930–1960." PhD diss., University of Wisconsin–Madison.

Horowitz, Roger. 1997. *Negro and White, Unite and Fight! A Social History of Industrial Unionism in Meatpacking, 1930–90*. Urbana: University of Illinois Press.

Howard, John C. 1970. "The Negro in the Lumber Industry." In *Negro Employment in Southern Industry, Report on the Racial Policies of American Industry*, ed. Herbert Northrup and Richard Rowan. Philadelphia: Wharton School of Finance and Commerce, Industrial Research Unit.

Howard, Walter T. 2001. "The National Miners Union: Communists and Miners in the Pennsylvania Anthracite, 1928–1931." *Pennsylvania Magazine of History and Biography* 125 (1/2): 91–124.

Howard, Walter T. 2007. *Black Communists Speak on Scottsboro: A Documentary History*. Philadelphia: Temple University Press.

Hoxie, Robert. (1915) 1966. *Trade Unionism in the United States*. New York: Russell & Russell.

Hudson, Hosea. 1972. *Black Worker in the Deep South: A Personal Record*. New York: International.

Hudson, Hosea and Nell Irvin Painter. 1979. *The Narrative of Hosea Hudson: His Life as a Negro Communist in the South*. Cambridge, MA: Harvard University Press.

Hudson, Roy. 1939. "The Path of Labor's United Action," *Communist* 18 (October): 10.

Huff, William Henry. 1944. "The New Charter of Slavery." *National Bar Journal* 2: 65–69.

Hughes, Cicero Alvin. 1982. "Toward a Black United Front: The National Negro Congress Movement." PhD diss., Ohio University.

Hughes, Jonathan R. T. 1990. *American Economic History*. 3rd ed. Glenview, IL: Scott Foresman.

Huntley, Horace. 1977. "Iron Ore Miners and Mine Mill in Alabama: 1933–1952." PhD diss., University of Pittsburgh.

Hyman, Owen James. 2012. "Corporate Organization and Social Control in the New South: Bogalusa, Louisiana, 1902–1980." MA thesis, Southeastern Louisiana University.

Hyman, Richard. 1973. *Marxism and the Sociology of Trade Unions*. London: Pluto Press.

ILWU. 2014. "Death of Nelson Mandela Recalls Decades of ILWU Support for Anti-Apartheid Struggle." *Dispatcher*. https://www.ilwu.org/death-of-nelson-mandela-recalls-decades-of-ilwu-support-for-anti-apartheid-struggle/. Accessed May 10, 2019.

Industrial Workers of the World. 1916. "Preamble and Constitution of the Industrial Workers of the World, Adopted Chicago, 1905." Chicago: Industrial Workers of the World.

Industrial Workers of the World. (1923) 2014. "I.W.W. Songs." 19th ed. [Little Red Songbook]. Chicago: Industrial Workers of the World.

Industrial Workers of the World. 2014. *Songs to Fan the Flames of Discontent: A Facsimile Reprint of the Nineteenth Edition (1923) of the 'Little Red Song Book*. Oakland, CA: PM Press.

Interchurch World Movement of North America, Bureau of Industrial Research. 1920. *Report on the Steel Strike of 1919*. New York: Harcourt, Brace and Howe.

Interchurch World Movement of North America, Bureau of Industrial Research. 1921. *Public Opinion and the Steel Strike: Supplementary Reports of the Investigators to the Commission of Inquiry, the Interchurch World Movement*. New York: Harcourt, Brace and Company.

Irons, Janet Christine. 2000. *Testing the New Deal: The General Textile Strike of 1934 in the American South*. Urbana: University of Illinois Press.

Isserman, Maurice. 1982. *Which Side Were You On?* Middletown, CT: Wesleyan University Press.

Jackson, Dan. 1953. "The I.W.A." MA thesis, University of California, Berkeley.

Jaffe, Philip. 1975. *The Rise and Fall of American Communism.* New York: Horizon.

James, Lee M. 1946. "Restrictive Agreements and Practices in the Lumber Industry, 1880–1939." *Southern Economics Journal* 13 (2): 115–25.

Jensen, Vernon H. 1945. *Lumber and Labor.* New York: Farrar & Rinehart.

Jensen, Vernon H. 1954. *Nonferrous Metals Industry Unionism, 1932–1954.* Ithaca, NY: Cornell University.

Jeszeck, Charles A. 1982. "Plant Dispersion and Collective Bargaining in the Rubber Tire Industry." PhD diss., University of California, Berkeley.

Johanningsmeier, Edward P. 1994. *Forging American Communism: The Life of William Z. Foster.* Princeton, NJ: Princeton University Press.

Johnson, Clyde. 1977. "CIO Oil Workers' Organizing Campaign in Texas, 1942–1943." In *Essays in Southern Labor History: Selected Papers, Southern Labor History Conference, 1976,* ed. Gary M. Fink and Merl E. Reed. Westport. CT: Greenwood Press.

Johnson, Timothy V. 2011. "'We Are Illegal Here': The Communist Party, Self-determination and the Alabama Share Croppers Union." *Science and Society* 75: 454–79.

Jones, G. T. 1933. *Increasing Return.* Cambridge: Cambridge University Press.

Jones, LeRoi. 1963. *Blues People: Negro Experience in White America and the Music That Developed from It.* New York: William Morrow.

Jones, William P. 2000. "Black Workers and the CIO's Turn Toward Racial Liberalism: Operation Dixie and the North Carolina Lumber Industry, 1946–1953." *Labor History* 41 (3): 279–306.

Jones, William P. 2005. *The Tribe of Black Ulysses: African American Lumber Workers in the Jim Crow South.* Urbana: University of Illinois Press.

Josephson, Matthew. 1952. *Sidney Hillman, Statesman of American Labor.* Garden City, NY: Doubleday.

Joshi, Chitra. 2003. *Lost Worlds: Indian Labour and Its Forgotten Histories.* Delhi: Permanent Black; Bangalore: Orient Longman.

Kaboub, Fadhel. 2013. "The End of Neoliberalism? An Institutional Analysis of the Arab Uprisings." *Journal of Economic Issues* 47 (2): 533–44.

Kahneman, Daniel. 2011. *Thinking, Fast and Slow.* New York: Farrar, Straus and Giroux.

Kampelman, Max M. 1957. *The Communist Party vs. the C.I.O.: A Study in Power Politics.* New York: Praeger.

Kane, Nancy Frances. 1988. *Textiles in Transition: Technology, Wages, and Industry Relocation in the U.S. Textile Industry, 1880–1930.* Westport, CT: Greenwood Press.

Katznelson, Ira. 2005. *When Affirmative Action Was White: An Untold History of Racial Inequality in Twentieth-Century America.* New York: W. W. Norton.

Katznelson, Ira. 2013. *Fear Itself: The New Deal and the Origins of Our Time.* New York: W. W. Norton.

Katznelson, Ira, Kim Geiger, and Daniel Kryder. 1993. "Limiting Liberalism: The Southern Veto in Congress, 1933–1950." *Political Science Quarterly* 108 (2): 283–306.

Keeran, Roger. 1974. "Communists and Auto Workers: The Struggle for a Union, 1919– 1941." PhD diss., University of Wisconsin–Madison.

Keeran, Roger. 1980. *The Communist Party and the Auto Workers Unions.* Bloomington: Indiana University Press.

Kelley, Robin D. G. 1990. *Hammer and Hoe: Alabama Communists During the Great Depression.* Chapel Hill: University of North Carolina Press.

Kelly, Brian. 1999. "Having It Their Way: Alabama Coal Operators and the Search for Docile Labor, 1908." In *It Is Union and Liberty: Alabama Coal Miners and the UMW,* ed. Edwin L. Brown and Colin J. Davis, 38–61. Tuscaloosa: University of Alabama Press.

Kendrick, John W. and Elliot S. Grossman. 1980. *Productivity in the United States: Trends and Cycles.* Baltimore: Johns Hopkins University Press.

Kendrick, John W., Kyu Sik Lee, and Jean Lomask. 1976. "National Wealth of the United States by Major Sector and Industry." Division of Economic Research, Conference Board.

Kennedy, Stetson. 1952. *New York Times*, November 5, 1952.

Kerr, Clark and Abraham Siegel. 1954a. "The Isolated Mass and the Integrated Individual: An International Analysis of the Inter-Industry Propensity to Strike." In *Industrial Conflict*, ed. Arthur Kornhauser, Robert Dubin, and Arthur Ross. New York: McGraw-Hill.

Kerr, Clark and Abraham Siegel. 1954b. *The Interindustry Propensity to Strike: An International Comparison*. New York: McGraw-Hill.

Key, V. O. 1984. *Southern Politics in State and Nation*. New ed. Knoxville: University of Tennessee Press.

Kienzle, Rick. 2012. "Sixteen Tons: The Story Behind the Legend." http://ernieford.com/SIXTEENTONS.html. Accessed January 16, 2014.

Kimeldorf, Howard Alex. 1985. "Reds or Rackets: Sources of Radical and Conservative Union Leadership on the Waterfront (Pacific Coast, Longshoremen, New York City)." PhD diss., University of California, Los Angeles.

Kimeldorf, Howard. 1988. *Reds or Rackets? The Making of Radical and Conservative Unions on the Waterfront*. Berkeley: University of California Press.

Kimeldorf, Howard. 1999. *Battling for American Labor: Wobblies, Craft Workers, and the Making of the Union Movement*. Berkeley: University of California Press.

Kirby, Jack T. 1983. "The Southern Exodus, 1910–1960: A Primer for Historians." *Journal of Southern History* 49 (4): 585–600.

Klehr, Harvey. 1984. *The Heyday of American Communism: The Depression Decade*. New York: Basic Books.

Klehr, Harvey, John Earl Haynes, and Kirill Mihailovic Anderson. 1998. *The Soviet World of American Communism*. New Haven, CT: Yale University Press.

Kling, Joseph Milton. 1983. "Making the Revolution—Maybe . . . Deradicalization and Stalinism in the American Communist Party, 1928–1935." PhD diss., City University of New York.

Klinkner, Philip A. 1992. "Race and the Republican Party: The Rise of the Southern Strategy in the Republican National Committee, 1960–1964." Presented at the 1992 Annual Meeting of the American Political Science Association, Chicago.

Koeltgen, Ewald. 1913. "I.W.W. Convention." *International Socialist Review* 14.

Kollros, James Carl. 1998. "Creating a Steel Workers Union in the Calumet Region, 1933 to 1945." PhD diss., University of Illinois at Chicago.

Korstad, Robert R. 2003. *Civil Rights Unionism: Tobacco Workers and the Struggle for Democracy in the Mid-Twentieth-Century South*. Chapel Hill: University of North Carolina Press.

Korstad, Robert and Nelson Lichtenstein. 1988. "Opportunities Found and Lost: Labor, Radicals, and the Early Civil Rights Movement." *Journal of American History* 75 (3): 786–811.

Krause, Paul. 1992. *The Battle for Homestead, 1880–1892: Politics, Culture, and Steel*. Pittsburgh: University of Pittsburgh Press.

Lahne, Herbert J. 1944. "The Cotton Mill Worker." PhD diss., Columbia University.

Lakatos, Imre. 1970. "Falsification and the Methodology of Scientific Research Programmes." In *Criticism and the Growth of Knowledge*, ed. Imre Lakatos and Alan Musgrave. Cambridge: Cambridge University Press.

Lambie, Joseph T. 1954. *From Mine to Market: The History of Coal Transportation on the Norfolk and Western Railway*. New York: New York University Press.

Lang, Clarence. 2009a. *Grassroots at the Gateway: Class Politics and Black Freedom Struggle in St. Louis, 1936–75*. Ann Arbor: University of Michigan Press.

Lang, Clarence. 2009b. "Freedom Train Derailed: The National Negro Labor Council and the Nadir of Black Radicalism." In *Anticommunism and the African American Freedom Movement: "Another Side of the Story,"* ed. Robbie Lieberman and Clarence Lang. New York: Palgrave Macmillan.

Larrowe, Charles P. 1972. *Harry Bridges: The Rise and Fall of Radical Labor in the United States*. New York: L. Hill.

Laslett, John H. M. 1996a. "A Model of Industrial Solidarity? Interpreting the UMWA's First Hundred Years, 1890–1990." In *The United Mine Workers of America: A Model of Industrial Solidarity?*, ed. John H. M. Laslett. University Park MD: Penn State University Press.

Laslett, John H. M., ed. 1996b. *The United Mine Workers of America: A Model of Industrial Solidarity?* University Park: Penn State University Press.

Leab, Daniel. 1967. "'United We Eat': The Creation and Organization of the Unemployed Councils in the 1930s." *Labor History* 8 (3): 300–15.

LeBlanc, Paul and Tim Davenport, eds. 2018. *The "American Exceptionalism" of Jay Lovestone and His Comrades, 1929–1940*. Chicago: Haymarket Books.

Leiserson, William Morris. 1959. *American Trade Union Democracy*. New York: Columbia University Press.

Lembcke, Jerry. 1978. "International Woodworkers of America: An Internal Comparative Study of Two Regions." PhD diss., University of Oregon.

Lembcke, Jerry and William M. Tattam. 1984. *One Union in Wood*. New York: International.

Lenin, Vladimir Il'ich. (1915) 1960. *What Is to Be Done?* Vol. 5 of *Collected Works*. 35 vols. Moscow: Foreign Languages Publishing House.

Lenin, V. I. (1917) 1964. *Lecture on the 1905 Revolution*. In vol. 23 of *Collected Works*. 45 vols. Moscow: Foreign Languages Publishing House.

Lenin, V. I. 1961. *Collected Works, Vol. 23:236–253*. Moscow: Progress Publishers.

Lens, Sidney. 1949. *Left, Right and Center, Conflicting Forces in American Labor*. Hinsdale, IL: H. Regnery.

Lens, Sidney. 1959. *The Crisis of American Labor*. New York: Sagamore Press.

Levenstein, Harvey A. 1981. *Communism, Anti-Communism, and the CIO*. Westport, CT: Greenwood Press.

Lewis, David. 1973. *Counterfactuals*. Cambridge, MA: Harvard University Press.

Lewis, David. 1986. *Philosophical Papers*, vol. 2. Oxford: Oxford University Press.

Lewis, Ronald L. 1987. *Black Coal Miners in America: Race, Class, and Community Conflict, 1780–1980*. Lexington: University Press of Kentucky.

Lichtenstein, Alexander C. 1996. *Twice the Work of Free Labor: The Political Economy of Convict Labor in the New South*. London: Verso.

Lichtenstein, Nelson. 1982. *Labor's War at Home: The CIO in World War II*. Cambridge: Cambridge University Press.

Lichtenstein, Nelson. 1995. *The Most Dangerous Man in Detroit: Walter Reuther and the Fate of American Labor*. New York: Basic Books.

Liebling, A. J. 1960. "The Wayward Press: Do You Belong in Journalism?" *New Yorker*.

Lippmann, Walter. 1922. *Public Opinion*. New York: Harcourt, Brace, and Co.

Lipset, Seymour Martin. 1981. *Political Man: The Social Bases of Politics*. Baltimore: Johns Hopkins University Press.

Little, Daniel. 2016. *New Directions in the Philosophy of Social Science*. London: Rowman & Littlefield International.

Lorence, James L. 1996. *Organizing the Unemployed: Community and Union Activists in the Industrial Heartland*. Albany, NY: SUNY Press.

Lorence, James L. 2009. *The Unemployed People's Movement: Leftists, Liberals, and Labor in Georgia, 1929–1941*. Athens: University of Georgia Press.

Lozovsky, Abraham. 1928. "Results and Prospects of the United Front (in Connection with the Coming Profintern, R.I.L.U., Congress)." *Communist International*, March 15.

Lubin, Isador. 1924. *Miners' Wages and the Cost of Coal: An Inquiry into the Wages System in the Bituminous Coal Industry and Its Effects on Coal Costs and Coal Conservation*. New York: McGraw-Hill.

Lynd, Staughton. 1972. "The Possibility of Radicalism in the Early 1930's: The Case of Steel. *Radical America* 6 (6): 37–64.

Magdoff, Harry. 1968. "The Age of Imperialism." *Monthly Review* 20 (2): 11–54.

Makalani, Minkah. 2004. "For the Liberation of Black People Everywhere: The African Blood Brotherhood, Black Radicalism, and Pan-African Liberation in the New Negro Movement, 1917–1936." PhD. diss., University of Illinois.

Mandel, Ernest. 1968. *Marxist Economic Theory*, vol. I. Trans. Brian Pearce. New York: Merlin Press.

Manley, John. 2005. "Moscow Rules? 'Red' Unionism and 'Class against Class' in Britain, Canada, and the United States, 1928–1935." *Labour/Le Travail* 56: 9–49.

Manley, John F. 1983. "Neo-Pluralism: A Class Analysis of Pluralism I and Pluralism II." *The American Political Science Review* 77 (2): 368–83.

Manning, Brian. 2017. "For Black Liberation Through Socialist Revolution: Race, Class and American Populism." *Workers Vanguard*, No. 1148.

Marks, Gary. 1989. *Unions in Politics: Britain, Germany, and the United States in the Nineteenth and Early Twentieth Centuries*. Princeton, NJ: Princeton University Press.

Marshall, F. Ray. 1967. *Labor in the South*. Cambridge, MA: Harvard University Press.

Martin, Ralph. 1947. "The CIO Takes a Long Lease in the South," *New Republic*, January 13.

Marx, Karl. (1847) 1976. *Poverty of Philosophy*. In *Karl Marx and Friedrich Engels: Collected Works*, vol. 6. New York: International.

Marx, Karl. (1852) 1979. "The Eighteenth Brumaire of Louis Bonaparte." In *Karl Mark and Friedrich Engels: Collected Works*, vol. 11. New York: International.

Marx, Karl and Friedrich Engels. 1948. *The Communist Manifesto*. New York: International.

Marx, Karl, and Friedrich Engels. 1968. "Wages, Price and Profit." In *Selected Works of Karl Marx and Friedrich Engels*. New York: International.

Marx, Karl and Friedrich Engels. 1969. *The Civil War in the U.S.* New York: International.

Marx, Karl and Friedrich Engels. 1988. *Marx Engels Werke*. Berlin: Institut fur Marxismus-Leninismus Beim.

McDonald, David J. 1969. *Union Man: The Life of a Labor Statesman*. New York: E. P. Dutton.

McElvaine Robert S. 1974. "Thunder Without Lightning: Working Class Discontent in the United States, 1929–1937." PhD diss., State University of New York, Binghamton.

McElvaine Robert S. 1984. *The Great Depression: America, 1929–1941*. New York: Times Books/Random House.

McLaurin, Melton Alonza. 1971. *Paternalism and Protest: Southern Cotton Mill Workers and Organized Labor, 1875–1905*. Westport, CT: Greenwood.

McLaurin, Melton Alonza. 1978. *The Knights of Labor in the South*. Westport CT: Greenwood.

Medvedev, Roy. 1971. *Let History Judge*. New York: Vintage.

Mehta, S. D. 1954. *The Cotton Mills of India, 1854–1954*. Bombay: Bombay Textile Association.

Meier, August, and Elliott M. Rudwick. 1979. *Black Detroit and the Rise of the UAW*. New York: Oxford University Press.

Melcher, Cody R. and Michael Goldfield. 2018. "Review of Rights Delayed: The American State and the Defeat of Progressive Unions, 1935–1950." *Journal of Labor and Society* 21 (2): 265–68.

Menon, Meena and Neera Akarkar. 2004. *One Hundred Years, One Hundred Voices: The Millworkers of Girangaon—An Oral History*. Calcutta: Seagull Books.

Meyerowitz, Ruth. 1985. "Organizing the United Automobile Workers: Workers at the Ternstedt General Motors Parts Plant." In *Women, Work, and Protest: A Century of U.S. Woman's Labor History*, ed. Ruth Milkman. Boston: Routledge.

Mezerik, A. G. 1947a. "The CIO Southern Drive." *Nation*, January 11.

Mezerik, Avrahm G. 1947b. "Dixie in Black and White." *Nation*, July 12, 40–42.

Mezerik, A. G. 1950. *Nation*, July 24.

Mikhailov, B. Y., N. V. Mostovets, and G. N. Sevostyanov, eds. 1977. *Recent History of the Labor Movement in the United States: 1918–1939*. Moscow: Progress.

Miller, Donald L., and Richard E. Sharpless. 1985. *The Kingdom of Coal: Work, Enterprise, and Ethnic Communities in the Mine Fields*. Philadelphia: University of Pennsylvania Press.

Miller, Richard W. 1987. *Fact and Method: Explanation, Confirmation and Reality in the Natural and the Social Sciences*. Princeton, NJ: Princeton University Press.

Millis, Harry Alvin. 1942. *How Collective Bargaining Works: A Survey of Experience in Leading American Industries.* New York: Twentieth Century Fund.

Minchin, Timothy J. 1997. *What Do We Need a Union For? The TWUA in the South, 1945–1955.* Chapel Hill: University of North Carolina Press.

Minutes of the Executive Board of the Congress of Industrial Organizations. 1946. March 15.

Mitchell, Broadus. 1921. *The Rise of Cotton Mills in the South.* Baltimore: Johns Hopkins Press.

Mitchell, Broadus. 1930. "The Present Situation in the Southern Textile Industry." *Harvard Business Review* 8 (3): 296–306.

Mittelman, B., Henry E. Hoagland, John B. Andrews, Selig Perlman, Don D. Lescohier, and Rebecca J. Bailey, 2008. *Matewan Before the Massacre: Politics, Coal, and the Roots of Conflict in a West Virginia Mining Community.* Morgantown: West Virginia University Press.

Morantz, Alison D. 2013. "Coal Mine Safety: Do Unions Make a Difference?" *Industrial and Labor Relations Review* 66 (1): 88–116.

Morgan, Edmund S. 1975. *American Slavery, American Freedom.* New York: W. W. Norton.

Morgan, Stephen L. and Christopher Winship. 2015. *Counterfactuals and Causal Inference: Methods and Principles for Social Research.* Cambridge: Cambridge University Press.

Mosimann, Nadja and Jonas Pontusson. 2017. "Solidaristic Unionism and Support for Redistribution in Contemporary Europe." *World Politics* 69 (3): 448–92.

Mumford, Lewis. 1934. *Technics and Civilization.* New York: Harcourt.

Murphy, Paul L., Kermit L. Hall, and David Klassen, eds. 1974. *The Passaic Textile Strike of 1926.* Belmont, CA: Wadsworth.

Muste, A. J. 1930. "The Crisis in the Miners' Union." In *Labor Age: The Voice of Progressive Labor*: 4–8.

Naison, Mark D. 1968. "The Southern Tenant Farmers Union and the CIO." *Radical America* 2 (5): 36–56.

Naison, Mark. 1973. "Claude and Joyce Williams: Pilgrims of Justice." *Southern Exposure* 1: 45–47.

Naison, Mark. 1983. *Communists in Harlem During the Depression.* Chicago: University of Chicago Press.

Naison, Mark. 1996. "The Southern Tenants Farmers' Union and the C.I.O." In *"We Are All Leaders": The Alternative Unionism of the Early 1930s*, ed. Staughton Lynd. Urbana: University of Illinois Press.

National Center for Science Education. 2013a. "YouGov Poll on Evolution." July 23.

National Center for Science Education. 2013b. "A New Poll on Climate from Pew." November 4. http://ncse.com/news/2013/11/new-poll-climate-from-pew-0015157. Accessed January 12, 2014.

National Science Foundation. 2017. "Top 20 Doctorate-Granting Institutions Ranked by Number of Minority U.S. Citizen and Permanent Resident Doctorate Recipients, by Ethnicity and Race of Recipient: 5-Year Total, 2011–15." https://www.nsf.gov/statistics/2017/nsf17306/data/tab9.pdf.

Needleman, Ruth. 2003. *Black Freedom Fighters in Steel.* Ithaca, NY: Cornell University Press.

Nelson, Bruce. 1990. *Workers on the Waterfront: Seamen, Longshoremen, and Unionism in the 1930s.* Urbana: University of Illinois Press.

Nelson, Bruce. 1996. "Class, Race and Democracy in the CIO: The 'New' Labor History Meets the 'Wages of Whiteness.'" *International Review of Social History* 41 (3): 351–74.

Nelson, Bruce. 2001. *Divided We Stand: American Workers and the Struggle for Black Equality.* Princeton, NJ: Princeton University Press.

Nelson, Daniel. 1988. *American Rubber Workers and Organized Labor, 1900–1941.* Princeton. NJ: Princeton University Press.

Nelson, James. 1955. *The Mine Workers' District 50: The Story of Gas, Coke, and Chemical Unions of Massachusetts and their Growth into a National Union.* New York: Banner Books.

Nelson, Steve. 1934. "How the Unemployed Councils Were Built in Lackawanna County." *Party Organizer* 7 (March).

Nichols, Claude W., Jr. 1959. "Brotherhood in the Woods: The Loyal Legion of Loggers and Lumbermen: A Twenty Year Attempt at 'Industrial Cooperation.'" PhD diss., University of Oregon.

Nolan, Dennis R. and Donald E. Jonas. 1977. "Textile Unionism in the Piedmont, 1901–1932." In *Essays in Southern Labor History: Selected Papers, Southern Labor History Conference, 1976*, ed. Gary M. Fink and Merl Elwyn Reed. Westport, CT: Greenwood Press.

Norrell, Robert J. 1986. "Caste in Steel: Jim Crow Careers in Birmingham, Alabama." *Journal of American History* 73 (3): 669–94.

Northrup, Herbert R. 1943. "The Negro and Unionism in the Birmingham, Ala., Iron and Steel Industry." *Southern Economic Journal* 10 (1): 27–40.

Northrup, Herbert Roof. 1944. *Organized Labor and the Negro*. New York: Harper and Brothers.

Norwood, Stephen H. 1997. "Bogalusa Burning: The War Against Biracial Unionism in the Deep South, 1919." *The Journal of Southern History* 63 (3): 591–628.

Nove, Alec. 1969. *The Soviet Economy: An Introduction*. New York: Praeger.

Nyden, Paul. 1974. *Black Coal Miners in the United States*. New York: American Institute for Marxist Studies.

Oates, Mary Josephine. 1969. "The Role of the Cotton Textile Industry in the Economic Development of the American Southeast: 1900–1940." PhD diss., Yale University.

O'Connor, Harvey. 1950. *History of Oil Workers International Union–CIO*. Denver: Oil Workers International Union.

Odum, Howard W. 1936. *Southern Regions of the United States*. Chapel Hill: University of North Carolina Press.

Oliver, Melvin L. and Thomas M Shapiro. 2006. *Black Wealth, White Wealth: A New Perspective on Racial Inequality*. Boca Raton, FL: CRC Press.

Ottanelli, Fraser M. 1991. *The Communist Party of the United States: From the Depression to World War II*. New Brunswick, NJ: Rutgers University Press.

Ovington, Mary White. 1920. "Bogalusa." *Liberator* (January).

Ozanne, Robert W. 1967. *A Century of Labor-Management Relations at McCormick and International Harvester*. Madison: University of Wisconsin Press.

Palmer, Bryan D. 2007. *James P. Cannon and the Origins of the American Revolutionary Left, 1890–1928*. Urbana: University of Illinois Press.

Palmer, Bryan. 2014. *Revolutionary Teamsters: The Minneapolis Truckers' Strikes of 1934*. Chicago: Haymarket Books.

Palmer, Bryan D. & Gaetan Heroux. 2016. *Toronto's Poor: A Rebellious History*. Toronto: Between the Lines Press.

Parry, Jonathan P., Jan Breman, and Karin Kapadia. 1999. *The Worlds of Indian Industrial Labour*. New Delhi: Sage Publications.

Peery, Nelson. 2007. *Black Radical: The Education of an American Revolutionary*. New York: New Press.

Perlman, Selig and Philip Taft. 1935. *History of Labor in the United States, 1896–1932*. New York: Macmillan.

Petras, James and Maurice Zeitlin. 1967. "Miners and Agrarian Radicalism." *American Sociological Review* 32 (4): 578–86.

Phelan, Craig. 1996. "John Mitchell and the Politics of the Trade Agreement, 1898–1917." In *The United Mine Workers of America: A Model of Industrial Solidarity?*, ed. John H. M. Laslett. University Park: Penn State University Press, 72–103.

Phelps, Christopher. 2012. "Herbert Hill and the Federal Bureau of Investigation." *Labor History* 53: 561–70.

Phelps, Christopher. 2013. "Response from Christopher Phelps to Trevor Griffey's Analysis." January 26. LAWCHA: Labor Online.

Phillips, Andy. 2002. *Quecreek Rescue*. Chicago: News and Letters.

Phillips, Kevin P. 1970. *The Emerging Republican Majority*. New Rochelle, NY: Arlington Press.

Pierce, Andrew J. 2013. "Radical Student Activism in the 1930s and Its Comparison to Student Activism During Occupy Wall Street." Senior Honors Projects, Paper 335, University of Rhode Island.

Pike, Robert E. 1967. *Tall Trees, Tough Men.* New York: W. W. Norton.

Piven, Frances Fox and Richard A. Cloward. 1977. *Poor People's Movements: Why They Succeed, How They Fail.* New York: Pantheon Books.

Pope, James Gray. 2003a. "The Western Pennsylvania Coal Strike of 1933, Part I: Lawmaking from Below and the Revival of the United Mine Workers." *Labor History* 44 (1): 15–48.

Pope, James Gray. 2003b. "The Western Pennsylvania Coal Strike of 1933, Part II: Lawmaking from Above and the Demise of Democracy in the United Mine Workers." *Labor History* 44 (2): 235–64.

Pope, Liston. 1942. *Millhands and Preachers: A Study of Gastonia.* New Haven, CT: Yale University Press; London: H. Milford, Oxford University Press.

Popper, Karl. 2002. *The Logic of Scientific Discovery.* New York: Routledge Classics.

Porter, Eduardo 2013. "For Insurers, No Doubts on Climate Change." *New York Times.*

Post, Charles. Forthcoming. "Explaining the Decline of Industrial Unionism in the North American Tire Industry, 1966–2008." Unpublished paper.

Potwin, Marjorie Adella. 1927. *Cotton Mill People of the Piedmont: A Study in Social Change.* New York: Columbia University Press.

Prago, Albert. 1976. "The Organization of the Unemployed and the Role of the Radicals, 1929–1935." PhD diss., Union for Experimenting Colleges and Universities.

Pratt, William C. 1988. "Rethinking the Farm Revolt of the 1930s." *Great Plains Quarterly* (Summer).

Pratt, William C. 1989. "Farmers, Communists, and the FBI in the Upper Midwest." *Agricultural History* 63 (3).

Preis, Art. 1964. *Labor's Giant Step: The First Twenty Years of the CIO, 1936–1955.* New York: Pathfinder Press.

Prickett, James R. 1973. "Communists and the Automobile Industry in Detroit before 1935." *Michigan History* 57: 185–208.

Prickett, James Robert. 1975. "Communists and the Communist Issue in the American Labor Movement, 1920–1950." PhD diss., University of California, Los Angeles.

Prickett, James R. 1981. "Communist Conspiracy or Wage Dispute? The 1941 Strike at North American Aviation." *Pacific Historical Review* 50 (2): 215–33.

Priest, Tyler and Michael Boston. 2012. "Bucking the Odds: Organized Labor in Gulf Coast Oil Refining." *Journal of American History* 99 (1): 100–10.

Public Broadcasting System. 2012. "Slavery v. Peonage," in *Slavery by Another Name.* Twin Cities Public Television. http://www.pbs.org/tpt/slavery-by-another-name/themes/peonage. Accessed July 7, 2015.

Putnam, Hilary. 1978. *Meaning and the Moral Sciences.* London: Routledge and Kegan Paul.

Rachleff, Peter J. 1989. *Black Labor in Richmond, 1865–1890.* Urbana: University of Illinois Press.

Ramsey, Ross. 2013. "Texans: Dinosaurs, Humans Walked the Earth at Same Time." In *Texas Tribune* (Austin).

Ramstad, Yngve and James L Starkey. 1995. "The Racial Theories of John R. Commons." *Research in the History of Economic Thought and Methodology* 13 (1): 1–74.

Raper, Arthur and Ira De A. Reid. 1941. *Sharecroppers All.* Chapel Hill: University of North Carolina Press.

Rawick, George P. 1957. "The New Deal and Youth." PhD diss., University of Wisconsin.

Reece, Florence. 1931. "Which Side Are You On?"

Reed, Merl E. 1969. "The IWW and Individual Freedom in Western Louisiana, 1913." *Louisiana History* 10: 61–69.

Reed, Merl. 1982. "Some Additional Material on the Coal Strike of 1943." *Labor History* 23 (Winter).

Regensburger, William Edward. 1987. "'Ground into Our Blood': The Origins of Working Class Consciousness and Organization in Durably Unionized Southern Industries, 1930–1946." PhD diss., University of California, Los Angeles.

Reich, Steven Andrew. 1998. "The Making of a Southern Sawmill World: Race, Class, and Rural Transformation in the Piney Woods of East Texas, 1830–1930." PhD diss., Northwestern University.

Rice, Charles Owen. 1989. "Confessions of an Anti-Communist." Labor History 30 (3): 449–63.

Rice, Charles Owen. 1996. Fighter with a Heart: Writings of Charles Owen Rice, Pittsburgh Labor Priest. Ed. Charles McCollester. Pittsburgh: University of Pittsburgh.

Richards, Paul David. 1978. The History of the Textile Workers Union of America, CIO, in the South, 1937 to 1945. Madison: University of Wisconsin.

Richmond, Al. 1972. A Long View from the Left: Memoirs of an American Revolutionary. New York: Dell.

Riesel, Victor. 1941. "Communist Grip on Our Defense." American Mercury 52 (February): 202–10.

Rimlinger, Gaston V. 1959. "International Differences in the Strike Propensity of Coal Miners: Experience in Four Countries." Industrial and Labor Relations Review 12 (3): 389–405.

Risser, Hubert E. 1958. The Economics of the Coal Industry. Lawrence: University of Kansas, School of Business, Bureau of Business Research.

Robeson, Paul. 1978. Paul Robeson Speaks. Ed. Philip S. Foner. Secaucus, NJ: Citadel Press.

Robinson, Donald L. 1979. Slavery in the Structure of American Politics, 1765–1820. New York: W. W. Norton.

Rochester, Anna. 1931. Labor and Coal. New York: International.

Rowan, Thomas. 1882. Coal. London, New York: E. and F. N. Spon.

Rosen, Dale. 1969. "The Alabama Share Croppers Union." Honors thesis, Radcliffe College.

Rosengarten, Theodore. 1974. All God's Dangers: The Life of Nate Shaw. New York: Knopf.

Rosenow, Michael. 2003. "Radicals in the Public Imagination: The Making of American Identity and the Great Steel Strike of 1919." Presented at the North American Labor History Conference, Detroit, MI.

Rosenzweig, Roy. 1975. "Radicals and the Jobless: The Musteites and the Unemployed Leagues, 1932–1936." Labor History 16 (1): 52–77.

Rosenzweig, Roy. 1976. "Organizing the Unemployed: The Early Years of the Great Depression, 1929–1933." Radical America 10 (4): 37–60.

Rosenzweig, Roy. 1979. "'Socialism in Our Time': The Socialist Party and the Unemployed, 1929–1936." Labor History 20 (4): 485–509.

Ross, James D., Jr. 2004. "'I Ain't Got No Home in This World': The Rise and Fall of the Southern Tenant Farmers' Union in Arkansas." PhD diss., Auburn University.

Rosswurm, Steve. 1992. "The Catholic Church and the Left-Led Unions: Labor Priests, Labor Schools, and the ACTU." In The CIO's Left-Led Unions, ed. Steve Rosswurm. New Brunswick, NJ: Rutgers University Press.

Rostow, W. W. 1978. The World Economy: History and Prospect. Austin: University of Texas Press.

Rothstein, Richard. 2017. The Color of Law: A Forgotten History of How Our Government Segregated America. New York: Liveright.

Rovere, Richard H. 1995. The Goldwater Caper. New York: Harcourt, Brace, and World.

Roy, Andrew. (1907) 1970. A History of the Coal Miners of the United States, From the Development of the Mines to the Close of the Anthracite Strike of 1902, Including a Brief Sketch of Early British Miners. Westport, CT: Greenwood Press.

Russian Institute. 1956. The Anti-Stalin Campaign and International Communism: A Selection of Documents Edited by Russian Institute, Columbia University. New York: Columbia University Press.

Salmond, John A. 2002. The General Textile Strike of 1934: From Maine to Alabama. Columbia: University of Missouri Press.

Sanders, M. Elizabeth. 1999. Roots of Reform: Farmers, Workers, and the American State, 1877–1917. Chicago: University of Chicago Press.

Saposs, David J. 1967. *Left Wing Unionism: A Study of Radical Policies and Tactics*. New York: Russell & Russell.

Sayles, John Cooper, dir. 1987. *Matewan*. Film. Cinecom Pictures.

Schatz, Ronald W. 1983. *The Electrical Workers: A History of Labor at General Electric and Westinghouse, 1923–1960*. Urbana: University of Illinois Press.

Schlesinger, Arthur M. 1949. *The Vital Center: The Politics of Freedom*. Boston: Houghton Mifflin.

Schlesinger, Arthur M. 1957. *The Age of Roosevelt*. Boston: Houghton Mifflin.

Schrecker, Ellen. 1998. *Many Are the Crimes: McCarthyism in America*. Boston: Little, Brown.

Scribner, Tom. 1966. "Lumberjack." In "Documents by Tom Scribner, IWW Documents Library." http://www.iww.org/history/library/Scribner/lumberjack. Accessed November 16, 2015.

Selvin, David F. 1996. *A Terrible Anger: The 1934 Waterfront and General Strikes in San Francisco*. Detroit: Wayne State University Press.

Sen, Amartya. 2005. *The Argumentative Indian: Writings on Indian History, Culture, and Identity*. New York: Farrar, Straus and Giroux.

Sen, Sukomal. 1977. *Working Class of India: History of Emergence and Movement 1830–1970*. Calcutta: K.P. Bagchi & Co.

Seymour, Helen. 1940. "The Organized Unemployed." MA diss., University of Chicago.

Shapiro, Harry H. 1964. "Involuntary Servitude." *Rutgers Law Review* 19 (65): 65–85.

Shifflett, Crandall A. 1991. *Coal Towns: Life, Work, and Culture in Company Towns of Southern Appalachia, 1880–1960*. Knoxville: University of Tennessee Press.

Shofner, Jerrell H. 1981. "Forced Labor in the Florida Forests, 1880–1950." *Journal of Forest History* 25 (1): 14–25.

Shogan, Robert. 2004. *The Battle of Blair Mountain: The Story of America's Largest Labor Uprising*. Boulder, CO: Westview Press.

Shorter, Edward and Charles Tilly. 1974. *The Shape of Strikes in France, 1830–1968*. New York: Cambridge University Press.

Shover, John L. 1965. *Cornbelt Rebellion, The Farmers' Holiday Association*. Urbana: University of Illinois Press.

Siegel, Morton. 1952. "The Passaic Textile Strike of 1926." PhD diss., Columbia University.

Silver, Beverly J. 2003. *Forces of Labor: Workers' Movements and Globalization Since 1870*. Cambridge: Cambridge University Press.

Singer, Alan Jay. 1982. "'Which Side Are You On?': Ideological Conflict in the United Mine Workers of America, 1919–1928." PhD diss., Rutgers University.

Singer, Alan J. 1996. "'Something of a Man': John L. Lewis, the UMWA, and the CIO, 1919–1943." In *The United Mine Workers of America: A Model of Industrial Solidarity?*, ed. John H. M. Laslett. University Park, MD: Penn State University Press.

Skotnes, Andor. 1991. "The Black Freedom Movement and the Workers' Movement in Baltimore, 1930–1939." PhD diss., Rutgers University.

Skotnes, Andor. 2013. *A New Deal for All? Race and Class Struggles in Depression-Era Baltimore*. Durham, NC: Duke University Press.

Smiley, Gene. 1983. "Recent Unemployment Estimates for the 1920s and 1930s." *Journal of Economic History* 43 (2): 487–93.

Smith, Robert S. 1960. *Mill on the Dan: A History of Dan River Mills, 1882–1950*. Durham, NC: Duke University Press.

Sofchalk, Donald G. 1977. "Labor Unions." In *Labor Unions*, ed. Gary M. Fink, 76–79. Westport, CT: Greenwood Press.

Solomon, Mark I. 1998. *The Cry Was Unity: Communists and African Americans, 1917–36*. Jackson: University Press of Mississippi.

Soule, George Henry. 1939. *Sidney Hillman, Labor Statesman*. New York: Amalgamated Clothing Workers of America.

Spero, Sterling Denhard and Abram Lincoln Harris. 1931. *The Black Worker: The Negro and the Labor Movement*. New York: Columbia University Press.

Spielmaker, Debra. 2014. "Growing a Nation: The Story of American Agriculture: Historical Timeline, 1930." U.S. Department of Labor, Utah State University Extension, and Letter Press Software. https.//www.agclassroom.org/gan/timeline/1930.htm. Accessed October 31, 2016.

Starobin, Joseph. 1972. *American Communism in Crisis: 1943–1957*. Berkeley: University of California Press.

Stein, Judith. 1993. "The Ins and Outs of the CIO." *International Labor and Working-Class History* 44 (Fall): 53–63.

Stein, Judith. 1998. *Running Steel, Running America: Race, Economic Policy and the Decline of Liberalism*. Chapel Hill: University of North Carolina Press.

Stepan-Norris, Judith and Maurice Zeitlin. 1996a. "Insurgency, Radicalism, and Democracy in America's Industrial Unions." *Social Forces* 75 (1): 1–32.

Stepan-Norris, Judith and Maurice Zeitlin. 1996b. *Talking Union*. Champaign: University of Illinois Press.

Stepan-Norris, Judith and Maurice Zeitlin. 2002. *Left Out: Reds and America's Industrial Unions*. Cambridge: Cambridge University Press.

Stevens, James. 1951. "The Frozen Logger." In *Folk Songs of North America*, ed. Alan Lomax. 120–21.

Stieber, Jack. 1959. *The Steel Industry Wage Structure: A Study of the Joint Union-Management Job Evaluation Program in the Basic Steel Industry*. Cambridge, MA: Harvard University Press.

Stone, David. 1973. "The IWA: The Red Block and White Block." Unpublished essay.

Stone, Katherine. 1974. "The Origins of Job Structures in the Steel Industry." *Review of Radical Political Economics* 6: 113–73.

Storch, Randi. 2007. *Red Chicago: American Communism at its Grassroots, 1928–35*. Urbana: University of Illinois Press.

Strange, Hannah. 2017. "Boats of Spanish Military Police Blocked by Catalan Ports as Unrest Grows." *Telegraph*, September 21. http://www.telegraph.co.uk/news/2017/09/21/boats-spanish-military-police-blocked-catala n-ports-unrest-grows/.

Streater, John Baxter. 1981. "The National Negro Congress, 1936–1947." PhD diss., University of Cincinnati.

Strong, D. S. 1972. "Alabama: Transition and Alienation." In *The Changing Politics of the South*, ed. W. C. Harvard, 427–71. Baton Rouge: Louisiana State University Press.

Suffern, Arthur E. 1926. *The Coal Miner's Struggle for Industrial Status: A Study of the Evolution of Organized Relations and Industrial Principles in the Coal Industry*. New York: Macmillan.

Sugar, Maurice. 1980. *The Ford Hunger March*. Berkeley: Meiklejohn Civil Liberties Institute.

Sumpter, Amy R. 2011. "Racial Identity, Spatial Mobility, and Labor in the Non-Plantation Rural South, 1880–1940." *Journal of Historical Geography* 37: 460–69.

Sundquist, James. 1983. *Dynamics of the Party System*. Washington, DC: Brookings Institution.

Swain, G. T. 2009. *The Blair Mountain War: Battle of the Rednecks*. Chapmanville, WV: Woodland Press.

Swearingen, Arthur Rodger. 1954. "The Communist Line in Japan." *Far Eastern Survey*, 56–61.

Sweeney, Vincent D. 1947. *The United Steelworkers of America, The First 10 years*. n.p.

Taft, Philip. 1957. *The A.F. of L.*, vol. 1: *In the Time of Gompers*. New York: Harper.

Taft, Philip. 1959. *The A.F. of L.*, vol. 2: *From the Death of Gompers to the Merger*. New York: Harper.

Taft, Philip. 1964. *Organized Labor in American History*. New York: Harper & Row.

Taft, Philip and Gary M. Fink. 1981. *Organizing Dixie: Alabama Workers in the Industrial Era*. Westport, CT: Greenwood Press.

Taft, Philip and Selig Perlman. 1935. In *History of Labor in the United States, 1896–1932*. 4 vols., vol. 3. Ed. John R. Commons, David J. Saposs, Helen L. Sumner, E. B. Mittelman, Henry E. Hoagland, John B. Andrews, Selig Perlman, Don D. Lescohier, Elizabeth Brandeis Raushenbush, and Philip Taft. New York: Macmillan.

Tattam, William Marquis. 1970. "Sawmill Workers and Radicalism: Portland, Oregon, 1929–1940." MA thesis, University of Oregon.

Taylor, Theman Ray. 1981. "Cyril Briggs and the African Blood Brotherhood: Another Radical View of Race and Class During the 1920s." PhD diss., University of California, Santa Barbara.

Temin, Peter. 1964. "Iron and Steel in Nineteenth-Century America, an Economic Inquiry." *American Federationist*, May.

Thompson, E. P. 1966. *The Making of the English Working Class.* New York: Vintage Books.

Thompson, Mindy. 1978. "The National Negro Labor Council: A History." American Institute for Marxist Studies, Occasional Paper No. 27.

Thoreau, Henry David. 1972. *The Maine Woods.* Ed. Joseph J. Modenhauer. Princeton, NJ: Princeton University Press.

Tindall, George Brown. 1967. *The Emergence of the New South, 1913–1945.* Baton Rouge: Louisiana State University Press.

Tippett, Thomas. 1931. *When Southern Labor Stirs.* New York: J. Cape and H. Smith.

Todes, Charlotte. 1931. *Labor and Lumber.* New York: International.

Tosstorff, Reiner. 2018. *The Red International of Labour Unions (RILU) 1920–1937.* Chicago: Haymarket Press.

Trauger, Donald B. 2002. *Horse Power to Nuclear Power: Memoir of an Energy Pioneer.* Franklin, TN: Hillsboro Press.

Trotsky, Leon. (1929) 1975. "The Tasks of the American Opposition." *Militant,* May 29, 1929. In *Writings of Leon Trotsky.* 1929. New York: Pathfinder.

Trotsky, Leon. (1930) 1971. "The Turn in the Communist International and the Situation in Germany," September 22.

Trotsky, Leon. "The Lessons of October." In *The Challenge of the Left Opposition: 1923–1925,* ed. Naomi Allen. New York: Pathfinder Press.

Trotsky, Leon. 1937. *The Revolution Betrayed: What Is the Soviet Union and Where Is It Going?* Garden City, NY: Doubleday, Doran and Co.

Trotsky, Leon. 1946. *The Transitional Program: The Death Agony of Capitalism and the Tasks of the Fourth International.* New York: Pathfinder Press.

Trotsky, Leon. 1957. *The Third International After Lenin.* New York: Pioneer.

Trotsky, Leon. 1969. "Communism and Syndicalism." In *On the Trade Unions.* New York: Merit.

Trotsky, Leon. 1971. *The Struggle Against Fascism in Germany.* New York: Pathfinder Press.

Truchil, Barry E. 1988. *Capital-Labor Relations in the U.S. Textile Industry.* New York: Praeger.

Tucker, Barbara M. 1984. *Samuel Slater and the Origins of the American Textile Industry, 1790–1860.* Ithaca, NY: Cornell University Press.

Tyler, Robert L. 1967. *Rebels of the Woods: The I.W.W. in the Pacific Northwest.* Eugene: University of Oregon Books.

Tyson, Timothy B. 2017. *The Blood of Emmett Till.* New York: Simon & Schuster.

Uchimura, Kazuko. 2007. "Miners Without Unions: Work and Labor Relations in West Virginia's Smokeless Coalfields, 1873–1935." PhD diss., Georgetown University.

Ulman, Lloyd. 1962. *The Government of the Steel Workers' Union.* New York: Wiley.

United States Census Bureau. 2013. "Comparison of Uninsured Rates Between States Using 3-year Averages: 2010 to 2012." http://www.census.gov/hhes/www/hlthins/data/incpovhlth/2012/tables.html.

U.S. Bureau of the Census. 1935. *Negroes in the U.S., 1920–1932.* Washington, DC.

U.S. Department of Labor. 1945. *Labor Unionism in American Agriculture.* Bulletin 836.

U.S. Senate, 76th Cong., 1st Sess., 1936–1941. "Violations of Free Speech and the Rights of Labor." This report and others based on hearings and reports by a subcommittee of the U.S. Senate Committee on Education and Labor headed by Senator Robert M. La Follette will be referred to as the "La Follette Committee Hearings."

Vallocci, Steve. 1990. "The Unemployed Workers Movement of the 1930s." *Social Problems* 37: 2.

Van der Linden, Marcel. 2008. *Workers of the World: Essays Towards a Global Labour History.* Leiden: Brill.

Walker, Thomas. 1982. "The International Workers Order: A Unique Fraternal Body." PhD diss., University of Chicago.

Wallerstein, Immanuel. 1985. *The Politics of World Economy: The States, the Movements, and the Civilizations*. Cambridge: Cambridge University Press.

Wallerstein, Immanuel. 2002. "The Itinerary of World-Systems Analysis; or, How to Resist Becoming a Theory." In *New Directions in Contemporary Sociological Theory*, ed. J. Berger and M. Zelditch, Jr. New York: Rowman & Littlefield.

Wallerstein, Immanuel. 2007. *World-Systems Analysis: An Introduction*. Durham, NC: Duke University Press.

Waltzer, Kenneth Alan. 1978. "The American Labor Party: Third Party Politics in New Deal-Cold War, 1936–1954." PhD diss., Harvard University.

Ward, Chris. 1990. *Russian's Cotton Workers and the New Economic Policy*. Cambridge: Cambridge University Press.

Ware, Norman. 1924. *The Industrial Worker, 1840–1860*. Boston.

Warren, Kenneth. 1973. *The American Steel Industry, 1850–1970*. Oxford: Clarendon Press.

Watson, Bruce. 2010. *Freedom Summer: The Savage Season That Made Mississippi Burn and Made America a Democracy*. New York: Viking.

Webb, Sidney and Beatrice Potter Webb. (1894) 1920. *The History of Trade Unionism*. London: Green.

Weber, Max. 1949. *The Methodology of the Social Sciences*. Trans. Edward A. Shils and Henry A. Finch. New York: Free Press.

Weir, Stan. 1972. "Class Forces in the 1970's." *Radical America* 6 (3): 31–77.

Weir, Stan. 1974. "Work in America: Encounters on the Job." *Radical America* 8 (4): 99–108.

Weir, Stan. 1996. "Unions with Leaders Who Stay on the Job." In *"We Are All Leaders": The Alternative Unionism of the Early 1930s*, ed. Staughton Lynd, 297–334. Urbana: University of Illinois Press.

Wellman, David T. 1995. *The Union Makes Us Strong: Radical Unionism on the San Francisco Waterfront*. Cambridge: Cambridge University Press.

Weyl, Nathaniel. 1932. "Organizing Hunger," *New Republic*, December 14, 117–20.

Whatley, Warren C. 1993. "African-American Strikebreaking from the Civil War to the New Deal." *Social Science History* 17 (4): 525–58.

White, Ahmed. 2016. *The Last Great Strike: Little Steel, the CIO, and the Struggle for Labor Rights in New Deal America*. Oakland: University of California Press.

Widgderson, Seth Marks. 1989. "The UAW in the 1950s." PhD diss., Wayne State University.

Wilensky, Harold L. 2002. *Rich Democracies: Political Economy, Public Policy, and Performance*. Berkeley: University of California Press.

Williams, T. Harry. 1969. *Huey Long*. New York: Knopf.

Williamson, John. 1969. *Dangerous Scot: The Life and Work of an American "Undesirable."* New York: International.

Wilson, James Q. 1973. *Political Organizations*. New York: Basic Books.

Woodward, C. Vann. 1951. *Origins of the New South, 1877–1913*. Baton Rouge: Louisiana State University Press.

Wright, Erik Olin. 2000. "Working-Class Power, Capitalist-Class Interests, and Class Compromise." *American Journal of Sociology* 105 (4): 957–1002.

Wright, Gavin. 1986. *Old South, New South: Revolutions in the Southern Economy Since the Civil War*. New York: Basic Books.

Wyche, Billy H. 1999. "Paternalism, Patriotism, and Protest in 'the Already Best City in the Land': Bogalusa, Louisiana, 1906–1919." *Louisiana History: The Journal of the Louisiana Historical Association* 40 (1): 63–84.

Zaremba, Joseph. 1963. *Economics of the American Lumber Industry*. New York: R. Speller.

Zieger, Robert H. 1990. "Showdown at the Rouge." *History Today* 40.

Zieger, Robert H. 1995. *The CIO, 1935–1955*. Chapel Hill: University of North Carolina Press.

Zieger, Robert H. 1996. "John L. Lewis and the Labor Movement, 1940–1960." In *The United Mine Workers of America: A Model of Industrial Solidarity?*, ed. John H. M. Laslett, 151–66. University Park: Penn State University Press.

Zieger, Robert H., Thomas J. Minchin, and Gilbert J. Gall. 2014. *American Workers, American Unions: The Twentieth and Early Twenty-First Centuries.* Baltimore: Johns Hopkins University Press.

Zirin, Dave. 2018. "Is It Okay to Watch Football?" *Jacobin Magazine.* https://jacobinmag.com/2018/02/is-it-okay-to-watch-football/. Accessed May 10, 2019.

Zumoff, Jacob A. 2014. *The Communist International and US Communism, 1919–1929.*

Zumoff, Jacob. A., 2015. "Hell in New Jersey: The Passaic Textile Strike, Albert Weisbord, and the Communist Party." *Journal for the Study of Radicalism* 9 (1): 125–69.

Archival Sources

Adolph Germer Papers. State Historical Society of Wisconsin, Madison.

AFL Region 8 Papers. Southern Labor Archives, Georgia State University, Atlanta.

Carry Haigher Collection. Southern Labor Archives. Georgia State University, Atlanta.

CIO Files of John L. Lewis. Archives of the United Mine Workers of America, Washington, DC.

Clinton S. Golden Papers. Steel Workers Organizing Committee Records. Pattee Library, Penn State University, State College.

Congress of Industrial Organizations Papers. Labor and Social History Records. Catholic University of America, Washington, DC.

David J. McDonald Papers, Steel Workers Organizing Committee Records. Pattee Library, Penn State University, State College.

District 20 Files. United Steelworkers of America Civil Rights Department, 1945–1971. Pattee Library, Penn State University, State College.

District 36 Files. United Steelworkers of America Civil Rights Department, 1945–1971. Pattee Library, Penn State University, State College.

Ernest Thompson Papers. Special Collections and University Archives, Rutgers University Libraries.

GSU Newspapers Collection. Southern Labor Archives. Georgia State University, Atlanta.

Henry Kraus Papers. Walter P. Reuther Library. Archives of Labor and Urban Affairs. Wayne State University, Detroit, MI.

Meyer Bernstein Papers. Historical Collections and Labor Archives, Special Collections Library. Pennsylvania State University.

Operation Dixie (OD). C.I.O. Southern Organizing Committee Papers, 1946–1953. William R. Perkins Library, Duke University, Durham, NC.

Oral History Projects. Pattee Library, Penn State University, State College.

Papers of the National Negro Congress. Manuscript Collections from the Schomburg Center for Research in Black Culture. New York Public Library.

Records of the International Woodworkers of America, 1936–1987. Library of the University of Oregon, Eugene.

Ruben Farr Collection. Birmingham Public Library, Birmingham, AL.

Steel Workers Organizing Committee Records. Pattee Library, Penn State University, State College.

Textile Workers of America Papers. Wisconsin Historical Society, Madison.

United Steelworkers of America Civil Rights Department, 1945–1971. Pattee Library, Penn State University, State College.

Western Federation of Miners/International Union of Mine, Mill & Smelter Workers collection. Special Collections & Archives, University of Colorado-Boulder Libraries.

INDEX

411